Human Rights in

Human Rights in Criminal Law

Ben Douglas-Jones KC
5 Paper Buildings

Daniel Bunting
Barrister, 2 Dr Johnson's Buildings

Paul Mason
Barrister, Doughty Street Chambers

Benjamin Newton
Barrister, Doughty Street Chambers

Bloomsbury Professional

LONDON • DUBLIN • EDINBURGH • NEW YORK • NEW DELHI • SYDNEY

BLOOMSBURY PROFESSIONAL

Bloomsbury Publishing Plc
50 Bedford Square, London, WC1B 3DP, UK
1385 Broadway, New York, NY 10018, USA
29 Earlsfort Terrace, Dublin 2, Ireland

British Library Cataloguing-in-Publication Data

A catalogue record for this book is available from the British Library.

ISBN: PB: 978 1 52651 951 1
Epdf: 978 1 52651 953 5
Epub: 978 1 52651 952 8

Typeset by Evolution Design and Digital (Kent)
Printed and bound by CPI Group (UK) Ltd, Croydon, CR0 4YY

To find out more about our authors and books visit www.bloomsburyprofessional.com. Here you will find extracts, author information, details of forthcoming events and the option to sign up for our newsletters

Foreword

I am delighted to write the Foreword for this timely work, of broad appeal and filling a gap in the literature. It has been produced by a distinguished, much-respected team of editors, in collaboration with a wide range of contributors.

As is apparent from its title, *Human Rights in Criminal Law* aims to provide a particular and specific focus on the impact of Human Rights law at every stage of the criminal justice process. Of great value, chapters begin with an introduction, putting the matter in context and bringing together domestic criminal law and procedure with the relevant Convention and Strasbourg jurisprudence.

This country has a proud record in the protection of human rights through both the common law and statute. By way of example, as observed in the introduction to Chapter 11, *Arrest and Detention*, citing Lord Hoffmann in *A and Others v SSHD* [2005] 2 AC 68, at [88]:

> 'Freedom from arbitrary arrest and detention, articulated in Magna Carta 1215, has been described as "a quintessentially British liberty, enjoyed by the inhabitants of this country when most of the population of Europe could be thrown into prison at the whim of their rulers".'

Complacency is, however, never warranted and Human Rights law has required us to re-examine areas taken for granted, from time to time improving our domestic procedures, to the benefit of both domestic law and the Strasbourg jurisprudence. Staying with my theme, the survey of the work of the European Court of Human Rights in Chapter 6 augments our knowledge of domestic law and protections, additionally revealing the very high regard displayed by the Strasbourg Court, rightly, for decisions from this jurisdiction.

When chairing the Independent Human Rights Act Review, I studied a vast amount of material on human rights, though nothing specifically focused on criminal law in the manner of this work. Had *Human Rights in Criminal Law* been available at the time, it would have been a most welcome addition to the learning. I commend this work.

Sir Peter Gross
January 2023

Preface

The law of human rights permeates every area of law. Achieving a confident command of the principles that apply in any given context is sometimes daunting for lawyers and academics alike. This is particularly so in the context of criminal law in England and Wales.

Our aim in publishing this book is to focus on the impact of human rights law at every stage of the criminal process. It traces the principal human rights issues that arise from protections that apply during an investigation, before a suspect even knows they are a suspect, to powers of arrest and search, and treatment at the police station. Further, it then considers every stage of the criminal court process up to any potential appeal before the domestic courts and the European Court of Human Rights.

The book is divided into four parts. Part 1 covers the fundamental principles of the European Convention on Human Rights and the Human Rights Act 1998, and their application in domestic law, particularly in relation to criminal trials and appeals. Parts 2 to 4 address the three broad phases of a criminal case – investigation, pre-trial and trial. They provide an analysis of human rights law in a structure that will be immediately familiar to those who have practised or studied criminal law.

We have been privileged in being able to bring together a great array of specialist authors from the Bar, solicitors' profession, judiciary and academia, whose work is focused on the *nexus* between criminal law and human rights. The authors are individuals of high repute in their respective fields, many with international reputations.

Our intention is that the book should stand as a dynamic interface between human rights, criminal law, professional practice and theory for practitioners and judges. We hope it will be a useful resource when seeking to marshal, reply to, or determine, sophisticated arguments at trial and on appeal, as well as meeting the needs of students and academics in areas such as criminal law and civil liberties.

Ben Douglas-Jones KC
Daniel Bunting
Paul Mason
Benjamin Newton

January 2023

Contents

General editors

Ben Douglas-Jones KC is a barrister at 5 Paper Buildings in London. He is also an attorney-at-law in Grenada, with rights of audience in the Eastern Caribbean Court of Appeal, a Deputy High Court Judge, Recorder of the Crown Court and Master of the Bench (Gray's Inn). He specialises in human rights, human trafficking and modern slavery, appeals, complex fraud, homicide, serious crime and regulatory law, including consumer and intellectual property. His human rights and appellate practice has seen him appear in many recent leading cases concerning human trafficking and refugees, and human rights in financial crime, including special court cases before three successive Lords Chief Justices. *Chambers and Partners* describes him as: 'An extremely talented barrister with exceptionally broad knowledge of the law, who can juggle the preparation of multiple complex cases concurrently'. Ben co-wrote the Crown Prosecution Service and Law Society Guidance on human trafficking and immigration crime and Judicial College Guidance on trafficking. He is a contributing editor of Southwell, Brewer and Douglas-Jones KC, *Human Trafficking and Modern Slavery: Law and Practice* (2nd Edn, Bloomsbury Professional, 2020) and an author of *Blackstone's Guide to the Consumer Rights Act 2015* (OUP, 2016). He provides domestic and international training on human rights in the context of judicial, practitioner and regulatory compliance training and has provided evidence to governmental committees on trafficking and transparency of supply chains. Ben has been a Gray's Inn advocacy trainer for many years.

Daniel Bunting is a barrister at 2 Dr Johnson's Buildings, prosecuting and defending in all areas of criminal law, with a special interest in criminal appeals, modern slavery and immigration offences (where he has appeared in many of the leading cases). He also practises in other areas including immigration law. He has regularly provided policy advice and has been instructed to provide advice to other lawyers in England and Wales and abroad. He has presented a number of lectures and seminars in a number of different areas of the law, and has regularly written for a variety of academic publications. He is a member of the Parole Board and sits as a Fee-Paid Judge in the Immigration Tribunal and Employment Tribunal.

Dr Paul Mason is a barrister at Doughty Street Chambers, where he specialises in defending serious criminal offences. He sits as a Fee-Paid Judge in the Employment Tribunal, Mental Health Tribunal and the Court of Protection. His publications include co-authoring *The Drug Offences Handbook* (Bloomsbury Professional, 2018) and contributor to *Taylor on Criminal Appeals* (OUP, 2022) and *The Routledge Companion to Media and Human Rights* (Routledge, 2017). Before coming to the Bar, Paul worked as a Research Assistant at the Law Commission. In his previous academic career, he was Director of Postgraduate Research and Senior Lecturer in the School of Journalism, Media and Culture at Cardiff University.

Benjamin Newton is a barrister at Doughty Street Chambers, due to be appointed as King's Counsel on 27 March 2023. He is instructed to defend those accused of the most serious and complex criminal offences, and regularly appears in high profile and legally significant cases. In 2019 he was awarded Crime Junior of the Year at the 2019 *Chambers and Partners* Bar Awards, and is noted by their guide to be 'widely acknowledged to be a standout defence junior at the general crime Bar' and 'valued for his wide-ranging experience in fraud cases'. His areas of particular expertise include financial crime, serious sexual offences, homicide, and terrorism. He has contributed to several significant publications on criminal law, including *Taylor on Criminal Appeals* (OUP, 2022) and regularly presents lectures and seminars. Benjamin also sits as a Recorder in the Crown Court, and as a Tribunal Judge in the Health, Education and Social Care Chamber of the First-tier Tribunal.

CONTRIBUTORS

Victoria Ailes is a barrister practising in public law and human rights matters at 6KBW College Hill. She was called to the bar in 2005 and has appeared in numerous human rights cases with a criminal justice focus at both domestic and international level, including notably *Al Khawaja and Tahery v United Kingdom*, *Taxquet v Belgium* and *Sanchez-Sanchez v United Kingdom*.

Farrhat Arshad is a barrister at Doughty Street Chambers. She specialises in the areas of Criminal Defence, Appeals and Public Law challenges by way of case stated and Judicial Review arising from the Criminal and Prison context. Farrhat is also a Crown Court Recorder sitting on the South-Eastern Circuit.

Peta-Louise Bagott is a barrister at Doughty Street Chambers. She specialises in crime, with a particular expertise in international crime. She was called to Bar of England and Wales in 2011, and prior to commencing pupillage worked on defence teams at the International Criminal Tribunal for the former Yugoslavia and the International Criminal Court. She is regularly instructed in complex, document heavy cases at the domestic level, as well as high-profile international cases.

Tayyiba Bajwa combines her criminal practice at Doughty Street Chambers with work in related areas of inquests, crime-related public law, prison law and actions against the police. She is instructed alone and as a led junior in a wide range of criminal cases, including serious violence, firearms and drug offences. She has particular expertise in challenging the convictions of victims of trafficking in the youth and adult courts. High profile public-law challenges on which she has acted include the operation of the Gangs Violence Matrix and the discriminatory application of anti-terrorism powers.

Denis Barry is a criminal barrister at 6KBW College Hill. He has two decades of experience in defending and prosecuting in serious criminal cases and has particular expertise in homicide, having appeared in a number of high-profile murder cases. He also has broad experience in organised crime and corruption offences, has appeared in many cases involving complex medical evidence (particularly those involving the mentally ill), and also cases involving the death of children. He is also a leading junior in the area of Consumer law.

Omran Belhadi is a criminal defence specialist at Doughty Street Chambers. He is regularly instructed both on his own and as a junior in cases of serious violence, firearms and large-scale drug offences. Prior to joining the Bar, Omran worked on human rights abuses in the context of national security during the War on Terror. He assisted on cases of torture and unlawful sharing of intelligence by the UK Government.

Steven Bird is the Managing Director of Birds Solicitors and is highly rated in the leading legal directories in criminal law. In 2016 he was admitted to the List of Counsel at the International Criminal Court. He is also a Director of Southwell & Partners, a specialist firm dealing with human trafficking cases. He is a Committee member of the London Criminal Courts Solicitors Association and Chairman of the Criminal Appeal Lawyers Association. He has contributed chapters to Taylor on Criminal Appeals, Human Trafficking and Modern Slavery: Law and Practice, The Drugs Offences Handbook, and The Confiscation Law Handbook.

Rupert Bowers KC leads the Business Crime & Investigations team at Doughty Street Chambers, maintaining a practice in financial crime and extradition, and data protection and information rights, with expertise in ancillary matters associated with criminal investigations and data breaches. He is one of the country's leading experts in challenging search warrants of all types, seizures of property and information and in challenging asset freezing orders.

Ian Brownhill is a barrister at 39 Essex Chambers, is His Majesty's Assistant Coroner for Kent and holds judicial roles with both the Football Association and the British Equestrian Federation. Ian works at the forefront of where criminal justice, mental health/capacity and safeguarding intersect. Ian has been instructed in a number of seminal cases in this area, including: *JB* [2021] UKSC 52 (capacity to engage in sexual relations); *WU* [2021] EWCOP 54 (coercive marriage); *EOA* [2021] EWCOP 20 (religious indoctrination); and *EG* [2020] EWHC 1457 (Admin) (prisoners who lack the mental capacity to conduct their parole processes).

Miranda Butler is a barrister at Landmark Chambers. She specialises in public law and has a particular interest in migration-related issues and human rights. She previously worked as a judicial assistant at the UK Supreme Court and European Court of Human Rights. She is also a member of the EHRC's panel of counsel and in 2020 was shortlisted for the Legal Aid Lawyer of the Year's 'Newcomer of the Year' award. In 2022 she co-founded the multi-award winning Ukraine Advice Project, which provides pro bono legal advice to those fleeing conflict in Ukraine.

Toby Cadman is the co-founder of the G37 Group and Joint Head of Guernica 37 Chambers. He is an established international law specialist in the areas of international criminal and humanitarian law, international commercial law, arbitration, and extradition law. He has provided advice and training to judges, prosecutors, lawyers and law enforcement agencies throughout the

Balkans, Middle East, North Africa and South Asia. He has appeared and been instructed in matters before the ICC, ICTY, International Crimes Tribunal Bangladesh, European Court of Human Rights, Bosnian State Court, the UN Human Rights Committee and the African Commission on Human and Peoples Rights.

Peter Carter KC practises law at Doughty Street Chambers. He has undertaken most types of criminal law work for defence and prosecution, with the emphasis on terrorism, homicide, trafficking and fraud. He has appeared in some of the major terrorist trials in the last 10 years. He created the Protocol for Special Counsel in Public Interest Immunity cases in R v Bourgass and others. He was a Special Adviser to the Joint Parliamentary Committee on the draft Modern Slavery Bill. He teaches advocacy domestically and internationally.

Joanne Cecil is a barrister at Garden Court Chambers with a practice encompassing serious crime, inquiries and public law with a civil liberties focus. She has a wealth of experience in representing children and is renowned for having been instructed in many test cases relating to children in the criminal justice system, resulting in significant changes in the law. She is also appointed to the 'A' panel of the Equalities and Human Rights Commission. Ranked as a leading junior in both crime and civil liberties in the legal directories, she is an elected Bencher of the Honourable Society of the Inner Temple and sits as a Recorder in both crime and family law.

Leslie Chinweze is a First-tier Tribunal Judge in the Immigration and Asylum Chamber. He qualified as a barrister and solicitor of the Nigerian Supreme Court in 1989, and was then admitted as a solicitor of the Law Society of England and Wales in 2000. For the next twenty years he was a Senior Crown Prosecutor and Solicitor Advocate for the Crown Prosecution Service, appearing in the Crown Court, the High Court and the Court of Appeal. Leslie served as a member of the Law Society's Immigration Law Committee between 2016 and 2019, and also sat for several years as a lay member on police misconduct tribunals.

Will Durrands is a barrister at 25 Bedford Row Chambers, London. His practice covers all aspects of criminal defence, with specialist experience in cases involving protest and public order offences engaging Convention rights.

Emma Fitzsimons is a barrister at Garden Court Chambers. She practises in immigration and public law, with a focus on human rights, asylum and trafficking. She regularly appears in cases in which Human Rights are engaged, particularly Articles 2, 3, 4 and 8. She was a member of the legal team in *VCL v United Kingdom* App No 77587/12, which achieved the profoundly important win against the government in human trafficking cases, establishing the extent of Article 4 operational measures duties in investigations. She is a contributing author to *Macdonald's Immigration Law and Practice* (10th Edn, LexisNexis, 2021).

Kate Goold has been a practising solicitor at London's leading criminal and human rights firms since 1996. She is described as a leading individual in crime, extradition and human rights by independent legal directories and has been named in The Best Lawyers in the United Kingdom guide for Criminal Law practice since 2020. Kate has been a partner at Bindmans LLP since 2014 and is particularly regarded for her skill in dealing with politically sensitive, high profile and controversial cases. Her notable cases are protecting journalists and their sources: *R (on the application of Miranda) v SSHD* 2016 EWCA Civ 6 and *The Shrewsbury Pickets* appeal.

Dr Lyndon Harris is a tenant at 6KBW College Hill practising in criminal and public law, appearing in the Crown Court, High Court and Court of Appeal (Criminal Division). He has a particular interest in sentencing and human rights, having worked at the Law Commission on the Sentencing Code project. He authors various texts on sentencing and regularly lectures to the professions. Formerly, Lyndon taught law at the University of Oxford and King's College, University of London. His academic work has been cited, with approval, by the Court of Appeal.

Deanna Heer KC, appointed Senior Treasury Counsel in 2022, is a highly experienced criminal barrister who is regularly instructed in the most serious and high-profile cases. For over a decade she has specialised in the prosecution of homicide offences at the Central Criminal Court. She frequently appears before the Court of Appeal in respect of appeals against conviction and advises the Attorney General on References to the Court of Appeal on questions of law and sentencing.

Christopher Jenkins is a barrister at 5 Paper Buildings, specialising in criminal law. Christopher prosecutes and defends across the full spectrum of offences, and has a particular interest in the interplay between human rights and the criminal law. Christopher also has particular experience and expertise in cases where defendants themselves have been the victim of trafficking and exploitation, and he has written and presented extensively on this subject throughout his time in practice.

Andrew Johnson is a barrister at 5 Paper Buildings. He has a broad practice, which includes prosecuting regulatory crime and acting in appeals involving alleged victims of trafficking before the Court of Appeal (Criminal Division). He appeared in *AAD* [2022] EWCA Crim 106, the leading case on the approach to victims of trafficking in the criminal courts. He sits as a Deputy District Judge (Magistrates' Courts) and as a Recorder of the Crown Court

Riel Karmy-Jones KC is a barrister specialising in crime. She has a high-profile practice which includes murder and manslaughter, serious organised crime, sexual offences, and modern slavery and human trafficking. She is a contributing editor to a number of legal texts, including *Archbold – Criminal Pleading, Evidence and Practice 2023* (Sweet and Maxwell, 2022); *Rook and Ward Sexual Offences: Law and Practice* (6th Edn, Sweet and Maxwell, 2021); *Young, Corker and Summers on Abuse of Process In Criminal Proceedings* (5th Edn, Bloomsbury Professional, 2022).

Kalvir Kaur is a solicitor at Freedom from Torture, with expertise in advocating for children, and for survivors of torture, trafficking and modern slavery. She is a Vital Voices Fellow 2017, recipient of the 2014 ECPATUK Children's Champion award and in 2008 was awarded Legal Aid Lawyer of the Year in the Immigration & Asylum category. She is accredited by the Law Society in immigration and asylum law at Advanced Level, and is an expert panel member for the Refugee Legal Clinic, University of London, and for ILPA Strategic Litigation Fund. She was a founding trustee of Asylum Research Consultancy.

Tim Kiely is a criminal barrister based at Red Lion Chambers. He has experience both prosecuting and defending in cases which involve allegations of serious violence; misconduct or failings by the police; and defendants or witnesses with acute vulnerabilities in terms of age, mental health or potential defences under the Modern Slavery Act. Currently he is on the counsel team instructed by the Metropolitan Police as part of the Undercover Policing Inquiry. Prior to joining chambers he also undertook work for the Capital Appeals Project, both assisting with casework and campaigning for the abolition of the death penalty in Louisiana.

Helen Law is a barrister at Matrix Chambers. Helen is an experienced criminal trial advocate with complementary expertise in advising on and litigating criminal justice and human rights issues in civil and public law proceedings, including failures in investigations/prosecutions and allegations of serious misconduct by state agencies. She has extensive experience of dealing with sensitive cases and vulnerable clients.

Dominic Lewis is an experienced criminal lawyer, with a healthy balance of prosecution and defence work. He practises from 5 Paper Buildings as a junior or leading junior, primarily in the field of financial crime. Alongside his criminal practice, Dominic is on the Attorney-General's panel of special advocates. As such he is regularly appointed to act on behalf of affected individuals in closed material proceedings across a range of fields, including terrorism, immigration, media and civil actions concerning breaches of Convention rights.

Sophie Nandy is a pupil at 25 Bedford Row Chambers. Prior to this, she studied law at Durham University and graduated with a master's degree from the University of Cambridge. As part of her master's studies, Sophie wrote a thesis testing the application of dialogue theory to *R (on the application of Miller and another) v Secretary of State for Exiting the European Union* [2017] UKSC 5 and its aftermath. In 2020, Sophie was awarded a Lord Denning Scholarship from the Honourable Society of Lincoln's Inn.

Kate O'Raghallaigh practises criminal law, extradition and public law in the field of criminal justice from Doughty Street Chambers. She is a versatile practitioner, being one of the few juniors in the country who specialises in terrorism work. Within crime and related civil work, Kate has particular expertise in terrorism, national security, contempt and the rights of children. She has a strong appellate and judicial review practice and regularly appears alone and led in the Court of Appeal, Administrative Court, and Privy Council.

Mary Prior KC is a leading Silk in criminal law who is known for having expertise in questioning of the vulnerable. She is ranked as a tier one Silk in *Legal 500*. She is a Bencher at Gray's Inn, Vice Chair in the Education Department for outreach, the elected silk representative of the CBA, Head of RASSO for the CBA and for the Midland Circuit. Mary's practice is in cases of homicide, exploitation of children and adults, organised crime and large scale sexual abuse cases. She trains barristers in how to question vulnerable witnesses and is a national and international speaker in criminal law.

Dr Aparna Rao specialises in criminal and civil fraud, with extensive experience in complex cases involving financial and technical matters. She is regularly instructed both on her own and as a junior in the Crown Court, First-tier Tribunal, and professional disciplinary tribunals. She qualified in 2009 in Australia, where she worked as an Associate to a Justice of the High Court of Australia (the final appellate court). She taught as a Lecturer in Law at the Australian National University in Canberra, and later tutored in Law at Oxford University while completing her DPhil on the topic of bad character in criminal trials.

David Rhodes is a barrister at Doughty Street Chambers, specialising in criminal defence. Recent instructions range from heavyweight allegations of homicide, serious violence and organised crime, to cases of rape and 'historical' sexual offences requiring a delicate touch; and from esoteric and intellectually challenging fraud work to criminal allegations arising from protests. David is a contributor to the leading textbooks, *Taylor on Criminal Appeals* (3rd Edn, OUP, 2022) and *The Law of Public Order and Protest* (OUP, 2010).

James Robottom is a barrister at Matrix Chambers. He has a multi-disciplinary practice which covers criminal law, public law and human rights law. He is a General Editor and author of *Coroners Investigations and Inquests* (LexisNexis, 2021). James' multi-disciplinary practice allows him to advise in complex claims where practice areas overlap. He has appeared in judicial review, civil and criminal proceedings at the highest level, unled at every level to the Court of Appeal, and led in the Supreme Court.

Nathaniel Rudolf KC is a member of 25 Bedford Row and is an acknowledged leader in the field of confiscation and restraint. He has appeared successfully at all levels in the Crown Court, Court of Appeal and Supreme Court. He has also lectured and written on money laundering and the proceeds of crime.

Miriam Smith is a barrister at 5 Paper Buildings. She practises in quasi-criminal public law, extradition and public inquiries.

Jack Sproson is a practising barrister and Member of Guernica 37 Chambers. Domestically, Jack regularly brings claims under the Human Rights Act and Equality Act and is experienced in judicial review proceedings, actions against the police, and criminal appeals work. Internationally, Jack advises on contemporaneous legal issues in live armed conflicts and has dealt with matters before the European Court of Human Rights, the UN Working Group on Arbitrary Detention, the International Criminal Court, and the Kosovo Specialist Chambers. Jack has also acted in respect of INTERPOL Red Notice appeals and is experienced in the area of business and human rights.

Monica Stevenson is a barrister with almost two decades' experience defending in criminal trials and practises from one of the leading chambers in London. She is instructed in a range of serious criminal cases and has undertaken working assignments for core participants to the Undercover Policing Inquiry and Post Office Horizon IT Inquiry. Before being called to the Bar, Monica lectured in her Masters' degree subject in International law. She has authored and co-authored articles for a range of legal publications, is accredited to provide training in the techniques of vulnerable witness cross-examination and assists with advocacy training at Middle Temple.

Laura Stockdale is a criminal defence barrister at Doughty Street Chambers. She specialises in criminal cases with a human rights aspect, including protestors exercising their rights to freedom of expression and assembly, and offenders subject to ancillary orders infringing their rights to privacy. She also practises in financial crime and professional discipline and regulation. Prior to moving to the UK, Laura practised as a solicitor in Australia at the Department of Public Prosecutions, and in the Supreme Court of New South Wales as a judicial assistant. She also previously worked at the International Criminal Tribunal for the former Yugoslavia in The Hague.

Áine Josephine Tyrrell is an interdisciplinary scholar whose current work explores how technology, privacy, and data protection intersect with human rights. Her interdisciplinary doctoral research at Stanford University examined counter-terrorism law post-9/11 in the UK, US, and France through the lens of performance. Prior to pursuing a career at the bar, she worked for a number of organisations around the world including the United Nations' World Food Program, UNESCO, and Stanford University. She has been published in various peer-reviewed journals and anthologies, including: Cultural Dynamics, The Drama Review, War on the Rocks, and Performing Statescraft: The Postdiplomatic Theatre of Sovereigns, Citizens, and States.

Anthony Vaughan is a barrister practising in human rights, administrative and equality law at Doughty Street Chambers, London. He represents people who have been victims of injustice at the hands of the State in a range of contexts, appearing in the civil and criminal courts, and in administrative tribunals. Anthony is on the Equality and Human Rights Commission's panel of specialist counsel, and is ranked as a leading junior by *Chambers and Partners* and *Legal 500* in immigration, and civil liberties and human rights. He writes and speaks widely on human rights and equality issues.

Tom Wainwright is a criminal defence barrister at Garden Court Chambers. He specialises in defending activists and has acted in some of the most high-profile protest cases of recent times, including the Colston Statue topplers, the Stansted 15 and the Rotherham 12. He has represented defendants arrested at demonstrations for Extinction Rebellion, Insulate Britain, Black Lives Matter, Occupy, student fees and many others. Tom has particular interest in the relationship between Article 10 and the criminal law and has spoken and published widely on the topic.

Katrina Walcott is a criminal barrister at Doughty Street Chambers. Prior to joining the Bar in 2019, she worked as a paralegal at leading criminal firm, Hickman & Rose. Katrina also previously worked in criminal and human rights law and policy research. She was a Research Assistant at the Law Commission for England and Wales (2019–2020), during which time she worked on the Hate Crime Review Consultation Paper. Katrina has also worked as a Law and Policy Researcher at JUSTICE and ARTICLE 19 and as a Human Rights Officer at The British Institute of Human Rights.

Colin Wells is a criminal defence barrister at 25 Bedford Row. His practice ranges from pre-charge criminal advisory, criminal defence work (specialising in fraud, money laundering, confiscation and related regulatory proceedings), criminal cost appeals. Chambers and Partners UK legal directory describes him as 'the go-to person on abuse of process matters.' Author of *Abuse of Process* (4th Edn, OUP, 2023). Reported appeal cases include Supreme Court: *SFO v Brian O'Brien* [2014] UKSC 23 SFO – prosecution, of £4.1 million 'boiler-room' fraud, contempt-extradition proceedings in the Supreme Court.

Mary Westcott (called 2007) is a highly respected extradition barrister with a background in criminal and public international law. She works at Doughty Street Chambers challenging extradition requests from far and wide, and advising in often complex related proceedings. She often represents especially vulnerable clients, successfully invoking the ECHR (recently, *Prusianiu v Romania* [2022] EWHC 1929 (Admin)). Mary has appeared alone and led in Divisional Court test cases, also led in the Supreme Court both for the defence (*Poland v Zakrzewski* [2013] 1 WLR 324) and for the requesting state (*Goluchowski & Sas v Poland* [2016] 1 WLR 2665).

Tara Wolfe works for the rehabilitation charity Freedom from Torture. She is a practising barrister with extensive experience in criminal law including murder, sexual violence, arson and terrorism, and in immigration and asylum law, representing appellants seeking protection in the UK. She has considerable experience representing vulnerable clients and witnesses, disadvantaged due to their age, mental health or past traumatic experiences. She taught on the Bar Professional Training Course at the University of the West of England, including designing and delivering the option on Immigration and Asylum law and taught Jurisprudence at the University of Bristol.

Zubier Yazdani is a solicitor and partner at Deighton Pierce Glynn solicitors. He is an expert in administrative law, civil liberties and human rights law. He has litigated in courts at all levels domestically as well as in the ECtHR and deals with cutting edge litigation. Zubier's core client group are children, young migrants and victims of trafficking. Zubier has a long standing commitment to social justice as reflected in the cases he has dealt with in his 20 years of practice.

Table of Statutes

[*All references are to paragraph number.*]

Table of Statutory Instruments

[All references are to paragraph number.]

Table of European Legislation

[All references are to paragraph number.]

Table of Cases

[*All references are to paragraph number.*]

B

D

E

F

G

K

L

M

O

P

Q

R

S

V

W

X

Y

Z

Part 1

ECHR and HRA

1 The Human Rights Act 1998 – introduction, overview, reservations and derogations

Miranda Butler

INTRODUCTION

1.1

The Convention for the Protection of Human Rights and Fundamental Freedoms (Rome, 4 November 1950) (ECHR) contains a broad range of substantive and procedural protections that are applicable in domestic criminal proceedings. Human rights will feature throughout criminal proceedings, from positive duties of investigation and protection prior to any suspect being identified, to safeguarding suspects' privacy, and then setting out extensive procedural protections for defendants in criminal trials and afterwards. It is also important to remember that it does not just provide rights for suspects and defendants, but also for victims and witnesses. Article 8 requires that the state take steps to protect a victim's private (and family) life that include having an adequate legal framework in place to protect them.

1.2

This chapter provides a broad introduction to how the ECHR and the Human Rights Act 1998 (HRA 1998) came into being, as well as an overview to the relevant procedural framework for the protection of human rights at a domestic level, and the rights protected. For more detail on any particular aspect, reference to the relevant subsequent chapter should be made.

1.3

Whilst the ECHR is a pan-European document, and the Human Rights Act applies to the United Kingdom as a whole, this book will look solely at English and Welsh criminal law and procedure (although there will be reference to Scottish cases).

HISTORICAL OVERVIEW

Origins of the ECHR

1.4

The horrors of the Second World War caused a profound shift in attitudes towards fundamental human rights on a trans-national level. On a global level, the Universal Declaration of Human Rights was adopted in 1948. This followed on from the 'four freedoms' (freedom of speech and worship, and freedom from fear and want) articulated by President Roosevelt in his 'State of the Union Address' from 1941. Eleanor Roosevelt (President Roosevelt's wife) chaired the UN Committee that produced the Universal Declaration. This was not legally binding but contains many of the freedoms that were later to be incorporated into regional treaties.

The Council of Europe

1.5

In 1949 the Treaty of London[1] was signed between ten Western European countries (including the United Kingdom). This contained no substantive provision for individual rights but set up the Council of Europe which consisted of representatives from the various signatory Governments (the Committee of Ministers) and the signatory Parliaments (the Consultative Assembly).

1.6

It was the Consultative Assembly, consisting of more than 100 Parliamentarians from the twelve members of the Consultative Assembly (Greece and Turkey having also signed up by then), which began to meet in August 1949 to draft what was to become the ECHR. Sir David Maxwell Fyfe KC, a Conservative party MP and former prosecutor at the Nuremberg trials, was the Chair of the Parliamentary Assembly's 'Committee on Legal and Administrative Questions' and the *rapporteur* of the drafting committee. He was also a leading member of the 'European Movement' that had already started work on drafting detailed proposals prior to the creation of the Council of Europe.

1.7

When the Council of Europe came into being, he and others produced a draft of the Convention in July 1949 which went through the Assembly and the Committee of Ministers. Two separate drafts were ultimately produced which, after much debate (not least within the UK Cabinet), were resolved in the Autumn of 1950.

1 The Statute of the Council of Europe (London, 5 May 1949).

Ratification of the ECHR

1.8

The final version of the Treaty was signed on 4 November 1950, with both the English and French versions being authoritative. There were three rights in particular (the right to peaceful enjoyment of property, the right to education and the right to free elections by secret ballot) on which there was no unanimous agreement to their inclusion. As a result, they were put into a separate Protocol (Protocol 1). Subsequent to that there have been a number of Protocols, making both procedural and substantive amendments. In 1951 the United Kingdom became the first country to ratify the ECHR. However, as a result of the dualist nature of the UK's legal system,[2] the ECHR was not directly enforceable in domestic law (at least until passage of the Human Rights Act 1998 (HRA 1998)). Pursuant to Article 46 of the ECHR, decisions of the ECtHR are binding on contracting states, but not directly binding on UK courts.

European Court of Human Rights

1.9

The European Court of Human Rights (ECtHR) was not established (pursuant to Article 19 ECHR) until January 1959. At that stage the European Commission of Human Rights had the sole power to bring a case to the ECtHR, thus acting as a filter mechanism.[3] A further barrier was that, by 1955, only five countries (Denmark, Iceland, Ireland, Sweden and West Germany) allowed for the right of individuals to bring a case to the Commission.

1.10

The first President of the ECtHR was Lord McNair, a British barrister and former Judge of the International Court of Justice. The Court first sat on 23 February 1959, with the first judgment being given in 1960.[4] Even then, there was only one case in 1961 and none brought at all in the years 1962–1965.

1.11

The first case related to the admissibility of a complaint by a member (or former member) of the IRA who had been detained without trial and was subsequently dismissed (albeit on the basis that Ireland had derogated from the

2 Recently reaffirmed in *R (SC and ors) v Secretary of State for Work and Pensions and ors* [2021] UKSC 26, [2021] 3 WLR 428.

3 The Commission was abolished by Protocol 11, which came into force in 1998. This Protocol also made the right of individual petition mandatory.

4 *Lawless v Ireland (No 1)* (Application no 332/57) 14 November 1960.

relevant right).[5] It was not until 1968 that the Court first found that there had been a violation of the ECHR.[6]

1.12

On 14 January 1966 the United Kingdom formally declared that it would recognise the right of individual petition, although at that point it would be for a trial period. Prior to this, the United Kingdom had first been the subject of an inter-state case that was brought by Greece in relation to the UK's attempt to use military force to put down an insurrection in Cyprus (the proceedings were subsequently dropped). It was only in 1975 that the United Kingdom 'lost' its first case at the ECtHR when the Court ruled[7] that for a prison to refuse to send a prisoner's letters to a solicitor and to the European Commission on Human Rights was a violation of Articles 6 and 8 of the Convention.

Membership of the Council of Europe

1.13

The Council of Europe has now expanded to 46 countries with Montenegro (2007) being the most recent signatory. The Russian Federation was a member from 1996 until it was expelled on 16 March 2022 following the invasion of Ukraine.

1.14

All members of the EEA are members. Apart from Russia, the only European countries that are not members are Belarus, Kazakhstan and the Vatican City. The European Union is not, itself, a party to the ECHR, although the Lisbon Treaty paved the way for this to happen at some point in the future.

THE CROWN DEPENDENCIES

1.15

The Channel Islands (the Bailiwicks of Jersey and Guernsey) and the Isle of Man are distinct legal territories and are not part of the United Kingdom. However, the reach of the ECHR was extended to both the Channel Islands and the Isle of Man by virtue of a Declaration registered with the Council of Europe on 23 October 1953. All three entities have their own legal systems, which are outside the scope of this book.

5 *Lawless v Ireland (No 3)* (Application no 332/57) 1 July 1961.
6 *Neumeister v Austria* (Application no 1936/63) 27 June 1968.
7 *Golder v United Kingdom* (1975) 1 EHRR 524

The Channel Islands

1.16

Laws similar to the Human Rights Act 1998 were introduced in both Bailiwicks (The Human Rights (Jersey) Law 2000 and the Human Rights (Bailiwick of Guernsey) Law 2000), although they were not brought into force until 2006. These are similar (but not identical) to UK law.

The Isle of Man

1.17

The Isle of Man's Human Rights Act 2001 came into force in 2006. It is along similar lines to the UK's Human Rights Act 1998.

THE ORIGIN OF THE HUMAN RIGHTS ACT

1.18

Although citizens of the United Kingdom had been able to petition the ECtHR (at least through the Commission) since 1966, this was a costly and lengthy process. When there were only a small handful of cases, this did not present a great problem. However, as the ECtHR began to receive thousands, then tens of thousands, of complaints, the position became increasingly untenable. In addition, as the number of cases before the ECtHR grew, the limitations of domestic law became increasingly clear.

Whilst the ECHR undoubtedly had an impact on jurisprudence, if a particular provision or decision under challenge was lawful in domestic law then a judge would not generally have the power to give effect to the ECHR. There have been a number of attempts to incorporate the ECHR, with the most recent, prior to 1997, being a Bill introduced by Lord Lester of Herne Hill QC in 1996, but all were unsuccessful.

1.19

The Labour Party Manifesto for the 1997 election contained the firm commitment that: 'Citizens should have statutory rights to enforce their human rights in the UK courts. We will by statute incorporate the European Convention on Human Rights into UK law to bring these rights home and allow our people access to them in their national courts'.

1.20

Having won that election, less than six months later, the new Government duly introduced a White Paper to 'bring rights home'.[8]

8 The HRA 1998 was proposed in a White Paper, *Rights Brought Home: The Human Rights Bill* (1997, Cm 3782).

The long title of the HRA 1998 is:

> An Act to give further effect to rights and freedoms guaranteed under the European Convention on Human Rights; to make provision with respect to holders of certain judicial offices who become judges of the European Court of Human Rights; and for connected purposes.

The aim of the HRA 1998 was to empower English and Welsh judges to apply human rights at the local level in the domestic courts. As well as being informed by the country's obligations under the ECHR, this would be informed by the Judges' particular understanding of domestic practice and procedure.

1.21

It should be noted that the human rights discussed in this chapter overlap in many places with the common law requirements of fairness, and other common law rights, which are beyond the scope of this book.

DEROGATIONS AND RESERVATIONS

Derogations under the ECHR

1.22

Article 15 (derogation in times of emergency) affords to the governments of States parties the possibility of derogating, in a temporary, limited and supervised manner, from their obligation to secure certain rights and freedoms under the Convention:

1. In time of war or other public emergency threatening the life of the nation any High Contracting Party may take measures derogating from its obligations under this Convention to the extent strictly required by the exigencies of the situation, provided that such measures are not inconsistent with its other obligations under international law.
2. No derogation from Article 2, except in respect of deaths resulting from lawful acts of war, or from Articles 3, 4 (paragraph 1) and 7 shall be made under this provision.
3. Any High Contracting Party availing itself of this right of derogation shall keep the Secretary General of the Council of Europe fully informed of the measures which it has taken and the reasons therefor. It shall also inform the Secretary General of the Council of Europe when such measures have ceased to operate and the provisions of the Convention are again being fully executed.

1.23

The use of Article 15 is governed by a number of procedural and substantive conditions. First, the right to derogate can only be invoked in time of war or other public emergency threatening the life of the nation. States are afforded a broad margin of appreciation in determining whether there is an emergency threatening the life of the nation.[9]

1.24

However, the Court will, in appropriate circumstances, go behind a country's derogation. In *Dareskizb v Armenia*, the Derogation of the Armenian Government in 2008 due to political unrest following a disputed election was not justified as whilst the situation:

> was undoubtedly very tense and could be considered a serious public order situation, the Court, nevertheless, considers that the Government failed to demonstrate convincingly and to support with evidence their assertion that the opposition demonstrations, which, moreover, were apparently confronted with a heavy-handed police intervention, could be characterised as a public emergency 'threatening the life of the nation' within the meaning of Article 15 of the Convention.[10]

1.25

A State may derogate from its obligations only to the extent strictly required by the exigencies of the situation. In *Piskin v Turkey*,[11] the applicant was working as an expert at the Ankara Development Agency but was dismissed on the grounds that he had links with a terrorist organisation following the declaration of a state of emergency in Turkey for the failed military coup of 15 July 2016, as well as the judicial review of that measure.

1.26

The applicant complained that neither the procedure leading to his dismissal, nor the subsequent judicial proceedings had complied with the guarantees of a fair trial and that he had been branded a 'terrorist' and 'traitor'. The Court held that there had been a violation of Articles 6(1) and 8. Regarding the derogation provided for by Article 15, the Court noted that the impugned Emergency Legislative Decree placed no restrictions on the judicial review to be exercised by the domestic courts following the termination of the employment contracts of the individuals concerned.[12] The Court pointed out that, even in the framework of a state of emergency, the fundamental principle of the rule of law had to prevail.

1.27

It would not be consistent with the rule of law, or the basic principles underlying Article 6(1) (namely that civil claims should be capable of being submitted to

9 Greer, S, 'The Margin of Appreciation: Interpretation and Discretion under the European Convention on Human Rights' (Council of Europe, 2000), 8. Available at: www.echr.coe.int/librarydocs/dg2/hrfiles/dg2-en-hrfiles-17(2000).pdf.

10 *Dareskizb v Armenia* (Application no 61737/08) 29 October 2021 at [62].

11 *Piskin v Turkey* (Application no 33399/18), 15 December 2020.

12 Ibid at [152].

a judge for an effective judicial review), if a State could, without restraint or control by the Convention enforcement bodies, remove from the jurisdiction of the courts a whole range of civil claims or confer immunities from civil liability on large groups or categories of persons.[13]

1.28

Accordingly, in view of the serious consequences for the Convention rights of those persons, where an emergency legislative decree did not contain any clear or explicit wording excluding the possibility of judicial supervision of the measures taken for its implementation, it always had to be understood as authorising the courts of the State to exercise sufficient scrutiny so that any arbitrariness could be avoided.[14] In those circumstances, the failure to observe the requirements of a fair trial could not be justified by the derogation, and, accordingly, the Court found that there had been a violation of Article 6(1).

1.29

The ECtHR has allowed derogations from certain Convention rights in the context of questioning or holding individuals suspected of terrorist activities. First, under Article 5 ECHR (right to liberty and security), States are not allowed to detain individuals for the sole purpose of intelligence gathering. However in *Murray v United Kingdom*, the Court held that where there is an '*honest suspicion on reasonable grounds*' of terrorist activity, an individual may be held and questioned.[15] Second, derogations cannot be incompatible with the State's other obligations under international law. Third, certain Convention rights do not allow for any derogation. Article 15(2) prohibits derogation in respect of the right to life (except in the context of lawful acts of war), the prohibition of torture and inhuman or degrading treatment or punishment,[16] the prohibition of slavery and servitude, and the rule of 'no punishment without law'. Finally, the State must keep the Secretary General of the Council of Europe fully informed.

1.30

In addition, there can be no derogation from Article 1, Protocol No 6 (abolishing the death penalty in peacetime), Article 1, Protocol No 13 (abolishing the death penalty in all circumstances), and Article 4, Protocol No 7 (right not to be tried or punished twice).

1.31

'War' is not formally defined in the Convention. It is likely that a formal state of war need not be declared, although the ECtHR have not determined this issue. In any event, even if there is not a formal declaration of war, the situation would very likely fall within the definition of 'public emergency'.

13 Ibid at [153].
14 Ibid.
15 *Murray v the United Kingdom* [GC] (Application no 14310/88), 28 October 1994.
16 *Ireland v the United Kingdom* (Application no 5310/71), 18 January 1978, at [163].

What is a public emergency?

1.32

In *Lawless v Ireland (No 3)*,[17] the ECtHR states that a public emergency for the purposes of Article 15 'refers to an exceptional situation of crisis or emergency which affects the whole population and constitutes a threat to the organised life of the community of which the State is composed'.

1.33

In *Denmark v Greece* ('The Greek Case'),[18] the European Commission of Human Rights stated that:

(i) the crisis or danger must be actual or imminent;

(ii) its effects must involve the whole nation;

(iii) the continuance of the organized life of the community must be threatened; and

(iv) the crisis or danger must be exceptional, in that the normal measures or restrictions, permitted by the Convention for the maintenance of public safety, health and order, are plainly inadequate.

The fact that the violence is regional, does not stop it affecting the whole nation.

1.34

Terrorism is a clear example of a public emergency that threatens the life of the nation. However, there is no reason in principle why other emergencies would not qualify, which could include natural disaster such as flooding, as well as a pandemic.

1.35

During the Covid-19 pandemic, a number of countries submitted derogations under Article 15.[19] At the time of writing, the ECtHR has not ruled on whether such a derogation would be permitted. The ECtHR has upheld the Romanian 'lockdown' as not being a breach of Article 5.[20] However, whilst Romania had entered a derogation, this was in relation to Article 2, Protocol 4 ('*Everyone lawfully within the territory of a State shall, within that territory, have the right to liberty of movement and freedom to choose his residence*') rather than Article 5. No issues relating to a breach of Article 2, Protocol 4, or the derogation had been raised.

---

17 *Lawless v Ireland (No 3)* (1961) EHRR 15.

18 *Denmark v Greece* (Application no 3321/67) & others, 24 January 1968.

19 Armenia, Albania, Estonia, Georgia, Latvia, Romania, Moldova, North Macedonia, San Marino and Serbia

20 *Terhes v Romania* (Application no 49933/20), 13 April 2021.

Derogations under the HRA 1998

1.36

Section 14 of the HRA 1998 provides a mechanism whereby government ministers may make an order incorporating any derogation made (or planned to be made) into the Act. Section 16 provides that derogations need the approval of Parliament. Derogations lapse after five years unless renewed for an additional five years.[21]

Derogations relied on by the UK

1.37

The UK has made two derogations, both of which have since been withdrawn.

1.38

The first was a derogation from Article 5(3) in respect of the detention of suspected terrorists in 1988 during the 'Troubles' in Northern Ireland. This was intended to permit the detention of suspected terrorists for up to seven days without judicial scrutiny. The ECtHR held in *Brannigan and McBride v UK*,[22] that this was reasonable in view of the nature of the emergency and the need to protect judges from a risk of violence.

1.39

The second was following the 9/11 terrorist attacks. Parliament enacted the Anti-Terrorism, Crime and Security Act 2001, which provided a power to detain foreign nationals without trial who had been certified as 'suspected international terrorists'.

1.40

The Government issued a notice of derogation under Article 15. The House of Lords accepted that there was an 'emergency threatening the life of the nation' but issued a declaration of incompatibility under the HRA 1998 on the grounds that the detention scheme discriminated unjustifiably against foreign nationals and quashed the derogation order made under section 14 of the HRA 1998.[23]

1.41

The ECtHR agreed with the House of Lords in relation to the declaration of incompatibility and found a violation of Article 5(1).[24] The ECtHR also ruled that it was for the Government to make its own assessment (as 'the guardian

---

21 HRA 1998, ss 17(1), (2).

22 *Brannigan and McBride v UK* (Application nos 14553/89 and 14554/89), 26 May 1993.

23 *A and ors v SSHD* [2004] UKHL 56

24 *A and ors v UK* [GC] (Application No 3455/05), 19 February 2009.

of its own people's safety') as to whether there is an emergency threatening the life of the nation, although this is a matter ultimately to be determined by the court.[25] The relevant part of the 2001 Act was repealed in 2005. Any derogations made are listed in Schedule 3 of the HRA 1998.

Reservations

1.42

Article 57 of the ECHR allows States to make reservations, namely, to choose at the time of signature or ratification not to be bound by specific provisions of the Convention:

1. Any State may, when signing this Convention or when depositing its instrument of ratification, make a reservation in respect of any particular provision of the Convention to the extent that any law then in force in its territory is not in conformity with the provision. Reservations of a general character shall not be permitted under this Article.
2. Any reservation made under this Article shall contain a brief statement of the law concerned

This makes it clear a reservation must be specific and clear.

Reservations relied upon by the UK

1.43

Article 2, Protocol 1 of the ECHR provides that States must respect the right of parents' religious and philosophical convictions in respect of education and teaching:

> No person shall be denied the right to education. In the exercise of any functions which it assumes in relation to education and to teaching, the State shall respect the right of parents to ensure such education and teaching in conformity with their own religious and philosophical convictions.

1.44

There were concerns in the United Kingdom that this would conflict with the principal of section 76 of the Education Act 1944 that 'pupils are to be educated in accordance with the wishes of their parents so far as that is compatible with the provision of efficient instruction and training and the avoidance of unreasonable public expenditure'.[26]

25 Ibid.
26 Repealed and replaced by the Education Act 1996, s 9.

1.45

When the United Kingdom agreed to be bound by this Article, Anthony Eden (the then Foreign Secretary) entered a reservation stating:

> I declare that, in view of certain provisions of the Education Acts in the United Kingdom, the principle affirmed in the second sentence of Article 2 is accepted by the United Kingdom only so far as it is compatible with the provision of efficient instruction and training, and the avoidance of unreasonable public expenditure.

Reservations under the HRA 1998

1.46

Section 15(1) of the HRA 1998 defines 'designated reservation' as:

(a) the United Kingdom's reservation to Article 2 of the First Protocol to the Convention; and

(b) any other reservation by the United Kingdom to an Article of the Convention, or of any protocol to the Convention, which is designated for the purposes of this Act in an order made by the Secretary of State.

1.47

Under section 17 of the HRA 1998, the government must keep reservations under review at least every five years. The Reservation to Article 2, Protocol 1 has been reviewed on a number of occasions but has been maintained since. To date, there have been no further reservations.

THE RIGHTS PROTECTED

1.48

Part 3 of this book below provides detailed consideration of all the rights in the ECHR and how they may arise in the criminal context. Set out below is a brief overview of the main ECHR rights that a criminal practitioner would need to be aware of.

Article 2 – the right to life

1.49

Article 2 entails an obligation of the State to conduct an independent and effective investigation when an individual has been killed as a result of the use of force by State agents[27] and in cases of suicide or near suicide in State

27 *McCann v the United Kingdom* (1996) 21 EHRR 97 at [161].

detention.[28] There is also a requirement for any investigation to be conducted with reasonable promptness and expedition.[29]

1.50

The ECtHR has also held that States have an obligation under Article 2 to take preventive operational measures to protect individuals identifiable as the potential target of a lethal act, such as witnesses in criminal proceedings.[30]

Article 3 – prohibition of torture, inhuman or degrading treatment or punishment

1.51

Article 3 is particularly significant for matters such as the use of force in law-enforcement action, the investigation of alleged offences and in the conduct of interrogations. This Article has played an important role in providing legal assurances to the victims of crimes, as well as improving due process for those accused of crime. For example, in relation to victims, a police failure to investigate allegations of rape breached Article 3.[31] A further example is that the CPS are required to take account of a victim's rights in deciding whether to proceed with a prosecution. The conditions of detention in a police station or a prison may constitute degrading treatment.[32]

1.52

The prohibition against Article 3 mistreatment includes a prohibition on removal (by way of extradition of otherwise) to a country where there would be such mistreatment.[33]

Article 5 – right to liberty and security

1.53

Article 5 has obvious implications for criminal proceedings. There is a strong presumption in favour of suspected offenders remaining at liberty.

28 *R (JL) v Secretary of State for Justice* [2008] UKHL 68, [2009] 1 AC 588.
29 *McCaughey v the United Kingdom* (2014) 58 EHRR 13.
30 *Van Colle v the United Kingdom* (2013) 56 EHRR 23; *A and B v Romania*, (Applications nos 48442/16 and 48831/16), 2 June 2020 at [118].
31 *Commissioner of the Metropolitan Police v DSD* [2018] UKSC 11, [2018] 3 All ER 369.
32 *RB (Algeria) (FC) and another v Secretary of State for the Home Department* [2009] UKHL 10, [2009] 2 WLR 512 at [112].
33 *Price v United Kingdom* (2002) 34 EHRR 241.

1.54

Article 5 imposes important obligations regarding initial apprehension and custody and the use and duration of detention on remand.[34] The ECtHR has set out principles to be applied in Article 5 challenges in a range of contexts, such as terrorism charges, hospitalisation and detention, and the period of imprisonment. In the case of bail in criminal cases, the ECtHR has held that national law must allow bail pending a criminal trial, unless certain conditions apply (generally those in the Bail Act 1976).

1.55

Police and other public authorities must ensure that any arrest or detention is lawful and is covered by one of the specified exceptions to the right to liberty. Further, it must be ensured that any arrest or detention is not excessive in the particular circumstances being dealt with; take all reasonable steps to bring a detained criminal suspect promptly before a judge; and take all reasonable steps to facilitate the detained person's right to challenge the lawfulness of their detention before a court.

Article 6 – right to a fair trial

1.56

Article 6 is at the heart of any consideration of human rights and the criminal process, including the critical right of a person accused to participate effectively in a criminal trial.[35] The rights enshrined therein must therefore be read holistically and interpreted purposively to ensure effective fairness in criminal proceedings. The courts will examine the criminal proceedings as a whole, having regard both to the rights of the defence but also the interests of the wider public, victims and witnesses.[36]

1.57

There are a number of procedural rights set out in Article 6, including an entitlement to a fair and public hearing, within a reasonable time. 'Public' includes both a public hearing and the public delivery of judgments.[37] The entitlement to a 'public hearing' has been held to necessarily imply a right to an oral hearing.[38] Equality of arms is an inherent feature of a fair trial.[39]

---

34 J McBride, *Human Rights and Criminal Procedure: The Case Law of the European Court of Human Rights* (Brussels, Council of Europe, 2018), 8.

35 *Murtazalieyeva v Russia* (Application no 36658/05), 18 December 2018, at [91].

36 *Schatschaschwili v Germany* (GC) [2015] ECHR 1113 at [100–101].

37 *Tierce and Others v San Marino* (Application nos 24954/94, 24971/94 and 24972/94), 25 July 2000 at [93].

38 *Döry v Sweden* (Application no 28394/95), 12 November 2002 at [37]

39 ECtHR, *Guide on Article 6 of the European Convention on Human Rights: Right to a fair trial (criminal limb)*, 30 April 2021, 34. Available at: www.echr.coe.int/documents/guide_art_6_criminal_eng.pdf.

1.58

Article 6(2) embodies the principle of the presumption of innocence. As well as including the fact that the burden of proof is on the prosecution, it requires that members of a court should not start with the preconceived idea that the accused has committed the offence charged.

1.59

Article 6(3)(a) provides that everyone charged with a criminal offence has the right to be informed promptly, in a language which they understand and in detail, of the nature and cause of the accusation against him.[40] Under Article 6(3)(b), everyone charged with a criminal offence has the right to have adequate time and facilities for the preparation of their defence.[41] Under Article 6(3)(c), everyone charged with a criminal offence has the right to defend themselves in person or through legal assistance of their own choosing, and if they do not have sufficient means to pay for legal assistance, to be given it free when the interests of justice so require.[42] Article 6(3)(d) provides that everyone charged with a criminal offence has the right to examine or have examined witnesses against him and to obtain the attendance and examination of witnesses on his behalf under the same conditions as witnesses against him. Under Article 6(3)(e), everyone charged with a criminal offence has the right to have the free assistance of an interpreter if they cannot understand or speak the language used in court. These rights are discussed in greater detail in the later chapters of this book.

Article 8 – right to private and family life

1.60

Article 8 sets important limits on the way in which offences can be investigated and evidence gathered. This is relevant to the restrictions which persons arrested and remanded in custody can be subjected and the publicity that can be given to certain aspects of criminal proceedings.

1.61

Although often seen through the context of the admissibility of evidence, a criminal practitioner needs to be aware that Article 8 arguments will often go beyond that (and beyond the four corners of the criminal trial) and it will be relevant in relation to a number of ancillary matters. For example, in *R (Catt)*

---

40 This has been described as an essential prerequisite for ensuring that the proceedings are fair: *Pelissier and Sassi v France* (Application no 25444/94), 17 December 1996 at [52].

41 What this entails will depend on the particular circumstances of the case, but the accused must have the opportunity to organise their defence in an appropriate way and must not be restricted in their ability to put all relevant arguments before the trial court: *Iglin v Ukraine* (Application no 39908/05), 12 January 2012 at [65]; *Gregačević v Croatia* (Application no 58331/09) 10 July 2012 at [51].

42 *Goddi v Italy* (1984) 6 EHRR 457. See also J B Rainey, E Wicks and C Ovey *Jacobs, White, and Ovey, The European Convention on Human Rights* 5th edn (OUP 2010), 291.

v Commissioner of Police of the Metropolis and another,[43] the Supreme Court found that the police's systematic collection and retention of previous convictions must be weighed by a principle of proportionality so that the rights of those previously convicted are not violated.[44] This concerned two individuals who had committed crimes years ago, who wanted to be removed from the national police database. The UKSC held that the systematic collection and retention by the police of data about the individuals disproportionately interfered with their right to privacy.

1.62

In *Gaugran v Chief Constable of the Police Service of Northern Ireland* [2015] UKSC 29, [2015] 2 WLR 1303,[45] the majority of the Supreme Court held that the indefinite retention of personal data (including DNA and fingerprint evidence) of a person convicted of a minor driving offence was compatible with Article 8 ECHR. Lord Kerr was the sole dissentient. His views were eventually endorsed by the ECtHR in *Gaughran v UK*,[46] which held that such retention was disproportionate, in particular because of its indefinite nature and the lack of link with the seriousness of the offending in question.

43 *R (Catt) v Commissioner of Police of the Metropolis and another* [2015] UKSC 9, [2015] 2 WLR 664.
44 Ibid at [33] and [60].
45 *Gaugran v Chief Constable of the Police Service of Northern Ireland* [2015] UKSC 29, [2015] 2 WLR 1303.
46 *Gaughran v UK* (Application no 45245/15), 13 June 2020.

2 Interpretation of the ECHR and the Human Rights Act 1998

James Robottom and Zubier Yazdani

INTRODUCTION

2.1

This chapter will provide an overview of the interpretative principles applied by the European Court of Human Rights (ECtHR) to the European Convention on Human Rights (ECHR), as well as to those set out in and developed by domestic courts under the Human Rights Act 1998 (HRA 1998).

THE EUROPEAN CONVENTION ON HUMAN RIGHTS – GENERAL PRINCIPLES OF INTERPRETATION

The Vienna Convention

2.2

As an international treaty, the interpretation of the Convention is guided by Articles 31 to 33 of the Vienna Convention on the Law of Treaties (Vienna, 23 May 1969).[1]

2.3

Article 31(1) of the Vienna Convention states that:

(i) A treaty shall be interpreted in good faith in accordance with the ordinary meaning to be given to the terms of the treaty in their context and in the light of its object and purpose.

Article 31(2) sets out that the context comprises a treaty's preamble and annexes, as well as certain agreements and instruments made in connection with it.

2.4

Article 32 states:

1 *Golder v United Kingdom* (1979–1980) 1 EHRR 524.

> **Supplementary means of interpretation**
>
> Recourse may be had to supplementary means of interpretation, including the preparatory work of the treaty and the circumstances of its conclusion, in order to confirm the meaning resulting from the application of article 31, or to determine the meaning when the interpretation according to article 31:
>
> (a) leaves the meaning ambiguous or obscure; or
>
> (b) leads to a result which is manifestly absurd or unreasonable.

2.5

Recourse may therefore be had to the *travaux préparatoires* to the ECHR. In accordance with Article 33 of the Vienna Convention, the English and French versions of the ECHR are equally authoritative, and the terms are presumed to have the same meaning in each.

Object and purpose of the ECHR

2.6

The 'main purpose' of the ECHR is said to be 'to lay down certain international standards to be observed by the Contracting States in their relations with persons under their jurisdiction'.[2] As a consequence, it is therefore 'necessary to seek the interpretation that is most appropriate in order to realise the aim and achieve the object of the treaty, not that which would restrict to the greatest possible degree the obligations undertaken by the Parties'.[3]

2.7

In *Ireland v United Kingdom*, the ECtHR held that:

> Unlike international treaties of the classic kind, the Convention comprises more than mere reciprocal engagements between contracting States. It creates, over and above a network of mutual, bilateral undertakings, objective obligations which, in the words of the Preamble, benefit from a 'collective enforcement'.[4]

2.8

The requirement under Article 31(1) of the Vienna Convention to interpret the terms of the treaty in their context means that the Convention must be read as a whole. Additionally, it should be interpreted in such a way as to promote

---

2 *Sunday Times v United Kingdom* (1979–1980) 2 EHRR 245 at [61], *Belgian Linguistics Case (Preliminary Objection)* (1967), Series A, No 5, p 19.

3 *Wemhoff v Germany* (1979–1980) 1 EHRR 55 at [8].

4 *Ireland v United Kingdom* (1979–1980) 2 EHRR 25 at [239].

internal consistency and harmony between its various provisions.[5] This may involve an analysis of the Protocols to the Convention as well as its Articles, although the requirements of a Protocol 'should not, in principle, be interpreted in such a way as to incorporate' its requirements 'in respect of states which have not ratified it.[6]

PARTICULAR INTERPRETATIVE TECHNIQUES

2.9

The ECtHR has developed a number of interpretative techniques designed to give effect to the object and purpose of the Convention.

Practical and effective

2.10

The ECHR 'is intended to guarantee not rights that are theoretical and illusory but rights that are practical and effective'.[7] Its object and purpose further 'require that its provisions be interpreted and applied so as to make its safeguards practical and effective'.[8]

2.11

In what is a departure from common practice for many common law lawyers, this may require an interpretation that goes beyond the wording of the article in question. As an example, in *Soering v United Kingdom*, the ECtHR held that although Article 1 of the ECHR sets the territorial reach of the Convention, and does not impose standards on external states, a decision to extradite a person to the US where he would be exposed to inhuman or degrading treatment 'would plainly be contrary to the spirit and intendment' of Article 3.[9] Further, Article 6(3)(c) ECHR requires the provision of the effective assistance from a lawyer, as opposed to simply one's nomination,[10] as the nominated lawyer may 'die, fall seriously ill, be prevented for a protracted period from acting or shirk his duties'.

5 *Austin v United Kingdom* (2012) 55 EHRR 14 at [54], *Stec and Others v the United Kingdom* (Application nos 65731/01 and 65900/01), 12 April 2006 at [48].
6 Ibid at [55].
7 *Marckx v Belgium* (1979–1980) 2 EHRR 330 at [31], *Airey v Ireland* (1979–80) 2 EHRR 305 at [24].
8 *Soering v United Kingdom* (1989) 11 EHRR 439.
9 Ibid at [88].
10 *Artico v Italy* (1981) 3 EHHR 1.

Creation of positive rights

2.12

The 'Practical and Effective' method of interpretation has played a significant role in developing the positive rights under the Convention. For instance, the procedural duty on the state to investigate killings by state agents,[11] and the requirement to put in place a spectrum of safeguards in national law to protect victims of human trafficking,[12] both came about because of a wider interpretation of the Convention than a plain reading of the words would suggest.

Broad construction

2.13

The terms of the ECHR are to be given a broad and purposive construction,[13] whereas exceptions and restrictions on its rights are to be interpreted narrowly. This principle applies not only to justifications relied upon by states for interferences with the qualified rights under Articles 8–11,[14] but also to specific exceptions to other rights, such as those on the right to life under Article 2[15] and the right to liberty under Article 5.

2.14

In relation to those exceptions, a wide interpretation 'would entail consequences incompatible with the notion of the rule of law from which the whole Convention draws its inspiration'.[16]

2.15

Article 18 of the ECHR states that the restrictions permitted under the specific rights to the Convention 'shall not be applied for any purpose other than those for which they have been prescribed'. Further, the ECtHR has stated that any conditions or limitations that are imposed on the exercise of a Convention right must not be allowed to *impair the essence of the right itself.*[17]

---

11 *Jordan v United Kingdom* (2003) 37 EHRR 2.

12 *Rantsev v Cyprus and Russia* (2010) 51 EHRR 1.

13 See, in respect of the right to a fair trial under Art 6, *Moreira de Azevedo v Portugal* (1991) 13 EHRR 721 at [66] and *De Cubber v Belgium* (1985) 7 EHRR 236 at [30].

14 See, in respect of Art 8, *Klass v Germany* (1979–1980) 2 EHRR 214 at [42]; in respect of Art 10, *Sunday Times v United Kingdom* at [65].

15 *McCann v United Kingdom* (1996) 21 EHRR 97 at [147–150].

16 *Engel v Netherlands* (1979–1980) 2 EHRR 387, at [37], see also *S v Denmark* (2019) 68 EHRR 17 at [73].

17 See, in respect of Art 6(1), *Ashingdane v United Kingdom* (1985) 7 EHRR 528 at [57].

Living instrument

2.16

It is an important principle that the Convention is 'a living instrument which should be interpreted in the light of present-day conditions'.[18] As a consequence, the interpretation of its provisions is not static over time, but develops in accordance with social and political progress, and commonly, accepted standards in Member States.[19] For example, the ECtHR held in 1978 that birching as a criminal punishment imposed by a court constituted degrading treatment contrary to Article 3 of the ECHR,[20] a view that may not have been shared in 1950. Likewise, despite the fact that human trafficking is not explicitly listed as being prohibited under Article 4 of the ECHR, in 2010 the ECtHR concluded that trafficking in itself is a violation of that Article.[21]

Stare Decisis

2.17

The interpretation of the Convention as a living instrument has meant that the ECtHR is willing to depart from its previous case law to provide greater rights protection.

2.18

In *Al Saadoon v United Kingdom*,[22] it was held that the express wording of Article 2 (which provides an exception to the right to life in the execution of a sentence of death imposed by the Court) had effectively been amended by the adoption of contracting states of Protocol 13 to the Convention (as well as state practice). The consequence was that there was an outright prohibition of the death penalty. A further example is *Sutherland v United Kingdom*.[23] There, the ECtHR held, contrary to its earlier finding in *X v United Kingdom*,[24] that the application of the offence of gross indecency to consensual sexual activity between 16- and 17-year-old males was a breach of Articles 8 and 14.

Autonomous terms

2.19

Although the terminology used in the Convention rights may correspond to a specific concept in domestic law, its provisions must be given an autonomous

18 *Tyrer v United Kingdom* (1979–1980) 2 EHRR 1 at [292].
19 Ibid at [31].
20 Ibid.
21 *Rantsev v Cyprus and Russia* (2010) 51 EHRR 1, *SM v Croatia* (2021) 72 EHRR 1 at [292].
22 *Al Saadoon v United Kingdom* (2010) 51 EHRR 9 relying on *Ocalan v Turkey* (2005) 18 BHRC 293 and departing from the position in *Soering v UK*.
23 *Sutherland v United Kingdom* (1997) 24 EHRR CD 22.
24 *X v United Kingdom* (1980) 19 DR 66.

interpretation to ensure that there is a uniformity of application across contracting states.

2.20

Of particular relevance for English criminal law is the context of due process rights. The ECtHR has established specific free-standing criteria for establishing whether any domestic proceedings are 'criminal' for the purposes of Article 6 of the ECHR. As a consequence, cases that domestic lawyers may consider to be civil in nature would attract Article 6 protection (and vice versa).[25]

IMPLIED RIGHTS

2.21

The ECtHR has consistently read into the Convention articles rights and obligations that are not set out in its original text. In accordance with Article 31(3)(c) of the Vienna Convention 'any relevant rules of international law applicable in the relations between the parties' shall be taken into account in determining the ordinary meaning of the ECHR's terms.

2.22

The ECtHR has frequently relied upon other international instruments in order to imply rights in the text of the Convention. In *Soering v UK*, the ECtHR cited the United Nations Convention Against Torture and Other Cruel, Inhuman or Degrading Treatment or Punishment (New York, 4 February 1985) and stated that the:

> fact that a specialised treaty should spell out in detail a specific obligation attaching to the prohibition of torture does not mean that an essentially similar obligation is not already inherent in the general terms of Article 3 of the European Convention.[26]

2.23

Noting that the International Covenant on Civil and Political Rights (New York, 16 December 1966), but not Article 6, contains a right against self-incrimination, the Court has read into the text of Article 6 the right to remain silent and the privilege against self-incrimination on the basis that they 'are generally recognised international standards which lie at the heart of the notion of a fair procedure'.[27]

25 *Engel v Netherlands* (1979–1980) 1 EHRR 647.

26 *Soering v UK* at [87].

27 *Saunders v United Kingdom* (1997) 23 EHRR 313 at [5] and [68].

2.24

Likewise, in *Rantsev v Cyprus and Russia*,[28] the ECtHR read the definition of human trafficking as that set out in the United Nations Palermo Protocol[29] and the Council of Europe Convention on Action Against Trafficking in Human Beings 2005[30] into Article 4.

POSITIVE OBLIGATIONS

The Convention as a source of state obligations

2.25

Importantly, the ECtHR has interpreted the Convention as placing positive, as well as negative, obligations upon state parties.

2.26

This originally derives from the general obligation in Article 1 of the ECHR to 'secure to everyone within their jurisdiction the rights and freedoms' in the Convention. In addition, it has been inferred from the specific terms of certain articles, such as the instruction that '[e]veryone's life shall be protected by law' in Article 2. This extends in certain circumstances to obligations to ensure that rights are not breached even as between private parties.[31]

Positive obligations and specific articles

2.27

Positive obligations have taken on particular significance in the ECtHR's case law since its landmark decision in *Osman v United Kingdom*[32] regarding the operational duty to protect life. The framework of the positive obligations under the unqualified rights – Articles 2, 3 and 4 – is broadly similar, each entails:

(1) a general duty to put in place a legislative and administrative framework to prohibit and punish conduct falling within the scope of the article and to protect victims from breaches;

(2) the duty, in certain circumstances, to take operational measures to protect victims, or potential victims; and

28 *Rantsev v Cyprus and Russia* (2010) 51 EHRR 1.

29 The Protocol to Prevent, Suppress and Punish Trafficking in Persons, especially Women and Children (New York, 12 December 2000), supplementing the United Nations Convention against Transnational Organised Crime (Palmero, 12 December 2000).

30 *Rantsev v Cyprus and Russia* (2010) 51 EHRR 1 at [295]

31 See, eg, in respect of the general duty under Art 4 *Siliadin v France* (2006) 43 EHRR 16; *Osman v United Kingdom* (2000) 29 EHRR 24 regarding the operational duty under Art 2; and *O'Keefe v Ireland* (2014) 59 EHRR 15 in respect of Art 3.

32 *Osman v United Kingdom* (2000) 29 EHRR 245.

(3) a procedural obligation to investigate situations of potential breach.[33]

2.28

Other Convention rights have also been construed as giving rise to specific positive obligations. Article 5(1), for instance, imposes a positive duty to take appropriate steps to provide protection against unlawful interference with the rights in question,[34] and Article 6 paragraphs (1) and (3) read together require Contracting States to take positive steps to enable an accused to examine or have examined witnesses against him.[35]

Limitations on positive obligations

2.29

The positive obligations under the Convention are not, however, unlimited. For example, the operational duty under Article 2 must be interpreted in a way which does not impose an impossible or disproportionate burden on the authorities when bearing in mind the difficulties involved in policing modern societies, the unpredictability of human conduct and the operational choices which must be made in terms of priority and resources.[36] The positive obligations under specific articles are dealt with in the relevant chapters of this book.

Interpreting qualified rights

2.30

The qualified rights under Articles 8–11 share a structure which means it is necessary to conduct a stepped analysis regarding whether an article has been breached. It must initially be shown there was an interference with the substantive right under the first paragraph in order for the Article to be engaged. Once that is satisfied, attention switches under the second paragraphs to assess whether the interference is 'as prescribed by' or 'in accordance with' the law.

2.31

Thirdly, it must be 'necessary in a democratic society' in pursuit of one of the aims set out in the Articles. The adjective 'necessary' must not be given too high a threshold. It is not synonymous with 'indispensable', but 'neither has it the flexibility of such expressions as "admissible", "ordinary", "useful", "reasonable" or "desirable"'. It implies the existence of a 'pressing social need'.[37] In particular, the interference must be 'proportionate to the legitimate aim pursued'.[38]

33 See *SM v Croatia* (Application no 60561/14), 25 June 2020 at [305–306].
34 *El-Masri v Macedonia* (2013) 57 EHRR 25 at [239].
35 *Sadak v Turkey* (2003) 36 EHRR 26 at [67].
36 *Osman v UK* at [116].
37 *Sunday Times v United Kingdom* at [59]; *Handyside v United Kingdom* (1979–1980) 1 EHRR 737 at [49].
38 *Handyside v UK* at [49]; *Sunday Times v UK* at [62].

Proportionality

2.32

A significant number of Articles to the Convention entail an assessment of proportionality. The term 'proportionality' is not actually used in the Convention, but since the Strasbourg Court's early case law, the concept of proportionality has gone on to play a central role in ECHR law and is 'inherent in the whole of the Convention'.[39]

2.33

The burden is on the state to establish that an interference is proportionate.[40] It is for the court to determine whether a particular measure is proportionate to the legitimate aim pursued and whether the reasons given by the national authorities to justify it are 'relevant and sufficient'.[41] In doing so it will assess 'whether a fair balance was struck between the demands of the general interest of the community and the requirements of the protection of the individual's fundamental rights'.[42]

2.34

The intensity of review will differ according to the right in issue and the context in which the question arises. In *Bank Mellat v Her Majesty's Treasury (No 2)*, Lord Reed observed that the ECtHR has described its approach to striking such a balance in different ways in different contexts, and in practice often approaches the matter in a relatively broad-brush way. By contrast the domestic courts have adopted a more structured approach to the assessment of proportionality of a given measure.[43] This is consistent with the structure of the Convention system and the principles of subsidiarity and the margin of appreciation.

SUBSIDIARITY AND THE MARGIN OF APPRECIATION

The principle of subsidiarity

2.35

The principles of 'subsidiarity' and the 'margin of appreciation' afforded to contracting states are referred to in the Preamble to the Convention and have important implications for principles of interpretation under the ECHR. The principle of subsidiarity dictates that it is primarily for the domestic legal systems of contracting states to safeguard human rights:

39 *Soering v United Kingdom* at [89].
40 *Smith and Grady v United Kingdom* (1999) 29 EHRR 493.
41 *Barthold v Germany* (1985) 7 EHRR 383.
42 *Sporrong and Lonroth v Sweden* (1982) 5 EHRR 35 at [69].
43 *Bank Mellat v Her Majesty's Treasury (No 2)* [2014] AC 700 at [70–74]. The approach to an assessment of proportionality undertaken by the domestic courts is at [74].

> The Convention leaves to each Contracting State, in the first place, the task of securing the rights and freedoms it enshrines. The institutions created by it make their own contribution to this task but they become involved only through contentious proceedings and once all domestic remedies have been exhausted.[44]

The ECtHR thus does not 'assume the role of the competent national authorities'. Its role is limited to ensuring the conformity of national measures with the Convention.[45]

2.36

States may therefore provide greater human rights protection than required by the ECHR. Article 53 provides that nothing in the Convention 'shall be construed as limiting or derogating from any of the human rights … which may be ensured' under national law.

Margin of appreciation

2.37

In theory, the concept of the margin of appreciation applies only to qualified rights, as there can be no room for state discretion in the protection of absolute rights. However, where the positive obligations under Articles 2, 3, and 4 are concerned, the ECtHR does afford states a margin of compliance. Thus, in *Lambert v France*, the Grand Chamber found that the legislative framework for withdrawal of medical treatment in France was such as to fall within the wide margin of appreciation afforded to states in the area of the end of life (under both Articles 2 and 8).[46]

2.38

Nevertheless, the margin of appreciation is of most significance to the assessment of the proportionality of a measure under qualified rights. Like the principle of subsidiarity, the concept of the margin of appreciation emphasises the primary role of national authorities in protecting rights under the Convention. In *James v United Kingdom*,[47] the ECtHR stated '[b]ecause of their direct knowledge of their society and its needs, the national authorities are in principle better placed than the international judge to appreciate what is 'in the public interest''.

2.39

Further, 'Under the system of protection established by the Convention, it is thus for the national authorities to make the initial assessment both of the existence of a problem of public concern warranting measures … and of the remedial action to be taken.' Contracting states therefore 'enjoy a certain

---

44 *Handyside v UK* at [48].

45 *The Belgian Linguistics Case* (1979–1980) 1 EHRR 252 at 10.

46 *Lambert v France* (2016) 62 EHRR 2 at [144–148].

47 *James v United Kingdom* (1986) 8 EHRR 123.

margin of appreciation'.[48] In *Handyside*, the ECtHR (in a judgment upholding the criminalisation of a publication under the Obscene Publications Acts as not being a breach of freedom of expression under Article 10 of the ECHR), emphasised that the margin 'is given both to the domestic legislator … and to the bodies, judicial amongst others, that are called upon to interpret and apply the laws in force'.[49]

2.40

The margin of appreciation is not unlimited, however. The ECtHR is empowered under the Convention to 'give the final ruling'[50] on whether a measure is reconcilable with the right in question. It therefore remains ultimately for the ECtHR to examine 'the interference complained of in the light of the case as a whole and determine whether it was 'proportionate to the legitimate aim pursued' and whether the reasons adduced by the national authorities to justify it are 'relevant and sufficient'.[51] The 'domestic margin of appreciation thus goes hand in hand with European supervision'.[52]

2.41

The margin of appreciation is not governed by hard or fast legal rules but varies dependent on context. Factors that may affect the width afforded to a state in respect of a given measure include: the nature of the right in question; the level of the interference with the right;[53] the nature and quality of the state's justification;[54] and the extent to which there is consensus among Member States as to how an issue is dealt with (the greater the consensus, the narrower the margin).[55]

THE HUMAN RIGHTS ACT 1998 – PRINCIPLES OF INTERPRETATION

The statutory scheme

2.42

Sections 2 to 4 of the Human Rights Act 1998 provide a self-contained scheme in relation to the interpretation of ECHR rights in English law. Subsection 3(1) states that:

48 Ibid at [46].
49 *Handyside v UK* at [48].
50 Ibid at [49].
51 *Vogt v Germany* (1996) 21 EHRR 205, at [52(iii)].
52 *Handyside v UK* at [49].
53 *Dudgeon v UK* (1982) 4 EHRR 149 at [61].
54 *Gafgen v Germany* (2011) 52 EHRR 1 at [175]; *Sunday Times v United Kingdom* at [59].
55 Ibid at [175].

> So far as it is possible to do so, primary legislation and subordinate legislation must be read and given effect in a way which is compatible with the Convention rights.

2.43

In *Poplar Housing and Regeneration Community Association Ltd v Donoghue*, Lord Woolf CJ stated:

> It is difficult to overestimate the importance of section 3 … Subject to the section not requiring the court to go beyond that which is possible, it is mandatory in its terms … When the court interprets legislation usually its primary task is to identify the intention of Parliament. Now, when section 3 applies, the courts have to adjust their traditional role in relation to interpretation so as to give effect to the direction contained in section 3.[56]

2.44

In interpreting domestic legislation under section 3, the first question is whether the 'natural' interpretation, the particular statute at issues would otherwise be a breach of the ECHR.[57] Section 3 applies to all legislation passed either before or after the HRA 1998.[58] It does not entitle a court to legislate,[59] but presupposes that 'not all provisions of primary legislation can be rendered Convention compliant'.[60]

The approach of the courts

2.45

The leading authority on the scope of the interpretative obligation under section 3 remains *Ghaidan v Mendoza*,[61] where the House of Lords articulated the limits of the duty in different ways.

2.46

A section 3 interpretation cannot 'adopt a meaning inconsistent with a fundamental feature of the legislation'. Whilst it can imply words into provisions, these must 'go with the grain of the legislation',[62] it cannot remove the very core and essence and pith and substance of the measure.[63]

56 *Poplar Housing and Regeneration Community Association Ltd v Donoghue* [2001] EWCA Civ 595, [2002] QB 48 at [72].
57 Ibid at [73].
58 HRA 1998, s 3(2)(a).
59 *Poplar Housing* at [72]
60 *In Re S (Children)(Care Order: Implementation of Care Plan)* [2002] UKHL 10, [2002] 2 AC 291 at [39].
61 *Ghaidan v Mendoza* [2004] UKHL 30.
62 Ibid at [33] per Lord Nicholls.
63 Ibid at [111] per Lord Rodger.

2.47

In *Ghaidan v Mendoza,* the House of Lords interpreted the words 'as his wife or husband' in the Rent Act 1977 to read '*as if they were his* wife or husband' in order to avert discrimination against a homosexual couple in breach of Articles 14 and 8.[64]

2.48

The limits of the section 3 function were demonstrated in *R (Anderson) v Secretary of State for the Home Department,*[65] where the House of Lords held that section 29 of the Crime Sentences Act 1997 (that gave the power to release mandatory life sentence prisoners to the Home Secretary) could not be read down so as to give the power to a judge or the parole board. To do so, Lord Bingham stated, 'would not be judicial interpretation but judicial vandalism'.[66]

The requirement to take Strasbourg authority into account

2.49

Section 2 of the HRA 1998 provides that:

> (1) A court or tribunal determining a question which has arisen in connection with a Convention right must take into account any—
>
> (a) judgment, decision, declaration or advisory opinion of the European Court of Human Rights,
>
> (b) opinion of the Commission given in a report adopted under Article 31 of the Convention,
>
> (c) decision of the Commission in connection with Article 26 or 27(2) of the Convention, or
>
> (d) decision of the Committee of Ministers taken under Article 46 of the Convention,
>
> whenever made or given, so far as, in the opinion of the court or tribunal, it is relevant to the proceedings in which that question has arisen.[67]

2.50

In *R (Ullah) v Special Adjudicator,*[68] Lord Bingham stated in relation to the duty under section 2 of the HRA that while Strasbourg case law is:

64 Ibid at [51].
65 *R (Anderson) v Secretary of State for the Home Department* [2002] UKHL 46.
66 Ibid at [30].
67 This not only includes all decisions and judgments of the ECtHR and Commission but also ECtHR advisory opinions and decisions of the Committee of Ministers taken under Art 46 of the Convention (see s 2(a)–(d)).
68 *R (Ullah) v Special Adjudicator* [2004] UKHL 26.

> not strictly binding … courts should, in the absence of some special circumstances, follow any clear and constant jurisprudence of the Strasbourg court. From this it follows that a national court subject to a duty such as that imposed by section 2 should not without strong reason dilute or weaken the effect of the Strasbourg case law… It is of course open to member states to provide for rights more generous than those guaranteed by the Convention, but such provision should not be the product of interpretation of the Convention by national courts, since the meaning of the Convention should be uniform throughout the states party to it. The duty of national courts is to keep pace with the Strasbourg jurisprudence as it evolves over time: no more, but certainly no less.[69]

2.51

The scope of the so called '*Ullah*' or 'mirror' principle, has been the subject of a much judicial and academic discussion, which is outside the remit of this text. In *R (AB) Secretary of State for Justice*, Lord Reed stated:

> … it is not the function of our domestic courts to establish new principles of Convention law. But that is not to say that they are unable to develop the law in relation to Convention rights beyond the limits of the Strasbourg case law. In situations which have not yet come before the European court, they can and should aim to anticipate, where possible, how the European court might be expected to decide the case, on the basis of the principles established in its case law.[70]

Horncastle and Al-Khawaja

2.52

There are clear occasions on which the domestic courts have been willing to interpret Convention rights beyond the limits of the Strasbourg case law in this way.[71] Where Strasbourg jurisprudence is 'clear and constant', English courts should follow it unless there are specific circumstances that justify a departure.[72]

2.53

One such specific circumstance was where the ECtHR has misunderstood principles of domestic law. In *R v Horncastle*,[73] a seven-judge panel of the Supreme Court declined to follow the decision of the ECtHR in *Al-Khawaja v*

---

69 *R (Ullah) v Special Adjudicator* at [20]. See also *R (Alconbury Developments Ltd) v Secretary of State for the Environment, Transport and the Regions* [2001] UKHL 23, [2003] 2 AC 295.

70 *R (AB) Secretary of State for Justice* [2021] UKSC 28, at [59]. See further *R (Elan-Cane) v Secretary of State for the Home Department* [2021] UKSC 56, [2022] 2 WLR 133.

71 See, as examples, *Rabone v Pennine Care NHS Trust* [2012] UKSC 2, [2012] 2 AC 72; *R (Limbuela) v Secretary of State for the Home Department* [2005] UKHL 66, [2006] 1 AC 396; *Re P (Adoption: Unmarried Couple)* [2008] UKHL 38, [2009] 1 AC 173.

72 *Manchester City Council v Pinnock (No 1)* [2010] UKSC 45, [2011] 2 AC 104 at [48].

73 *R v Horncastle* [2009] UKSC 14, [2010] 2 AC 373.

United Kingdom,[74] that there would be a breach of Article 6 of the ECHR where hearsay evidence was the 'sole or decisive' evidence in a prosecution:[75]

> The requirement to 'take into account' the Strasbourg jurisprudence will normally result in the domestic court applying principles that are clearly established by the Strasbourg court. There will, however, be rare occasions where the domestic court has concerns as to whether a decision of the Strasbourg court sufficiently appreciates or accommodates particular aspects of our domestic process. In such circumstances it is open to the domestic court to decline to follow the Strasbourg decision, giving reasons for adopting this course. This is likely to give the Strasbourg court the opportunity to reconsider the particular aspect of the decision that is in issue, so that there takes place what may prove to be a valuable dialogue between the domestic court and the Strasbourg court. This is such a case.

2.54

The Supreme Court held that where it was satisfied that the ECtHR had insufficiently appreciated or accommodated a particular aspect of the domestic process, a domestic court could decline to follow that decision. It considered that, in *Al-Khawaja v UK*, the ECtHR had failed to understand the extent to which the hearsay provisions of the Criminal Justice Act 2003, which had to be read as a complete Code, provided sufficient safeguards to ensure defendants received a fair trial in compliance with Article 6.

2.55

Other circumstances that may justify a departure from clear and constant Strasbourg jurisprudence include where it is 'inconsistent with some fundamental substantive or procedural aspect' of English law, where it overlooks or misunderstands some argument or point of principle,[76] or where the ECtHR is simply wrong.[77] In determining this question, a relevant factor is likely to be whether there is Grand Chamber Strasbourg authority on the issue.[78]

The authority of the Supreme Court and the House of Lords remains binding on lower courts, even where subsequent ECtHR case law establishes an incompatibility, although the Court of Appeal may depart from its previous decisions to prevent an ECHR breach.[79]

74 *Al-Khawaja v United Kingdom* (2009) 49 EHRR 1.
75 *R v Horncastle* at [11], per Lord Phillips.
76 *Manchester CC v Pinnock* at [48].
77 *R (Hallam) v Secretary of State for Justice* [2019] UKSC 2, [2020] AC 279.
78 *Poshteh v Kensington and Chelsea Royal London Borough Council* [2017] UKSC 36, [2017] AC 624 at [36].
79 *R (RJM) v Secretary of State for Work and Pensions* [2008] UKHL 63, [2009] 1 AC 311.

RETROSPECTIVITY

2.56

The general rule is that Convention rights cannot be relied upon under the HRA 1998, nor proceedings brought under it unless the act or omission complained of took place after its coming into force on 2 October 2000. However, there is an exception where an individual wishes to invoke his Convention rights in proceedings that have been brought at the instigation of a public authority. Then Convention rights may be invoked in defence under the HRA 1998 'whenever the act in question took place'.[80]

2.57

Such instances will include the vast majority of criminal proceedings. In *R v Lambert*,[81] the House of Lords held that this retrospective application does not apply to appeals where the trial took place prior to October 2000. In *R v Kansal (No 2)*,[82] a majority of the House of Lords held that *R v Lambert* had been wrongly decided but declined to depart from it and it remains good law.

80 HRA 1998, subs 7(1) and 22(4).
81 *R v Lambert* [2001] UKHL 37.
82 *R v Kansal (No 2)* [2001] UKHL 62.

3 The Human Rights Act 1998 – substance

Helen Law

INTRODUCTION

3.1

This chapter sets out an overview of the substantive provisions of the Human Rights Act 1998 (HRA 1998) where those provisions are not dealt with in more detail elsewhere in this book.

SECTION 1: THE CONVENTION RIGHTS

3.2

Section 1(1) states:

> In this Act 'the Convention rights' means the rights and fundamental freedoms set out in—
>
> (a) Articles 2 to 12 and 14 of the Convention,
>
> (b) Articles 1 to 3 of the First Protocol, and
>
> (c) Article 1 of the Thirteenth Protocol,
>
> as read with Articles 16 to 18 of the Convention.

Those Articles are set out in Schedule 1 to the HRA 1998.[1]

The status of the 'Convention Rights' under the HRA 1998

3.3

Contrary to popular public perception, the HRA 1998 does *not* incorporate the ECHR into English law. Instead, it creates a new set of rights under English law which take as their framework the comparable, but distinct rights which exist under the ECHR.

1 See HRA 1998, s 1(3).

3.4

The consequence is that there are some differences between some of the substantive rights under the ECHR and the rights of the same name under the HRA 1998 in English law. Whilst there was some doubt about this in the initial case law after the Act came into force, Lord Nicholls *In re McKerr*[2] explained:

> Having had the advantage of much fuller arguments I respectfully consider that some of these courts, including the Divisional Court in the Hurst case[3] and the Court of Appeal in the Khan case,[4] fell into error by failing to keep clearly in mind the distinction between (1) rights arising under the Convention and (2) rights created by the Human Rights Act by reference to the Convention.
>
> These two sets of rights now exist side by side. But there are significant differences between them. The former existed before the enactment of the Human Rights Act 1998 and they continue to exist. They are not as such part of this country's law because the Convention does not form part of this country's law. That is still the position. These rights, arising under the Convention, are to be contrasted with rights created by the Human Rights Act. The latter came into existence for the first time on 2 October 2000.
>
> They are part of this country's law. The extent of these rights, created as they were by the Human Rights Act, depends upon the proper interpretation of that Act. It by no means follows that the continuing existence of a right arising under the Convention in respect of an act occurring before the Human Rights Act came into force will be mirrored by a corresponding right created by the Human Rights Act. Whether it finds reflection in this way in the Human Rights Act depends upon the proper interpretation of the Human Rights Act.

3.5

It is for this reason that the much-used description that the HRA 'incorporates' the ECHR rights into English is, as Lord Hoffmann explained in *McKerr*, at para 65:

> … a misleading metaphor. What the Act has done is to create domestic rights expressed in the same terms as those contained in the Convention. But they are domestic rights, not international rights. Their source is the statute, not the Convention. They are available against specific public authorities, not the United Kingdom as a state. And their meaning and application is a matter for domestic courts, not the court in Strasbourg.

---

2 *In Re McKerr* [2004] UKHL 12, [2004] 1 WLR 807 [at 26].

3 *Hurst v Coroner for the Northern District of London* [2003] EWHC 1721 (Admin), [2004] UKHRR 139.

4 *R (Khan) v Secretary of State for Health* [2003] EWCA Civ 1129, [2004] 1 WLR 971.

The regular use of 'incorporation' by the English courts cannot be taken as intended to undermine the constitutional and legislative position as described in *McKerr*: see Kerr J in *R (Minton Morrill) v Lord Chancellor*.[5] The term is used merely as a 'convenient shorthand'.

The omission of Article 13

3.6

Article 13 is the right to an effective remedy for a breach of a Convention Right. It is not included in Schedule 1 to the HRA 1998 because its function is to ensure that there is a direct and effective remedy in the English courts for violations of the Convention Rights. If the HRA 1998 or the Court's application of it fails to provide an effective remedy, an individual can still bring a claim for violation of Article 13 (and the underlying Convention Right) in the ECtHR.

3.7

The UK has been found to be in violation of Article 13 on 34 occasions between 1959 and 2020.[6] In recent years, that has included failures in the domestic law regime under the HRA 1998 (see, eg, *Hammerton v UK*[7] and *SW v UK*[8] concerning the exclusion of damages for judicial acts done in good faith under section 9(3)[9]) and breach of Rule 39 interim measures granted by the ECtHR (see, eg, *Al-Saadoon & Mufdhi v UK*[10] in the context of Articles 2 and 3).

INTERPRETATION AND INCOMPATIBILITY

Sections 2–3 – interpretation

3.8

The question of the interpretation of both Convention right, and interpretation in domestic law, has been considered in full in Chapter 2. The HRA 1998 was designed to strike a balance, preserving Parliament's sovereignty over the enactment and amendment of statutes through the compatibility procedure in sections 4, 5, 10 and 19, whilst giving the Courts a 'powerful tool' of construction in section 3, the use of which is not optional but obligatory.[11]

5 *R (Minton Morrill) v Lord Chancellor* [2017] EWHC 612 (Admin), at paras 26–27.
6 See www.echr.coe.int/Documents/Stats_violation_1959_2020_ENG.pdf.
7 See *Hammerton v UK* [2016] ECHR 272.
8 See *SW v UK* [2021] ECHR 541.
9 See Chapter 4 on Remedies.
10 *Saadoon & Mufdhi v UK* (2010) 51 EHRR 9.
11 See Lord Nicholls in *Re S (Children) (Care Order: Implementation of Care Plan)* [2002] UKHL 10, [2002] 2 AC 291 at paras 37–39.

3.9

The House of Lords decision in *Ghaidan v Godin-Mendoza*[12] remains the leading authority on the interpretation of section 3. Lord Nicholls explained, at paragraph 30, that the section is of:

> an unusual and far-reaching character … [and]… may require a court to depart from the unambiguous meaning the legislation would otherwise bear. In the ordinary course the interpretation of legislation involves seeking the intention reasonably to be attributed to Parliament in using the language in question. Section 3 may require the court to depart from this legislative intention, that is, depart from the intention of the Parliament which enacted the legislation.

3.10

In *Sheldrake v DPP*,[13] a case concerning the legality of reverse burdens of proof in criminal proceedings, Lord Bingham summarised, at paragraph 28, the key principles from *Ghaidan*:

> **First**, the interpretative obligation under section 3 is a very strong and far reaching one, and may require the court to depart from the legislative intention of Parliament. **Secondly**, a Convention-compliant interpretation under section 3 is the primary remedial measure and a declaration of incompatibility under section 4 an exceptional course. **Thirdly**, it is to be noted that during the passage of the Bill through Parliament the promoters of the Bill told both Houses that it was envisaged that the need for a declaration of incompatibility would rarely arise. **Fourthly**, there is a limit beyond which a Convention-compliant interpretation is not possible, such limit being illustrated by R(Anderson) v Secretary of State for the Home Department [2003] 1 AC 837 and Bellinger v Bellinger (Lord Chancellor intervening) [2003] 2 AC 467.
>
> In explaining why a Convention-compliant interpretation may not be possible, members of the committee used differing expressions: such an interpretation would be incompatible with the underlying thrust of the legislation, or would not go with the grain of it, or would call for legislative deliberation, or would change the substance of a provision completely, or would remove its pith and substance, or would violate a cardinal principle of the legislation (paras 33, 49, 110–113, 116). All of these expressions, as I respectfully think, yield valuable insights, but none of them should be allowed to supplant the simple test enacted in the Act: 'So far as it is possible to do so …' While the House declined to try to formulate precise rules (para 50), it was thought that cases in

12 *Ghaidan v Godin-Mendoza* [2004] UKHL 30, [2004] 2 AC 557.
13 *Sheldrake v DPP* [2004] UKHL 43, [2005] 1 AC 264.

which section 3 could not be used would in practice be fairly easy to identify.[14]

Sections 4, 5 and 10 – declarations of incompatibility

3.11

Where there is an apparent incompatibility between a legislative provision and the HRA 1998 and it is not possible to use the interpretative power under section 3 to remedy it, certain courts may make a declaration of incompatibility under section 4, which provides:

> (1) Subsection (2) applies in any proceedings in which a court determines whether a provision of primary legislation is compatible with a Convention right.
>
> (2) If the court is satisfied that the provision is incompatible with a Convention right, it may make a declaration of that incompatibility.
>
> (3) Subsection (4) applies in any proceedings in which a court determines whether a provision of subordinate legislation, made in the exercise of a power conferred by primary legislation, is compatible with a Convention right.
>
> (4) If the court is satisfied—
>
> (a) that the provision is incompatible with a Convention right, and
>
> (b) that (disregarding any possibility of revocation) the primary legislation concerned prevents removal of the incompatibility, it may make a declaration of that incompatibility.
>
> (5) In this section "court" means—
>
> (a) the Supreme Court;
>
> (b) the Judicial Committee of the Privy Council;
>
> (c) the Court Martial Appeal Court;
>
> (d) in Scotland, the High Court of Justiciary sitting otherwise than as a trial court or the Court of Session;
>
> (e) in England and Wales or Northern Ireland, the High Court or the Court of Appeal.
>
> (f) the Court of Protection, in any matter being dealt with by the President of the Family Division, the Chancellor of the High Court or a puisne judge of the High Court.
>
> (6) A declaration under this section ("a declaration of incompatibility")—

---

14 See also Baroness Hale in *Gilham v Ministry of Justice* [2019] UKSC 44, [2019] 1 WLR 5905, at para 39.

(a) does not affect the validity, continuing operation or enforcement of the provision in respect of which it is given; and

(b) is not binding on the parties to the proceedings in which it is made.

In any case where the Court is considering whether to make a declaration of incompatibility, the Crown is entitled to be informed of that and has the right to be joined to the proceedings to make submissions.[15]

3.12

Section 4 is a power of last resort. As Lord Steyn described it in *Ghaidan,* the making of a declaration under section 4 'must always be an exceptional course' because the section 3 power confers a strong – but nonetheless rebuttable – presumption in favour of a Convention compliant interpretation.[16] Section 4 only provides a power, and does not impose an obligation, to make a declaration where there is an established incompatibility. A declaration is a discretionary remedy, but 'will be influenced by the usual considerations which apply to the grant of declarations'.[17]

3.13

Whilst in practice it will be rare for an incompatibility to be found but no declaration to be made, this is not impossible. Examples include where the legislation in issue is in relation to legislation that is obsolete[18], or where the question is one that involves the resolution of complex political or social issues that is best left for Parliament.[19] It will not be sufficient for the government to assert that steps are already being taken to remedy the incompatibility, or to ask for a period of time to do so. The appropriate course is still for the declaration to be made.[20]

3.14

Conversely, the Courts have not ruled out the possibility of making a declaration where there is a breach on the face of the legislation but where the factual basis in the particular case is not made out. As Lord Hoffmann explained in

---

15 HRA 1998, s 5.

16 *Ghaidan* [50].

17 *Donoghue v Poplar Housing and Regeneration Community Association Ltd* [2001] EWCA Civ 595, [2002] QB 48.

18 *R (Rusbridger) v Attorney General* [2003] UKHL 38, [2004] 1 AC 357, where the House of Lords declined to make a declaration which was sought by the applicant, editor of *The Guardian*, despite the existence of an incompatibility with a piece of criminal legislation concerning treason that was essentially obsolete. Lord Rodger (who was in the minority on other aspects of the decision, but in the majority, with Lord Walker and Lord Hutton, on this issue) explained that it was not for the Courts to 'spring-clean' the statute book and making a declaration in this case would serve no purpose other than furthering the applicant's campaigning.

19 *R (Nicklinson) v Ministry of Justice* [2014] UKSC 38, [2015] AC 657. Mr Nicklinson had been left paralysed from the neck down following a stroke and wished to end his life but could not do so without assistance. As an alternative to a declaration that would permit a doctor in assisting his suicide, he sought a declaration that 'the current state of the law' was incompatible with his Art 8 rights.

20 *Bellinger v Bellinger* [2003] UKHL 21, [2003] 2 AC 467, [51–55].

R (Nasseri) v Secretary of State for the Home Department,[21] whilst it would be rare to do so:

> I would not therefore wish to exclude the possibility that in a case in which a public authority was not, on the facts, acting incompatibly with a Convention right, the court might consider it convenient to make a declaration that if he had been so acting, a provision of primary legislation which made it lawful for him to do so would have been incompatible with Convention rights.

3.15

The power to issue declarations of incompatibility is limited to the higher courts (s 19(5)), so there is no power for a magistrates or crown court to make such an order.

3.16

A potential way around this lack of power is illustrated by the approach of the applicant (at that point a criminal defendant) in *R v DPP ex parte Kebilene*.[22] The defendant was charged with a terrorism offence which required the DPP's consent and which contained a reverse burden of proof. He stood trial after the HRA 1998 had received the Royal Assent, but before it came into force. Before the Crown Court he argued that the reverse burden violated Article 6. The Crown Court agreed but had no power to issue a declaration of incompatibility (that provision not even yet being in force and in any event not available to the Crown Court).

3.17

As a result, Mr Kebilene then asked the DPP to reconsider his decision to consent to the prosecution in light of the Crown Court's ruling that it violated Article 6. The DPP refused and Mr Kebilene challenged *that* refusal by way of judicial review. He ultimately lost in the House of Lords, but only because the House found that judicial review was unnecessary where there was a remedy in the Crown Court as the relevant offence could be read as imposing an evidential presumption and not a reverse burden. As of December 2020, declarations of incompatibility had been made in only 43 cases, of which nine were subsequently overturned on appeal.[23]

3.18

Where a declaration is made, the offending legislation remains in force exactly as before (see s 4(6)), but the relevant Minister is granted the power under s 10 to take remedial action. That same power is triggered where it appears to

---

21 *R (Nasseri) v Secretary of State for the Home Department* [2009] UKHL 23, [2010] 1 AC 1, at para 19.

22 *R v DPP ex parte Kebilen [1999] UKHL 43, [2000] 2 AC 326.*

23 *The Government's Independent Human Rights Act Review*, Joint Committee on Human Rights (8 July 2021, HC 89) at [124].

the Minister that a finding of the ECtHR means that a provision of domestic legislation is incompatible with the HRA 1998 (ss 10(1)(b)).

3.19

If triggered, section 10(2) provides that:

> If a Minister of the Crown considers that there are compelling reasons for proceeding under this section, he may by order make such amendments to the legislation as he considers necessary to remove the incompatibility.

3.20

Where the incompatibility is in subordinate legislation, section 10(3) confirms that the remedial power extends to the relevant primary legislation where necessary.

3.21

Schedule 2 of the HRA 1998 sets out further detail about the remedial power. It confirms that the Minister is granted the power to amend primary legislation, including beyond that which contains the incompatible provision (para 1(2)), and that the remedial order may have the same extent as the original legislation (para 1(3)).

3.22

Draft remedial orders must be laid before both Houses of Parliament, unless the urgent procedure is to be followed where the order can be made and then subsequently amended (s 10(4) and Sch 2 paras 2–4).

Section 19 – statements of compatibility

3.23

Any Bill which reaches its Second Reading after 24 November 1998[24] requires the sponsoring government minister to make a statement under section 19 to the effect either that the Bill is compatible with the HRA 1998 or that a statement of compatibility cannot be made, but the government wishes to proceed with the Bill in any event. The latter course has only been taken on '*very few occasions*' in the past two decades.[25]

24 Section 19 was brought into force by the Human Rights Act 1998 (Commencement) Order 1998 (SI 1998/2882).

25 *The Government's Independent Human Rights Act Review*, Joint Committee on Human Rights, HC 89 (2021) at para 100.

SECTION 6 – PUBLIC AUTHORITIES

3.24

Section 6(1) sets out the key duty under the HRA 1998, namely that it is unlawful for a public authority to act in a way which is incompatible with a Convention right. Section 6 covers failure to act as well as positive acts, with the exception of any failure to introduce or make any legislation or remedial order (s 6(6)).

3.25

Section 6 does not fully define 'public authority', but section 6(3)(a) confirms that it includes a court or tribunal. It follows that any court seized of a criminal case is obliged to act compatibly with the defendant's rights under the HRA 1998. Whilst Articles 5 and 6 might be the most visible and relevant rights, as the subsequent chapters of this book illustrate, many (if not all) of the Convention rights may be brought into play by criminal proceedings.

3.26

Section 6(3)(b) continues the definition of 'public authority' to include 'any person certain of whose functions are functions of a public nature but does not include either House of Parliament or a person exercising functions in connection with proceedings in Parliament'.

3.27

Section 6(5) qualifies this last category by confirming that '[i]n relation to a particular act, a person is not a public authority by virtue only of subsection (3)(b) if the nature of the act is private'.

3.28

In *Aston Cantlow v Wallbank*,[26] the House of Lords adopted the language of 'core public authorities' to reflect those entities who are obviously public in nature and 'hybrid public authorities' to reflect those bodies some of whose functions are of a public nature. The precise delineation between those two concepts and the circumstances in which a hybrid authority will be carrying out a public rather than private function has been the source of much litigation. Lord Nicholls said:[27]

> What, then, is the touchstone to be used in deciding whether a function is public for this purpose? Clearly there is no single test of universal application. There cannot be, given the diverse nature of governmental functions and the variety of means by which these functions are discharged today. Factors to be taken into account include the extent

26 *Aston Cantlow v Wallbank* [2003] UKHL 37, [2004] 1 AC 546.
27 *Cantlow v Wallbank* at [12].

to which in carrying out the relevant function the body is publicly funded, or is exercising statutory powers, or is taking the place of central government or local authorities, or is providing a public service.

3.29

In *YL v Birmingham City Council*,[28] the majority of the House of Lords[29] held that a private care home caring for a person placed there by a local authority was not acting in its public capacity when caring for that person. The care home was a hybrid public authority which performed public functions in so far as regulation and supervision of its actions by primary legislation were concerned, but in the day-to-day task of caring for the resident, it was performing a private function. In reaching this view, the House was guided by the Strasbourg jurisprudence.

3.30

A useful summary taken from *Aston Cantlow* and *YL* of the factors to be used when determining whether an entity was a hybrid public authority exercising public functions within the meaning of section 6(3)(b) can be found in the judgment of Coulson J (as he then was) in *TH v Chapter of Worcester Cathedral*:[30]

(a) Is the body performing a task which a 'core' public authority is under a duty to perform, and which has been delegated to it?

(b) To what extent is the function of a governmental nature and/or a part of public administration?

(c) Does the body have any special statutory powers in relation to the function in question?

(d) To what extent is the body supported or subsidised from public funds?

(e) To what extent is the body democratically accountable?

(f) Would the allegations, if made against the United Kingdom, render it in breach of its international law obligations?

3.31

There is no doubt that the CPS and the police (at least when they are acting in relation to a criminal investigation) are public authorities. With other prosecuting authorities, many will fall within the definition of public authority. With governmental agencies (HMRC for example) and local authorities there will be little doubt. Even with private bodies, those that prosecute regularly (such as the RSPCA) will often be deemed to be performing a public act and will therefore fall within the definition.

28 *YL* v Birmingham City Council [2007] UKHL 27, [2008] 1 AC 95.

29 Lords Mance, Scott and Neuberger.

30 [2016] EWHC 1117 (Admin) at para 64.

3.32

In any event, as was discussed during the passage of the HRA 1998 through Parliament, even where there is a 'truly private' prosecution brought by, for example, Tesco,[31] whilst the prosecutor will not be a public authority, the Court that hears the case will be, and must therefore take account of the principles of the ECHR. Whilst that may mean that, in the Tesco example, a suspect would not be able to rely on the HRA 1998 in relation to some matters, it is unlikely to make any practical difference.

SECTIONS 7–9 – PROCEEDINGS AND REMEDIES

3.33

Section 7 of the HRA 1998 sets out the circumstances in which a person can either bring a claim for breach of the Convention rights or rely upon the rights in legal proceedings. It is now attenuated in the context of claims concerning the actions of armed forces overseas by section 7A. Limitations in relation to claims for breach against the judiciary are set out in section 9. The operation of section 8 concerns the remedies which can be granted by a Court where there has been a breach of the Convention rights. These are considered in further detail in Chapter 4.

SECTION 11 – EXISTING RIGHTS

3.34

Section 11 provides express protection for existing rights, both substantive and procedural. The higher Courts have repeatedly pointed out that the common law often goes as far as and sometimes goes further than the rights protected under the HRA 1998. Lord Mance in *Kennedy v Information Commissioner*[32] stressed that:

> Since the passing of the Human Rights Act 1998, there has too often been a tendency to see the law in areas touched on by the Convention solely in terms of the Convention rights. But the Convention rights represent a threshold protection; and, especially in view of the contribution which common lawyers made to the Convention's inception, they may be expected, at least generally even if not always, to reflect and to find their homologue in the common or domestic statute law.

31 HC Deb 24 June 1998 vol 314, 1055.
32 [2014] UKSC 20, [2015] AC 155 at para 46.

> Not surprisingly, therefore, Lord Goff of Chieveley in Attorney General v Guardian Newspapers Ltd (No 2) [1990] 1 AC 109 , 282–284 and the House in Derbyshire County Council v Times Newspapers Ltd [1993] AC 534, 551E both expressed the view that in the field of freedom of speech there was no difference in principle between English law and article 10.
>
> In some areas, the common law may go further than the Convention, and in some contexts it may also be inspired by the Convention rights and jurisprudence (the protection of privacy being a notable example). And in time, of course, a synthesis may emerge. But the natural starting point in any dispute is to start with domestic law, and it is certainly not to focus exclusively on the Convention rights, without surveying the wider common law scene.

SECTIONS 12–13: PARTICULAR REGARD TO THE RIGHTS TO FREEDOM OF EXPRESSION AND THOUGHT, CONSCIENCE OR RELIGION

3.35

Section 12 sets out specific requirements in relation to the granting of any remedy which may '*affect the exercise of the Convention right to freedom of expression* (ss 12(1)–12(3)). It requires the Court to have particular regard to the importance of the right to freedom of expression when the issue concerns journalistic, literary or artistic material, or conduct connected to that material (s 12(4)).

3.36

Section 13 requires a Court to have particular regard to the importance of the right to freedom of thought, conscience and religion in determining any issues which may touch upon it.

ARTICLES 16–18 ECHR – RESTRICTIONS ON RIGHTS

Article 16

3.37

This states:

> **Restrictions on political activity of aliens**
>
> Nothing in Articles 10, 11 and 14 shall be regarded as preventing the High Contracting Parties from imposing restrictions on the political activity of aliens.

3.38

Article 16 is extremely unlikely to arise in practice. As was noted by the ECtHR in 2015, it 'reflects an outdated understanding of international law' and must be strictly interpreted.[33]

3.39

In 1995 the ECtHR ruled[34] that a citizen of an EU Member State could not be considered to be an 'alien' for the purposes of Article 16 (although this conclusion rested, in part, on the applicant being an MEP).

Article 17

3.40

Article 17 states:

> **Prohibition of abuse of rights**
>
> Nothing in this Convention may be interpreted as implying for any State, group or person any right to engage in any activity or perform any act aimed at the destruction of any of the rights and freedoms set forth herein or at their limitation to a greater extent than is provided for in the Convention.

The purpose of Article 17 was to safeguard the previous rights and prevent groups from using the ECHR to weaken or undermine the rights of others.[35] An example is *Norwood v United Kingdom*[36] where the applicant, a Regional Organiser for the BNP, had been convicted of a racially aggravated Public Order Act offence for displaying several extremely Islamophobic posters. His complaint that this breached his Article 10 rights was rejected as:

> Such a general, vehement attack against a religious group, linking the group as a whole with a grave act of terrorism, is incompatible with the values proclaimed and guaranteed by the Convention, notably tolerance, social peace and non-discrimination. The applicant's display of the poster in his window constituted an act within the meaning of Article 17, which did not, therefore, enjoy the protection of Articles 10 or 14.

3.41

Like all restrictions in rights, it must be strictly applied. The test is also a high one, so that:[37]

---

33 *Perincek v Switzerland* (Application no 27510/08) 15 October 2015.
34 *Piermont v France* (1995) 20 EHRR 301.
35 *Zdanoka v Latvia* (Application no 58278/00) 15 March 2006.
36 *Norwood v United Kingdom* (Application no 23131/03) 16 November 2004.
37 *Forstater v CGD Europe & Oths* [2022] ICR 1, EAT.

> it is only those beliefs that would be an affront to Convention principles in a manner akin to that of pursuing totalitarianism, or advocating Nazism, or espousing violence and hatred in the gravest of forms, that should be capable of being not worthy of respect in a democratic society. Beliefs that are offensive, shocking or even disturbing to others, and which fall into the less grave forms of hate speech would not be excluded from the protection.

The ECtHR will often consider it as an aid to interpretation of qualified rights as well as applying it directly.[38] This was the approach taken by the House of Lords in upholding a conviction under the Communications Act for a constituent who had left a series of extremely racist messages on the office phone of his MP.[39]

Article 18

3.42

Article 18 states:

> **Limitation on use of restrictions on rights**
>
> The restrictions permitted under this Convention to the said rights and freedoms shall not be applied for any purpose other than those for which they have been prescribed.

This means that a state will be in violation of the ECHR if it restricts a qualified right on grounds other than one permitted under the Convention. There can be no freestanding Article 18 breach, it can only be found in conjunction with a breach of another article.

3.43

So, where an individual is detained pending trial due to the lack of respect that she had shown the Court, this was not a permitted reason under Article 5, and there was a violation of Article 18 taken with Article 5.[40] This is not an Article of the ECHR that has featured extensively in English and Welsh law and is also unlikely to arise in practice in the criminal courts.

---

38 A useful summary of the occasions on which Article 17 has been used by the ECtHR is available at: www.echr.coe.int/Documents/Guide_Art_17_ENG.pdf, p 43.

39 *DPP v Collins* [2006] UKHL 40, [2006] 1 WLR 2223 at [14].

40 *Tymoshenko v Ukraine* (Application no 49872/11) 30 April 2013.

4 The Human Rights Act 1998 – procedure and remedies in domestic law

Toby Cadman and Jack Sproson

INTRODUCTION

4.1

This chapter sets out an overview of procedural aspects of the Human Rights Act 1998 (HRA 1998), as well as details of what remedies can be applied for, and awarded, for a breach.

PROCEDURE

The impact of the Human Rights Act 1998

4.2

As noted in Chapter 3, the HRA 1998 did not create or replace the human rights and civil liberties regime in the United Kingdom. That both pre-dates and continues to develop in parallel to the statutory regime as a matter of common law. Proceedings brought with an (actual or perceived) ignorance to the common law risks attracting condemnation and concern from the judiciary, which has stressed that 'it was not the purpose of the Human Rights Act that the common law should become an ossuary'.[1]

4.3

Nonetheless, the HRA has changed how those rights and freedoms are litigated in practice, which has given rise to a new procedural framework containing a list of positive rights and entitlements[2] and incorporated a far greater jurisprudential foundation on which claims may be formulated. Courts and

1 *Kennedy v Information Commissioner* [2014] UKSC 20, [2015] AC 455 at [46]. *See also*, *R (Guardian News & Media Ltd) v City of Westminster Magistrates' Court* [2012] EWCA 420, [2012] 3 All ER 551 at [88].

2 Prior to the introduction of the HRA 1998, civil liberties in UK common law were primarily defined negatively, ie, that where an individual was not *prohibited* from engaging in conduct by law, they were seen to be *permitted* to do so. For that reason, fundamental freedoms were therefore not 'positive rights but an immunity from interference by others' – *Wheeler v Leicester City Council* [1985] AC 1054 at [1065].

Tribunals are permitted to consider[3] (and in many cases bound to follow) any clear and constant jurisprudence of the ECtHR.[4]

4.4

Where there is conflicting Strasbourg jurisprudence, 'a real judicial choice'[5] must be made as to the applicability of the Convention to any particular case. Where there is no Strasbourg jurisprudence on a particular point, UK courts will interpret the relevant provisions. This may include an interpretation that exceeds the protections presently afforded to those provisions as a matter of Strasbourg jurisprudence.[6]

Who has standing to bring a claim?

The meaning of 'victim'

4.5

Under section 7 of the HRA 1998, a person may bring proceedings against a public body, or body performing a public function, where they are a 'victim' of a Convention violation committed by that body. For the purposes of section 7 of the HRA 1998, someone is a 'victim' of an unlawful act if they fall within definition set out in Article 34 of the Convention:[7]

> [t]he Court may receive applications from any person, non-governmental organisation or group of individuals claiming to be the victim of a violation by one of the High Contracting Parties of the rights set forth in the Convention or the Protocols thereto. …

4.6

As is considered further in Chapter 6 in relation to the ECtHR, Article 34 does not permit claims '*in abstracto*',[8] meaning that a victim must generally have suffered harm to have standing under the Convention and, by extension, the Human Rights Act. This is a material distinction from the position in relation to judicial review proceedings, which allow a broader range of groups to bring claims in relation to public interest issues as long as they establish their 'sufficient interest' in those proceedings. Individuals may attain victim status in exceptional circumstances where they can show that a future violation will affect them

---

3 HRA 1998, s 2.

4 *R (Alconbury) v Secretary of State for the Environment* [2001] UKHL 23, [2003] 2 AC 295 at [26]; *R (Ullah) v Special Adjudicator* [2004] UKHL 26, [2004] 2 AC 323 at [20].

5 *R (Alconbury) v Secretary of State for the Environment.*

6 *Metropolitan Police Commissioner v DSD* [2018] UKSC 11, [2018] 3 All ER 369 at [78]. *See also, Moohan v Lord Advocate* [2014] UKSC 67, [2015] AC 901 at [105].

7 HRA 1998, s 7(7).

8 *Centre For Legal Resources on behalf of Valentin Câmpeanu v Romania* [2014] ECHR 789, (Application no 47848/08), 17 July 2014 at [101].

personally.[9] Victimhood for the purposes of the ECHR encompasses either 'direct' or 'indirect' victims.

Direct victim

4.7

A 'direct' victim is an individual who has been 'directly affected' by a particular measure or course of conduct. Harm does not have to be actually inflicted which means that, in certain circumstances, it may be sufficient to bring a claim against legislation incompatible with a Convention right on the basis that the legislation forced an individual to modify their behaviour protected by that right, even in the absence of substantive punishment.[10]

Indirect victim

4.8

An 'indirect' victim is an individual that has suffered secondary but proximate harm at the hands of a public body. The pool of individuals falling within this definition is small and is intended to encompass claims by close relatives, such as parents or other next of kin, on account of supposed Convention violations, usually (if not exclusively) in circumstances where the 'direct victim' is deceased or missing.[11] Outside this restricted pool of individuals, claims brought on the basis of indirect victimhood may encounter difficulty.

Claims by corporate bodies

4.9

Victims for the purposes of the Convention and the Human Rights Act need not only be natural and may also be legal persons.[12] In such cases, it is possible, for example, that the legal person (eg, a business) is treated as the primary victim and the owner (a natural person) as an indirect victim, although indirect victimhood in this case will usually be contingent upon it being proven either

9 *Senator Lines GMBH v Fifteen Members of the European Union* (Application no 56672/00), 10 March 2004.

10 *Tănase v Moldova* [2010] ECHR 446.

11 See, eg, *Giuliani & Gaggio v Italy* [2011] ECHR 513.

12 Companies in the United Kingdom have long had a distinct legal personality. See, eg, Interpretation Act 1978, s 5 and Sch 1 ('*"person" includes a body of persons corporate or unincorporate*'). This Act repealed and replaced the Interpretation Act 1889, where s 19 states '... *the expression 'person' shall, unless the contrary intention appears, include any body of persons corporate or unincorporate*'. The Interpretation Act 1978, s 2 specifically provides for this definition to criminal offences. The same position is true of Art 34 of the Convention, which envisages the possibility of companies being entitled to, inter alia, rights under Arts 6, 8, and Protocol 1 – see, eg, *OAO Neftyanaya Kompaniya Yukos v Russia* [2011] ECHR 1342 (43,000 pages disclosed four working days before a trial); *Société Colas Est & Others v France* [2002] ECHR 421; *Kin Stib and Majkic v Serbia* [2010] ECHR 616.

that the business and its owner/shareholders are so closely linked as to make distinguishing between the two artificial.[13]

Who can a claim be brought against?

4.10

As discussed in Chapter 3, a claim in domestic law can only be brought against a 'public authority'. An applicant will have to be advised in relation to this in many cases, particularly in cases of 'hybrid' public bodies (bodies that are by nature private, but nonetheless have been delegated authority to perform public functions) will be more complex, given that 'at first sight the Human Rights Act might seem to have nothing to do with [them]'.[14]

Claims against 'hybrid' or private bodies

4.11

In formulating their claim, prospective litigants will thus be required to engage in a fact specific enquiry and must remain aware of the fact that in 'borderline cases … the decision is very much one of fact and degree'.[15]

4.12

Where would-be litigants are seeking to bring a claim against purely private bodies (ie, those that are not core public bodies and are not performing a public function at the time concerned with the relevant conduct) the Human Rights Act 1998 and the Convention rights incorporated by it will not be directly applicable. Those rights may, however, retain relevance in some cases based on the doctrine of 'indirect horizontal effect', which will arise in cases where a claim between two private actors gives rise to interests capable of falling within the corpus of rights protected by the Convention, as incorporated by the HRA 1998, and the court or tribunal, as a public body, is obliged to act compatibly with those rights.

4.13

An example would be an allegation of breach of confidence between two private parties. Notwithstanding that neither party was a public body, the court itself (as a public body) is obliged to have regard to the jurisprudence concerning the right to privacy under Article 8 of the Convention. As a result, whilst this

13 *See Kin Stib and Majkic v Serbia*. Note, however, that the general position remains that a natural person who is a shareholder will not necessarily be a 'victim' for the purposes of the ECHR in order to exercise a right that a company has. See *Agrotexim and Others v Greece* (1996) 21 EHRR 250.

14 *Agrotexim and Others v Greece* at [4].

15 *Poplar Housing and Regeneration Community Association Ltd and Secretary of State for the Environment v Donoghue* [2001] EWCA Civ 595, [2002] QB 48 at [66].

did not give rise to a new cause of action between private parties under the HRA 1998, it did allow the Convention to have 'indirect horizontal effect'.[16]

Raising a Human Rights Act claim

4.14

Section 7 of the HRA 1998 envisages separate yet parallel regimes for litigants to raise questions relevant to Convention rights. Section 7(1) states:

> (1) A person who claims that a public authority has acted (or proposes to act) in a way which is made unlawful by section 6(1) may—
>
> (a) bring proceedings against the authority under this Act in the appropriate court or tribunal, or
>
> (b) rely on the Convention right or rights concerned in any legal proceedings,
>
> but only if he is (or would be) a victim of the unlawful act.

Proceedings under section 7(1)(a)

4.15

Almost all proceedings under section 7(1)(a) can be brought in any court for compensation or other judicial remedy under the HRA 1998 itself. This includes by way of judicial review. The exception is for proceedings where the impugned conduct is in the form of a judicial act (for example, a judgment).[17] In that case, proceedings may only be brought by way of appeal, through judicial review, or in other such forum as expressly prescribed by relevant rules.[18]

Proceedings under section 7(1)(b)

4.16

Under section 7(1)(b), Convention points may also be 'raised' within the contexts of other, independent causes of action where the opposing party is a public authority. This includes a defendant in a criminal case.

---

16 *Campbell v MGN* [2004] UKHL 22, [2004] 2 All ER 995, also *Mckennitt v Ash* [2006] EWCA Civ 1714, [2008] QB 73.

17 HRA 1998, s 9(1).

18 Except where it is a claim 'in respect of a judicial act' in which case the claim must be brought in the High Court, Civil Procedure Rules 7.11.

Convention claims in a criminal case

4.17

Convention rights are embedded into English and Welsh criminal law. The Criminal Procedure Rules contain, as an overriding objective, an obligation to deal with cases 'justly'. This specifically includes 'recognising the rights of a defendant, particularly those under Article 6'.[19]

4.18

The Criminal Procedure Rules have a specific provision for the procedure to be followed where a party wishes to invite the Court of Appeal[20] (or the High Court in relation to extradition[21]) to make a declaration of incompatibility. However, many points that are Convention questions are dealt with under domestic law. So, a defendant who is aggrieved at being held on remand has the remedy of a bail application whilst the defendant who is aggrieved at the length of time he has been on remand will likely have reached a Custody Time Limit application before he could argue a separate breach of Article 5.

4.19

Further, someone who is convicted after considerable delay need not raise a distinct Article 6 argument for sentence. The delay can be relied upon in mitigation in general, and a reduction in sentence given, without a formal finding of a breach of the reasonable time requirement[22] (although see below as to the approach taken by the ECtHR and the advantages in such a finding). This would not preclude any ancillary proceedings under the civil law for an alleged Convention breach.

REMEDIES UNDER THE HUMAN RIGHTS ACT 1998

Judicial remedies available for a breach

Overview of remedies available

4.20

Where a breach of a Convention right is established, section 8 of the HRA 1998 gives courts the ability to 'grant such relief or remedy, or make such an order, within its powers as it considers just and appropriate'.[23] This includes those available to the courts at common law, including damages or other orders (eg, quashing, mandatory, or prohibitive).

19 Criminal Procedure Rules, r 1.1-2(d).
20 CPR r 36.12.
21 CPR r 50.28.
22 *See, Dyer v Watson* [2002] UKPC D 1, [2004] AC 379 for an overview.
23 HRA 1998, s 8(1).

4.21

Judicial acts committed in good faith should not attract damages otherwise than to compensate a person to the extent necessary in Article 5(5) of the Convention or to compensate a person for an action contrary to Article 6 when the person is detained and, but for the action, they would not have been.[24]

4.22

A breach of a Convention right (most often Article 6) may have an impact on a criminal trial. For example, successfully establishing a breach of Article 6 may lead to the exclusion of evidence under section 78 of the Police and Criminal Evidence Act 1984,[25] whilst circumstances involving a breach of relevant procedural time requirements may attract just satisfaction including, *inter alia*, an order to expedite the hearing (if the breach is identified before the hearing), a public acknowledgment of the Article 6 violation, release on bail (if in custody), a stay of proceedings, a reduction in sentence (if applicable),[26] or compensation (if acquitted).[27]

Hammerton v UK

4.23

In *Hammerton v UK*,[28] the domestic courts had found that an applicant had spent extra time in prison following procedural errors during his committal proceedings (for contempt of court in a family case), in breach of his rights under Article 6 of the Convention. However, he was unable to obtain damages to compensate for the breach because section 9(3) of the HRA 1998 did not allow damages to be awarded in proceedings under that Act in respect of a judicial act done in good faith, except to compensate a person to the extent required by Article 5(5) of the Convention.

4.24

At the ECtHR the breach of Article 6 was upheld, but it was found by the Strasbourg Court that the applicant's inability to receive damages in the domestic courts in the particular circumstances of his case led to a violation of the right to an effective remedy under Article 13 of the Convention. The applicant received €8,400 in respect of non-pecuniary damages.[29]

---

24 HRA 1998, s 9(3).

25 See, eg, *A and Others v Secretary of State for the Home Department* [2005] UKHL 71, [2006] 2 AC 221, at [53].

26 A reduction in sentence will not generally deprive a defendant of their status as a 'victim' for the purposes of the ECHR, except where made in an 'express and measurable' manner by a Court in recognition of the delay – *Eckle v Germany* (1982) 5 EHRR 1. In *Beck v Norway* [2001] ECHR 404, the Court's reduction of a sentence from four to two years, where at least one year was due to a two-year delay caused by the change of investigators, was sufficient redress to mean that there was no breach of Article 6 even though the exact reduction 'could have been more precise'.

27 *AG Reference (No 2 of 2001)* [2003] UKHL 68, [2004] 2 AC 72.

28 *Hammerton v UK* (2016) 63 EHRR 23.

29

4.25

Following the judgment, a remedial order was made (through the non-urgent procedure under s 10 of the HRA 1998) to enable damages to be awarded under the Act in respect of judicial acts done in good faith where the judicial act is incompatible with Article 6, and the breach of Article 6 causes the person to be (i) detained when they would not otherwise have been, or (ii) subjected to a longer period of detention than had the breach not been committed.[30]

Damages for Convention breaches

Awarding damages in the domestic court

4.26

Damages, however, may be awarded only by a court which has power to award damages (or to order the payment of compensation) in civil proceedings.[31] They are not to be awarded unless, taking account of all the circumstances of the case (including any other relief or remedy granted, or order made, in relation to the act in question and the consequences of any decision in respect of that act) the court is satisfied that the award is necessary to afford just satisfaction to the person in whose favour it is made.[32] In determining whether, or in what amount, to award damages, the court must take into account the principles applied by the European Court of Human Rights in relation to the award of compensation under Article 41 of the Convention.[33]

4.27

The remedial framework in this regard was summarised in *R v Secretary of State for the Home Department ex parte Greenfield (FC)*,[34] where it was noted that:

> …under article 41 there are three pre-conditions to an award of just satisfaction: (1) that the Court should have found a violation; (2) that the domestic law of the member state should allow only partial reparation to be made; and (3) that it should be necessary to afford just satisfaction to the injured party. There are also pre-conditions to an award of damages by a domestic court under section 8: (1) that a finding of unlawfulness or prospective unlawfulness should be made based on breach or prospective breach by a public authority of a Convention right; (2) that the court should have power to award damages, or order the payment of compensation, in civil proceedings; (3) that the court should be satisfied, taking account of all the circumstances of the particular case, that an award of damages is necessary to afford just satisfaction to the person in whose favour it is made; and (4) that the

30 The Human Rights Act 1998 (Remedial) Order 2020 (SI 2020/1160), Art 2.

31 HRA 1998, s 8(2).

32 HRA 1998, s 8(3).

33 HRA 1998, s 8(4).

34 *R v Secretary of State for the Home Department ex parte Greenfield* (FC) [2005] UKHL 14, [2005] 1 WLR 673.

court should consider an award of damages to be just and appropriate. It would seem to be clear that a domestic court may not award damages unless satisfied that it is necessary to do so, but if satisfied that it is necessary to do so it is hard to see how the court could consider it other than just and appropriate to do so. In deciding whether to award damages, and if so how much, the court is not strictly bound by the principles applied by the European Court in awarding compensation under article 41 of the Convention, but it must take those principles into account. It is, therefore, to Strasbourg that British courts must look for guidance on the award of damages.

The approach of the ECtHR

4.28

In approaching awards, the Strasbourg Court's primary focus will be on the just satisfaction needed in order to ensure '*restitutio in integrum*' (a complete reparation for damage derived from the breach).[35] In many cases, this may not even involve the award of damages *per se*, with the finding of a violation having been deemed sufficient to remedy the prejudice to an applicant:

> The Court recalls that it is well established that the principle underlying the provision of just satisfaction for a breach of Article 6 is that the applicant should as far as possible be put in the position he would have enjoyed had the proceedings complied with the Convention's requirements. The Court will award monetary compensation under Article 41 only where it is satisfied that the loss or damage complained of was actually caused by the violation it has found, since the State cannot be required to pay damages in respect of losses for which it is not responsible.[36]

Calculation of monetary awards

4.29

Nonetheless, the court has been willing to accept that in some cases declaratory remedies are insufficient to remedy the otherwise irremediable prejudice caused to an applicant and has therefore been willing to award pecuniary (eg, for loss of earnings,[37] medical expenses[38]) or non-pecuniary losses (eg, for distress,[39]

---

35 Examples include *Vidal v Belgium* (Application no 14/1991/266/337), 22 April 1992 at [8], *Polskiego v Poland* [2004] ECHR 433 at [47]; *Edwards and Lewis v United Kingdom* [2003] ECHR 381 at [49]; *Pelissier and Sassi v France* (1999) 30 EHRR 715 at [80]; *Zielinski and Others v France* [1999] 31 EHRR 532 at [79]; *Davies v United Kingdom* (2002) 35 EHRR 720 at [34]

36 *Kingsley v United Kingdom* (2002) 35 EHRR 10 at [40].

37 See, eg, *Young, James and Webster v United Kingdom* (1983) 5 EHRR 201; *Smith and Grady v United Kingdom* [2000] ECHR 384.

38 See, eg, *Aksoy v Turkey* (1997) 23 EHRR 553; *Ilhan v Turkey* [2000] ECHR 354.

39 See, eg, *H v France* (1990) 12 EHRR 74.

frustration,[40] inconvenience,[41] or humiliation[42]). The Court may also make awards in respect of costs and expenses.[43] Even where awards in damages are made, however, the Strasbourg Court's approach to *quantum meruit* has generally been a cautious one, with awards being modest and commonly resistant to the award of exemplary damages, which may otherwise significantly inflate the value of the claim.[44]

4.30

Generally, the Court's calculation of *quantum meriut* will be conducted with reference to numerous factors, including, *inter alia*, the seriousness of the violation,[45] the conduct of the respondent.[46] Also relevant may be contextual factors relevant to the applicant.[47] To justify an award of damages, the Court will also require clear evidence of a causal link[48] between the violation and the loss and will not generally entertain damages claims that are unduly speculative.[49] However, the Court's actual eventual award is often based on an 'equitable assessment' that is not directly bound by prior precedent, meaning that the precise breakdown and reasons for awards is therefore difficult to decipher with any degree of certainty.[50]

The domestic approach to damages

4.31

Although the unpredictability of awards at Strasbourg is less common in domestic courts, who often prefer to take a more factually grounded, forensic, approach, the broad principles used at Strasbourg are mirrored in domestic authority, which has confirmed the position that 'where an infringement of an individuals' human rights has occurred, the concern will usually be to bring the infringement to an end and any question of compensation will be of

40 See, eg, *Van der Leer v Netherlands* [1990] 12 EHRR 567.

41 See, eg, *Olsson v Sweden* (No 2) [1992] 17 EHRR 134.

42 See, eg, *Young, James and Webster v United Kingdom* [1981] 4 EHRR 38.

43 ECHR, Practice Direction, Just Satisfaction of Claims (3 June 2022)

44 Ibid. Note, however, that multiple violations in a case will lead to a higher award as will the factors discussed below, such as the conduct of the respondent – see, eg, *M and C v Romania* [2011] ECHR 1452 at [154].

45 For example, violations of Arts 2 and 3 as 'the most fundamental' Convention provisions will evidently be considered serious and may be likely to attract a higher level of damages (*Al-Sadoon and Mufdhi v UK* (2010) 51 EHRR 9).

46 Particularly serious, egregious, or 'offensive' breaches may attract higher awards – see, eg, *Halford v United Kingdom* (1997) 24 EHRR 523.

47 Such as whether the violation was made more serious on account of factors such as the applicant's age – see, eg, *Kostovska v the Former Yugoslav Republic of Macedonia* [2006] ECHR 622.

48 See, eg, *Shesti Mai Engineering OOD and Others v Bulgaria* (Application no 17854/04), 20 September 2011 at [114].

49 See, eg, *Turek v Slovakia* (2006) EHHR 861.

50 See, eg, *Varnava and others v Turkey* [2008] ECHR 30 at [224]; *Al-Skeini and Ors v United Kingdom* (2011) 53 EHRR 18.

secondary, if any, importance'.[51] In relation to the amount of awards, domestic jurisprudence has also made it clear that:

> the 1998 Act is not a tort statute. Damages need not be ordinarily awarded to encourage high standards of compliance by member states, since they are already bound under international law to perform their duties under the Convention in good faith…the purpose of incorporating the Convention in domestic law through the 1998 Act was not to give victims better remedies at home than they could recover in Strasbourg but to give them the same remedies without the delay and expense of resort to Strasbourg.[52]

Prospective litigants must therefore remain cautious about the limited damages available in most claims under the HRA 1998 and the Convention, more generally, should a financial remedy be their primary priority.

Examples of damages awarded

4.32

This limited availability of damages can be seen in HRA 1998 claims involving deprivation(s) of liberty in contravention of Article 5 of the Convention. Cases involving frustration and anxiety as a result of violations of Article 5(4) in parole proceedings have attracted modest awards, with awards of £1,000 not being uncommon for up to two years of delay in parole reviews,[53] although it is possible that the presence of procedural unfairness will increase these awards slightly.[54]

4.33

Loss of liberty more generally, particularly in cases where the lawful basis for an individuals' detention has expired, may attract higher awards. In *Kolanis v United Kingdom*,[55] it was found that an applicant would have been released from detention in a psychiatric hospital 12 months earlier had procedures been in conformity with Article 5(4), leading to an award of €6,000.

4.34

In *Johnson v United Kingdom*,[56] the applicant had been detained in a psychiatric hospital in breach of Article 5(1) for a period of three-and-a-half years. The court observed that the delay in his release could not be attributed entirely to the authorities: some delay was inevitable as a suitable hostel placement had

---

51 *R (Mambakasa) v Secretary of State for the Home Office; R(N) v Secretary of State for the Home Office* [2003] EWHC 319. (Admin) [2004] QB 1124, at [56]. *See also*, *R v Secretary of State for the Home Department ex parte Greenfield* at [9].

52 *R v Secretary of State for the Home Department ex parte Greenfield* at [19].

53 See *Oldham v United Kingdom* (2001) 31 EHRR 34.

54 *Mooren v Germany* (2010) 50 EHRR 23 (increase to £3,000 for frustration arising from the unfairness).

55 *Kolanis v United Kingdom* (2006) 42 EHRR 12.

56 *Johnson v United Kingdom* (1999) 27 EHRR 296.

to be found and, in addition, the applicant had contributed to the delay by his refusal to co-operate. Having regard to those factors, the court awarded £10,000. In a domestic case a loss of liberty claims will often be accompanied by heads of claim falling under the tort of 'false imprisonment'. Those claims will typically attract significantly higher damages and can give a misleading view of what a typical HRA 1998 claim will attract.

4.35

Indeed, this basic observation is apparent when referencing some of the higher awards granted as a result of breaches of other Convention rights. In *Van Colle v Chief Constable of Hertfordshire*,[57] the Court was concerned with a serious case in which the claimants were the parents of a witness murdered due to inadequate police protection. This had happened despite multiple pleas for such protection and an escalating pattern of witness intimidation which was then followed by a failure to observe the witness protection protocol. Taking account of the minor disciplinary sanction imposed on the officer concerned, the Court awarded damages under the HRA 1998 of £15,000 for the victims' distress leading up to his death and £35,000 for the claimants' grief and suffering. Despite the seriousness of this case and the comparatively large award granted as a result, the award is much less than those brought under another compensatory head of claim (such as false imprisonment). For that reason, in many cases practitioners may be well advised to consider seeking tortious or other statutory bases for their claims, especially if the award of damages is a primary consideration for their clients.

57 *Van Colle v Chief Constable of Hertfordshire* [2006] EWHC 360 (QB).

5 Criminal appeals

Steven Bird and Colin Wells

INTRODUCTION

5.1

Human rights, as provided for in the European Convention of Human Rights (ECHR), feature throughout criminal proceedings, from positive duties of investigation and protection, to safeguarding suspects' privacy, and setting out extensive procedural protections for defendants in criminal trials.

5.2

This chapter provides an overview of the appeals structure and then considers the human rights aspects of the criminal appellate jurisdiction. There are a variety of procedural avenues available to those who, in criminal proceedings, wish to challenge human rights breaches. The exact route depends on the Court involved and, to an extent, on tactical decisions made by a prospective appellant. Whilst it will focus on appeals to the Court of Appeal on indictment, most of the Article 6 principles apply equally to appeals to the Administrative Court. The same does not apply to appeals to the Crown Court from the magistrates' court where the nature of the appeal (as a re-hearing) means that, in general, the rules for first instance trials apply.

OVERVIEW OF AVENUES OF APPEAL

Appeals from the magistrates' court

5.3

A person aggrieved by a decision of the magistrates' court has three means of challenge to that decision available:

(a) appeal to the Crown Court;

(b) appeal to the High Court by way of case stated; and

(c) application to the High Court for judicial review

Appeals to the Crown Court

5.4

It should be noted that an appeal to the Crown Court can only be pursued by a convicted defendant, whereas the other two routes of appeal are open to the prosecutor in the magistrates' court.

5.5

A decision made by a magistrates' court may be challenged by the defence on appeal (whether against conviction or sentence) by way of rehearing at the Crown Court under section 108 of the Magistrates' Courts Act 1980, as governed by Part 34 of the Criminal Procedure Rules. If a defendant convicted in the magistrates' court appeals to the Crown Court, any further appeal to the High Court on a point of law should be by way of case stated and not judicial review.[1]

5.6

The procedure on appeal to the Crown Court is governed by Part 34 of the Criminal Procedure Rules 2020. An appeal against the magistrates' decision must be lodged on notice, in writing within 15 business days of the date of sentence (or committal for sentence), to a court officer of the magistrates' court and to any other party to the appeal, stating the grounds of appeal. The appeal to the Crown Court is a complete rehearing. There is no obligation on the prosecution to put their case in the same way as in the lower court and, if convicted, the sentence is at large in that it is not limited to the sentence imposed on in the magistrates' court.

Appeals to the Administrative Court – case stated

5.7

An appeal from the magistrates' court by way of case stated to the High Court is provided for in sections 111 to 114 of the Magistrates' Courts Act 1980, Part 35 of the Criminal Procedure Rules and the Civil Procedure Rules, Part 52. The essence of the procedure is an appeal on a point of law. As noted, this is available to both the prosecution and defence.

5.8

An application to state a case must be made within 21 days of the 'day on which the court sentences or otherwise deals with the offender'. CrimPR Part 35 provides a uniform procedure for an application to state a case whether it be from the magistrates' court or from the Crown Court under s 28 of the Senior Courts Act 1981.

---

1 *Gloucester Crown Court, ex parte Chester* [1998] COD 365.

5.9

Under s 28A(3) of the Senior Courts Act 1981, the court may 'reverse, affirm or amend' the decision of the magistrates' court, or remit the case with its opinion, or make any other order (including an order as to costs) as it sees fit. The Divisional Court may quash an acquittal with a direction that the magistrates' court convicts and then proceeds to sentence. Alternatively, the court may simply substitute a conviction for the previous acquittal and proceed to sentence itself.

5.10

Where a defendant invites the magistrates' court to 'state a case' for the opinion of the High Court under s 111 of the Magistrates' Courts Act 1980, the right of appeal to the Crown Court ceases to exist. For that reason, a convicted defendant must make a tactical decision as to whether he would wish to have 'another bite of the cherry' at the Crown Court (and run the risk of the evidence coming out in such a way that the legal point he wished to run no longer arises). The applicant may challenge the decision to refuse to state a case by way of judicial review.[2]

Appeals to the Administrative Court – judicial review

5.11

Decisions of the magistrates' court (and those of the Crown Court which are not concerned with matters relating to trial on indictment) are susceptible to judicial review by means of quashing orders, mandatory orders and prohibiting orders. The procedure to be followed on an application for judicial review is governed by section 31 of the Senior Courts Act 1981, along with Part 54 of the Civil Procedure Rules and Practice Direction. Rule 54.5(1) of the Civil Procedure Rules provides that a claim form must be filed promptly and, in any event, not later than three months after the grounds to make the claim first arose.

5.12

The principal grounds upon which judicial review may be sought are:

(a) error of law on the face of the court record;

(b) excess of jurisdiction; and

(c) breach of natural justice.

5.13

The Administrative Court's judicial review jurisdiction is supervisory rather than appellate. It is concerned with procedure and the decision-making process,

2 *Reigate Justices, ex parte Counsell* (1983) 148 JP 193; *Ealing Justices, ex parte Woodman* [1994] Crim LR 372.

and not with the merits of the original case. The Administrative Court, will not substitute its own decision for that of the body under review – it will only intervene and quash a decision which was:[3]

> ... so plainly irrational and untenable that no reasonable bench of justices, properly directed, could have reached it. That is, of course, a very high standard for an applicant to meet.

5.14

Any appeal from the High Court in a criminal cause or matter, either in relation to an appeal by way of case stated or a judicial review, is direct to the Supreme Court. For a full explanation of the origins and meaning of the phrase 'criminal cause or matter' see *Belhaj v DPP*.[4]

5.15

The refusal by the Crown Court to stay proceedings on the grounds of abuse of process cannot be challenged in the Administrative Court, as it concerns a matter on indictment. For example, judicial review is not available for challenges to the application for dismissal or for a stay of proceedings in cases committed under section 51 of the Crime and Disorder Act 1998. Section 29 of the Supreme Court Act 1981 has been held to be compatible with the Article 6 right to a fair trial, as a defendant has a right to appeal a Crown Court decision to the Court of Appeal Criminal Division.

Appeals from the Crown Court

At first instance

5.16

To challenge a Crown Court conviction or sentence an appeal lies (with permission) to the Court of Appeal (Criminal Division).[5] The Court will allow an appeal against conviction if they think the conviction is unsafe and will dismiss it in other cases. In relation to an appeal against sentence, the test under section 9 of the Criminal Appeal Act 1968 is much wider than that for an appeal against conviction. Although the jurisdiction is often said to be 'wrong in law or manifestly excessive', the Court is willing to act on a variety of bases, including on information subsequent to the imposition of a perfectly proper sentence.[6]

3 *R v Willesden Justices ex p Clemmings* (1988) 87 Cr App R 280.
4 *Belhaj v DPP* [2018] UKSC 33, [2018] 3 WLR 435.
5 All references in this chapter to the Court of Appeal are to the Criminal Division of the Court of Appeal.
6 See, as an example, *Newsome* [2019] EWCA Crim 921.

Prosecution appeals from the Crown Court

5.17

Prosecution rights of appeal in relation to trials on indictment exist for:[7]

- rulings in preparatory hearings in serious fraud cases and long and complex cases; and
- judges' rulings in relation to all trials on indictment, at any stage prior to the start of the judge's summing-up (other than applications to discharge a jury).

This right of appeal requires leave (of the first instance judge or the Court of Appeal) and the prosecution must accept that, if the appeal is unsuccessful – either because the ruling is confirmed on appeal, leave is refused, or the appeal is abandoned) – the accused is acquitted of the relevant offence.

5.18

There is also provision for appeals against any evidential rulings which significantly weaken the prosecution case (limited to 'qualifying' offences) which apply both before and at trial (up to the opening of the case for the defence). An unsuccessful appeal against an evidential ruling would not automatically lead to an acquittal of the accused and can only do so if the prosecution indicates that it does not intend to proceed with the prosecution. It should be noted that this provision is not yet in force, and no date for implementation has been set.

5.19

The Court of Appeal may not reverse a ruling on appeal under the Criminal Justice Act 2003 provisions unless it is satisfied:

- that the ruling was wrong in law;
- that the ruling involved an error of law or principle; or
- that the ruling was a ruling that it was not reasonable for the judge to have made.

Appeals to the Supreme Court

Appeals from the Court of Appeal

5.20

Sections 33 and 34 of the Criminal Appeal Act 1968 allow either the prosecution or defence to appeal a decision of the Court of Appeal to the Supreme Court, but only if the Court of Appeal or the Supreme Court itself considers that the appeal involves a point of law of general public importance which should

7 They are set out in full at Criminal Justice Act 2003, ss 57–74.

be considered. In addition, the Court of Appeal must certify that the appeal involves a question concerning a point of law of general public importance.

5.21

An application to the Court of Appeal for leave to appeal to the Supreme Court must be made by the party seeking to appeal no more than 28 days after the decision, or the date on which the court gives the reasons for its decision, whichever is later. Time begins to run on the day of the decision and not the day following the decision.

5.22

Where the Court of Appeal is of the view that the prospective appeal raises no point of law of public importance, it may decide so on the papers.[8] A refusal to allow oral submissions will not amount to a violation of a person's rights under Article 6 of the ECHR.[9] A refusal by the Court of Appeal to certify a question cannot be appealed.

5.23

In *Dunn*,[10] the Court of Appeal concluded that the fact that the question of whether an appeal that has failed before it raises a point of law of public importance is decided by the Court itself does not offend either Articles 6 or 14 of the ECHR. In addition, the existence of such a filter mechanism is not a breach of Article 6. Practice Direction 12 of the Supreme Court Practice Directions provides comprehensive instruction in respect of appeals to the Supreme Court concerning criminal proceedings.

From the High Court in a criminal cause or matter

5.24

Section 1(1)(a) of the Administration of Justice Act 1960 provides that any appeal from the High Court in a criminal cause or matter will be direct to the Supreme Court, thereby leapfrogging the Court of Appeal. A similar leave process to that operating in the Court of Appeal applies, the Divisional Court must certify that the appeal involves a point of law of general public importance and leave to appeal must be granted by either the Divisional Court or the Supreme Court.

8 *Daines* [1961] 1 All ER 290.
9 *Steele* [2006] EWCA Crim 2000, [2007] 1 WLR 222.
10 *Dunn* [2010] EWCA Crim 1823, [2011] 1 WLR 958.

APPLICATION OF THE ECHR TO APPEALS

Does the ECHR apply to appeals?

5.25

In relation to many criminal appeals, the Article 6 'right to a fair trial' arguments feature heavily in the appellant jurisprudence. For a detailed examination of the application of Article 6 to the criminal trial process, which will then feature in an appeal, see Chapter 24. Article 6 does not provide a right to an appeal[11] and Parliament is entitled to legislate to exclude a right of appeal even where similar cases would have an appeal mechanism.[12] However, where a national authority does provide for an appeal process, that must be compliant with Article 6.[13] The Court of Appeal is entitled to have regard to time limits set out in legislation, provided there is the capacity for flexibility in suitable circumstances.[14] The ability to grant permission out of time would satisfy this. An applicant cannot use Article 13 as a means to appeal an alleged breach of Article 6,[15] as Article 13 has not been incorporated to UK law.

Prosecution right of appeal

5.26

Whilst the lack of a right of appeal by an unsuccessful prosecutor has historically long been held in England and Wales to be a fundamental principle (and, even where such a right has been provided, it should be strictly construed), there is nothing objectionable under the ECHR about the prosecution having such a right. This includes, in principle, a case where an appeal court reverses an acquittal and imposes a conviction.[16] However, that would generally only be where the Court is considering a question of law.[17] However, Article 6 does not give a Prosecutor any right to appeal.[18] This extends to a victim, although they may be able to lodge a collateral challenge against the CPS (or other body).[19]

---

11 There is such a right in criminal matters in Art 2, Protocol 7:

1. Everyone convicted of a criminal offence by a tribunal shall have the right to have his conviction or sentence reviewed by a higher tribunal. The exercise of this right, including the grounds on which it may be exercised, shall be governed by law.

2. This right may be subject to exceptions in regard to offences of a minor character, as prescribed by law, or in cases in which the person concerned was tried in the first instance by the highest tribunal or was convicted following an appeal against acquittal.

However, this has only been ratified by a small number of countries, not including the United Kingdom.

12 *R (Langley) v Preston Crown Court* [2008] EWHC 2623 (Admin), [2009] 1 WLR 1612.

13 *Delcourt v Belgium* (1979–1980) 1 EHRR 355.

14 *Maresti v Croatia* [2009] ECHR 981.

15 *Kudla v Poland* (2002) 35 EHRR 11.

16 *Arnarsson v Iceland* (2003) 39 EHRR 426.

17 *Lamatic v Romania* [2020] ECHR 848.

18 *Ramsahi v The Netherlands* (2008) 46 EHRR 43.

19 *R (Waxman) v CPS* [2012] EWHC 133 (Admin).

Specific aspects of an appeal

The test on appeal

5.27

The test adopted by the Court of Appeal on appeal against conviction, namely the safety[20] of the conviction, as discussed in *Chalkley and Jeffries*,[21] was considered by the European Court in *Condron v United Kingdom*[22] in the context of the right to silence under Article 6. The ECtHR was critical of the fact that the Court of Appeal was required to focus on the safety of conviction, observing that:

> the question whether or not the rights of the defence guaranteed to an accused under Article 6 were secured in any given case cannot be assimilated to a finding that his conviction was safe in the absence of any enquiry into the issue of fairness.

5.28

In *R v Togher*,[23] the Court of Appeal has held that denial of a fair trial will often result in a conviction being regarded as unsafe. However, it is important to note that a breach of Article 6 will not necessarily mean a conviction will be quashed by the Court of Appeal, as the safety of the conviction is still the primary concern of the appellant court.[24] In those circumstances, the Court of Appeal will look at the nature and consequence of a breach.[25] For example, a conviction by a Court or Tribunal that is not independent or impartial will inevitably be unsafe, however strong the case against the appellant is or however unmeritorious the appeal would be otherwise.[26] On the other hand, where there is a breach of the reasonable time requirement this is unlikely to mean that the conviction is, as a whole, unsafe,[27] unless there is substantive prejudice that has been caused by the delay. There are a number of other ways in which the Court of Appeal can mark the breach, most often by way of a reduction in sentence.

5.29

Issues surrounding breaches of Article 6 often feature in cases of entrapment. The use of evidence obtained by entrapment ('as a result of police incitement'), may deprive a defendant of their Article 6 and common law right to a fair trial.

---

20 Innocence is not the test: see *Pope* [2013] 1 Cr App R 14 at 214. A guilty plea does not necessarily preclude the 'safety' test being considered: see *Hamilton v Post Office Ltd* [2021] EWCA Crim 577 at [69].

21 *Chalkley and Jeffries* [1998] 2 All ER 155.

22 *Condron v United Kingdom* (2001) 31 EHRR 1.

23 *R v Togher* [2001] 3 All ER 463.

24 *Lyons v United Kingdom* (2003) 37 EHRR 313.

25 *Abdurahman* [2019] EWCA 2239, [2020] 1 Cr App R 27 – in that case the EHCR found a breach of Art 6 as legal advice being wrongly withheld from a suspect. On a CCRC referral the Court of Appeal disagreed with that finding, but said that even had there been a breach, it would not have rendered the conviction unsafe.

26 *Abdiiokov & Oths* [2007] UKHL 37, [2008] 1 All ER 315.

27 *Tapper v DPP* [2012] UKPC 26, [2012] 1 WLR 2712.

The origins are in the ECtHR's judgment in *Teixeira de Castro v Portugal*,[28] where the court considered entrapment and Article 6. In that case a person with no previous drugs record, who was persuaded by police officers to buy heroin on their behalf, had not had a fair trial because 'the two officers did not confine themselves to investigating his criminal activity, but instead incited the commission of the offence, which would not have been committed without their intervention'.

5.30

Subsequent to *Teixera v Portugal*, the House of Lords decision in *R v Looseley and Attorney General's Reference (No 3 of 2000)*[29] provides the leading domestic authority on state executive entrapment, although implemented in the United Kingdom via the principles of section 78 and/or abuse of process. The decision is fact specific and depends on a number of factors including, but not limited to, the previous criminality of the defendant. It is not sufficient for there to have been entrapment, but there must also be conduct on the part of the authorities that brought the administration of justice into disrepute such as to merit a stay of proceedings.

5.31

Where evidence has been lost or destroyed and the defence has been deprived of a potential opportunity to advance its case, the court in protecting fair trial rights has a discretion to stay proceedings. The court, when considering an abuse application based on the non-availability of evidence, must consider the relevance of the material, whether it should have been preserved, why it was destroyed (in terms of bad faith, serious fault or incompetence) and alternative trial remedies.[30]

Delay in the appeal hearing

5.32

A delay in hearing an appeal by the Court of Appeal can lead to a violation of Article 6, even where the first instance proceedings were conducted in a timely manner.[31] Similar principles apply in an appeal to the Administrative Court. A delay of six months for the Recorder in the Crown Court to prepare the draft case stated and, after comment were received 'promptly', a further unexplained delay of 10 months, was a breach of the reasonable time requirement that could properly be reflected in a reduction in sentence (but not in relation to the period of disqualification in that case).[32]

---

28 *Teixeira de Castro v Portugal* [1998] 28 EHRR 101.

29 *R v Looseley and Attorney General's Reference (No 3 of 2000)* [2001] UKHL 53.

30 For more details on this topic see guidance given in *R v Feltham Justices, ex parte Ebrahim* [2001] EWHC Admin 130, [2001] 1 WLR 1293 and subsequent cases.

31 *Webber* [2002] EWCA Crim 2782.

32 *Myers v DPP* [2008] EWHC 594 (Admin), [2002] 2 All ER 902.

Effective participation in the appeal

Oral arguments at appeal

5.33

The ECtHR has repeatedly emphasised the importance of defendants in criminal proceedings being able to participate in an oral hearing.[33] However, the question of whether there is a breach of Article 6 must be resolved by looking at proceedings as a whole. For that reason, something that may appear to be a breach if taken in isolation, will not be so if the proceedings are considered together.

5.34

There is nothing objectionable about a filter (or 'sift') mechanism such as exists in the Court of Appeal. At that stage, the question is not the safety of the conviction, but whether there are arguable grounds. For that reason, Article 6 does not require an oral hearing, especially as an applicant will have been convicted after an oral hearing and, if the appeal has potential merit, there will be an oral hearing at that point. Where the case proceeds to a full hearing, the practice in United Kingdom Courts means that an appellant will almost always have the opportunity (in person or through an advocate) to address the Court in oral argument. This is likely higher than the minimum requirement in Article 6, although where the Appeal Court had 'to make a full assessment of the question of the applicant's guilt or innocence', Article 6 required an oral hearing to assess the evidence of the appellant.[34]

5.35

Taking the proceedings as a whole can mean that consideration is given to the whole duration of the case. For example, Article 6 does not require that there was an oral hearing to determine a minimum tariff set by the Lord Chief Justice as there had previously been an oral hearing in setting the sentence. This was the case even though the tariff was set some nine years after the trial.[35]

Presence at appeal

5.36

The nature of the issues being considered on appeal, and the extent to which an appellant is legally represented, are relevant factors when deciding whether an appellant has a right to be present. This is linked, but separate to, the question of whether an oral hearing is needed. It is clear that an appellant is not necessarily entitled to be present during any hearing of an appeal.[36] However, where

33 *Delcourt v Belgium*, at [27].

34 *Ekbatani v Sweden* (1988) 13 EHRR 504. See also *Sigurthor Arnarsson v Iceland* (2003) 39 EHRR 426.

35 *R (Dudson) v SSHD* [2005] UKHL 52. A subsequent application to the ECHR was declared to be 'manifestly ill-founded' – *Dudson v United Kingdom* [2009] ECHR 1308.

36 *Prinz v Austria* (2001) 31 EHRR 12.

there are factual issues to be considered and decided by the Appeal Court, the appellant generally has a right to be present to enable the court to form a 'new assessment of [his] personality and character'.[37]

5.37

This is not absolute, so in *Nawaz*,[38] the applicant, who was seeking to appeal his conviction, informed the Court that he had Covid-19 two days before the hearing (although he intended to come anyway) but applied for an adjournment for fresh legal representation. An order was made to exclude him from the Royal Courts of Justice (on public health grounds) partly on the basis that there was no automatic right to attend.

Legal aid

5.38

The interests of justice test contained within Article 6(3)(c) means that the state is not required to provide legal aid to all appellants. A merits test can be compatible with Article 6(3)(c). In *Monnell and Morris v United Kingdom*,[39] the European Court commented that:

> The interests of justice cannot … be taken to require an automatic grant of legal aid whenever a convicted person, with no objective likelihood of success, wishes to appeal after having received a fair trial at first instance in accordance with Article 6.

This illustrates that compliance with Article 6 in the context of an appeal is assessed by looking at the proceedings as a whole. The fact that legal aid was provided at trial was a factor that was to be taken into account when determining whether the denial of legal aid on appeal is compatible with Article 6.

5.39

This was further considered in *Granger v United Kingdom*.[40] The European Court noted that the importance and significance of the issues (a term of five years' imprisonment) and the complexity of the arguments meant that the appellant would have been unable to participate effectively and put his case without legal representation to be provided under legal aid. As a consequence, a violation of Article 6(3)(c) was found.

---

37 *Cooke v Austria* (2001) 31 EHRR 11.
38 *Nawa* [2020] EWCA Crim 1715.
39 *Monnell and Morris v United Kingdom* (1988) 10 EHRR 205.
40 *Granger v United Kingdom* [1990] ECHR 6.

Right to reasons

5.40

In general, the right to have reasons for a decision is part of Article 6.[41] There is no fixed rule as to how detailed these reasons must be, all will depend on the circumstances of the case and the stage of the proceedings. However, whilst they may be short, they must not be formulaic and must address any 'specific pertinent and important points' raised by an applicant. Whilst an Appeal Court can simply endorse the decision and reasoning of the lower court,[42] that is generally undesirable and, in cases where the challenge is a lack of reasons or particular factual matters are raised (such as the admissibility of evidence) this will need to be addressed.[43]

5.41

The ECtHR recognises the distinct position of juries and has held that the 'framework' of the trial, which includes speeches of prosecution and defence setting out the respective cases and then directions from the Judge, and the remedy of an appeal, is sufficient for a defendant to know the basis on which he is convicted and no further reasons are needed.[44]

Retrials

5.42

There is no prohibition in the ECHR preventing a retrial where a conviction appeal is allowed. Whilst there is a specific provision in Protocol 7,[45] this would not assist an appellant in the Court of Appeal and, as stated above, it has not been adopted by the United Kingdom.

THE APPLICATION OF ARTICLE 5

5.43

Whilst many people convicted of a crime will serve a prison sentence, it will be rare that Article 5 (the right to liberty) will apply. Article 5(1) and (2) specifically provide for the detention of someone subject to a prison sentence or by the

41 *Moreira Ferreira v Portugal (No 2)* [2017] ECHR 658.

42 *Garcia Ruez v Spain* (1999) EHHR 589.

43 *Shabelnik v Ukraine (No 2)* [2017] ECHR 499.

44 *Judge v United Kingdom* [2011] ECHR 367.

45 **Right not to be tried or punished twice**

1. No one shall be liable to be tried or punished again in criminal proceedings under the jurisdiction of the same State for an offence for which he has already been finally acquitted or convicted in accordance with the law and penal procedure of that State.

2. The provisions of the preceding paragraph shall not prevent the reopening of the case in accordance with the law and penal procedure of the State concerned, if there is evidence of new or newly discovered facts, or if there has been a fundamental defect in the previous proceedings, which could affect the outcome of the case.

order of a Court. It is not permissible for a challenge to a conviction or sentence to be made under the guise of an Article 5 challenge to the ensuing detention.[46] The fact that a conviction or sentenced was subsequently overturned does not retrospectively make the detention 'unlawful' for the purposes of Article 5.[47] An order by the Court of Appeal for a 'loss of time' direction does not contravene Article 5.[48]

46 *Benham v United Kingdom* (1996) 22 EHRR 293.
47 *Krzycki v Germany* (1978) DR 13.
48 *Monnell v United Kingdom* (1988) 10 EHRR 205.

6 The European Court of Human Rights

Victoria Ailes

INTRODUCTION

6.1

The history and early years of the court are set out in Chapter 1. This chapter aims to provide an overview of the court's current procedures from the point of view of litigants seeking to take a case to the European Court of Human Rights (ECtHR).

6.2

Further detail may be found in the ECHR itself (which from Article 19 onwards deals with the constitution and procedures of the court), the Rules of Court and the Practice Directions. In addition, the Registry of the ECtHR produces guidance documents on a wide range of procedural and substantive areas.

Constitution of the Court

The Court

6.3

The Court is currently composed of 46 Judges, one representing each member state of the Council of Europe.[1] They are elected by the Parliamentary Assembly of the Council of Europe for a non-renewable term of nine years from a shortlist of three candidates provided by the country concerned.[2] Though nominated by their home nation, the judges are expected to act impartially.

6.4

For administrative purposes, the judges are divided into five sections each of nine or 10 judges. These are constituted for a period of three years (meaning that the judges of a particular section will consistently work together until the sections are re-formed at the end of that period). Sections are geographically

1 There were 47 until the expulsion of the Russian Federation in March 2022. The Russian Judge ceased sitting on 16 September 2022 when Russia ceased to be a party to the ECHR.
2 ECHR, Arts 22–23.

and gender balanced, as well as reflecting the different legal systems of the judges.[3] Each section has a president and vice-president.

6.5

Cases are assigned to a section when they are received by the court. Judicial formations for decision making are derived from the judges of the section as needed: a single judge, three judges for a committee decision and seven judges for a Chamber decision. The national judge for the respondent state will never act as the single judge, but will sit *ex officio* on any Chamber, even if not a member of the section to which the case has been assigned. The section President presides over every Chamber formed within his/her section.

6.6

The official languages of the Court are English and French. While all judges of the court have an 'active' knowledge of at least one of those languages (and at least a 'passive' knowledge of the other), most are not working in their first language.

6.7

The judges are supported by the Registry, which is responsible for administrative functions including the processing of applications, communication with the parties, preparing files and analytical notes, translation and ensuring the accessibility of the court's case law.

THE APPLICATION PROCESS

Commencing proceedings

6.8

Proceedings in the ECtHR are instituted by making an application under Article 34 of the Convention and Rule 47 of the Rules of Court. The application form is available on the court website. The most significant information required by the form is a 'concise and legible'[4] 'statement of facts' a 'statement of alleged violations of the Convention and relevant arguments' and a statement dealing with admissibility. The information sought in these boxes on the form is commonly provided by cross-referring to a separate document (much as is the case with pleadings in a domestic claim form) and indeed the Rules of Court make provision for such a document: it must be presented in numbered paragraphs on paginated A4 paper not exceeding 20 pages, must use at least a 12 pt type and must have margins of at least 3.5cm.[5]

3 Rules of Court, Rule 25.2.

4 Rules of Court, Rule 47(1)(e) and (f).

5 There appears in practice to be no sanction for non-compliance with these rules.

6.9

The application must be accompanied by a paginated bundle of relevant documents including judgments in any domestic proceedings, with a detailed explanation for the failure to include any omitted document. It is important to note, when ensuring that an application is submitted within time (see below), that the application form requires the original signatures of both the applicant and their lawyer (if the applicant is represented).[6] A separate document authorising the lawyer to act as legal representative will not be accepted.[7] If an application is rejected as incomplete, the Court destroys the file. A complete application must therefore be resubmitted with all relevant documents attached, even if they have previously been provided.

Representation (agents and legal representatives)

6.10

An applicant is permitted (but not required) to have legal representation when making an application to the ECtHR. The ECtHR does not grant legal aid, however, for the making of the initial application or before a case is communicated to the government. This is a significant omission, given that the written application is generally the applicant's only opportunity to explain why the application has, at the very least, sufficient merit to be communicated to the government for their observation – a hurdle which the court's own statistics show that a majority of cases do not clear.

6.11

Legal representation is not only permitted but is also generally required under Rule 36 of the Rules of Court once an application has been communicated and/or held admissible. The representative may be any 'advocate authorised to practise in any of the Contracting Parties and resident in the territory of one of them, or any other person approved by the President of the Chamber'.[8] The court may at this stage grant legal aid (either of its own motion or on application).

6.12

In order for an applicant to obtain legal aid, it is necessary to satisfy the President of the Chamber, firstly, that legal aid is necessary for the proper conduct of the case before the Chamber and, secondly, that the applicant has insufficient means to meet all or part of the costs entailed. Legal aid may be granted for more than one representative in appropriate cases. Any grant will continue in force should

6 Rules of Court, Rule 47(1)(c).

7 An 'authority form' is available on the ECHR website but is intended only for circumstances where an applicant obtains or changes legal representation after the application has been submitted.

8 Rules of Court, Rule 36(4)(a). The 'advocate' who completes the form is usually a solicitor and need not be the advocate at any hearing or the person who settled the application. There is no apparent bar on a barrister from signing, although consideration would need to be given as to whether this constituted 'litigation' for the purposes of the Legal Services Act 2007, Sch 2, para 4.

the matter go to the Grand Chamber. Payments are by way of a lump sum which is to be regarded as a contribution towards the costs of representation.

6.13

No court fee is charged and, irrespective of the outcome, an applicant is never ordered to pay the government's legal costs.

6.14

Member States are represented before the court through their 'Agent',[9] assisted by advocates and/or advisers.[10] From the government's perspective, an application to the ECtHR is by no means the continuation of the domestic proceedings; it involves the question of whether the Member State has complied with its treaty obligations. For that reason, in UK cases the Agent is a lawyer from the Foreign, Commonwealth and Development Office. Although the Agent will seek information as necessary from any relevant prosecuting authority or public authority, the proceedings are conducted by the United Kingdom Government.

Process on receipt

The preliminary examination stage

6.15

Once the application is lodged, Rule 54(1)–(2) of the Rules of Court provide:

1. The Chamber may at once declare the application inadmissible or strike it out of the Court's list of cases. The decision of the Chamber may relate to all or part of the application.
2. Alternatively, the Chamber or the President of the Section may decide to:
   (a) request the parties to submit any factual information, documents or other material considered by the Chamber or its President to be relevant;
   (b) give notice of the application or part of the application to the respondent Contracting Party and invite that Party to submit written observations thereon and, upon receipt thereof, invite the applicant to submit observations in reply;
   (c) invite the parties to submit further observations in writing.

The ECtHR has a highly developed set of rules for the admissibility of applications covering both procedural and substantive issues, which are considered in more detail below.

9 Rules of Court, Rule 35.

10 Non-legal persons in proceedings before the ECtHR are also required to appoint an agent.

6.16

This stage of the proceedings is referred to by the court as the 'preliminary examination' of admissibility. Rule 54A permits the Chamber to decide that the admissibility and merits of an application should be determined together under Article 29(1). Although the court can make a decision on admissibility at any stage, its general practice is to leave admissibility and merits to be determined together rather than make a separate decision that an application is admissible. Decisions on admissibility at the 'preliminary examination' stage are therefore usually negative.

The communication stage

6.17

If it is not struck out or ruled inadmissible at the preliminary examination stage, the court will give notice of the application to the Respondent government. The UK Government generally has no knowledge that an application to the ECtHR has even been made until it is formally 'communicated' by the court, unless the grant of interim relief or some other step has required the court to draw it to its attention.

6.18

The communication of an application is an important stage in the procedure. Communication of a case indicates that the application is of sufficient merit not to have been struck out or immediately declared inadmissible (which is the fate of the great majority of applications). It is usually the stage at which the ECtHR publishes information about the case on its website and triggers rights to legal aid and use of 'eComms'. It commences the non-contentious and contentious phases of proceedings (see below). Upon communicating a case, the Court will produce and publish a 'Statement of Facts' and 'Questions to the Parties'. This document will occasionally also require parties (or even, in cases involving cross-border issues, other Member States) to provide further information or documents to the Court.

Electronic filing

6.19

The Court operates an Electronics Communications Service (eComms). If applicants opt to use it, then the Court will send and accept documents electronically in text-searchable pdf format. However, this service is available only after an application has been communicated to the government. It follows that it cannot be used to make the original application. The court also refuses to accept applications for interim relief electronically, even if made at a time when the applicant is otherwise using eComms.[11] The Court does *not* accept

11 Practice Direction on Electronic Filing by Applicants.

electronic signatures on eComms documents, and any signed document filed electronically should be a scan of a wet ink signature, the original of which should be retained.

Third-party interveners

6.20

The communication stage is also the stage at which third parties may seek to intervene. If a case involves the nationals of another Member State, then that state has the right to intervene in the case and the court will contact it at the same time as the Respondent. The Council of Europe Commissioner for Human Rights also has the right to intervene in any case. In addition, any other Member State or any 'person concerned' may seek permission to do so.

6.21

Third- party interventions are often made by other Member States with similar national laws to those under challenge, as well as by non-governmental organisations and charities with an interest in the relevant subject matter. An application should be made, in writing, no later than 12 weeks after notice of the case has been given to the respondent State.[12]

The non-contentious phase

6.22

Upon communication of an application to the respondent government, the case next enters a 12-week 'non-contentious' phase, with a view to encouraging the parties to enter into a 'friendly settlement' under Article 39. 'Friendly settlement' involves an agreement between the parties disposing of the application without it being adjudicated upon by the court.

6.23

The court used to carry out this phase in parallel with the exchange of proceedings. However, since 1 January 2019, it has expanded the scope of its 'friendly settlement' programme and now writes to parties as a matter of course when the case is communicated to the Respondent government and invite them to make proposals for 'friendly settlement'. This process is part of the Court's package of measures to try to manage its case load.

6.24

This communication of a proposal to enter into a friendly settlement can come as a surprise to defendants in criminal cases, given that it is often outside the power of the government (and certainly the defendant) to rectify any alleged

12 Rules of Court, Rule 44.

violation of the Convention. For example, once the domestic courts have ruled on any appeal the government has no legal basis for disregarding that ruling.

6.25

However, a communication inviting the parties to make proposals for a friendly settlement should not be taken to imply that the court has formed any particular view of the merits, or that the case is one which is particularly likely to be amenable to settlement. These proposals are made irrespective of whether there is any realistic, or even lawful, basis on which settlement could be achieved.[13] In many cases, therefore, the UK Government and the applicant merely indicate that there is nothing that could be done to achieve a friendly settlement. If there is a prospect of reaching a friendly settlement, the court is likely to agree to proposals to extend the non-contentious phase beyond the initial 12 weeks. Where Friendly Settlement negotiations are carried out, they are confidential and without prejudice to the parties' arguments in the contentious proceedings (and thus should not be referred to in them).

6.26

The court expects to be involved in the Friendly Settlement process. Proposals for friendly settlements are sent to the court (and not conducted solely in *inter partes* correspondence). The court may also be proactive and may, for example, set a timetable for negotiations or make its own proposals for resolution of the dispute. If it considers that a proposal for friendly settlement has been unreasonably refused by an applicant, the court may strike the application out of its list (as long as the government accepts that there has been a violation of the Convention). If a Friendly Settlement is reached, the case is struck out of the court's list, and a short summary and description of the accommodation reached is published on its website.[14]

The contentious phase

6.27

If attempts to achieve a Friendly Settlement fail, the case proceeds to the 'contentious phase'. This involves the court setting a timetable for the provision of written observations by the government on the application, followed by a reply by the Applicant. Save in expedited cases, the parties are often given 12 weeks. In providing their written observations, the parties should bear in mind that the ECtHR directs oral hearings extremely rarely. The vast majority of cases, therefore, are conducted entirely on the papers and this written document will be the only opportunity either party will have to set out their arguments before the case is decided.

---

13 See Rules of Court, Rule 62(1), which describes the procedure that the Registrar will enter into in mandatory terms.

14 Rules of Court, Rule 62(3).

6.28

The Practice Direction on Written Pleadings covers the form and content of the parties' observations. The same rules as to font size, margins, etc, apply as to documents annexed to the application. The Practice Direction requires the pleadings to use headings corresponding to those which are used in the court's own decisions and judgments (ie, 'Facts'/'Domestic law [and practice]'/'Complaints'/'Law' followed by 'Preliminary objection on …', 'Alleged violation of Article …', as the case may be).

6.29

The statement of facts and questions provides the framework for the parties' observations. As to the facts, neither party should address facts which are undisputed (and in appropriate cases, the parties should simply state that the statement of facts prepared by the Registry is not disputed). As for the issues, the parties should present their legal arguments under the appropriate headings and provide an answer to each of the questions posed by the court under a separate heading.

6.30

While the parties are not precluded from raising issues not covered in the statement of issues, the Court's questions typically reflect the legal issues which arise in the case based on the Court's existing case law.

6.31

The applicant is often invited to submit any claim for 'just satisfaction' at the same time as written observations in reply to the government's. The law and procedure in relation to claims for 'just satisfaction' are set out below.

Evidence

6.32

Either party, and any intervener, may annex documents to their pleadings. In most cases, the most crucial (and sometimes the only) documents are the decisions and orders of the domestic courts.

6.33

Parties should also provide any domestic statutory materials or case law which is necessary for the judges (only one of whom will be from the United Kingdom) to understand the relevant domestic law and practice. In explaining the domestic position, it is important to bear in mind that not all Council of Europe states have jury systems, that many adopt inquisitorial rather than adversarial procedures, and that most rules of criminal evidence are unique to the common law tradition.

6.34

It is unnecessary to provide the court with copies of its own case law.

6.35

It is almost invariably inappropriate and ill-advised for applicants to make statements or obtain new evidence (such as expert reports) for the purpose of an application to the Strasbourg Court. The Court has held that, consistent with the principle of subsidiarity, it is not its function to substitute its own judgment for that of the national courts, or to act as a 'fourth instance appeal'.[15]

6.36

Any new evidence will, in most cases, be disregarded at best. At worst it may give rise to an objection that the application is inadmissible because the applicant is raising matters in respect of which domestic remedies have not been exhausted. While exceptionally, the court has power to take investigative measures by sending a delegation to a country to take evidence from witnesses, those measures exist to address situations in which the domestic authorities have failed to investigate and are unlikely ever to be implemented in connection with decisions arising from any well-functioning legal system.

6.37

The UK Government is not under a duty of disclosure equivalent to that of the Crown in domestic criminal proceedings, but the Strasbourg Court can ask it to provide information and documents, and regards it as bound to comply under Article 38 of the Convention (which requires High Contracting Parties to 'furnish all necessary facilities' in connection with its examination of the case).

Issuing of the judgment

Judgment

6.38

Occasionally a chamber will hold an oral hearing. Since most oral hearings are convened for cases before the Grand Chamber, the procedure is dealt with below.

6.39

The judges will deliberate in private. Following their deliberations, a judgment will then be prepared. Most judgments are unattributed judgments of the court, although individual judges are entitled to provide concurring or dissenting opinions. The delay between deliberation and the giving of judgment is, by the

15 *Edwards v the United Kingdom* (1992) 15 EHRR 417 at [34].

standards of the domestic courts, slow. However, the court has a priority policy for speeding up the processing of certain cases.

6.40

In the first priority category are obviously urgent applications (such as cases involving ongoing deprivation of liberty and risks to life or health). In the second category are cases raising important questions of general interest or capable of having an impact on the effectiveness of the Convention system. Applications alleging violations of the 'core rights' (Arts 2, 3, 4 and 5(1)) are in the third category, with the remaining categorisations pertaining to ease of decision making and prospects of success. This means that the lapse of time between pleadings and judgment can vary significantly between cases.

6.41

The court does not inform the parties of the outcome of proceedings before judgment is given. However, it will usually notify the parties in advance of the date and time when its judgment is to be published on the court's website. A Chamber judgment does not become final until the possibility of a referral to the Grand Chamber is exhausted.

6.42

The court will not reopen its own final decisions on the basis that a subsequent development of the court's jurisprudence suggests that the case would now be determined differently. A procedure exists, however, to reopen a decision if new facts emerge which were not known to the court or to the party applying to reopen the decision and could not reasonably have been known; any such application must be made within six months of the facts coming to light.[16]

Pilot judgment procedure

6.43

The court may operate a 'pilot judgment procedure' to deal with 'repetitive cases' or where a 'structural or systemic problem or other similar dysfunction'[17] gives rise to a large number of applications against the same country. A pilot judgment not only resolves the application under consideration but also halts pending proceedings in similar cases for a period after it is given. The hope is that the Member State will use this time to set up domestic procedures to provide compensation or redress and, by these means, remedy the violation and compensate the victims, so that any remaining cases need not be individually considered by the court.

16 Rules of Court, Rule 80.
17 Rules of Court, Rule 61.

6.44

The United Kingdom was made subject to the pilot judgment procedure when some 2,500 cases concerning prisoner voting rights were brought following the Grand Chamber decision in *Hirst (No 2) v United Kingdom*[18] in 2005. In *Greens and MT v United Kingdom*,[19] the court issued a pilot judgment which noted that every comparable case satisfying the admissibility criteria would give rise to a violation of the Convention.[20]

6.45

The Court may also stay proceedings without implementing a pilot judgment procedure, if a lead case is expected to resolve a novel point of ECHR law or to be relinquished or referred to the Grand Chamber.

THE GRAND CHAMBER

Overview

6.46

Any case before the ECHR may, in principle, be transferred to the Grand Chamber, either by the Court itself[21] (relinquishment of jurisdiction) or upon acceding to a request by one of the parties[22] (referral). In practice, it is only the most exceptional cases – typically around 20–25 per year – that are considered by the Grand Chamber; there have been even fewer in recent years.

6.47

The Grand Chamber comprises 17 of the court's 46 judges. It must always include the President and Vice-Presidents of the court, the section presidents and the national judge corresponding to the respondent State. With the exception of the section president and the national judge, it will not include any judge who was involved in any Chamber decision.[23] The remaining judges are selected by drawing lots.

Referral criteria

6.48

Any party to a case may request referral to the Grand Chamber within three months of a Chamber judgment. In the absence of any such request, the Chamber judgment becomes final.[24] Article 43 provides:

18 (2006) 42 EHHR 41.
19 (2011) 53 EHRR 21.
20 Ibid at [116].
21 ECHR, art 30.
22 ECHR, art 43.
23 ECHR, art 26(5).
24 ECHR, art 43(1).

Referral to the Grand Chamber

1. Within a period of three months from the date of the judgment of the Chamber, any party to the case may, in exceptional cases, request that the case be referred to the Grand Chamber.
2. A panel of five judges of the Grand Chamber shall accept the request if the case raises a serious question affecting the interpretation or application of the Convention or the Protocols thereto, or a serious issue of general importance.
3. If the panel accepts the request, the Grand Chamber shall decide the case by means of a judgment.

6.49

The period during which a request for referral may be made begins on the day after delivery of the Chamber judgment and runs to midnight (Central European Time) three calendar months thereafter. The three months cannot be extended and run irrespective of when the Chamber judgment becomes known to the parties. It expires even if the last date on which a request may be made falls on a weekend, bank holiday or period of judicial recess.

6.50

Article 43(1) appears to suggest that a request for referral should only be made by one of the parties 'in exceptional cases'. However, this is an unenforceable rule, at least insofar as applicants are concerned. In practice, the panel appears to treat the 'in exceptional cases' formulation as being part of the test which it must apply. The panel does not give reasons for granting or refusing a request for referral. However, the Court has published guidance indicating the principles that have emerged in the panel's practice over the years.[25] This provides some insight into the Court's interpretation of Article 43(2) and suggests that cases which are referred to the Grand Chamber are likely to belong to one of the following categories:

1. *Cases affecting case law consistency*: the panel sees its fundamental role as ensuring that Chamber judgments are consistent with the established case law of the Court and will refer cases in order to resolve emerging conflicts between section decisions.
2. *Cases which may be suitable for development of the case law*, such as those raising issues going beyond the scope of the existing case law or highlighting a change in society that might suggest a need to re-examine questions on which the Court has previously ruled.

25 *Practice followed by the Panel of the Grand Chamber when deciding on requests for referral under Article 43 of the Convention, 2 June 2021*, European Court of Human Rights.

3. *Cases which are suitable for clarifying the principles set forth in the case law,* which may involve explaining and clarifying concepts which lacked specificity or had been misunderstood.
4. *Cases in which the Chamber decision involves a significant development of existing case-law,* for example by finding a violation in circumstances which, in the past, had not generally led to such a conclusion.
5. *Cases raising a serious question affecting the application of the Convention,* such as where there is a structural or systemic problem or other dysfunction necessitating a substantial change to domestic law or practice in the respondent State.
6. *Cases concerning 'new' issues* which have not previously been examined by the Court.
7. *Cases raising a 'serious issue of general importance'*: the Court assesses the importance of the issue at a European or global rather than a national level.
8. *Cases with 'significant repercussions'*: these may relate to historical, geopolitical or religious issues which are at the centre of a sensitive national, European or global debate. They may also concern a specific incident or crime that has attracted exceptional media attention.

6.51

A request for referral should include detailed reasons by reference to the above categories, since it will be examined solely on the basis of the Chamber judgment and the contents of the request. The fact that a case might appear to fit one of the above categories does not mean that the case will be referred to the Grand Chamber. Referral is never a formality and the vast majority[26] of requests are refused. However, a case not fitting any of the categories will almost certainly not be accepted. In particular, the panel will not refer a case simply because they disagree with the Chamber's reasoning or with the final outcome of the case. The panel will also routinely refuse requests for referral which challenge:

1. Decisions that a complaint is inadmissible.
2. The amount of an award of just satisfaction.
3. The Chamber's assessment of the facts.
4. Isolated errors or omissions in the discharge of a state's obligation to ensure an effective investigation under Articles 2, 3 or 4.
5. The 'normal' application of well-established Convention case law.

26 Over 95% of referrals are refused.

Oral hearings

6.52

Hearings are ordinarily held in public and are broadcast on the Court's website. It is permissible, but not required, to wear robes. Advocates from the United Kingdom do not usually do so.

6.53

The length of submissions will be communicated to the parties prior to the hearing. Usually, it will be no more than 30 minutes for each party, followed by 10 minutes for each party in reply.

6.54

Submissions may be made (with permission) in any of the official languages of any Member state of the Council of Europe and will be simultaneously translated into the Court's official languages (English and French). Advocates are required to submit their speaking notes the day before the hearing in order to assist the interpreters and should be aware that some of the judges may be listening to their submissions in translation. Submissions are not usually interrupted.

6.55

At the conclusion of the parties' submissions, the President will invite the judges to ask any questions they have for the parties. Once all questions have been asked, there will be a break to allow the advocates to take instructions and prepare their answers to the questions. The parties are then given the opportunity to make their replies, encompassing an answer to the judges' questions and any response to the other party's submissions. Following the hearing, the matter proceeds to judgment as set out at **6.50–6.56** above, save that any decision of the Grand Chamber is final as soon as it is given.

Admissibility

Introduction

6.56

Most applications to the ECtHR are never communicated to the respondent government or examined on their merits at all. This is because most fail one of the Court's admissibility criteria. The ECtHR takes a strict approach to admissibility, not least because its caseload would be unmanageable if it did not. To be admissible, an application must:

- be made by a 'victim' of the alleged violation;
- not be anonymous;
- not be made until the applicant has exhausted their domestic remedies;

- be made within time (now four months) of exhausting those remedies;
- deal with matters within the ECtHR's jurisdiction;
- not be manifestly ill-founded;
- not be repetitious and abusive;
- demonstrate that the applicant has suffered a 'significant disadvantage'.

The parties and 'victim status'

6.57

To bring a claim in the ECtHR a person must be a 'victim' of an alleged act. Article 34 of the Convention provides:

> The Court may receive applications from any person, non-governmental organisation or group of individuals claiming to be the victim of a violation by one of the High Contracting Parties of the rights set forth in the Convention or the Protocols thereto. The High Contracting Parties undertake not to hinder in any way the effective exercise of this right.

6.58

The court's task is not to review the relevant law and procedure *in abstracto* but to determine whether the manner in which they were applied to, or affected, the applicant gave rise to a violation of the Convention.[27] A victim, in its the autonomous meaning under the Convention, is someone who has been 'directly affected by the impugned measure'.[28] 'Victim' need not denote a victim of crime: a criminal defendant who has an unfair trial would be a 'victim' of a violation of Article 6. The test is applied 'with some degree of flexibility and without excessive formalism'.[29] Anyone subject to offence-creating legislation may be a 'victim' if they are affected by it: so, for example, a homosexual man had 'victim status' in respect of a challenge to legislation in Northern Ireland criminalising homosexual acts between consenting adults.[30] The court also takes a flexible approach to 'victim status' in cases involving covert investigative techniques, where an applicant may not know to what extent they have been affected by the measure in question.[31]

6.59

An application can only be submitted and pursued by a victim who is alive. However, in some circumstances (especially those which concern the death or disappearance of the direct victim) a family member can be considered to be

27 *Roman Zakharov v Russia* (Application no 47143/06), 4 December 2015.
28 *Burden v United Kingdom* (2008) 47 EHRR 38.
29 *Gorraiz Lizaragga v Spain* [2007] 45 EHRR 45.
30 *Dudgeon v United Kingdom* (Application no 7525/76), 22 October 1991.
31 *Roman Zakharov v Russia*.

an 'indirect victim'.[32] Whilst an organisation that has been created to represent people who are victims of an act is not itself a 'victim',[33] NGOs and other interested groups may be given permission to submit 'third-party interventions'.

Anonymity

6.60

Article 35(2)(a) of the ECHR provides that the Court shall not deal with any application that is anonymous. This principle requires that the ECtHR should be able to identify the applicant or applicants in order for the application to be admissible. This principle does not prevent the Court from making an order directing that the identity of the applicants should not be disclosed to the public.[34] A request for anonymity may be made at any time (but will normally be made at the time of the initial application) and should be accompanied by a statement of reasons explaining why the ordinary rule of public access should be disapplied.

Exhaustion of domestic remedies

6.61

Fundamental to the working of the ECHR is the principle of subsidiarity. In the first instance it is for Member States to safeguard and enforce the rights enshrined by the Convention. It follows that the ECtHR will not consider any application until the applicant has first exhausted any domestic remedy that may be available. If there is no effective remedy that can be sought before a national authority for a violation of ECHR rights, that would, in itself, be a violation of Article 13 of the Convention.

6.62

In proceedings in the United Kingdom, the exhaustion of domestic remedies will involve bringing a claim before the domestic courts or making the arguments in ongoing proceedings (such as a criminal trial). It will then be necessary to exhaust any appeal rights – including, importantly, taking any available steps to attempt an appeal to the Supreme Court. The court has held that where a litigant relied on advice from counsel that a case had been determined on issues of fact and did not raise an issue of general public importance and that therefore it was not amenable to further appeal to the Supreme Court, his failure to seek certification of a point of law of general public importance nevertheless amounted to a failure to exhaust domestic remedies.[35]

---

32 *Centre for Legal Resources (acting on behalf of Valentin Campeanu) v Romania* [2014] ECHR 789.

33 *Nencheva v Bulgaria* [2013] ECHR 554.

34 Rules of Court, Rule 47(4).

35 *Bahmanzadeh v United Kingdom* (Application no 35752/13), 25 January 2016.

6.63

Applicants must comply with domestic time limits and procedures. An applicant who has not appealed where there was a right to do so cannot claim to have exhausted domestic remedies because such an appeal would now be out of time. Good practice dictates that any human rights arguments that may in due course be pursued before the ECtHR should be run directly and explicitly before the domestic courts. This will ensure that it is clear that domestic remedies have been exhausted.

6.64

However, the ECtHR has held that the requirement to exhaust domestic remedies must be applied with some degree of flexibility and without excessive formalism.[36] The test is therefore whether the complaint has been raised 'at least in substance' in the domestic courts.[37] This does not invariably require that matters argued before the domestic courts should have been formulated as human rights arguments, provided that the complaint made before the domestic courts was fundamentally the same.

Time limits

6.65

Article 35(1) of the ECHR states:

> The Court may only deal with the matter … within a period of four months from the date on which the final decision was taken.[38]

The court applies this rule strictly and an application made out of time will normally be held inadmissible without even being communicated to the respondent government.

6.66

The 'final decision' under Article 35(1) is the date on which domestic remedies are finally exhausted. In the United Kingdom, this will typically be the date on which any Supreme Court judgment is handed down, or a decision precluding any further appeal (such as a decision refusing permission to appeal or a decision refusing to certify a point of law of general public importance). In rare cases, an applicant may rely on the date when they became aware of the exhaustion of domestic remedies, if this was later. However, the knowledge of a

36 *Gherghina v Romania* [GC], (Application no 42219/07), 9 July 2015 at 87.

37 *Vučković v Serbia* [GC], (Applications nos 17153/11, 17157/11, 17160/11, 17163/11, 17168/11, 17173/11, 17178/11, 17181/11, 17182/11, 17186/11, 17343/11, 17344/11, 17362/11, 17364/11, 17367/11, 17370/11, 17372/11, 17377/11, 17380/11, 17382/11, 17386/11, 17421/11, 17424/11, 17428/11, 17431/11, 17435/11, 17438/11, 17439/11, 17440/11 and 17443/11), 25 March 2014, at 69–77.

38 The time limit was six months until 1 August 2021. The principles have not otherwise changed and any case law referring to the six-month period will now apply with equal force to the four-month rule.

legal representative is treated as the knowledge of the applicant.[39] Time begins to run on the day after the final decision and expires four calendar months later (irrespective of the number of days in the relevant months, and irrespective of whether it falls on a weekend or public holiday).

6.67

A completed application form, signed by the applicant, must be sent by post within the relevant time limit. The date which the Court will rely on for the purposes of considering limitation will be the date of the postmark on the letter. Applications sent by other means (eg, by fax) will not be treated as bringing an otherwise out of time application within time.

Jurisdiction

6.68

The Convention imposes obligations on Contracting Parties to safeguard and not to interfere with the rights which it guarantees. It follows that the ECtHR only has jurisdiction where the violation of the Convention alleged is committed by, or at least attributable to, the Contracting State. Where this is not so, the Court may find the application inadmissible '*ratione personae*' (ie, because of the party against which it is brought).

6.69

Jurisdiction under the Convention is primarily territorial, based on the requirement under Article 1 that states should 'secure to everyone within their jurisdictions' the ECHR rights. There is extensive case law on the scope of extra-territorial jurisdiction under Article 1, especially in the context of military operations in other countries and in cases involving extradition or deportation. Any dispute as to the extent of Article 1 in these contexts will inevitably be considered together with the merits of the application.

6.70

However, where conduct complained of does not fall within the ECHR's territorial jurisdiction, it may be held inadmissible either *'ratione loci'* (because of the place where it arose) or *'ratione personae'* (because the Contracting Party against which the case is brought is not the right party, it being a matter outside their jurisdiction).

6.71

A case will be inadmissible *'ratione temporis'* (because of the time) if the violation alleged arose before accession to the Convention. This will rarely apply to cases against the United Kingdom, which has been bound by the Convention since 3 September 1953.

---

39 *Çelic v Turkey 68853/17.*

Manifestly ill-founded applications

6.72

Article 35(3)(a) of the Convention requires the Court to hold an application inadmissible if it is 'manifestly ill-founded'. This will be the case if a preliminary examination of its substance does not disclose any appearance of a violation of the rights guaranteed by the Convention. An application may be rejected as manifestly ill-founded at any stage, including by a single judge acting under Article 27 of the Convention. Any decision by a single judge that an application is manifestly ill-founded is final. The absence of any such decision at the outset, however, is not equally determinative; the question whether an application is 'manifestly ill-founded' is one which often remains live until the Chamber gives judgment.

Fourth Instance cases

6.73

The Court is not a court of 'fourth instance' (ie, it is not simply an opportunity for a further appeal after the applicant has had a first instance decision, an appeal and possibly a further appeal to a supreme or constitutional court in the domestic courts). The Court has therefore held that, consistent with the principle of subsidiarity, it is not its function to substitute its own judgment for that of the national courts, or to act as a fourth instance appeal.[40] It will reject as inadmissible an invitation to adjudicate on questions of domestic law, although it will examine the compatibility of domestic law with the Convention. Likewise, it will ordinarily reject any invitation to re-examine the facts of the case in a situation where the court has made findings in domestic proceedings. In particular, the admissibility of evidence is a matter for regulation by national law and the national courts and that the Court's only concern is to examine whether the proceedings have been conducted fairly.[41]

6.74

One form of inadmissible complaint which arises frequently is an attempt by applicants to rely on the procedural rights in Article 6 of the Convention as if they were substantive rights. This would typically be a complaint that a trial was 'unfair' simply because the answer which it produced was (the applicant suggests) wrong. Applications on this basis are likely to be dismissed as inadmissible under the fourth instance doctrine (provided that the applicant had the benefit of adversarial proceedings, that the court considered the arguments which the parties wished to raise, and that it gave reasons for its decision).

40 *Edwards v the United Kingdom* (1992) 15 EHRR 417 at [34].
41 *Gäfgen v Germany* (Application no 22978/05), 3 June 2010 at [162].

Unsubstantiated complaints

6.75

An application may be dismissed as manifestly ill-founded where it does not contain a statement of facts in compliance with Rule 47 of the Rules of Court, or where those facts cannot be substantiated. In most cases, the ECtHR will base its decision on the factual findings of the domestic courts, and it is therefore unnecessary to provide it with the evidence on which the courts made those findings. However, the parties are often requested by the Court to provide particular factual information, and where the applicant omits or refuses to do so, the sanction may be that the application is held to be inadmissible.

No appearance of a violation

6.76

In some cases, the court will determine that there is no appearance of a violation. In such a case the application is manifestly ill-founded simply because the result is, in light of the court's case law, clear. Often this is either because there have been a lot of similar cases or that, although the circumstances are novel, the ECHR principles are particularly clear.

6.77

The court will also reject applications which are incoherent, far-fetched or have clearly been invented, or where it is impossible to make sense of the alleged violations of the Convention in the context of the pleaded facts (although such applications are also likely to be inadmissible on other grounds, such as the failure to exhaust domestic remedies).

Repetitious complaints

6.78

Article 35(2)(b) of the ECHR provides that the court will not deal with any application that:

> is substantially the same as a matter that has already been examined by the Court or has already been submitted to another procedure of international investigation or settlement and contains no relevant new information.

6.79

This principle is a counterpart to the domestic law concept of *res judicata*: the reference to 'substantially the same… matter' is a reference to applications that involve essentially the same persons, facts and complaints. The purpose of the rule is to ensure finality of proceedings. For this reason, the court does not apply this admissibility criterion as flexibly as others:[42] it will not look at substantially the same case twice.

6.80

The ECtHR may agree to consider an application which is based on substantially new factual information (which may include a change in domestic law) but will not revisit cases where a subsequent development in the court's jurisprudence calls into question its previous decision. The ECHR may also hold inadmissible an application which would lead to parallel proceedings before multiple international courts or tribunals.

Abuse of right

6.81

Article 35(3)(a) of the ECHR establishes that an application which is 'an abuse of the right of individual application' is inadmissible. Such applications may include those which mislead the court, use particularly inappropriate language (going beyond merely cutting, polemical or sarcastic observations) which is not withdrawn and for which there is no apology, and those which are vexatious or devoid of any real purpose. However, the Court has emphasised that holding an application inadmissible on the grounds that it is an abuse of right is an exceptional measure.[43]

Significant disadvantage

6.82

Article 35(3)(b) of the Convention provides that an application is inadmissible if the Court considers that:

> the applicant has not suffered a significant disadvantage, unless respect for human rights as defined in the Convention and the Protocols thereto requires an examination of the application on the merits.

6.83

This head of inadmissibility was added in 2010 with the intention of helping the Court to managing its case load by introducing what amounts to a *de minimis* principle. While this *de minimis* threshold would theoretically need to be cleared with respect to any of the rights protected by the Convention, the Court has held that it is difficult to imagine circumstances in which complaints under Articles 2 or 3 would be dismissed on the basis that the victim had suffered no significant disadvantage. The Court is also yet to dismiss an application under Article 5 on the basis that there has been no significant disadvantage.

---

42 *Harkins v the United Kingdom* (Application no 71537/14), 10 July 2017 at [52]–[54].

43 *Mirolubovs v Latvia* (Application no 798/05), 15 September 2009.

6.84

The question whether there has been a significant disadvantage is one which is required to be considered in light of both the objective fact and the victim's subjective perception. 'Significant disadvantage' does not require pecuniary loss, but in circumstances where the disadvantage is financial, the Court appears, without having bound itself to an inflexible rule, to have set the threshold for significant disadvantage at around €500.[44] Equally, it will have regard to the applicant's circumstances when assessing the significance of any financial loss. The Court will nevertheless examine a case on its merits if respect for human rights requires it to do so. This has to date included cases in which:

1. A novel issue of principle arises which requires to be determined.
2. The issues are of widespread interest or there are potential systemic problems.
3. The issues raise serious questions affecting the application or interpretation of the Convention or important questions concerning national law.
4. There is an alleged lack of effective remedy in the domestic legal system.

REMEDIES

Introduction

6.85

Article 41 of the Convention states:

> If the Court finds that there has been a violation of the Convention or the Protocols thereto, and if the internal law of the High Contracting Party concerned allows only partial reparation to be made, the Court shall, if necessary, afford just satisfaction to the injured party.

6.86

'Just satisfaction' is a concept which encompasses both pecuniary and non-pecuniary damages, as well as costs and expenses. The court does not always award just satisfaction and will sometimes hold that the finding of a violation of the Convention is sufficient to constitute 'just satisfaction' on its own, since a public finding in a judgment binding on the government is itself a powerful form of redress.

6.87

In addition to the obligation to pay any specific award of damages, expenses and costs ordered in light of a finding of a violation, Member States are under an obligation to 'abide by the final judgment of the court in any case in which

44 *Practical Guide on Admissibility Criteria*, 30 April 2022.

they are parties'.[45] This means that they are required both to take steps to end the specific violation suffered by the applicant (and where possible, to put him back in the situation in which he would have been had the violation not occurred) and to take general measures to prevent future similar violations in similar situations. The Committee of Ministers supervises the execution of final judgments.[46]

Procedure

6.88

A specific claim for an award of just satisfaction must be made under Rule 60 of the Rules of Court. The court will not award an applicant more than they have specified in the claim.

6.89

It is not necessary to include a claim for just satisfaction in the application itself. The court will usually inform the applicant of the time frame for submitting the claim at the same time that the case is communicated to the respondent government. This will often be at the same time as any response to the observations made by the government.

6.90

The claim must be made in accordance with the court's direction for an award to be made. For that reason, even if an application has been included in the application it will have to be re-submitted in response to the direction of the court. It is also essential that the application should be accompanied by sufficient supporting evidence. It is for the applicant to make out their claim and there is not usually an opportunity to supplement supporting evidence at a later stage.

6.91

There is generally no opportunity to make submissions on just satisfaction once it is known whether there is a finding of a violation (and if so on what basis), so the written application should contain full details of the basis of the claim. The respondent government will be given an opportunity to respond in writing to the claim. The decision on just satisfaction will be included in the judgment. The respondent government is ordinarily required to make payment within three months of a judgment becoming final (which may be up to three months after it has been handed down).

45 ECHR, art 46(1).
46 ECHR, art 46(2).

Pecuniary damages

6.92

The court approaches pecuniary damages in accordance with the principle of *restitutio in integrum*. It will award pecuniary damages for losses already suffered, as well as for any expected future loss. The Court will usually make financial awards in euros irrespective of the nationality of the applicant and the currency in which a claim is expressed. Pecuniary damages can only be claimed where there is a direct causal link between the violation of the ECHR and the damages sought. If damages are incapable of precise assessment, the court will make as accurate an estimate as it can based on the information before it, although it will not seek further information. In some cases, a combined award will be made covering both pecuniary and non-pecuniary loss. The court may also consider whether there is an opportunity to reopen domestic proceedings or to obtain compensation at a national level, rather than make any award.

Non-pecuniary damages

6.93

An award in respect of non-pecuniary damage reflects the need to make redress for a breach of fundamental human rights. By its nature, it is incapable of precise assessment, but the amount of damages broadly reflects the gravity of the violation and the importance of the right infringed. The court may also take into account any redress already provided or available to the applicant. In addition, in choosing the level of award, the court may take some account of local economic conditions. This means that practitioners should not place undue reliance on awards made to victims in other Member States with a different cost of living. The assessment of damages is a less rigorous process than it is in the domestic courts in the United Kingdom. There is little guidance, as well as some apparent inconsistency, in the amounts awarded in individual cases. In addition, awards can often seem low in comparison with damages awarded by domestic courts in England and Wales.

Costs and expenses

6.94

Successful applicants can claim costs and expenses which they can evidence that they have actually incurred in the proceedings. Legal costs should be particularised in an itemised invoice or schedule of work. Evidence must be provided to establish that the sum claimed is a sum which the applicant is contractually obliged to pay their lawyers (and not simply the amount the representatives would like to be paid if their fees are covered by the award of just satisfaction). Any award of legal aid will be deducted from the amount claimed.

6.95

Where a violation of more than one article of the ECHR is alleged, it may be helpful to set out the legal costs by reference to the time and cost incurred in addressing each, since only the costs and expenses incurred in making successful complaints will be recovered. The amount claimed may not be awarded if the ECtHR considers that it is unreasonable and excessive. This will be assessed largely by comparison with other costs claims from the same jurisdiction.

Other remedies

6.96

Judgments of the court have no direct effect in domestic law. Where an applicant succeeds, for example, in establishing a violation of the Article 6 right to a fair criminal trial, the judgment does not itself overturn the conviction. A defendant who believes their case should be quashed in consequence of a judgment of the court will typically need to invite the Criminal Cases Review Commission to refer his case to the Court of Appeal or Crown Court (which is applicable) as a first appeal will usually have occurred when domestic remedies were exhausted.

6.97

It cannot be assumed that a finding of a violation of the Convention will automatically lead to the domestic courts quashing a criminal conviction. In some instances (for example, if it is held to be a violation of the Convention that particular conduct is criminal at all) it may do so. However, some procedural defaults (such as a failure to ensure a trial within a reasonable time) may not call into question the safety of a conviction.

Interim relief

Introduction

6.98

Rule 39 of the Rules of Court provides that the court may:

> at the request of a party or of any other person concerned, or of their own motion, indicate to the parties any interim measure which they consider should be adopted in the interests of the parties or of the proper conduct of the proceedings.

Grant of relief

6.99

The threshold condition for a grant of Interim relief is an 'imminent risk of irreparable harm'. Like the final remedies available under the ECHR, an order for interim relief has no direct effect in domestic law but the United Kingdom is bound by its treaty obligations to take whatever interim measure the Court requests.[47] The most commonly granted form of interim relief granted in a criminal law context is an order preventing removal in extradition proceedings where human rights issues (especially issues under arts 2 or 3) are raised.

6.100

There have been a number of cases in which the court has ordered an interim measure to ensure that a prisoner has access to appropriate medical care,[48] but interim relief is not used to grant any form of bail pending the outcome of the Strasbourg proceedings. Interim measures have also occasionally been granted to ensure the right of access to a court.[49] It is not possible to appeal against or challenge a refusal to grant interim relief.

Procedure for applying for interim relief

6.101

An application for Rule 39 relief, where appropriate, should be made as soon as possible after the final decision of the domestic courts. It is not necessary first to have made an application under Article 34. The application is made in writing and submitted by post or fax.[50]

6.102

The Court has struggled with the volume of applications for interim measures[51] and, in light of the need to manage its workload, takes a strict approach to the procedural rules. In particular, it is essential for applicants to include the reasons why interim relief should be granted directly on the application and to attach relevant documents and domestic decisions, as the Court will not contact applicants to request missing reasons or documents.[52] It is insufficient to cross-refer to any Article 34 application or other document on the case file. The application for interim relief should explain clearly the nature of the risk and the Convention rights said to have been violated. Applicants should consider any recourse they may have in domestic law before applying for interim measures and may, in some cases, be able to reach agreement with the government on interim measures without the need for a court order.

47 Although specific provision for interim relief is only found in the Rules of Court, the ECtHR has held that the obligation to comply with interim measures derives from Article 34 and that such orders have binding legal effect: *Mamatkulov and Askarov v Turkey* (Application no 46827/99), 4 February 2005.

48 See, eg, *Paladi v Moldova* [GC] [2009] ECHR 450.

49 *Ocalan v Turkey* (2003) 37 EHRR 10.

50 The Court will *not* accept applications by email.

51 See *President's statement on Rule 39 requests to suspend deportation* (2011).

52 Practice Direction on interim measures (2011).

6.103

Applications for interim relief may take at least a business day for the Court to process.[53] If immediate and irreversible action (for example, extradition) is likely in the event of a negative domestic decision, such that the application for interim relief cannot be processed in the time between the decision and the step against which relief would be sought, the court will accept an application for interim relief made prior to the final decision of the domestic courts which is expressed to be conditional on that final domestic decision being negative.[54]

53 It is important to be alert to the public holidays and other dates when the Registry is closed, which may include approximately a week over the Christmas period as well as other dates which are not UK bank holidays.

54 Practice Direction on interim measures.

Part 2

Criminal investigation

7 Entrapment, surveillance and covert policing

Denis Barry

INTRODUCTION

7.1

The areas of entrapment, surveillance and covert policing most frequently engage ECHR Articles 6, 8 and 10, the critical concepts to consider being proportionality and lawfulness. There are a range of statutes that are explicitly designed to ensure that the actions of state actors in the UK are ECHR compliant. As much was the purpose of the Regulation of Investigatory Powers Act 2000 (RIPA). The same is true for Part III of the Police Act 1997 and section 5 of the Intelligence Services Act 1994, which provide a statutory framework under which covert surveillance or property interference activity can be authorised and conducted compatibly with the ECHR.

7.2

RIPA in particular was designed to ensure that the law clearly covered the purposes for which powers can be used, which authorities could use the power, who should authorise the use of the power, the use that could be made of the material gained, independent judicial oversight, and a means of redress for the individual. It is important to emphasise the fact that RIPA of itself did not make anything unlawful *per se* – section 80 made that explicit.

7.3

The Investigatory Powers Act 2016 is specifically concerned with privacy, as is clear from section 1(1). It also deals, among other things, with the interception of communications, equipment interference, the acquisition and retention of communications data, bulk personal datasets.[1]

1 See *R (on the application of National Council for Civil Liberties (Liberty)) v Secretary of State for the Home Department* [2020] 1 WLR 243; *Privacy International v Sec of State for Foreign and Commonwealth Affairs* [2021] 2 WLR 1333; *Big Brother Watch and others v UK* (Application nos 58170/13, 62322/14 and 24960/15) and *R (On the Application of Schofield) v Sec of State for Home Department* [2021] EWHC 902 (on the bar of the use of intercept material in criminal cases).

ENTRAPMENT

7.4

The background to this area was comprehensively addressed in *R v Syed*.[2] Common law jurisdictions deal with the issue of entrapment slightly differently: in the USA entrapment is a substantive defence: a matter for the jury. In Canada the remedy is a stay.[3] In Australia, the trial judge has a discretion to exclude evidence. In New Zealand the court has an inherent jurisdiction to exclude evidence to prevent an abuse.[4]

7.5

In the leading case of *R v Looseley*,[5] Lord Nicholls described the difficulty of drawing the line between acceptable and unacceptable conduct:

> It is simply not acceptable that the state through its agents should lure its citizens into committing acts forbidden by the law and then seek to prosecute them for doing so. That would be entrapment. That would be a misuse of state power, and an abuse of the process of the courts.

7.6

It is obviously not as simple as that. Lord Steyn in *R v Latif*,[6] explained that the issue of entrapment posed the 'perennial dilemma':

> If the court always refuses to stay such proceedings, the perception will be that the court condones criminal conduct and malpractice by law enforcement agencies. That would undermine public confidence in the criminal justice system and bring it into disrepute. On the other hand, if the court were always to stay proceedings in such cases, it would incur the reproach that it is failing to protect the public from serious crime.

7.7

Syed explored whether there is any real distinction between the jurisprudence of the ECHR and the domestic court. It was a terrorism case reliant on online conversations between the defendant and security service personnel, without which the Crown would not have had a case.

---

2 *R v Syed* [2019] 1 WLR 2459.

3 *Ahmad v R (British Columbia Civil Liberties Association and others intervening); Williams v R (Same and another intervening)* [2020] 5 LRC 173, Supreme Court of Canada.

4 *R v Syed* at [67].

5 *R v Looseley* [2002] 1 Cr App R 29.

6 *R v Latif* [1996] 1WLR 104 at [112].

7.8

The Court of Appeal rejected the submission that the Strasbourg jurisprudence required a new approach, different from *Looseley*, to be taken to the topic of alleged entrapment. It held that domestic disclosure procedures, fortified by the prosecutor's continuing duty as to disclosure, are not in any way non-compliant with Article 6, for the following four reasons:[7]

1 The rationale for both the domestic and European law is the same: the concern for the integrity of the criminal justice system. As a result, ends do not necessarily justify means. Criminal proceedings amounting to an affront to the public conscience on account of the improper conduct of state agents may be stayed. Were it otherwise, the administration of justice would be brought into disrepute. A balance has to be struck, and there are limits as to what is accepted by way of police, intelligence or security work. The propositions for those limits come equally from ECHR and domestic authority.

2 The working definitions of entrapment are the same. Though there may be distinctions between the wording used, these are distinctions without a material difference.

3 Efforts to construct differences between the two approaches based on an unduly literal reading of the language of judgments are misplaced and to be discouraged. As a result, the distinction in both systems becomes clear. That distinction is between on the one hand state agents doing no more than presenting a defendant with an unexceptional opportunity to commit a crime and on the other the state punishing an individual for a crime which the state itself has instigated. These matters are always fact specific.

4 The same logic applies to the issues of disclosure, which is often important in the context of cases where there is a suggestion of entrapment.

7.9

This was predicated on the fact that a careful analysis of the distinctions between the ECHR and domestic authority had already been completed by the House of Lords in *Loosley*. Their Lordships had already examined with care in particular *Teixeira de Castro v Portugal*[8] and concluded that its 'statement of principle' was not 'divergent from the approach of English law'.

7 *R v Syed* at [108]–[111].

8 *Teixeira de Castro v Portugal* (1999) 28 EHRR 101.

Convention background

7.10

Teixeira was concerned with an applicant whose conviction had been mainly based on statements of police officers who had incited the commission of the offence. The Court emphasised that the admissibility of evidence was primarily a matter for national law and what the Court was concerned with was whether the proceedings, as a whole, were fair. The problem in that case was that the relevant officers exercised an influence such as to incite the commission of the offence. Without the actions of the officers there is nothing to suggest that the offence would have been committed. There was therefore a violation of Article 6(1). The Court has been concerned in the past with the disclosure exercise in such cases, especially when the facts involved public interest immunity hearings. Strasbourg cases decided before the decision in *R v H*[9] should be approached with caution, as *Syed* made plain.[10]

7.11

Ramanauskas v Lithuania[11] described some 'general principles', including the definition of police incitement:

> Police incitement occurs where the officers involved – whether members of the security forces or persons acting on their instructions – do not confine themselves to investigating criminal activity in an essentially passive manner, but exert such an influence on the subject as to incite the commission of an offence that would otherwise not have been committed, in order to make it possible to establish the offence, that is, to provide evidence and institute a prosecution.

7.12

The Court said that there was an obligation for a thorough examination as to whether the prosecution has incited a criminal act. Such enquiries should include the reasons why the operation had been mounted, the extent of the police's involvement in the offence, and the nature of any incitement or pressure that had been applied.

7.13

In *Syed*, the Court also considered the European Court of Human Rights (ECtHR)'s decisions in *Bannikova v Russia*[12] and *Veselov v Russia*.[13] The former suggests that the following factors should be considered carefully:

---

9 *R v H* [2004] 2 AC 134.

10 See *Edwards and Lewis v United Kingdom* (2005) 40 EHRR 24 and *Syed* at [94].

11 *Ramanauskas v Lithuania* (2010) 51 EHRR 11 at [49–61].

12 *Bannikova v Russia* (2010) 18757/06.

13 *Veselov v Russia* (2012) 23200/10.

(a) whether there were objective suspicious that the applicant had been involved in criminal activity or was predisposed to commit a criminal offence;

(b) whether the authorities could demonstrate good reasons for mounting the covert operation; and

(c) whether undercover agents merely joined the criminal acts or, in fact, instigated them.

7.14

In *Veselov*, the role of domestic courts was summarised as follows:

> Any arguable plea of incitement places the courts under an obligation to examine it in a manner compatible with the right to a fair hearing. The procedure to be followed must be adversarial, thorough, comprehensive and conclusive on the issue of entrapment, with the burden of proof on the prosecution to demonstrate that there was no incitement. [...] The scope of the judicial review must include the reasons why the covert operation was mounted, the extent of the police's involvement in the offence and the nature of any incitement or pressure to which the applicant was subjected.[14]

The main principles

7.15

The following principles may be taken from *Looseley* and *Moore & Burrows*,[15] cited with approval in *Syed:*

(a) It is not acceptable that the state through its agents should lure its citizens into committing acts forbidden by the law and then seek to prosecute them for doing so. Such conduct would be entrapment, a misuse of state power and an abuse of the process of the courts.

(b) By recourse to the principle that every court has an inherent power and duty to prevent abuse of its process the courts can ensure that executive agents of the state do not so misuse the coercive law enforcement functions of the courts and thereby oppress citizens of the state.

(c) However, the investigatory technique of providing an opportunity to commit crime should not be applied in a random fashion or be used for wholesale virtue-testing without good reason. The greater the degree of intrusiveness, the closer the court will scrutinise the reason for using it.

---

14 See also *Furcht v Germany* (2015) 61 EHRR 25.
15 *Moore & Burrows* [2013] EWCA Crim 85.

(d) The use of proactive techniques are required more and are hence more appropriate in some circumstances than others; the secrecy and difficulty of detection and the manner in which the particular criminal activity is carried on being relevant considerations.

(e) In deciding what is acceptable, regard is also to be had to the defendant's circumstances, including his vulnerability.

7.16

In *Syed*,[16] Lord Justice Rix cited with approval the analysis of Professor Ormerod[17] in identifying five factors as of particular relevance:

- *Reasonable suspicion* of criminal activity as a legitimate trigger for the police operation. This works as a control for testing the good faith of the police. Suspicion need not be centred on a particular individual: it could be on a particular place.
- *Authorisation and supervision* of the operation as a legitimate control mechanism. This is relevant to the question of whether the state has overstepped the mark of legitimate detection into the creation of crime. To allow policemen or controlled informers to undertake entrapment activities carries obvious dangers.
- *Necessity and proportionality* of the means employed to police particular types of offence. This may depend on the type of offence since 'consensual' crimes such as the supply of drug require undercover operations as an essential ingredient in the process of detection.
- '*Unexceptional opportunity*' meaning 'Did the undercover officer cause the crime, or merely provide an opportunity to commit it with the officer rather than someone else? In this context it should be remembered that since (for example) ordinary members of the public do not become involved in large-scale drug dealing, the appropriate standards of behaviour in such cases become problematic.
- *Authentication of the evidence*. The significance of an unassailable record is very important.[18]

The burden of proof in entrapment cases

7.17

Syed[19] considered in a limited way (it not being determinative of the appeal) where the burden lies in such cases. The appellant suggested that *Ramanauskas*[20]

16 (2019) 1 WLR 2459 at [89].
17 In 'Recent Developments in Entrapment' [2006] *Covert Policing Review* 65.
18 See *R v Chandler* [2002] EWCA Crim 91.
19 *R v Syed* at [112].
20 *Ramanauskas v Lithuania* at [70].

was authority for the proposition that the State bears the burden to demonstrate that there was no breach of Article 6, the Court having there held:

> It falls to the prosecution to prove that there was no incitement, provided that the defendant's allegations are not wholly improbable. In the absence of any such proof, it is the task of the judicial authorities to examine the facts of the case and to take the necessary steps to uncover the truth in order to determine whether there was any incitement. Should they find that there was, they must draw inferences in accordance with the Convention.

7.18

However, the Court in *Syed* found this paragraph to be 'not entirely straightforward' and reiterated the conventional understanding that the burden in English law 'rests on the accused to make good the charge of abuse'.

7.19

The alternative remedy is an application under section 78 of the Police and Criminal Evidence Act 1984, where the burden of proof is not applicable because that test involves an exercise of discretion. The European decisions are 'more obviously geared to differently articulated criminal systems',[21] in which there is often judicial oversight of operations. There is also no defence of entrapment, as there is in other jurisdictions.

Entrapment by private citizens

7.20

The position where the entrapment is not by a state agent has been considered in a series of cases[22] involving undercover journalists, regulatory proceedings and, most recently in *R v TL*,[23] in which a member of the public posed as a child to collect evidence against the appellant. The Lord Chief Justice explained:

> In both domestic jurisprudence (see the *Health Care Professionals* case) and in Strasbourg when looking at conduct for the purposes of article 6 (see the *Shannon* case) there is a recognition that the conduct of a private citizen may in theory found a stay of proceedings as an abuse of process. As Goldring J recognised in the former case, no question of the state seeking to rely upon evidence which flows from its own misuse of power arises. The underlying purpose of the doctrine of abuse of process is not present. None the less, a prosecution needs evidence;

21 Per Roderick Munday in his commentary on *R v Syed* at CLW/19/03/2.

22 See *R v Shannon* [2001] 1 Cr App R 12, *R v Hardwicke and Thwaites* [2001] Crim LR 220, *R v Marriner* [2002] EWCA Crim 2855, *Hasan v GMC* [2003] UKPC 5, *Council for the Regulation of Health Care Professionals v GMC* and *Saluja* [2007] 1 WLR 3094.

23 *R v TL* [2018] 1 WLR 6037.

> and it is not inconceivable that given sufficiently gross misconduct by a private citizen, it would be an abuse of the court's process (and a breach of article 6) for the state to seek to rely on the product of that misconduct. The issue would be the same: would the prosecution be 'deeply offensive to ordinary notions of fairness' or 'an affront to the public conscience' or 'so seriously improper as to bring the administration of justice into disrepute'. In other words, as Goldring J put it, 'so serious would the conduct of the non-state agent have to be that reliance upon it in the court's proceedings would compromise the court's integrity'. He observed that there had been no reported case in which such activity has founded a successful application for a stay. Like him, we do not find that surprising. Given the absence of state impropriety, the situations in which that might occur would be rare.

7.21

There has been a growth in 'internet vigilante' cases and it has been suggested that it may be a matter of time before such a group could be regarded as falling within the definition of covert human intelligence sources.[24]

SURVEILLANCE

7.22

Part II of RIPA is concerned with surveillance and human intelligence sources. Surveillance is defined by section 48(2) as:

> (a) monitoring, observing or listening to persons, their movements, their conversations or their other activities or communications;
>
> (b) recording anything monitored, observed or listened to in the course of surveillance; and
>
> (c) surveillance by or with the assistance of a surveillance device.

In *Re A Complaint of Surveillance*,[25] the Investigatory Powers Tribunal suggested that the correct approach to the topic was to regard surveillance as bearing the ordinary English meaning.

Authorisations

7.23

Codes of Practice[26] issued pursuant to section 71, stipulate the way in which authorisations are to be granted and make it plain that Convention Rights are

---

24 See commentary on *R v TL* in Criminal Law Week CLW/18/33/1.

25 *Re A Complaint of Surveillance* [2014] 2 All ER 576.

26 See www.gov.uk/government/publications/covert-surveillance-and-covert-human-intelligence-sources-codes-of-practice.

at the heart of the authorisation process[27] because Articles 6 and 8, as well as Article 1 of the First Protocol are obviously engaged. The Code emphasises that this is particularly important where the prosecution seeks to protect the use of surveillance techniques through public interest immunity procedures. The Act does not make a failure to obtain an authorisation a criminal offence, but the explanatory notes accompanying the Act (see para 180) recognise that such a failure may mean that the law enforcement agency had acted unlawfully under section 6 of the Human Rights Act 1998.[28]

7.24

If the relevant authorisations are in place, then, pursuant to section 27, surveillance and the use of a covert human intelligence source is lawful for all purposes.[29] Authorisations must be reviewed frequently. Those granting them should be mindful of unforeseen changes to the reason why an authorisation was given. The Protection of Freedoms Act 2012 inserted section 32A,[30] which requires a Justice of the Peace to approve any authorisations for a local authority under section 29. Section 43 of RIPA provides general rules as to the grant, renewal and duration of authorisations.

DIRECTED SURVEILLANCE

7.25

Directed surveillance is that which is covert (ie, with an intention to be secret[31]) but not intrusive and is undertaken:

(a) for the purposes of a specific investigation or a specific operation;

(b) in such a manner as is likely to result in the obtaining of private information about a person (regardless of whether the person has been specifically identified for the purposes of the investigation or operation); and

(c) otherwise than by way of an immediate response to events or circumstances the nature of which is such that it would not be reasonably practicable for an authorisation under this Part to be sought for the carrying out of the surveillance.

27 See, eg, the Code for Covert Surveillance and Property Interference at 2.7.

28 The purpose of RIPA was further considered in *Mc E v Prison Service of NI* [2009] 2 WLR 782 at [34] and [70].

29 But see *Chatwani and Orsa v National Crime Agency* [2015] Lloyd's Rep FC 659 at [15] re the duty of candour in such applications.

30 As a result of the Home Office Review into Counter-Terrorism and Security Powers in 2011 and *Paton v Poole Borough Council* IPT/09/01/C.

31 *R (on the application of Butt) v Secretary of State for the Home Department* [2019] EWCA Civ 256.

7.26

The last section is designed to ensure that CCTV cameras or an officer on routine patrol do not require authorisations, for example *R v Rosenberg*[32] in which the Court of Appeal found that CCTV installed by a neighbour did not engage RIPA since it was not done at the behest of the police.[33]

7.27

Directed surveillance obviously engages Article 8, therefore authorisations are required under section 28 from an appropriately designated person. Such authorisations must be proportionate and necessary, under one of the grounds in section 28(3). The authorised conduct must be carried out 'for the purposes of the investigation or operation specified or described in the authorisation' (s 28(4)(b)). Schedule 1 sets out the authorities that may carry out directed surveillance.

7.28

In *R v Khan*,[34] authorisation was provided under RIPA for recording equipment to be installed in police vans due to transport the defendants for the purpose of ensuring that that there was sufficient evidence to charge. At the time of the recording the defendants had, in fact, been charged, therefore the recording was outside the authority given. The Court of Appeal said that, as a result, the Court should focus on whether the material should be excluded pursuant to section 78 of PACE:

> … if the behaviour of the police in the particular case amounts to an apparent or probable breach of some relevant law or convention, common sense dictates that this is a consideration which may be taken into account for what it is worth. Its significance, however, will normally be determined not so much by its apparent unlawfulness or irregularity as upon its effect, taken as a whole, upon the fairness or unfairness of the proceedings.

7.29

The Court in *Khan* specifically noted that the ECtHR has consistently held that issues of admissibility of evidence obtained unlawfully are for the national courts to decide based on principles of fairness and cited with approval the review by Lord Hobhouse in *R v P*.[35] The rationale for this (and similar decisions) is:

(a) Article 8 is a qualified right: inference with the right in accordance with law for the prevention of crime is not a breach.

---

32 *R v Rosenberg* [2006] EWCA Crim 6.

33 See also *R v Loveridge* [2001] EWCA Crim 973 (defendants recorded covertly for identification purposes and art 8); *R v Mason* [2002] EWCA Crim 385 (covert recording in cells), *R v Button* [2005] EWCA Crim 516 (where a correct authorisation not granted).

34 *R v Khan* [2013] EWCA Crim 2230. See also *R v Plunkett* [2013] 1 WLR 3121 and *R v Bond (Anthony)* [2020] EWCA Crim 1596, discussed at 9.22.

35 *R v P* [2002] 1 AC 146. See also *Schenk v Switzerland* (1991) 13 EHRR 242 (1988).

(b) Article 19 makes it plain that the role of the Court is to 'ensure the observance of the engagements undertaken by the Contracting Parties'. That is the reason why rules of admissibility are a matter for national courts.[36]

(c) Even in circumstances where there has been a breach of Article 8, section 78 of PACE is not concerned with providing remedies for such a breach. The Court is concerned only to consider the overall fairness of the trial process.

7.30

In *Mc E v Prison Service of NI*,[37] a remand prisoner sought an assurance that their consultations would not be monitored; no such assurance was forthcoming; likewise, when a consultant psychiatrist asked for the same. The House of Lords held that RIPA did permit covert surveillance of communications of persons in custody, provided that the surveillance was carried out in accordance with the Act and the Code of Practice and did not violate Convention rights. Directed surveillance in such circumstances was unlawful, however, and violated Article 8. Consequently, the authorisation for surveillance had to be made at the enhanced level such as pursuant to the intrusive surveillance provisions.[38]

7.31

As Lord Phillips observed, the case involved the tension between the importance of covert surveillance in the fight against terrorism and serious crime and the importance of LPP. He further noted that the relevant Strasbourg jurisprudence[39] covers interception of communications, covert surveillance and the right to private consultation with a lawyer. The cases demonstrate that there is no absolute prohibition on surveillance in any of these situations. Both Articles 6 and 8 may be engaged. So far as Article 6 is concerned, surveillance on communications between lawyer and client will not necessarily interfere with the absolute right to a fair trial.

Intrusive surveillance

7.32

The distinctions between directed and intrusive surveillance are important because the latter requires a different type of authorisation. There is a deliberate overlap between the provisions in RIPA governing intrusive surveillance and those in Part III of the Police Act 1997 and section 5 of the Intelligence Services Act 1994 which govern entry to, or interference with, property.

---

36 At [41] to [46].

37 *Mc E v Prison Service of NI* [2009] 2 WLR 782.

38 This led, in turn, to amendments to the Codes – see **9.19**.

39 See *Klass v Germany* (1978) 2 EHRR 214; *Weber and Saravia v Germany* (Application no 54934/00), 29 June 2006, *Huvig v France* (1990) 12 EHRR 528, *Kruslin v France* (1990) 12 EHRR 547, *Kopp v Switzerland* (1998) 27 EHRR 91, *S v Switzerland* (1991) 14 EHRR 670.

7.33

Surveillance is intrusive if it is covert surveillance that is carried out in relation to anything taking place on any residential premises, or in any private vehicle, involves the presence of an individual on the premises, or in the vehicle, or is carried out by means of a surveillance device. This kind of surveillance may take place by means either of a person or device located inside residential premises or a private vehicle of the person who is subject to the surveillance, or by means of a device placed outside which consistently provides a product of equivalent quality and detail as a product which would be obtained from a device located inside.[40]

7.34

Intrusive surveillance is governed by a distinct regime with stricter controls, requiring a higher level of authorisation. The initial authorisation has to be given by a designated senior officer. Pursuant to section 36 of RIPA it is not to take effect until its grant has been approved by a surveillance commissioner and written notice of the approval has been given. Under section 32(3) of RIPA the authorisation may only be given if it is necessary in the interests of national security, for the purpose of preventing or detecting serious crime, or in the interests of the economic well-being of the UK. This contrasts with the much broader grounds for directed surveillance under section 28(3).

COVERT HUMAN INTELLIGENCE SOURCES

7.35

As defined by section 27(8) of RIPA, someone is a covert human intelligence source (CHIS) if that person establishes or maintains a personal or other relationship with a person for the covert purpose of:

(a) facilitating the obtaining of information or to provide access to any information to another person; or

(b) covertly disclosing information obtained by the use of such a relationship or as a consequence of the existence of such a relationship.

7.36

Surveillance is covert if, and only if, it is carried out in a manner that is calculated to ensure that persons who are subject to the surveillance are unaware that it is or may be taking place (s 27(9)(a)). A purpose is covert, in relation to the establishment or maintenance of a personal or other relationship, if and only if

40 Covert Surveillance and Property Interference Code of Practice at 3.19 onwards. The Code further addresses the meaning of residential premises at 3.23. See also 9.28.

the relationship is conducted in a manner that is calculated to ensure that one of the parties to the relationship is unaware of the purpose (s 27(9)(b)).[41]

7.37

Allan v UK[42] related to a long-standing police informant who spoke to the appellant whilst he was in his cell. The ECtHR considered other international authorities on the topic,[43] which demonstrate that the critical factor is to be able to demonstrate sound operational decision making. The Court held that, in determining whether a procedure such as that deployed had extinguished the right to silence, the relevant factors to be examined were the nature and degree of the compulsion, the existence of any relevant safeguards, and the use to which the material obtained was put. In this case the persistent questioning led to the equivalent of an interrogation without any of the normal safeguards and was not in accordance with law; there had therefore been a breach of Article 8.

7.38

In *Wilson v Commissioner of the Metropolis*,[44] which concerned an undercover officer having sexual relationships, confirmed that the CHIS authorisation system in RIPA was in accordance with law pursuant to Article 8(2), although the claimant's Article 8 rights had been violated. There were also breaches of Articles 10 and 11.

Authorisation of covert human intelligence sources

7.39

In order for an authorisation to be granted it must be necessary and proportionate. The grounds upon which it can be necessary, pursuant to section 29(3) of RIPA are the same, and therefore as broad, as for directed surveillance (s 28(3)).

7.40

The Code identifies (at 3.5) elements of proportionality that should be considered, including the need to balance the scope of the activity against the proposed gravity and extent of the perceived crime or harm, collateral intrusion, and the need to evidence, as far as reasonably practicable, what other methods have been considered and why they were not (or not successfully) implemented. The Code also sets out the information to be provided in an authorisation (at 5.11).

41 Further explanation as to establishing, maintaining and using a relationship is provided in the Covert Human Intelligence Sources Code of Practice at 2.15.

42 *Allan v UK* (2003) 36 EHRR 12.

43 *R v Herbert* [1990] 2 SCR 151, *R v Broyles* [1991] 3 SCR 595, *R v Liew* [1999] 3 SCR 227, *R v Swaffield* and *R v Pavic* [1998] HCA 1.

44 *Wilson v Commissioner of the Metropolis* [2021] 9 WLUK 354.

7.41

Authorising officers also need to consider the risk of interference with the private and family life of persons who are not the intended subjects of the CHIS activityThe Code also deals in detail (at 8.26 onwards) with the various types of privileged information (for example journalistic material or that protected by LPP).

COVERT HUMAN INTELLIGENCE SOURCES (CRIMINAL CONDUCT) ACT 2021

7.42

This Act is concerned with authorisations for the security and intelligence agencies, law enforcement agencies and a limited number of other public authorities to participate in criminal conduct where it is necessary and proportionate to do so for a limited set of specified purposes. It amended section 29 of RIPA to include a new section 29B: a requirement for a judicial commissioner to be notified of a grant or cancellation of such a 'criminal conduct authorisation'. There are specific safeguards for the vulnerable and juveniles. The threshold is the same for intrusive surveillance, rather than directed surveillance or the more standard CHIS.

7.43

A criminal conduct authorisation may not be granted unless it is necessary, proportionate to what is sought to be achieved, and arrangements exists that satisfy such requirements as may be imposed by the Secretary of State. In considering whether those requirements are satisfised, the person must take into account whether what is sought to be achieved could not be reasonably achieved by other conduct which would not constitute crime.

8 Interception of communications

Rupert Bowers KC

INTRODUCTION

8.1

Often, and for good reason, legislative change lags behind social change and any shift in public attitudes. In the context of the interception of communications the speed at which technology advances presents a problem as the law struggles to keep pace.

8.2

The overwhelming majority of criminal prosecutions now involve evidence gathered from computers, mobile phones and other devices which include text and voice messages. Much of this evidence will be obtained from the devices themselves which are seized in the course of searches of either the person or of premises. However, as the prosecutions across the globe that rely in large part on evidence obtained from the EncroChat server in France has demonstrated, the remote interception of communications plays an ever-increasing part in the investigation and prosecution of serious crime, as well as the gathering of intelligence.

8.3

It is axiomatic that the interception, extraction and recording of personal communications interferes with the right to respect for private life and the right to respect for correspondence.[1] Any such interference must be proportionate and in accordance with the law, serve a legitimate interest and be necessary in a democratic society to fall within the Article 8(2) exception. While the Strasbourg jurisprudence in relation to Article 8 has shaped domestic laws governing interception by public authorities across Europe, with the same principles concerning the accessibility and foreseeability tests under the legality condition of Article 8(2) applying to indiscriminate bulk interception techniques as those targeted at individuals, no breach of Article 8 rights could serve to render otherwise admissible evidence inadmissible in this jurisdiction, the remedy for such a breach lying outwith the criminal process. Neither could a breach of Article 8 be said to render a fair trial impossible in accordance with

1 *Liberty and others v United Kingdom* (2009) 48 EHRR 1 at [63].

Article 6. Any breach of Article 8 would be a matter that could be prayed in aid upon an application to exclude evidence pursuant to section 78 of the Police and Criminal Evidence Act 1984 (PACE), however unlawfully obtained evidence is admissible subject to the exclusionary provisions of section 78.

8.4

The Investigatory Powers Act 2016 (IPA) changed the regime for the interception of a communications on a grand scale. It provides for a range of intrusive powers all of which engage the citizen's right to privacy but in terms of some of the wider powers, such as the bulk collection of communications data, give rise to particular issues relating to the collateral intrusion into the privacy of those who are not targets of any investigation. The ability to intercept communications in this way, and on this scale, necessitated the introduction of control and independent oversight in the shape of the judicial approval of warrants by Judicial Commissioners of the Investigatory Powers Commissioners Office (IPCO).

HISTORICAL CONTEXT

8.5

The interception of communications is not a new phenomenon, but it has become an increasingly complex area given the sophistication of communication methods. Whilst the state has always possessed the ability to intercept letters under disparate powers, legislative formality only arrived in 1985 following the case of *Malone v United Kingdom*.[2] The ECtHR found that our domestic law lacked the necessary legal certainty and that the interception of Mr Malone's telephone calls amounted to a breach of Article 8. One need only compare the central pieces of legislation to see how the interception of communications has burgeoned in the near past. The consequently enacted Interception of Communications Act 1985 (IOCA) was but 15 pages long and its successor, the Regulation of Investigatory Powers Act 2000 (RIPA) contained 25 sections in Part I. In the same compass of time, the Investigatory Powers Act 2016 (IPA) has increased the number of provisions tenfold.

8.6

Unsurprisingly, IOCA was of its time. It could not have anticipated the myriad ways in which electronic communication would take place in the future. It was directed at the interception of telephone calls and post, which were the types of interference challenged in *Malone*. Section 1 of IOCA created an offence of intentionally intercepting a communication 'in the course of transmission', a phrase which forms an integral part of the definition of 'interception' in section 4(1) of the IPA. The procedure for authorising interception under IOCA remained essentially unchanged, involving the issuance of warrants by

2 *Malone v United Kingdom* (1985) 7 EHRR 245.

the Secretary of State. However, IOCA introduced a regime which governed the issue, duration and form of warrants and created a tribunal in the form of a Commissioner to which complaint could be made by those affected.

8.7

RIPA was, at least in part, the legislative response to the decision of the ECtHR in *Halford v UK*.[3] Mrs Halford was a senior police officer who had been given the private use of one of the telephones comprised in the internal telephone network of Merseyside police. The system was not a part of the public network. Mrs Halford alleged that her communications had been intercepted. The interception was unwarranted because there was no interference with a public network, so it fell outside the scope of IOCA; however, the Court held that the interference engaged Article 8(1) and could not fall within Article 8(2) for this reason.

8.8

There had been significant advances in communication technology since the introduction of IOCA so rather than amend IOCA piecemeal to include private communication systems, which were increasing rapidly by that time, a decision was taken to replace IOCA in entirety and to introduce RIPA which would cover comprehensively not only all forms of interception and associated data gathering but also covert surveillance and the decryption of encrypted material.

8.9

The catalyst for the IPA was the litigation against government agencies spawned by the revelations made by the former National Security Agency contractor Edward Snowden in relation to the bulk interception of communications data under what was known as Operation Tempora. The IPA followed the ill-fated Data Retention and Investigatory Powers Act 2014 (DRIPA) which permitted the state's retention of data following the case of *Digital Rights Ireland v Minister for Communications, Marine and Natural Resources*,[4] in which the ECJ held that the EU legislature had exceeded the limits of the principle of proportionality in relation to Articles 7, 8 and 52(1) by adopting the Data Retention Directive. DRIPA was enacted swiftly, with little scrutiny, to fill that void, receiving Royal Assent on 17 July 2014.

8.10

It was not long before it was challenged. David Davis and Tom Watson, respectively Conservative and Labour Members of Parliament at that time, sought a declaration that sections 1 and 2 of DRIPA were incompatible with Articles 7 and 8 of the Convention for the reasons given in the *Digital Rights Ireland* case. The Home Secretary appealed the decision and the Court of Appeal referred questions for preliminary ruling to the ECJ which held that

---

3 *Halford v UK* (1997) 24 EHRR 523.

4 *Digital Rights Ireland v Minister for Communications, Marine and Natural Resources* [2014] 3 WLR 1607.

the Convention rights in play precluded legislation which provided for access to retained traffic and location data by national authorities when this was not retained for the purposes of combatting serious crime or where the right to access is not subject to prior judicial scrutiny and authorisation. This was the death knell for the short-lived DRIPA, which was repealed on 31 December 2016 to be replaced by the IPA, an Act of 272 sections and 10 Schedules which runs to over 500 pages.

8.11

The complex provisions of the IPA, so far as they relate to the prosecution of serious criminal offences, came under scrutiny for the first time from 2020 in the raft of prosecutions that followed the takedown of the encrypted mobile phone network known as EncroChat which, according to the National Crime Agency, was used exclusively by the criminal fraternity.

PRIVATE COMMUNICATIONS AS EVIDENCE AT A CRIMINAL TRIAL

8.12

As the commission of crime now routinely involves the use of messaging on any number of different platforms it is inevitable that the legislation and Codes of Conduct thereto, which seek to strike the balance between privacy and the investigation of crime, will be more complex.

8.13

This is not a chapter about all of the issues involved in surveillance (covert or overt) or the interception or extraction of communications, many of which relate to the gathering of intelligence, but rather how the right to privacy of communication enjoyed by every individual can be lawfully interfered with in the wider public interest of the investigation and prosecution of serious crime and how the interception and extraction of communications, and the lawfulness thereof, impacts upon the right to a fair trial if those communications are introduced as evidence in a criminal trial. That said, communications that are intercepted or obtained in the course of an intelligence-gathering exercise which then leads to a criminal investigation would be subject to the disclosure provisions contained in the Criminal Procedure and Investigations Act 1996 and any applications that may be made for non-disclosure of otherwise disclosable communications on the basis of public interest immunity.

8.14

Section 56 of the IPA replaced section 17 of RIPA which, in turn, had replaced section 6 of IOCA. The provisions are to the same effect and driven by policy. During their currency these provisions prohibited the disclosure of communications intercepted into legal proceedings. There are a number of exceptions, which are contained in Schedule 3 of the IPA. In relation to criminal proceedings Schedule 3, paragraph 2 provides that there may be disclosure of a communication that falls within s 6(1)(c) IPA which defines 'lawful authority' to intercept a communication as including:

> (c) in the case of a communication stored in or by a telecommunication system, the interception—
>
> (i) is carried out in accordance with a targeted equipment interference warrant under Part 5 or a bulk equipment interference warrant under Chapter 3 of Part 6,
>
> (ii) is in the exercise of any statutory power that is exercised for the purpose of obtaining information or taking possession of any document or other property, or
>
> (iii) is carried out in accordance with a court order made for that purpose.

8.15

The effect of section 6(1)(c) is that provided communications are harvested whilst being 'stored' in or by the telecommunication system as opposed to being intercepted 'in the course of its transmission' (see IPA, s 4(1)) and that there is an underlying authority or power for obtaining the communications, then the communications are not caught by the prohibition in section 56 and are admissible as evidence in a criminal trial. The scope of the prohibition in section 56(1) is broad:

> (1) No evidence may be adduced, question asked, assertion or disclosure made or other thing done in, for the purposes of or in connection with any legal proceedings or Inquiries Act proceedings which (in any manner)—
>
> (a) discloses, in circumstances from which its origin in interception-related conduct may be inferred—
>
> (i) any content of an intercepted communication, or
>
> (ii) any secondary data obtained from a communication, or
>
> (b) tends to suggest that any interception-related conduct has or may have occurred or may be going to occur.

This is subject to Schedule 3 (exceptions).

8.16

The potential effect of section 56 cannot be underestimated. If it applies then there is no way back for a prosecuting authority as, unlike section 78 of PACE, there is no element of discretion to be considered by the Court in relation to the effect on the fairness of any trial in admitting the evidence; the communications are inadmissible as a strict operation of law. The policy that lies behind the prohibition in section 56 and its predecessors is not driven by any consideration of whether a defendant may receive a fair trial (as many a defendant has thought) but by a desire to protect intelligence-gathering techniques. This is why the scope of the prohibition extends to even asking any questions or making an assertion in relation to the subject matter covered by section 56(1).

8.17

This prohibition has been the subject of litigation both recently, in EncroChat cases, and historically. It has now been extended to 'secondary data' to reflect the introduction of that new concept in the IPA. 'Interception-related conduct' is another new concept introduced by the IPA and is defined in section 56(2). Other European jurisdictions draw no distinction between communications that are harvested 'in the course of transmission' and those that are 'stored'. The Council of Europe Criminal Law Convention on Corruption recommended that signatory states adopt 'such legislative measures as may be necessary … including those permitting the use of special investigative techniques' to facilitate the gathering of evidence and confiscation of proceeds.[5]

8.18

While the interception and extraction of communications are necessary tools for combatting serious crime and terrorism, there is a plain difference between the use of those communications and associated data as intelligence, and its use as evidence. Section 56 patrols that distinction. It is increasingly difficult, however, to understand why the prohibition exists in relation to communications intercepted 'in the course of transmission' and not to those harvested from some 'storage' cache on a device or other part of the telecommunications system by a similarly covert technical method. As the analysis of the case of *A, B, D and C* below shows, the courts are (perhaps understandably) reluctant to find that communications have been intercepted in the course of transmission so that the prohibition in section 56 precludes their use in evidence. All communications must exist somewhere between the point of sending and the point of receipt. Along the course of the transmission of a message it will be temporarily stored at any given moment in time on the sending or receiving handset (if a mobile network) or at various junctions, such as servers, in between. How the law regards 'in the course of transmission' may not[6] coincide with the view of a technical expert.

8.19

Any determination of whether section 56(1) applies requires a consideration of the flow of sections 3, 4 and 6 of the IPA. Section 3(1) creates an offence of unlawful interception if a person intentionally intercepts a communication[7] 'in the course of its transmission' in the UK by means of, *inter alia*, a public

5 Criminal Law Convention on Corruption, Article 23, https://polis.osce.org/council-europe-criminal-law-convention-corruption
6 And in the case of *A, B, D and C* it does not.
7 See IPA, s 261(2).

telecommunications system[8] (s 3(1)(a)(i)). Section 4(1) of the IPA provides that a person will intercept a communication in the course of its transmission if that person does a 'relevant act' in relation to the system and the effect of that act is to make any content of the communication available at a 'relevant time', to a person who is not the sender or the intended recipient of it.

8.20

The 'relevant act[s]' are set out in section 4(2) of the IPA and include modifying or interfering with the telecommunications system or its operation (s 4(2)(a) and (3)). Section 4(4) defines 'relevant time' in relation to a communication and means any time *while* the communication is being transmitted (s 4(4)(a)) and 'any time when the communication is stored in or by the system (whether before or after its transmission)' (s 4(4)(b)). That a stored communication is capable under the IPA of being intercepted 'in the course of its transmission' appears, at first blush, counter-intuitive, but the purpose of the two provisions can only be to distinguish the point in time at which a communication is collected.

8.21

The interception of a communication is carried out in the UK if that interception is carried out by 'conduct' within the UK (s 4(8)(a)) *and* the communication is intercepted either in the course of transmission by means of a public telecommunications service (s 4(8)(b)(i)), *or* if transmission is through a private telecommunication system where the sender or recipient is in the UK (s 4(8)(b)(ii)). Parliament chose not to define, and so not to restrict, the meaning of 'conduct' within the IPA. There is no reason for 'conduct' to be interpreted as synonymous with 'overt act'.

8.22

The interception of a communication as described above may only occur lawfully in the circumstances set out in section 6 of the IPA.

8.23

The domestic higher courts have long held that communications intercepted by foreign jurisdictions are admissible in evidence in our domestic courts, subject to section 78 of PACE, provided that the interception does not take place at the behest of the UK authorities. This is regardless of the distinction drawn by our domestic legislation between communications that are 'stored' and those that are 'live'.[9] The House of Lords in *P*, approving the decision in *Aujla*, held that although the proposed use in evidence in an English criminal trial of calls intercepted abroad involved an interference with the Article 8 rights of the accused, no breach existed because all that had been done in the other

8 See IPA, s 261(9).

9 See *R v Aujla* [1998] 2 Cr App R 16; *R v P* [2002] 1 AC 145; *R v Knaggs* [2018] EWCA Crim 1863.

country was pursuant to statutory authority and subject to judicial supervision. Importantly, as was stated in *Knaggs* at paragraph 170:

> …there was no rule of public policy, independent of statute, that intercept should not be used in a criminal trial; and that, where secrecy was not required in the public interest, it was *'necessary in a democratic society'* within article 8(2) for all relevant and probative evidence including intercept evidence obtained abroad, to be admissible to assist in the apprehension and conviction of criminals and ensure that their trial was fair.

8.24

It is the trial process, including the ability to invoke section 78 of PACE, which ensures the fairness of the trial.

PRIVILEGED COMMUNICATIONS

8.25

While Article 8 protects the secrecy of all communications, privileged communications enjoy special protection under the law of England and Wales. The protection is well known and fundamental[10] and is recognised and safeguarded in other areas of criminal investigative process such as the obtaining of search warrants under PACE. However, protecting privileged material under a regime of interception presents far more difficulty than in a search and seizure operation, and unlike under the search warrant regime, legally privileged material may be deliberately acquired and examined.

8.26

Chapter 1 of Part 2 of the IPA provides for both the deliberate acquisition of Legal Professional Privilege material and its selection for examination after its acquisition, regardless of whether it was obtained deliberately or incidentally. Sections 26 to 29 provide additional safeguards for different categories of privileged or protected material. These are for Members of Parliament (s26), legal privilege (s 27), confidential journalistic material (s 28) and the sources of journalistic material (s 29). In the case of a Member of Parliament,[11] the Secretary of State may not issue a targeted interception warrant or a targeted examination warrant the purpose of which is to intercept communications sent by or to a Member of Parliament without the approval of the Prime Minister.

10 See *Three Rivers District Council and Others v Governor and Company of the Bank of England (No 3)* [2003] 2 AC 1.

11 IPA, s 26(3) includes members of the devolved legislatures.

8.27

So far as legally privileged material is concerned, any application for a targeted interception warrant, mutual assistance warrant or targeted examination warrant which has as at least one of its purposes the interception or examination of LPP material, the application must state that purpose and the warrant may only issue if there are 'exceptional and compelling circumstances that make it necessary'. In consideration of this criterion section 27(6) steers the decision maker. Such a warrant may not be issued unless:

(a) the public interest in obtaining the information that would be obtained by the warrant outweighs the public interest in the confidentiality of items subject to legal privilege;

(b) there are no other means by which the information may reasonably be obtained; and

(c) in the case of a warrant considered necessary as mentioned in section 20(2)(b) or (3) or (as the case may be) section 21(4), obtaining the information is necessary for the purpose of preventing death or significant injury.

8.28

If the *only* reason such a warrant is sought is for the purpose of preventing or detecting serious crime, then it may not be issued (s 20(2)(b)). This will obviously rule out such warrants for the majority of criminal investigations and limit their use to matters which are in the interests of national security (s 20(2)(a)) and the economic well-being of the UK so far as those are relevant to the same (s 20(2)(c)). If such a warrant is issued, there are further safeguards as to how that material may be retained and handled in sections 53–57 and 150–154. Sections 55 and 153 of the IPA deal specifically with legally privileged material and make it a requirement for the Investigatory Powers Commissioner to be informed if such material is intercepted or to be examined and makes provision for their oversight and direction of the same.

8.29

However, any communications harvested pursuant to the warrants set out above could not be used in evidence for the reasons explained already. The state's use of legally privileged material is therefore limited to intelligence in these circumstances.

8.30

As will already be clear this is not the case if communications are not caught by the prohibition in section 56. If the communications sought are not intercepted in the course of transmission but instead are gathered pursuant to a targeted equipment interference warrant issued pursuant to section 99 of the IPA, then those communications will be admissible in evidence by virtue of the exception to section 56 contained in paragraph 2 of Schedule 3 to the IPA. Unlike other warrants for interception under the IPA which may only be sought by the intelligence services, warrants for equipment interference under Part 5 may be both sought and issued by the police and all the usual authorities charged with the investigation of criminal offences if the responsible 'law enforcement chief' is satisfied with the criteria in s 106(1):

(a) the law enforcement chief considers that the warrant is necessary for the purpose of preventing or detecting serious crime;

(b) the law enforcement chief considers that the conduct authorised by the warrant is proportionate to what is sought to be achieved by that conduct;

(c) the law enforcement chief considers that satisfactory arrangements made for the purposes of sections 129 and 130 (safeguards relating to disclosure etc.) are in force in relation to the warrant; and

(d) except where the law enforcement chief considers that there is an urgent need to issue the warrant, the decision to issue the warrant has been approved by a Judicial Commissioner.

8.31

That the issuance of a targeted equipment interference warrant requires review and approval by a Judicial Commissioner operating on the principles of judicial review adds an additional safeguard. Similar safeguards relating to privileged communications as apply to targeted interception and targeted examination warrants are contained in sections 111–114. Legally privileged material may be sought if it is necessary for the purpose of preventing or detecting serious crime but *not* if the only reason it is sought is because it is necessary in the interests of the economic well-being of the UK so far as those interests are relevant to national security. Pursuant to section 131 the Investigatory Powers Commissioner has the same oversight over how legally privileged material may be treated.

ENCROCHAT

8.32

The takedown of the encrypted EncroChat mobile phone network by a multi-national team including the UK authorities was hailed by the National Crime Agency as a 'massive breakthrough' in the fight against serious organised crime. The hacking of the network in France by an EU Joint Investigations Team ('JIT') comprised of the French and Dutch[12] led to the dissemination of captured communications to other European countries via Europol and has led to hundreds of arrests and prosecutions in the UK for offences of murder, drug trafficking and firearms.

12 The United Kingdom were not permitted to be a part of the JIT because it was about to leave the EU following the Brexit referendum.

8.33

The prosecution of these offences has come with legal challenges to the admissibility of the EncroChat evidence with the prohibition contained in section 56 at the heart of that litigation. Various aspects of the interception of messages sent via the EncroChat network and intercepted in France have been challenged to date in *R (on the application of C) v DPP*[13] in relation to the European Investigation Order, the legal instrument under the authority of which the captured messages and data were transferred to the authorities in the UK, and to the mechanism and lawfulness of the data capture in *R v A, B, D and C.*[14] Applications are also pending before the Investigatory Powers Tribunal at the time of writing in relation to the lawfulness of the warranty obtained by the NCA.

8.34

The Court in *A, B, D and C* examined the circumstances of when a communication may be said to be 'in the course of transmission' for the purposes of section 4(4)(a) of the IPA and so inadmissible in evidence by operation of section 56, and when it may be said to be 'stored' for the purposes of section 4(4)(b) IPA, making it admissible through and exception in Schedule 3 of the IPA if the correct warranty is in place. The decision might certainly surprise those who are technically savvy in this area. The crucial evidence at first instance was given by an expert called by the defence to the effect that while the communications may have been exfiltrated from the handset of the sending device this could only have been after the phone operator had pressed 'send' and sent a message on its journey to the recipient, and before it had completed its journey to the recipient's device.[15] Any reader of the judgment could be forgiven for believing that they were reading a treatise on existential philosophy, for the kernel of the judgment on this issue (appearing from paragraph 61) is that a communication may be both 'stored' and 'in the course of transmission' at the same time. At paragraph 62 the Court identified the crucial question involved:

> …The statutory question for any court determining if section 4(4B) applies is this: was the communication stored in or by the system at the time when it was intercepted?

8.35

The answer to this question would surely *always* be 'yes', at least on an existential level, since the communication must exist and be held somewhere on the telecommunications system at all times if it is to exist at all. Given the way in which it approached the matter the Court held it was unnecessary to 'define exactly when transmission starts and ends'.

---

13 [2020] 4 WLR 158.

14 [2020] 2 WLR 1301.

15 The Court disagreed with the expert on this point, holding that it was purely a matter of statutory interpretation.

CONCLUSION

8.36

Those involved in serious criminal activity cannot expect those criminal endeavours to be protected by their general right to enjoy privacy of correspondence. While s 56 of the IPA of course gives no expectation of the same, its provisions must surely be reviewed. If this jurisdiction were to remove the distinction between communications 'in the course of transmission' and those 'stored' in step with other European jurisdictions who draw no such distinction, then the regime could be simplified. This would not mean that secret and sensitive covert techniques would suddenly be laid bare for public scrutiny. Those techniques could still be protected, as they are in any event with the general ability to apply for non-disclosure on the grounds of Public Interest Immunity, while allowing all intercept evidence to be admitted in evidence subject to the provisions of section 78 of PACE in any given case.

8.37

As was recognised by the June 2020 investigation report of the Information Commissioner's Office:[16]

> The right to a fair trial is an absolute right, and the right to privacy and the protection of personal data have to be considered in this context. For the public to have confidence in the criminal justice process, it is important that a public authority gives due deference and proper weight to individuals' right to privacy.

8.38

The EncroChat litigation has highlighted the potential issues that arise where data is obtained overseas and heavily encrypted. The Supreme Court case of *KBR v SFO*[17] has also drawn into sharp focus the jurisdictional limits of the courts' interpretation of legislation in line with perceived public policy aims. It is for the government, and then Parliament, to address these issues.

16 Mobile phone data extraction by police forces in England and Wales. Available at: https://ico.org.uk/media/about-the-ico/documents/2617838/ico-report-on-mpe-in-england-and-wales-v1_1.pdf.
17 [2021] UKSC 2.

9 Interference with property

Omran Belhadi

INTRODUCTION

9.1

Interference with property and equipment is governed by overlapping statutes and codes of practice. These include: the Intelligence Services Act 1994 (IS 1994), the Police Act 1997 (PA 1997), the Regulation of Investigatory Powers Act 2000 (RIPA 2000) and the Investigatory Powers Act 2016 (IPA 2016).

9.2

Two relevant codes of practice also exist. The Covert Surveillance and Property Interference Revised Code of Practice, August 2018 (Property Interference Code) relates to powers under IS 1994, PA 1997 and RIPA 2000.[1] The Equipment Interference Code of Practice, March 2018 (Equipment Interference Code) relates to powers under IPA 2016.[2]

9.3

Unlike material obtained through interception of communications, material obtained through interference with property can be used as evidence. It remains subject to rules on admissibility and the exercise of a trial judge's discretion to exclude under section 78 of the Police and Criminal Evidence Act 1984 (PACE).

LEGAL FRAMEWORK

Interference with property

9.4

IS 1994 governs the use of powers to interfere with property by the intelligence services. This includes the Security Service (SyS), the Secret Intelligence Service (SIS) and Government Communications Headquarters (GCHQ). None of the intelligence services are permitted to apply for warrants which relate to property within the British Islands unless it is in relation to conduct which

---

1 See www.gov.uk/government/publications/covert-surveillance-and-covert-human-intelligence-sources-codes-of-practice.

2 See www.gov.uk/government/publications/equipment-interference-code-of-practice.

involves serious crime. Serious crime has the same definition across the relevant statutes, namely:

> it involves the use of violence, results in substantial financial gain or is conduct by a large number of persons in pursuit of a common purpose, or
>
> the offence or one of the offences is an offence for which a person who has attained the age of twenty-one and has no previous convictions could reasonably be expected to be sentenced to imprisonment for a term of three years or more.[3]

9.5

PA 1997 governs the powers of the police. In addition, RIPA 2000 regulates intrusive surveillance activities which is broad enough to encompass interference with property.[4] The legislative framework follows the same principles regardless of the statute or agency.

9.6

First, interference must be necessary for a purpose specified in statute. For the intelligence agencies and any authorisation of intrusive surveillance under RIPA 2000 this includes the protection of national security, the economic well-being of the UK or the prevention and detection of serious crime.[5] For the police this includes the prevention and detection of serious crime or preventing or detecting the use of unmanned aircraft in the commission of a relevant offence.[6] Necessity is subjective and objective. The authorising officer or Secretary of State must hold a genuine belief the intrusion is necessary. It must also be objectively necessary. The phrase national security has 'sufficient precision' such that interference in the name of national security is in accordance with law.[7] Similarly, the phrase 'economic well-being' met the requirements of foreseeability and was sufficiently precise.[8]

9.7

Second, interference must be proportionate.[9] This requires an assessment of whether the aim to be achieved can be achieved by less intrusive means.[10] The Property Interference Code states that the following elements of proportionality should be considered:[11]

---

3 IS 1994, s 5(3B); PA 1997, s 93(4), RIPA 2000, s 81(2),(3).

4 See further Chapter 7.

5 IS 1994, s 5(2)(a); RIPA 2000, s 32(2)(a) and (3).

6 PA 1997, s 93(2)(a).

7 *Harman and Hewitt v The United Kingdom (No 2)* (Application no 20317/92), 1 September 1993.

8 *Christie v The United Kingdom* (1994) 78-A DR 119; *C v Police and Secretary of State* IPT/03/32/H, 14 November 2006.

9 IS 1994 s 5(2)(b); PA 1997, s 93(2)(b); RIPA 2000, s 32(2)(b).

10 Ibid, s 5(2A); Ibid, s 93(2B); Ibid, s 32(4).

11 Property Interference Code of Practice para 4.7.

- balancing the size and scope of the proposed activity against the gravity and extent of the perceived crime or harm;
- explaining how and why the methods to be adopted will cause the least possible intrusion on the subject and others;
- considering whether the activity is an appropriate use of the legislation and a reasonable way, having considered all reasonable alternatives, of obtaining the information sought; and
- evidencing, as far as reasonably practicable, what other methods had been considered and why they were not implemented or have been implemented unsuccessfully.

9.8

Third, it must be authorised using the authorisation process set down by statute and the Code. For the intelligence services, the Secretary of State may grant an equipment interference or intrusive surveillance authorisation.[12] For police and NCA applications for property interference or intrusive surveillance warrants this requires a senior authorising officer or a designated deputy.[13]

9.9

Applications must be made in writing.[14] They must provide the reasons for necessity, the nature of the surveillance, the residential premises or private vehicle targeted, the identities of the subject, an explanation of the information sought, details of any collateral intrusion or confidential information that is likely to be obtained and the reasons for proportionality.[15]

9.10

Any law enforcement warrant for intrusive surveillance requires approval of a Judicial Commissioner.[16] Law enforcement warrants for property interference require approval of a Judicial Commissioner in the following situations:[17]

- where the property specified is a bedroom in a hotel, dwelling, or office premises; or
- the action is likely to result in acquiring:
  - legally privileged material;
  - confidential personal information; or
  - confidential journalistic information.

12 IS 1994, s 5(2).
13 PA 1997, s 93(5); RIPA 2000, s 32(6).
14 IS 1994, s 6; PA 1997, s 95(1); RIPA 2000, s 43(1)(b).
15 Property Interference Code of Practice paras 6.5 and 7.7.
16 RIPA 2000, s 36.
17 PA 1997, s 97(2).

9.11

Agencies may obtain combined authorisations for the interference with property and intrusive surveillance.[18] For example, to fit a listening device into a suspect's vehicle a property interference warrant would be required, whilst the material recovered by that listening device would then constitute intrusive surveillance. The necessity and proportionality of each must be considered separately.

Interference with equipment

9.12

IPA 2016 contains powers for intelligence and law enforcement agencies to interfere with equipment. A targeted equipment interference warrant can only be obtained for the purposes of obtaining communications, equipment data, or other information.[19] Equipment data is defined as:

- systems data, which is 'data that enables or facilitates, or identifies or describes anything connected with enabling or facilitating, the functioning of any' system identified in section 263(4) of the IPA 2016; or
- identifying data which falls within the definition of section 100(2) of the IPA 2016.

9.13

The purpose of a targeted equipment interference warrant is more limited than a property interference warrant. If, for example, the police wished to covertly obtain fingerprints from a suspect's telephone they would need to use a property interference warrant. Targeted equipment interference warrants are governed by the same principles as property interference and intrusive surveillance warrants. They must be necessary, proportionate and authorised (IPA 2016, ss 102–106). For law enforcement the necessity can only attach to serious crime. For intelligence agencies, it attaches to national security, the economic well-being of the UK and serious crime. Proportionality is assessed in a manner similar to property interference and intrusive surveillance. The Equipment Interference Code includes as a factor the consideration of whether interference remains proportionate where there is a risk for the privacy and security of other users of equipment and systems such as the internet.[20]

9.14

Authorisation can only be granted by personnel approved by statute. For law enforcement agencies this means the Chief Constable or an appropriate delegate.[21] For intelligence agencies this means the Secretary of State (IPA 2016,

18 Property Interference Code of Practice, para 7.4.
19 IPA 2016, s 99(2).
20 Equipment Interference Code para 4.20.
21 IPA 2016, Sch 6.

s 102). The applications must contain similar levels of detail to those for property interference and intrusive surveillance. Any application for targeted equipment interference must be approved by a Judicial Commissioner (IPA 2016, s 108).

9.15

There may be overlap between a targeted equipment interference warrant and an intrusive surveillance authorisation because the conduct that is permissible under a targeted equipment interference warrant could constitute surveillance for the purposes of RIPA 2000. A separate authorisation for intrusive surveillance is not required where a targeted equipment interference warrant is obtained. Where there is no overlap – such as where a police force wishes to install a camera inside a property to monitor a suspect's activity – a separate authorisation is required.[22]

Specific material

9.16

Certain material receives enhanced protection under the statutory schemes. There is no prohibition on interference with property or equipment which would result in the collection of legally privileged material. Instead, limits are placed on what can be done with this material. Where warrants are sought specifically to examine or collect legally privileged information they will only be granted in exceptional and compelling circumstances. Such circumstances cannot exist unless the public interest in obtaining the information outweighs the public interest in preserving confidentiality and there is no other means of obtaining the information.[23] They can only be issued 'for the purpose of preventing death or significant injury or in the interests of national security'.[24] Section 14 of the IPA 2016 provides that where legally privileged information is sought, only a targeted equipment interference warrant may be issued and not one under RIPA 2000 or a property interference warrant.

9.17

By virtue of the 2010 Legal Consultations Order, any surveillance of part of premises used for legal consultation is to be treated as intrusive surveillance.[25] This means it is subject to the more rigorous requirements of intrusive surveillance over directed surveillance. The locations where such surveillance may be carried out include: prisons, police stations, immigration detention, places of detention under the Mental Health Act 2003, places of business of any legal adviser and any place used for the sitting of courts, tribunals, inquests and inquiries.[26]

---

22 Equipment Interference Code paras 3.17–3.20.
23 IPA 2016, s 112(4).
24 Equipment Interference Code para 9.50.
25 Property Interference Code paras 9.65–9.68.
26 Ibid, para 3.28 – for background see 7.32.

9.18

Other confidential material, such as journalistic material, confidential information about health or information about a constituent can also be collected whether by property or equipment interference. Such information is not considered confidential if it is 'is exchanged with the intention of furthering a criminal purpose'.[27] Where its collection is incidental, mitigation steps should be taken.[28] It should only be kept as long as is necessary and proportionate. Its collection is only permissible if it is specifically necessary and proportionate.

Use of material in criminal cases

9.19

Unlike material obtained through interception of communications, any material obtained because of property or equipment interference is admissible. It remains, however, subject to the usual rules on admissibility. Challenges to admissibility can attack the necessity and proportionality of the surveillance.

9.20

In *R v Plunkett and another*,[29] the police identified the defendants, each of whom was serving a prison sentence for unrelated matters, as suspects in a serious violent domestic burglary. They were brought to the police station for three separate interviews in the same van, which contained a listening device, and were left alone for 15 minutes at the end of each journey, during which they made incriminating remarks. The Court of Appeal found that the surveillance was necessary and proportionate. The trial judge had been right not to exercise his discretion to exclude it because there had been no deception, bad faith, coercion or intimidation on the part of the police. They had merely given the defendants an opportunity to communicate with each other.

9.21

In *R v Bond (Anthony)*,[30] covert recordings were again made in the back of a police van during transportation to the police station for interviews under caution. The Court of Appeal held that although the authority should not have been granted, the breach was mitigated by the fact that all officers acted in the genuine belief the authority was correctly in place. There was no breach of PACE Code C which prevented questioning at a location other than the police station and, again, all the police did was provide an opportunity for conversation. In any event there was no injustice to the defendants because experts were instructed to set out what could be heard. They could, and did, give evidence of what could be heard and explain any adverse comments.

27 Ibid, para 9.29; Equipment Interference Code paras 9.40 and 9.79.

28 Ibid, para 9.32; Ibid, para 9.40.

29 *R v Plunkett and another* [2013] 1 WLR 3121.

30 *R v Bond (Anthony)* [2020] EWCA Crim 1596.

9.22

Challenges to admissibility can also focus on the inadequacy of disclosure and the true nature of the capabilities. In *R v GS and others*,[31] the prosecution sought to adduce recordings of conversations between three of the defendants. The Court of Appeal held that RIPA 2000 and PA 1997 prevented the Court from inquiring into the lawfulness of an approved authorisation for directed or intrusive surveillance. The court held the lawfulness may, but does not necessarily, affect any decision as to admissibility. The role of the Commissioner was not to determine admissibility. The trial judge had therefore been correct in not ordering the disclosure of the material placed before the surveillance commissioners when seeking approval for authorisations and renewals. Prosecution's counsel's duty to ensure proper disclosure acted as a sufficient safeguard and if there was material submitted to the commissioners which was disclosable it could be disclosed.

9.23

The *GS* case should not be interpreted as barring any challenge, in the criminal courts, to the legality of the relevant warrants. As subsequent cases have demonstrated, challenges are entertained to necessity and proportionality. *GS* is authority for the principle that the Judicial Commissioner's decision is not open to challenge in the criminal courts. It does not prevent challenge of the police officers authorising the relevant warrants.

9.24

In *R v Allsopp and others*,[32] recordings of conversations between two defendants were challenged on two grounds. First, the defence argued that redacted authorisations signed by the judicial commissioner and granted on the basis that the defendants were suspected of involvement in dealing controlled drugs, were insufficient disclosure from which to challenge. The Court held that the trial judge's assessment of public interest immunity was sufficient and there was no need to disclose more. Second, the defence argued that what occurred was interception and not property interference. The police used a mobile telephone that could be activated and de-activated remotely and could record ambient conversations between parties; the conversations were then drawn into the mobile telephone. The Court of Appeal rejected the argument that this constituted interception and found that this method was no different from a police officer overhearing the conversation and recording it verbatim.

9.25

In *R v A and others*[33] the EncroChat servers based in France were compromised by the police using malware, allowing them access to the contents of EncroChat devices including conversations between parties. The precise nature of the

31 *R v GS and others* [2005] EWCA Crim 887.

32 *R v Allsopp and others* [2005] EWCA Crim 703.

33 *R v A and others* [2021] 2 WLR 1301. See also the discussion at 8.33.

malware has never been shared with defence teams, but it was unprecedented because it gave law enforcement across Europe near real time access to conversations between members of organised criminal groups and individuals involved in serious criminality. In the UK the information from EncroChat was obtained from French police and Europol by using targeted equipment interference warrants under the Investigatory Powers Act 2016. The Court held that the question of whether material was intercepted or stored did not 'require a minute examination of the inner workings of every system in every case.' Parliament had not chosen the relevant time when interception took place by reference to the location of the information on the device at the time of extraction. Because of the speed at which technology develops, the 'statutory scheme must work, whatever the technical features of the system in question'. The terms 'transmission' and 'stored' should be given ordinary English definitions. The Court's task was to understand the system and decide whether, as a matter of ordinary language, material was transmitted or stored when extracted. The Court did not find it necessary to set out the expert evidence which was inconsistent in its conclusions. The IPA 2016 does not use technical language. The experts 'have an important role in explaining how a system works, but no role whatever in construing an Act of Parliament'.

9.26

A challenge may also be mounted on the location of the surveillance. In *R v Nicholas Roderick Walters*,[34] covert surveillance was undertaken, while he was on remand, of conversations between the defendant and his visiting partner. The defence argued, first, that the surveillance was disproportionate. The officer who authorised the surveillance was not called to give evidence at trial and thus was not challenged on proportionality. The Court of Appeal held that, in the absence of forensic challenge, the Court could not substitute an officer's judgement as to what further evidence might be obtained instead of surveillance. The defence also argued that the visiting cubicle which was placed under surveillance in prison required an intrusive surveillance warrant on the basis that it was a substitute or an extension of the prison cell. The Court of Appeal found this argument 'far-fetched'; the cubicle was an open plan public area, offering only a very limited degree of privacy in relation to other inmates, there were security cameras and signs indicating their presence. It was not a space used for residential or living purposes.

Practical considerations

9.27

The possibility of property interference, intrusive surveillance and targeted equipment interference gives rise to practical considerations for criminal practitioners.

34 *R v Nicholas Roderick Walters* [2004] EWCA Crim 987.

(a) The existence of material derived from interference with property or equipment would not always be obvious to defence practitioners. It will be obvious when incriminating material is served. It will not be obvious where surveillance or interference is carried out and yields either nothing or exculpatory information. The CPIA Code of Practice, CPS Disclosure Manual and Attorney General's Guidelines on Disclosure envisage the existence of a sensitive schedule of unused material.[35] 'Sensitive' is defined as 'any material the disclosure of which would give rise to a real risk of serious prejudice to an important public interest'. That schedule is provided to the prosecutor who must then decide whether material is disclosable in whole or in part, disclosable but subject to public interest immunity, or not disclosable. While the defence is provided with a schedule of non-sensitive material as a matter of course, the same is not true of a sensitive schedule.

(b) The role of prosecution counsel is crucial in ensuring a fair trial. Where there is material resulting from property interference, intrusive surveillance or targeted equipment interference, prosecution counsel is solely responsible for ensuring any disclosable material is brought to the attention of the defence and the court. The defence is hampered by not having access to the sensitive schedule of unused material. Prosecution counsel's failure to bring disclosable material to the attention of the court and defence can result in injustice.[36]

(c) Even where authorisations are unlawful, the evidence may remain admissible. It is therefore incumbent on legal advisers to ensure that suspects are aware from an early stage of the possibility of their discussions with co-defendants, fellow prisoners, and social visitors being recorded.

35 CPIA Code of Practice, paras 6.14–6.17; CPS Disclosure Manual, Ch 8; Attorney General's Guidelines on Disclosure, paras 66–70 and 117–122.

36 *R v Conrad Jones* [2014] EWCA Crim 1337.

10 Search and seizure

Leslie Chinweze

INTRODUCTION

10.1

'The right to privacy and respect for personal property are key principles of the Human Rights Act 1998 (HRA 1998). Powers of entry, search and seizure should be fully and clearly justified before use because they may significantly interfere with the occupier's privacy. Officers should consider if the necessary objectives can be met by less intrusive means'.[1]

10.2

The power to search premises and seize property will engage Article 8 of the European Convention on Human Rights (the Convention). Article 8(1) provides that everyone has a right to respect for their private and family life, their home and correspondence. Article 1 of the First Protocol of the Convention extends this right to the peaceful enjoyment of possessions.

10.3

Unlike absolute rights from which there can be no derogation, the right to respect for private and family life and property can be restricted in the public interest. Thus Article 8(2) states:

> There shall be no interference by a public authority with the exercise of this right except such as is in accordance with the law and is necessary in a democratic society in the interests of national security, public safety, or the economic well-being of the country, for the prevention of disorder or crime, for the protection of health or morals, or for the protection of the rights and freedoms of others.

10.4

Similarly, Article 1 of the First Protocol provides:

> No one shall be deprived of his possessions except in the public interest and subject to the conditions provided for by law by the general principles of international law.

---

1 Police and Criminal Evidence Act 1984, Code B, para 1.3: Code of practice for searches of premises by police officers and the seizure of property found by police officers on persons or premises.

10.5

The fact that a search or seizure of property is undertaken in good faith will not necessarily mean it complies with the Convention, if it is not in accordance with the law or necessary in a democratic society. In *Keegan v United Kingdom*,[2] the police obtained a search warrant and forcibly entered a house to search for stolen money. The suspect no longer lived in the property and the occupier sought damages for breach of her Article 8 right for respect for her privacy. The European Court of Human Rights (ECtHR) held that although the entry and search of the claimant's property had been in accordance with the law and in pursuit of the legitimate aim of preventing crime and disorder it was not necessary in a democratic society. The police had made no reasonable enquiries to verify the identity of the resident of the address. It was not a defence for the police to assert they had acted in good faith as the aim of the Convention was to protect individual rights against the abuse of power, however motivated or caused.

10.6

Through the Police and Criminal Evidence Act 1984 (PACE), the UK has sought to ensure that powers of search and seizure are compliant with the Convention. Part II of PACE sets out the statutory framework governing powers of entry, search and seizure. Further guidance is contained in PACE Code B, the Code of Practice governing the searching of premises and seizure of property by police officers. Further, paragraph 1.3A of Code B provides that officers must use their powers of search and seizure fairly and without unlawful discrimination. Thus, Code B reinforces Article 14 of the Convention, which provides that the rights and freedoms in the Convention shall be secured without discrimination on grounds such as sex, race, colour, language, religion, political or other opinion, national or social origin, association with a national minority, property, birth, or other status.

SEARCHES

10.7

Save in certain specified circumstances, section 8 of PACE requires a police constable to obtain a warrant from a Justice of the Peace[3] to enter any premises and conduct a search. The application is made *ex parte* and supported by an information in writing.[4] Section 15(4) requires a constable to answer on oath any question the justice or judge hearing the application asks of him.

2 *Keegan v United Kingdom* (2007) 44 EHRR 33.

3 By virtue of the Courts Act 2003, s 66 a recorder, circuit judge and Judge of the High Court can also issue a warrant under PACE, s 8 as they have the same powers as a justice of the peace in relation to criminal causes or matters.

4 PACE, s 15(3).

10.8

'Premises' has an extended definition under section 23 of PACE and includes any place, as well as vehicles, aircrafts, tents and movable structures.

10.9

Section 8(1)(a)–(d) of PACE provides that before a warrant is issued, a justice must be satisfied that there are reasonable grounds for believing that:

(i) an indictable offence has been committed;

(ii) there is material on the premises which is likely to be of substantial value (whether by itself or together with other material), to the investigation of the offence;

(iii) the material is likely to be relevant evidence; and

(iv) the material does not consist of, or include items subject to legal privilege, excluded material or special procedure material.

10.10

All four of the above conditions must be met. In addition, section 8(1)(e) of PACE requires that a justice must also be satisfied that any one of the conditions specified in section 8(3) apply, these are:

(i) that it is not practicable to communicate with any person entitled to grant entry to the premises;

(ii) that even though it is practicable to communicate with a person entitled to grant entry to the premises, it is not practicable to communicate with any person entitled to grant access to the evidence;

(iii) that entry to the premises will not be granted unless a warrant is produced; and

(iv) that the purpose of a search may be frustrated or seriously prejudiced unless a constable arriving at the premises can secure immediate entry.

10.11

The conditions that must be met before a search warrant is issued have been strictly construed. In *Redknapp v Commissioner of Police for City of London*,[5] police obtained warrants to search the home of a football manager for evidence of conspiracy to defraud, false accounting and money laundering. The application was supported by a form which set out the four conditions in section 8(3) and directed the deletion of whichever condition was not applicable. The police failed to delete any of the four alternatives. The Divisional Court held that the search warrants had been issued unlawfully. Latham LJ, giving the judgment of the court said:

5 *Redknapp v Commissioner of Police for City of London* [2008] EWHC 1177 (Admin).

> The obtaining of a search warrant is never to be treated as a formality. It authorises the invasion of a person's home. All the material necessary to justify the grant of a warrant should be contained in the information provided on the form …
>
> The application for the warrant did not identify which of the conditions in section 8(3) was being relied on … I am not prepared to infer from the contents of the statement that the magistrate must have been told, or that there is enough in the statement to indicate that there was material before the magistrate which could have justified him in concluding that at least one of the conditions was met. As I have already said, it is wholly unsatisfactory, where the validity of such a warrant is in issue, to be asked to rely on anything other than the application itself … As the conditions set out in 8(3) have accordingly not been met, the warrant was unlawfully issued.

Application for a search warrant (section 15)

10.12

Section 15(2)(2A) of PACE provides that a constable applying for a warrant shall state:

(i) the grounds on which he makes the application;

(ii) the enactment under which the warrant would be issued; and

(iii) if relevant, the grounds on which he seeks entry on more than one occasion and whether he seeks a warrant authorising an unlimited number of entries, or if not, the maximum number of entries desired.

10.13

Section 15(6)(b) states that the warrant should identify, as far as is practicable, the articles or persons to be sought. A warrant when issued should specify the name of the applicant, the date on which it is issued, the enactment it is issued under and identify as far as practicable the articles or persons sought.[6] A warrant which fails to specify with sufficient precision the articles or people sought is likely to be quashed. In *R (on the application of Van der Pijl) v Kingston Crown Court*,[7] the Divisional Court held that a search warrant to search a property to find suspects in that did not identify the suspects by name was in breach of section 15(6)(b) of PACE, even though the suspects were named in supporting material. The warrant had to be judged exclusively by its own terms and it had failed to specify with sufficient precision the persons sought.

---

6 PACE, s 15(6).

7 *R (on the application of Van der Pijl) v Kingston Crown Court* [2013] 1 WLR 2706.

10.14

A warrant to search premises does not give the police the power to search persons found in the premises, unless the police are acting under a specific statutory power, such as the Misuse of Drugs Act 1971 or the Firearms Act 1964.[8]

10.15

If the application is to search one or more sets of premises, the warrant must set out the number of premises it is reasonably practical to specify. It must also state the identity of the person who is in occupation or control of the premises and why it is necessary to search more premises than can be reasonably specified. A warrant must specify if multiple entries are authorised and whether such entries are unlimited or limited to a specified maximum number.[9]

Execution of search warrants (section 16)

10.16

Section 15(1) of PACE provides that an entry on or search of premises under a warrant is unlawful unless it complies with the provisions of sections 15 and 16.

10.17

In *R v Chief Constable of Lancashire ex p Parker* [1993],[10] the Divisional Court held that section 15(1) refers to the '*composite*' process of entering and searching a property. For that process to be lawful the application for the warrant must comply with section 15 and its execution with section 16. Section 15(1) has been strictly interpreted. In *Parker*, the occupants of premises searched by police were supplied with uncertified photocopies of the schedules attached to the warrant when certified copies should have been provided. The Court held that the warrant had not been lawfully produced and the police were deprived of the authority to retain any of the materials seized. The applicants were entitled to have the material seized returned to them immediately.

10.18

Section 16 of PACE provides the following safeguards:

- a warrant may authorise a person to accompany a constable who is executing it. The person has the same powers as a constable but can only exercise those powers in the company of and under the supervision of a constable (s 16(2) and (2A));
- a warrant must be executed within three months of the date of its issue (s 16(3));

8 *Hepburn v Chief Constable of Thames Valley* [2002] EWCA Civ 1841.
9 PACE, s 15(2)(b) (2A) (5A).
10 [1993] QB 577.

- the entry and the search must be at a reasonable hour, unless it appears to the constable executing it that the purpose of search may be frustrated (s 16(4));
- where either the occupier of premises to be searched or some other person who appears to be in charge of the premises is present, a constable seeking to execute a warrant must identify himself to the occupier and, if the constable is not in uniform, produce documentary evidence that he is a constable. He must also produce the warrant and supply a copy of it to the occupier or person who appears to be in charge of the premises (s 16(5)–(7));
- if a warrant authorises a search of all premises connected to an occupier, premises which are not specified may not be searched unless an officer of at least the rank of inspector has authorised the search in writing (s 16(3A));
- premises may not be entered or searched for a second or subsequent time under a warrant, unless an officer of at least the rank of inspector has authorised it in writing (s 16(3B));
- a search under a warrant may only be conducted to the extent required for the purpose for which the warrant was issued (s 16(8)); and
- a constable executing a warrant shall endorse it with the articles or persons sought, including whether any articles were seized, other than those that were sought (s 16(9)).

10.19

In *R (on the application of Hoque) v City of London Magistrates' Court*,[11] search warrants were issued to HMRC officers. The warrants allowed an officer to remove from the claimant's home and business premises 'any form of evidence deemed relevant to the investigation, or which was of evidential value'. The Court held that the warrants were unlawfully issued as they afforded the officer too wide a discretion and failed to identify the nature of the investigation or the limits of the search. The searches carried out in pursuance of the warrant were declared to be unlawful and damages were awarded to the claimant.

PACE Code B

10.20

Further protections of the right to privacy and respect for property are set out in the Code B of PACE:

- no search under warrant may continue, once the items specified in the warrant have been found (paragraph 6.9A);

11 *R (on the application of Hoque) v City of London Magistrates' Court* [2014] EWHC 725 (Admin).

- searches must be conducted with due consideration for the property and privacy of the occupier and cause no more disturbance than necessary (paragraph 6.10);
- the occupier should be allowed to have a friend, neighbor, or other person witness the search, unless the officer in charge reasonably believes that this would hinder the investigation or endanger officers, or other people (paragraph 6.11).

Limitations

10.21

Despite the safeguards there are limitations that make it difficult for an individual to challenge the issue of a search warrant. There is, for instance, no provision in PACE requiring a warrant to state the grounds on which it has been issued. Nor is it necessary for the purposes of compliance with the HRA 1998 for a magistrates' court to record its reasons for issuing a search warrant, *R (on the application of Cronin) v Sheffield Justices*.[12] As the procedure for obtaining a search warrant is *ex parte*, police are entitled to conceal from the subject of the warrant the information that formed the basis for the application. In *R (on the application of Haralambous) v St Albans Crown Court*,[13] the claimant was provided with a redacted copy of the information sworn in support of an application for a warrant to search his home. The Court rejected the argument that because the warrant was a serious invasion of his right to privacy, he was entitled to have sight of the material which formed the basis of the application. It held that this would frustrate Parliament's intention to establish a relatively simple system for the issuing of search warrants, and an entitlement to automatic disclosure of material police used to apply for a warrant would be at odds with the public interest in the investigation and prosecution of crime.

10.22

There is also no rule in English law excluding evidence obtained from an unlawful search. Instead, section 78 of PACE gives a court the discretion to exclude evidence if, having regard to all the circumstances, its admission would have such an adverse effect on the fairness of the proceedings that it ought not to be admitted. Thus, evidence obtained from an unlawful search would be admissible if a court decided that the fairness of proceedings was not sufficiently adversely affected by its admission.

---

12 *R (on the application of Cronin) v Sheffield Justices* [2003] 1 WLR 752.
13 *R (on the application of Haralambous) v St Albans Crown Court* [2016] 1 WLR 3073.

Special categories of material

10.23

Section 9(2) of PACE provides that a warrant cannot be issued under section 8 to search for items which are the subject of legal privilege, excluded material, or special procedure material that consists of documents or records.

Items subject to legal privilege

10.24

Items subject to legal privilege are defined as communications between a professional legal adviser and his client, or any person representing that client, that are made in connection with the giving of legal advice (PACE, s 10(1)). Communications made in connection with, in contemplation of, or for the purpose of legal proceedings are covered by legal privilege, as are items enclosed with or referred to in such communications, when they are in possession of a person who is entitled to possess them. Items held with the intention of furthering a criminal purpose, are not subject to legal privilege.

10.25

The absolute prohibition on a search for items subject to legal privilege is consistent with the right to privacy and respect for personal property enshrined in the Convention. In *Niemietz v Germany*,[14] German authorities searched the law offices of the applicant to identify the writer of an insulting letter who had used a false name; a criminal offence in Germany. The ECtHR found there had been a violation of Article 8: even if the search had the legitimate aim of preventing crime, it was not proportionate because it impinged on professional secrecy (the equivalent of legal privilege).

Excluded material

10.26

Excluded material is defined as personal records, human tissue or fluid taken for the purposes of diagnosis or medical treatment and journalistic material held in confidence (PACE, s 11). Personal records are defined as documentary or other records concerning a person living or dead, which relate to their physical or mental health or spiritual counselling given to a person for their personal welfare by a voluntary organisation or an individual who, by reason of their office, occupation or order of a court, has responsibility for that person's welfare and supervision (PACE, s 12). Thus, excluded material would include items such as medical records or counselling notes.

---

14 *Niemietz v Germany* (1992) 16 EHRR 9.

Special procedure material

10.27

Special procedure material is defined as material, other than items subject to legal privilege and excluded material, which is in the possession of a person who acquired or created it in the course of a trade, business, profession or other occupation or for the purpose of any paid or unpaid office and who holds it subject to an express or implied undertaking to hold it in confidence or subject to a restriction contained in any enactment (PACE, s 14). Special procedure material would include bank statements or documents that are restricted from disclosure under the Official Secrets Act 1989.

10.28

A constable who wishes to obtain access to excluded or special procedure material must make an application to a Circuit Judge under Schedule 1 of PACE (s 9(1)). The procedure does not apply to items that are subject to legal privilege.

10.29

Whilst it is difficult for an individual to challenge a warrant issued under section 8 of PACE, an application for excluded or special procedure material is subject to a very different regime. Pursuant to Schedule 1, paragraph 7 of PACE, the application must be made on notice, to either a Circuit Judge or District Judge (para 17). The judge must be satisfied that one of two sets of access conditions are satisfied before they order access to or production of the material or issue a warrant (para 1).

10.30

The first set of access conditions which relate only to special procedure material,[15] is that there must be reasonable grounds for believing:

- an indictable offence has been committed;
- there is special procedure material on the premises specified in the application;
- the material is likely to be of substantial value to the investigation;
- the material is likely to constitute relevant evidence;
- other methods of obtaining the material are bound to fail or were tried without success; and
- it is in the public interest to provide access or produce the material.

15 PACE, Sch 1, para 2.

10.31

The second set of conditions applies to both special procedure and excluded material:[16]

- that there are reasonable grounds for believing that there is material which consists of or includes excluded material or special procedure material on the premises;
- but for section 9(2) of PACE, a warrant authorising the search could have been granted under an enactment other than Schedule 1; and
- the issue of a warrant would have been appropriate.

10.32

If the special procedure or excluded material is in electronic format, it must be provided in a form which is legible and can be taken away.[17] Once a notice under Schedule 1 has been served on any person he shall not, until the application is dismissed, abandoned or the order complied with, conceal destroy or dispose of the material except with the leave of a judge or written permission of a constable.[18]

10.33

The procedure in Schedule 1 was described as '*very vigorous*' in *R (on the application of S and others) v Chief Constable of the British Transport Police.*[19] The police applied for warrants under Schedule 1 to search the home address of a solicitor for special procedure material which was on a computer and mobile phone. The information in support of the warrant did not set out any of the facts or matters on which it was said the first set of conditions were met. The warrant was therefore quashed as having been issued unlawfully.

10.34

The consequences for an individual whose home has been searched and property seized can be severe, regardless of whether the power is exercised under section 8 or Schedule 1 to PACE. It is a matter for continued debate whether more can be done to align the two procedures to ensure a fair balance is struck between the legitimate aim of preventing crime and the protection of an individual's right for respect for their privacy and their property under the Convention.

---

16 PACE, Sch 1, para 3.

17 Ibid, Sch 1, para 5.

18 Ibid, Sch 1, para 11.

19 *R (on the application of S and others) v Chief Constable of the British Transport Police* [2014] 1 All ER 268 at [45].

Search without a warrant

10.35

A search of a premises without warrant will be unlawful unless it is reasonably required by one of the purposes set out above in section 17 of PACE, which provides that a constable may enter and search any premises, without a warrant, for the following purposes:

- executing a warrant of arrest arising out of criminal proceedings, arresting a person for an indictable offence or for certain specified offences;
- the arrest of a child or young person who has been remanded to local authority or youth detention accommodation;
- the arrest of someone who is unlawfully at large; and
- to save life and limb or prevent serious damage to property.

10.36

In addition, section 17(1)(6) preserves the common law power under which a constable can enter premises without a warrant to prevent a breach of the peace.

10.37

In *R v Veneroso*,[20] police officers entered the address of the next-of-kin of the victim of a road traffic accident. Inside the property they found evidence of drugs offences. The Court of Appeal held the search was in clear breach of Article 8, as the entry and search had not been effected to save life and limb or prevent serious damage to property. Accordingly, the public interest in bringing the defendant to trial did not outweigh the need to protect his right to privacy. As evidence from an unlawful search will not automatically be excluded (PACE, s 78) *Veneroso* must be seen on its own particular facts; the Court may well have reached a different conclusion had the officers found evidence of terrorist offences.

10.38

A search of premises without a warrant can also be affected under section 18 of PACE, which permits an officer to enter premises occupied or controlled by a person under arrest for an indictable offence, as long as the officer has reasonable grounds for believing evidence relating to the indictable offence or some other arrestable offence is on the premises. The search can only be to the extent that is reasonably required for the purpose of discovering the evidence sought (s 18(3)).

20 *R v Veneroso* [2002] Crim LR 306.

10.39

A constable also has the power under section 32(2)(b) of PACE to enter and search any premises that a person under arrest for an indictable offence was in at the time or immediately before their arrest. The phrase 'at the time of arrest' has been construed to mean immediate or close in time to an arrest. In *R v Badham*,[21] a search of premises made more than three hours after the suspect's arrest was held to be unlawful, as it was not made at the time of the arrest. The court also held there was no open-ended right to go back and search premises following an arrest. As in the case of section 18, the search must be to the extent that is reasonably required for the purpose of discovering evidence of an offence (PACE, s 32(3)).

SEIZURE

10.40

A constable who is lawfully on any premises may seize anything on the premises which they reasonably believe has been obtained as a consequence of the commission of an offence or is evidence of an offence and the constable reasonably believes that it is necessary to seize the item in order to prevent it being concealed, lost, damaged, altered, or destroyed (PACE, s 19). Police may also seize evidence found on the premises of a person under arrest for an indictable offence (PACE, s 18), or obtained through stop and search (PACE s 1(6)).

10.41

Any property seized from a person brought to a police station where there are grounds to believe that the property might be used to cause injury, damage property, interfere with evidence or effect escape can also be seized but must be returned when the person is released from custody (PACE, s 22(3)).

10.42

Where police believe that information in electronic format and accessible from the premises is evidence of an offence and will otherwise be concealed, lost, tampered with or destroyed, they can require the information to be produced in a form in which it is visible and legible and can be taken away (PACE, s 19(4)). The power covers information stored on a phone or computer. A suspect who refuses to divulge the passwords to such items could risk prosecution for obstructing an officer in the exercise of their duty.

10.43

The power of seizure does not extend to items which a constable reasonably believes are subject to legal privilege (PACE, s 19(6)), however section 50 of

21 *R v Badham* [1987] Crim LR 202.

the Criminal Justice and Police Act 2001 gives an officer who is conducting a lawful search the power to take material away from the premises if it is not reasonably practical to determine its relevance at the scene. If the officer believes that the material he seeks to examine also contains material he is not entitled to seize and it is not practicable to separate the material on the premises, he may remove all of it to determine which material he is entitled to retain. Factors such as the length of time it would take to examine the material, the number of persons required to carry out the examination and whether property would be damaged if the examination is carried out on the premises, are all relevant to the decision whether material is taken away for examination.

10.44

Seizure of property is a last resort. No article may be retained by police if a photograph or copy would be sufficient (PACE, s 22(4)) and an owner can also make an application under section 1 of the Police (Property) Act 1897 for the return of their property (expressly preserved by PACE, s 22(5)). Seized property can only be retained by police for as long as is necessary to use it as evidence in a trial, facilitate an investigation or forensic examination or to establish the lawful owner (PACE, Code B, para 7.14). Once these purposes no longer apply, the property must be returned.

10.45

In *Chief Constable of Merseyside Police v Joseph Patrick Owens*,[22] police investigating an offence of arson seized a video tape from Mr Owens' CCTV system. The video appeared to show the person who caused the fire but, as an identification could not be made, the case was closed. The police refused to return the video tape, believing that Mr Owens would use the tape to track down the arsonist and take revenge. It was held that the powers of the executive to seize and retain goods were carefully controlled by the courts, and privacy and possessions were not to be invaded except for the most compelling reasons. There was nothing in PACE to suggest that property could be retained for any other purpose, such as the prevention of crime, so the video was to be returned forthwith.

10.46

When seizing large quantities of goods, police must consider each item separately and decide whether there are reasonable grounds for believing the material should be seized (PACE, Code B, para 7.7). Reasonable steps should also be taken to accommodate an interested person's request to be present when his property is seized, as long as this does not harm the investigatory process (PACE, Code B, para 7.8A).

22 *Chief Constable of Merseyside Police v Joseph Patrick Owens* [2012] EWHC 1515 (Admin).

CONCLUSION

10.47

In *Foxley v UK*,[23] the ECtHR said the implementation of measures that interfere with an individual's fundamental human rights must be accompanied by adequate and effective safeguards which ensure the minimum impairment possible.

10.48

In relation to powers of search and seizure the Police and Criminal Evidence Act 1984 seeks to protect Convention rights of respect for privacy and peaceful enjoyment of property whilst also enabling the effective investigation and prosecution of crime. As can be seen from this chapter, the courts are particularly vigilant to ensure this balance is struck as fairly and as effectively as possible.

23 *Foxley v UK* (2001) EHRR 25.

11 Arrest and detention

Kate O'Raghallaigh

INTRODUCTION

11.1

The right to protection from arbitrary arrest and detention is a fundamental feature of English common law and is of the 'first rank'[1] of protections of the physical security of an individual. Freedom from arbitrary arrest and detention, articulated in Magna Carta 1215, has been described as 'a quintessentially British liberty, enjoyed by the inhabitants of this country when most of the population of Europe could be thrown into prison at the whim of their rulers'.[2] The ECtHR has consistently held that the right to liberty and security of the person is of the highest importance in a 'democratic society' and is necessary 'to secure the rule of law'.[3]

THE SCHEME OF ARTICLE 5 ECHR

11.2

The right to liberty and security of person enshrined in Article 5 is not coextensive with the common law protection from false imprisonment. Whilst the tort of imprisonment encompasses a person being made to stay in a particular place by another person, whether by means of physical barriers, threats of force or of legal process, the concept of a deprivation of liberty within the meaning of Article 5 is 'very different and much more nuanced', requires a 'multi-factorial approach' and is 'distinct' from the concept of restriction of physical liberty.[4] In short, there can be imprisonment at common law without there being a deprivation of liberty for the purposes of Article 5.

The purpose of Article 5

11.3

Article 5 protects the right to liberty and security of person, fundamentally protecting the individual from arbitrary detention, and requires judicial

1 *McKay v United Kingdom* (2007) 44 EHRR 41 at [30].
2 *A and ors v SSHD* [2005] 2 AC 68 at [88], per Lord Hoffmann.
3 *Winterwerp v Netherlands* (1979–80) 2 EHRR 387 at [39]; *Brogan v United Kingdom* (1989) 11 EHRR 117 at [58].
4 *R (Jalloh) v SSHD* [2021] AC 262 at [29].

oversight. It is not concerned with mere restrictions on liberty of movement, which are governed by Article 2 of Protocol No 4 and which can be justified in the public interest.[5]

11.4

The notion of arbitrariness in Article 5 extends beyond lack of conformity with national law. Thus, a deprivation of liberty may be lawful in terms of domestic law but nevertheless still arbitrary and contrary to the Convention. There is no global definition of what amounts to arbitrariness for the purposes of Article 5; what may or may not amount to arbitrariness will vary depending on the type of detention involved and its context.

11.5

For example, detention will be arbitrary where, despite complying with national law, there has been an element of bad faith or deception on the part of the authorities.[6] The condition that there be no arbitrariness also requires that the detention must genuinely conform with the purpose of the restrictions permitted by Article 5(1).[7] There must therefore be some relationship between the ground of permitted deprivation of liberty relied on and the place and conditions of detention.[8] It is through that relationship that Article 5 touches upon, and to some extent is capable of regulating, the location and/or conditions of detention.[9]

The concept of deprivation of liberty

11.6

Article 5 will not be engaged unless there has been a deprivation of liberty: 'Its place in the scheme of other unqualified rights shows that it deals with literal physical restraint.'[10] The paradigm case is 'classic detention in prison'[11] and outside that paradigm the absolute nature of the right requires 'a more exacting examination of the relevant criteria'.[12]

---

5 *Engel v Netherlands* (1979–80) 1 EHRR 647 at [58]; *Guzzardi v Italy* (1980) 3 EHRR 333 at [92]. The UK has not ratified Article 4 of the Fourth Protocol.

6 *Bozano v France* (1987) 9 EHRR 297 at [59]–[61]; *Saadi v United Kingdom* (2008) 47 EHRR 17 at [74].

7 *Winterwerp v The Netherlands (*1979) 2 EHRR 387; *Bouamar v Belgium* (1989) 11 EHRR 1.

8 *Bouamar v Belgium* (1987) 11 EHRR 1 at [50]; *Aerts v Belgium* (2000) 29 EHRR 50 at [46]; *Enhorn v Sweden* (2005) 41 EHRR 30 at [42]. See also *Ashingdane v UK* (1985) 7 EHRR 528 and *Mayeka v Belgium* (2008) 46 EHRR 449.

9 *R (Idira) v SSHD* [2016] 1 WLR 1694.

10 *Austin v Commissioner of Police of Metropolis* [2009] 1 AC 564 at [16].

11 *Guzzardi v Italy* (1981) 3 EHRR 333 at [95]; *Austin v Commissioner of Police of Metropolis* [2009] 1 AC 564 at [18, 20, 41 and 52]; *Austin v United Kingdom* (2012) 55 EHRR 14 at [59]; *Archer v Commissioner of Police of Metropolis* [2021] EWCA Civ 1662, para 67.

12 *Austin v Commissioner of Police of the Metropolis* (2009) 1 AC 564 at [18].

11.7

The difference between deprivation of and restriction upon liberty is 'merely one of degree or intensity, and not one of nature or substance'.[13] In determining whether the threshold between restriction and deprivation of liberty has been crossed, the starting point must be the person's 'concrete situation'[14] and '[a]ccount must be taken of a whole range of criteria such as the type, duration, effects and manner of execution or implementation of the penalty or measure in question'.[15]

11.8

The analysis of whether there has been a deprivation of liberty within the meaning of Article 5 can involve an objective and a subjective element.[16] Relevant objective factors to be considered may include the possibility of leaving the restricted area, the degree of supervision and control over the person's movements, the extent of isolation and the availability of social contacts.[17]

11.9

In *Gillan v Commissioner of Police of the Metropolis*,[18] the appellant was stopped and searched pursuant to section 44 of the Terrorism Act 2000, which permitted the police to stop and search members of the public at random for articles that could be used in connection with terrorism. The House of Lords held that the section 44 procedure did not involve a deprivation of liberty under Article 5. The procedure was brief (20 minutes) and the appellant had not been handcuffed or moved to another location. Lord Bingham held: 'I do not think, in the absence of special circumstances, such a person should be regarded as being detained in the sense of being confined or kept in custody; he was more properly to be regarded as being detained in the sense of being kept from proceeding or kept waiting. There is no deprivation of liberty.'[19]

11.10

The case was considered by the ECtHR in *Gillan v United Kingdom*.[20] The Court unanimously held that, whilst section 44 had a basis in domestic law, there were insufficient safeguards so as to offer the individual adequate protection against arbitrary interference and there had been a violation of Article 8. In relation to Article 5, the Court held that, whilst there had been an element of coercion inherent in the search which was indicative of a deprivation of liberty, given

13 *Guzzardi v Italy* (1981) 3 EHRR 333, para 93.
14 *Engel v. Netherlands* (1979–80) 1 EHRR 647 at [59].
15 *Guzzardi v Italy* (1981) 3 EHRR 333 at [92]; *Ashingdane v UK* (1985) 7 EHRR 528 at [30]; *Austin v United Kingdom* [2012] 55 EHRR 14 at [57].
16 *Storck v Germany* (2006) 43 EHRR 6 at [74]; *Stanev v Bulgaria* (2012) 55 EHRR 22 at [117].
17 *Storck v Germany* ibid at [73].
18 *Gillan v Commissioner of Police of the Metropolis* [2006] 2 AC 307.
19 Ibid, at [25].
20 *Gillan v United Kingdom* (2010) 50 EHRR 45.

the finding of a breach of Article 8, it was not necessary to decide that question definitively.[21]

11.11

In *Secretary of State for the Home Department v JJ*,[22] a case concerning non-derogating control orders issued under section 1(2)(a) of the Prevention of Terrorism Act 2005, the House of Lords held that the extensive restrictions imposed by the control orders on six individuals amounted to deprivations of liberty. The restrictions included curfews for 18 hours per day and extensive restrictions on residence and communication with others. In finding that the cumulative effect of the control orders amounted to a deprivation of liberty, Lord Hoffmann asked:

> Why is deprivation of liberty regarded as so quintessential a human right that it trumps even the interests of national security? In my opinion, because it amounts to a complete deprivation of human autonomy and dignity. The prisoner has no freedom of choice about anything. He cannot leave the place to which he has been assigned. He may eat only when and what his gaoler permits. The only human beings whom he may see or speak to are his gaolers and those whom they allow to visit. He is entirely subject to the will of others.[23]

11.12

Lord Hoffmann recognised that some deviation from the paradigm case may occur without the interference ceasing to be to a deprivation of liberty. In the view of the majority of the House of Lords, the circumstances of the appellants in *JJ* approximated sufficiently closely to detention in an open prison that there had been a deprivation of liberty within the meaning of Article 5.[24]

The Austin litigation

11.13

Since *JJ*, the purpose of Article 5 has assumed considerable importance in the courts' analysis of whether a deprivation of liberty has occurred and whether such detention conforms with Article 5. The absence of arbitrariness has become something of a regulating principle, as part of a notable shift towards a 'pragmatic approach' which accommodates the imperatives of modern policing.

21 Ibid, at [57].

22 *Secretary of State for the Home Department v JJ* [2008] 1 AC 385.

23 Ibid, at [37].

24 For two other control order cases in which the House of Lords and Supreme Court reviewed control orders under Art 5, see *SSHD v MB* [2008] 1 AC 385 and *SSHD v AP* [2011] 2 AC 1.

11.14

This is particularly the case in the context of the use of police powers to prevent and control public disorder. In *Austin v Commissioner of Police of the Metropolis*,[25] the House of Lords considered the appeal of a protester who took part in a large demonstration in central London. The police had pursued a policy of 'containment' or 'kettling' in order to prevent violence, injury and damage and imposed a cordon around the crowd before conducting a controlled dispersal which took several hours to complete. The appellant, whilst inside the cordon, had no access to food or toilet facilities. It was accepted before the House of Lords that the sole purpose of the cordon was to maintain public order, that it was proportionate to that need and that those within the cordon were not deprived of their freedom of movement arbitrarily.

11.15

Crucially, however, none of the justifications for interference with an individual's liberty contained in Article 5(1)(a)–(e) were clearly applicable. The key question was whether it was relevant to have regard to the overall *purpose* for which the person's freedom of movement had been interfered with. Lord Hope, with whom the other members of the House of Lords agreed, concluded that measures of crowd control which involve a restriction on liberty will not engage Article 5(1) unless they are carried out in bad faith or go beyond what is reasonably required for the purpose for which they were undertaken. In other words, where there has been an interference with liberty but none of the exhaustive criteria in Article 5(1)(a)–(e) are applicable, the absence of arbitrariness, presence of good faith and proportionate duration of the interference will operate to thwart the engagement of Article 5. This was 'a pragmatic approach to be taken which takes full account of all the circumstances'.[26]

11.16

The House of Lords' reasoning in *Austin* was confirmed by the ECtHR in *Austin v United Kingdom*,[27] where the Grand Chamber held that Article 5 'cannot be interpreted in such a way as to make it impracticable for the police to fulfil their duties of maintaining order and protecting the public, provided that they comply with the underlying principle of Article 5, which is to protect the individual from arbitrariness'.[28] The Court did not consider that commonly occurring restrictions on movement, as long as they are unavoidable, necessary to avert a real risk of serious injury or damage and are kept to the minimum duration required for that purpose, amount to a deprivation of liberty within the meaning of Article 5(1).[29]

25 *Austin v Commissioner of the Police of the Metropolis* [2009] UKHL 5.
26 Ibid, at [34].
27 *Austin v United Kingdom* (2012) 55 EHRR 14.
28 Ibid, at [56].
29 Ibid, at [59]. See also *De Tommaso v Italy* (2017) 65 EHRR 19 and *Nada v Switzerland* (2013) 56 EHRR 18. For an arguably conflicting analysis, see *Rozkhov v Russia (No 2)* (Application no 38898/04), 31 January 2017.

11.17

The shift towards a 'pragmatic approach' which was central to the outcome in the *Austin* litigation is a key feature of two subsequent domestic cases: *R (on the application of Roberts) v Commissioner of Police of the Metropolis*[30] and *R (on the application of Hicks) v Commissioner of Police of the Metropolis.*[31] In *Hicks*, the claimants were arrested in London on the morning of a royal wedding on the grounds that their arrests were necessary to prevent anticipated breaches of the peace. They were each detained at a police station but, once the wedding was over and the police considered that the risk of a breach of the peace had passed, they were released without charge. The claimants argued that there had been a deprivation of liberty which was not permitted by Article 5(1)(b) or (c), relying on the decision in *Ostendorf v Germany*[32] in which the Court held that Article 5(1)(c) was incapable of authorising purely preventive detention and that the person concerned must be suspected of having already committed a criminal offence.

11.18

Having cited the 'pragmatic approach' articulated in Austin and stating that 'it is necessary to keep a grasp of reality',[33] the Supreme Court in Hicks unanimously held that the claimants' detention fell within Article 5(1)(c), but that the detention was justified. Lord Toulson, with whom all members of the Court agreed, held that Article 5(1)(c) is capable of applying to detention for preventive purposes:

> If the police cannot lawfully arrest and detain a person for a relatively short time (too short for it to be practical to take the person before a court) in circumstances where this is reasonably considered to be necessary for the purpose of preventing imminent violence, the practical consequence would be to hamper severely their ability to carry out the difficult task of maintaining public order and safety at mass public events. This would run counter to the fundamental principles [of Article 5].[34].

EXCEPTIONS AND GUARANTEES

11.19

Freedom from arbitrary detention is guaranteed through a list of six exceptions to the right to liberty with attendant safeguards contained in Article 5(1)(a)–(f).[35] It has repeatedly been held that the list of exceptions is exhaustive and is to

30 *R (on the application of Roberts) v Commissioner of Police of the Metropolis* [2016] 1 WLR 210.

31 *R (on the application of Hicks) v Commissioner of Police of the Metropolis* [2017] AC 256.

32 *Ostendorf v Germany* (15598/08) 34 BHRC 738; [2013] Crim LR 601.

33 *Hicks* at [30].

34 Ibid at [31]

35 This chapter is generally concerned with exceptions (a)–(e), because (f) has limited general bearing on criminal proceedings.

be narrowly construed.[36] It has been held that the six permitted grounds, having been formulated in relation to peacetime conditions, do not readily adapt to a military context involving a non-Convention state and are to be seen not as exhaustive, but as illustrations of the exercise of the power to detain in the course of either an international or a non-international armed conflict.[37]

Article 5(1)(a): Detention following conviction by a competent court

11.20

Article 5(1)(a) permits the detention of a person after conviction by a competent court and pursuant to a procedure prescribed by law. It applies to any 'conviction' which results in a deprivation of liberty pronounced by a court, regardless of the domestic legal character of the offence in question.[38] Article 5(1)(a) does not require a 'lawful conviction' but only speaks of 'lawful detention'[39] and has been held to authorise all deprivations of liberty consequent on a properly imposed sentence of imprisonment. There must be a sufficient causal connection between the conviction and the deprivation of liberty at issue.[40]

11.21

The term 'competent court' requires that the court is established by law,[41] is independent of the executive and of the parties to the case and guarantees judicial procedure. The ECtHR has held that: 'The forms of the procedure need not be identical in each of the cases where the intervention of a court is required. In order to determine whether a proceeding provides adequate guarantees, regard must be had to the particular nature of the circumstances in which such proceeding takes place'.[42] If a conviction is the result of proceedings which were 'manifestly contrary to the provisions of Article 6 or the principles embodied therein', the resulting deprivation of liberty will not be justified under Article 5(1)(a).[43]

11.22

The ECtHR has rejected claims brought under Article 5 where custody decisions reached in accordance with a prescribed procedure have later been

36 *Selahattin Demirtas v Turkey (No 2)* (Application no 14305/17), 22 December 2020 (GC), para 312; *S v Denmark* (2019) 68 EHRR 17, para 73.

37 *Serdar Mohammed v MoD (No 2)* [2017] AC 821. See also *Hassan v United Kingdom* (2014) 38 BHRC 358 and *Al-Jedda v United Kingdom* (Application no 27021/08), 7 July 2011, (2011) 53 EHRR 23.

38 *Engel v The Netherlands* (1979–80) 1 EHRR 647 at [68].

39 *Webster v Lord Chancellor* [2015] EWCA Civ 742 at [42]; *Brooks v Independent Adjudicator* [2016] EWCA Civ 1033 at [30].

40 *James v United Kingdom* (2013) 56 EHRR 12 at [189].

41 *Yefimenko v Russia* (Application no 152/04), judgment of 12 February 2013 at [109].

42 *De Wilde, Ooms and Versyn v. Belgium* (ibid) at [78]

43 *Othman v United Kingdom* (2012) 55 EHRR 1 at [233] and [259]; *Willcox v United Kingdom* (2013) 57 EHRR SE16 at [95]; *Willcox v Hurford v United Kingdom* (2013) 57 EHRR SE16 at [95].

reversed. In *R (on the application of Brooks) v Independent Adjudicator*,[44] the Court of Appeal held that the detention of a young offender did not breach Article 5(1) where the award of additional days had been quashed after the days had been served because they had been imposed in accordance with a judicial procedure prescribed by law.[45]

Article 5(1)(b): Detention to enforce court orders or legal obligations

11.23

Article 5(1)(b) permits the lawful arrest or detention of a person for non-compliance with the lawful order of a court or to secure the fulfilment of any obligation prescribed by law. The first element of permitted detention is straightforward and has been held to apply to the failure to pay a court fine,[46] a refusal to undergo a court-ordered blood test,[47] breach of conditions of bail[48] and breach of a bind-over to keep the peace.[49]

11.24

In respect of the latter element, Article 5(1)(b) permits the detention of a person to compel them to fulfil a *specific and concrete obligation*[50] already incumbent on them and which they have failed to satisfy. In order to be covered by Article 5(1)(b), an arrest and detention must be aimed at, or directly contribute to, securing the fulfilment of that obligation and not be punitive in character. As soon as the relevant obligation has been fulfilled, the basis for detention will cease to exist.[51]

Article 5(1)(c): Arrest and detention on suspicion of a criminal offence

11.25

Article 5(1)(c) permits:

> the lawful arrest or detention of a person effected for the purpose of bringing him before the competent legal authority on reasonable suspicion of having committed an offence or when it is reasonably considered necessary to prevent his committing an offence or fleeing after having done so;

---

44 *R (on the application of Brooks) v Independent Adjudicator* [2016] EWCA Civ 1033.

45 Ibid, at [27], [29], [30]–[32].

46 *Velinov v the former Yugoslav Republic of Macedonia* (Application no 16880/08), 19 December 2013; *Airey v Ireland (Application* no 6289/73), 7 July 1977, DR 8.

47 *X v Austria*, (Application no 8278/78), 13 December 1979, DR 18.

48 *Gatt v Malta* (Application no 28221/08), 27 July 2010.

49 *Steel and Others v the United Kingdom* (1999) 28 EHRR 603.

50 *Engel v The Netherlands* (1979–80) 1 EHRR 647 at [69].

51 *S v Denmark* (2019) 68 EHRR 17 at [80]–[81].

11.26

The purpose for which a person is to be brought before the court must be in respect of a criminal offence,[52] the concept of which has an autonomous Convention meaning independent of its domestic classification.[53]

11.27

It would appear that Article 5(1)(c) no longer excludes purely preventive detention: in *R (on the application of Hicks) v Commissioner of Police of the Metropolis,* the Supreme Court disagreed with the majority decision in *Ostendorf v Germany*,[54] in which the ECtHR held that German legislation aimed exclusively at preventing offences was purely preventive from the outset and its use was not justified under Article 5(1)(c).

Reasonable suspicion

11.28

A reasonable suspicion of having committed an offence is a condition *sine qua non* for the validity of arrest and detention. Article 5(1)(c) speaks of a 'reasonable suspicion' rather than a genuine and *bona fide* suspicion.[55] The 'reasonableness' of the suspicion on which an arrest must be based forms an essential part of the safeguard against arbitrary arrest and detention. What may be regarded as 'reasonable' will depend upon all the circumstances. The ECtHR 'has insisted on the need for the authorities to furnish some facts or information which would satisfy an objective observer that the person concerned may have committed the offence in question'.[56]

11.29

In *O'Hara v Chief Constable of the Royal Ulster Constabulary*,[57] Lord Steyn described the requirement of 'reasonable suspicion' in Article 5(1)(c) as 'contemplating a broader test' than in domestic law, in that the test under Article 5(1)(c) is not confined to matters present in the mind of the arresting officer.[58] Thus, an arrest will be unlawful in domestic law where the arresting officer was acting on the directions of his superiors, without more. Reasonable suspicion is, however, distinct from *prima facie* proof.[59] Thus, the standard required for 'reasonable suspicion' is low: 'suspicion in its ordinary meaning is a state of conjecture or

52 *Ciulla v Italy* (1991) 13 EHRR 346.
53 *Steel v UK* (1999) 28 EHRR 603 at [48]–[49]; *Benham v UK* (1996) 22 EHRR 293 at [64].
54 *Ostendorf v Germany* (2013) Crim LR 7.
55 *Fox, Campbell and Hartley v United Kingdom* (1991) 13 EHRR 157 at [31].
56 *James v United Kingdom* (2013) 56 EHRR 12 at [193].
57 *O'Hara v Chief Constable of the Royal Ulster Constabulary* [1997] AC 286.
58 Ibid, at p 292.
59 *Dumbell v Roberts* [1944] 1 All ER 326; *Hussien v Chhong Fook Kam* [1970] AC 942; *O'Hara v United Kingdom* (2002) 34 EHRR 32 at [36].

surmise where proof is lacking … Suspicion arises at or near the starting point of an investigation of which the obtaining of prima facie proof is at the end'.[60]

11.30

Whilst one of the aims of Article 5(1)(c) is to limit the period of detention before a detainee's first court appearance, the scope of Article 5(1)(c) is not limited to detention pending the first court hearing. In *Zenati v Commissioner of Police of the Metropolis*,[61] the Court of Appeal confirmed that Article 5(1)(c) does not permit detention when the investigating authorities no longer have a reasonable suspicion that the alleged offence has been committed.[62] Because a detained person is detained by order of the court it follows that there is a duty, where the investigating authorities cease to have a reasonable suspicion that the detained person committed the offence in question, to bring the relevant facts to the attention of the court as soon as possible.[63]

Article 5(1)(d): Detention of minors

11.31

Article 5(1)(d) extends to anyone under the age of 18[64] and permits:

> the detention of a minor by lawful order for the purpose of educational supervision or his lawful detention for the purpose of bringing him before the competent legal authority.

11.32

The general scheme of pre-charge detention in England and Wales is governed by Part IV and Code C of the Police and Criminal Evidence Act 1984 (PACE).[65] Under that regime, where practicable, steps should be taken to identify the person responsible for the welfare of any child or young person taken into custody and to inform that person of the fact of the arrest and place of detention.[66]

11.33

Section 38(1)(b) of PACE provides the grounds on which a child may be detained pre-charge. Pursuant to s 38(1)(b)(ii), an arrested child may be denied release on the ground that it is reasonably believed to be in their own interests to do so. In *Archer v Commissioner of Police of the Metropolis*,[67] the Court of Appeal held that

60 *Hussien v Chong Fook Kam* at 948; see also *O'Hara v United Kingdom* at [38].
61 *Zenati v Commissioner of Police of the Metropolis* [2015] EWCA Civ 80.
62 Ibid, at [16].
63 Ibid, at [20].
64 *Koniarska v United Kingdom*, (Application no 33670/96), 12 October 2000.
65 Anyone who appears to be under 18, shall, in the absence of clear evidence that they are older, be treated as a juvenile for the purposes of the PACE Codes: see Code C, at [1.5] and Note 1L.
66 PACE Code C at [3.13 and 3.15].
67 *Archer v Commissioner of Police of the Metropolis* [2021] EWCA Civ 1662.

section 38(1)(b)(ii) could not justify a child's detention in circumstances where none of the limbs of Article 5(1)(c) were made out, but that section 38(1)(b)(ii) was not inherently incompatible with Article 5. The Court of Appeal held that, in the context of that case, Article 5(1)(d) added nothing to the protection inherent in Article 5(1)(c).[68]

11.34

The Court of Appeal in *Archer* further held that the combination of section 38 of PACE and section 21 of the Children Act 1989 make clear that there are very limited circumstances to justify the detention of children at police stations. Moreover, whilst the pre-trial detention of juveniles is not inherently contrary to the ECHR, pre-trial detention of juveniles for their own protection should be the exception and not the rule.[69]

11.35

As to the conditions of detention for children, section 38(6) of PACE makes special provision for children who are to be kept in police detention to be moved to local authority accommodation. The local authority has a discretionary power to provide secure accommodation which should be exercised in so far as it is practicable to do so, in order to further the policy objective of preventing children from being detained in police cells.[70] Moreover, the statutory prohibition on the association of children with adults in police detention would appear to be absolute.[71]

Article 5(1)(e): Detention of persons suffering from infectious diseases, persons of unsound mind, alcoholics, drug addicts, and vagrants

11.36

Article 5(1)(e) permits the detention of persons suffering from infectious diseases, persons of unsound mind, alcoholics, drug addicts, and vagrants. The rationale for this is that they may be considered to pose a danger to public safety or their own interests may necessitate their detention.[72]

11.37

In relation to infectious diseases, the essential criteria when assessing the lawfulness of the detention of a person are whether the spreading of the infectious disease is dangerous to public health or safety and whether detention

68 Ibid at [27].
69 Ibid at [125].
70 *R(M) v Gateshead Metropolitan Borough Council* [2006] QB 650; *R(BG) v Chief Constable of West Midlands Constabulary and Birmingham City Council* [2014] EWHC 4374 (Admin).
71 See the Children and Young Persons Act 1933, s 31 and *R (on app of T) v MoJ* [2013] EWHC 1119 (Admin).
72 *Guzzardi v Italy* (1981) 3 EHRR 333 at [98].

of the person infected is the last resort to prevent the spreading of the disease. If these criteria are not fulfilled, the deprivation of liberty will not conform to Article 5(1)(e).[73]

11.38

Particular emphasis is also placed in this context on the need for legal certainty and for concepts such as 'vagrant' or 'alcoholic' to be clearly defined in the national law. The Convention does not contain a definition of the term 'vagrant' however the ECtHR has held that, in principle, someone with no fixed abode, no means of subsistence and no regular trade or profession may fall within the Article 5(1)(e) exception.[74]

Article 5(2): Right to be informed promptly of the reasons for arrest

11.39

Article 5(2) guarantees a person the right to 'be informed promptly, in a language which he understands, of the reasons for his arrest and of any charge against him'. This guarantee contains the essential safeguard that any person arrested should know why they are being deprived of their liberty. Article 5(2) is therefore an integral part of the scheme of Article 5.[75]

11.40

The constraints imposed by 'promptness' will be satisfied where the arrested person is informed of the reasons for their arrest within a few hours.[76] Article 5(2) is reflected in section 28 of PACE which, subject to certain requirements of practicability, provides that no arrest is lawful unless the person arrested is informed of the ground for arrest at the time of, or as soon as practicable after, the arrest.

Article 5(3)

11.41

Article 5(3) guarantees that:

> Everyone arrested or detained in accordance with the provisions of paragraph 1(c) of this Article shall be brought promptly before a judge or other officer authorised by law to exercise judicial power and shall be entitled to trial within a reasonable time or to release pending trial. Release may be conditioned by guarantees to appear for trial.

---

73 *Enhorn v Sweden* (2005) 41 EHRR 30 at [44].

74 *De Wilde, Ooms and Versyp v Belgium (No 2)* (1979–80) 1 EHRR 373 at [68].

75 *Khlaifia and Others v Italy* (Application no. 16483/12) [GC], 15 December 2016 at [115].

76 *Kerr v the United Kingdom* (2000) 29 EHRR CD184; *Fox, Campbell and Hartley v the United Kingdom* (1991) 13 EHRR 157 at [42].

11.42

The protection embraces two stages of criminal proceedings: the initial period of detention following the person's arrest and the period pending trial before a criminal court during which the suspect may be detained or released with or without conditions. The protection in Article 5(3) confers distinct rights in respect of each stage of proceedings.[77]

11.43

The means by which the Article 5(3) protection finds expression in domestic law is essentially through the array of provisions contained in Part IV of PACE 1984, the Bail Act 1976, the Prosecution of Offences Act 1985, the Prosecution of Offences (CTL) Regulations 1987 (as amended) and the Criminal Procedure and Investigations Act 1996, including the relevant Codes of Practice.

Article 5(3): Right to be brought promptly before a judicial authority

11.44

In relation to the first limb, there must be judicial control of the arrest or detention of a suspect and on the first appearance of an arrested individual this must be prompt: 'the Court's case law establishes that there must be protection of an individual arrested or detained on suspicion of having committed a criminal offence through judicial control. Such control serves to provide effective safeguards against the risk of ill-treatment, which is at its greatest in this early stage of detention, and against the abuse of powers bestowed on law enforcement officers or other authorities for what should be narrowly restricted purposes and exercisable strictly in accordance with prescribed procedures.'[78]

The strict time constraint imposed by this requirement leaves little flexibility in interpretation, and the review of detention must be automatic and cannot depend upon the detained person making an application.[79]

11.45

The judicial officer must offer the requisite guarantees of independence from the executive and the parties and they must have the power to order release after reviewing the lawfulness the arrest and detention. The requirement to review the legality of detention at first appearance before a judicial officer is not to be confused with the power to grant bail. The question of bail can only

77 *TW v Malta* (2000) 29 EHRR 185 at [49]; *McKay v UK* (2007) 44 EHRR 41 at [31].

78 *McKay v UK* (ibid) at [32].

79 Ibid, paras 32–36; *Brogan v United Kingdom* (A/145-B) (1989) 11 EHRR 117, para 62. In *Brogan*, periods of more than four days' detention without appearance before a judge were in violation of Art 5(3) even in the special context of terrorist investigations.

arise if the person's detention is in accordance with law. The question of bail therefore falls under the second rather than the first limb of Article 5(3).[80]

Article 5(3): Right to trial within a reasonable time

11.46

The core focus of the second limb of Article 5(3) is that pre-trial detention does not exceed a reasonable time. The second limb of Article 5(3) does not give judicial authorities a choice between either bringing an accused to trial within a reasonable time or granting them bail pending trial. The presumption of innocence applies until conviction and the purpose of Article 5(3) requires a person's provisional release once their continuing detention ceases to be reasonable.[81] 'Continued detention can be justified in a given case only if there are specific indications of a genuine requirement of public interest which, notwithstanding the presumption of innocence, outweighs the rule of respect for individual liberty.'[82]

11.47

A court monitoring the detention of an individual who has been arrested on suspicion of the commission of an offence must conduct the proceedings with particular expedition or special diligence.[83] The gravity of the charges cannot by itself serve to justify long periods of detention on remand.[84] Whilst the obligation of special diligence falls upon the national court, the conduct of investigating authorities is not irrelevant. If delay on the part of the investigating or prosecuting authorities causes a court to fail to conduct proceedings with special diligence, then those who cause the delay will be responsible for the breach of Article 5(3).[85] Thus, if the investigating authorities fail to bring to the attention of the court material information of which the court should be made aware when reviewing a detention, this may have the effect of causing a decision by the court to refuse bail to be in breach of Article 5(3).[86]

11.48

Under domestic law, the principal check on pre-trial detention beyond the provisions of the Bail Act 1976 is the regime of custody time limits (CTL) enacted by the Prosecution of Offences Act 1985 and the Prosecution of Offences (Custody Time Limits) Regulations 1987.[87] The maximum period

80 Ibid, at [36] and [39].

81 *Neumeister v Austria* (A/37) (1979–80) 1 EHRR 91 at [4]; *McKay v UK* (2007) 44 EHRR 41 at [41].

82 *Kudla v Poland* (2002) 35 EHRR 11, at [110]; *McKay v UK* (2007) 44 EHRR 41 at [42].

83 *Stogmuller v Austria* (1979–80) 1 EHRR 155, para 5; *Zenati v Commissioner of Police of the Metropolis* [2015] EWCA Civ 80 at [42].

84 *Ilijkov v Bulgaria* (Application no 33977/96), 21 September 1990; *Ječius v. Lithuania*, (Application no 34578/97), 1 December 1997 at [93].

85 *Zenati v Commissioner of Police of the Metropolis* [2015] EWCA Civ 80 at [43].

86 Ibid, at [44].

87 Prosecution of Offences (Custody Time Limits) Regulations 1987 (SI 1987/299).

of custody (subject to the bringing of further charges) is currently 182 days between the time the accused is sent for trial in the Crown Court and the start of the trial.[88] This period may be extended by a court at any time prior to expiry, but only if the court is satisfied of various statutory conditions or that there is some other 'good and sufficient cause' and that the prosecution has acted with 'all due diligence and expedition'.

11.49

It has been held that the CTL regime 'in fact imposes a more rigid formula for the extension of custody time limits than Strasbourg does with regard to the reasonable time guarantee under article 5(3)'.[89] Thus, in domestic law, the question which arises under Article 5(3) is not whether there has been a specific period of delay but whether 'the total length of the detention pending trial appear[s] excessive'.[90]

11.50

A list of non-exhaustive principles and safeguards which applies to the extension of a custody time limit in the context of the Covid-19 pandemic was set out by a Divisional Court in *R (on the application of DPP) v Woolwich Crown Court*.[91] An adjournment caused by the lack of legal representation during action by the Criminal Bar Association may, in principle, constitute a good and sufficient reason to extend a CTL, but whether it did was a case-specific consideration.[92]

Article 5(4): Right to Challenge Lawfulness of Detention

11.51

Article 5(4) provides that 'everyone who is deprived of his liberty by arrest or detention shall be entitled to take proceedings by which the lawfulness of his detention shall be decided speedily by a court and his release ordered if the detention is not lawful'.

11.52

This is essentially the mechanism by which the Convention confers the right to *habeas corpus*, by providing detained persons with the right to actively seek a judicial review of their detention. Article 5(4) also secures the right to have the lawfulness of detention decided 'speedily' by a court and to have release ordered if the detention is not lawful.

---

88 See reg 5(6B).
89 *Regina (O) v Crown Court at Harrow* [2007] 1 AC 249 at [63].
90 Ibid, at [60].
91 *R (on the application of DPP) v Woolwich Crown Court* [2020] EWHC 3243 (Admin) at [44].
92 *R (on the Application of DPP) v Bristol Crown Court* [2022] EWHC 2415 (Admin).

11.53

Article 5(4) does not confer a right to release on parole. Where a person is deprived of their liberty pursuant to a conviction by a competent court, the supervision required by Article 5(4) is incorporated in the decision by the court at the conclusion of judicial proceedings.[93]

11.54

The ECtHR has held that no Article 5(4) review is required in the case of mandatory life sentences which are purely punitive in nature. However, in cases where the grounds justifying deprivation of liberty are susceptible to change over time, the possibility of recourse to a body satisfying the requirements of Article 5(4) is required.[94] In several cases against the United Kingdom, therefore, the Court found that Article 5(4) guarantees prisoners sentenced to life imprisonment the right to a remedy to determine the lawfulness of their detention once they have served the 'tariff' *or* punitive element of the sentence.[95]

11.55

In *James v United Kingdom*,[96] the ECtHR held that the UK's failure to provide rehabilitation courses to indeterminate sentenced prisoners, such as would enable them to satisfy the Parole Board of a reduction in their risk, rendered their detention arbitrary and unlawful contrary to Article 5(1) and that their release was required pursuant to Article 5(4). In *Kaiyam v SSHD*,[97] however, the Supreme Court declined to follow *James v UK*, holding that, whilst a duty to facilitate release could be implied as part of the overall scheme of Article 5, it was an ancillary duty which did not affect the lawfulness of detention.

11.56

The 'court' to which the detained person has access for the purposes of Article 5(4) does not have to be a court of law of the classical kind. It must, however, be a body of 'judicial character' offering certain procedural guarantees, including independence of the executive and of the parties to the case, and the same qualities of independence and impartiality as are required of the 'tribunal' required by Article 6[98]: 'In order to constitute such a "court" an authority must provide the fundamental guarantees of procedure applied in matters of deprivation of liberty. If the procedure of the competent authority does not provide them, the State could not be dispensed from making available to the person concerned a second authority which does provide all the guarantees of judicial procedure.'[99]

---

93 *De Wilde, Ooms and Versyp v Belgium* (1979–80) 1 EHRR 373 at [76].

94 *Kafkaris v Cyprus* (2011) 53 EHRR SE14 at [58].

95 *Stafford v United Kingdom:* (2002) 35 EHRR 32; *Wynne v United Kingdom* (2004) 38 EHRR 42; *Waite v United Kingdom* (2003) 36 EHRR 54.

96 *James v United Kingdom* (2013) 56 EHRR 12.

97 *Kaiyam v SSHD* [2015] AC 1344.

98 *Stephens v Malta (No 1),* (2010) 50 EHRR 7 at [95]; *Bas v Turkey* (Application no 66448/17), 3 March 2020 at [266].

99 *De Wilde, Ooms and Versyp v Belgium* (1979–80) 1 EHRR 373 at [76].

12 Collection and retention of personal data

Dr Aparna Rao

INTRODUCTION

12.1

In the age of the General Data Protection Regulation (GDPR), analysis of the rights surrounding our personal data merits its own book. The law is emerging and evolving – many aspects are as yet untested in the courts of England and Wales. The consequence is that guidance and suggestions surrounding the collection, processing, and retention of personal data are subject to regular revision. For those attempting to navigate this new world in the context of a criminal investigation, it can be difficult to know where the legitimate use of personal data ends and liability begins.

12.2

This chapter focuses on the way in which law enforcement authorities in England and Wales – primarily the police forces, Crown Prosecution Service (CPS), Director of Public Prosecutions (DPP), and HM Courts and Tribunals Service (HMCTS) – collect and handle personal data in the context of criminal proceedings.[1] In particular it examines:

- How and when can personal data be collected?
- How can it be used, shared, and retained?
- What safeguards exist?

12.3

The Police and Criminal Evidence Act 1984[2] (PACE) governs the collection, destruction, retention, use and other regulation of certain evidential material. Unlike the newer GDPR regime, its operation is guided by case law to assist us in determining the boundaries and protections surrounding personal data.

---

1 The intelligence services are dealt with in a different Part of the DPA.
2 As amended by the Protection of Freedoms Act 2012 (PFA).

12.4

The GDPR – a creature of EU law – still provides the foundational structure for processing and retention of personal data within England and Wales. The Data Protection Act 2018 (DPA) was extensively amended following the Data Protection, Privacy and Electronic Communications (Amendments etc) (EU Exit) Regulations 2019, which effectively created a creature known as 'the UK GDPR'. This is a shorthand for the original EU GDPR Regulation[3] as it forms part of the law of England and Wales, Scotland and Northern Ireland by virtue of section 3 of the European Union (Withdrawal) Act 2018 (see DPA, s 3(10)). The shorthand 'GDPR' for our purposes means the relevant parts of the UK GDPR and the DPA. Where possible, references will be to the DPA.

12.5

Part 2 of the DPA applies to the processing of data that is conducted by non-law enforcement authorities, or data processed by a law enforcement authority but not in that capacity.[4] Part 3 applies to processing by a law enforcement authority for law enforcement purposes.

12.6

The Information Commissioner's Office (ICO) is the body that oversees the implementation of the DPA and has the power to impose penalties for breaches. It maintains Guidance on the General Data Protection Regulation (GDPR).[5] In the absence of court-approved interpretations, it provides the most reliable statements on the meaning and application of the DPA. The National Police Chiefs' Council (NPCC) maintains its own policy documents in respect of GDPR and PACE obligations; these and local force policies should be consulted where appropriate.

12.7

PACE is the domain of the police forces. The Part 3 powers under which the police and courts operate have the effect of placing the GDPR on an abstract level, with the precise rules being contained within PACE.

WHAT IS PERSONAL DATA?

12.8

The DPA offers the following definitions:

---

3 (EU) 2016/679 of 27 April 2016.

4 For example, according to the ICO, a police force processing data about its employees' criminal records for human resources purposes, or sharing data with victim support services, needs to comply with the UK GDPR: https://ico.org.uk/for-organisations/guide-to-data-protection/guide-to-the-general-data-protection-regulation-gdpr/criminal-offence-data/what-is-criminal-offence-data/#whatis.

5 See https://ico.org.uk/for-organisations/guide-to-data-protection/.

'Personal data' means 'any information relating to an identified or identifiable living individual' (DPA, s 3(2)).

'Identifiable living individual' means 'a living individual who can be identified, directly or indirectly, in particular by reference to—

(a) an identifier such as a name, an identification number, location data or an online identifier, or

(b) one or more factors specific to the physical, physiological, genetic, mental, economic, cultural or social identity of the individual' (DPA, s 3(3)).

'Data subject' means 'the identified or identifiable living individual to whom personal data relates' (DPA, s 3(5)).

12.9

There is no exhaustive list of what constitutes personal data. It will be context dependent. Sometimes the data, most obviously a name, *directly* identifies a person. However, data that by itself cannot identify a living individual may still do so in combination with other data, in which case it may become personal data (*indirect* identification). There is no clear test for determining when that possibility becomes real enough that the first piece of data becomes personal data. For example, a document giving (i) a defendant's profession and (ii) the school their child attends, may be sufficient for the staff of that school to identify that defendant even if the document does not contain the defendant's name. On the other hand, if the defendant's profession is extremely common, or the school is a large one, a combination of (i) and (ii) may not be sufficient. 'Identifying' an individual does not mean that the data must lead directly to the individual's name.

12.10

As a guide, personal data includes tangible and intangible information, such as:

- Name, date of birth, details of relatives, employment, state-issued identification (eg, passport/driving licence/NI numbers).
- Photographs and videos.
- Electronic addresses, such as email addresses, IP addresses, cookies, browser records.
- Physical locations, including both home and work addresses, schools, medical treatment facilities, prisons.
- Financial information, bank statements, credit card details, credit checks, purchase histories.
- Special category data.
- Criminal offence data.

Special category data

12.11

The GDPR imposes particular rules for the handling of special category data and criminal offence data. As a base rule, Article 9(1) of the UK GDPR specifies that the processing of the following personal data is prohibited:

- Personal data revealing racial or ethnic origin.
- Personal data revealing political opinions.
- Personal data revealing religious or philosophical beliefs, or trade union membership.
- Genetic data. This includes DNA, whether partly or wholly sequenced and, possibly, DNA of someone related to an individual (as this permits family identification of others).
- Biometric data for the purpose of uniquely identifying an individual, including fingerprints, facial recognition, eye (iris) scan and retinal analysis, voice recognition, ear shape recognition, keystroke analysis, handwriting analysis, gait and gaze analyses. The ICO states that digital photographs are not automatically biometric data.
- Data concerning health, including mental and physical health, treatment, medication, type of medical service provided.
- Data concerning an individual's sex life or sexual orientation.

12.12

Confusingly, processing special category data is also known as 'sensitive processing' for the purposes of law enforcement authorities under section 35(8) of the DPA. There are then various exceptions to this prohibition, explored below. For statutory definitions of DNA, fingerprints, and similar terms, see PACE section 65.

Criminal offence data

12.13

The processing of criminal offence data is also prohibited except 'under the control of official authority or when the processing is authorised by domestic law providing for appropriate safeguards for the rights and freedoms of data subjects …'.[6]

6 UK GDPR, Art 10(1).

12.14

By s 11(2) of the DPA 'references to personal data relating to criminal convictions and offences or related security measures include personal data relating to—

(a) the alleged commission of offences by the data subject, or

(b) proceedings for an offence committed or alleged to have been committed by the data subject or the disposal of such proceedings, including sentencing.'

12.15

The ICO states that the words 'relating to criminal convictions and offences …' should be 'interpreted broadly' so as to include data 'linked to criminal offences, or which is specifically used to learn something about an individual's criminal record or behaviour'.[7]

12.16

Importantly, the criminal offence data rule only applies to non-Part 3 processing. Thus, the majority of processing conducted by the police, CPS and criminal justice bodies will *not* fall within this rule and will instead be covered by Part 3.

12.17

Criminal offence data includes:

- Data relating to convictions, allegations, sentences, and evidence underlying these.
- Personal data of victims, complainants, and witnesses.
- The ICO suggests that '*related security measures*' in Article 10(1) includes penalties, conditions or restrictions placed on an individual as part of the criminal justice process (eg, cautions, bail conditions, probation requirements), or civil measures which may lead to a criminal penalty if not followed (such as CBOs).

12.18

The Police National Computer (PNC) contains much of this information where it relates to defendants/suspects. It is not a creature of statute, except insofar as it gives effect to section 27 of PACE and, more recently, Article 10(1) of the UK GDPR. Its status is opaque; its public face appears to be ACRO (which stands for the ACPO Criminal Records Office). ACPO is itself an acronym of the 'Association of Chief Police Officers', which has now been superseded by the NPCC. ACRO is now overseen by an independent board with representatives from the NPCC and the Home Office and is subject to freedom of information legislation. The PNC is considered by courts to be the authoritative source of information on convictions, cautions, penalties and

7 See https://ico.org.uk/for-organisations/guide-to-data-protection/guide-to-the-general-data-protection-regulation-gdpr/criminal-offence-data/what-is-criminal-offence-data/.

associated matters. However, it also contains information not falling within section 27 of PACE, such as pending proceedings and bail conditions.

12.19

A Police National Database (PND) is to be distinguished from the PNC. The PND is a system for police forces to store information and intelligence concerning a wide range of matters connected with policing. It is not a formal record of an individual's offending. In *Catt v United Kingdom*,[8] the ECtHR held that the indefinite retention of personal data on databases of this sort, where there was no actual conviction or record of offence, was a disproportionate interference with Article 8 rights. The ECtHR's decision is in conflict with the Supreme Court's decision in the same case in 2015,[9] which held that the interference was proportionate.The trend of domestic UK law has been towards permitting the making and keeping of records of criminal activity; including keeping crime reports,[10] keeping surveillance logs,[11] and sharing information between various authorities.[12]

PROCESSING BY LAW ENFORCEMENT AUTHORITIES (PART 3 POWERS)

12.20

Part 3 gives competent authorities the power to process criminal offence data (and indeed other personal data) for the primary purpose of law enforcement. Pursuant to section 31 this means 'the prevention, investigation, detection or prosecution of criminal offences or the execution of criminal penalties, including the safeguarding against and the prevention of threats to public security'.

12.21

Schedule 7 to the DPA sets out the list of competent authorities. It includes:

- Police forces of various types across the UK.
- Authorities that investigate the police (such as Ombudsmen).
- Government departments and statutory bodies that investigate and prosecute (such as His Majesty's Revenue & Customs, the Serious Fraud Office, Financial Conduct Authority and the Criminal Cases Review Commission).
- Probation services, parole boards, prison authorities and secure transport services.

8 *Catt v United Kingdom* (2019) 69 EHRR 7.

9 *R (Catt) v Association of Chief Police Officers of England, Wales and Northern Ireland* [2015] AC 1065. And see *R (Butt) v SSHD* [2019] 1 WLR 3873 which distinguished the ECHR decision.

10 *R (CL) v Chief Constable of Greater Manchester* [2018] EWHC 3333 (Admin).

11 *Kinloch v HM Advocate* [2013] 2 AC 93.

12 *R (M) v Chief Constable of Sussex* [2021] EWCA Civ 42.

- The Director of Public Prosecutions.
- The Information Commissioner.
- Courts and Tribunals.

12.22

All such authorities are permitted to process personal data for section 31 purposes, in accordance with the six law enforcement data protection principles in sections 35 to 40 of the the DPA:

(1) Processing of personal data for any of the law enforcement purposes must be lawful and fair.

(2) The law enforcement purpose for which personal data is collected on any occasion must be specified, explicit and legitimate, and personal data collected must not be processed in a manner that is incompatible with the purpose for which it was originally collected.

(3) Personal data processed for any of the law enforcement purposes must be adequate, relevant and not excessive in relation to the purpose for which it is processed.

(4) Personal data processed for any of the law enforcement purposes must be accurate and, where necessary, kept up to date, and every reasonable step must be taken to ensure that personal data that is inaccurate, having regard to the law enforcement purpose for which it is processed, is erased or rectified without delay.

(5) Personal data processed for any of the law enforcement purposes must be kept for no longer than is necessary for the purpose for which it is processed. Appropriate time limits must be established for the periodic review of the need for the continued storage of personal data for any of the law enforcement purposes.

(6) Personal data processed for any of the law enforcement purposes must be processed in a manner that ensures appropriate security of the personal data, using appropriate technical or organisational measures (and, in this principle, 'appropriate security' includes protection against unauthorised or unlawful processing and against accidental loss, destruction or damage).

12.23

These are intended to allow for effective investigation and prosecution while preserving individual rights and dignities. To date there is little analysis or case law to indicate whether this has been successful.

12.24

Part 3 authorities may process special category data (sensitive processing) and criminal offence data. There are no additional requirements for the processing of criminal offence data. Special category data can only be processed if the section 35(4) and (5) conditions are satisfied. In practice this will mean that one of the conditions in Schedule 8 of the DPA is satisfied, which are broad and encompass the kinds of activities that law enforcement authorities might be expected to engage in. In *R (Bridges) v Chief Constable of South Wales*,[13] the Court held that the force's use of Automated Facial Recognition had not been DPA-compliant, but that in principle (with the correct framework and policies in place) the use of such technology was a lawful interference with Article 8 rights.

12.25

The cumulative effect of Part 3 and Schedule 8 is that law enforcement authorities can (where consistent with the six principles above) process all personal data necessary for the investigation, prosecution, trial, and sentencing of crimes. For an example of the wide scope of the provisions, see *R (YZ) v Chief Constable of South Wales Police*,[14] where evidence relating to charges of which the defendant was acquitted could nonetheless be retained on the PNC for 100 years. For a different view, see *R (II) v Commissioner of Police*,[15] holding that the continued retention data collected about a child's alleged radicalisation risk was in breach of their Article 8 rights and sections 35 and 39 of the DPA.

12.26

Schedule 2 sets out a number of specific provisions (paragraph 1) which do not apply to personal data processed for certain law enforcement purposes (paragraph 2), or certain disclosure purposes (paragraph 5(3)).[16]

12.27

Personal data retained by UK authorities may be shared with the relevant authorities of other countries. The process is overseen by the Forensic Information Database Service (FINDS), which published an updated International DNA and Fingerprint Exchange Policy for the UK on 24 December 2020.[17] The interaction between the DPA and the Mutual Legal Assistance principles was recently examined in *R (Elgizouli) v SSHD*.[18]

12.28

Individual subject access rights are, in large part, constrained by the purpose of Part 3. Thus, the right to object and the right to data portability do not apply. The general right to be informed about the collection and use of one's personal data does not apply where necessary and proportionate to avoid prejudicing the prevention, detection, investigation or prosecution of criminal offences or the

13 [2020] EWCA Civ 1058, [2020] 1 WLR 5037.
14 [2021] EWHC 1060 (Admin).
15 [2020] EWHC 2528 (Admin).
16 As to which, see *Mircom Ltd v Virgin Media Ltd* [2019] EWHC 1827 (Ch) and *Lucky Technology Limited v HMRC* [2021] UKFTT 0055 (TC).
17 See also the DPA, Pt 3 Ch 5, concerning Transfers of Personal Data to Third Countries.
18 [2020] EWHC 2516 (Admin), [2021] 3 All ER 247, and see *CJ v Secretary of State* [2019] UKUT 00126 (IAC) concerning video link hearings between jurisdictions.

execution of criminal penalties.[19] However, this does not justify a blanket refusal *R (Dalton) v CPS*.[20]

12.29

The accountability and governance provisions in Part 3, Chapter 4 are, again, largely aspirational in nature. The more practical aspects include common-sense measures such as secure storage and transmission of data, limiting the scope and number of groups permitted to access data, and monitoring access, erasure, and transmission of data.

12.30

Because of the nature of law enforcement activities, the most reliable safeguard in place is likely to be self-reporting of breaches to the ICO. Reports must be made if a breach is likely to result in a risk to the rights and freedoms of individuals.[21] As law enforcement processing regularly encompasses a significant quantity of special category and criminal offence data, a breach is more likely to result in a risk to the rights and freedoms of individuals.

PROCESSING BY NON-LAW ENFORCEMENT AUTHORITIES (PART 2 POWERS)

12.31

Some entities working within the criminal justice system (notably solicitors and barristers) are not law enforcement authorities (unless *employed* by a law enforcement authority). Thus, they must generally operate under one of the Part 2 lawful bases for processing which are contained within Article 6 of the UK GDPR:

(a) the data subject has given consent to the processing of his or her personal data for one or more specific purposes;

(b) processing is necessary for the performance of a contract to which the data subject is party or in order to take steps at the request of the data subject prior to entering into a contract;

(c) processing is necessary for compliance with a legal obligation to which the controller is subject;

(d) processing is necessary in order to protect the vital interests of the data subject or of another natural person;

(e) processing is necessary for the performance of a task carried out in the public interest or in the exercise of official authority vested in the controller;

19 DPA, s 44(4).
20 [2020] EWHC 2013 (Admin), [2020] 1 WLR 5329.
21 DPA, s 67(2).

(f) processing is necessary for the purposes of the legitimate interests pursued by the controller or by a third party, except where such interests are overridden by the interests or fundamental rights and freedoms of the data subject which require protection of personal data, in particular where the data subject is a child.

12.32

Section 8 of the DPA defines Article 6(1)(e) public interest as including the administration of justice.

12.33

For defence lawyers, consent will be the most common basis for processing the client's data. Processing of the data of others involved in the case such as complainants is not directly covered in any of the provisions but may reasonably be expected to be included in (e). Similarly, the work of prosecuting counsel instructed and not employed by the CPS or other prosecuting authority, is not explicitly covered in the provisions. Again, the public interest and administration of justice might reasonably be considered to cover this work.

Special category data

12.34

Processing special category data under Part 2 requires both a lawful basis under Article 6 of the UK GDPR and a separate condition for processing under Article 9. The latter includes:

(a) explicit consent;

...

(f) Processing necessary for the establishment, exercise or defence of legal claims or whenever courts are acting in their judicial capacity – this would appear to cover the majority of work by legal representatives.

(g) Reasons of substantial public interest (see DPA 2018, Pt 2, Sch 1).

Criminal offence data

12.35

The base rule in Article 10 applies to Part 2 processing of criminal data. Under s 10(5) and (6) criminal offence data can only be processed under Part 2 if a specific condition for processing in Schedule 1 of the DPA 2018 is satisfied. That list of conditions is extensive and includes processing where necessary for the administration of justice (para 7) and legal claims (para 33). The latter is likely to cover legitimate activities of solicitors and barristers prosecuting and defending criminal cases:

This condition is met if the processing—

(a) is necessary for the purpose of, or in connection with, any legal proceedings (including prospective legal proceedings),

(b) is necessary for the purpose of obtaining legal advice, or

(c) is otherwise necessary for the purposes of establishing, exercising or defending legal rights.

COLLECTION AND RETENTION

12.36

The PACE regime encompasses the Act itself (Part II seizure provisions ss 19–22; and Part V, ss 53–65B inclusive), PACE Code C (Requirements for the detention, treatment and questioning of suspects not related to terrorism in police custody) and PACE Code H (relating to terrorism).

12.37

All powers and responsibilities granted by this regime operate alongside the DPA regime. Thus, for example, a DNA sample taken from a suspect under PACE must be retained and processed not only in accordance with PACE but also in accordance with the DPA. As yet, there is little guidance on interaction or lacunae between the two.

12.38

On 31 October 2013, PACE protections were enhanced (by amendments made by the PFA), in the wake of the decisions in *S and Marper v United Kingdom*[22] and *R (GC) v Commissioner of Police*,[23] from which he following general principles arise:

- Indiscriminate and indefinite retention of material may be a disproportionate interference with Article 8 rights.
- Retention should be proportionate to the nature of the data and the circumstances in which it was collected (eg, a serious or unusual crime would warrant lengthier retention).
- Retention should be secure and restricted.
- There should be time limits on retention or scheduled reviews.
- There should be a process for subjects to apply for destruction/deletion of the data.

---

22 (2009) 48 EHRR 50.

23 [2011] UKSC 21, [2011] 1 WLR 1230.

12.39

The principles in *S and Marper* are also applicable to the retention of photographs.[24] The amended PACE regime, permitting indefinite retention of fingerprints, photographs and DNA profiles of convicted persons has been held to be a proportionate infringement of Article 8 rights.[25] The regime consists of a fairly complicated set of rules that apply to the collection and retention of personal data depending on the nature of the offending/allegation/investigation, the type of data, the location of the collection and retention, and the subject's circumstances.

Types of offences

12.40

A 'recordable offence' is one in respect of which the Secretary of State has by regulation made provision for recording in national police records (PACE, s 27). The list is contained in the National Police Records (Recordable Offences) Regulations 2000.[26] It includes convictions, cautions, reprimands and warnings in respect of any offence punishable with imprisonment and certain other specified offences. By implication, the record of the offence also includes the sentence for that offence. Where a conviction is recordable, the defendant's conviction for any other offence of which he is convicted in the same proceedings also becomes recordable. The Rehabilitation of Offenders Act 1974 does not affect the meaning of 'recordable offence' in respect of Part V of PACE.[27]

12.41

A 'qualifying offence' is one specified in section 65A of PACE. Section 65A sets out a lengthy list of offences (and ancillary offences) that are qualifying offences, in respect of which the collection and retention of personal data is subject to fewer restrictions. As well as the most serious kinds of offending it also includes offences of exposure and certain public order offences.

12.42

By section 63F of PACE, an 'excluded offence' means a recordable offence

(a) which—

  (i) is not a qualifying offence,

  (ii) is the only recordable offence of which the person has been convicted, and

24 *R (C) v Commissioner of Police* [2012] 1 WLR 3007.

25 *Gaughran v Chief Constable of the Police Service of Northern Ireland* [2016] AC 345.

26 SI 2000/1139.

27 PACE, s 65B(2).

(iii) was committed when the person was aged under 18, and

(b) for which the person was not given a relevant custodial sentence of five years or more.

Although not formally defined, a 'minor offence' is also a term used within PACE,[28] essentially meaning a recordable offence that is not a qualifying offence.

Intimate and non-intimate samples

12.43

Taking intimate samples requires authorisation from an appropriately senior officer (at present an inspector), and the consent in writing of the subject.[29] The only exception appears to be in relation to road traffic accident. Section 7A of the Road Traffic Act 1988 permits a blood sample to be taken from someone who appears incapable of giving valid consent, however, the sample cannot be analysed without the person's subsequent consent.[30] If the person dies before giving such consent, the sample ceases to be personal data for the purposes of the GDPR. A non-intimate sample may be taken without consent.[31]

12.44

Fingerprints, like photographs, do not seem to fall into either the definition of intimate or non-intimate samples. They are not quantities of something taken for analysis, but rather *copies* of identifying features. In any event, both can be taken without consent.[32] Fingerprints are retained in the UK National Fingerprint Database (IDENT1). A DNA sample can be intimate or non-intimate depending on where it is taken from. DNA profiles retained under any of the retention powers referred to in section 63D must be recorded on the National DNA Database.[33] This is now supervised by the National DNA Database Strategy Board.

12.45

Samples taken under PACE must be destroyed within six months, subject to renewal authorised by a court.[34] This is not the same as a DNA profile *derived from* a sample, which is subject to the section 63D provisions below. If a sample or section 63D material appears to have been taken unlawfully or in connection with an arrest in circumstances where the arrest was unlawful or based on

28 See, eg, PACE, ss 63H, 63K and 63KA.
29 Ibid, s 62.
30 RTA 1988, s 7A(4).
31 PACE, s 63.
32 Ibid, ss 61 and 64A.
33 Ibid, s 63AA.
34 Ibid, s 63R.

mistaken identity it must be destroyed.[35] Destruction of section 63D material includes the destruction of any copies, unless appropriately anonymised.[36]

Section 63D material

12.46

Special rules apply to fingerprints and DNA profiles (known as 'section 63D material') which are, by default, to be destroyed unless a power to retain applies. Retention is permitted in a number of circumstances.

(a) Where the offence in question is being investigated or results in a conviction/caution/penalty etc:

   (i) If the material is taken in connection with the investigation of an offence in which it is suspected that the person to whom the material relates has been involved, until the conclusion of the investigation or any proceedings arising (s 63E).

   (ii) If convicted of a recordable offence, indefinitely (s 63I).

   (iii) Where a penalty notice is issued under section 2 of the Criminal Justice and Police Act 2001, retention for two years from the taking of the material (s 63L).

   (iv) If the material is or may become disclosable under the Criminal Procedure and Investigations Act 1996 (CPIA) regime (s 63U(5)). However, use of the material is restricted to the offence in connection with which the material was taken.

(b) Where the offence in question does *not* result in a conviction/caution/penalty etc:

   (i) For national security purposes, indefinitely (s 63M).

   (ii) If the person involved is subsequently arrested for, charged or convicted of a different offence (there appears to be no requirement for any connection with the original offence), material taken in connection with the investigation of the original offence is to be considered as taken in connection with the new offence (s 63P).

   (iii) If the person is arrested/charged with a qualifying offence but not convicted of that offence, for a specified period of time (at the moment three years from the taking of the material), which may be extended for a further two years by a court. This changes to indefinite retention if the person becomes (or has already been) convicted of a recordable offence before the material is required to be destroyed (s 63F), but not if that recordable offence is an excluded offence.

35 Ibid, ss 63D(2) and 63R(2).
36 Ibid, s 63Q.

(iv) If a person consents to the giving of the material, and has been or is convicted of a recordable offence, indefinitely (with some exceptions) (s 63N(4)). This provision seems particularly broad, as there is no requirement that the material have any relation to the recordable offence.

(v) The Commissioner for the Retention and Use of Biometric Material (a role created under the PFA) can give permission for retention in certain circumstances (s 63G).

(vi) Where a person is arrested for or charged with a minor offence, and has no previous recordable offences, the material cannot be retained (s 63H). There is a more complicated regime for persons under the age of 18 (s 63K).

12.47

Where particular terrorism-related offences are concerned, section 63D does not apply.[37] Where the police are acting under immigration law, the protections do not prevent the use of personal data to identify someone[38]. Where the material is taken from one person, but relates to another person, sections 63D–63T do not apply.[39] Thus, it would seem that a DNA sample of cells taken from the complainant which actually came from the body of the attacker, do not fall within the regime.

Use of material

12.48

Pursuant to section 63T of PACE:

(1) Any material to which section 63D, 63R or 63S applies must not be used other than—

(a) in the interests of national security,

(b) for the purposes of a terrorist investigation,

(c) for purposes related to the prevention or detection of crime, the investigation of an offence or the conduct of a prosecution, or

(d) for purposes related to the identification of a deceased person or of the person to whom the material relates.

(2) Material which is required by section 63D, 63R or 63S to be destroyed must not at any time after it is required to be destroyed be used—

37 Ibid, s 63U.
38 Ibid, s 63U(7).
39 Ibid, s 63U(6).

(a) in evidence against the person to whom the material relates, or

(b) for the purposes of the investigation of any offence.

12.49

In practice, this is a broad definition. There is no blanket restriction on material collected for one purpose being used for a different purpose. There are some specific restrictions (eg, ss 63R(11) and 63U(5A)). Additionally, section 22 of PACE is subject to section 63T.[40]

12.50

Police may still undertake 'speculative searches' with the authority of the responsible chief officer of police.[41] A 'speculative search' in relation to a person's fingerprints or samples, means such a check against other fingerprints or samples or against information derived from other samples.[42] The check can be made against data held by a broadly defined set of law-enforcement authorities[43] including the NDNAD.

12.51

A sample may be retained if it is likely to be needed for the purposes of disclosure to a defendant (this does not appear to be restricted to the defendant whose sample it is).[44]

12.52

Less intimate, and generally less personal, data can be retained for longer. Thus, impressions of footwear may be retained 'for as long as is necessary for purposes related to the prevention or detection of crime, the investigation of an offence or the conduct of a prosecution'.[45] Photographs and videos may be retained without any specified limit.[46] It may also be used by, or disclosed to, any person for any purpose related to the prevention or detection of crime, the investigation of an offence or the conduct of a prosecution or to the enforcement of a sentence but see *Mengesha v Commissioner of Police*[47] for limits to section 64A.

40 See *Re Z (Children) Application for Release of DNA Profiles* [2015] 1 WLR 2501.
41 PACE, ss 63A, 63D(5) and 63R(13).
42 Ibid, s 65.
43 Ibid, s 63A(1A).
44 Ibid, s 63R(7)(a).
45 Ibid, s 63S.
46 Ibid, s 64A(4).
47 [2013] EWHC 1695 (Admin).

13 Victims of crime

Kalvir Kaur and Tara Wolfe

INTRODUCTION

13.1

The relationship between a victim's rights, criminal law and rights enshrined in the ECHR is one that continues to evolve, with scope remaining in practice for greater implementation and active promotion of enshrined rights for better protection of victims at the investigatory stage. For victim reassurance and continued co-operation, the initial interaction with the criminal justice process can be the defining aspect.[1] Valuing victim's rights and ensuring all action is compliant with those rights can be central to the success of the investigatory process and any subsequent prosecution.

13.2

In the 2016 Victim's Commissioner's review, *What works in supporting victims of crime*,[2] the following themes emerged:

(a) Timely and accurate information and effective methods of communication with victims, both in delivering information and listening to their needs. The basic provision of timely information can assist victims in coping with the impact of victimisation. A lack of information can only act to aggravate these symptoms and in many cases can result in victims disengaging with the criminal process and withdrawing their co-operation.

(b) The quality of service that victims get from criminal justice professionals and associated agencies is often a more important factor in victim satisfaction than the final outcome of their case. Perceptions of fair treatment, including knowledge of and access to entitlements, increases victims' perceptions of legitimacy and aids compliance.

(c) Co-located multi-agency partnership working across statutory and voluntary sectors can provide effective support for victims in terms of information sharing. It can assist in reducing the duplication of tasks, so that the process is less confusing for victims.

---

1 See HMIC & HMCPSI *Living in fear – the police and CPS response to harassment and stalking* 5 July 2017 https://www.justiceinspectorates.gov.uk/hmicfrs/wp-content/uploads/living-in-fear-the-police-and-cps-response-to-harassment-and-stalking.pdf.

2 Victims' Commissioner and the University of Portsmouth *What works in supporting victims of crime: A rapid evidence assessment* March 2016. Available at: https://victimscommissioner.org.uk/document/what-works-in-supporting-victims-of-crime-a-rapid-evidence-assessment/.

(d) A single point of contact or advocate is an effective way to provide victims with a combination of the information and support required to help regain a sense of autonomy that the crime has taken from them.

13.3

This chapter considers the existing framework of protection for victims with an examination of the key caselaw and the duties arising out of Articles 2, 3, 4 and 8 of the European Convention on Human Rights (ECHR) during the investigative stage. It then focuses on investigative interviewing techniques which serve to complement and supplement existing models, offering practical insight into techniques to allow interviewing at the investigative stage to be conducted through a victim-centred lens.

VICTIMS OF CRIME

13.4

The development of victim's rights within the criminal justice system has been slow to evolve. In our adversarial system, strengthening of the rights of victims has sparked fear of a corresponding deterioration in the rights of defendants. However, recent years have seen a radical shift, as is evidenced by Part 2 of the Youth Justice and Criminal Evidence Act 1999, which was pivotal in radically reforming the way in which evidence is gathered and presented, enabling access to justice for the most vulnerable of victims. Furthermore, *R v Killick*[3] led to the introduction in 2013 of the Victim's Right to Review scheme when a decision is taken not to prosecute.

13.5

There is now widespread recognition that those who are competent to give evidence should be assisted in doing so; justice cannot be achieved without ensuring the meaningful participation of victims. The evidence obtained during the investigative stage determines whether an offender can be brought to justice, the framework in which the offence is charged and how it will be presented at the trial. Effective investigation is that which can establish the relevant facts and which relies on adequate safeguards and procedures to ensure that victims can understand the process, be heard and understood.

Legal framework

13.6

Victim's rights were first articulated at international level in the Declaration of Basic Principles of Justice for Victims of Crime and Abuse of Power 1985[4]

3 *R v Killick* [2011] EWCA Crim 1608.
4 UN 40/34.

followed by the UN Convention Against Transnational Organized Crime and the three related Protocols.[5] But such rights, being soft law, are not enforceable and, as such, do not provide meaningful protection to victims of crime. The EU Directive established minimum standards for the rights of victims.[6] It has been given effect in the Code of Practice for Victims of Crime in England and Wales, (the Victim's Code) 2021, which sets out the minimum level of service victims can expect at every stage of the justice process, regardless of whether they choose to report the crime or not.

13.7

Thus far, efforts to create a legally enforceable set of rights through legislation have not been successful.[7] Equally, the courts have declined to find that the provisions of the 1999 Act concerning special measures for vulnerable witnesses impose implied statutory duties on the police in the conduct of criminal investigations.[8] It is the human rights framework that provides a mechanism by which victim's rights are given effect.

Who is a victim?

13.8

Consistent with the international and regional instruments, the Victim's Code defines a victim widely as 'a person who has suffered harm, including physical, mental or emotional harm or economic loss which was directly caused by a criminal offence or a close relative or close family member of a person whose death was directly caused by a criminal offence'. Significantly, there is no requirement that the crime be reported to the police nor that the perpetrator is identified or prosecuted.

13.9

The first right of the Code is arguably the most significant for the investigative stage of the process and provides:

> You have the Right to be helped to understand what is happening and to be understood. In considering appropriate measures, service providers must consider any relevant personal characteristics which may affect your ability to understand and to be understood. All service providers must communicate in simple and accessible language and all

5 Protocol to Prevent, Suppress and Punish Trafficking in Persons, Especially Women and Children; Protocol against the Smuggling of Migrants by Land, Air and Sea; and Protocol against the Illicit Manufacturing and Trafficking in Firearms, Their Parts and Components and Ammunition adopted by General Assembly Resolution 55/255 of 31 May 2001.

6 Preserved by the European Union (Withdrawal) Act 2018.

7 See Victims of Crime Etc (Rights, Entitlements and Related Matters) 2015.

8 *R (on the application of AB) v Chief Constable of Hampshire Constabulary and the Secretary of State for Justice* [2019] EWHC 3461.

translation or interpretation services must be offered free of charge to the victim.

13.10

This reflects Articles 3 (the right to understand and be understood) and 5 (the right of victims when making a complaint) of the EU Directive. In practical terms, a victim, regardless of their personal characteristics or vulnerabilities, must be provided with the support and assistance required to enable effective communication, consistent with the duty to make reasonable adjustments under the Equality Act 2010.

DUTY TO PROPERLY INVESTIGATE

Protecting the right to life: Article 2

13.11

It is now beyond contention that there is a positive obligation on the state to protect the right to life through adequate and effective operational measures during the investigation of criminal complaints. As established in *Osman v UK*, the obligation exists in circumstances which 'the authorities knew or ought to have known at the time of the existence of a real and immediate risk to the life of an identified individual or individuals from the criminal acts of a third party and that they failed to take measures within the scope of their powers which, judges reasonably, might have been expected to avoid that risk'. This test was endorsed by the House of Lords in the case of *Van Colle v Chief Constable of Hertfordshire.*[9] The threshold is high, but nevertheless the prerequisite to the authorities being able to make the assessment of whether there is a real and imminent risk to life, is that the victim is provided with the opportunity of giving their account.

Systemic and operational failings: Articles 3 and 8

13.12

First and foremost, a victim must be entitled to bring proceedings in law. In *X v Netherlands*,[10] the ECtHR considered the inability of a 16-year-old rape victim with learning difficulties to lodge a complaint due to the severity of their disability, and the fact that their father was not able to lodge a complaint on their behalf. The Court held that the impossibility of instituting criminal proceedings amounted to a violation of Article 8. The state was required to change the law in order to ensure access to justice for those most vulnerable of victims.

9 [2008] UKHL 50.

10 (1986) 8 EHRR 235.

13.13

Recent jurisprudence illustrates how this principle has informed practice, indicative of a significant shift in approach. In the case of *R v Watts*,[11] the four victims of serious sexual misconduct were profoundly disabled and wheelchair bound: three with cerebral palsy and one tetraplegic with an acquired brain injury. Various special measures were employed to enable the four women to provide their account to the police by way of a recorded Achieving Best Evidence interview, including the use of an electronic device with images and the interpretation of eye movements. The defendant was ultimately convicted. As commented by Mr Justice Mackay, 'less than half a generation ago the criminal courts would not have contemplated attempting to receive evidence from persons in the position of these complainants'.

13.14

The duty to investigate not only encompasses systemic failures but also operational failings. In *MC v Bulgaria*,[12] a 14-year-old victim reported that they had been raped by two men. The authorities declined to prosecute on the basis there was no evidence of physical violence and they had not resisted the attack. The ECtHR found that 'states have a positive obligation inherent in articles 3 and 8 of the Convention to enact criminal law provisions effectively punishing rape and to apply them in practice through effective investigation and prosecution'. The state not only has a negative duty not to inflict ill-treatment contrary to Article 3 of the ECHR but also has a positive obligation to protect its citizens from such ill-treatment through adequate enforcement mechanisms.[13]

13.15

This approach was endorsed in *D v Commissioner of Police of the Metropolis*,[14] the Supreme Court finding a general duty on the police under article 3 to conduct an effective investigation into serious criminal conduct whether the crime has been carried out by the state or private individuals.[15] There is an obligation to take all reasonable steps to secure the evidence related to the incident, including a detailed account of the allegation from the victim. However, the threshold is very high; only 'conspicuous or substantial' or 'egregious' operational errors in the investigative process will be actionable. Where the police are found to have done what they reasonably could to establish whether a crime has been committed and to identify the perpetrator, there will be no breach. Therefore, in practice it is likely that very few victims will be successful in challenging operational failings in the investigative process.

---

11 [2010] EWCA Crim 1824.

12 *Van Colle v Chief Constable of Hertfordshire* (2005) 40 EHRR 20.

13 *Assenov v Bulgaria* (1998) 28 EHRR 652, para 102.

14 *D v Commissioner of Police of the Metropolis* [2019] AC 196.

15 Commissioner of Police of the *Metropolis v DSD* [2018] UKSC 11.

Victim as defendant: Article 4

13.16

Victims of trafficking who find themselves in the criminal justice system are entitled to an enhanced set of enforceable rights at the investigatory stage. *VCL v United Kingdom*[16] marked the first occasion the ECtHR had an opportunity to consider the interplay between Article 4 and the decision to prosecute in the context of trafficking. The police had failed to route potential victims of trafficking into a safeguarding-led process which would have enabled the authorities to better identify them as a victim of trafficking and therefore entitled to various rights under the Council of Europe's Anti-Trafficking Convention (CEAT).

13.17

The Court held that the state's positive obligations under Article 4 must be construed in light of the CEAT. In circumstances in which the authorities are aware or ought to have been aware of circumstances giving rise to a possibility of the suspect being a victim of trafficking, there is a positive duty to take operational measures to protect victims or potential victims. In recognition of their vulnerabilities, the victims should be assessed promptly by a suitably qualified professional. This assessment must take place prior to the decision to prosecute is made. Only in this way can the twin aim of protecting the victim from further harm and facilitating their recovery be met.

INTERVIEWING TECHNIQUES

13.18

One of the critical elements of the investigative stage is interviewing of witnesses[17] and victims continue to face difficulties, often with a gender element,[18] when reporting crimes committed against them. Whilst the PEACE[19] model remains an important practical tool, as new techniques and skills become available it is appropriate to incorporate them to supplement the model so that it may evolve, reflect current learning and assist interviewers to be as skilled as possible in eliciting reliable evidence whilst fostering an empowering environment for the victim to engage in the process. Trauma-informed interviewing can therefore strengthen the fundamental rights of witnesses at the investigative stage.

16 *VCL v United Kingdom* (2021) 73 EHRR 9.

17 European Union Agency for Fundamental Rights: *Crime, Safety and Victims' Rights* 2021. Available at: https://fra.europa.eu/sites/default/files/fra_uploads/fra-2021-crime-safety-victims-rights_en.pdf.

18 'No support': domestic abuse survivors on feeling ignored by police *Guardian*, 17 September 2021. Available at: www.theguardian.com/society/2021/sep/17/no-support-domestic-abuse-victims-on-being-ignored-by-police.

19 Planning and preparing, Engage and explain, Account, Clarify and challenge, Closure, Evaluation.

Trauma-informed interviewing

13.19

Trauma-informed interviewing techniques are becoming more widely understood and their benefit recognised. Effective, trauma-informed interviewing techniques aim not only to strengthen capacity and efficiency of interviewers but also foster public trust in (and cooperation with) the criminal justice system, decrease unreliable information, improve respect for the rights of persons in heightened situations of vulnerability, safeguard dignity of the victims and advance the application of safeguards and due process guarantees to all persons being interviewed.

13.20

Trauma-informed interviewing techniques have been described as the tools for considering what type of questions should be asked and how to ask them in order to get the most coherent and detailed account without retraumatising; to learn how a victim-centred approach can give victims a voice in the justice system and help remove victim stigmatisation. Additionally, recognising the unequal power dynamic, trauma-informed interviewing techniques seek to avoid putting the victim in a powerless situation which may lead to personal boundaries being violated.[20]

Rapport-based, non-coercive interviewing

13.21

Complementing trauma-informed interviewing, rapport-based, non-coercive interviewing seeks to:[21]

(a) stimulate communication between the interviewer and the interviewee;

(b) facilitate memory retrieval;

(c) increase the accuracy and reliability of information provided;

(d) enable exploration of the veracity of information provided;

(e) increase the likelihood of information-rich and genuine admissions; and

(f) reduce the risk of eliciting false information or false confessions.

13.22

Establishing and maintaining rapport is an adaptive skill which enables better communication. It is achieved by the interviewer establishing a connection

20 HEUNI *RE-JUST Final Conference: Towards a victim-centred criminal justice system. Talking about trauma* 17 September 2021. Available at: https://heuni.fi/-/towards-a-victim-centred-criminal-justice-system.

21 Association for the Prevention of Torture: *Principles on Effective Interviewing for Investigations and Information Gathering* May 2021. Available at: www.apt.ch/sites/default/files/publications/PoEI_final_2021.06.pdf.

with the victim based on trust and respect for human dignity. This requires demonstration of genuine empathy as well as reassuring them that they will receive fair treatment, free of discrimination and untainted by stereotypes. Rapport-based techniques offer the victim autonomy over what they do or do not say and facilitate a positive interaction between the parties thereby increasing the likelihood of collecting accurate information. Ways to facilitate rapport by the interviewer include the use of behaviours such as establishing common ground and using active listening skills.

13.23

Incorporating this learning to make interview techniques trauma-informed, rapport-based and victim-centred, requires consideration of how alternative techniques may complement each other. One such technique is cognitive interviewing.

Cognitive interviewing

13.24

Cognitive interviewing is an interviewing technique which allows for a trauma-informed, victim-centred approach.[22] To apply this method the following principles should be adhered to:

(a) Create an optimum environment for the victim.

(b) Personalise the interview.

(c) Improve communication by helping the victim to give a complete account.

(d) Acknowledge the victim's psychological needs.

13.25

In *The Cognitive Interview of Children*, Teresa Jaśkiewicz-Obydzińska and Ewa Wach of the Institute of Forensic Expert Opinions, Kraków,[23] explain how cognitive interviewing can be employed in the case of children. The principles can, however, be readily modified and applied to adults. When interviewing, it is advised that the interviewer should:

(a) Sit naturally.

(b) Express friendliness and support.

(c) Use eye contact frequently but do not stare.

(d) Speak slowly using short sentences and pauses.

---

22 RE Geiselman, RP Fisher, DP MacKinnon and HL Holland 'Eyewitness Memory Enhancement in the Police Interview: Cognitive Retrieval Mnemonics Versus Hypnosis' (1985) 70(2) *Journal of Applied Psychology* 401–412.

23 See www.canee.net/files/The%20Cognitive%20Interview%20of%20Children.pdf.

(e) Express your attending: nodding, 'aha' but not evaluative terms such as 'that's right'.

(f) Praise them for their efforts.

(g) Avoid rapid movements or chaotic style of speaking.

(h) Not interrupt.

(i) Allow breaks.

(j) Show patience.

13.26

For this to be an effective technique, the interview should follow the following phases:

13.27

Phase 1: The opening phase (during which the interview is personalised). This will serve to break down perceived barriers of hierarchy and authority. Explain the goals of the interview. Owing to the unequal power dynamic, the need to give the instruction to tell everything becomes extremely important here. This is a critical stage; the opening communication, tone, body language, what is said and what is not said and whether active listening is employed all create the important first impression which may dictate the extent of engagement by the victim for the remainder of the interview.

13.28

Phase 2: Free narrative account and re-instating the context. At this phase, they are asked to describe their memories of the event, paraphrasing their last thought without adding any detail and without interrupting them, or asking any specific questions. Encouragement is given to try to remember additional detail, which can be assisted using non-specific prompts. They should also be asked to re-instate the context, both physical and environmental. To ensure this phase is effective an interviewer should:

(a) Ask them to listen to the instruction carefully.

(b) Emphasise that you want them to recall all details of the event.

(c) Give them enough time to reinstate the context.

(d) Ask questions slowly, making intentional pauses.

(e) Ask one question at a time.

(f) Not continue the interview before they re-establish the context.

13.29

Phase 3: Asking questions. Cognitive interviewing tells us asking questions is associated with activating imaginative pictures in the mind. Asking a question makes them use an imaginative picture and 'read out' the required information.

For example, if they are asked to describe a perpetrator, a picture of the perpetrator will emerge in their consciousness. If the next question concerns the same picture, for example 'What was the perpetrator wearing?' they will continue to use the same picture. However, if the next question concerns another imaginative picture, for example, 'Who else was with the perpetrator?' the first picture will be abandoned and they will evoke another picture corresponding to the question. We are told every single act of evoking a new representation interrupts the process of memory scanning and requires some mental effort. If we then ask a question relating to the first picture, this act of hopping from representation to representation increases inaccuracy. Thus, for practical purposes, it appears for effective application of this method, the interviewer should seek to exhaust questions relating to one issues before moving to the next.

13.30

Phase 4: *Closure.* The final phase should be used to summarise what they have said, to be advised of next steps and thanked for their time and effort. They should be asked if there is anything more they wish to tell. The aim of closure is that they leave the interview in a positive frame of mind; to help this it is useful to revert to neutral topics discussed in the rapport phase.

13.31

Throughout, being acutely aware of conducting the interview underpinned by the principle to do no harm means awareness of the psychological impact on the victim, of not only answering questions but also disclosing the details of the incident and being able to identify any harm and have in place appropriate support which can address their needs.

Remote interviews

13.32

The Covid-19 pandemic meant face-to-face interviewing was not always possible and digital communication came to be relied upon instead. Guidance on best practice and factors for consideration[24] include:

(a) Only interviewing remotely if necessary and appropriate with reference to the needs and psychological and capacity profile of the witness.

(b) Maintaining the security of the witness including forward planning and consideration of the need for any psycho-social support.

24 See: *Interviews with Victims and Witnesses During the Covid-19 Pandemic: Revised Guidance* June 2020 www.staffsscb.org.uk/wp-content/uploads/2020/07/250620-Chiefs-Operational-Brief-Interviews-with-Victims-and-Witnesses-revised-guidance.pdf and Institute for International Criminal Investigations: *IICI Guidelines on Remote Interviewing* August 2021 https://iici.global/0.5.1/wp-content/uploads/2021/08/IICI-Remote-Interview-Guidelines.pdf.

(c) Using only highly trained, competent and experienced interviewers to conduct remote interviews.

(d) Awareness of the high risk of being unable to properly sense non-verbal communication cues, even with good-quality digital platforms.

(e) The challenge of the necessary use of a third party, such as an interpreter, in terms of security and the dynamics of the relationship.

(f) The importance of the location of the remote interview, with consideration to avoid transference of distress into a safe, personal place with which it may then be associated.

13.33

Clearly, successful rapport build when conducting remote interviews is much more difficult, however, with the possibility of this method of interviewing becoming more frequent at the investigative stage, the need to constantly adapt, modify and reflect on skills and best practice becomes paramount.

14 Human trafficking

Tayyiba Bajwa

INTRODUCTION

14.1

Modern slavery and human trafficking is an increasing and evolving issue in the criminal jurisdiction. In 2021, 12,727 potential victims of modern slavery were referred to the National Referral Mechanism (NRM); a 20% increase on the preceding year.[1] Notwithstanding the large numbers of referrals into the NRM, the identification, recognition and protection of victims of trafficking in the criminal justice system continues to present difficulties. The protection of such victims within the criminal justice system and the ability of that system to safeguard the rights of such victims remains an ongoing challenge. Following the enactment of the Modern Slavery Act 2015 (MSA), the non-punishment principle derived from international legal instruments has, however, been placed on a statutory footing in the form of the section 45 defence.

PROHIBITION OF MODERN SLAVERY AND HUMAN TRAFFICKING

Key instruments

14.2

The UK is party to a number of international agreements prohibiting modern slavery and trafficking:

- Article 4 of the European Convention on Human Rights (ECHR) provides that no one shall be held in slavery or servitude and no one shall be required to perform forced or compulsory labour. Article 4 does not itself refer to trafficking, but the European Court of Human Rights (ECtHR) has made it clear that trafficking, as defined in the Protocol to Prevent, Suppress and Punish Trafficking in Persons, especially Women and Children (Palermo Protocol) and the Council of Europe Convention on Action against Trafficking in Human Beings ('ECAT'), falls under

1 Home Office, 3 March 2022, see www.gov.uk/government/statistics/modern-slavery-national-referral-mechanism-and-duty-to-notify-statistics-uk-end-of-year-summary-2021.

the scope of Article 4.[2] It is incorporated into domestic law by virtue of Schedule 1 of the Human Rights Act 1998 (HRA 1998).

- The Protocol to Prevent, Suppress and Punish Trafficking in Persons, especially Women and Children ('Palermo Protocol'), the purpose of which is to prevent and combat trafficking, protect and assist victims of trafficking and promote cooperation among State Parties to the Protocol.
- Council of Europe Convention on Action against Trafficking in Human Beings (ECAT), the purpose of which is to prevent and combat trafficking, to protect the human rights of victims, as well as to ensure effective investigation and prosecution, and to promote international co-operation on action against trafficking. ECAT has not been incorporated into domestic law,[3] but the obligations arising under the ECAT have been implemented by a variety of measures,[4] including the MSA, published guidance[5] and the creation of the National Referral Mechanism (NRM).
- Prior to the UK's withdrawal from the European Union, the EU Trafficking Directive ('Directive') had direct effect in English law.[6]

Definition of trafficking

14.3

Human trafficking has three components:[7]

(i) *the action*: there must be an act such as recruitment, transportation, transfer, harbouring or receipt of persons which involves an element of movement (that need not involve crossing a border);

(ii) *the means*: the action must be achieved through a means such as a threat or use of force, coercion, abduction, fraud, deception, abuse of power or vulnerability; and

(iii) *the purpose*: for the purpose of exploitation which includes forced criminality, sexual exploitation, forced labour or domestic servitude, slavery, financial exploitation or organ removal.

---

2 *Rantsev v Cyprus* (2010) 51 EHRR 1 at [282]; *SM v Croatia* (2021) 72 EHRR 1 at [292] – [296].

3 The UK signed ECAT on 23 March 2008 and ratified it on 17 December 2008.

4 *MS (Pakistan) v Secretary of State for the Home Department* [2020] 1 WLR 1373 at [20].

5 Home Office, *Modern Slavery: Statutory Guidance for England and Wales (under s 49 of the Modern Slavery Act 2015) and Non-Statutory Guidance for Scotland and Northern Ireland*, 20 September 2022. Available at: www.gov.uk/government/publications/modern-slavery-how-to-identify-and-support-victims.

6 For a discussion of the Directive's effect following Brexit, see, eg M Southwell, P Brewer and B Douglas-Jones KC, *Human Trafficking and Modern Slavery Law and Practice* 2nd edn (Bloomsbury Professional, 2020), p 3.

7 Statutory Guidance, pp. 17–24. Southwell, Brewer and Douglas Jones KC, *Human Trafficking and Modern Slavery Law and Practice* ibid, pp 4–13; *SM v Croatia* at [113]–[114], [155]–[156], [290].

14.4

Adults must satisfy all three components of the definition to be defined as victims of trafficking; children (those who are under 18 at the time of trafficking) are deemed victims of trafficking where there is an act and purpose, they do not have to satisfy the 'means' requirement.[8]

14.5

Trafficking and exploitation can take many forms. One area that has come to the fore for criminal practitioners in recent years is county lines and child criminal exploitation. County lines is a term used to describe gang involvement in drug supply using dedicated mobile phone lines; county lines drug operations often exploit children and vulnerable persons to move and store drugs and money.[9] These cases can be complex, with potential victims of trafficking only coming to the authorities' attention following arrest or charge for involvement in criminal activity.[10]

REQUIREMENT TO CRIMINALISE AND EFFECTIVELY PUNISH

14.6

Article 4 of the ECHR entails a positive obligation on states to penalise and prosecute effectively any act aimed at maintaining a person in a situation of slavery, servitude or forced or compulsory labour.[11] To ensure compliance with this obligation, states are required to put in place a legislative and administrative framework to prevent and punish trafficking and protect victims.[12] The ECtHR has specifically linked this to the obligations under Article 5 of the Palermo Protocol and Articles 18–23 of ECAT which require punishment, prevention and protection.

14.7

The requirement to criminalise is realised in English law under the two statutory offences created by MSA 2015: section 1 criminalises slavery, servitude

---

8 ECAT, art 4(c); Statutory Guidance, pp 17–18. *MS (Pakistan) v Secretary of State for the Home Department* at [18].

9 Home Office, 'Criminal Exploitation of Children and Vulnerable Adults: County Lines', published 11 July 2017, updated 7 February 2020. See www.gov.uk/government/publications/criminal-exploitation-of-children-and-vulnerable-adults-county-lines; National Crime Agency, County Lines, see www.nationalcrimeagency.gov.uk/what-we-do/crime-threats/drug-trafficking/county-lines.

10 Children's Society, 'Counting lines – responding to children who are criminally exploited' (July 2019), See www.childrenssociety.org.uk/information/professionals/resources/counting-lives.

11 *Siladin v France* (2006) 43 EHRR 16 at [89] and [112]. See also, *CN v United Kingdom* (2013) 56 EHRR 24 [66] – [69].

12 *Rantsev v Cyprus* at [285].

or forced and compulsory labour and section 2 criminalises human trafficking.[13] The scope of both offences are drawn by reference to the jurisprudence of the European Court of Human Rights defining what constitutes slavery, servitude, compulsory labour and exploitation.[14] Section 4 of MSA 2015 creates a further offence of committing any offence with intent to commit an offence of human trafficking under section 2, the purpose being to capture those offenders who commit offences with intent to aid or abet trafficking (eg those who provide forged documents to enable trafficking, or those who kidnap or falsely detain victims of trafficking).

REQUIREMENT TO INVESTIGATE AND IDENTIFY VICTIMS OF TRAFFICKING

14.8

There is an obligation under Article 10 of ECAT[15] and Article 4 of the ECHR to identify victims of trafficking. The scope of the obligation to investigate has been articulated clearly by the ECtHR in *Rantsev v Cyprus*,[16] holding that Article 4:

> …entails a procedural obligation to investigate situations of potential trafficking. The requirement to investigate does not depend on a complaint from the victim or next-of-kin: once the matter has come to the attention of the authorities they must act of their own motion. For an investigation to be effective, it must be independent from those implicated in the events. It must also be capable of leading to the identification and punishment of individuals responsible, an obligation not of result but of means. A requirement of promptness and reasonable expedition is implicit in all cases but where the possibility of removing the individual from the harmful situation is available, the investigation must be undertaken as a matter of urgency. The victim or the next-of-kin must be involved in the procedure to the extent necessary to safeguard their legitimate interests.

14.9

The Article 4 duty is engaged wherever state authorities are aware, or ought to be aware, of circumstances giving rise to a credible suspicion that an identified

13 Section 4 also creates an offence of committing any offence with intent to commit an offence of human trafficking under section 2. The purpose of the section 4 offence is to capture those offenders who commit offences with intent to aid or abet trafficking (eg, those who provide forged documents to enable trafficking, or those who kidnap or falsely detain victims of trafficking).

14 See *R v K(S)* [2013] QB 82. which concerned the precursor offence to MSA 2015, s 1 under the Asylum and Immigration (Treatment of Claimants etc) Act 2004, s 4. In addition, the ILO indicators of forced labour may be relevant, see eg, *Hounga v Allen* [2014] 1 WLR 2889 [48]–[49].

15 See also, CETS, *Explanatory Report to the Council of Europe Convention on Action against Trafficking in Human Beings*, para 127, see https://rm.coe.int/16800d3812.

16 *Rantsev v Cyprus* at [288].

individual had been, or was at real and immediate risk of being, trafficked or exploited.[17] In *R (TDT) v SSHD*,[18] the Court of Appeal held that this threshold is relatively low and can arise from generic information such as Home Office country reports.

14.10

The duty to investigate may require a criminal investigation; if this is the case the investigation must take place with reasonable speed and diligence and authorities must take all reasonable steps to secure evidence.[19] In the context of a criminal investigation, police are under a duty to pursue all reasonable lines of enquiry, and as a public body fall subject to the Article 4 obligation.[20] As a consequence of this procedural duty under Article 4 and Article 10 ECAT the failure to identify a victim of trafficking, the failure to remove an identified individual from a situation of trafficking, the failure to have their claim properly investigated and the failure to consider properly and fairly whether a person has been trafficked constitute actionable breaches of their fundamental rights.[21]

14.11

Article 3 of the ECHR prohibits torture, inhuman and degrading treatment where such treatment crosses the 'minimum level of severity' and similarly gives rise to a procedural obligation to investigate.[22] If authorities fail to conduct an effective investigation into serious offences against the person or credible claims of serious crimes, that failure may constitute a breach of the Article 3 rights of the victim of crime.

14.12

In addition to the obligations under the ECHR and ECAT, section 52 of the MSA 2015 also requires specified public authorities to notify the Home Office about any potential victims of trafficking .[23] Notification can be via a referral to the National Referral Mechanism (NRM) or, for those who do not consent to a referral, by otherwise notifying the Home Office of the existence of a potential victim.

---

17 *VCL v United Kingdom* (2021) 73 EHRR 9 at [152].

18 *R (TDT) v SSHD* [2018] 1 WLR 4922 [34] [38] [47].

19 *J v Austria* (Application no 68216/12), 17 January 2017 at para 107.

20 Criminal Procedure and Investigations Act (CPIA) 1996, Revised CPIA Code of Practice, March 2015, para 3.5.

21 *R (on the application of SF) v SSHD* [2016] 1 WLR 1439; *VCL v United Kingdom* at para 152.

22 *Ireland v UK* (1979–80) 2 EHRR 25; *Metropolitan Police Commissioner v DSD* [2019] AC 196.

23 The public authorities currently subject to this duty are (a) a chief officer of police for a police area, (b) the chief constable of the British Transport Police Force, (c) the National Crime Agency, (d) a county council, (e) a county borough council, (f) a district council, (g) a London borough council, (h) the Greater London Authority, (i) the Common Council of the City of London, (j) the Council of the Isles of Scilly, (k) the Gangmasters Licensing Authority.

The National Referral Mechanism

14.13

The NRM is the identification mechanism for victims of trafficking in the UK. It was established by the Home Office in April 2009 to provide the framework for identifying and referring potential victims of modern slavery and ensuring they receive the appropriate support. Potential victims of trafficking may be referred into the NRM by a designated 'first responder'.[24] Adults must consent to be referred but consent is not required to refer children.[25]

14.14

Legal practitioners are not first responders. However, where concerns arise that a defendant in criminal proceedings may be a victim of trafficking, practitioners can approach a suitable first responder to make a referral provided they have the client's consent; consent is always required for a legal practitioner to make contact with a first responder regardless of whether the client is an adult or a child because instructions received consistent with indicators of trafficking are subject to legal professional privilege.[26]

14.15

The Single Competent Authority (SCA) must first make a decision about whether there are reasonable grounds to suspect that a person may be a victim of modern slavery – the 'reasonable grounds' decision. The threshold for this decision is 'suspect but cannot prove'.[27] A positive reasonable grounds decision triggers a 45-day recovery and reflection period[28] and a requirement for the SCA to investigate and make a 'conclusive grounds' decision about whether an individual is a victim of trafficking; a positive conclusive grounds decision, made after investigation applies a standard of the balance of probabilities.[29]

14.16

Individuals, and those acting on their behalf, including first responders and legal advisers, can ask the SCA to review a negative decision. The discretion to reopen negative decisions must be exercised in accordance with the obligations under ECAT and the ECHR to identify victims.[30] It is also possible to challenge negative decisions by way of judicial review provided such challenges

24 First responders are the Home Office, local authorities, Health and Social Care Trusts, the police, the National Crime Agency, Trafficking Awareness Raising Alliance, Migrant Help, Kalayaan, Gangmasters Licensing Agency, Medaille Trust, the Salvation Army, Barnardo's, the National Society for the Prevention of Cruelty to Children, Unseen UK, New Pathways, BAWSO and the Refugee Council.

25 Statutory Guidance, Annex E: see www.gov.uk/government/publications/modern-slavery-how-to-identify-and-support-victims.

26 Youth Justice Legal Centre, Child Criminal Exploitation, December 2020.

27 Statutory Guidance, Annex E.

28 ECAT, art 12 requires that, during this period, victims are assisted in their physical, psychological and social recovery.

29 *R(MN) v Secretary of State for the Home Department* [2021] 1 WLR 1956; Statutory Guidance, Annex E.

30 *R (DS) v Secretary of State for the Home Department* [2020] Imm AR 409.

are brought promptly and in any event within three months of the relevant decision.[31]

14.17

Although a reasonable grounds decision should be taken within five days of receipt of the referral and the conclusive grounds decision at least 45 days after the reasonable grounds decision, [32] increasingly decisions are taking months, if not years.[33] The High Court concluded before the pandemic that the significant delays in making decisions were not sufficiently significant and widespread as to be systematic, therefore the delay itself is not unlawful.[34]

FAIR TRIAL GUARANTEES

14.18

Article 6 of the ECHR guarantees the right to a fair trial. The right to a fair trial requires that legal representation for the defendant be able to secure without restriction the fundamental aspects of a defence; that includes the ability to discuss the case, organise the defence, collect evidence favourable to the defendant, support for a defendant in distress, preparation for questions and checking the defendant's conditions of detention.[35]

Failure to investigate and Article 6 ECHR

14.19

In *R v O*,[36] the Court of Appeal expressly linked the obligation to identify victims of trafficking with the right to a fair trial finding that the appellant in that case had not been given a fair trial because neither the defence nor the prosecution had investigated the appellant's account of trafficking. This finding has been confirmed by the ECtHR in *VCL v UK*,[37] the Grand Chamber concluding that evidence concerning an accused's status as a victim of trafficking is a 'fundamental aspect' of the defence which an accused should be able to secure without restriction and that the failure by the state to conduct a timely assessment of whether the applicants in that case had prevented them from securing evidence which may have constituted a fundamental aspect of their defence in breach of Article 6. The Court further emphasised that the failure of defence lawyers to identify indicators of trafficking did not absolve the state

31 See further, Southwell, Brewer and Douglas Jones KC, *Human Trafficking and Modern Slavery Law and Practice*, pp. 80–92.
32 Statutory Guidance, p.87.
33 See www.gov.uk/government/statistics/modern-slavery-national-referral-mechanism-and-duty-to-notify-statistics-uk-end-of-year-summary-2021.
34 *R (O and H) v Secretary of State for the Home Department* [2019] EWHC 148 (Admin) at [112].
35 *Dvorski v Croatia* (2016) 63 EHRR 7 at [108].
36 *R v O* [2008] EWCA Crim 2835 at [26].
37 *VCL v UK* (2021) 73 EHRR 9, at [196]–[200].

of its obligation to do so and further emphasised that the state was not entitled to rely upon the 'shortcomings of legal aid [defence] counsel' as a defence to a potential breach of Article 6 where those shortcomings amount to a manifest failure to provide effective representation.

Conduct of the trial

14.20

The Equal Treatment Bench Book[38] emphasises that victims of modern slavery are 'likely to be vulnerable witnesses, considerably damaged by their experiences and wary of authority figures. They will often have a profound sense of powerlessness and worthlessness inculcated in them by those holding them in thrall'. It is important to remember that defendants may well be victims and these considerations must apply equally to defendants and witnesses.[39] One aspect of protecting victims of trafficking prosecuted for criminal offences may be an application for anonymity. The Crown Court, for trials on indictment, can make an order protecting the identity of defendants under the age of 18,[40] however, there is no specific power to anonymise adult defendants during trial. Where a victim (or potential victim) of trafficking has been charged with others, it may be that other co-defendants were involved with their exploitation or trafficking. If that is the case application can be made for the victim of trafficking to be tried separately.[41]

THE NON-PUNISHMENT PRINCIPLE

14.21

Article 26 of the ECAT sets out the non-punishment principle and provides that State Parties shall 'provide for the possibility of not imposing penalties on victims for their involvement in unlawful activities, to the extent that they have been compelled to do so'.[42] This is echoed in Article 8 of the Directive.[43] The non-punishment principle does not give rise to a general prohibition on the prosecution of victims of trafficking but rather requires a fact sensitive case-by-case assessment of whether it is appropriate to prosecute a victim of trafficking.

14.22

The ECtHR considered the relationship between Article 4 and the non-punishment principle in *VCL v United Kingdom*.[44] The Grand Chamber

38 See Equal Treatment Bench Book, July 2022, p.205. Available at: www.judiciary.uk/about-the-judiciary/diversity/equal-treatment-bench-book/.

39 See, eg, Criminal Practice Direction I, 3E, 3F, 3G in relation to special measures and intermediaries.

40 Youth Justice and Criminal Evidence Act 1999, s 45.

41 Indictments Act 1915, s 5(3) and Crim PR 3.29.

42 See further: CETS, *Explanatory Report to the Council of Europe Convention on Action against Trafficking in Human Beings*, para 272.

43 Recital (14) of the Preamble to the Directive.

44 *VCL v United Kingdom* at [158]–[162].

concluded that although there is no general prohibition on the prosecution of victims of trafficking, such prosecutions may breach the State's obligations to take operational measures to protect such individuals under Article 4 as prosecution is injurious to victims' recovery and may leave them vulnerable to being re-trafficked. The Court observed that, pursuant to Article 4, states have an obligation as soon as they 'are aware, or ought to be aware, of circumstances giving rise to a credible suspicion that an individual suspected of having committed a criminal offence may have been trafficked or exploited' to ensure that such individuals should be promptly assessed by 'individuals trained and qualified to deal with victims of trafficking'.

14.23

This principle is consistent with CPS Guidance which requires prosecutors to advise the investigating law enforcement agency to investigate the suspect's trafficking/slavery situation and to consider referring the suspect to the NRM. The Guidance goes on to provide that '[a]n NRM referral should always be made unless the law enforcement agency is in possession of clear and sufficient evidence to prove that the suspect is not a victim of trafficking/slavery'.[45] If a credible suspicion of trafficking arises post charge, then CPS Guidance provides that prosecutors should seek an adjournment and a referral through the NRM.

14.24

In relation to any decision to prosecute, the Grand Chamber in *VCL* was clear that such decisions should 'insofar as possible – only be taken once a trafficking assessment has been made by a qualified person'. The Court further held[46] that:

> Once a trafficking assessment has been made by a qualified person, any subsequent prosecutorial decision would have to take that assessment into account. While the prosecutor might not be bound by the findings made in the course of such a trafficking assessment, the prosecutor would need to have clear reasons which are consistent with the definition of trafficking contained in the Palermo Protocol and the Anti-Trafficking Convention for disagreeing with it.

14.25

Prior to the MSA 2015, the non-punishment principle was not reflected in domestic legislation but was given effect by the courts primarily by means of CPS guidance, the common law defence of duress and abuse of process.[47] In cases falling under MSA 2015, the non-punishment principle is reflected in CPS policy, the common law defence of duress and the defence under section 45.

45 See www.cps.gov.uk/legal-guidance/human-trafficking-smuggling-and-slavery.

46 *VCL v United Kingdom* at [161].

47 See summary of authorities in *R v GS* [2018] 4 WLR 167 at [76].

CPS policy – the four-stage test

14.26

The CPS guidance on the prosecution of potential victims of trafficking sets out a four-stage test prosecutors must apply in deciding whether to prosecute an individual who might be a victim of trafficking or slavery.[48]

- *Is there a reason to believe the person is a victim of trafficking?* Pursuant to this obligation, prosecutors are required to consider, regardless of their admissibility at trial, decisions issued by the Single Competent Authority assessing whether an individual is a victim of trafficking.[49] Prosecutors are required to subject such assessments to thorough examination, considering the cogency of the evidence on which the SCA relied as well as considering other expert evidence.[50] The Grand Chamber has since made it clear that prosecutors would need to have 'clear reasons' for disagreeing with assessments made by qualified persons.[51]
- *Is there clear evidence of duress?* The common law defence of duress can apply to victims of trafficking but is very narrowly drawn and requires that the individual has a reasonable, genuinely held belief that there was a threat of death or serious injury to the defendant, or a member of their immediate family or a person to whom they reasonably regard themselves as responsible.[52] The defendant's criminal conduct must have been directly caused by the threat and a sober person of reasonable firmness, having the same characteristics as the defendant would have responded in the same way.[53] Prior to the introduction of the statutory defence (below), the court had refused to extend duress in cases involving victims of trafficking.[54]
- *Is there clear evidence of a section 45 defence?* This defence is discussed in greater detail below. The CPS Guidance makes it clear that 'no charges should be brought' if there is 'sufficient evidence' that suggests that:

  (i) the suspect is a genuine victim of trafficking or slavery;

  (ii) the other conditions in section 45 are met; and

  (iii) the offence is not an excluded offence under Schedule 4.
- *Is it in the public interest to prosecute?* In assessing the public interest, the CPS guidance requires consideration of:

  (i) the seriousness of the offence and the culpability of the offender – the 'more serious the offence, the greater the dominant force needed

48 See www.cps.gov.uk/legal-guidance/human-trafficking-smuggling-and-slavery. For comprehensive discussion of the application of this test, see. Southwell, Brewer and Douglas Jones KC, *Human Trafficking and Modern Slavery Law and Practice*, Chapter 5.

49 *R v AAD, AAH and AAI* [2022] EWCA Crim 106.

50 *R v VSJ* [2017] 1 WLR 3153 at [39]; *R v L* [2014] 1 All ER 113 at [28].

51 *VCL v United Kingdom* at [162].

52 *R v Hasan* [2005] 2 A.C. 467 at [21]–[23].

53 *R v Graham* (1982) 74 Cr App R 235, CA at 241.

54 *R v van Dao* [2012] EWCA Crim 1717 at [33]; *R v N* [2012] 1 Cr App R 35 at [54].

to reduce the criminality or culpability to the point where it is not in the public interest to prosecute';[55]

(ii) the level of compulsion which includes consideration of the vulnerability of the defendant and whether the compulsion was continuing;[56] and

(iii) the nexus between the crime committed and the trafficking.[57]

Section 45 defence

14.27

Pursuant to section 45 of the MSA 2015, which came into force on 31 July 2015, slavery or trafficking victims may have a defence to certain offences:

(1) A person is not guilty of an offence if—

(a) the person is aged 18 or over when the person does the act which constitutes the offence;

(b) the person does that act because the person is compelled to do it;

(c) the compulsion is attributable to slavery or to relevant exploitation; and

(d) a reasonable person in the same situation as the person and having the person's relevant characteristics would have no realistic alternative to doing that act.

(2) A person may be compelled to do something by another person or by the person's circumstances.

(3) Compulsion is attributable to slavery or to relevant exploitation only if—

(a) it is, or is part of, conduct which constitutes an offence under section 1 or conduct which constitutes relevant exploitation; or

(b) it is a direct consequence of a person being, or having been, a victim of slavery or a victim of relevant exploitation.

(4) A person is not guilty of an offence if—

(a) the person is under the age of 18 when the person does the act which constitutes the offence;

(b) the person does that act as a direct consequence of the person being, or having been, a victim of slavery or a victim of relevant exploitation; and

55 *R v VSJ* [2017] 1 WLR 3153 at [20].
56 *R v GS* at [76].
57 Ibid.

(c) a reasonable person in the same situation as the person and having the person's relevant characteristics would do that act.

(5) For the purposes of this section 'relevant characteristics' means age, sex and any physical or mental illness or disability; 'relevant exploitation' is exploitation (within the meaning of section 3) that is attributable to the exploited person being, or having been, a victim of human trafficking.

(6) In this section references to an act include an omission.

(7) Subsections (1) and (4) do not apply to an offence listed in Schedule 4.

14.28

The defence applies only to events post-dating 31 July 2015[58] and cannot operate as a defence to those offences listed in Schedule 4 to the MSA 2015. In all other cases, it is for the defendant to raise evidence of each element of the defence and for the prosecution to disprove one or more of those elements to the criminal standard.[59]

14.29

As set out in section 45(4) children must only show that they did the act as a direct consequence of being a victim of trafficking and that a reasonable person in the same situation as the person and sharing their characteristics would have done the act. By contrast, adult defendants are additionally required to demonstrate that they have been compelled to do the act. Compulsion is not defined within the narrow confines of the defence of duress[60] and must be seen in the context of the trafficking and exploitation to which the defendant has been subject.[61]

14.30

In advancing the section 45 defence, the conclusive grounds decision itself is not admissible because SCA caseworkers cannot properly be considered experts to the standard required in a criminal trial and decisions are not issued in accordance with CrimPR 19.[62] This does not, however, preclude reliance upon conclusive grounds decisions in appeals against conviction or in abuse of process applications.[63]

---

58 *R v CS* [2021] EWCA Crim 134 at [59]–[73]. For offences before 31 July 2015 the earlier jurisprudence remains applicable. Where the offending straddles a period before 31 July 2015 it is arguable that one reading of the Modern Slavery Act 2015 (Commencement No. 1, Saving and Transitional Provisions) Regulations 2015, paragraph 2, looked at together with paragraph 3, is that the defence would apply to the whole of that period, notwithstanding that it only came into force on 31 July 2015. This point has not been decided.

59 *R v MK* [2018] EWCA Crim 667, [2019] QB 86 at [45].

60 *R v LM* [2011] 1 Cr App R 12.

61 CETS, *Explanatory Report to the Council of Europe Convention on Action against Trafficking in Human Beings*, para 273.

62 *R v Brecani* [2021] 2 Cr App R 12 at [54].

63 *R v AAD, AAH and AAI* [2022] EWCA Crim 106 at [79] and [142].

14.31

Reliance therefore needs to be placed upon the material underlying the conclusive grounds decision and/or other sources of evidence to raise the defence, such as asylum and immigration or social services records. The defence may also seek to adduce expert evidence from psychiatrists, country experts or trafficking experts. Care must be taken, however, as to the instruction of appropriate experts who have access to all relevant information and direct interaction with the defendant. The Court in *Brecani* was openly critical of the trafficking expert relied upon in that case raising queries about whether they possessed sufficient knowledge of modern slavery and suggesting that their 'opinion was reached without consideration of core relevant information'.

14.32

In addition to expert and documentary evidence, cross-examination of the officer in the case about the investigative steps taken by the police in relation to the alleged trafficking, the nature of the relevant form of exploitation and how such exploitation can manifest in a criminal context (eg the role of hierarchy in a county lines drug operation – will be crucial).[64]

Abuse of process

14.33

Prior to the enactment of the section 45 defence, the abuse of process jurisdiction under the criminal law was used to seek a stay of a prosecution to ensure that the non-punishment principle under Article 26 of the ECAT was respected.[65] Such applications were made on the basis that the decision to prosecute had not been properly carried out, and had the decision been taken properly then there would or might well have been a decision not to prosecute.[66]

14.34

In *R v AAD, AAH and AAI*,[67] the Court addressed a number of points of principle including whether it remained possible to argue that a prosecution was an abuse of process, and concluded:

(i) the limb two abuse of process jurisdiction remains available in principle in all VOT cases following the 2015 Act, and whether or not they are Schedule 4 cases;

(ii) such jurisdiction is 'special' only in the sense that it falls to be exercised in the context of a particular sensitivity required to be applied to VOT prosecutions, having regard to international obligations and specific CPS

64 Southwell, Brewer and Douglas Jones KC, *Human Trafficking and Modern Slavery Law and Practice*, pp. 274–275.

65 *R v L(C)* [2014] 1 All ER 113.

66 *R v M(L)* [2011] 1 Cr App R 12, at [19].

67 *R v AAD, AAH and AAI* at [142].

guidance. The core requirements of unfairness and oppression and illegality (inherent in almost every limb two case) remain central to applications for a stay in a VOT context;

(iii) mere disagreement with a decision to prosecute, following due regard given by the prosecution to the CPS guidance and to any conclusive grounds decision, gives no basis whatsoever for an application for a stay. Decisions to prosecute are for the CPS. Decisions on disputed facts or evaluations of fact are for the jury; and

(iv) if (in what will be likely to be a most exceptional case) there has been a failure to have due regard to CPS guidance or if there has been a lack of rational basis for departure by the prosecution from a conclusive grounds decision then a stay application may be available. It will then be assessed by the court, by way of review on grounds corresponding to public law grounds.

Sentencing victims of trafficking

14.35

When a victim of trafficking is convicted of an offence, even following an unsuccessful section 45 defence, the background of trafficking and exploitation and other related evidence (eg, psychological reports) remains acutely relevant as mitigation and speaks to culpability.[68]

REMEDIES FOR VICTIMS OF TRAFFICKING

14.36

Article 13 of the ECHR requires that individuals have a right to an effective remedy for breaches of their rights under the ECHR. It remains an unfortunately common occurrence that victims of trafficking and exploitation are not recognised as such in the criminal justice system; it is very important that *prima facie* unsafe criminal convictions of those who are or may be victims of trafficking are challenged promptly to ensure that any violations of their rights under the ECHR are promptly remedied. This is of particular practical importance where such individuals face concurrent immigration proceedings and where a criminal conviction may result in an order for deportation or otherwise interfere with the victim's access to permanent residence, education or employment.[69]

68 See, eg, *R v L* [2014] at [14].
69 Immigration Act 1971, s 3(6). See, eg, *R v GB* [2020] EWCA Crim 2.

Appeal from the magistrates' court

14.37

A defendant only has an automatic right of appeal to the Crown Court in relation to their conviction if they pleaded not guilty.[70] A defendant who pleaded guilty can therefore only appeal against conviction in very limited circumstances, such as where the guilty plea was equivocal or the product of duress.[71] Historically, practitioners have used section 142 of the Magistrates' Courts Act 1980, relying upon *R (Williamson) v City of Westminster Magistrates' Court*,[72] to re-open cases where victims of trafficking have, often on erroneous advice or in the absence of recognition of their status as a victim, entered guilty pleas in the magistrates' court. However, in *H v DPP*,[73] the Divisional Court considered the case of a youth charged with offences including possession of a knife in a public place and possession of significant amounts of heroin and cocaine with intent to supply who had pleaded guilty in the magistrates' court. Following a post-conviction NRM referral, he applied under section 142(2) to reopen his case, but the Divisional Court upheld the refusal of his application on the basis that the magistrates' court has no power to allow a plea of guilty to be vacated under section 142 once the defendant had been sentenced in the Crown Court. The Court went on to specifically distinguish *Williamson* and conclude that 'an argument that a defendant failed to adduce evidence which might have led to an acquittal or failed generally to pursue a defence that it is later asserted was available (such as modern slavery or self-defence) is not something that falls within section 142(2) of the 1980 Act'. In the view of the Divisional Court, challenges to convictions following a guilty plea in the magistrates' court should be dealt with by application to the Criminal Cases Review Commission. This decision does not sit easily with the right under Article 13 of ECHR and the ECtHR's decision in *VCL*,[74] given the significant delays contingent in applications to the CCRC.

Appeal from the Crown Court

14.38

Those defendants who are convicted in the Crown Court can apply for leave to appeal against conviction to the Court of Appeal Criminal Division (CACD), the test being whether the conviction is unsafe.[75] A victim of trafficking can seek to argue that a conviction following a guilty plea is unsafe, applying the considerations set out in *R v Tredget*,[76] applied to trafficking appeals in *AAD*.[77]

70 Magistrates' Courts Act 1980, s 108.

71 *R v Rochdale Justices ex p Allwork* [1981] 3 All ER 434; *R v Marylebone Justices ex p Westminster City Council* [1971] 1 All ER 1025.

72 *R (Williamson) v City of Westminster Magistrates' Court* [2012] 2 Cr App R 24.

73 *H v DPP* [2021] 1 WLR 2721.

74 *VCL v United Kingdom* (2021) 73 EHRR 9 at [174] [183] [200] [205]–[209].

75 Criminal Appeal Act 1968, s 2.

76 *R v Tredget* [2022] 4 WLR 62.

77 *R v AAD, AAH and AAI* at [155]–[157].

Victims of trafficking may also seek to appeal against their sentence where mitigation relating to their status as a victim was not placed before or considered by the sentencing court.

14.39

The Court has the power to grant anonymity to an appellant who is a victim of trafficking under section 11 of the Contempt of Court Act 1981. Relevant rights include the right to life (Article 2), prohibition on torture (Article 3), prohibition on slavery (Article 4) and right to family life and privacy (Article 8).[78] These will need to be weighed against the need for open justice and the right to freedom of information under Article 10.[79] In *R v L*,[80] the Court of Appeal gave guidance as to the application of section 11 in this context and considered that it would be desirable, in principle, for the CACD to follow the practice of the Court of Appeal Civil Division and Immigration Tribunal of anonymising the applicant in cases raising international protection issues.

Criminal Cases Review Commission (CCRC)

14.40

Individuals who have been convicted on indictment, sentenced following conviction or convicted by a magistrates' court may apply to the CCRC to have their case referred to the Crown Court or Court of Appeal as appropriate.[81] The CCRC has investigative powers and can request the production of documents or other material 'which may assist the Commission in the exercise of any of their functions'.[82] The CCRC can only make a reference to the Court of Appeal where it considers that (i) there is a real possibility that the conviction, verdict, finding or sentence would not be upheld were the reference to be made; (ii) because of an argument, or evidence, not raised in the proceedings which led to the conviction, verdict, finding or sentence, or in the case of against it; and (iii) an appeal has been determined or leave to appeal refused.[83] It is therefore clear that an application should only be made to the CCRC from a conviction in the Crown Court if the conventional right of appeal to the Court of Appeal has been exhausted.

78 *R v O* [2019] EWCA Crim 1389; *R v GB* [2020] EWCA Crim 2.

79 See, eg, *A v BBC* [2015] AC 588; *Re Guardian News and Media Ltd* [2010] 2 AC 697.

80 *R v L* [2017] EWCA Crim 2129.

81 Criminal Appeal Act 1995, ss 9 and 11.

82 Ibid, s 17.

83 Ibid, s 13.

Compensation

14.41

Article 15 of the ECAT requires Member States to provide compensation for victims.[84] These obligations are met under domestic law through several mechanisms:

- compensation orders.[85]
- slavery reparation orders made pursuant to section 8 of the MSA 2015 may also require a defendant to pay compensation to the victim;
- compensation via the Criminal Injuries Compensation Scheme.[86]
- the Miscarriage of Justice Application Scheme (for those who have been wrongfully convicted and punished).[87]

14.42

Victims may also seek to assert their rights to an effective remedy under Article 13 by pursuing a claim for damages for breach of the HRA 1998 against a public body. Such claims have a short limitation period of one year, subject to the court finding it equitable to extend the period.[88]

84 See also International Covenant on Civil and Political Rights, art 14(6) and the Seventh Protocol of the ECHR, art 3.
85 Powers of Criminal Courts (Sentencing) Act 2000, ss 130–133.
86 Criminal Injuries Compensation Scheme 2012.
87 Criminal Justice Act 1988, s 133.
88 HRA 1998, s 7(5). See, eg, *OOO v Commissioner of Police for the Metropolis* [2011] HRLR 29.

Part 3

Pre-trial issues

15 Extradition

Kate Goold and Mary Westcott

INTRODUCTION

15.1

Extradition is the legal transfer of a person in custody for the purpose of criminal prosecution, sentencing, or enforcing a custodial sentence previously imposed. Contrast deportation, which is the removal of a person from a country on a court's recommendation, or for the public good. Extradition proceedings are treated as a sub-set of general crime, but the process does not involve a finding of guilt or innocence, so Article 6(2)–(3) of the European Convention on Human Rights (ECHR) is not directly engaged.[1] Article 5(1)(f) of the ECHR specifically includes an exception arising from lawful detention pending extradition.

15.2

Most specialist extradition law developed in this jurisdiction arises from so-called 'export' proceedings (ie, people arrested in this jurisdiction, wanted for prosecution or custodial punishment elsewhere). 'Import' extradition requests issued by this jurisdiction justifying arrest elsewhere, bring people before our courts. The initial preparation of an extradition request does not involve proceedings in open court, with proceedings becoming public only after a person's arrest.

15.3

Human rights issues are a crucial part of challenging 'export' extradition, especially relevant to protections under Articles 2, 3, 5, 6 and 8 of the ECHR. The focus of this chapter is on 'import' work, where criminal practitioners are most likely to encounter extradited persons outside the sphere of the specialist extradition courts considering 'export' requests.[2]

15.4

Extradition itself is a serious interference with a person's liberty. After extradition, a person can expect to experience the myriad human rights issues that would occur during any criminal case, examined in other chapters. There

1 *Trabelsi v Belgium* (2015) 60 EHHR 21, [60].
2 Following arrest or provisional arrest in the UK, the Extradition Act 2003 (EA 2003) requires production in custody at Westminster magistrates' court for an 'initial hearing' (EA 2003, ss 3–8, 71–74E).

are, however, some specific concerns for the extradited person either inherent to the extradition process (Is the offence extraditable?) or if the process has not been followed (eg, in the case of 'disguised extradition' and specialty),[3] which could result in a subsequent trial being stayed as an abuse of process.

15.5

Statistics suggest encountering a case that has involved extradition is increasingly likely over the last decade.[4] It remains to be seen to what extent that trend is reversed with reduced travel following increased digital working, loss of freedom of movement and changes to our extradition machinery as a result of the United Kingdom's departure from the European Union.[5] There is speculation that the loss of real-time information-sharing systems[6] will reduce efficiencies, which will also reduce the arrests of extradition defendants, although the new arrangements still allow for cooperation with bodies such as Eurojust and Europol.[7]

MUTUAL TRUST AND HUMAN RIGHTS

15.6

There is an ingrained tension between the policy-driven need for reciprocity integral to extradition and the need to respect fundamental human rights, with expectations and standards differing internationally. By definition, extradition is 'a form of international cooperation in criminal matters, based on comity (rather than any overarching obligation under international law), intended to promote justice'.[8] That cooperation requires a certain degree of acceptance of the criminal justice systems of other countries, including different views of offences and appropriate prosecution and punishment. On the other hand, the absolute nature of fundamental rights and varying international standards potentially challenge mutual respect between jurisdictions. If human rights are effectively protected, that risks preventing effective extradition, in turn fettering the rights of the victims of crime.

15.7

The EA 2003 ensures that before any 'export' extradition decision is made, that decision is also deemed compatible with a requested person's Convention

3 See 15.27 onwards.

4 The National Crime Agency publishes annual arrest and surrender data (www.nationalcrimeagency.gov.uk/what-we-do/how-we-work/providing-specialist-capabilities-for-law-enforcement/fugitives-and-international-crime/european-arrest-warrants).

5 See 15.11.

6 For example, the pan-European Schengen Information System II (SIS II) database is no longer accessible to the UK. For further context see E Grange and R Niblock, *Extradition Law: A Practitioner's Guide* 3rd edn (Legal Action Group, 2021).

7 House of Lords European Union Committee 'Beyond Brexit: policing, law enforcement and security' (House of Lords EU Committee), 26 March 2021 at [85]–[87].

8 *A Review of the United Kingdom's Extradition Arrangements* (Baker Review), 2011.

rights.[9] When considering whether to extradite, the extraditing jurisdiction holds part of the responsibility for subsequent breach of fundamental rights, at least for the purposes of Article 3 of the ECHR.[10]

15.8

Successive reviews of UK extradition arrangements have concluded that the statutory human rights bars to extradition provide 'appropriate protection against prospective human rights violations' in requesting territories'.[11] Further, 'domestic courts have interpreted the human rights bar in accordance with the principles developed and applied by the European Court of human rights in the context of extradition'.[12]

15.9

Extradition requests involving countries that are, for example, signatories to the ECHR, are traditionally not as problematic due to shared human rights standards. Against that, countries including the UK have actively provided sanctuary for people sought by oppressive regimes for political prosecutions. Provisions allowing for extra-territorial extradition offences and consideration of the appropriate forum in which to prosecute are one way of addressing this problem.

15.10

The public bodies arranging for 'import' extradition are arguably subject to obligations to ensure they are not the instigators of human rights violations (eg, to avoid detention in degrading conditions in the requested territory at their behest).[13] It is understood that risk assessments of sorts are routinely carried out by UK authorities as part of UK extradition requests to some territories, but it will likely take litigation in order to scrutinise and understand the precise approach taken, which likely varies case by case.

EXTRADITION MACHINERY

15.11

The machinery behind extradition proceedings partly dictates the way in which human rights issues arise. The consequences of recent significant amendments are not yet clear and will doubtless be clarified by case law. The EA 2003 is the principal national instrument, dividing requesting countries between

9 EA 2003, ss 21 and 87.
10 *Soering v United Kingdom* (1989) 11 EHRR 439; *Saadi v Italy* (2009) 49 EHHR 30.
11 Baker Review 2011 at [11.8]; also House of Lords Select Committee on Extradition law, 'Extradition: UK law and practice', 10 March 2015, [60]–[61].
12 Baker Review 2011 at [11.9].
13 See Chapters 27, 28 and 29.

Category 1[14] and Category 2 territories,[15] with Parts 1 and 2 of the Act applying respectively. Part 3 of the EA 2003 deals with 'import' extradition requests from Category 1 and 2 territories (ss 142–150), although it is the royal prerogative rather than the EA 2003 which allows requests to Category 2 territories.[16]

15.12

The EA 2003 has been amended to reflect the new surrender arrangements following the UK's departure from the European Union. Part 3 also governs requests for extradition from Norway and Iceland and further practical aspects. The key new instrument that relates to Category 1 countries is Part III, Title VII of the Trade and Cooperation Agreement 2021 (TCA) between the United Kingdom of Great Britain and Northern Ireland, of the one part, and the European Union and the European Atomic Energy Community of the other part.

15.13

After a person is arrested abroad based on a UK request, the extradition process will follow the legislation of the territory in question. Almost all national extradition arrangements have certain requirements for an extradition offence, regarding maximum possible custodial penalties or penalties imposed.[17] Extradition requests do not universally have to prove the case against the requested person via a *prima facie* case, although there are frequently requirements of 'dual criminality' for any qualifying extradition offence.[18]

15.14

A 'political offence' exception is common in extradition arrangements aimed at protecting people from unjust prosecution,[19] with the TCA providing for national opt outs and an exception for terrorism offences. Specialty protection[20] is also frequently explicitly guaranteed, designed to ensure a person is only dealt with in the requesting territory for the offences for which they were extradited (see further below), in addition to provisions designed to prevent double jeopardy commonly featuring. There are further differences in the process depending on whether a person is arrested in a Category 1 or Category 2 territory, especially in the likely level of mutual trust to be extended to a Category 1 territory

14 27 EU Member States and Gibraltar.

15 The relevant territories are defined by The Extradition Act 2003 (Designation of Part 2 Territories) Order 2003 (SI 2003/3334).

16 *Barton v The Commonwealth of Australia* [1974] 131 CLR 477.

17 For definition of an extradition offence see EA 2003, s 148.

18 Or 'Double criminality' which means the underlying conduct would be criminal in both requesting and requested countries, excluding, for example, certain matters that might otherwise be treated as merely civil offending in some jurisdictions (unpaid child maintenance), or not at all (homosexual activity).

19 A combination of the 'double criminality' extradition offence requirements and protections against discrimination preserved this in UK legislation (EA 2003, ss 13, 64–65, 81, 137–138 and 148) also TCA arts 599–602.

20 Or 'speciality', see *Hilali v Central Court of Criminal Proceedings No 5 of the National Court, Madrid* [2006] EWHC 1239 (Admin); EA 2003, ss 17, 95, 146–147; and TCA, art 625 also refers.

and some 'trusted' Category 2 countries.[21] In both scenarios, the EA 2003 dovetails with Article 6 of the ECHR in that it provides for prompt return after extradition to the UK back to the country of arrest, free of charge.[22]

Category 1

15.15

With exceptions for transitory arrangements, the end of 2020 heralded the end of the European Arrest Warrant (EAW) in the UK, to be replaced by a new system applicable to Category 1 territories under the TCA. The resulting extradition tool, colloquially a 'TCA warrant', has requirements broadly similar to an EAW.[23] EAWs remain relevant due to the transitory provisions allowing continuing force in certain circumstances and because the EAW continues to prevail across the European Union, built on the cornerstone of mutual recognition and trust.[24] It is therefore no coincidence that the new TCA arrangements closely echo the EAW system, presumably with the aim of harmony firmly in mind.

15.16

The formal principle of mutual recognition underlying the EAW no longer applies, but shared human rights standards remain. Article 524 of the TCA provides for cooperation based on:

> Member States' long-standing respect for democracy, the rule of law and the protection of fundamental rights and freedoms of individuals, including as set out in the Universal Declaration of Human Rights and in the European Convention on Human Rights …

The TCA includes a principle of proportionality,[25] but this and other rights will be conferred on the subject of the extradition process in accordance with domestic law because the TCA is an international agreement and its provisions have not been directly incorporated into domestic law. Where there are differences between TCA provisions and the EA 2003, the starting point is domestic law. CJEU decisions in TCA cases are no longer binding.[26] At the time of writing the status of the TCA in some Member States had temporarily halted extradition to the UK, but the CJEU has recently confirmed Ireland is

21 See recent amendments to the Category 2 'export' provisional arrest scheme which allow for arrest in this country based on a document other than an arrest warrant (such as an Interpol Red Notice) if properly certified by the NCA, relating to a 'serious' offence and emanating from a designated 'trusted' country (EA 2003, ss 74A–74E and Sch A1) including the United States.

22 EA 2003, s 153.

23 EA 2003, s 2, TCA, art 606 and as-yet-unused waivers of dual criminality with the result that this is required in every TCA warrant at present.

24 With every other Member State still following the underlying Council Framework Decision on the EAW and the surrender procedures between Member States (2002/584/JHA).

25 TCA, art 597 applies equally to accusation and conviction cases.

26 *Polakowski v Westminster Magistrates' Court* [2021] EWHC 53 (Admin), [2021] 1 WLR 2521 at [32].

bound by the new arrangements and the authors are not aware of any other challenges.[27]

15.17

An outgoing TCA warrant must be issued by an 'appropriate judge' on application from a constable or 'appropriate person' (EA 2003, s 142(1)).[28] Further, there are requirements for reasonable grounds for believing that the accused has committed the extradition offence and there is an underlying domestic warrant (s 142(2)) with parallel provisions applicable to a convicted person (s 142(2A)). There are further procedural requirements, including for certification by the National Crime Agency, providing the TCA warrant contains the prescribed information and was issued by an appropriate 'Judicial Authority' (EA 2003, s 2).[29] An 'appropriate person' who may apply for a TCA warrant includes designated members of the Serious Fraud Office, the DPP and 'any Crown Prosecutor and any counsel or solicitor instructed by the Crown Prosecution Service for the purposes of the case concerned' (s 142(9)).[30]

15.18

One practical change in the TCA system is that, so far, 12 Category 1 territories have used the option to refuse to extradite their own nationals to the UK (TCA, art 603),[31] with others only agreeing to do so on condition that their own nationals will be returned following extradition to complete any custodial sentence.[32] UK nationals do not enjoy the same protection and are unlikely to do so,[33] which has led to speculation about fundamental inequality in a system that is supposed to be based on reciprocity.[34]This is the context for the call made by the House of Lords in 2021 for a government explanation about:

> the extent to which UK citizens subject to [TCA warrants] … will be able to rely upon the rights set out in the Agreement in UK courts" and to provide the rationale for the apparent imbalance … between the rights enjoyed and enforceable by citizens in the EU before their national courts in comparison to those who are resident in the UK.[35]

27 [2022] 1 WLR 1975 (C-479/21 PPU).

28 EA 2003, s 149.

29 Also with a wide-ranging power to refuse to certify an extradition request based on 'national security' (EA 2003, ss 208(2)–(4)).

30 Extradition Act 2003 (Part 3 Designation) Order (SI 2003/3335) as amended by Extradition Act 2003 (Part 3 Designation) (Amendment) Order (SI 2005/1127).

31 Austria, Croatia, the Czech Republic, Finland, France, Germany, Greece, Latvia, Poland, Slovakia, Slovenia and Sweden. See http://data.parliament.uk/DepositedPapers/Files/DEP2021-0194/Letter_Kevin_Foster_to_Lord_Ricketts_UK_EU_security_cooperation.pdf, 5 March 2021.

32 Denmark, Estonia, Hungary, Lithuania, Netherlands, Portugal and Romania. *Ibid*

33 According to the answers of Kevin Foster MP, Parliamentary Under Secretary of State (Minister for Future Borders and Immigration) to the House of Lords EU Committee, 26 March 2021 at [135].

34 Professor Mitsilegas answers to the House of Lords EU Committee, 26 March 2021 at [138].

35 House of Lords EU Committee, 26 March 2021 at [141].

15.19

Embodied within TCA is also the option to suspend the agreement 'in the event of serious and systemic deficiencies within one Party as regards the protection of fundamental rights of the principle of the rule of law', including 'personal data' (art 693). That is plainly a very high bar, but noteworthy given mounting rule of law criticisms of some Member States such as Poland and Hungary.

Category 2

15.20

UK extradition requests directed towards other countries are made under the Royal Prerogative as required by the relevant extradition treaty[36] or, in rare cases, an *ad hoc* arrangement if there is no treaty. The Foreign and Commonwealth Office provides an online register of treaties.[37] *Ad hoc* arrangements require the Secretary of State to recognise third country requests using a memorandum of understanding, after which it will follow the same process as a Category 2 territory request.[38] *Ad hoc* 'import' requests have been made by the UK to countries such as Afghanistan, Bahrain, Rwanda, Taiwan and Pakistan.

15.21

The UK Government has openly recognised the need for caution surrounding cooperation in certain contexts. For example, the Home Secretary referred to some countries 'where we will have very real concerns about the conditions in which somebody who was extradited … would be treated' and 'there will be decisions for us in relation to human rights and safeguards and the judicial systems of other countries' which will 'change over time'.[39] The Lords, however, were satisfied that the Courts were able to deal with 'countries of concern' effectively.[40]

Key actors

15.22

Various public bodies will have acted in a person's extradition case prior to arrival in the UK, when the person will be before a criminal court in the ordinary way. The Crown Prosecution Service (CPS)[41] is the most prominent and will be bound by their own code prior to any charging decision in the usual

36 These can be bilateral or multilateral, see EA 2003, s 193 regarding International Conventions and Extradition Act 2003 (International Conventions) Order 2005 (SI 2005/46).
37 See https://treaties.fco.gov.uk/responsive/app/consolidatedSearch/.
38 EA 2003, s 194.
39 House of Lords Select Committee on Extradition Law, 10 March 2015 at [392].
40 Ibid at [393].
41 It is the duty of the DPP to conduct 'any' extradition proceedings and to advise on 'proposed proceedings' per s 3(2)(ea)– (eb). For Scotland see the Procurator Fiscal Service and for Northern Ireland, the Crown Solicitor's Office.

way. It is at that juncture that the CPS may consider far-reaching considerations including the appropriate forum for prosecution and modern-day slavery or trafficking allegations.[42]

15.23

It is understood that, consistent with the old EAW approach, TCA warrants are prepared by the relevant CPS area, using a local court, whereas requests to Category 2 territories will usually be prepared using the specialist CPS Extradition Unit, International Justice and Organised Crime Division. The Serious Fraud Office also has the power to prepare extradition requests in addition to investigatory powers. The National Crime Agency (NCA) is the designated central authority for the certification of TCA warrants.[43] The NCA also has a role in communicating requests between jurisdictions, including diffusion of requests on to international information systems. Specialist CPS extradition prosecutors hold the primary responsibility for preparing requests to Category 2 territories. These requests are then transmitted to the Home Office for further consideration and transmission to the requesting jurisdiction via diplomatic channels.

15.24

The Secretary of State (the Home Secretary) is responsible for certifying Category 2 requests, with the Act requiring that all incoming extradition meet certain statutory requirements.[44] The government's legal department acts as the private solicitor on behalf of the Secretary of State in these matters. There is not yet clear guidance from case law on the extent to which risk assessments by these bodies before and during 'import' extradition may discharge culpability for human rights violations.

15.25

Police and intelligence agencies frequently provide detail such as the possible location and future movements of a person, particularly if it is necessary to target a request to a certain country which applies to most Category 2 requests. This may generate unused material relevant to disclosure schedules in subsequent proceedings, in addition to the extradition request itself (which should have been provided during the extradition proceedings). The extradition process is closely linked but distinct from requests for mutual legal assistance in criminal matters.[45] Both will frequently precede and run in parallel between states and others, using the Home Office, Europol and Interpol. Both processes are notorious for delays and bureaucracy, possibly compounded by the UK's departure from the EU.

---

42 The operation of forum considerations has been the subject to controversy, eg see Dr Paul Arnell and Gemma Davies (2020) 'The Forum Bar in UK Extradition Law: An Unnecessary Failure' in 84(2) *Journal of Criminal Law* 142–62.

43 TCA, art 605.

44 EA 2003, s 70.

45 Many of which have also been radically altered with the UK's departure from the EU, often meaning reliance by default on the European Convention on Mutual Legal Assistance 1959.

15.26

The House of Lords expressed regret about the UK's 2021 loss of the Schengen Information Sharing System II, leaving a 'significant gap in terms of lost capacity''[46] and noted the work being done to try to improve the efficiency of Interpol systems. The Lords noted the likely increased use of Interpol warrants but emphasised that that 'it is essential that cooperation … is tied to respect for the [convention] rights … and respect for data protection rules' ([31]).[47]

SPECIALTY AND ABUSE OF PROCESS

15.27

Specialty 'is a principle that an extradited person shall not be tried or punished for any offence other than the offence or offences for which he had been extradited'.[48] A person extradited into this jurisdiction enjoys statutory specialty rights, with certain exceptions.[49]

15.28

Possible remedies for asserted breach of specialty rights at subsequent trial include a stay based on abuse of process or applying to quash certain counts. Demonstrating the precise nature of the preceding extradition will be vital. For example, in *R v Seddon*[50] pursuing a Bail Act 1976 offence which was not included in the EAW breached specialty. Although a speciality waiver could have been requested,[51] the preferred approach was to specifically refer to the Bail Act offence as one of the extradition offences. A 'passing reference' was insufficient. *R v Jones (Royston)*[52] [2011] EWCA Crim 107 followed a similar approach in relation to the prosecution for a 'failure to surrender' which had not been included in the EAW.[53] However, 'lesser offences', subsumed within the extradition request, are permitted.

15.29

Depending on the applicable surrender framework, if a person has consented to as opposed to challenged extradition, they may have renounced their specialty right.[54] Further, specialty lapses after 45 days, which has been construed as starting from the point of being given the opportunity to leave the country.[55] The

46 House of Lords EU Committee, 26 March 2021 at [85]–[87].
47 See also [118]–[119] as, without data sharing meeting EU standards, the UK is unlikely to enjoy the third-party status it has negotiated with Eurojust and Europol.
48 *Bowen v Secretary of State for Home Department* [2016] EWHC 1400 (Admin) at [10].
49 EA 2003, ss 146, 151A and 151B which include voluntary waiver of specialty.
50 *R v Seddon* [2009] EWCA Crim 483.
51 EA 2003, s 146(3)(c).
52 *R v Jones (Royston)* [2011] EWCA Crim 107.
53 More recently followed in *R v Farber* [2019] EWCA Crim 1716 and *R v Shepherd* [2019] 2 Cr App R 26.
54 TCA, art 611 as opposed to EA 2003, s 45(3) and 125(5) as amended in 2015.
55 EAW Framework Decision, art 27 and TCA, art 625(3)(a) but, contrast EA 2003, ss 55(9), 146(4) and 146(5) for alternative starting points.

same specialty principle, however, does not prevent a prosecutor, in the context of a continuing offence, from adducing evidence about events pre-dating the extradition offences on the indictment as a means to prove those extradition offences. That is because matters of evidence fall outside the specialty rule and are for the courts of the requesting state.

15.30

Two important points of interpretation arise from CJEU case law, casting a broad definition of the same factual nexus of an offence (meaning a seemingly separate offence might be disclosed in the request after all)[56] and confirming specialty is not actually breached until an additional punishment is imposed.[57]

DISGUISED EXTRADITION

15.31

Disguised, or veiled, extradition, is the process of transfer to a territory for trial or punishment outside a lawful extradition process. If lawful extradition procedures are not followed, the court may stay proceedings against that person as an abuse of process. Whether proceedings will be stayed will depend on the facts, the seriousness of the charge and the degree of illegality involved in bringing the defendant to the UK. The court will be required to weigh up the public interest in ensuring that those who are charged with grave crimes should be tried and the competing public interest in not giving the impression that the court will adopt the approach that the end justifies the means.[58] Cases where it is appropriate to order a stay will be rare.[59]

15.32

In *R v Horseferry Road Magistrates Court Ex p Bennett (No 1)*[60] proceedings were stayed where it was established that collusion between South African and British authorities had resulted in the defendant's forcible return to the UK under the pretext of deportation to New Zealand, enabling their arrest at Heathrow and subsequent prosecution for dishonesty offences. In *R v Mullen*,[61] the Court of Appeal held that the unlawful deportation to forcibly return the defendant to the UK was such a 'degradation of the lawful administration of justice' that the prosecution was unlawful and the conviction was therefore quashed, despite the seriousness of the offence. The Court of Appeal commented that if the CPS had voluntarily disclosed material regarding the unlawful deportation at trial, as they should have, the defendant could have successfully argued for proceedings

56 EA 2003, s 146(3) regarding confiscation see *R v Di Sephano* [2017] 4 WLR 166.

57 *Leymann and Pustovarov* (Case C-388–08PPU) EU:C:2008:669; [2008] ECR I-8993.

58 *R v Latif* [1996] 1 WLR 104 per Lord Steyn 112–113.

59 *R v Jama* 14 July 2008 (unreported). See C Nicholls, C Montgomery and J Knowles (2013) *The Law of Extradition and Mutual Assistance* (Oxford University Press at [12.76].

60 *R v Horseferry Road Magistrates Court Ex p. Bennett (No1)* [1994] 1 AC 42.

61 *R v Mullen* [1999] 3 WLR 777.

to be stayed as an abuse of process. Contrast *R v Latif (Khalid)*,[62] where it was held not to be an abuse of process for an undercover customs officer to trick a defendant to enter the jurisdiction with a consignment of drugs.

15.33

If detention follows disguised extradition this may amount to unlawful and arbitrary detention.[63] Disguised extradition is distinct from extraordinary rendition, which also involves an unlawful transfer between jurisdictions, but with the purpose of detention or interrogation outside the normal legal process where there is a real risk of a breach of Article 3 of the ECHR.[64] Conversely, there could be legitimate reasons, such as resources or intelligence about frequent travel, for an active decision to wait for a person to enter the jurisdiction voluntarily rather than pursue an extradition request.

UNDERTAKINGS, GUARANTEES, ASSURANCES AND ARTICLE 3 ECHR

15.34

Representatives should be astute as to whether assurances have been offered as part of the extradition process. Some countries[65] will only extradite their nationals if there has been an undertaking to return the person to their home country in order to complete any penalty. There are also requirements for undertakings that might be given by the Secretary of State to promptly return a person, in custody, following extradition (eg, if the process has interrupted a custodial sentence in the requested jurisdiction) but these are subject to human rights considerations.[66]

15.35

If a defendant is extradited to the UK and the Secretary of State has given an undertaking to the extraditing territory that they will remain in custody until the conclusion of proceedings, bail can only be granted in 'exceptional circumstances'.[67] The TCA provides for various 'guarantees' from the requesting state, 'if there are substantial grounds for believing that there is a real risk to the protection of the fundamental rights of the requested person' (Art 604(c)).

15.36

This follows what has become routine in 'export' cases, where if there are credible fears of human rights violation following extradition, frequently assurances

62 *R v Latif (Khalid)* [1996] 1 WLR 104.
63 *Bozano v France* (1987) 9 EHRR 297.
64 See, eg, *El-Masri v Former Yugoslav Republic of Macedonia* [2012] ECHR 39630/09 and *Babar Ahmad and Others v UK* (dec.), nos 24027/07, 11949/08 and 36742/08, at [113], 6 July 2010).
65 Eg, The Netherlands and Belgium.
66 EA 2003, ss 153A–153D.
67 EA 2003, s 154.

about conditions of detention, particularly living space, are deployed. The House of Lords found arrangements in place for monitoring such assurances were 'flawed'[68] and questioned 'whether the UK can be as certain as it should be that it is meeting its human rights obligations'.[69] It is feasible that similar assurances may have been provided as part of the extradition process bringing a person to the UK, particularly with rising criticism of certain UK conditions of detention,[70] or if a person is ill (eg, making air travel unsafe).

15.37

More generally, in an era of professed common human rights standards, some have doubted whether exchange of specific assurances placing certain people in a better position than others, is anachronistic,[71] but the use of assurances is seen as 'indispensable' by the Supreme Court.[72]

PRACTICAL CONSIDERATIONS

15.38

Representatives are reminded that the context of extradition reaches far beyond the law and facts of a case into the realm of what is politically expedient at the time, especially noting that key actors are not limited to the courts. Notwithstanding these somewhat opaque points, the following practical considerations recur.

15.39

Extradition proceedings will necessarily generate material from both the UK and the foreign territory; the usual duty of disclosure review applies[73] and may be essential to ensure a fair trial. Representatives are advised to obtain disclosure of materials arising from the extradition process (as above), not least to advise on possible remedies if a breach of specialty rights or disguised extradition is alleged, but also in relation to more straightforward matters such as bail and any exculpatory reply given on the extradition arrest.

15.40

Import extradition may require early disclosure in accordance with common law, prior to the formal statutory disclosure duties. When justice and fairness may require immediate disclosure will vary on the particular case circumstances.[74]

---

68 Baker Review, 2015 at [89].

69 Ibid at [90].

70 See, eg UN Special Rapporteur, Close Supervision Centre conditions 'may amount to torture', 10 May 2021. See www.ohchr.org/en/NewsEvents/Pages/DisplayNews.aspx?NewsID=27076&LangID=E.

71 UN Human Rights Council (2018) *Report of the Special Rapporteur on Torture, and Other Cruel, Inhuman or Degrading Treatment or Punishment*, 23 November 2018.

72 *Zabolotnyi v Hungary* [2021] UKSC 14 at [44], approving *Shankaran v India* [2014] EWHC 957 (Admin).

73 Including unused extradition material.

74 *R v DPP ex parte Lee* [1999] 2 All ER 737.

UK escort officers should ensure they obtain all material when they collect the wanted person and provide this to the disclosure officer for review and scheduling. The way in which material was obtained in the requested jurisdiction may result in further applications under sections 76 and 78 of the Police and Criminal Evidence Act (PACE) 1984 applications to exclude evidence, of particular relevance in countries where the rule of law is considered to be fragile.

15.41

Most national extradition arrangements provide for representation in the requested country during the extradition process.[75] Prompt and effective liaison with foreign lawyers can be crucial to assist with representations that might be made to the CPS about pursuing the UK case, notwithstanding the full code test should already have been met. It may assist in subsequent applications if it can be shown that a person cooperated prior to extradition and/or was granted the equivalent of conditional bail in the executing country.

15.42

Crediting 'time served' awaiting extradition is not required by Article 5 of the ECHR[76] but is explicitly provided for nationally[77] and frequently within extradition instruments.[78] Sections 240ZA and 243 of the CJA 2003 apply whatever foreign state a person has been extradited from so if no extradition instrument applies, UK domestic law ensures time spent in custody overseas awaiting extradition will be credited. Under section 327(3) of the Sentencing Code, the judge must specify in open court the number of days for which the prisoner was so kept in custody.[79] Section 243 of the Criminal Justice Act 2003 also applies to those unlawfully at large after trial but before sentence. In *Farber*, the judge fell into error by expressly failing to consider time spent in custody pending extradition. Complications can, however, arise where a person is detained for more than one reason.[80]

15.43

Those involved in extradition will benefit from advice about how to live with and ideally challenge associated restrictions, such as Interpol Red Notices, which can bite deep into a person's personal and business life. If certified, Red Notices can now have direct effect in the UK in some circumstances to justify

75 See, eg, TCA, arts 609 and 617.

76 *Zandbergs v Latvia* (Application no 71092/01), 20 December 2011 at [63].

77 CJA 2003, ss 240ZA and 243 and *R v Farber* [2019] EWCA Crim 1716 at [27]–[29].

78 TCA art 624 for Part 1 cases (previously Framework Decision, art 26); for Part 2 cases on the Recommendations of the Committee of Ministers governed by the European Convention on Extradition, see Nicholls, Montgomery and Knowles, (2013) *The Law of Extradition and Mutual Assistance*.

79 Sentencing Act 2020.

80 CJA 2003, s 240Z(4).

provisional arrest.[81] Certain territories have been accused of inappropriate use of Interpol Red Notices,[82] leading to a proportionality check of sorts with the introduction of a $10,000 dollar bad cheque threshold. The first point of challenge is usually the national arrest warrant underlying a Red Notice, but representations to the Commission for the Control of Interpol's Files (CCF) have also led to notices being withdrawn, with some anonymised examples published.[83]

---

81 See Extradition (Provisional Arrest) Act 2020 (E(PA)A 2020) which allows provisional arrest for 'serious extradition offences' following a request from trusted extradition partners listed in the EA 2003 (currently Australia, Canada, Iceland, Liechtenstein, New Zealand, Norway, Switzerland and the USA).

82 D Calvert-Smith, B Keith, and R Davies (2021) *Undue Influence: The UAE and Interpol.* Available at: www.5sah.co.uk/knowledge-hub/news/2021-04-08/the-report-undue-influence-the-uae-and-interpol-now-published.

83 See www.interpol.int/en/Who-we-are/Commission-for-the-Control-of-INTERPOL-s-Files-CCF/CCF-sessions-and-decisions.

16 Bail

Farrhat Arshad

INTRODUCTION

16.1

The scope of this chapter is the right to bail post-charge and pre-trial.[1] The right to apply for bail pending trial is provided for in Article 5 of the European Convention on Human Rights (ECHR)[2] and in the Bail Act 1976 (the Act). This chapter begins with a brief outline of the provisions of the Bail Act 1976. It then moves to a substantive consideration of the Convention jurisprudence, focusing primarily on Article 5 of the Convention and also considers the interpretation of the Convention by the domestic courts.

THE BAIL ACT 1976

16.2

The Act provides a general right to bail[3] unless the accused falls within one of the exceptions to that general right as set out in the Act. Section 4 provides that a person brought before a magistrates' court or a Crown Court charged with a criminal offence, has a right to be released on bail, except as provided in Schedule 1 to the Act. The general right to bail under section 4 does not apply to persons accused of homicide or rape in certain circumstances.[4] If section 25 applies, the person shall be granted bail if the court (or constable) is of the opinion that there are exceptional circumstances which justify it.

The exceptions to bail

16.3

Schedule 1, paragraph 2 sets out the exceptions to bail. These are:

(1) If the Court is satisfied that there are substantial grounds for believing that the defendant, if released on bail, would fail to surrender to custody, commit an offence whilst on bail, interfere

1 Detention pre-charge is dealt with in Chapter 11.
2 Other provisions of the Convention are also of relevance, in particular art 2, Fourth protocol (freedom of movement) and art 6(2) (the presumption of innocence).
3 Bail Act 1976, s 4 and Sch 1.
4 Criminal Justice and Public Order Act 1994, s 25.

with witnesses or otherwise obstruct the course of justice, whether in relation to themselves or any other person;

(2) If the offence is an indictable offence or an offence triable either way and it appears to the court that the defendant was on bail in criminal proceedings on the date of the offence;

(3) If the court is satisfied that the defendant should be kept in custody for their own protection or, if they are a child or young person, for their own welfare;

(4) If they are in custody in pursuance of a sentence of a court or a sentence imposed by an officer under the Armed Forces Act 2006;

(5) If it has not been practicable to obtain sufficient information for the purpose of taking the decisions required for want of time since the institution of the proceedings against the defendant;

(6) If, having previously been released on bail in, or in connection with, the proceedings, the defendant has been arrested in pursuance of section 7 (failure to surrender or alleged breach of bail.)

(7) If the defendant is charged with murder, the defendant may not be granted bail unless the court is of the opinion that there is no significant risk of the defendant committing, while on bail, an offence that would, or would be likely to, cause physical or mental injury to any person other than the defendant;

(8) If they are aged 18 or over, a drug test shows the presence of a specified Class A drug (and other conditions apply).

16.4

Once a custody time limit has expired without extension, the Crown Court is obliged to order the defendant's release on bail.

Bail conditions

16.5

Subsections 3(4)–(7) of the Act set out the conditions which may be attached to the grant of bail in criminal proceedings. Whilst two specific types of condition are listed as security[5] and surety, section 3(6) is much broader. It states that '[A person granted bail in criminal proceedings] may be required … to comply, before release on bail or later, with such requirements as appear to the court to be necessary':

(a) to secure that he surrenders to custody;

(b) to secure that he does not commit an offence whilst on bail;

5 Bail Act 1976, s 3(4).

(c) to secure that he does not interfere with witnesses or otherwise obstruct the course of justice;

(d) for his own protection or, if he is a child or young person, for his own welfare or in his own interests;

(e) to secure that he makes himself available for the purpose of enabling inquiries or a report to be made to assist the court in dealing with him for the offence;

(f) to secure that before the time appointed for him to surrender to custody, he sees his legal adviser.

16.6

Where bail is refused or conditions on the grant of bail are imposed, the court is required to give reasons for its decision.[6]

ARTICLE 5 AND THE GUARANTEED PROTECTIONS

16.7

Pre-trial detention is just one of the forms of detention that Article 5 is concerned with. The relevant parts of Article 5 that apply to pre-trial detention and the consideration of release pending trial, are 5(1)(c), 5(3) and 5(4).[7]

Detention is necessary

16.8

Article 5(1)(c) should be read together with Article 5(3), 'which forms a whole with it'.[8] Detention pursuant to Article 5(1)(c) must be a proportionate measure to achieve the stated aim.[9] The onus is on the domestic authorities to convincingly demonstrate that detention is necessary.

16.9

The necessity test under the second limb of Article 5(1)(c) requires that measures less severe than detention must be considered and found to be insufficient to safeguard the individual or public interest. The offence in question has to be of a serious nature, entailing danger to life and limb or significant material damage. In addition, the detention should cease as soon as the risk has passed, which called for monitoring, the duration of the detention being also a relevant factor.[10]

---

6 Ibid, s 5.

7 Article 5(5) the right to apply for compensation where there has been arrest or detention in breach of art 5 also applies to pre-trial detention.

8 *Ciulla v Italy* (1991) 13 EHRR 346, at [38]; See also *Aquilina v Malta* (2000) 29 EHRR 185, at [47].

9 *Ladent v Poland* hudoc (2008) at [55]–[56].

10 *S, V and A v Denmark* (2019) 68 EHRR 17 at [161].

Prompt judicial review

16.10

Article 5(3) guarantees the right of an arrested person to be brought before a judge or other judicial officer 'promptly' after an arrest. No exceptions are possible even if there has been prior judicial involvement.[11] This judicial oversight must be automatic and would be insufficient if it was only triggered by the detainee making an application.[12] This is one of the features that distinguishes the safeguard in Article 5(3) from that in Article 5(4). The purpose of the safeguard of judicial scrutiny in 5(3) might otherwise be defeated.[13]

16.11

The judge or other comparable officer must consider 'lawfulness issues and whether or not there is a reasonable suspicion that the arrested person has committed an offence'.[14] There is no general rule in Convention jurisprudence that hearings on the lawfulness of detention must be held in public.[15]

16.12

The purpose of prompt judicial control was succinctly explained in *McKay v UK*:[16]

> The judicial control on the first appearance of an arrested individual must above all be prompt, to allow detection of any ill-treatment and to keep to a minimum any unjustified interference with individual liberty. The strict time constraint imposed by this requirement leaves little flexibility in interpretation, otherwise there would be a serious weakening of a procedural guarantee to the detriment of the individual and the risk of impairing the very essence of the right protected by this provision.

16.13

Whilst Convention jurisprudence has not laid down precise time limits in *Brogan v UK*,[17] detention of four days and six hours was found to be a breach of Article 5(3).[18] In *McKay*, the Grand Chamber proceeded on the understanding that four days was the 'maximum' period of time that could elapse before a review. Article 5(3) may still be breached before this if there are no special

11 *Bergmann v Estonia* hudoc (2008) at [45].

12 *McKay v UK* (2007) 44 EHRR 41 at para 34; *Varga v Romania,* hudoc (2008) at [52]; *Burzo v Romania* hudoc (2009) at [107].

13 *Aquilina v Malta* (2000) 29 EHRR 185 at [49]; *Niedbala v Poland* (2001) 33 EHRR 48 at [50].

14 *McKay v UK* (2007) 44 EHRR 41.

15 *Reinprecht v Austria* (2007) 44 EHRR 39; *Lebedev v Russia* (2008) 47 EHRR 34 at [82] and [94].

16 *McKay v UK* (2007) 44 EHRR 41 at [33].

17 *Brogan v UK* (1989) 11 EHRR 117.

18 Under the Prevention of Terrorism (Temporary Provisions) Act 1984.

circumstances preventing the authorities from bringing the arrested person before a judge sooner,[19] or if the detainees have particular vulnerabilities.[20]

Competent legal authority

16.14

The 'competent legal authority' in s 5(1)(c)) has been held to have the same meaning as 'judge or other officer authorised by law'.[21] In English law the requirement is satisfied by bringing an accused before a magistrate. Two qualities that 'other officer authorised by law' must have are independence and impartiality. They must be able to make a legally binding decision as to detention or release.[22] An officer will not be impartial if he is 'entitled to intervene in the subsequent criminal proceedings as a representative of the prosecuting authority'.[23] Impartiality involves an objective as well as a subjective element.

16.15

Whilst it is not obligatory that a lawyer be present,[24] exclusion of a lawyer may adversely affect the applicant's ability to present his case.[25]

Review of the merits of detention, assessment and the power to release

16.16

The judge or officer must consider the issues going to the lawfulness of detention and the existence of 'reasonable suspicion'.[26] The review is not limited to lawfulness but must be sufficiently wide that it encompasses the circumstances militating for or against detention.[27] The facts upon which suspicion is based should amount to 'facts or information which would satisfy an objective observer that the person concerned may have committed the offence'.[28] A failure by the

---

19 *Gutsanovi v Bulgaria* hudoc (2013) at [154]–[159]; *Ipek and Others v Turkey* hudoc (2009) at [36]–[37]; and *Kandzhov v Bulgaria* hudoc (2008) at [66].

20 See *Ipek and Others v Turkey* (2009) – breach held where the detainees were minors without legal representation and appearance before judge was three days and nine hours after arrest. See also *Gutsanovi v Bulgaria* (2013) – the time period was three days, five hours and thirty minutes; detainee was psychologically frail.

21 *Lawless v Ireland (No 3)* (1979–80) 1 EHRR 15; *Schiesser v Switzerland* (1979–80) 2 EHRR 417.

22 *Ireland v UK* (1978) 2 EHRR 25 at [199].

23 *Huber v Switzerland* hudoc (1990) at [43] (This was a development from *Schiesser*, which only required that the 'officer' did not actually take part in the prosecution case.); See also *Brincat v Italy* (1993)16 EHRR 591 at [20].

24 *Schiesser v Switzerland* at [36].

25 *Lebedev v Russia* at [83]–[91].

26 See *Schiesser v Switzerland* at [31]; *Pantea v Romania* (2005) 40 EHRR 26 at [231]; and *Aquilina v Malta* (2000) 29 EHRR 185 at [47]; *McKay v UK* (2007) 44 EHRR 41 at [40]; and *Oral and Atabay v Turkey* hudoc (2009) at [41].

27 *Aquilina v Malta* (2000) 29 EHRR 185 at [52].

28 *Fox, Campbell and Hartley v The United* Kingdom (1991) 13 EHRR 157 at [32]. See also *Demirtas v Turkey (No 2)* hudoc (2020) at [314]; *Mammadov v Azerbaijan* hudoc (2014) at [88]; *Erdagoz v Turkey* (2001) 32 EHRR 19 at [51].

authorities to make a genuine inquiry into the basic facts of a case in order to verify whether a complaint was well-founded disclosed a violation of Article 5(1)(c).[29] The fact that a suspicion is merely held in good faith is insufficient.[30] If there are no reasons to justify detention, the 'officer' must have the power to make a binding order for the detainee's release.[31] For a review to be compliant with Article 5(4) there must be a proper assessment of whether bail has been denied legitimately.[32] If the detention has been made by the order of a court, there is no need for a separate Article 5(4) review. However, it may be required for an administrative decision to continue to detain someone and Article 5(4) may require a review of detention after a certain time and at reasonable intervals thereafter.

'Right to trial within a reasonable time or to be released pending trial'

16.17

The second limb of Article 5(3) does not give the authorities a choice between either bringing an accused to trial within a reasonable time or granting them provisional release pending trial.[33] Until conviction, they must be presumed innocent; and the purpose of Article 5(3) is to require their provisional release if their continuing detention ceases to be reasonable. Whether it is reasonable for an accused to remain in detention must be assessed on the facts of each case. Continued detention can be justified only if there is a genuine public interest requirement which outweighs the respect for individual liberty laid down in Article 5.[34]

16.18

The responsibility falls in the first place to the national judicial authorities to ensure that, in a given case, the pre-trial detention of an accused person does not exceed a reasonable time. Therefore they must, paying due regard to the principle of the presumption of innocence, examine all the facts arguing for or against the existence of the demand of public interest justifying a departure from the rule in Article 5 and must set them out in their decisions on the applications for release. Reasonable suspicion will not, of itself, justify continued detention of that person beyond the initial review hearing and pending trial of the criminal offence.[35]

---

29 *Stepuleac v Moldova* hudoc (2007) at [73]; *Elci and others v Turkey* hudoc (2003) at [674]; *Moldoveanu v the Republic of Moldova* hudoc (2021) at [52]–[57].

30 *Gusinskiy v Russia* (2005) 41 EHRR 17 at [53]; *Sabuncu and Others v Turkey* hudoc (2020) at [145].

31 *Assenov and Others v Bulgaria* (1999) 28 EHRR 652 at [146]; *Nikolova v Bulgaria* (2001) 31 EHRR 3 at [49]; *Niedbala v Poland* (2001) 33 EHRR 48 at [49]; and *McKay v UK* (2007) 44 EHRR 41 at [40].

32 *Tymoshenko v Ukraine* (2014) 58 EHRR 3 at [279]–[282].

33 *Wemhoff v Germany* (1979–80) 1 EHRR 55.

34 Ibid.

35 Ibid. See also *Merabishvili v Georgia* hudoc (2017) at [222]; *Buzadji v The Republic of Moldova* hudoc (2016) at [102].

16.19

Where grounds do justify the continued deprivation of liberty, Article 5(3) may still be infringed, if the accused's detention is prolonged 'beyond a reasonable time' because the proceedings have not been conducted with the necessary expedition. The period to be considered is from the day the accused is taken into custody until the charge is determined.[36] The guarantee in Article 5(3) requires that in respect of a detained person the authorities show 'special diligence in the conduct of the proceedings'.[37] The factors to be taken into account in assessing whether trial within a reasonable time has taken place are the complexity of the case, the conduct of the accused, and the efficiency of the national authorities.[38]

RELEASE PENDING TRIAL

Grounds for continued detention

16.20

As both the right to liberty and the presumption of innocence are in play here, it is for the State to establish that one or more grounds for detention applies. In *Merabishvili v Georgia*,[39] it was emphasised that, 'those risks must be duly substantiated, and the authorities' reasoning on those points cannot be abstract, general or stereotyped'.[40] Automatic denial of bail will be a violation of Article 5(3).[41] Any burden on the detained person to show why he should be released will be in breach of Article 5(4).[42]

16.21

In *R (O) v Crown Court at Harrow*,[43] it was held that section 25(1) of the Criminal Justice and Public Order Act 1994 merely served to remind the court of the risks normally posed by defendants to whom it applied. The Court found that section 25 had no substantive effect upon the way in which bail applications (prior to the expiry of a custody time limit) would fall to be determined. This would only assume relevance where the court, having considered the matter under the 1976 Act, was left unsure as to bail. It was necessary that section 25 be read down under section 3 of the Human Rights Act 1998 to that extent.

---

36 *Kalashnikov v Russia* (2003) 36 EHRR 34 at [110].

37 *Herczegfalvy v Austria* (1993) 15 EHRR 437 at [71]; *Buzadji v The Republic of Moldova* hudoc (2016) at [87]; and *Idalov v Russia* hudoc (2012) at [140]. See also Chapter 12 at [18.16]

38 *Neumeister v Austria (No 1)* (1968) 1 EHRR 91 and *Kemmache v France* (1992) 14 EHRR 520 at [60]. The Court had already found a breach of the right to bail in both cases.

39 hudoc (2017) at [234].

40 *Merabishvili* at [222].

41 *Caballero v UK* (2000) 30 EHRR 643, in relation to the unamended first iteration of CJPOA 1994, s 25. However, the Court has recognised that sometimes the 'unavailability of bail' can be 'self-evident' – *Khodorkovskiy v Russia* (2011) 53 EHRR 32 at [196], although even in such circumstances detention should not be automatic.

42 *Iljikov v Bulgaria* hudoc (2001); See also *Bykov v Russia* hudoc (2009) at [64].

43 *R (O) v Crown Court at Harrow* [2006] UKHL 42; [2007] 1 AC 249; See also *O'Dowd v UK* (2012) 54 EHRR 8.

16.22

Convention jurisprudence has identified four principal grounds upon which a national court may justify the refusal of bail under Article 5(3):[44]

(1) Risk of failure to appear for trial.

(2) Risk of interference with the course of justice.

(3) Commission of further offences.

(4) The preservation of public order or the defendant's own protection.

16.23

However, these grounds must be viewed alongside the fact that bail conditions can be imposed or other 'preventative measures' taken. Therefore, an individual should only be detained if their release would lead to a real risk that harm under one of the grounds for detention will occur *and* if the imposition of bail conditions or other reasonable preventative measures cannot either stop or reduce to an acceptable level that risk.[45]

16.24

Minors should only be detained pre-trial as a measure of last resort. Any period of detention should be as short as possible. Where detention is strictly necessary, minors should be kept apart from adults.[46]

THE GROUNDS JUSTIFYING DETENTION

(1) Failure to appear for trial

16.25

The risk of absconding can justify detention and whilst the severity of the sentence that the defendant may expect if convicted is relevant to the assessment of risk of absconding, 'the need to continue the deprivation of liberty cannot be assessed from a purely abstract point of view, taking into consideration only the gravity of the offence'.[47] The test to be applied is set out in *Stögmüller v Austria*:[48]

> 'there must be a whole set of circumstances, particularly, the heavy sentence to be expected or the accused's particular distaste of detention, or the lack of well-established ties in the country, which give reason to suppose that the consequences and hazards of flight will seem to him to be a lesser evil than continued imprisonment.'

44 *Buzadji v The Republic of Moldova* hudoc (2016) at [88]; *Tiron v Romania* hudoc (2009) at [37]; *Smirnova v Russia* (2004) 39 EHRR 31 at [59]; *Piruzyan v Armenia* (2015) 61 EHRR 22 at [94].

45 *Jablonski v Poland* (2003) 36 EHRR 27 at [84].

46 *Nart v Turkey* hudoc (2008) at [31]; and *Guvec v Turkey* hudoc (2009) at [109].

47 *Idalov v Russia* hudoc (2012) at [145]; *Panchenko v Russia* hudoc (2005) at [106]. See also *Letellier v France* (1992) 14 EHRR 83 at [43].

48 *Stögmüller v Austria* (1979–80) 1 EHRR 155 at [15].

16.26

Other relevant factors to be borne in mind are, 'those relating to the character of the person involved, his morals, his home, his occupation, his assets, his family ties and all kinds of links with the country in which he is being prosecuted'.[49]

16.27

The mere absence of a fixed residence does not give rise to a danger of flight.[50] The strength of the evidence against the accused cannot alone justify lengthy detention.[51] In *Gault v UK*,[52] it was held impermissible for the Court of Appeal to have detained the accused after her conviction had been overturned and pending the retrial. In refusing bail pending the retrial on the grounds of risk of absconding (despite the applicant having been on bail during the original proceedings), the Court of Appeal had borne in mind that she had been previously convicted of the offence. The Strasbourg Court held that that persistence of reasonable suspicion was not in itself a relevant and sufficient reason for the refusal of bail. It could not be said that there was a greater risk of absconding before the re-trial than had been the case before the previous trial. If the risk of absconding is the only justification for the detention, release pending trial should be ordered if it is possible to ameliorate the risk by the imposition of adequate and enforceable bail conditions.[53]

16.28

Convention jurisprudence has established that the danger of flight 'necessarily decreases as the time spent in detention passes by'.[54] Article 5(3) therefore carries a duty to reconsider this ground at regular intervals and to check that the grounds remained valid at later stages of the proceedings.[55]

(2) Interference with the course of justice

16.29

A well-founded fear that the accused, if released, will interfere with the course of justice is a permissible ground for detention.[56] Examples of interference with justice include interference with witnesses,[57] warning or collusion with other suspects,[58] or destruction of evidence.[59] The risk asserted by the authorities

49 *Neumeister v Austria (No 1)* (1968) 1 EHRR 91; *Becciev v Moldova* (2007) 45 EHRR 331 at [58].
50 *Sulaoja v Estonia* (2006) 43 EHRR 36 at [64].
51 *Dereci v Turkey* hudoc (2005) at [38].
52 *Gault v UK* (2008) 46 EHRR 48.
53 *Wemhoff v Germany* (1979–80) 1 EHRR 55; *Merabishvili v Georgia* hudoc (2017) at [223].
54 *Neumeister v Austria (No 1)* (1968) 1 EHRR 91, para 10. See also *Wemhoff v Germany* (1979–80) 1 EHRR 55; *Tomasi v France* (1993) 15 EHRR 1.
55 *Bykov v Russia* hudoc (2009).
56 *Wemhoff v Germany* at [13]–[14].
57 *Letellier v France* (1992)14 EHRR 83.
58 *Wemhoff v Germany*.
59 Ibid.

must be identifiable and substantiated with evidence.[60] A generalised risk is insufficient. The mere fact of a charge of conspiracy or organised crime is insufficient to justify detention.[61]

16.30

The longer the detention continues and the more the investigation makes progress, the less likely that interference with justice will remain a good reason for detention.[62] It has been frequently recognised in the Strasbourg jurisprudence that once an investigation is completed, any risk of interference with the investigation will have lessened.[63] In *Letelllier v France*,[64] the Court stated that whilst 'a genuine risk of pressure being brought on the witnesses may have existed initially' this risk had 'diminished and indeed disappeared with the passing of time'. Another matter weighing against a finding of sufficient risk is where a defendant has previously been on bail without suggestion of interference with the course of justice.[65]

(3) Commission of further offences

16.31

The detention of the accused on the basis of the prevention of crime has been held to be compatible with Article 5(3).[66] There must be shown good reasons to believe that the accused, if released, will commit an offence or offences of the same serious kind with which he is already charged.[67] The anticipated offence must be serious[68] and the risk of repetition genuine.[69] A risk of further offences cannot automatically be assumed from the fact that the accused has a criminal record. The Court must consider whether any previous convictions are 'comparable, either in nature or in the degree of seriousness' to the charges preferred against the accused'.[70]

(4) The preservation of public order and protection of the accused

16.32

It was confirmed in *Letellier v France*[71] that the preservation of public order could be a valid ground for refusing bail but should only be used in 'exceptional

60 *Clooth v Belgium* (1992) 14 EHRR 717 at [44].
61 *Starokadomskiy v Russia* hudoc (2008) at [72].
62 *Clooth at* [43].
63 *Kemmache v France* (1992) 14 EHRR 520; *Kalashnikov v Russia* (2003) 36 EHRR 34.
64 *Letelllier v France* (1992) 14 EHRR 83.
65 *Matznetter v Austria* (1979–80) 1 EHRR 198.
66 Ibid. See also *Toth v Austria* (1992) 14 EHRR 551; *B v Austria* (1991) 13 EHRR 20; and *Clooth v Belgium* (1992) 14 EHRR 717.
67 However, in *Clooth* at para 40, the Court used a different formula, stating that the danger of repetition must be a plausible one.
68 *Matznetter.*
69 *Toth v Austria* (1992) 14 EHRR 551.
70 *Clooth v Belgium* (1992) 14 EHRR 717 at [40]; *Lyubimenko v Russia* hudoc (2009) at [74].
71 (1992) 14 EHRR 83.

circumstances'. The Court stated that it ought to be confined to offences of particular gravity and where there was a sufficient factual basis to support the contention that public disorder would be caused by the defendant's release. Where the decision to refuse bail on this ground takes into account only the gravity of the offence the test is not satisfied.[72]

16.33

In *IA v France*,[73] it was said that there may be cases in which, '... the safety of a person under investigation requires his continued detention for a time at least. However, this can only be so in exceptional circumstances having to do with the nature of the offences concerned, the conditions in which they were committed and the context in which they took place ...'. However, this proposition was firmly rejected in *Lelievre v Belgium*.[74] Strasbourg jurisprudence does not generally consider the protection of the detainee themselves a valid ground for pre-trial detention. There is therefore a tension between Strasbourg jurisprudence and the position in domestic law.

CONDITIONS OF BAIL

16.34

Article 5(3) provides that release 'may be conditioned by guarantees to appear for trial'. Where, therefore, the attachment of conditions could overcome the reasons for detention, bail should be granted.[75] As bail conditions are capable of engaging a wide range of Convention rights, consideration of appropriate conditions should be as exacting a task as the consideration of whether bail can be granted.[76] Whilst consideration of each case on its merits is still necessary, the following conditions have been seen as legitimate by the Court:

(a) residence;[77]

(b) surrender of travel and driving documents;[78] and

(c) a surety and/or a security.[79]

16.35

The factors to be taken into account when setting the amount of security or surety for bail were considered in *Mangouras v Spain*.[80] The applicant contended that the €3m set for bail in his case had been excessive and had been fixed

72 *Letellier*.
73 *IA v France* hudoc (1998) at [108].
74 *Lelievre v Belgium* hudoc (2007) at [104].
75 *Wemhoff v Germany* (1979–80) 1 EHRR 55; *Poplawski v Poland* hudoc (2008); *Idalov v* Russia hudoc (2012) at [140].
76 *Iwanczuk v Poland* (2004) 38 EHRR 8 at [66].
77 *Schmid v Austria* (1985) 44 DR 195.
78 *Stögmüller v Austria* (1979–80) 1 EHRR 155.
79 *Neumeister v Austria (No 1)* (1968) 1 EHRR 91.
80 *Mangouras v Spain* (2012) 54 EHRR 25.

without his personal circumstances being taken into consideration. The Grand Chamber collated the general principles.[81] In particular, as the guarantee provided for by Article 5(3) is designed to ensure the appearance of the accused at the hearing, its amount must be assessed principally by reference to the means of the accused and his relationship with the persons who are to provide the security. The amount set for bail must be justified in the decision fixing bail.[82] The fact that a detainee remains in custody after bail has been granted indicates that the domestic courts have not taken the necessary care in fixing appropriate bail.[83]

'Deprivation of liberty' and bail conditions

16.36

The imposition of bail conditions can violate an individual's rights in certain circumstances. However, the distinction between restrictions upon freedom of movement serious enough to fall within Article 5 and those subject only to Article 2 of the Fourth Protocol (freedom of movement) is 'merely one of degree or intensity, and not one of nature or substance'.[84] When assessing whether the required 'degree or intensity' of restriction exists, regard must be had to 'a whole range of criteria such as the type, duration, effects and manner of implementation of the measure in question'.[85] In *Creanga v Romania*,[86] the Court said that '*in determining whether or not there has been a violation of Convention rights it is often necessary to look beyond the appearances and the language used and concentrate on the realities of the situation …*'.[87]

16.37

In the Strasbourg jurisprudence, house arrest for 24 hours a day has been held to be a deprivation of liberty within the meaning of Article 5(1).[88] However, closer to home, a distinction was drawn by the Scottish High Court of Justiciary between physical detention and a 22 hour a day curfew, the Court finding that the curfew did not engage Article 5. [89]

81 Ibid at paras 78–81.

82 *Georgieva v Bulgaria* hudoc (2008) at [15; 30-31].

83 *Gafà v Malta* hudoc (2018) at [73]. See also *Kolakovic v Malta* hudoc (2015) at [74].

84 *Guzzardi v Italy* (1981) 3 EHRR 333 at [93].

85 Ibid at [92].

86 *Creanga v Romania* (2013) 56 EHRR 11 at [91]. The Court added that the characterisation or lack of characterisation given by a State to a factual situation cannot decisively affect the Court's conclusion as to the existence of a deprivation of liberty.

87 Ibid at [92].

88 *NC v Italy* hudoc (2002) at [33] where it was 'undisputed' and *Nikolova v Bulgaria (No 2)* hudoc (2004) at [60] where the Court stated there was 'no doubt' that house arrested constituted deprivation of liberty; *Pekov v Bulgaria,* hudoc (2006).

89 *McDonald v Procurator Fiscal, Elgin,* (2003) SCCR 311; [2003] 3 WLUK 565; *The Times,* 17 April 2003.

PROCEDURAL PROTECTIONS

Equality of arms

16.38

The equality of arms principle inherent in Article 6 applies to bail hearings.[90] This includes a right to disclosure of prosecution evidence for the purposes of making a bail application.[91] In *Becciev v Moldova*,[92] the Court stated that 'where there is evidence which prima facie appears to have a material bearing on the issue of the continuing lawfulness of the detention, it is essential, for compliance with Article 5(4), that the domestic courts examine and assess it'.[93] As a reasonable suspicion that the accused person has committed an offence is a condition *sine qua non* for the lawfulness of the continued detention, the detainee must be given an opportunity effectively to challenge the basis of the allegations against him. This may require the court to hear witnesses whose testimony appears to have a bearing on the continuing lawfulness of the detention.[94]

16.39

In *R (DPP) v Havering Magistrates' Court; R (McKeown) v Wirral Borough Magistrates' Court*,[95] the Divisional Court was required to consider the procedural protections where a breach of bail was alleged.[96] The Court held that such hearings did not involve the determination of a criminal charge within Article 6(1) and Article 5 did not require the facts underlying the justice's decision to be proved to the criminal standard, nor that the justice should be restricted to the consideration of admissible evidence. It was sufficient that the Justice took proper account of the quality of the material before him and afforded the defendant a proper opportunity to answer the material by cross-examining the witness and giving oral evidence in person.

16.40

Equality of arms is not ensured if the applicant, or his counsel, is denied access to documents which are essential to effectively challenge the lawfulness of his detention.[97] However, as long as the detainee had sufficient knowledge of the evidence that formed the basis for his pre-trial detention and therefore had an opportunity to effectively challenge his detention even if they had not been

90 *Woukam Moudefo v France*, Commission Report of 8 July 1987 (Application no 10868/84), 11 October 1998; *Ovsjannikov v Estonia* hudoc (2014) at [72].

91 *Lamy v Belgium*, (1989)11 EHRR 529; *Wloch v Poland* (2002) 34 EHRR 229.

92 *Becciev v Moldova* (2007) 45 EHRR 331.

93 Citing *Chahal v UK* at [130]–[131] and *Hussain v UK*, judgment of 21 February 1996 at [60].

94 *Turcan v Moldova* hudoc (2007) at [67]–[70].

95 *R (DPP) v Havering Magistrates' Court; R (McKeown) v Wirral Borough Magistrates' Court* [2001] 2 Cr App R 2, DC.

96 Pursuant to Bail Act 1976, s 7.

97 *Ragip Zarakolu v Turkey* hudoc (2020) at [59]–[61]; *Ovsjannikov v Estonia* hudoc (2014) at [72]; *Korneykova v Ukraine* hudoc (2012) at [68]; *Fodale v Italy* (2008) 47 EHRR 43 at [41].

allowed unlimited access to the investigation file, Article 5(4) would not be violated.[98]

16.41

In *R (KS) v Northampton Crown Court*,[99] the Court of Appeal found that where the evidence supporting the objections has not been fully disclosed to the defence (on grounds of public interest immunity) the judge should consider appointment of a Special Advocate where any refusal of bail would be founded in part, at least, on the closed material. An urgent duty of disclosure arises where the investigating authorities cease to have reasonable suspicion that a detainee is guilty of the charge for which he has been remanded.[100]

Reasons

16.42

The Convention requires an independent, critical assessment by the judge or judicial officer[101] and that this has taken place should be clear from the reasons given. If a particular ground has been relied upon it is necessary for this to be expressly stated in the decision of the domestic authorities.[102] 'Relevant and sufficient' reasons must be accepted by the Court to justify continued detention.[103] It is these reasons that the Court will have regard to when considering any alleged violation:

> 'It is essentially on the basis of the reasons given in these decisions and of the true facts mentioned by the applicant in his applications for release and his appeals that the Court is called upon to decide whether or not there has been a violation of Article 5 para. 3 (art. 5-3)'.[104]

16.43

In *Gault v UK*,[105] the Court had to consider the reasoning of the Court of Appeal in refusing bail. The Court found a 'lack of clarity' and noted that 'it would certainly have been desirable for the Court of Appeal to have recorded more detailed reasoning as to the grounds for the applicant's detention'.

98 *Atilla v Turkey* hudoc (2021) at [151]–[154].
99 *R (KS) v Northampton Crown Court* [2010] EWHC 723 (Admin); [2012] 1 WLR 1.
100 *Zenati v Commissioner of Police of the Metropolis* [2015] EWCA Civ 80; [2015] 2 WLR 1563.
101 *Tase v Romania* hudoc (2008) – 'Quasi-automatic prolongation of detention contravenes Article 5(3)' at [40] *and Khodorkovskiy v Russia* (2011) 53 EHRR 32 at [202].
102 *Trzaska v Poland* hudoc (2000) at [66].
103 *Wemhoff v Germany* (1979–80) 1 EHRR 55.
104 *Tomasi v France* (1993) 15 EHRR 1.
105 *Gault v UK* (2008) 46 EHRR 48.

17 The right to representation

Laura Stockdale

OVERVIEW

17.1

The right to representation guarantees the assistance of a lawyer to any person charged with a criminal offence. As such, it performs a vital role in ensuring the fairness of criminal proceedings. A defendant does not face the might of the state alone and the complexity of criminal law is explained to them. It is regarded as one of the 'fundamental features of a fair trial'.[1]

17.2

The first section of this chapter considers the right to representation as it is embodied in Article 6(3)(c) of the European Convention of Human Rights (ECHR). The second section considers the right in the investigation and pre-trial stages of criminal proceedings. The third section deals briefly with the right to representation at the trial and appellate stages.[2]

ARTICLE 6(3)(C) OF THE ECHR

17.3

The right to representation is guaranteed by Article 6(3)(c) of the ECHR. It states that:

> 'Everyone charged with a criminal offence has the following minimum rights…(c) to defend himself in person or through legal assistance of his own choosing or, if he has not sufficient means to pay for legal assistance, to be given it free when the interests of justice so require'.

17.4

The Article has three principal rights:

(a) the right to defend oneself;

---

1 *Salduz v Turkey* (2009) 49 EHRR 19 at [51].

2 See further Chapter 24.

(b) the right to choose one's legal representation; and

(c) the right to be provided with free legal representation in certain circumstances.

17.5

There are three structural issues concerning Article 6(3)(c) which have affected the approach to the right to representation taken by the European Court of Human Rights (ECtHR). The first issue is the relationship between Article 6(3)(c), which is one of the minimum guarantees for persons charged with criminal offences, and the general right to 'a fair and public hearing' in Article 6(1). The question arises whether the right to representation in Article 6(3)(c) is an independent right or is merely part of the general right to a fair trial.[3]

17.6

The ECtHR has held repeatedly that Article 6(3)(c) is 'one element, amongst others, of the concept of a fair trial in criminal proceedings contained in paragraph (1)'.[4] In two more recent cases, the Grand Chamber has made statements strongly suggestive of Article 6(3)(c) not being independent of Article 6(1). In *Ibrahim v The United Kingdom*,[5] the Grand Chamber held that:

> The minimum rights listed in Article 6(3) can be viewed, therefore, as specific aspects of the concept of a fair trial in criminal proceedings in Article 6(1)… However, those minimum rights are not aims in themselves: their intrinsic aim is always to contribute to ensuring the fairness of the criminal proceedings as a whole.[6]

17.7

Further, in *Simeonovi v Bulgaria*[7] the Grand Chamber stated that:

> Article 6(3)(c) does not therefore secure an autonomous right but must be read and interpreted in the light of the broader requirement of fairness of criminal proceedings, considered as a whole, as guaranteed by art.6(1) of the Convention.[8]

These statements, perhaps together with the recent consistent approach of the ECtHR to consider alleged violations of Article 6(3)(c) 'taken together' with Article 6(1), suggest the right to representation is merely an aspect of the general right to a fair trial.

---

3 R Goss, *Criminal Fair Trial Rights: Article 6 of the European Convention on Human Rights* (Hart Publishing, 2020) 119.

4 *Imbroscia v Switzerland* (1993) 17 EHRR 441 at [37]. See also *Salduz v Turkey* at [50] and *Dvorski v Croatia* (2016) 63 EHRR 7 at [76].

5 *Ibrahim v The United Kingdom* (13 September 2016, unreported), ECtHR (Grand Chamber).

6 Ibid at [251].

7 *Simeonovi v Bulgaria* (2018) 66 EHRR 2.

8 Ibid at [113].

17.8

The second structural issue is that Article 6(3)(c) (as well as the other components of Article 6) is an unqualified right as there is no express limitation clause setting out when infringements are justified. A question arises over the exact nature of the right to representation in Article 6(3)(c), in other words, the extent to which it is an absolute or limited right. The ECtHR has held that the right to representation in Article 6(3)(c) is not an absolute right and can be restricted in various circumstances. In both *Salduz v Turkey*[9] and *Dvorski v Croatia*[10] the Grand Chamber stated that the right to representation in Article 6(3)(c) was not absolute.[11] In *Ibrahim* it noted that Article 6(3)(c) was 'unqualified' but held that 'what constitutes a fair trial cannot be the subject of a single unvarying rule but must depend on the circumstances of the particular case'.[12]

17.9

As will be seen throughout this chapter, the ECtHR's general approach to determining alleged violations of Article 6(3)(c) is to consider the alleged violation within the entire criminal proceedings to determine if the applicant's fair trial rights have been unduly prejudiced. This approach has been described as an 'unstructured … balancing approach'[13] and will be referred to as the whole of proceedings test.[14] Not only does this approach confirm that Article 6(3)(c) is not an absolute right, but also reinforces that the right to representation is not independent of the right to a fair trial.

17.10

The third structural issue is that Article 6(3)(c) includes certain implied rights, such as the right to confidential communication with a lawyer[15] and the right to be notified of the right to access a lawyer.[16] The recognition of such implied rights is based on the need to ensure that the right to representation is 'practical and effective'.[17] In contrast to the above, the recognition of implied rights in Article 6(3)(c) suggests the right to representation does have independent force. These various structural issues concerning Article 6(3)(c) have affected the ECtHR's approach to the right to representation which, overall, has weakened this right. It is hoped that in future cases the ECtHR will reconsider the above issues to ensure the right to representation – a fundamental aspect of the right of a fair trial – is more robust.

9 *Salduz v Turkey* (2009) 49 EHRR 19
10 *Dvorski v Croatia* (2016) 63 EHRR 7.
11 *Salduz v Turkey* at [51]; *Dvorski v Croatia*, ibid at [78]–[79].
12 *Ibrahim v The United Kingdom* at [250].
13 Goss, *Criminal Fair Trial Rights*, p. 204.
14 Ibid at p. 124.
15 *S v Switzerland* (1991) 14 EHRR 670 at [48]; *Brennan v The United Kingdom* (2002) 34 EHRR 18 at [58].
16 *Ibrahim v The United Kingdom* at [272]; *Beuze v Belgium* (2019) 69 EHRR 1 at [129].
17 *S v Switzerland* ibid at [48]; *Ibrahim v The United Kingdom*, ibid.

THE INVESTIGATION AND PRE-TRIAL STAGE

General principles

17.11

The right to representation arises during the investigation and pre-trial stage of criminal proceedings. Although Article 6 is engaged when a person is subject to a 'criminal charge', this phrase has an autonomous meaning in ECtHR jurisprudence that includes events before a criminal charge is formally laid. The protections of Article 6 are afforded from the moment a person has been 'substantially affected' by authorities because of a suspicion that they have been involved in criminal activity, such as when they are arrested or questioned by police about an offence.[18] Article 6(3)(c) applies during the investigation and pre-trial stage 'so far as the fairness of the trial is likely to be seriously prejudiced by an initial failure to comply' with the right.[19] In *Ibrahim*, the Grand Chamber highlighted the ways in which an investigation may impact upon a subsequent criminal trial. It stated that not only does the evidence obtained determine how the prosecution put its case at trial, but also, in many cases, a defendant's initial response to police questioning has consequences for their defence at trial.[20] In *Beuze v Belgium*,[21] the Grand Chamber stated that the right to representation at the investigation and pre-trial stage fulfils the following aims: it ensures the right to a fair trial including the principle of equality of arms; it provides a counterweight to the vulnerability to suspects in police custody (particularly given the increasingly complex rules on criminal procedure and evidence) and safeguards against ill-treatment and coercion by the police; and it ensures respect for the right to remain silent and not to incriminate oneself.[22]

Content of the right to representation

17.12

Article 6(3)(c) does not specify the content of the right to representation at the investigation and pre-trial stage.[23] The manner in which Article 6(3)(c) applies during an investigation and before trial will depend upon the special features and circumstances of the case.[24] Nevertheless, the right to representation at the initial stages must be 'practical and effective'.[25] Merely assigning a lawyer to a

18 *Simeonovi v Bulgaria* at [110]–[111].

19 *Imbroscia v Switzerland* at [36]; *Murray v The United Kingdom* (1993) 17 EHRR 441 at [62]; *Salduz v Turkey* at [50]; *Dvorski v Croatia* at [76]; *Ibrahim v The United Kingdom* at [253]; *Simeonovi v Bulgaria*, ibid at [114].

20 *Ibrahim v The United Kingdom* at [254]. For example, the Criminal Justice and Public Order Act 1994, s 34 permits a court or jury to draw inferences from a defendant's failure in an interview under caution to mention any fact later relied upon at trial which they could reasonably have been expected to mention.

21 *Beuze v Belgium* (2019) 69 EHRR 1.

22 Ibid at [125]–[128].

23 Ibid at [131].

24 *Imbroscia v Switzerland* at [38]; *Murray v The United Kingdom* at [62]; *Ibrahim v The United Kingdom* at [253].

25 *Artico v Italy* (1980) 3 EHRR 1 at [33]; Imbroscia *v Switzerland* at [38]; *Salduz v Turkey* at [51]; *Beuze v Belgium* at [131].

suspect or defendant does not ensure the effectiveness of legal representation.[26] Whilst the conduct of any defence is 'essentially a matter between a defendant and his representative', where a lawyer engaged to represent a person fails to provide effective representation during the pre-trial stage, state authorities will be required to intervene where the failure is 'manifest or sufficiently brought to their attention'.[27]

17.13

As a first step for the right to be 'practical and effective' a suspect or defendant must be aware of their right to representation. Accordingly, the ECtHR has held that 'inherent' in the right to representation is a right to be notified of this right and that a person must be 'immediately informed' of its content.[28] This right to notification may be regarded as an implied right. In *Beuze*, the Grand Chamber set out the following 'minimum requirements' of the right to representation at the pre-trial stage:

> First, as the Court has already stated, suspects must be able to enter into contact with a lawyer from the time when they are taken into custody. It must therefore be possible for a suspect to consult with his or her lawyer prior to an interview or even where there is no interview. The lawyer must be able to confer with his or her client in private and receive confidential instructions.
>
> Secondly, the Court has found in a number of cases that suspects have the right for their lawyer to be physically present during their initial police interviews and whenever they are questioned in the subsequent pre-trial proceedings. Such physical presence must enable the lawyer to provide assistance that is effective and practical rather than merely abstract, and in particular to ensure that the defence rights of the interviewed suspect are not prejudiced.[29]

17.14

In relation to the first minimum requirement that discussions between a detainee and their lawyer are confidential, the ECtHR has previously stated that 'if a lawyer were unable to confer with his client and receive confidential instructions from him without surveillance, his assistance would lose much of its usefulness'.[30] The Court has rejected arguments that monitoring of legal consultations were necessary either to prevent collusion amongst defence lawyers,[31] or to prevent information being passed to suspects still at large.[32] A lack of confidentially has amounted to a violations of Article 6(3)(c) both on

26 Imbroscia *v Switzerland* ibid at [38]; *Salduz v Turkey* ibid at [51]; *Beuze v Belgium* ibid at [132].
27 *Imbroscia v Switzerland* at [41].
28 *Ibrahim v The United Kingdom* at [272]; *Beuze v Belgium* at [129].
29 *Beuze v Belgium* at [133]–[134] [citations omitted].
30 *S v Switzerland* at [48]; *Brennan v The United Kingdom* at [58].
31 *S v Switzerland* ibid at [49].
32 *Brennan v The United Kingdom* at [59].

its own,[33] as well in conjunction with Article 6(1).[34] In relation to the second minimum requirement, the ECtHR has long held that Article 6 requires a person to benefit from the assistance of a lawyer during questioning by police,[35] particularly where domestic laws attach consequences to a suspect's responses to police questioning at a subsequent trial.[36]

17.15

The requirement for a lawyer to be physically present during a police interview is more recent.[37] However, in *Doyle v Ireland*,[38] the Chamber held that the lack of physical presence of the applicant's lawyer had to be placed in context when assessing the extent of the restriction to the right to representation.[39] In that case the extent of the restriction arising from the absence of the applicant's lawyer during his police interviews was 'relative' given that he had access to his lawyer before the first interview, he had requested and was granted access to his lawyer at any time after that interview, and all the interviews were video recorded.[40]

17.16

A lawyer must but also be allowed to 'actively assist' a suspect during the police interview.[41] A lawyer must be permitted to intervene to ensure respect for the suspect's rights and to assist the suspect until the end of questioning, including when any statements or record are signed.[42] Police must also refrain from questioning if a suspect has invoked their right to be assisted by a lawyer.[43] In *Soytemiz v Turkey*[44] the Chamber found a violation of the applicant's right to representation where police had terminated the interview after the applicant's lawyer had tried to assist the applicant and had coerced the applicant to sign the interview record after removing the applicant's lawyer from the room.[45]

17.17

In *Ambrose v Harris*,[46] the Supreme Court considered three cases in which each of the appellants, who had been cautioned but not arrested or detained in custody, had responded to police questions without legal representation in light

33 *S v Switzerland* at [51].

34 *Brennan v The United Kingdom* at [58]–[63]; *Öcalan v Turkey* (2005) 41 EHRR 45 at [132]–[133].

35 *Murray v The United Kingdom* at [63]; *Magee v The United Kingdom* (2001) 31 EHRR 35 at [41]; *Brennan v The United Kingdom* at [45]; *Salduz v Turkey* at [52], [54], [55]; *Dvorski v Croatia* at [76]; *Ibrahim v The United Kingdom* at [255].

36 See 17.11 above and footnote 18.

37 *Šebalj v Croatia* (28 June 2011, unreported), ECtHR (Chamber) at [251]–[254] and [257]; *Erkapić v Croatia* (25 April 2013, unreported) ECtHR (Chamber) at [80]–[81] and [89]. See also *Doyle v Ireland* (23 May 2019, unreported), ECtHR (Chamber) at [79]–[80] and [101].

38 *Doyle v Ireland* (23 May 2019, unreported), ECtHR (Chamber).

39 Ibid at [83].

40 Ibid.

41 *Soytemiz v Turkey* (27 November 2018, unreported), ECtHR (Chamber) at [44]–[46].

42 Ibid.

43 Ibid.

44 Ibid.

45 Ibid at [47] and [57]–58].

46 *HM Advocate v M; HM Advocate v G* [2011] 1 WLR 2435.

of the ECtHR's jurisprudence. In the first case, the appellant had been sitting the passenger seat of a car seemingly intoxicated. He told police that he had the car keys in his pocket. In the second case, the appellant had been questioned by police at his home and admitted to being involved in a fight at a pub. In the third case, the appellant had been handcuffed following a struggle during the execution of a search warrant of his flat. He then responded to questions about items seized during the search. The Supreme Court held that in the first two cases there was no requirement to provide the appellants with legal representation,[47] but that the circumstances of the third case were sufficiently coercive that the appellant should have been provided legal representation; as a result, his responses to questioning were inadmissible at trial.[48]

17.18

Beyond these minimum requirements, the presence of a lawyer may be required during identification procedures;[49] reconstructions of events;[50] and searches of property.[51] Further, the right to representation may require that meetings with lawyers are not limited in frequency or duration where a criminal case is large and complex[52] and that lawyers have access to the case file with sufficient time to prepare the defence case before trial.[53] However, the right to representation does not extend to testing procedures or the compulsory provision of information following suspected road traffic offences.[54]

Domestic law

17.19

The right to representation for persons detained in custody is contained in section 58 of the Police and Criminal Evidence Act 1984 (PACE), which entitles a detainee to request to consult a solicitor privately at any time.[55] Following a request, they must be permitted to consult a solicitor as soon as practicable.[56] Requests for legal assistance must also be recorded in the custody record.[57] Part 6 of Code C of PACE provides further detail of the right representation for detainees. In particular, the Code states that all detainees must be informed of their right to consult privately with a solicitor and that free representation is available.[58]

---

47 Ibid at [68]–[70].

48 Ibid at [71].

49 *Türk v Turkey* (5 September 2017, unreported), ECtHR (Chamber) at [47].

50 Ibid; *Mehmet Duman v Turkey* (23 November 2019, unreported), ECtHR (Chamber) at [41].

51 *Ayetullah Ay v Turkey* (7 October 2020, unreported) ECtHR (Chamber) at [135] and [163].

52 *Öcalan v Turkey* at [134]–[135].

53 Ibid at [145]–[147]. But see also *AT v Luxemburg* (9 April 2015, unreported), ECtHR (Chamber) at [79]–[84] where a lawyer did not have a right to 'unlimited access' to the criminal case file.

54 *Халасъ Sršen v Croatia* (22 January 2019, unreported), ECtHR (Chamber) at [42]–[45]. See also *Kennedy v CPS* [2002] EWHC 2297 (Admin) at [3].

55 PACE 1984, s 58(1).

56 Ibid, s 58(4).

57 Ibid, s 58(2).

58 PACE, Code C at [6.1].

17.20

Where a detainee has consulted a solicitor, they can request that solicitor to be present during the interview, unless certain exceptions apply.[59] A solicitor can only be required to leave the interview where their conduct prevents the police from properly putting questions to the suspect.[60] Where a juvenile or vulnerable detainee wishes to consult a solicitor the necessary arrangements should be made without waiting for an appropriate adult.[61] If a juvenile or vulnerable detainee does not wish to consult a solicitor, the appropriate adult has the right to request for solicitor if they consider it to be in the best interests of that detainee.[62] However, the detainee cannot be forced to see a solicitor if they do not wish to do so.[63]

Restriction of the right to representation

17.21

The right to representation may be restricted in certain circumstances by delaying access to a lawyer during the investigation or pre-trial stage. Previously, any restriction had to be 'for good cause' and a violation of Article 6(3)(c) in conjunction with Article 6(1) was found where the restriction 'in light of the entirely of the proceedings, has deprived the accused of a fair hearing'.[64] Where a person is questioned by police without a lawyer, a key factor the application of this test will be the admission into evidence of their answers to police at the trial. In *Salduz*, the test was reformulated. First, there had to be compelling reasons for the restriction and secondly, the restriction did not unduly prejudice the right to a fair trial.[65] *Ibrahim* provided further clarification on this two-part test. The four applicants in that case had been convicted of criminal offences related to the detonation of bombs in London on 21 July 2005 as part of a planned terrorist attack. In relation to the requirement for 'compelling reasons', the Grand Chamber held that restrictions are only permitted in 'exceptional circumstances' and must be of a temporary nature and based on the individual circumstances of the case.[66] It also held that relevant considerations were whether the decision to restrict legal advice had a basis in domestic law and whether the

59 Ibid at [6.8]. See also 17.27-17.30.

60 Ibid at [6.9]–[6.11].

61 Ibid at [6.5].

62 Ibid.

63 Ibid.

64 *Murray v The United Kingdom* at [63]; *Magee v The United Kingdom* at [41]; *Brennan v The United Kingdom* at [45].

65 *Salduz v Turkey* at [55]. The ruling in *Salduz* was applied by the Supreme Court of the United Kingdom in *Cadder v HM Advocate* [2010] 1 WLR 2601 at [48]–[51] in the interpretation of sections of the Criminal Procedure (Scotland) Act 1995 concerning the rights of detainees. However, unlike PACE 1984, the Scottish legislation did not provide a right to representation prior to a police interview.

66 *Ibrahim v The United Kingdom* at [258].

scope and content of any restriction were sufficiently circumscribed by law to guide operational decision making.[67]

17.22

In relation to the assessment of whether the defendant's rights have been unduly prejudiced, the Grand Chamber held that 'a holistic assessment of the entirety of the proceedings must be conducted to determine whether they were 'fair' for the purposes of Article 6(1)'.[68] This is reiteration of the whole of proceedings test. Whilst a lack of compelling reasons is not alone sufficient for a violation of Article 6,[69] a standard of 'very strict scrutiny' is applied to the fairness assessment in such situations and the lack of compelling reasons 'weighs heavily in the balance when assessing the overall fairness of proceedings'.[70] The Grand Chamber also set out a list of non-exhaustive factors to be considered when assessing the impact of procedural failings at the pre-trial stage on the overall fairness of criminal proceedings.[71] These were:

(a) Whether the applicant was particularly vulnerable, for example, by reason of his age or mental capacity.

(b) The legal framework governing the pre-trial proceedings and the admissibility of evidence at trial, and whether it was complied with; where an exclusionary rule applied, it is particularly unlikely that the proceedings as a whole would be considered unfair.

(c) Whether the applicant had the opportunity to challenge the authenticity of the evidence and oppose its use.

(d) The quality of the evidence and whether the circumstances in which it was obtained cast doubt on its reliability or accuracy, taking into account the degree and nature of any compulsion.

(e) Where evidence was obtained unlawfully, the unlawfulness in question and, where it stems from a violation of another Convention Article, the nature of the violation found.

(f) In the case of a statement, the nature of the statement and whether it was promptly retracted or modified.

(g) The use to which the evidence was put, and in particular whether the evidence formed an integral or significant part of the probative evidence upon which the conviction was based, and the strength of the other evidence in the case.

---

67 Ibid. A statutory restriction that has general application and is mandatory will not remove the need for authorities to assess whether there are compelling reasons in an individual case: *Beuze v Belgium* at [142]. Further, a restriction resulting from the general practice of police or other authorities will not constitute compelling reasons: *Simeonovi v Bulgaria* at [130]; *Doyle v Ireland* at [84].

68 Ibid at [263].

69 Ibid at [262].

70 Ibid at [262]–[264].

71 Ibid at [274].

(h) Whether the assessment of guilt was performed by professional judges or lay jurors, and in the case of the latter the content of any jury directions.

(i) The weight of the public interest in the investigation and punishment of the particular offence in issue.

(j) Other relevant procedural safeguards afforded by domestic law and practice.

17.23

In *Ibrahim,* the Grand Chamber distinguished between the first three applicants whose access to a lawyer had been delayed as part of a 'safety interview'[72] and the fourth applicant who did not have access to a lawyer because he was interviewed as a witness. The Grand Chamber held that the authorities had compelling reasons to delay access to a lawyer for the first three applicants given the 'urgent need to avert serious adverse consequences for life, liberty or physical integrity'.[73] However, compelling reasons had not been proved by the UK Government in respect of the fourth applicant since there was no record of the reasons why he was not cautioned when his interview was suspended temporarily.[74] The Grand Chamber also held that the rights of the first three applicants had not been unduly prejudiced by admission of their interviews, as the cautions given had informed them of their right to remain silent and as they had challenged the admission of the interviews at trial and appeal.[75] However, the rights of the fourth applicant had been unduly prejudiced and a violation of Article 6 was found.[76] The Court of Appeal (Criminal Division) in *R v Abdurahman*[77] subsequently considered the safety of the conviction of the fourth applicant in *Ibrahim* in light of the Article 6 violation. The Court of Appeal criticised the Grand Chamber's approach to the fairness assessment that it described as creating 'a strong presumption of irretrievable prejudice' in cases where compelling reasons to restrict the right to representation and notification of that right were lacking, which detracted from a 'multifactorial and holistic' fairness assessment.[78] However, the approach in *Ibrahim* had been subsequently confirmed by the Grand Chamber in *Simeonovi* and *Beuze* whose judgments were not referred to by the Court of Appeal.[79]

72 A safety interview was shorthand for an interview conducted urgently for the purpose of protecting life and preventing serious damage to property under the Terrorism Act 2000, Sch 8, para 8: *Ibrahim v The United Kingdom* (at [23], [188]–[190] and [193]–[198].

73 *Ibrahim v The United Kingdom*, ibid at [259], [276]–[279]. The Grand Chamber noted, however, that a general risk of leaks would not constitute compelling reasons at [259].

74 Ibid at [298]–[300].

75 Ibid at [280]–[294].

76 Ibid at [311].

77 *R v Abdurahman* [2020] 4 WLR 6.

78 Ibid at [111(b)], [116].

79 *Simeonovi v Bulgaria* at [118]; *Beuze v Belgium* at [144]–[145].

17.24

The Court of Appeal disagreed with the Grand Chamber's finding of an absence of compelling reasons in the fourth applicant's case given the urgent need to obtain information about the perpetrators of the terrorist attack.[80] The Court also disagreed with outcome of the Grand Chambers' fairness assessment on the basis that the fourth applicant's initial statement had been voluntary; he did not retract that statement; he challenged its admissibility at both the *voir dire* and appeal; and there was other overwhelming evidence against him.[81] Such different reasoning between the Grand Chamber and Court of Appeal highlights the problems associated with the whole of proceedings test (given its unstructured balancing approach), as well as with the exceptional treatment of crimes occurring in a terrorist context.

17.25

As stated above, the principles set out in *Ibrahim* were subsequently confirmed by the Grand Chamber in two cases. First, in *Simeonovi*,[82] where the Grand Chamber held that the applicant's rights had not been unduly prejudiced since no evidence had been obtained during the period that he lacked access to a lawyer and, further, his failure to make any statement had no impact on later criminal proceedings. Secondly, in *Beuze*,[83] where the Grand Chamber held that the applicant's rights had been unduly prejudiced since he had given detailed statements without a lawyer present to police which 'substantially affected' his defence, even though they were not self-incriminating in the narrow sense.[84] Further, these statements were admitted at trial without proper consideration; formed an integral part of the evidence upon which the applicant's conviction was based; and the jury were not given directions on how to assess them.[85] Finally, the appeal court had failed to assess the consequences of a lawyer's absence for the applicant's defence.

17.26

In *Dvorski*, the issue before the Court was not the delay of access to a lawyer, but denial of the applicant's choice of a lawyer during the interview and throughout the criminal proceedings. Whilst in custody, the applicant had repeatedly asked for a particular lawyer to represent him but had not been told by police when that lawyer attended the police station. During the interview in which he made a confession the applicant was represented by a different lawyer appointed by the authorities. In such circumstances, the Grand Chamber held that that a less stringent test applied: (i) were there 'relevant and sufficient reasons' to deny the

80 *R v Abdurahman* at [114].

81 Ibid at [118]–[123].

82 *Simeonovi v Bulgaria* at [136]–[138].

83 Ibid.

84 *Beuze v Belgium* at [193]. See also *Bjarki H Deigo v Iceland* (15 March 2022, unreported), ECtHR (Chamber) at [57]–[58] where the Chamber held that the applicant's answers to police questions without a lawyer 'substantially affected' his position given the factually and legally complex nature of allegations of financial crime.

85 Ibid.

applicant the lawyer of his choosing; and (ii) in light of the proceedings as a whole, whether the rights of the defence had been 'adversely affected'.[86] A violation of Articles 6(1) and (3)(c) was found based on the above circumstances, as well as the fact that the applicant's confession had been admitted at the trial and the domestic courts had failed to take remedial measures.[87]

Domestic law

17.27

Section 58 of PACE sets out the circumstances in which the right to representation for detainees may be delayed. A delay, which cannot exceed 36 hours,[88] is only permitted where a person is detained for an indictable offence and has been authorised by an appropriate officer with a reasonable belief that exercising the right to consult a solicitor will (a) lead to interference with evidence or other persons, (b) lead to alerting other suspects not yet arrested, or (c) hinder the recovery of any property obtained or the value of the benefit from criminal conduct.[89]

17.28

A person must be informed of the reasons for a delay to comply with their request to consult a solicitor and those reasons must be recorded on the custody record.[90] Code C of PACE states that a detainee who wants legal advice must not be interviewed (or continue to be interviewed) until they have received such advice, except if in any of the following circumstances:

(a) the statutory grounds for delaying legal advice apply;

(b) an appropriate officer has reasonable grounds for believing that the consequent delay would have the same effect as set out in section 58 of PACE, or that awaiting the arrival of a solicitor would cause unreasonable delay to the investigation;

(c) the solicitor nominated by the detainee cannot be contacted or declines to attend and the detainee does not ask for the Duty Solicitor; or

(d) the detainee changes their mind about wanting legal representation.[91]

17.29

If a person is not provided with legal advice prior to their interview, no adverse inferences may be drawn from their silence to police questioning.[92] A failure to comply with section 58 of PACE or the provisions of Code C of PACE does

86 *Dvorski v Croatia* at [81]–[82].
87 Ibid at [112].
88 PACE 1984, s 58(5).
89 Ibid at s 58(6), (8), (8A).
90 Ibid at s 58(9).
91 PACE, Code C [6.6].
92 Criminal Justice and Public Order Act 1994, s 34(2A). See also PACE, Annex C of Code C.

not automatically result in answers to police questions being excluded at trial, however, it may form the basis of an admissibility challenge under section 78 of PACE, as demonstrated by the case law discussed in the previous section.[93] Further, in *HM Advocate v P*,[94] the Supreme Court held there was no absolute rule preventing the admission at trial of evidence obtained from information disclosed during an interview where a person did not have legal representation, and that the admissibility of such evidence would be determined in accordance with the general rules of evidence.[95]

17.30

There is a separate statutory regime governing the right to representation for persons arrested on suspicion of terrorist offences.[96] Schedule 8, paragraph 7 of the Terrorism Act 2000 contains the right to representation for such persons and paragraph 8 sets out the circumstances in which the right to representation may be delayed.

Waiver of the right to representation

17.31

A person may waive their right to representation at the investigation or pre-trial stage of criminal proceedings. As the ECtHR has held on numerous occasions, there is nothing in the letter or spirit of Article 6 which prevents a person from waiving, either explicitly or tacitly, their right to a fair trial.[97] In *Simenonvi*, the Grand Chamber summarised the requirements for a waiver of Article 6 rights to be effective:

> [I]f it is to be effective for Convention purposes, such a waiver must be established in an unequivocal manner and be attended by minimum safeguards commensurate to its importance. Such a waiver need not be explicit, but it must be voluntary and constitute a knowing and intelligent relinquishment of a right. Before an accused can be said to have implicitly, through his conduct, waived an important right under art. 6, it must be shown that he could reasonably have foreseen what the consequences of his conduct would be. Moreover, the waiver must not run counter to any important public interest.[98]

93 *Kennedy v CPS* [2002] EWHC 2297 (Admin) at [14].
94 *HM Advocate v P* [2011] 1 WLR 2497.
95 Ibid at [19]–[34].
96 Terrorism Act 2000, s 41.
97 *Pishchalnikov v Russia* (24 December 2009, unreported) ECtHR (Chamber) at [77]; *Dvorski v Croatia* at [100]; *Simeonovi v Bulgaria* at [115].
98 *Simeonovi v Bulgaria* ibid at [115].

17.32

Most importantly, given that the right to representation is one of the fundamental rights in Article 6, any waiver must meet the 'knowing and intelligent' standard.[99] For a waiver to meet this standard, it will be highly relevant whether a person was notified of their right to representation.[100] In *Simeonnovi*, the failure to notify resulted in any implicit waiver by the applicant being ineffective.[101] Yet for an express waiver to be effective there is no requirement for a person to have received prior legal advice.[102]

17.33

In *Zachar and Čierny v Slovakia*,[103] the applicants, who were charged with drug offences, waived their rights to representation during pre-trial proceedings. Later in those proceedings, when the applicants were represented by lawyers, the charges were amended to the aggravated form of the drug offences, thereby increasing the penalty. The Chamber held the failure by authorities to inform the applicants, prior to their initial waiver, of the risk that the charges would be amended resulted in those waivers not being attended by the minimum safeguards.[104]

17.34

Documents signed by a person in custody may be relevant to establishing the effectiveness of a waiver. Whilst such documents have probative value, they are not an end in themselves and must be examined by a court in light of all the circumstances.[105] In particular, a printed waiver formula may pose a challenge to ascertaining whether a person's decision to waive their right to representation was free and informed.[106] In *Akdağ v Turkey*,[107] the Chamber held that a record signed by the applicant with the printed words 'no lawyer sought' and a box marked 'X' was insufficient in the circumstances to constitute a valid waiver.[108]

17.35

The vulnerabilities of a person in custody may also be relevant to assessing a waiver's validity. Additional protection should be provided for illiterate persons in custody.[109] In *Akdağ*, the failure by domestic courts to examine whether the applicant was illiterate contributed to the Chambers' finding that the validity of the applicant's waiver had not been demonstrated.[110] An initial waiver of

99 *Pishchalnikov v Russia* at [78]; *Dvorski v Croatia* at [100].
100 *Simeonovi v Bulgaria* at [118].
101 Ibid at [127]–[128].
102 *McGowan v B* [2011] 1 WLR 3121 at [45] (Lord Hope).
103 *Zachar and Čierny v Slovakia* (21 July 2015, unreported), ECtHR (Chamber).
104 Ibid at [72]–[74].
105 *Akdağ v Turkey* (17 September 2019, unreported), ECtHR (Chamber) at [54].
106 Ibid.
107 Ibid.
108 Ibid at [50], [54]–[59], [61]. See also *Bozkaya v Turkey* (5 September 2017, unreported), ECtHR (Chamber) at [42], [48].
109 *Akdağ v Turkey* at [57].
110 Ibid at [57] [59[and [61].

the right to representation is no longer effective if a person later requests the assistance of a lawyer.[111] An ineffective waiver of the right to representation may be rectified during the subsequent trial. Accordingly, an examination of the fairness of the entire criminal proceedings is required before a violation of Article 6 is found.[112] This is again an example of the whole of proceedings test.

17.36

In domestic law, Code C of PACE sets out what officers should do in circumstances where a detainee declines to exercise their right to representation. These steps assist in establishing whether a waiver is effective. First, an officer should point out that the right to representation includes the right to speak with a solicitor on the telephone.[113] The basis for this requirement is to ensure that a detainee does not decline legal advice based on an apprehension that their time in custody will be delayed as a result.[114] It is suggested that best practice also requires officers to explain that legal advice is free.[115] Where a detainee continues to decline legal advice, the officer should ask for their reasons and record any reasons given on the custody record.[116]

TRIAL AND APPEAL STAGE

17.37

The right to representation continues throughout the trial and appellate stages of criminal proceedings. This section briefly considers the three distinct rights provided by Article 6(3)(c) during these later stages, namely, the right to represent oneself, the right to a lawyer of one's own choosing, and the right to free legal representation.[117]

17.38

At the outset it must be reiterated that none of these rights are absolute. The rights to self-representation and choice of lawyer are implicitly subject to an interests of justice test; the ECtHR has repeatedly held that a defendant's wishes may be overridden where there are relevant and sufficient grounds that it is in the interests of justice to do so.[118] In *Correia de Matos v Portugal*,[119] the Grand Chamber summarised the principles from previous ECtHR cases as follows:

111 *Artur Parkhomenko v Ukraine* (16 February 2017, unreported), ECtHR (Chamber) at [81].
112 *Türk v Turkey* at [53]–[54].
113 PACE, Code C [6.5].
114 *McGowan v B* at [49].
115 Ibid at [51].
116 PACE, Code C [6.5].
117 See Chapter 23.
118 In respect of the right to self-representation see: *Galstyan v Armenia* (2010) 50 EHRR 25 at [91]–[90]; *Correia de Matos v Portugal* (2018) 44 BHRC 319 at [121]–[122]. In respect of the right to a choice of lawyer see: *Croissant v Germany* 16 EHRR 135 at [29]; *Meftah v France* (26 July 2002, unreported), ECtHR (Grand Chamber) at [45]; *Mayzit v Russia* (2006) 43 EHRR 38 at [66]; *Dvorski v Croatia* (at [79]. See also *R (Howe) v South Durham Magistrates' Court* [2004] EWHC 362 (Admin) at [24]–[25].
119 *Correia de Matos v Portugal* (2018) BHRC 319

> (a) Article 6 §§ 1 and 3 (c) does not necessarily give the accused the right to decide himself in what manner his defence should be assured; (b) the decision as to which of the two alternatives mentioned in that provision should be chosen, namely the applicant's right to defend himself in person or to be represented by a lawyer of his own choosing, or in certain circumstances one appointed by the court, depends, in principle, upon the applicable domestic legislation or rules of court; (c) Member States enjoy a margin of appreciation as regards this choice, albeit one which is not unlimited.[120]

17.39

Meanwhile, the right to free legal representation is subject to the explicit limitations in Article 6(3)(c) of 'not ha[ving] s sufficient means' and the 'interests of justice'.[121] Relevant to the assessment of the interests of justice are the seriousness of the offence and the severity of sentence; the complexity of the case; and the defendant's personal situation, particularly whether they were able to present their case in an adequate manner.[122] Where deprivation of liberty is at stake, the interests of justice in principle call for legal representation.[123]

17.40

The right to representation at the trial and appeal stages requires that legal assistance is 'practical and effective'.[124] Merely assigning a lawyer to a person charged with a criminal offence does not ensure the effectiveness of legal representation as a lawyer 'may die, fall seriously ill, be prevented for a protracted period from acting or shirk his duties'.[125] However, given the independence of the legal profession, the conduct of the defence is essentially a matter between a defendant and their lawyer (whether provided free by the state or privately engaged) and state authorities are only required to intervene where the failure to provide effective representation is manifest or sufficiently brought to their attention in another way.[126]

---

120 Ibid at [143].

121 The Legal Aid, Sentencing and Punishment of Offenders Act 2012, Pt 1 includes the statutory regime for the provision of free legal representation in the United Kingdom. Section 17 of that Act states that qualifications for criminal legal aid are based on an individual's financial resources (as addressed in s 21) and the interests of justice.

122 *Quaranta v Switzerland* (24 May 1991, unreported), ECtHR (Chamber) at [33]–[36]; *Benham v The United Kingdom* (1996) 22 EHRR 293 at [60]–[64].

123 *Benham v The United Kingdom* ibid at [61]; *Hammerton v The United Kingdom* (2016) 63 EHRR 23 at [142]. Note the Sentencing Act 2020, s 226(3) which states that a court may not pass a sentence of imprisonment unless the offender is legally represented (or has failed or is ineligible on financial grounds to benefit from relevant representation as defined in s 226(7–8)), or the offender has previously been sentenced to imprisonment by a court (a suspended sentence is to be disregarded for this provision: see s 226(5)).

124 *Artico v Italy* at [33].

125 Ibid.

126 *Kaminski v Austria* (1989) 13 EHRR 36 at [65]; *Ebanks v The United Kingdom* (2010) 51 EHRR 2 at [72]–[73].

17.41

The right to representation may extend to appeal proceedings. The manner in which the Article 6(3)(c) rights are applied at this stage depend on the special features of the proceedings, including the whole of the criminal proceedings and the role of the appellate court.[127]

CONCLUSION

17.42

The right to representation in the early stages of criminal proceedings requires, at the very least, persons in custody to receive confidential legal advice and to have a lawyer present when questioned by police. Whilst the right is not absolute, it may only be restricted in limited circumstances and the threshold for an effective waiver is high, demonstrating the crucial role of legal representation in guaranteeing a host of other fair trial rights, including the right to silence and the privilege against self-incrimination, and the equality of arms between defence and prosecution.

127 *Monnell and Morris v The United Kingdom* (1987) 10 EHRR 205; *Granger v The United Kingdom* (1990) 12 EHRR 469 at [44]. In *Monnell and Morris* it was not in the interests of justice to grant the applicants free representation when seeking leave to appeal since there was no objective likelihood of success of the appeal and the leave to appeal procedure enabled the applicants participate, particularly by providing written submissions on the issue of loss-of-time orders. In contrast, in *Granger*, it was in the interests of justice to grant the applicant free representation during an appeal against his conviction of perjury given it involved issues of importance and complexity to which the applicant could not respond.

18 Delay

Monica Stevenson

INTRODUCTION

18.1

Delay has begun to feature in criminal cases more often in recent years. For various reasons this trend looks set to continue. In criminal proceedings, delay is instituted in one of two ways. First, the prosecution of historic allegations owing to delayed reporting or the discovery of new evidence. Secondly, police investigations and legal proceedings which, though commenced in time, have, for one reason or another, become protracted and drawn out.

18.2

At the time of writing, the Human Rights Act 1998 remains in force and makes it unlawful for any public body to act in a manner incompatible with the European Convention on Human Rights (ECHR). Enshrined in the Convention is of course the right to a fair trial, which includes the right to trial 'within a reasonable time'.

18.3

Recognition of the importance of efficiency in due process is long-standing and was acknowledged as far back as the Magna Carta, which stated: '…we will not deny or defer to any man either justice or right'. In the UK, the criminal justice system has developed different ways to manage the effects of delay, with the appropriate remedy depending on the impact of deferment in the individual case.

18.4

Since the Covid-19 pandemic, delay in the criminal justice system has almost become normalised. Whilst the courts continued to operate during lockdown, they did so at a reduced capacity meaning that a backlog of court cases which existed *before* the cataclysmic events of the Pandemic, has now increased significantly.

18.5

Delays in the criminal process stem from other developments. These include the growing practice of suspects 'released under investigation' (RUI) following the implementation of the Policing and Crime Act 2017. This legislation introduced the presumption of release without bail and was intended to stop criminal suspects languishing on police bail for extended periods of time. The legal changes did not, however, cater for how RUI would operate in practice. Nor did it create any time incentives for the police to work towards.

18.6

A joint inspection report from the *HM Crown Prosecution Service Inspectorate and HM Inspectorate of Constabulary and Fire & Rescue Services*[1] found that criminal investigations involving RUI suspects were generally taking longer and were often subject to less scrutiny than those involving bail. The same report found RUI cases were often being given less priority and discovered '… worrying examples of suspects who had been RUI for many months, and sometimes years, without hearing anything from the police'.[2] The report went on to note that: 'It is usually only in cases where the suspect or their legal representative has contacted the police for information that they are told anything about the progress in the investigation.'[3] The Police Crime Sentencing and Courts Act 2022 has instituted some changes to pre-charge bail and RUI. This includes removing the statutory presumption to release suspects without bail as well as adjusting time limits for pre-charge bail periods. At the time of writing, the College of Policing has completed a public consultation on draft statutory guidance for pre-charge bail and RUI.

18.7

Anecdotal evidence suggests that delays have also arisen from problems with postal requisitions not being sent to or received by RUI suspects. Other factors inducing delay in criminal proceedings include reduced police budgets, with forces left to prioritise the progression of cases. The collation of evidence from third parties, such as social service or medical records has also impacted on the efficiency and progress of criminal investigations.

18.8

Arguably, the single biggest reason for delay in criminal investigations is the collation of digital forensic evidence, with checks of electronic devices (such as computers and mobile phones) routinely taking several months to complete. These challenges facing the criminal justice system are exacerbated by a sustained lack of funding, as well as political and public attention.

18.9

This chapter considers delay in the context of the right to a fair trial and the factors to be considered by criminal practitioners when dealing with this issue.

---

1 11 December 2020.
2 Ibid, p 15.
3 Ibid.

THE EFFECT OF DELAY IN CRIMINAL PROCEEDINGS

18.10

In *Porter v Magill*,[4] it was said that: 'The two possible effects of delay are an unsafe verdict and other damage for the appellant.'[5] Questions regarding the effect of delay may be raised before *or* after the decision of the tribunal. In the case of *Porter*, Lord Kennedy observed that *before* the tribunal decision:

> '… it will be necessary to consider the danger of an unreliable verdict and the danger of other damage caused to the litigant by delay. Both can be dealt with either by way of a stay of the proceedings or order for a speedy trial'.[6]

18.11

Delay in the context of a criminal case can induce a host of different results, all of which criminal practitioners should be alive to early on when considering this issue. Any assessment of the effect of delay on the right to a fair trial will always be fact specific.

18.12

However, below is a non-exhaustive list of the type of problems which can be engendered by delay:

(a) the loss or non-availability of exculpatory evidence;

(b) the loss or destruction of documentation (such as third-party records, CCTV and contemporaneous notes);

(c) the death of witnesses and/or difficulty in tracing witnesses;

(d) changes to the locus (crime scene) and difficulties inspecting the same;

(e) the loss of forensic evidence/forensic opportunities;

(f) the impairment of witness recollection due to the passage of time;

(g) the risk of collusion between witnesses/contamination of witnesses;

(h) a lack of continuity in police investigations with key tasks not being completed;

(i) anxiety for the defendant as a result of the proceedings hanging over them/increased periods of time spent in custody pending trial; and

(j) the undermining of public confidence and trust in the criminal justice system itself.

---

4 *Porter v Magill* [2001] UKHL 67.

5 Ibid at [32].

6 Ibid at [33].

THE RIGHT TO TRIAL 'WITHIN A REASONABLE TIME'

The European Convention on Human Rights

18.13

The right to a trial within a reasonable time is enshrined in Articles 5(3) and 6 of the Convention. Article 5(3) provides that: 'Everyone arrested or detained shall be brought promptly before a judge or other officer authorised by law to exercise judicial power and shall be entitled to trial within a reasonable time or to release pending trial.' Article 6 of the ECHR states: 'In the determination of their [his] civil rights and obligations, or of any criminal charge against him, everyone is entitled to a fair and public hearing within a reasonable time by an independent and impartial tribunal.'

18.14

In *Attorney General's Reference (No 2 of 2001)*,[7] the House of Lords observed that Article 6(1) 'creates rights which, although related, are separate and distinct'.

18.15

The 'reasonable time requirement' is therefore a separate guarantee, distinct from the other components which make up a fair trial such as the right to a fair and public hearing, and the right to a hearing by an independent and impartial tribunal. In the above case, the House of Lords also noted that: 'It does not follow that the consequences of a breach, or a threatened or prospective breach of each of these rights is necessarily the same.'[8]

'Trial within a reasonable time' – The underlying logic

18.16

Several ECHR cases have addressed the underlying rationale of the right to trial 'within a reasonable time'. In *Kart v Turkey*,[9] the ECHR stated that:

> While there is no right under Article 6 of the convention to a particular outcome of criminal proceedings, or therefore to a formal conviction or acquittal following the laying of criminal charges, there is an indisputable right to have one's case heard by a court within a reasonable time, once the judicial process has been set in motion. That right is based on the need to ensure that accused persons do not have

7 *Attorney General's Reference (No 2 of 2001)* [2003] UKHL 68.
8 Ibid, at [12].
9 *Kart v Turkey* (Application no 8917/05), 3 December 2009.

to remain too long in a state of uncertainty as to the outcome of the criminal accusations against them.[10]

18.17

In *Attorney General's Reference (No 2 of 2001)*, it was noted that the purpose of the 'reasonable time requirement' was '... to ensure that criminal proceedings, once initiated, are prosecuted without undue delay and to preserve defendants from the trauma of awaiting trial for inordinate periods'.[11]

18.18

Plainly, the indulgence of excessive procedural delay could give license to the deliberate abuse of state power; with drawn-out proceedings designed to punish citizens or pressure them into admitting allegations. In *Mills (Kenneth Anthony) v HM Advocate*,[12] Lord Steyn acknowledged a further issue, namely that systemic tolerance of delays could see an erosion of public trust and confidence in the integrity of the legal system.

The 'reasonable time requirement' – breaches

18.19

Both European and UK case law have made clear that a breach of the right to trial 'within a reasonable time' does not automatically compromise the fairness of the trial process. Cases such as *Zarb v Malta*[13] and *Scordino v Italy*[14] indicate that breaches of the 'reasonable time requirement' can be corrected during the proceedings, whether by way of compensation, reduction in sentence or public address.

18.20

In *Porter*, the House of Lords confirmed that it is not necessary to demonstrate a 'specific prejudice' in order to establish a breach of the reasonable time guarantee. The conjoined Scottish appeal of *Dyer v Watson*[15] – which was the first UK case to consider the issue of delay in the framework of Article 6 – saw the Privy Council (PC) issue guidance on the application of the reasonable time guarantee.

18.21

The Council confirmed that the starting point was to consider the period of time which had elapsed. Only where the lapse of time gave rise to 'real concern'

---

10 Ibid, at [68].
11 *Attorney General's Reference (No 2 of 2001)* at [27].
12 *Mills (Kenneth Anthony) v HM Advocate* [2002] UKPC D2 at [14].
13 *Zarb v Malta* (Application no 16631/04), 9 July 2013, [2006] ECHR 689.
14 *Scordino v Italy (No 1)* [2006] ECHR 276.
15 *Dyer v Watson* [2004] 1 AC 379.

would it be necessary to go on to consider a possible infringement of the Convention rights. The court said that unless the delay is:

> … one which, on its face and without more, gives grounds for real concern it is almost certainly unnecessary to go further, since the Convention is directed not to departures from the ideal but to infringements of basic human rights. The threshold of proving a breach of the reasonable time requirement is a high one, not easily crossed.[16]

18.22

Where the time which has passed does raise a potential breach of the 'reasonable time guarantee' the courts should then go on to consider the facts and circumstances of the individual case, as well as the explanation or justification of the prosecution for any delay.

18.23

With respect to the actions of the prosecuting authority, both the European and UK courts have had to straddle a line between not indulging the incompetence or inertia of prosecuting authorities whilst recognising that all legal systems suffer delays and work to deliver justice to victims as well as defendants. In *Dyer* it was said that:

> This was recognised by the court in *Sporrong and Lönnroth v Sweden* (1982) 5 EHRR 35, 52 when, in para 69 of its judgment, it referred to the striking of a fair balance between the demands of the general interest of the community and the requirements of the protection of the individual's fundamental rights, the search for which balance was said to be inherent in the whole of the Convention.[17]

'Reasonable time' – When does the clock begin and end ticking?

18.24

In considering the question of when time starts to run, the European Court of Human Rights (ECtHR) has had to cater for the different 'procedural regimes' of individual Member States. As a result, European human rights jurisprudence has resisted laying down any fixed rule about timing, the effect of which could be to defeat the overall aim of the 'reasonable time requirement'.

18.25

In *Attorney General's Reference (No 2 of 2001)*, the House of Lords acknowledged this dilemma of the European Court, observing (at [27]) that:

16 Ibid at [52].
17 Ibid at [16].

> In seeking to give an autonomous definition of 'criminal charge' for Convention purposes, the European Court has had to confront the problem that procedural regimes vary widely in different member states and a specific rule appropriate in one might be quite inappropriate in another. Mindful of this problem, but doubtless seeking some uniformity of outcome in different member states, the Court has drawn on earlier authority to formulate a test in general terms. It is found in paragraph 73 of the Court's judgment in *Eckle v Republic of Germany* (1982) 5 EHRR 1.

The 'starting point'

18.26

European case law shows this is the time when the accused is officially notified or substantially affected by proceedings taken against them. In *Eckles v Republic of Germany*,[18] it was said that in criminal matters the 'reasonable time' referred to in Article 6(1) begins to run as soon as a person is 'charged' but it went on to observe that the starting point '… may occur on a date prior to the case coming before the trial court, such as the date of arrest, the date when the person concerned was officially notified that he would be prosecuted or the date when preliminary investigations were opened'.[19]

18.27

In *Wemhoff v Germany*,[20] the court held that the time started from stage of the applicant's arrest. By contrast, in *Kaleja v Latvia*,[21] the starting point was found to be the questioning of the applicant on suspicion of having committed the offence. In *Attorney General's Reference (No 2 of 2001)*, the House of Lords was asked to consider the question of when 'reasonable time' began for the purpose of UK law and stated as follows:

> As a general rule, the relevant period will begin at the earliest time at which a person is officially alerted to the likelihood of criminal proceedings against [them]. 'Arrest will not ordinarily mark the beginning of the period.' 'An official indication that a person will be reported with a view to prosecution may, depending on all the circumstances, do so'.[22]

18.28

The House of Lords judgment went on to approve the Court of Appeal's determination that '… the period will ordinarily begin when a defendant is

18 *Eckles v Republic of Germany* (1982) 5 EHRR 1.
19 Ibid, at [73].
20 *Wemhoff v Germany* (Application no 2122/64), 27 June 1968, [1968] ECHR 2.
21 *Kaleja v Latvia* (Application no 22059/08), 5 October 2017.
22 *Attorney General's Reference (No 2 of 2001)* at [27]–[28].

formally charged or served with a summon' whilst noting that it would be 'wise to avoid laying down any inflexible rule'.[23]

18.29

The end period for the calculation of 'reasonable time' in criminal matters will be until the conclusion of any appeal.[24] This can include an appeal against a confiscation order.[25]

THE ASSESSMENT OF 'REASONABLE TIME'

18.30

European human rights jurisprudence has not identified any cut-off point in terms of 'reasonable time' and, similarly in *R v E*,[26] the Court of Appeal confirmed that there is no overall time period which is determinative of an application to stay proceedings on the grounds of delay.

18.31

In *Boddaert v Belgium*,[27] a case involving a time period of six years, two months, and 22 days, the ECtHR noted that: 'The reasonableness of the length of proceedings is to be determined with reference to the criteria laid down in the Court's case-law and in the light of the circumstances of the case, *which in this instance call for an overall assessment*.'[28]

18.32

Whilst efficiency may be evidenced at some stages of the legal process, it is the overall length of time which falls to be considered. In *Dobbertin v France*,[29] for example, it was recognised that the final stages of the proceedings had been conducted 'at an acceptable speed' but that the total length of the proceedings nonetheless exceeded a 'reasonable time' such that it amounted to a breach of Article 6. In this case it was found that the domestic courts had been slow to resolve two issues. First, in taking nine months to determine the validity of an indictment and more than two years before an order commissioning experts was quashed. Second, the applicant was committed for trial over ten years after his arrest by the police.

18.33

The ECtHR has focused on the following factors when addressing the issue of delay as an alleged breach of the Convention.

23 Ibid.
24 See *Eckles v Republic of Germany* (1982) 5 EHRR 1.
25 See *Neuemister v Austria* (Application no 1936/63), 7 May 1974, [1974] ECHR 1.
26 *R v E* [2008] EWCA Crim 604.
27 *Boddaert v Belgium* (1992) (65/1991/317/389), 27 October 1992.
28 Ibid at [360], emphasis added.
29 *Dobbertin v France* (Application no 13089/87), 25 February 1993.

The complexity of the case

18.34

Delay must be considered with regard to the complexity of a case. However, whilst a case may have challenging aspects, the court will not indulge lengthy periods of 'unexplained activity'.[30] European jurisprudence has considered the complexity of a case a factor when assessing the alleged breaches of the 'reasonable time guarantee'. However, in *Attorney General's Reference (No 1 of 1990)* the Court of Appeal made clear that: 'Delay due merely to the complexity of the case or contributed to by the actions of the defendant himself should never be the foundation for a stay'.[31]

The applicant's conduct

18.35

Whilst the accused is not compelled to cooperate with judicial authorities and is permitted to put the State to proof, the extent to which an applicant has contributed to delay will be a factor for consideration. The court would consider the conduct of the applicant to see if any delay complained about was caused by their actions, or whether any of the applicant's conduct was designed to delay proceedings and cause deliberate obstruction to the resolution of matters. In *Sociedade de Construções Martins & Viera & Others*,[32] the ECtHR stated at [48] that:

> As to the applicant's conduct, the Court reiterates that Article 6 does not require a person charged with a criminal offence to cooperate actively with the judicial authorities (see, among other authorities, *Corigliano v. Italy*, 10 December 1982, § 42, Series A no. 57). It also considers that defendants cannot be blamed for taking full advantage of the resources and tools afforded by national law in the defence of their interests (see *Kolomiyets v. Russia*, no. 76835/01, § 25-31, 22 February 2007). Nonetheless, the applicant's conduct, in itself legitimate, constitutes an objective fact which cannot be attributed to the respondent State, and which must be considered for the purpose of determining whether or not the reasonable time referred to in Article 6 § 1 has been exceeded (see *Eckle v. Germany*, 15 July 1982, § 82, Series A no. 51).

30 See, eg, *Adiletta v Italy* (20/1990/211/271-273), 24 January 1991.

31 *Attorney General's Reference (No 1 of 1990)* [1992] QB 630 at [1].

32 *Sociedade de Construções Martins & Viera & Others* (Application no 56637/10), 30 October 2014.

The conduct of the relevant authorities

18.36

A further principle relevant to the assessment of reasonable time is the balance to be struck between the rights of the accused and the other objectives of the justice process. In the case of *Boddaert* the ECtHR noted that:

> Article 6 commands that judicial proceedings be expeditious, but it also lays down the more general principle of the proper administration of justice. In the circumstances of the case, the conduct of the authorities was consistent with the fair balance which has to be struck between the various aspects of this fundamental requirement.[33]

18.37

Whilst ECHR Member States have a duty to ensure their legal system gives effect to Convention rights, the ECtHR also recognises that delay is a feature of even a healthy and functioning legal system. Whilst case workloads and limited resources will not be sufficient justification for delay, the State will not be liable for delays caused by the applicant or their legal team: *Konig v Germany*.[34] Member States will also not be held responsible for delays caused by prosecuting agents or the court where they breach.[35]

18.38

In *Bell v DPP of Jamaica*,[36] the Privy Council approved four factors first articulated by Judge Powell in the American case of *Barker v Wingo*,[37] cited as being of relevance to the issue of delay, which were:

(a) the length of the delay;

(b) the explanation given for the delay by the prosecuting authority;

(c) the responsibility of the accused for asserting his right to have his case tried; and

(d) the prejudice caused to the accused person by virtue of the delay.

18.39

In *Dyer*, the Privy Council noted that the second and third factors were to be found, with only slight variations, in the jurisprudence of the Strasbourg court. As regards the first factor – the length of delay – it was said that it was clear from Strasbourg jurisprudence that '… it too takes the view that until there is some delay which is presumptively prejudicial there is no need for an inquiry into the

---

33 *Boddaert v Belgium* (1992) (65/1991/317/389) at [39].
34 *Konig v Germany* [1978] ECHR 3; (1978) 2 EHRR 170.
35 *Eckles v Republic of Germany* (1982) 5 EHRR 1.
36 *Bell v DPP of Jamaica* [1985] AC 937.
37 *Barker v Wingo* 407 US 514.

question whether the delay was "unreasonable"'.[38] The fourth factor (prejudice to the accused) was the real difference with the factors considered relevant by the European court, with there being no requirement in the context of the Article 6(1) guarantee for the defendant to demonstrate 'prejudice'.

REMEDIES FOR DELAY

18.40

European case law confirms that a range of remedies exist for delay, with the appropriate one depending on the nature of the breach and the stage at which the breach is established. In *Porter*, the subject of appropriate remedies was discussed and it was said that:

> An award of damages may well be a more appropriate remedy for damage caused to a litigant by an unduly delayed trial. This is clearly so where the litigant has been acquitted or found not liable. While in the case of an unsuccessful litigant no doubt the quashing of the decision will be welcome it does not as such provide any relief which is commensurate with the loss which has been suffered.[39]

18.41

A list of possible remedies for delay include the following:

(a) a stay of the proceedings as an abuse of process;

(b) the quashing of a conviction;

(c) the exclusion of evidence pursuant to sections 78 or 82 of the Police and Criminal Evidence Act 1984;

(d) a judicial direction to a jury about the effects of delay and prejudice to the defendant;

(e) a judicial direction to a jury concerning the risk of collusion between witnesses;

(f) the severance of one or more counts from the indictment;

(g) the release of the accused on bail or a variation of bail conditions;

(h) delay as a feature of mitigation, leading to a reduction in the overall sentence; and

(i) the discontinuance of a prosecution/review of decision.

38 *Dyer v Wilson* [2004] 1 AC 379 at [90].
39 *Porter v Magill* at [33].

The common law and delay

18.42

Whilst European jurisprudence has informed UK appellate case law on the issue of delay, the power to deal with this issue is not an invention of the Convention. Though the common law does not set time limits for the commencement of criminal proceedings, the court does have 'inherent powers' to stay the proceedings, where delay can be said to amount to an abuse of the court process. The House of Lords in *Attorney General's Reference (No 2 of 2001)* noted that the power of the domestic courts to stay proceedings on the grounds of delay '… rests, in Convention terms, on the fair trial guarantee and not on the reasonable time requirement'.[40]

18.43

The inherent powers of the court to deal with unreasonable delay was expressly acknowledged by the Privy Council in *Bell v DPP of Jamaica* in which it was stated:

> Their Lordships do not in any event accept the submission that prior to the Constitution the law of Jamaica, applying the common law of England, was powerless to provide a remedy against unreasonable delay, nor do they accept the alternative submission that a remedy could only be granted if the accused proved some specific prejudice, such as the supervening death of a witness. Their Lordships consider that, in a proper case without positive proof of prejudice, the courts of Jamaica would and could have insisted on setting a date for trial and then, if necessary, dismissing the charges for want of prosecution. Again, in a proper case, the court could treat the renewal of charges after the lapse of a reasonable time as an abuse of the process of the court.

18.44

The absence of any 'time guillotine' at common law means that – save for those offences where the charging of offences is regulated by statute – the UK courts can and do litigate allegations which are decades old. This commonly includes the prosecution of historic sexual offences as well as other charges, such as murder cases where new forensic evidence is obtained.

40 *Attorney General's Reference (No 2 of 2001)* at [17].

STAYING THE PROCEEDINGS AS AN ABUSE OF PROCESS AND DELAY

18.45

The leading authority on abuse applications based on delay remains that of *Attorney General's Reference (No 1 of 1990)*.[41] In this case, the Court of Appeal was asked to consider whether proceedings could be stayed on the ground of prejudice resulting from delay, even where the delay was not caused by any fault on the part of the prosecution. Whilst this question was answered in the affirmative, the CA made clear that even in cases where delay was occasioned by prosecutorial failings, the imposition of a permanent stay of the proceedings '… should be the exception rather than the rule'.

18.46

The Court went on to state that:

> No stay should be imposed unless the defendant shows on the balance of probabilities that owing to the delay, he will suffer serious prejudice to the extent that no fair trial can be held, in other words that the continuance of the prosecution amounts to a misuse of the process of the court. In assessing whether there is likely to be prejudice and if so whether it can properly be described as serious, the following matters should be borne in mind: first, the power of the judge at common law and under the Police and Criminal Evidence Act 1984 to regulate the admissibility of evidence; secondly, the trial process itself, which should ensure that all relevant factual issues arising from delay will be placed before the jury as part of the evidence for their consideration, together with the powers of the judge to give appropriate directions to the jury before they consider their verdict.

18.47

The acknowledgement in this judgment that '… decisions in this type of case will very much depend on their own facts' was said by the Court of Appeal in *CPS v F*,[42] to be:

> …based on the narrowest of grounds, the inability of the court 'to anticipate in advance all the infinitely variable circumstances which may arise in the future'. In short, it represented the practical application of the sensible rule that in the operation of the criminal justice system it is never wise to say 'never'. In reality the occasions when this situation will arise are likely to be almost vanishingly rare.[43]

41 *Attorney General's Reference (No 1 of 1990)* (1992) 95 Cr App R (S) 296.
42 *CPS v F* [2011] EWCA Crim 1844.
43 Ibid, at [16]

18.48

It is noteworthy that this guideline case was handed down eight years *before* the implementation of the Human Rights Act 1998 and is silent about Article 6, with defence submissions having relied instead on Clause 29 of the Magna Carta. The judgment was issued at a time when applications based on delay were said to have 'increased alarmingly', with the final paragraph of the judgment expressing the hope that there would be a 'significant reduction in such applications'. Despite this, in *R v F* the Court of Appeal noted that the judgment '… continues to provide the benchmark' on abuse arguments based on delay.[44]

18.49

R v S (SP)[45] saw the Court of Appeal re-state the principles set out in *Attorney General's Reference (No 1 of 1990)* and confirm the following principles of relevance to applications to stay the proceedings based on delay:[46]

> 'i. Even where delay is unjustifiable, a permanent stay should be the exception rather than the rule
>
> ii. Where there is no fault on the part of the complainant or the prosecution, it will be very rare for a stay to be granted
>
> iii. No stay should be granted in the absence of serious prejudice to the defence so that no fair trial can be held
>
> iv. When assessing possible serious prejudice, the judge should bear in mind his or her power to regulate the admissibility of evidence and that the trial process itself should ensure that all relevant factual issues arising from delay will be placed before the jury for their consideration in accordance with appropriate direction from the judge
>
> v. If, having considered all these factors, a *judge's assessment is that a fair trial will be possible, a stay should not be granted.'*

18.50

In *F(S)* it was confirmed that an application to stay on the grounds of delay must be determined in accordance with *Attorney-General's Reference (No 1) of 1990* and such applications will not succeed unless, exceptionally a fair trial is no longer possible owing to prejudice to the defendant occasioned by the delay which cannot fairly be addressed in the normal trial process. The explanation or justification for the delay was said to be relevant, only insofar as it bore on that question.

---

44 Ibid, at [38].
45 *R v S (SP)* [2006] EWCA Crim 756.
46 *Attorney General's Reference (No 2 of 2001)* at [21].

DELAY AND HALF-TIME SUBMISSIONS

18.51

In *CPS v S* the Court of Appeal also decried the conflation of the tests for abuse of process and application of the *Galbraith*[47] principles stating:

> In our judgment any suggestion that, on the basis of delay, the judge may be responsible for assessing whether in advance of a conviction, the conviction would be unsafe, is based on a misunderstanding of the principles in both *Galbraith* and *Attorney-General's Reference No 1 of 1990*. The judge, of course, is responsible for the conduct of the trial. That responsibility extends to deciding whether the trial should be stayed because it would constitute an abuse of process, applying the principles relevant to that question, and the distinct, separate question, whether at the end of the prosecution case, the jury should be directed to return a "not guilty" verdict or verdicts on Galbraith principles. These are distinct features of the trial process and neither of these separate responsibilities of the judge should be elided with each other, or with the equally distinct responsibilities of the jury.[48]

DELAY AND SEXUAL OFFENCES

18.52

In the same case, the Court of Appeal resisted any suggestion that there should be a different approach for sexual assault cases, noting that in the overwhelming majority of historic sex allegations the reasons for the delayed complaint, and whether and how the delay is explained or justified, bore directly on the *credibility* of the complainant, which remained an issue for the jury.

18.53

The appellate cases on delay and abuse emphasise that when assessing such applications, the court should have regard to the power of the judge at common law and under PACE 1984 to regulate the admissibility of evidence. The Court of Appeal said in *Attorney General's Reference (No 1 of 1990)* that the trial process itself '… should ensure that all relevant factual issues arising from delay will be placed before the jury as part of the evidence for their consideration, together with the powers of the trial judge to give appropriate directions to the jury before they consider their verdict'.[49]

---

47 *R v Galbraith* [1981] 2 All ER 2016.

48 *CPS v S* [2011] EWCA Crim 1844, 2011 WL 2747935, see para.39

49 *Attorney General's Reference (No 1 of 1990)* [1992] 1 QB 630 CA p 7.

DELAY AS A FACTOR OF MITIGATION

18.54

Where delay is not so severe as to justify a termination of the proceedings, it may form mitigation which warrants some adjustment to the sentence to be passed. The *Sentencing Guideline for Overarching Principles* identify 'delay since apprehension' as a mitigating feature, stating that: 'Where there has been an unreasonable delay in proceedings since apprehension which is not the fault of the offender, the court may take this into account by reducing the sentence *if this has had a detrimental effect on the offender*' [emphasis added].

18.55

In *Mills,* Lord Hope recognised that delay could, in an appropriate case, justify an adjustment to sentence with it causing two elements of prejudice to the appellant: 'One was the anxiety resulting from prolongation of the proceedings. The other was that his life had changed during the period of the delay.'[50]

18.56

In *R v Prenga*, the Court held:

> We start by considering the nature and extent of the discretion to adjust otherwise lawful sentences where required to achieve justice. It is, in this regard, well established that a sentencing judge may reduce the sentence that would otherwise be imposed to achieve justice and to reflect exceptional factors. The paradigm illustration flows out of the requirement in ECHR article 6 that proceedings must be concluded within a reasonable time. Where proceedings are unduly delayed that delay may count as a mitigating factor in appropriate circumstances. The threshold is necessarily a high one.[51]

50 *Mills (Kenneth Anthony) v HM Advocate* [2002] UKPC D2 at [54].
51 *R v Prenga* [2017] EWCA Crim 2149.

19 The media

Áine Josephine Tyrrell

INTRODUCTION

19.1

One of the fundamental principles underpinning domestic legislature is open justice or that justice should be administered in public. Hence, proceedings are open to the public, evidence is communicated publicly, and the media is permitted to publish fair, accurate, and contemporaneous reports of proceedings.[1] However, with the rise of the internet and of social media, there has been an increase in excessive and unethical media coverage of criminal cases. The 'trial by media' phenomenon sees coverage infringing on the presumption of the accused's innocence by stating premature judgements, disclosing unflattering personal details or evidence at the pre-trial stage, or otherwise using prejudicial language when describing the defendant.[2]

19.2

As public authorities bound by the Human Rights Act 1998, the courts have a duty to act in accordance with the European Convention of Human Rights (ECHR).[3] However, with respect to media reporting of criminal proceedings, tensions exist between the right to freedom of expression under Article 10 of the ECHR, the right to a public hearing under Article 6 and an individual's right to privacy under Article 8. Thus, it is the Court's duty to balance a person's right to a private life against the rights of the media and the public in each case such that any restriction they place on the public's right to public proceedings is proportionate, necessary, and convincingly established.[4]

---

1 This commitment is reflected in Criminal Procedure Rules 2020, r 6.2(1). See also Judicial College (2022), *Reporting Restrictions in the Criminal Courts,* September 2022. Available at: www.judiciary.uk/guidance-and-resources/reporting-restrictions-in-the-criminal-courts-4th-edition-update/.

2 ARISA Project (2021) 'Balance the Tight to a Fair Trial with the Public's Right to Know' in *The Presumption of Innocence and the Media Coverage of Criminal Cases: Case Study Analysis*, Center for the Study of Democracy. Available at: https://arisa-project.eu/the-presumption-of-innocence-and-the-media-coverage-of-criminal-cases-2/12/.

3 Human Rights Act 1998, s 6(1).

4 *Re S (A Child) (Identification: Restrictions on Publication)* [2005] 1 AC 593; *Re Trinity Mirror plc* [2008] EWCA Crim 50

ARTICLE 10: FREEDOM OF EXPRESSION

19.3

Article 10 of the ECHR reads as follows:

> 10(1): 'Everyone has the right to freedom of expression. This right shall include freedom to hold opinions and to receive and impart information and ideas without interference by public authority and regardless of frontiers.'[5]
>
> 10(2): 'The exercise of these freedoms, since it carries with it duties and responsibilities, may be subject to such formalities, conditions, restrictions or penalties that are prescribed law and are necessary in a democratic society, in the interests of national security, territorial integrity or public safety, for the prevention of disorder or crime, for the protection of health or morals, for the protection of the reputation or rights of others, for preventing the disclosure of information received in confidence, or for maintaining the authority and impartiality of the judiciary.'[6]

19.4

These principles have been incorporated into domestic law via the Human Rights Act 1998, Article 10. Parliament has also recognised the importance of protecting the media from liability for contempt of court and defamation in the exercise of their function of providing the public fair, accurate and contemporaneous reports of court proceedings through section 4(1) of the Contempt of Court Act 1981 and section 14 of the Defamation Act 1996.

19.5

For its part, the judiciary has also recognised the value transparency brings to the quality of justice and how the media, as public watchdog, bolsters public confidence in the justice system in common law.[7] In *R v Legal Aid Board ex parte Kaim Todner (A firm)*, Lord Woolf MR described the importance of the media for criminal proceedings:

> The need to be vigilant arises from the natural tendency for the general principle to be eroded and for exceptions to grow by accretion as the exceptions are applied by analogy to existing cases. This is the reason it is so important not to forget why proceedings are required to be subjected to the full glare of a public hearing. It is necessary because the public nature of the proceedings deters inappropriate behaviour on the part of the court. It also maintains the public's confidence in

---

5 Convention for the Protection of Human Rights and Fundamental Freedoms (European Convention on Human Rights, as amended) (ECHR).

6 Ibid.

7 *Observer and Guardian v UK* (1992) 14 EHRR 153 at [59].

> the administration of justice. It enables the public to know that justice is being administered impartially. It can result in evidence becoming available which would not become available if the proceedings were conducted behind closed doors or with one or more of the parties' or witnesses' identity concealed. It makes uninformed and inaccurate comment about the proceedings less likely … Any interference with the public nature of court proceedings is therefore to be avoided unless justice requires it. However, Parliament has recognised there are situations where interference is necessary.[8]

The strict liability rule

19.6

The media's role as a public watchdog is bound by the strict liability rule. Conduct is regarded as being in contempt of court if, regardless of the author's intent, it interferes, or risks interfering or prejudicing, the course of justice in live proceedings.[9] The rule only applies once the first step in the proceedings has been taken. That concerns a suspect has been placed under arrest.

19.7

In practice, the provisions of the Contempt of Court Act 1981 mean that ignorance of the law or of the existence of reporting restrictions/their substance is not a defence if contempt is committed[10]. It is also important to note that the breadth of the definition of 'publication' provided in section 2(1) of the Contempt of Court Act 1981 means strict liability applies to traditional newspapers and broadcasts as well as to online media and individual social media users.[11]

Restrictions on reporting: CrimPR and CPS guidelines

19.8

Similarly, the Crown Prosecution Service (CPS) has published legal guidance for prosecutors on reporting restrictions to safeguard against the media or online content prejudicing the outcome of an ongoing/active proceedings. Throughout these guidelines, the CPS emphasises that Article 10 is a *qualified* right (my emphasis) meaning interference may be appropriate 'where this is necessary and proportionate in pursuit of a legitimate aim such as the protection

8 *R v Legal Aid Board ex parte Kaim Todner (A firm)* [1999] QB 966 [977].
9 Contempt of Court Act 1981, s 1.
10 'Restrictions on Reporting' (Judicial College) 13.
11 Ibid.

of the rights of others to a fair trial (Article 6, ECHR), or to privacy (Article 8, ECHR)'.[12]

19.9

This Guidance echoes Part 6 of the Criminal Procedure Rules (CrimPR), which sets out the procedure for imposing restrictions on media reporting, on public access to hearings, and/or withholding information from the public during an otherwise public hearing.[13] This also specifies where and how the court can vary or remove a statutory restriction on reporting, where it can order a trial in private, and when the court can allow recording or other electronic communication during a hearing.[14]In deference to the open justice principle, the CrimPR highlight how, in exercising these powers, the court must have regard to a number of factors. These include dealing with criminal cases in public and allowing a public hearing to be reported to the public.

ARTICLE 6: RIGHT TO A PUBLIC TRIAL

19.10

As discussed further in Chapter 24, Article 6 has been incorporated into UK domestic law via the Human Rights Act 1998, specifically Schedule 1, sections 1 to 4. Section 1 is of particular relevance here as it reads:

> '1. In the determination of his civil rights and obligations or of any criminal charge against him, everyone is entitled to a fair and public hearing within a reasonable time by an independent and impartial tribunal established by law. Judgment shall be pronounced publicly but the press and public may be excluded from all or part of the trial in the interests of morals, public order or national security in a democratic society, where the interests of juveniles or the protection of the private life of the parties so require, or to the extent strictly necessary in the opinion of the court in special circumstances where publicity would prejudice the interests of justice.'

19.11

In *Global Torch v Apex Global Management Ltd* [2013] 1 WLR 2993 (CA), the Court held that hearings in public and media reporting were fundamental to open justice and, as such, Articles 6 and Article 10 of the ECHR would generally trump witnesses' and parties' rights under *Article 8*. However, in *Hauschildt v Denmark*,[15] the European Court of Human Rights recognised that a campaign

12 Crown Prosecution Service (May 2022), *Contempt of Court, Reporting Restrictions and Restrictions on Public Access to Hearings*, London: HMSO.

13 CrimPR 2020, r 6.1–6.5.

14 Ibid.

15 *Hauschildt v Denmark* (Application no 10486/83), 24 May 1989 .

of extremely negative press during and about a criminal case may impact the fairness of the trial and, more particularly, the impartiality of the jury.

Restrictions on reporting under section 11 of the Contempt of Court Act 1981

19.12

It is for this reason that the domestic courts can withhold material from the public where they are satisfied that publication of certain matters or details would impede the administration of justice. Where the Court decides to exercise said power in criminal proceedings, it may make directions under section 11 of the Contempt of Court Act 1981. The principles on which such a departure from the open justice rule is permitted were identified by Lord Diplock in *AG v Leveller Magazine* [1979] AC 440:

> However, since the purpose of the general rule is to serve the ends of justice it may be necessary to depart from it where the nature or circumstances of the particular proceeding are such that the application of the general rule in its entirety would frustrate or render impracticable the administration of justice or would damage some other public interest for whose protection Parliament has made some statutory derogation from the rule.

19.13

In *Re Times Newspapers; R v Abdulaziz* [2016] EWCA Crim 887, the *Times* appealed against an order made under section 11 of the Contempt of Court Act 1981 by relying on section 159(1) of the Criminal Justice Act 1988.[16] In dismissing the appeal, the Gross LJ clarified that:

> [O]pen justice is a fundamental principle of the common law; the test for departure is one of necessity – nothing less will do [...] For the Court to have power to give directions prohibiting the publication of a "matter", the Court must first have (1) allowed the matter to be withheld from the public in proceedings before the Court; and (2) have had power to allow that matter to be thus withheld [...] [D]irections prohibiting publication are thus linked to the purpose for which the matter was withheld in the first place.[17]

16 Section 159(1) of this Act states: 'A person aggrieved may appeal to the Court of Appeal, if that court grants leave, against – (a) an order under section [...]11 of the Contempt of Court Act 1981 made in relation to a trial on indictment; [...] (c) any order restricting the publication of any report of the whole or any part of the trial on indictment or any such ancillary proceedings.'

17 These principles are reflected in CrimPD 2020 6B.4 which states that orders to this effect must stipulate whether the making of or the specific terms of the order may be reported, not to mention whether this itself is prohibited; care must be taken that information heard *in camera* and subject to a restriction is not inadvertently mentioned in open court.

Thus, it is not appropriate for the Court to withhold matters under section 11 because of the defendant's discomfort or feelings.[18] Similarly, section 11 cannot be used to prevent damage to reputation to or financial losses for the defendant.[19]

19.14

In *Osman v United Kingdom* [1998] 29 EHRR 245, a section 11 order was sought on the grounds of Article 2 of the ECHR:[20] the claimant submitted that his identification would expose him to real and immediate risk to his life and, as such, the state's duty to protect was engaged. The Court held that, in such cases, the courts would consider whether the fear is well-founded.[21] The applicant would have to provide evidence of how the publication of their name/address would create or materially increase the risk of death or serious injury.[22]

Statutory restrictions on reporting

19.15

Outside section 11 of the Contempt of Court Act 1981, there are a number of automatic restrictions that relate to media reports of interim and pre-trial hearings in criminal proceedings. Some of these include:

(a) unsuccessful dismissal proceedings made in the Crown Court cannot be reported until the conclusion of the trial';[23]

(b) reporting on special measure directions, directions relating to the accused's use of 'live link', or prohibitions preventing an accused from cross-examining a witness in person cannot be reported until the conclusion of proceedings;[24]

(c) section 41 of the Criminal Procedure and Investigations Act 1996 and section 8C of the Magistrates' Courts Act 1980, relate to restricting the reporting on the admissibility of evidence or legal issues until the end of the trial;

(d) section 52A of the Crime and Disorder Act 1998 states that, when a suspect appears in the magistrates' court and the court decides to send the matter to the Crown court, there is an automatic reporting restriction preventing the reporting of that decision bar certain specified facts, namely the name of the accused, the court, and the charges they face;

---

18 *Evesham Justices ex parte McDonagh* [1988] QB 553.

19 See: *R v Dover JJ ex parte Dover District Council* 156 JP 433, DC.

20 Article 2 of the ECHR is the 'Right to Life' such that 'everyone's right to life shall be protected by law'.

21 *Re Officer L* [2007] UKHL 36.

22 'Restrictions on Reporting' (Judicial College) 27.

23 'Reporting in Criminal Proceedings: Guidance for Journalists' *Attorney General's Office*. Available at: www.ipso.co.uk/media/ 1717/ anonymity-principles-guide-v2.pdf.

24 Ibid.

(e) section 71 of the Criminal Justice Act 2003 prohibits the reporting of prosecution appeals against rulings that terminate proceedings from the moment the prosecution informs the court of their intention to appeal. These restrictions apply in Crown Court, Court of Appeal or Supreme Court proceedings. Only certain specified factual information is exempt such as the identification of the court, judge, defendant, witnesses, lawyers, place and date etc;[25] and

(f) section 49 of the Children and Young Persons Act 1933 states that, whilst the media is permitted to attend hearings in youth court,[26] they cannot publish information that may lead to a minor's identification – whether witness, victim, or accused. This prohibition extends to appeals that were originally heard in the youth court as well as to proceedings in the magistrates' court pertaining to breaches, revocation, and/or amendment of youth rehabilitation orders.[27]

Breaches of these restrictions are criminal offences and may also amount to contempt of court. As with section 11 orders, the Court may lift automatic reporting restrictions but only upon concluding it is in the interests of justice to do so.

Defendants under 18

19.16

In *McKerry v Teesdale and Wear Valley Justices,* Lord Bingham, CJ emphasised that the Court must also have regard to particular considerations when deliberating whether to restrict public access to proceedings and/or media reporting when the defendants are under 18.[28] The considerations, and related domestic and international instruments, are:

(a) duties under section 37 of the Crime and Disorder Act 1998 to consider the principle aim of the youth justice system: to prevent offending by children and young persons;

(b) obligations under section 44 of the CYPA 1933 to have regard to the welfare of the child or young person;

(c) The Right to Privacy under Article 8 of the ECHR, particularly as it is interpreted in the UN Convention of the Rights of the Child and the UN Standard Minimum Rules for the Administration of Justice 1985[29] (the Beijing Rules); and

25 'Reporting on Criminal Proceedings' (Judicial College) 16.

26 It is important to note that proceedings in the Youth Court are not open to the general public.

27 Attorney General's Office, 4.

28 *McKerry v Teesdale and Wear Valley Justices* [2001] EMLR 5.

29 United Nations Standard Minimum Rules for the Administration of Justice (The Beijing Rules) (adopted 29 November 1985) UNGA Res 40/33.

(d) Obligations under Article 3 of the UN Convention on the Rights of the Child, that requires the 'best interests of the child' to be a 'primary consideration' though, admittedly, not necessarily the prevalent one.[30]

19.17

In the case of *T v United Kingdom and V v United Kingdom*,[31] the ECtHR considered whether two defendants – both of whom were just 11 years of age at the time of the trial – received a fair trial in light of the extremely high levels of interest their case had generated amongst the press. The domestic proceedings had taken place in open, adult court despite the defendants' age and no special restrictions were placed on media reporting. While the UK relied on Article 6 of the ECHR and the importance of public trials for the transparent administration of justice in their defence, the ECtHR held that the proceedings could have been conducted in a more appropriate court better protect the two minors' privacy without sacrificing the need for open justice. The Court held that this, coupled with the excessive media coverage and other factors, meant that the applicants had not received a fair hearing, which was in breach of Article 6.

Postponement orders and discretionary restrictions

19.18

It is also within the courts' power to hold proceedings in private. Needless to say, such measures severely impact the general public's right to be informed and, as such, are only to be adopted in exceptional circumstances.[32]

19.19

The courts will typically attempt to prevent any prejudice to a trial process by adopting less extreme measures. Discretionary reporting restrictions such as postponement orders under section 4(2) of the Contempt of Court Act 1981 are prime examples of lesser measures. These are typically made when disputed applications to admit evidence or other matters are discussed in open court but without the jury present. This means that any publication of these matters could prejudice the proceedings.[33] Similarly, if there are two or more trials taking place which are connected, publication of fair, accurate and contemporaneous reports on one trial could prejudice the other, connected proceedings. It is important to note that a court can only order the postponement of fair, accurate and contemporaneous reports under section 4(2) meaning it has no power

30 UN Convention on the Rights of the Child (adopted 20 November 1989, entered into force 2 September 1990) UNGA Res 44/25.

31 *T v United Kingdom and V v United Kingdom* (Application no 24724/94), 16 December 1999.

32 *AG v Leveller Magazine* [1979] AC 440, 450; *R v Times Newspapers Ltd* [2009] 1 WLR 1015.

33 'Restrictions on Reporting' (Judicial College) 30.

to suppress the publication of other matters such as those not admitted into evidence or prejudicial comments relating to the proceedings.[34]

19.20

The Court of Appeal has a similar power to postpone media reports on proceedings under section 82 of the CJA 2003, when this reporting could prejudice the administration of justice in a retrial. In these orders the Court can specify the postponement period and the order typically expires following the conclusion of the trial.[35]

19.21

When deciding whether to issue a postponement order, the court must adopt a three-stage approach as detailed by Longmore LJ in *R v Sherwood (ex p the Telegraph Group plc)*.[36] The Judicial College summarised this approach as follows:

(1) Would reporting give rise to a substantial risk of prejudice to the administration of justice in the relevant proceedings (ie, the current proceedings or proceedings that are pending or imminent)? If not, no order should be made.

(2) Is a section 4(2) order necessary? It will only be necessary if it would eliminate the risk and the risk could not satisfactorily be overcome by some lesser restriction.

(3) If there is no other way of eliminating the perceived risk of prejudice, is the degree of risk tolerable as being 'the lesser of two evils' balancing the competing public interests in a fair trial and open justice under Articles 6 and 10 of the ECHR?[37]

The courts should also consider whether an order under section 45(4) of the SCA 1981 would be sufficient to prevent the identified risk – (eg, postponing the identification of certain persons involved in the trail or particular matters in the case).

19.22

Outside of postponement orders, other lesser measures invoked to avoid private hearings include allowing a witness to give evidence from behind a screen, giving the judge the witness's name via hand-passed note, identifying a witness by a pseudonym (usually a letter of the alphabet) and/or prohibiting the publication of a witness's true name via an anonymity order under section 11 of the Contempt of Court Act 1981. In the event that hearing parts of a case in private proves unavoidable, the Judicial College has advised that the courts

34 *Galbraith v Her Majesty's Advocate, High Court of Justiciary,* 7 September 2000, adopted by the Court of Appeal *in R v B* [2006] EWCA Crim 2692 at [24]–[25].

35 Ibid.

36 [2001] EWCA Crim 1075 and approved by the Privy Council in *Independent Publishing Co Ltd* [2005]1 AC 190 at [69].

37 *R v Sherwood (ex p the Telegraph Group plc)* [2001] EWCA Crim 1075 at [31]–[32].

should revert to proceedings in open court as soon as privacy is no longer necessary.[38]

ARTICLE 8: RIGHT TO RESPECT FOR PRIVATE AND FAMILY LIFE[39]

19.23

In *R (Rai) v Crown Court at Winchester*, Warby, LJ stated that any restriction on the open justice and freedom of expression principles will not only be exceptional, but the burden of proof is on the party seeking the restriction: 'they must establish it is a necessity on the basis of clear and cogent evidence'.[40] Many of the restrictions that can be made have already been detailed in the previous sections. There are, however, a few remaining that should be noted. In the following cases information that would likely lead to the identification of a victim and/or complainant cannot be published from the moment that the allegation is made:

(a) section 1 of the Sexual Offences (Amendment) Act 1992, which provides lifelong anonymity to complainants and victims of sexual offences;[41]

(b) section 122A of the Anti-Social Behaviour, Crime and Policing Act 2014 and section 4A of the Female Genital Mutilation Act 2003 afford victims and complainants of forced marriage and female genital mutilation lifelong anonymity;

(c) section 2 of the Modern Slavery Act 2015 imposes a lifetime ban on reporting any matter likely to lead to the identification of a victim of human trafficking offences. These offences do not need to be sexual in nature but involve a person arranging or facilitating the travel of another person within or between countries with a view to their being exploited;[42] and

(d) section 13 of the Education Act 2011 amended the Education Act 2002 to provide anonymity to a teacher when an allegation is made by a pupil at their school (or someone on a pupil's behalf) against them stating that they have committed a criminal offence. Section 13 prevents publications from identifying the teacher until proceedings against them have been initiated.

---

38 'Restrictions on Reporting' (Judicial College) 12.

39 See Chapter 30.

40 *R (Rai) v Crown Court at Winchester* [2021] EWCA Civ 604 at [22]. See also *re S (FC) (a child) (Appellant)* [2004] UKHL 47.

41 In *R (Press Association) v Cambridge Crown Court* [2012] EWCA Crim 2434 [15]–[17], the Court found that SOA 1992 does not restrict the naming of a defendant or of witnesses other than the complainant in a sex case.

42 Modern Slavery Act 2015, s 1 states that 'exploitation' includes domestic servitude, sexual exploitation, forced labour, organ harvesting, or any other service if secured through the use of force, threats, or deception.

19.24

It should be noted that whereas youth victims, witnesses, and defendants' anonymity is protected by statutory provisions when proceedings are held in the youth court, their anonymity is not automatically protected in criminal proceedings held in the adult magistrates' court or the Crown Court unless the proceeding falls under the statutory provisions listed above. However, the courts can impose discretionary reporting restrictions to prevent their identification in the media under sections 45 and 45A of the Youth Justice and Criminal Evidence Act 1999. Whereas section 45 orders expire once the party turns 18 (unless a further order is made), orders made under section 45A can impose lifelong anonymity on a youth victim or witness.

19.25

Under section 46 of the YJCEA 1999, the courts can also impose lifetime anonymity on an adult witness and/or victim, or on the identification of children if this identification would lead to the identification of an adult witness. The Judicial College indicated that there is no statutory provision that confers the Court with powers to order lifelong anonymity for a criminal defendant, regardless of whether they are an adult or a minor.[43] One of the few exceptions is the High Court's power to grant an injunction – referred to as the 'Venables jurisdiction' – under section 6(1) of the HRA 1998 [44] and section 37 of the Senior Courts Act 1981.[45]

19.26

Venables was the first instance in which the 'Venables jurisdiction' was recognised. Dame Elisabeth Butler-Sloss P granted a lifelong injunction to protect Jon Venables and Robert Thompson, two eleven-year-old defendants who had become notorious by virtue of being convicted of the murder of James Bulger, aged two. The Court held:

> In the present case the reason for advancing that special quality [of protection] is that, if the information was published, the publication would be likely to lead to grave and possibly fatal consequences. In my judgement, the court does have the jurisdiction, in exceptional cases, to extend the protection of confidentiality of information, even to impose restrictions on the press, where not to do so would be likely to lead to serious physical injury, or to the death, of the person seeking that confidentiality, and there is no other way to protect the applicants other than by seeking relief from the court.[46]

---

43 'Restrictions on Reporting' (Judicial College) 36.

44 HRA 1998, s 6(1) states: 'It is unlawful for a public authority to act in a way which is incompatible with a Convention right.'

45 SCA 1981, s 37(1) and (2) state: '(1) The High Court may be order (whether interlocutory or final) grant an injunction or appoint a receiver in all cases in which it appears to the court to be just and convenient to do so; (2) Any such order may be made either unconditionally or on such terms and conditions as the court thinks just.'

46 *Venables v News Group Newspapers* [2001] Fam 430 at [81].

19.27

The Judiciary College has underscored that the exercise of the Venables jurisdiction is rare and has, to date, typically been used to protect the new identities of notorious offenders upon their release.[47] It has been invoked when the defendant's identification in the media places them at real and immediate risk of death or serious injury, thus engaging the state's duty to protect under Articles 2 and 3 of the ECHR.[48]

19.28

Finally, *Sir Cliff Richard OBE v British Broadcasting Company and The Chief Constable of South Yorkshire*[49] points to another (ongoing) privacy debate, this one relating to anonymity for suspects of offences. In 2014, Sir Cliff Richard, the popular singer, was a suspect in an investigation of historic child sexual abuse. Sir Cliff was neither arrested nor charged as part of the South Yorkshire Police's investigation, yet the raid that was conducted on his private residence in 2014 was covered by the BBC and resulted in a media furore.

19.29

In bringing the claim, Sir Cliff claimed that both the BBC and the SYP violated his right to privacy under Article 8; he claimed substantial damages because both his life and his finances had been irrevocably impacted by the media attention the BBC had spawned. In weighing Article 8 against Article 10 considerations, Mann, J ultimately held that, as a matter of general principle, a suspect in a police investigation has a reasonable expectation of privacy:

> It seems to me that on the authorities, and as a matter of general principle, a suspect has a reasonable expectation of privacy in relation to a police investigation, and I so rule. As a general rule is it understandable and justifiable (and reasonable) that a suspect would not wish others to know of the investigation because of the stigma attached. It is, as a general rule, not necessary for anyone outside the investigating force to know, and the consequences of wider knowledge have been made apparent in many cases. If the presumption of innocence were perfectly understood and given effect to, and if the general public was universally capable of adopting a completely open- and broad-minded view of the fact of an investigation so that there was no risk of taint either during the investigation or afterwards (assuming no charge) then the position might be different. But neither of those things is true. [50]

47 'Restrictions on Reporting' (Judicial College) 36.

48 *Ibid.*

49 *Sir Cliff Richard OBE v British Broadcasting Company and The Chief Constable of South Yorkshire [2018] EWHC 1837 (Ch)*

50 Ibid, at [248].

19.30

Since this time, the campaign group FAIR (Falsely Accused Individuals for Reform) has renewed its calls for making the naming of sexual offence suspects pre-charge a criminal offence.[51] Critics, however, are concerned that such an amendment would not only undermine Articles 6 and 10, but would also undermine sexual offence victims' belief in the police and the criminal justice system. [52]

19.31

In *Alaedeen Sicri v Associated Newspapers Limited*, a case was brought against newspapers for their coverage of Mr Sicri's arrest in connection with the Manchester Arena bombing. Warby J reaffirmed that an individual under investigation has a reasonable expectation of privacy in respect of information 'that they have come under suspicion by the state[.]' [53]Most recently, *Bloomberg LP v ZXC*,[54] the Supreme Court built upon the general principle articulated above and in *Murray v Express Newspapers Ltd*:[55]

> [W]e understand that the reference to a general rule or general starting point means that once it is established that the relevant information was that a person, prior to being charged, was under criminal investigation then the correct approach is for a court to start with the proposition that there will be a reasonable expectation of privacy in respect of such information.

51 David Brown 'Cliff Richard plea to MPs for suspect anonymity' (*The Times*, 9 June 2022). Available at: www.thetimes.co.uk/ article/cliff-richard-appeal-women-mps-support-anonymity-suspects-cchxk0pkb.
52 'Sir Cliff Richard urges anonymity for sex offence suspects' (*BBC News*, 8 June 2022). Available at: www.bbc.co.uk/news/uk-politics-61737406.
53 *Alaedeen Sicri v Associated Newspapers Limited* [2020] EWHC 3541 (QB) at [75].
at [75].
54 *Bloomberg LP v ZXC* [2022] UKSC 5 at [70].
55 *Murray v Express Newspapers Ltd* [2009] Ch 481. Particularly the Court's formulation of the so-called 'Murray factors'.

20 Disclosure

David Rhodes and Katrina Walcott

INTRODUCTION

20.1

Disclosure is one of the most fundamental and contentious, aspects of the right to a fair trial.[1] Article 6(3)(b) of the European Convention on Human Rights (ECHR) guarantees the accused 'adequate time and facilities for the preparation of his defence', which includes access to material which may undermine the prosecution case or assist his case. There must be an 'equality of arms'. Yet, in an adversarial system, the prosecution is responsible for collecting that material and making the initial assessment as to whether it is relevant and should be disclosed or withheld in the public interest. This chapter explores the tensions inherent in that paradox and the ways in which the domestic and Strasbourg courts have defined a range of principles to ensure the law is compatible with the Convention.

20.2

While there is an absolute right to a fair trial under Article 6(1), and as the European Court (ECtHR) has acknowledged, the entitlement to disclosure of relevant evidence is not an absolute right. It may be limited in pursuit of legitimate aims, such as the protection of national security or rights of others. Notwithstanding, such restrictions on the rights of the defence should be strictly necessary and counterbalanced by procedural safeguards to ensure the accused is protected.[2]

DISCLOSURE AND THE REQUIREMENTS OF THE CONVENTION

20.3

The principal authority from Strasbourg on the question of pre-trial disclosure is *Jespers v Belgium*[3] in which the Commission expounded the principle of' 'equality of arms'. The applicant was accused of attempted murder – he

1 See Lord Steyn comments in *R v Winston Brown* [1995] 1 Cr App R 191, CA, at 198.

2 *Rowe and Davis v UK* (2000) 30 EHRR1, para 61. *See also Jasper v UK* (2000) 30 EHRR 441, paras 43 and 52.

3 *Jespers v Belgium* (1981) 27 DR61.

complained that the prosecuting authorities withheld a 'special folder' containing relevant information. The Commission placed considerable importance on the disparity of resources and power between the prosecution and the defence in criminal cases. Considering the meaning of 'facilities' in Article 6 (3)(b), the Commission found that an 'equality of arms' could only be achieved if the prosecution was under a duty to use its police machinery, considerable technical resources and means of coercion to gather evidence in favour of the accused as well as evidence against him.

20.4

This judgment has far-reaching significance. Note first, that the duty of disclosure must begin *early* in the proceedings for the purpose of preparing the defence case. In *R v DPP, ex parte Lee*,[4] the Court held that disclosure begins early because some material, such as the previous convictions of a complainant, could reasonably assist the defence when applying for bail. Moreover, disclosure of the names of potential eyewitnesses which the Crown does not seek to rely on, might enable the defence team to interview those witnesses and make preparations for trial, whereas the value of that information might be significantly reduced if disclosure is delayed.

20.5

Secondly, the duty of disclosure under Article 6 is not limited to information which might exonerate the accused. It extends also to relevant material which might assist him in obtaining a reduction in sentence.[5] This extends to material which might support an application to exclude evidence, or to stay proceedings as an abuse of process, or which might lead to a finding of incompatibility with the Convention.[6] The emphasis in *Jespers*, on the greater resources of the State and entitlement and potential access to all relevant material, provides a foundation for applications to stay proceedings as an abuse of process. This occurs where prosecuting authorities have failed to secure and disclose evidence which could have been collected had they properly discharged its obligations. This has become a frequent occurrence in respect of digital material and has also formed the basis for many high-profile appeals.[7] Notwithstanding this, it will be necessary to establish that the prosecution was under a duty to obtain that material and failed to make reasonable inquiries which subsequently compromises the fairness of the trial.[8]

---

4 *R v DPP, ex parte Lee* [1999] 2 Crim App R 304 – the issue was whether the duty of primary disclosure under the Criminal Procedure and Investigations Act 1996 (CPIA) arose before the committal proceedings.

5 *See A-G Guidelines on Disclosure*, May 2022, para 139.

6 *R v H and C* [2004] 2 AC 134, HL.

7 *See Hamilton v Post Office Ltd* [2021] EWCA Crim 577 – 39 appellants were held not to have received a fair trial due to the failure of the private prosecutor to disclose key information about the reliability of computer system data which formed the basis of the prosecution.

8 *See R v Feltham Magistrates' Court, ex p Ebrahim; Mouat v DPP* [2001] 2 Cr App R 23 and *R v Hewitt* [2020] EWCA Crim 1247.

20.6

Accordingly, failure by prosecuting authorities to disclose relevant material to the defence before the trial does not *automatically* lead to a violation of Article 6. In *Edwards v United Kingdom*,[9] the European Court held that it was the fairness of the proceedings as a whole mattered, and those proceedings included the appeal stage. In *Edwards*, the applicant complained that his right to a fair trial had been violated because the prosecution had not disclosed at trial that the victim failed to select his photograph in a police album and, the discovery of their neighbour's fingerprints at the scene. The Court of Appeal held that the newly disclosed material did not cast any doubt over the safety of the conviction. The European Court concluded that the appeal stage had cured the defect in the disclosure process because it afforded the accused the opportunity to know and challenge the previously undisclosed material. The 'equality of arms' was restored. Accordingly, there was no violation of Article 6.[10]

20.7

Furthermore, in *Preston v United Kingdom*,[11] the applicants complained of the non-disclosure of telephone intercept material obtained pursuant to the Interception of Communications Act 1985. The Commission rejected the applicants' complaint of a breach of Article 6 as they had failed to establish how the material could have assisted the defence case which had not been used by the prosecution during the trial as had merely been the starting point of the police investigation.

20.8

The failure by the prosecution to disclose evidence such that it compromises the fairness of the trial has been further considered in domestic case law. In *R v DS and Another*,[12] a decision to stay proceedings due to serious failings in the disclosure of unused evidence was overturned. Thomas LCJ held that alternative sanctions, such as a wasted costs order against the CPS or police, was the more proportionate and appropriate response. Distinguishing this case from *R v Boardman*,[13] it was concluded that a fair trial would be possible especially as the documents not disclosed were of 'limited materiality' and that there was a public interest in trying this case.[14]

20.9

In summary, the Strasbourg jurisprudence provides that fair disclosure is an inseparable part of the right to a fair trial. The key principle is that there should be an 'equality of arms' so that material uncovered by the prosecution during an

9 *Edwards v United Kingdom* (1992) 15 EHRR.417.

10 The European Court reached similar conclusions in *IJL, GMR and AKP v UK* (2001) 33 EHRR 1 and *Dowsett v UK* (2004) 38 EHRR 41.

11 *Preston v United Kingdom* (1997) EHRR 695.

12 *R v DS and Another* [2015] EWCA Crim 662.

13 *R v Boardman* [2015] EWCA Crim 175.

14 *R v DS and Another* [2015] EWCA Crim 662 at [70]–[72].

investigation is subject to an adversarial process. However, the failure to disclose will not always result in a breach of Article 6. The European Court nonetheless seeks to impose a positive and wide-ranging obligation on the prosecuting authorities to gather and disclose material which enables the accused to respond effectively to the charges laid against him. It is against this background that we now turn to examine the way in which the domestic law complies with Convention standards.

THE DEVELOPMENT OF DOMESTIC LAW

20.10

In parallel with the development of the Convention standards of disclosure and a fair trial, English law has witnessed a widening and then narrowing of the duty of disclosure. Criminal proceedings in England and Wales have been subject to a number of disclosure regimes in recent times. As the starting point for any argument about disclosure, it is important to determine which regime applies. For any alleged offence for which a criminal investigation began before 1 April 1997, only the common law principles apply. For cases in which the criminal investigation[15] began between that date and 4 April 2005, the Criminal Procedure and Investigations Act 1996 (CPIA) will apply. Where the criminal investigation began on or after 4 April 2005, CPIA 1996, as amended by the Criminal Justice Act 2003 (CJA) will apply. The revised code of practice, brought into operation on 31 December 2020, applies to criminal investigations which began on or before that date.

20.11

Furthermore, a number of additional guidance documents have been published, to be read in conjunction with the CPIA and Code of Practice. For instance, the most recent revised *Attorney General's Guidelines on Disclosure* took effect from 25 July 2022,[16] to replace the previous 2020 edition as well as the Supplementary Guidelines on Digital Material, issued in 2013.[17]

The common law prior to CPIA 1996

20.12

It is vital to understand the historical development of the law of disclosure. Prior to CPIA 1996, disclosure was dependant on the common law and the fairness of the police and prosecutors concerned.[18] Unfortunately, such a spirit of fair play

15 The meaning of 'criminal investigation' is defined broadly in CPIA 1996, s 1(4).

16 Attorney General's Office, *A-G Guidelines on Disclosure*, (May 2022).

17 Practitioners should also consider the *Judicial Protocol on the Disclosure of Unused Material in Criminal Cases*, which took effect in December 2013. Other guidance documents include the *CPS/Police Disclosure Manual* (CPS Disclosure Manual), December 2018 and Part 15 of the Criminal Procedure Rules (October 2020) and Criminal Practice Direction IV, [15A.1–2].

18 *See* Lord Denning in *Dallison v Caffery* [1965] 1 QB 348 at 369.

did not always abound. In the early 1990s numerous grave miscarriages of justice came to light which highlighted the deficiencies of such a trusting approach.

20.13

The 'catalogue of non-disclosure' in the case of *R v Ward*[19] proved a watershed. At the height of the IRA's bombing campaign in the early 1970s, Judith Ward was convicted of several charges of murder and causing explosions. The Crown's case rested mainly on her alleged confessions and on scientific evidence of traces of nitro-glycerine found on her person and property. Twenty years later, it was discovered that the prosecution had concealed scientific expert evidence which significantly undermined that evidence. It also became apparent that there existed little or no guidance for investigating officers as to the retention and recording of 'unused' material and whether to bring that information to the attention of the prosecution or defence.

20.14

The Court of Appeal condemned the 'woefully deficient' disclosure and set down a wide-ranging test which centred on the defendant's right to a fair trial.[20] More importantly, the Court stressed that the decision as to whether information should be withheld in the public interest was always for the Court, not the police or the prosecutor, to determine. With echoes of *Jespers*, the Court of Appeal acknowledged the 'undoubted inequality' of resources and access to forensic scientists as between prosecution and defence, could only be remedied by a wide-ranging duty of disclosure on the prosecution which 'extends to anything which may arguably assist the defence'.

20.15

That broad scope was then defined in *R v Keane*[21] with the 'materiality' test:

> '…that which can be seen on a sensible appraisal by the prosecution (1) to be relevant or possibly relevant to an issue in the case; (2) to raise or possibly raise a new issue whose existence is not apparent from the evidence which the prosecution proposes to use; (3) to hold out a real (as opposed to fanciful) prospect of providing a lead which goes to (1) or (2)'.

CPIA 1996

20.16

CPIA 1996, together with the subsequent Code of Practice,[22] provided for the first time a statutory framework governing the retention, recording and

---

19 *R v Ward* (1993) 96 Cr App R 1, CA.
20 Ibid, at [674].
21 *R v Keane* [1994] 2 All ER 478.
22 Issued under CPIA 1996, s 23.

disclosure of unused material, placing clear duties on the police and prosecutors.[23] It also had the clear objective of bringing about a significant restriction of the prosecution's common law duty of disclosure to roll back the broad and inclusive scope of *Ward* and *Keane*.

20.17

CPIA 1996 adopts a multi-stage process of disclosure. Section 3 provides for the initial stage of disclosure, imposing a duty on the prosecution to automatically disclose to the accused any prosecution material[24] not previously disclosed. This section, as amended by the CJA 2003, provides a unified and objective test for the prosecution to apply to unused evidence. This is whether material 'might reasonably be considered capable of (a) undermining the prosecution case or (b) assisting the case for the accused'.[25]

20.18

The second stage deals with the defence duties of disclosure and is detailed in sections 5–7A of CPIA. The defendant is required to serve a defence statement,[26] setting out the general nature of the defence and the matters in issue between the prosecution and defence. Following this, the prosecution must disclose any further material which has not been previously disclosed but might assist that defence case.[27] Under section 7A, the prosecution is under a continuing duty of review,[28] following the service of the defence statement and throughout the proceedings. Should the Crown fail to disclose further such material, then the accused can apply to the court under section 8 of CPIA 1996 for an order of specific disclosure.[29] The *Judicial Protocol on the Disclosure* emphasises that defence requests for specific disclosure of unused material which are not referable to any issue identified in the defence case statement should be rejected.[30] The CPIA regime subsequently provides for the making of comments by the prosecution and the drawing of adverse inferences where the accused advances a defence at trial in terms which differ from the content of the defence case statement.[31]

20.19

Several amendments to CPIA (some not yet in force) impose further duties of disclosure on the defence and give rise to questions of compatibility with the Convention. Notably, the defence is under a duty to notify the court and prosecutor as to any witnesses it intends to call and the identifying information

23 CPIA 1996 is supplemented by the *A-G Guidelines: Disclosure* – originally published in November 2000 and subsequently updated in 2005, 2013, 2020 and 2022.
24 *See* CPIA 1996, s 3(2) for the definition of 'prosecution material'.
25 Ibid, s 3(1)(a)
26 Ibid, s 6A. The defence case statement muse be served in Crown Court cases. For cases in the magistrates' court this is voluntary.
27 Ibid, s 7A.
28 Ibid.
29 The procedure for making s 8 applications is set out in the Criminal Procedure Rules 2020, r 15.5.
30 (December 2013), para 26.
31 CPIA 1996, s 11.

of such witnesses.[32] The notification of such details is designed to abolish trial by ambush. Other amendments, not yet in force, impose a requirement on the defence to disclose material, such as a defence statement, to any co-accused;[33] and to notify the prosecution of names of experts consulted by the defence even if not relied upon.[34] It also imposes a duty to provide an updated defence statement.[35] All of these duties may be enforced by way of sanctions for failure to disclose,[36] including further adverse inferences.

Development of disclosure in practice – post-CPIA 1996

20.20

In recent years, there have been significant developments in the law and application of disclosure in practice. There are numerous sources of guidance to help us better understand and apply disclosure. It is important to consider the context in which these developments were made, their impact and subsequent human rights issues involved.

20.21

There have been numerous editions of the *A-G Guidelines*. The most significant changes were introduced in 2013 and thereafter in 2020. The guidelines are not designed to be an unequivocal statement of the law although they assist practitioners to understand and apply statutory disclosure, which is maintained as good law.[37] Most recently, the *Guidelines* have aimed to alleviate the well-known failings in the application of disclosure in practice and re-emphasise the importance of disclosure, underlining the accused's right to a fair trial under Article 6 of the Convention.[38]

Issues with the application of disclosure

20.22

Despite the introduction of the 2013 *A-G Guidelines*, updating the *Code of Practice* in 2015 and further guidance documents issued to clarify and ensure the effective the application of CPIA 1996, there remained issues with disclosure in practice. Failings in the disclosure process led to the well-publicised breakdown of prosecutions and successful appeals.[39] The guidelines had previously done

32 Ibid, s 6C as inserted by CJA 2003, s 34.
33 Ibid, s 5(5A), (5B) and (5D), inserted by CJA 2003, s 33(1) (not yet in force).
34 Ibid, s 6D, inserted by CJA 2003, s 35 (not yet in force).
35 Ibid, s 6B, inserted by CJA 2003, s 33(3) (not yet in force).
36 Ibid, s 11 as inserted by CJA 2003, s 39 (not yet in force).
37 Geoffrey Cox QC MP, '*Review of the Efficiency and Effectiveness of Disclosure in the Criminal Justice System*' (November 2018), pp 10–13.
38 Attorney General's Office *A-G Guidelines on Disclosure*, (May 2022), at [1].
39 *Blackstone's Criminal Practice 2022*, D9.1.

little to address the problems with disclosure of voluminous and sensitive digital material, with which prosecuting authorities must increasingly contend.

20.23

The primary concern remains whether a defendant can receive a fair trial. In *R v Allan,*[40] the defence made repeated requests for disclosure of the complainant's phone records which were frequently dismissed as irrelevant. Furthermore, the police later admitted they struggled to deal with the volume of phone download and wrongly assured themselves they had analysed its entirety. Following *Allan,* various other cases were publicised which revealed the same issues[41] leading to a widescale CPS review of disclosure in rape and sexual assault cases in England and Wales in June 2018.[42] The CPS, along with the College of Policing, subsequently committed to a *National Disclosure Improvement Plan.*[43]

The guidelines

20.24

A subsequent *Review of the Efficiency and Effectiveness of Disclosure in the Criminal Justice System,* published in 2018, conducted a widescale examination of disclosure practices, guidelines, and legislation. It made several practical recommendations which were incorporated into the subsequent *A-G Guidelines.*

20.25

One of the important stated principles is that prosecutors should apply a 'thinking manner' to disclosure, so that it is not reduced to a box-ticking exercise. This means viewing material as part of context of the case as a whole; what the likely issues may be; and the impact on reasonable lines of inquiry, when making decisions about disclosure, rather than in isolation.[44] Outside the 'thinking approach', the 2020 revision introduced the rebuttable presumption practice. This pertains to categories of material presumed to meet the disclosure test, therefore it *should* and *must* be disclosed unless there is good reason not to do so.[45]

40 *See 'A Joint Review of the Disclosure Process in the Case of R v Allan: Findings and recommendations for the Metropolitan Police Service and CPS London'* (January 2018), pp 4–6.

41 *See* Dargue, 'An analysis of disclosure failings in murder appeals against conviction 2006–2018' (2020) Crim LR 707, 707–09.

42 Around 47 out of 3,637 cases reviewed were stopped during the process because of issues with the disclosure of unused material. In many cases, communications evidence, such as text messages and social media, were being examined late in the process and after charge.

43 NPCC, College of Policing and CPS (January 2018).

44 Attorney General's Office, *A-G Guidelines on Disclosure,* (May 2022), para 4.

45 Ibid, at [86]–[92].

20.26

Investigators and disclosure officers should apply the four R's: to *retain* and *record* relevant material, to *review* it and to *reveal* this material to the prosecutor.[46] As always, investigators are expected to maintain clear communication with the prosecution and a full log of disclosure decisions must be kept.[47] Schedules must contain clear and accurate descriptions so that prosecutors can identify important material.[48]

20.27

Disclosure Management Documents (DMDs), are prepared by the prosecutor and outline the 'strategy and approach' to disclosure.[49] They are designed to assist the court with case management and facilitate early defence engagement with the disclosure process.[50] They are especially important in the context of digital material.[51] DMDs should be served on the defence and court at an early stage and are considered 'living documents' to be updated as the case progresses.[52] DMDs are compulsory for all Crown Court cases and may be prepared for magistrate and youth court cases where beneficial.[53]

20.28

The *A-G Guidelines* emphasise the importance of the defence involvement in the process. Defence statements are described as being an 'integral' part of the process to ensure the prosecutor, court and other interested parties are alive to the relevant issues.[54] Where further disclosure is requested and is not relevant to issues set out in the initial defence statement, a further or amended defence statement is required.[55]

DISCLOSURE AND THE COMPATIBILITY WITH THE CONVENTION

20.29

A principle ongoing issue in recent times has been the compatibility of disclosure with Article 6 as well as with Article 8, the right to a private life. The recent *A-G Guidelines* encourage prosecuting authorities to be wary of the impact of their enquiries on an individual's right to privacy as well as other parties

46 Ibid, at [8].
47 Ibid, at [6] and [110].
48 Ibid, at [60]–[61]. See also Annex A, which contain specific provision for the recording and retention of digital material.
49 Ibid, at [93]. See also Annex C which provides a template for DMDs.
50 Ibid, at [94].
51 Ibid, at [58].
52 Attorney General's Office, *A-G Guidelines on Disclosure,* (May 2022), [86] and [97].
53 Ibid, at [96].
54 Ibid, at [123].
55 Ibid, at [131].

who may be subject of that material.[56] Disclosure of sensitive digital material is used as an example for which a careful balance needs to be struck.[57] The *Guidelines* provide a list of principles to be abided by.[58] Prosecuting authorities are reminded that pursuing a reasonable line of inquiry will not always justify obtaining personal information about a complainant or witness.

20.30

Investigators and prosecutors are reminded that where there is a conflict between Article 6 and 8 rights, the absolute nature of the right to a fair trial should be considered. Indeed, intrusion into privacy rights may be unavoidable and justifiable where it is no more than necessary.[59]

20.31

The *A-G Guidelines*, draw from the judgment in *R v Bater-James and Another*,[60] which addressed the issue of Article 8 and disclosure of digital material. In this case, the Court emphasised that complainants' right to privacy under Article 8 is not waived because a complaint is made. The Protocol holds that: 'The court, as a public authority, must ensure that any interference with the right … is in accordance with the law, and is necessary in pursuit of a legitimate public interest.'[61]

20.32

The Court subsequently warned investigators against 'fanciful or inherently speculative researches' of a complainant or witness's digital material, holding they must only seek to obtain and review this material where there was 'good cause' to do so.[62] The Court highlighted that there was no presumption that a complainant's device should be 'inspected, retained or downloaded' in sexual assault cases.[63] Consideration should be given to alternative sources of the information sought, where possible.[64] Notably, the Court recommended the use of key search terms of electronic downloads to necessarily narrow the parameters of examination.[65]

20.33

Furthermore, the Court recommended that complainants be updated about how their device will be copied, for how long it will be required and what will be extracted.[66] In following *R v PR*,[67] the Court provided that 'careful

56 Ibid, at [11].
57 Ibid, at [12].
58 Ibid, at [11]–[13].
59 Ibid at [13(h)].
60 *R v Bater-James and Another* [2020] EWCA Crim 790.
61 Ibid, at [47].
62 Ibid, at [70].
63 Ibid, at [77].
64 Ibid.
65 Ibid, at [82].
66 Ibid, at [92].
67 *R v PR* [2019] EWCA Crim 1225.

judicial direction' regarding destroyed material may alleviate concerns about the defendant's ability to receive a fair trial.[68] It was further provided that careful cross-examination may overcome the 'uncooperative stance' of a witness.[69] The Court stressed the important distinction between speculation about missing or unrecoverable documents and that which 'represents a significant and demonstrable chance of amounting to decisive or strongly supportive evidence' for the defence case.[70]

PUBLIC INTEREST IMMUNITY (PII)

20.34

The prosecution's duty of disclosure is also in conflict with the right to a fair trial in the arena of public-interest immunity. In particular, the procedure by which immunity is claimed, PII arises where the Crown is in possession of material which may pass the disclosure test, however there are legitimate public interest reasons for withholding it. For example, to protect the identity of a valuable police informer or to keep secret the methods of the police. As it is material which the prosecution does not want the defence to see, the opportunity for adversarial argument about whether the material should be disclosed or for testing the merits of the prosecution's claim of PII is very limited.

20.35

The ultimate decision-making process takes place in the absence of the accused and his representatives. Essentially, the judge is asked by the prosecution to decide not whether the evidence is relevant (it is), but rather just how helpful it would be to the defence. Often the judge must speculate how the defence might be conducted if the evidence were disclosed without hearing any effective representation by the defence. The question is whether this procedure offends the principle of an 'equality of arms'.

20.36

Considering Judge Pettiti's dissenting comments in *Edwards v United Kingdom,*[71] the central topic is whether there is an adversarial element in the decision-making process to provide the accused with adequate procedural safeguards. Until the early 1980s, in English law, decisions on disclosure and the claim to PII was largely left to the judgment of the police and prosecuting authorities which had disastrous effects. These shortcomings were exposed in *R v Ward,*[72] in which the Court of Appeal strongly held it was for the court and not the

68 Ibid, at [66].
69 *R v Bater-James and Another* at 790.
70 Citing Treacy LJ in *R v R D* [2013] EWCA Crim 1592, 15.
71 *Edwards v United Kingdom* (1993) 15 EHRR 417, CA.
72 *R v Ward* (1993) 96 Cr App Rep 1, at 57.

prosecution to decide where the balance lies in terms of PII disclosure in order to ensure fair proceedings.[73]

20.37

In *Rowe and Davis v United Kingdom,*[74] the applicants argued they had not received a fair trial because the identity of an informant whose evidence was crucial to the prosecution case, was withheld under PII. The European Court held there had been a violation of Article 6(1) due to the withholding of this evidence, without disclosing this to the trial judge. The Court nonetheless maintained that the right to disclosure was not 'absolute' and would need to be balanced with 'competing interests' such as the need to protect vulnerable witnesses or police secret methods.[75] Echoing *Ward*, the Court held that where the prosecution seeks to act as judge in their own cause, this is a violation of Article 6. Additionally, the Court found that the fact the material had been revealed to the Court of Appeal in an *ex parte* hearing could not cure the unfairness.[76]

20.38

In *Jasper v United Kingdom,*[77] it was narrowly held the *ex parte* procedure itself did not necessarily breach Article 6(1). In contrast to *Rowe and Davis,* the material in question was submitted to the trial judge at an *ex parte* hearing of which the defence had been on notice though, unaware of the category of material.[78] The Court were satisfied that the defence were informed and able to make submissions and participate in the decision-making process so far as possible.[79]

Special counsel

20.39

In *Jasper,* the dissenting opinions expressed the view that the *ex parte* procedure alone was insufficient to safeguard the right to a fair trial as the defence had not been able to advance submissions before the judge.[80] The dissenting opinion subsequently endorsed the system of 'special counsel'. Such counsel would make arguments on behalf of the defence regarding the relevance of the undisclosed evidence; test the strength of the prosecution claim and safeguard against bias without having to disclose the evidence in question. In *Edwards and Lewis v United Kingdom,*[81] the trial judges were tribunals of fact and were

73 Ibid, at [60].
74 *Rowe and Davis v United Kingdom* (2000) 30 EHRR 480.
75 Ibid, at para 61.
76 Ibid, at para 65. See also *Atlan v UK* (2002) 34 EHRR 33.
77 *Jasper v United Kingdom* (2000) 30 EHRR 441. See also *Fitt v UK* (2000) 30 EHRR 1 – decided on similar facts on the same day.
78 See 'Type 2' hearing under the Court of Appeal guidelines in *R v Davis, Johnson and Rowe* [1993] All ER 643, 647–48.
79 *Jasper v United Kingdom* (2000) 30 EHRR 441 at [55].
80 Ibid, at p 26.
81 *Edwards and Lewis v United Kingdom* (2005) 30 EHRR 24 (Grand Chamber decision).

shown PII material *ex parte,* which was damaging to the defence. The European Court held that this offended the 'equality of arms' principle and supported the introduction of suggestion of 'special independent counsel' and proposed in the *Auld Report.*[82]

20.40

This issue was comprehensively dealt with by the House of Lords in *R v H and* C.[83] Lord Bingham rejected the argument that Convention jurisprudence required the appointment of special counsel in every case. He held that this would 'place the trial judge in a straitjacket'.[84] Notwithstanding, the use of special counsel was approved, subject to the demonstrable necessity for them in the interests of justice and fairness to the defendant.[85] Indeed, such an appointment would always be 'exceptional' and Lord Bingham provided a series of questions to assist the courts when dealing with 'any issue of derogation from the golden rule of full disclosure'.[86] A number of cases have dealt with the necessity of special counsel since *R v H and C,* such as *R v Chisholm (John)* which deals with use of special counsel in an appeal against conviction.[87]

20.41

The full procedure for prosecutors making PII applications is set out in a Criminal Practice Direction.[88] Material which may be subject to a PII is to be recorded in a 'sensitive' schedule by investigators.[89] The CPIA Code of Practice provides a non-exhaustive list of material which may be 'sensitive'.[90] The *A-G Guidelines 2022* provide further guidance about how sensitive unused material should be scheduled and examined.[91]

CONCLUSION

20.42

Disclosure is at the heart of the right to a fair trial. Yet because the entitlement to disclosure is not an absolute right, there remains a grey area in which competing interests will seek to withhold relevant evidence and restrict the right of the accused. The scope and interpretation of that grey area will continue to provide

82 *The Review of the Criminal Courts in England and Wales by Lord Justice Auld* (September 2001). See paras 193–97, in particular para 194.
83 *R v H and C* (2005) 30 EHRR 24 (Grand Chamber decision), para 33.
84 Ibid, at [33].
85 Ibid, at [22].
86 Ibid, at [36].
87 *R v Chisholm (John)* (2010) EWCA Crim 258. In *obiter,* the court suggested that in many of these cases, the judge will read material which will abolish the need for special counsel.
88 See Crim PD 15.3(2) and (3)(a)(iii).
89 CPS, *Disclosure Manual: Chapter 8 – The Sensitive Material Schedule,* (October 2021) – defines 'sensitive' material as that which would 'give rise to a real risk of serious prejudice to an important public interest' if disclosed.
90 See CPIA Code of Practice (March 2015), 6.14.
91 Attorney General's Office, *A-G Guidelines on Disclosure,* (May 2022), [66]–[69].

the potential for future miscarriages of justice of the kinds outlined in this chapter, as well as a crucible for robust legal argument.

20.43

Practical experience shows that a great deal of court time continues to be taken up by defence applications chasing up outstanding disclosure by the prosecution, or in legal argument about whether a failure to disclose relevant material has impugned the fairness of the trial.

20.44

Although in recent times, there has been development in the framework for the fair disclosure in practice, the problem may always be that we operate in an adversarial system, in which prosecutors decide what should and should not be passed on to the defence. A fair trial depends upon the fairness and integrity of the police from the moment an investigation begins and police properly undertaking all reasonable lines of enquiry. It depends also on the diligence and integrity of prosecutors, conscientiously ensuring timely disclosure is made to the defence.

20.45

And yet, as we have seen with 'special counsel', that adversarial system is also the solution to the problem. The key to the balance of competing interests is always to ensure that there remains 'an equality of arms' and the decision-making process is subjected to adversarial argument.

21 Human rights and the law of criminal responsibility

Riel Karmy-Jones KC and Timothy Kiely

21.1

In any criminal matter that turns on whether a defendant had the requisite intent to commit the offence (the so-called *mens rea* or 'guilty mind'), close attention must be paid to the personal characteristics and antecedents of the accused. Attributes such as youth, mental capacity, disability or disorder and other influences such as addiction, or even personal circumstances,[1] may impact on their intention to commit the crime, to the extent that sometimes culpability will be reduced or even eliminated. In such cases, the question of intention inevitably involves direct consideration of a number of Convention Rights, particularly those protected by Articles 5 and 6: the right to liberty and security; and the right to a fair trial respectively. In this chapter we look at how human rights considerations come into play in cases involving the young, and those whose mental capacity is in question.

21.2

From a human rights perspective, the right to a fair trial under Article 6 will be closely scrutinised in all cases involving young defendants. The younger the accused, the more robust the safeguards imposed by the court will need to be to ensure that they receive a fair trial, which should include that all measures are taken to make certain not only that the conduct of the proceedings is fair, but that the child or young person is themselves properly able to understand the proceedings, and to participate in them. The issues are dealt with in Chapter 23.

INSANITY AND FITNESS TO PLEAD

21.3

Defendants who, for various reasons, might have mental health or developmental conditions which affect their ability to take part in court proceedings are an obvious source of concern with respect to their Article 6 rights. The Strasbourg

1 See, eg, Modern Slavery Act, s 45 discussed in Chapter 13.

case of *Stanford v United Kingdom*[2] makes it clear that Article 6, read as a whole, 'guarantees the right of an accused to participate effectively in a criminal trial', including to hear and follow proceedings, to examine witnesses or to have access to an interpreter if proceedings are in a language they do not understand.

21.4

In England and Wales, the relevant test regarding fitness to plead still derives from the nineteenth-century case of *R v Pritchard,*[3] which set out four main criteria for deciding whether a defendant was fit to plead and stand trial:

(a) whether they are able to instruct a solicitor or counsel;

(b) whether they are fit to plead to the indictment (ie, they understand the nature of the charges against them);

(c) whether they are able to challenge a juror; and

(d) whether they are able to both understand and give evidence.

21.5

The defence of insanity, meanwhile, is provided for under section 2(1) of the Trial of Lunatics Act 1883 – the outdated and, for many people, offensive language of 'lunacy' being but one illustration of the problems with this area of the law, which are discussed further below. The legal test necessary to make out the defence of insanity is set out in the case of *R v McNaughten*,[4] and begins from the presumption that every man is sane and knows the law of the land. Thereafter, to raise it, the defence must show that at the time of doing the act the defendant was 'labouring under such a defect of reason, from a disease of the mind, as not to know the nature and quality of the act he was doing; or, if he did know it, that he did not know he was doing what was wrong'[5] and then to prove it, on the balance of probabilities. A 'disease of the mind' is not the same as a temporary abnormality, for example a 'psychotic episode', which may flow from the effects of voluntarily imbibed substances.[6]

21.6

Of course, societal understandings of mental health have developed considerably since *Pritchard* and *McNaughten* were decided, but nonetheless, the cases remain good law.[7] The legal burden remains on the prosecution to prove to the criminal standard that an offence was committed, but the finding of insanity or of unfitness to plead does not of itself amount to a finding of guilt in a criminal charge, and generally Strasbourg judgments have found these provisions to be

---

2 *Stanford v United Kingdom* [1994] ECHR Series A No 282-A (23 Feb 1994) at [26].

3 *R v Pritchard* (1836) 7 C&P 303.

4 *R v McNaughten* (1843) 8 ER 718.

5 Ibid, p 722.

6 See *R v Coley; McGhee; Harris* [2013] EWCA Crim 223; [2013] Crim LR 923.

7 *McNaughten* was approved in *R v Sullivan* [1984] AC 156, HL, and has been applied in more recent cases, eg *R v Oye* [2013] EWCA Crim 1725 regardless of whether the evidence indicates that the defendant suffered from delusions.

compliant with Article 6.[8] Nevertheless, concern for the rights and dignity of court users with mental and other health conditions has meant that the legal framework surrounding both the insanity defence and fitness to plead has recently become a subject of extensive discussion and debate.

21.7

Fitness to plead is governed by section 4 of the Criminal Procedure (Insanity) Act 1964, which provides that the question of fitness is one to be determined by the court without the jury, as soon as it arises but, if expedient, at any time before the opening of the case for the defence and that the decision must be based on the evidence of two or more registered medical practitioners, one of whom is duly approved. In 2016 the Law Commission published a lengthy report on the current fitness to plead regime,[9] recommending among other things that the *Pritchard* criteria be replaced by a statutory test aimed at establishing whether or not the defendant lacked the 'capacity to participate effectively' in the trial process.[10] It specifically did not require that the capacity be linked with a medical condition, such as a mental health diagnosis (the so-called 'diagnostic threshold').[11] Positive comparisons were drawn with civil law, where the decision around a litigant's capacity to engage is based largely on their ability to understand, retain relevant information, and communicate a decision to their representatives or the court.

21.8

Where a defendant is determined to be unfit to plead, and so unfit to properly be able to participate in their trial, the court may nevertheless ask a jury to determine whether the defendant did the act or omission which is said to constitute the offence. This will usually be after a form of trial where the defendant has had little input into the way their defence has been run, or the challenges made to the evidence. If the jury finds that that they did commit the act, the court has the power to order a wide range of disposals, from an absolute discharge under section 5 of the Criminal Procedure (Insanity) Act to hospital or guardianship orders under section 37 of the Mental Health Act (MHA) 1983, which bring with them an automatic restriction on an offender's liberty (admission to a hospital will be mandatory in cases where the penalty is fixed by law, as for example with murder).

21.9

This can cause questions to arise under Article 5. Article 5(1) does make explicit provision for derogation from the rights which it protects in certain situations and 'in accordance with a procedure prescribed by law'. This includes (among other things) when someone is being sentenced following conviction for a

8 See, eg *H v United Kingdom Application* 15023/98 and *Robinson v United Kingdom* (Application no 20858/92), 5 May 1993.

9 Law Commission (2016) *Unfitness to Plead, Vol 1: Report*, Law Com No 364, London: HMSO.

10 Law Commission (2016) *Unfitness to Plead, Vol 2: Draft Legislation*, Law Com No 364, London: HMSO.

11 *T and V v United Kingdom* (2000) 30 EHRR 121 at [327].

criminal offence, or detained on suspicion of committing an offence, and the lawful detention of persons of 'unsound mind',[12] even in circumstances where they have not committed a crime (such provisions also exist for those suffering from alcohol dependence or homelessness).[13] The Convention itself contains no definition of 'unsound mind', however case law tends to focus on the criteria elaborated in the 1979 case of *Winterwerp v Netherlands*,[14] which broadly set out that there must be a 'true mental disorder' of a kind or degree warranting confinement in a hospital, clinic or other appropriate institution, thereby paralleling our domestic case law's nomenclature, 'disease of the mind'.

21.10

The essential means by which people's liberties are restricted may begin as (arguably) 'necessary' measures, for example, to prevent harm to themselves or others. It may even be something which the detained person themselves seeks and complies with. That the detention nonetheless still has the potential to tip over into violations of Article 5 is demonstrated in judgments such as that in *Ashingdane v United Kingdom,*[15] where a patient on an open ward was regarded as being 'detained' for Article 5 purposes.[16] There the appellant was not free at any point to leave the hospital ward where they were being housed and was placed under continuous supervision. This was enough of itself, the Strasbourg Court found, to raise potential questions about deprivation of liberty and would be so even if the detained person had volunteered for their own detention, as 'the distinction between deprivation of, and restriction upon, liberty is merely one of degree and not one of nature or substance'.[17] The Court thus made it clear that where a person lacks the mental capacity to make properly informed decisions about their care, restrictive measures that deprive them of their liberty may well violate Article 5.

21.11

It is therefore imperative that those authorities with the power to make assessments of a person's mental health do so considering the rights guaranteed by Article 5. Similarly, that those with the power to impose restrictions on their freedom do so with Article 5 at the forefront of their minds, so to avoid unacceptable deprivations of liberty. The case law shows the perils involved in making such a determination when the nature of the care required by a particular applicant is not always clear-cut. Two related approaches, both of which came before the Strasbourg Courts, are worth mentioning here: *Johnson v United Kingdom,*[18] and *Kolanis v United Kingdom.*[19]

---

12 Art 5(1)(e).
13 Though 'vagrancy' is the word used in the Convention.
14 *Winterwerp v Netherlands* (1979–80) 2 EHRR 387.
15 *Ashingdane v United Kingdom* (1985) 7 EHRR 528.
16 See also *HL v United Kingdom* (2005) 40 EHRR 32.
17 Ibid, at [89].
18 *Johnson v United Kingdom* (1999) 27 EHRR 296.
19 *Kolanis v United Kingdom* (2006) 42 EHRR 12.

21.12

In *Johnson,* an appellant argued successfully that his Article 5 rights were being violated by his ongoing detention at Rampton High Secure Hospital in spite of the fact that medical evidence established that the symptoms of his illness had disappeared. The Mental Health Review Tribunal (MHRT) sought to justify their continued detention while a suitable hostel was sought for the appellant's conditional release on the grounds that the national authorities could determine for themselves, based on 'relevant circumstances', whether continued detention or supervision was necessary for the protection of the public. While the Strasbourg Court was prepared to accept that the Tribunal did have the authority to make such determinations even when medical evidence showed that symptoms of a mental illness had disappeared (since this did not always mean that a complete recovery has taken place), they also found that the authority did *not* have the powers to ensure that such a hostel would be procured, and so the appellant released, within a reasonable period of time. The result was that the appellant had been detained in hospital at a time when one of the *Winterwerp* criteria had simply fallen away and their continued detention could not be justified.

21.13

The case of *Kolanis* concerned an appellant whose mental health condition was subject to control by medication and which, in the Court's view, warranted a somewhat different approach. Following their conviction for assault occasioning grievous bodily harm, the appellant had been detained in a hospital for a time before having their case assessed by the MHRT. The assessment resulted in a sentence of conditional discharge, the terms of which were that they should have a designated residence (their home or that of their parents), and that they should cooperate with a designated supervising consultant psychiatrist. In the event, finding such a supervisor proved impossible, and when the appellant was finally discharged nearly two years after her conviction into a resettlement project hostel, she claimed that the conditions imposed by the MHRT had resulted in a violation of her Article 5 rights. The Strasbourg Court disagreed, noting that there could be '*no question*'[20] of interpreting Article 5 in such a way as to require a mentally unsound defendant to be released immediately if the conditions of their discharge could not be met. They did, however, find that the review process had not taken place 'speedily' enough for there not to be a violation under Article 5(4)).

21.14

In both cases, the approaches taken by the lower court reflected the perceived need to prioritise the safety of the public, arguably at the expense of the rights of the offender and consideration of their situation (as in *Johnson*). This emphasis on the protection of the public risks obscuring the power which the criminal justice system, and other arms of the State, can bring to bear on people with

20 Ibid, at [H7].

mental health issues. Even when robust safeguards exist, for example in the form of a regular review of the lawfulness of detention (as mandated by Article 5(4)), people with severe mental health conditions are uniquely vulnerable users of the criminal justice system and are inherently poorly equipped to protect themselves.

21.15

This vulnerability is reflected in recent statistics concerning deaths in custody or following contact with the police. According to the Independent Office for Police Conduct (IOPC), in the year 2019/2020 nearly two-thirds of the deaths recorded were in respect of people who had been identified as having mental health concerns, including bipolar depression, schizophrenia, psychosis, anxiety and suicidal or self-harming tendencies.[21] Police officers and other officials may understandably, in the moment, be more concerned with removing the 'danger' of the mentally unwell person than with that person's welfare, but sometimes the consequences are tragic.

21.16

A consciousness of this over-representation in the statistics has led to some positive actions. For example, the Policing and Crime Act 2017 includes provisions, effective from December of the same year, removing the use of police cells as 'places of safety' for those under the age of 18 who are detained under sections 135 and 136 of the MHA. As a result there has been a steady decline in the number of police stations being used as 'places of safety' for those experiencing mental health crises.[22] This is but a small step in the right direction and there is much farther to go. Meanwhile those who suffer from acute mental health issues remain in a precarious situation when facing proceedings in the criminal justice system; this remains a subject of concern.

DIMINISHED RESPONSIBILITY[23]

21.17

The defence of diminished responsibility applies only in the case of a defendant charged with murder. Under section 2 of the Homicide Act 1957,[24] such a defendant may instead be found guilty of manslaughter, if they were suffering from 'an abnormality of mental functioning' which has arisen from a 'recognised medical condition', provides an explanation for the defendant's conduct and which substantially impaired their ability to either understand the nature of their conduct, form a rational judgement or exercise self-control. As with insanity, the

21 *Deaths During or Following Police Contact: Statistics for England and Wales 2019/20*. Available at https://policeconduct.gov.uk/sites/default/files/Documents/statistics/deaths_during_following_police_contact_201920.pdf.

22 *Deaths During or Following Police Contact: Statistics for England and Wales 2019/20* notes a 98% reduction since 2013.

23 See also Chapter 22.

24 As amended by the Coroners and Justice Act 2009.

burden of proof is on the defence to show that diminished responsibility is made out. However, uniquely, it also imposes not simply an evidential burden on the defendant (leaving it for the prosecution to prove the defence does *not* apply) but a legal one, as per section 2(2), 'it shall be for the defence to prove that the person charged is by virtue of this section not liable to be convicted of murder'.

21.18

In practice, the partial defence of diminished responsibility relies on three factors. First, that the accused accepts the fact of their role in the killing. In *R v Curran* [2021] EWCA Crim 1999, the Court of Appeal noted as follows:

> We do not go so far as to say that a defendant will only be able to pursue a partial defence of diminished responsibility in circumstances where he or she personally admits the actus reus and also an intention to kill or commit grievous bodily harm. There will be circumstances … where defendants do rely upon the partial defence, and yet do not themselves give evidence at trial. We are aware of the same. However, in such cases we note that there is necessarily an evidential basis upon which the partial defence is mounted. Be that an account by the defendant in interview with police or psychiatrists, or a contemporaneous narrative eyewitness account of the assault leading to death, and which provides the context for a psychiatric opinion as to the impact of or link between the likely abnormality of mind and the assault.

21.19

The second factor is that they have sufficient insight to recognise that they suffer from both a recognised medical condition and consequently an abnormality of mind that caused them to act as they did. Thirdly, that they are willing to co-operate with psychiatric assessments[25] to show as much, as medical evidence is necessary for the defence to succeed:

> The etiology of the abnormality of mind (namely, whether it arose from a condition of arrested or retarded development of mind or any inherent causes or was induced by disease or injury) does … seem to be a matter to be determined on expert evidence …[26]

21.20

Thus, the process of obtaining the relevant psychiatric reports relies heavily on the co-operation of the accused – the very person who may be suffering from 'an abnormality of mind'. However, if the accused refuses to accept either the fact of their 'recognised medical condition' or that their mental functioning has in any way been impaired, their approach to the psychiatric assessments

25 Here it must be remembered that a defendant must consent to any form of medical examination – see, eg, *R v Lambert and Ali* [2002] QB 1112 as per Lord Woolfe at [18].

26 See *R v Byrne* [1960] 2 QB 396; *R v Dix* (1982) 74 Cr App R 306, CA, and *R v Bunch* [2013] EWCA Crim 2498.

may result in an inconclusive or skewed outcome. In other words, they may not be wholly truthful in their answers to the experts' questions but may respond in a manner which they have learned is more socially acceptable. If they are consequently deemed to have 'malingered' in their answers, this can be interpreted as an indication that they have understood the nature of their conduct, are able to form a rational judgement and so their responsibility is not diminished. However, there seems to be little or no recognition that the very 'malingering' may be part and parcel of the medical condition and consequent to the abnormality of mind.

21.21

It seems wrong, in principle, to put the reins of the partial defence in the hands of the defendant who may, as a result of their difficulties, neither want to drive it, nor appreciate the direction of travel. Defence counsel may also be at something of a disadvantage in such a situation as they are limited in what they can do to assist their client, their duty being fearlessly to follow their client's instructions, however ludicrous they may appear to be.

21.22

Furthermore, the approach to the defence seems to run against an explicit provision of Article 6(2), one which embodies the so-called 'Golden Thread' of justice in the English and Welsh legal tradition: 'everyone charged with a criminal offence shall be presumed innocent until proved guilty according to law'. Unlike the reverse burdens imposed on those seeking to determine defences such as insanity, diminished responsibility effectively places the defendant in the position of being presumed guilty of murder, and this is many times more invidious a position to be in than would ordinarily justify such an exception. If the defence fails, after all, then a defendant faces the prospect of life imprisonment, there being little that a judge can do as far as mental health disposal is concerned post-conviction.

21.23

However, as with insanity and other fitness-to-plead issues, Strasbourg judgments have tended to support the conclusions of courts in England and Wales that the reverse burden of proof is not, of itself, at odds with Article 6. In *Robinson v United Kingdom*,[27] the Commission found that the presumption that a defendant knew what they were doing, absent evidence of some kind of mental impairment, was generally a matter for the defence to dispute (a point previously made by Woolf CJ in the authority of *R v Lambert and Ali* when he noted that the defendant could not be required to submit to medical or psychological examination).[28] The issue of whether the defendant's mental state diminished their responsibility was, according to these judgments, naturally the proper domain of the defence, and the argument that section 2(2) was in conflict with Article 6(2) such as to infringe it unacceptably was deemed manifestly ill-founded.

27 *Robinson v United Kingdom* (Application no 20858/92), 5 May 1993.
28 *R v Lambert and Ali* [2002] QB 1112 at [18].

21.24

This debate found extensive consideration in a case which straddled an amendment of the Homicide Act in 2010. *R v Foye*[29] concerned an appellant who was, at the time of their offending conduct, serving a life sentence for murder at a secure institution dedicated to psychiatric treatment. Foye had admitted (eventually) to killing one of his cellmates by wrestling him to the ground and repeatedly stamping on his head. Before trial he had also vandalised his cell and severed both ears from his own head. Three consultant psychiatrists agreed to a diagnosis of dissocial or psychopathic personality disorder, with one of them noting that there may have been a psychotic element to the killings – Foye had purportedly harmed himself to stop himself from hearing voices. As such, the issue at trial was whether his condition (which certainly came within the ambit of an 'abnormality' of mind) had substantially impaired his 'mental responsibility' for the killing (a broader form of words than the more specific provisions of the amended Act, as outlined in the opening paragraph of this section). His defence was that he was unable to resist his homicidal thoughts, whereas the prosecution focused on his planning of the killings to indicate that, notwithstanding his condition, he was nevertheless responsible. In the event, the defence failed and Foye was convicted of murder.

21.25

On appeal, the Court of Appeal rejected the submissions both that the defendant's Article 6 rights had been violated by the reserve legal burden and that the trial judge ought to have 'read down' the provisions of the Act to impose an evidential burden only. Faced with the argument that the presumption of innocence had been undermined, the Court found instead that the presumption was not infringed upon at all, since the defendant was only being called upon to establish an 'exception or an excuse' to a killing which was already accepted as having happened, rather than seeking to prove or disprove one or more of the elements of the offence. Moreover, they concluded that a merely evidential burden on the defence might be nearly impossible for the prosecution to disprove, since to do so they would have to show that the defendant's own state of mind and grasp of his surroundings was not as he claimed it had been.

21.26

Notwithstanding the findings of the courts on this defence, the human rights implications of the reverse burden are worth considering in terms of how they co-exist with other defences to murder, in particular that of provocation under section 3 of the same Act, where the defendant bears only an evidential burden. In its report on the subject in 2006, the Law Commission, despite finding that members of the judiciary seemed evenly split on whether to impose an evidential burden only,[30] did not recommend any changes to the current regime

29 *R v Foye* [2013] EWCA Crim 475.

30 Law Commission (2004) *Final Report on Partial Defences to Murder* (Law Com 290), London: HMSO at [5.88].

(indeed, it also recommended imposing a similar burden on those seeking to establish a defence of duress, though this has yet to be implemented).[31]

21.27

Diminished responsibility defences also present an interesting point of contrast with the current age of criminal responsibility. Since section 2 of the Homicide Act refers specifically to an 'arrested or retarded development of mind' as the necessary condition for a such a defence to be available, it seems that this might allow an adult with, for example, the mental age of a 10-year-old to rely on a defence of diminished responsibility where a child would be precluded from doing so on the basis of the presumption that any child over the age of 10 can be guilty of any offence.

21.28

It is clear that how the courts in England and Wales regard those who come before them, and the question of the degree to which the accused are judged to be 'responsible' for their criminal conduct before proceedings have even begun, remains a vexed area. There has been a considerable amount of public discussion and debate on the interplay between human rights and criminal justice in England and Wales which tends to view the former as an encumbrance, a form of judicial interference in what are, more properly, political issues. The recent Independent Human Rights Act Review,[32] chaired by Sir Peter Goss and published in October 2021, was established in December 2020 'to examine the operation of the Human Rights Act 1998 in two main areas: first, the relationship between domestic courts and the European Court of Human Rights (the ECtHR); secondly, the impact that the HRA has had on the relationship between the Judiciary, the Government and Parliament'. Amongst other things, the Review considered the concept of 'the margin of discretion' that exists in UK domestic law, which 'refers to the respect and weight that the UK courts give to domestic decision making by Government and Parliament when considering the application of Convention rights to such decisions …'.[33]

21.29

Citing the evidence given by Lord Justice Laws with approval, the Review concluded that the margin of discretion:

> ensures that a proper balance is maintained within the UK between the three Branches of the State: … the margin of discretionary judgment enjoyed by the primary decision maker, though variable, means that the court's role is kept in balance with that of the elected arms of government; and this serves to quieten constitutional anxieties that the

31 Law Commission (2006) *Murder, Manslaughter and Infanticide* (Law Com No 304), London: HMSO, Ch 8.

32 See https://assets.publishing.service.gov.uk/government/uploads/system/uploads/attachment_data/file/1040525/ihrar-final-report.pdf.

33 Ibid, Part 3 at [21].

Human Rights Act draws the judges onto ground they should not occupy.[34]

21.30

The Review did not consider the effects of the Convention rights on the more immediate questions of a defendant's responsibility for a crime. However, it was commissioned against a political background where human rights concerns were routinely cited as, among other things, impediments to the deportation of 'foreign-born criminals' or unfair impositions on British armed services personnel operating overseas. During his inaugural speech to the Conservative Party Conference on 5 October 2021, the Justice Secretary Dominic Raab commented on the need to, as he put it, 'restore some common sense' to the justice system and remove the ability of 'dangerous criminals' to exploit it, such as in the case of a man who had purportedly been convicted of assaulting his ex-partner but who had avoided deportation by 'abusing human rights laws'. A House of Commons debate specifically on 'the Deportation of Foreign National Offenders' was led by Conservative MP Simon Clarke on 2 February 2021, where supposedly obstructive interpretations of the Human Rights Act 1998 were cited with frequency.

21.31

There is a certain irony, then, that possibly the most high-profile instance in recent years of the diminished responsibility defence being utilised successfully was in *R v Blackman*, the case of the Royal Marine Alexander Blackman[35] who fatally shot a wounded Taliban insurgent in the chest at close range when deployed in Afghanistan. His appeal to have his conviction for murder quashed and substituted with manslaughter by reason of diminished responsibility drew enthusiastic comment from several observers known largely for their hostility to human rights as mediated through the courts, including from sources such as the *Daily Mail* newspaper. Clearly, when it comes to the fight around access to human rights and legal protections, some candidates can command more sympathy than others.

21.32

It is likely that there will never be a legal system which is able to avoid having to grapple, in some way, with the issue of reverse burdens, the detention of mentally ill court users, or the difficult task of doing justice by defendants who might be too young or too gripped by acute mental health issues to navigate the system fairly. Being accused of a crime, and having to submit to legal processes, will necessarily entail infringements on certain rights. We suggest that, in all cases, the loadstar ought to be that in any criminal justice process, at all points before, during and after trial, those caught up in the system should be afforded the essential rights that come, first and foremost, with being human.

34 Ibid, at [23].
35 *R v Blackman* [2017] EWCA Crim 190.

22 Mental health and capacity

Ian P Brownhill

INTRODUCTION

22.1

The number of people in the criminal justice system who have issues in respect of their mental health or mental capacity is not known.[1] Those who have severe mental illness are shown, statistically, more likely to be the victim of crime compared to those without.[2]

22.2

As many as 60% of adult offenders are estimated[3] to have suffered a traumatic brain injury.[4] In one case, the Administrative Court held, 'prisoners lacking capacity to participate in their parole review is not theoretical and that there is a need to be addressed'.[5] Despite the high levels of contact that people will mental health and capacity issues have with the criminal justice system, there is not a single legislative framework which addresses the huge variety of matters which arise. Rather, there is a challenge to co-ordinate the various pieces of legislation and existing case law. The case law coming from not only the criminal courts but also the Court of Protection, the Upper Tribunal and the Administrative Court.

1 See the Criminal Justice Joint Inspection Report of November 2021. Available at: www.justiceinspectorates.gov.uk/cjji/wp-content/uploads/sites/2/2021/11/Mental-health-joint-thematic-report.pdf.

2 See At *Risk, Yet Dismissed*. Available at: www.mind.org.uk/media-a/4121/at-risk-yet-dismissed-report.pdf.

3 See Parsonage. Available at: https://barrowcadbury.org.uk/wp-content/uploads/2016/07/Traumatic-brain-injury-and-offending-an-economic-analysis.pdf.

4 For more on offending following brain injury see H Kent, J Tonks, and H Williams with I Brownhill, 'Paediatric Outcomes after Traumatic Brain Injury: Social and Forensic Risk Management in Multidisciplinary Treatment Approaches' in P Moore, S Brifcani and A Worthington *Neuropsychological Aspects of Brain Injury Litigation: A Medicolegal Handbook for Lawyers and Clinicians* (Abingdon, Taylor and Francis, 2021).

5 See para [74] of the decision of May J in *EG, R (On the Application Of) v The Parole Board of England and Wales* [2020] EWHC 1457 (Admin) (9 June 2020).

PREVENTING OFFENDING

Protecting persons with mental health and capacity issues from crime

22.3

Whilst the criminal justice system's primary focus is to look at events which have already happened, the civil justice system is able to look prospectively and determine whether steps may be taken to protect a person from becoming the victim of crime.

22.4

Outside of the courts, public authorities have the duty to safeguard adults at risk of abuse or neglect. The Care Act 2014 sets out the statutory responsibilities for the integration of care and support arrangements between health and local authorities. Local authorities in England and Wales have the statutory responsibility for safeguarding. Put simply, safeguarding adults means protecting an individual's rights to live in safety, free from abuse and/or neglect. The safeguarding duty is not limited to those with mental health or capacity issues. Rather, an adult at risk is any person who is aged 18 years or over and at risk of abuse or neglect because of their need for care and/or support.

22.5

The statutory duty includes the duty to enquire (or require others to do so) if it believes an adult is experiencing or is at risk of, abuse or neglect. That enquiry should identify whether any action needs to be taken to stop abuse or neglect. That action will vary on a case-to-case basis; the guidance which accompanies the Care Act 2014 emphasises that where there is reason to suspect criminal activity then the police should be involved at an early stage.[6] Where a person is assessed as lacking capacity to make decisions as to contact with their alleged abuser, then a best-interests decision may be made that they do not have contact. Ultimately, that best-interests decision may be made into an enforceable court order by the Court of Protection.

22.6

In *Re SF (Injunctive Relief)*,[7] Keehan J was concerned with a young woman, SF who had a diagnosis of autism spectrum disorder and had learning disabilities. She resided in a supported living establishment where she received one-to-one support 24 hours a day. In September 2019, her carers became aware that SF was communicating with several men via social media and the internet. Further, it became apparent that some of these men were attending her placement and sexually exploiting her. Only one of those men was identified and the local authority applied for an injunction against him to prevent him from attending

6 See *Care and Support Statutory Guidance* at [14.83].
7 *Re SF (Injunctive Relief)* [2020] EWCOP 19.

SF's accommodation. Keehan J concluded that the combination of section 47(1) of the Mental Capacity Act 2005 and section 37(1) of the Senior Courts Act 1981 allowed the court to grant injunctive relief.[8]

22.7

Other preventative orders are available which do not depend on the adult-at-risk's capacity, for example domestic violence protection orders,[9] forced marriage protection orders[10] and female genital mutilation protection orders.[11] The common law also provides a safety net for adults who are able to make their own decisions but are subject to some form of coercion or undue influence.[12] The inherent jurisdiction of the High Court may be invoked to 'allow the individual to be able to regain their autonomy of decision making'.[13] If there is no other statutory mechanism which can be used, the High Court may invoke[14] the inherent jurisdiction to make orders against the person who is the source of the undue influence or coercion.

PREVENTING PERSONS WITH MENTAL HEALTH AND CAPACITY ISSUES FROM COMMITTING CRIME

22.8

The fact that there is an issue with a person's mental health or mental capacity does not necessarily[15] exclude them from having a preventative or ancillary order imposed upon them by the criminal courts.[16] Similarly, the fact that a person has no criminal conviction is not a bar to restrictions being imposed to prevent the commission of offences.

22.9

The Mental Health Act 1983 provides a means of compulsorily admitting a person to hospital and detaining them there, if the conditions set down in the Act are met.[17] Admission for assessment or treatment under sections 2 and 3 of the Act does not depend on a person committing a criminal offence.

---

8 This approach, and the approach of the Court of Protection more generally in respect of injunctions, is explored in the decision of the Court of Appeal in *G, Re (Court of Protection: Injunction)* [2022] EWCA Civ 1312.

9 Crime and Security Act 2010, ss 24–33.

10 Family Law Act 1996, ss 63A–63CA.

11 Female Genital Mutilation Act 2003, Sch 2.

12 See Munby J in *Re SA (Vulnerable Adult with Capacity: Marriage)* [2005] EWHC 2942 (Fam) at [77].

13 See Lieven J in *London Borough of Croydon v KR & Anor* [2019] EWHC 2498 (Fam) at [40].

14 For procedural matters see *Mazhar v Birmingham Community Healthcare Foundation NHS Trust & Ors* [2020] EWCA Civ 1377.

15 However, it is unlikely to be enforceable if the nature of the individual's mental health or capacity is such that they do not understand or cannot retain the prohibitions contained within a preventative/ancillary order.

16 Albeit it is always important to be clear about the source of the restrictions which are being imposed: *The Queen on the Application of Smith v Derbyshire County Council* [2008] EWHC 3355 (Admin).

17 Mental Health Act 1983, ss 2–5.

22.10

Put simply, an admission for assessment[18] may be made on the basis that a person is suffering from a mental disorder which warrants their detention in hospital for assessment and they ought to be detained in the interests of their own health or safety *or* with a view to the protection of others. The protection of others does not necessarily mean the public at large, it could simply be a risk of harm to a particular person or group of persons.[19]

22.11

Admission to hospital is not the only means of preventing persons with mental health issues from committing offences. There exists an additional power of guardianship.[20] An application for guardianship does not depend on the individual committing an offence. Guardianship requires that the person is suffering from a mental disorder, and it is necessary for their welfare of the protection of others. It remains a relative rarity. The guardian can require that the person lives in a particular place, attend medical or other appointments and meets with their psychiatrist or other mental health professionals. It is an offence if other people prevent the person from complying with the requirements of their guardianship order. However, the power of guardians is relatively limited. The guardianship cannot authorise a deprivation of liberty nor can they require a person to take medication unless they consent to do so. In cases where the person lacks the mental capacity to make decisions as to their care and support arrangements, it may well be preferable to use the Mental Capacity Act 2005.[21]

22.12

Unlike the Mental Health Act 1983, the Mental Capacity Act does not contain any statutory provision for imposing restrictions on a person in order to protect the public. However, the interpretation of the Act has included public protection elements in best interests analysis. The oft quoted passage is taken from the decision of Moor J in *Y County Council v ZZ*:[22]

> I have come to the clear conclusion, for all the reasons given by the various doctors, that it is lawful as in Mr ZZ's best interests to deprive him of his liberty in accordance with the local authority care plan, pursuant to schedule A1 of the Mental Capacity Act 2005. I make that declaration. In doing so, I am following the advice of the expert professionals who know Mr ZZ so well. Indeed, the Official Solicitor accepts, on his behalf, that I should do so. I make it clear to Mr ZZ that I have no doubt that the restrictions upon him are in his best interests. They are designed to keep him out of mischief, to keep him safe and healthy, to keep others safe, to prevent the sort of situation where the

18 For full text see the Mental Health Act 1983, s 2.

19 See judgment of Harrison J in *R v Northwest London Mental Health NHS Trust Ex p. Stewart* (1996) 39 BMLR 105.

20 Mental Health Act 1983, s 7.

21 See *C v Blackburn with Darwen Borough Council & Ors* [2011] EWHC 3321 (Fam).

22 *Y County Council v ZZ* [2012] EWCOP B34 at [49].

relative of a child wanted to do him serious harm, which I have no doubt was very frightening for him, and they are there to prevent him from getting into serious trouble with the police.

22.13

The paragraph is controversial.[23] It has been read by some as allowing a broad imposition of restrictions on a person who does not have capacity to make decisions as to their care and support arrangements in order to prevent criminality. Arguably, those restrictions may be more onerous than those imposed on a person who has committed an offence. Whatever the merits of the arguments, it is now clear that the Supreme Court has concluded[24] that decisions of the Court of Protection may have the effect of protecting the public.[25]

22.14

Whilst one of the purposes of the Mental Capacity Act 2005 is to promote the autonomy of the person and, unlike the Mental Health Act 1983, public protection is not one of its express purposes, the operational obligations of the Court of Protection itself.[26] The need for consistency across the whole of the justice system, including the criminal justice system, means that the issue will continue to arise in cases.

INVESTIGATIONS

As a witness to a crime

22.15

There is, on occasion, the misconception that a person with mental health issues or mental capacity cannot act as a witness in a criminal investigation and subsequent proceedings. This misconception is compounded by a mismatch between the criminal and civil legal frameworks. A person is competent[27] to act as a witness in a criminal trial if they are able to understand the questions put to them and are able to give answers which are understood. However, that test is distinct from whether a person has the mental capacity to participate in an ABE interview, for example.[28] Similarly, a lack of competence to give evidence in a criminal court does not prevent a civil court considering evidence from the same witness as to the same incident.[29]

23 For more see I Brownhill, *The Myths and Mistakes of Capacity and Criminality*. Available at: https://openjusticecourtofprotection.org/2020/09/18/the-myths-and-mistakes-of-capacity-and-criminality/.

24 See Lord Stephens in *A Local Authority v JB (Rev 1)* [2021] UKSC 52 at [92]–[93].

25 The decision of Judd J in *DY v A City Council & Anor* [2022] EWCOP 51 confirms that the Deprivation of Liberty Safeguards contained in Schedule A1 to the Mental Capacity Act 2005 may be used to authorise a care plan which has the effect of protecting the public from an individual who cannot consent to those arrangements.

26 Human Rights Act 1998, s 6.

27 Youth Justice and Criminal Evidence Act 1999, s 53.

28 For more as to the difference between competence, capacity to consent to being interviewed and procedural considerations see the decision of McFarlane J in *LB of Enfield v SA, FA, KA* [2010] EWHC 196 (Admin).

29 See the decision of HHJ Rogers in *A County Council v AB* [2016] EWCOP 41.

22.16

One alarming feature is the number of criminal investigations which result in no further action on the basis that a witness with mental health or capacity issues is deemed not to be credible. This is despite the Crown Prosecution Service's own guidance which states, 'care must be taken with a suggestion that a person's mental health condition affects their credibility and reliability such that there is insufficient evidence to proceed'.[30] Those witnesses who are suffering from a mental disorder, as defined by the Mental Health Act 1983, or have a significant impairment of intelligence and social functioning[31] qualify for special measures when giving evidence in court. The Court of Appeal[32] has been clear that that a court should take every reasonable step to encourage and facilitate the attendance and participation of vulnerable witnesses.

As a suspect

22.17

The investigation of crimes suspected to have been committed by persons with mental health or capacity issues is often considered to be difficult. The balance to be struck between the public interest in diverting a defendant with significant mental illness from the criminal justice system against safeguarding the public (and those who provide services to people with mental health or capacity issues) is often controversial.

22.18

There is some debate as to whether there is a requirement for an application to made to the Court of Protection ahead of the police interviewing a person who is subject to extant proceedings before that court. This debate is based on a misunderstanding as to the decision of McFarlane J in *LB of Enfield v SA*.[33] That judgment is focused on the ability of a person to consent to an interview as a witness *not* as a defendant.

22.19

In relation to wards of the court (which appears a fair comparator), Sir James Munby P was clear,[34]: 'there is not and never has been any principle or rule that judicial consent is required before the police can interview a ward of court'. There is no requirement of law which requires the Court of Protection to consent to a person who lacks capacity to be interviewed for the police an offence. The only exception to this, perhaps, is where a person is invited to a voluntary interview at the police station and could not understand, retain, use

30 *Mental Health: Victims and Witnesses with Mental Health Conditions and Disorders.*
31 See Youth Justice and Criminal Evidence Act 1999, s 16(2).
32 *R v Lubemba* [2014] EWCA Crim 2064.
33 *LB of Enfield v SA* [2010] EWHC 196 (Admin).
34 *Re Ward of Court (Wardship: Interview)* [2017] EWHC 1022.

or weigh the information they have to be given[35] before deciding whether to engage in the voluntary interview.

22.20

The fact that a person has a diagnosis of a mental illness will not automatically render them unfit to be interviewed.[36] Rather, the focus is upon assessing whether the interview may harm the person, or anything done in respect of the interview process may render the evidence given unreliable. Those interviewing are instructed to seek the advice of healthcare professionals. If a person is suspected as being vulnerable, then they are to be treated as such and provided with access to an appropriate adult.

Fitness to plead and stand trial

22.21

Fitness to plead remains one of the most controversial areas. It refers to a defendant's ability to understand and participate in the legal process and is accepted by most as being a prerequisite to a fair trial. The controversy remains despite the Law Commission's report on the subject.[37] At the core of the debate is the nineteenth-century approach to participation in the criminal process for defendants with mental health and capacity issues. That approach is incongruent with other domestic civil courts which apply an approach based, generally, on whether a person has capacity to conduct the proceedings.

22.22

The legal test for unfitness to plead is derived from the common law, as set down by Alderson B in the 1836 case of *Pritchard*.[38] This case, and those which follow it have set down the criteria as to whether someone is fit to plead which have come to be known as the *Pritchard* criteria. A defendant had to be able to:

(a) plead to the indictment;

(b) understand the course of proceedings;

(c) instruct a lawyer;

(d) challenge a juror; and

(e) understand the evidence.

If an accused was found to lack any one of these abilities that would be sufficient for him or her to be found unfit to plead.

35 See [3.21A] of Code C of the PACE Codes of Practice.
36 See [4] of Annex G of PACE Code C.
37 Law Commission – *Unfitness to Plead Law Commission Report Vol. 1* , No. 364 12 January 2016.
38 *R v Pritchard* (1836) 7 C & P 303, 173 ER 135.

22.23

That legal test advanced further in *M (John)*.[39] That decision, which pre-dates the enactment of the Mental Capacity Act 2005, held that a defendant was unfit to plead if any one or more of the following was beyond his capability:

(a) understanding the charge(s);

(b) deciding whether to plead guilty;

(c) exercising his or her right to challenge jurors;

(d) instructing solicitors and/or advocates;

(e) following the course of the proceedings; and/or

(f) giving evidence in his or her own defence.

22.24

This is distinct to the test which would be applied in civil proceedings which is underpinned by the decisions which follow *Masterman-Lister v Brutton & Co*[40] and the application of sections 2 and 3 of the Mental Capacity Act 2005. The application of the *Pritchard* criteria leads to the situation whereby someone who might be found to lack capacity to conduct proceedings in a civil court is found to be fit to plead in a criminal court.[41] The alignment with the law in the civil courts is not the only concern. There is an additional concern as to whether the *Pritchard* criteria are compatible with the 'effective participation' provision required by Article 6 of the ECHR.

22.25

The requirements of this provision are set out in *SC v United Kingdom* as follows:[42]

> 'effective participation' in this context presupposes that the accused has a broad understanding of the nature of the trial process and of what is at stake for him or her, including the significance of any penalty which may be imposed. It means that he or she, if necessary with the assistance of, for example, an interpreter, lawyer, social worker or friend, should be able to understand the general thrust of what is said in court. The defendant should be able to follow what is said by the prosecution witnesses and, if represented, to explain to his own lawyers his version of events, point out any statements with which he disagrees and make them aware of any facts which should be put forward in his defence.

39 *M (John)* [2003] EWCA Crim 3452.

40 *Masterman-Lister v Brutton & Co* [2003] 3 All ER 162.

41 For an example of this, see a defendant who was suffering from delusions which may have impacted his ability correctly to appraise, believe, weigh up and validly use information: *Moyle* [2008] EWCA Crim 3059.

42 *SC v United Kingdom* (2005) 40 EHRR 10 (Application no 60958/00) 15 June 2004 at [29].

22.26

The Law Commission's proposed solution to these concerns is found in the Criminal Procedure (Lack of Capacity) Bill. That proposal is not universally endorsed. Some[43] have questioned the lack of a consistent diagnostic threshold[44] within the law of diminished responsibility, a reformed insanity defence and a test for lack of capacity in criminal courts and suggested that such a diagnostic threshold could be used to promote consistency. Others argue that a diagnostic threshold is not necessary and the supposed objectivity that such a criterion adds is illusory.[45]

PATIENTS CONCERNED IN CRIMINAL PROCEEDINGS

The application of Article 5

22.27

A mentally disordered person may come within Article 5 for reasons unconnected with their mental health, for example, following conviction or arrest on suspicion of crime (Article 5(1)(a) and (c)). The involvement of the criminal court will mean that in some cases a mentally disordered person will also be detained by virtue of other parts of Article 5(1). Where the person is detained, whether on remand or after conviction for purposes of psychiatric assessment or treatment, then Article 5(1)(e) will apply in addition to Articles 5(1)(a) or (c)

Powers to remand

22.28

The criminal courts have powers[46] to remand a person to a hospital for the report on their mental condition. In the Crown Court[47] that power arises where a person is awaiting trial for an offence or has been arraigned for an offence (but not sentenced) which is punishable with imprisonment. In the magistrates' court[48] the power arises where any person has been convicted of an offence punishable by imprisonment or where a person consents to such remand. To remand a person for assessment, the court must be satisfied that the accused person is suffering a mental disorder following receiving evidence from

43 See H Howard (2016) 'Lack of Capacity: Reforming the Law on Unfitness to Plead' 80 *Journal of Criminal Law* 428. Available at: www.https://doi.org/10.1177/0022018316675544.

44 Meaning a requirement that the defendant is found to have some form of diagnosis of disorder or some other qualifying condition before he can be said to lack the capacity to participate.

45 See J Mason, *Unfitness to Plead, Insanity and the Law Commission: Do We Need a Diagnostic Threshold?* (2021) 85(4) *The Journal of Criminal Law* 268–279.

46 Mental Health Act 1983, s 35.

47 Ibid, at s 35(2)(a).

48 Ibid, at s 35(2)(b).

a registered medical practitioner and that it would be impracticable to obtain such a report were the person bailed.[49]

22.29

In addition, the Crown Court has the power[50] to remand a person to hospital, rather than custody, for treatment if two registered medical practitioners give evidence that a person is suffering from a mental disorder which makes it appropriate for the person to detained in hospital for medical treatment and that appropriate treatment is available for that person.

Hospital or guardianship order

22.30

A hospital order[51] may be made which sends a person to hospital instead of prison upon conviction. The Crown Court or magistrates' court may give a hospital order if convicted of an imprisonable offence and two registered medical practitioners have given evidence that the person has a mental disorder that means you should be in hospital for treatment, and appropriate treatment is available. A guardianship order may be made where a local authority (or alternative guardian)[52] consents to their appointment and it is considered to be the most appropriate disposal in the circumstances. When sentencing to hospital, the judge must have regard to section 37(4) of the Mental Health Act 1983, which requires that she should be satisfied on evidence provided by an approved clinician with overall responsibility for the person's case that there is a bed available for them within 28 days of the order being made. If the judge does not have such regard, then the sentence is invalid.[53]

22.31

Where the Crown Court has made a section 37 hospital order, it may also impose restriction on discharge.[54] This is known as a 'Restriction Order'. Before the Crown Court makes such an order it must be satisfied having regard to the nature of the offence, the antecedents of the offender and the risk of his committing further offences if set at large, that it is necessary for the protection of the public from serious harm so to do. Those restrictions limit the ability of the person to be discharged and limits their ability to obtain leave[55] from the hospital without the involvement of the Secretary of State for Justice.[56] These

49 Ibid, at s 35(3).
50 Ibid, at s 36.
51 Ibid, at s 37.
52 Ibid, at s 37(6).
53 *R. v Ellerton (Mark William)* [2022] EWCA Crim 194.
54 Mental Health Act 1983, s 41.
55 Any rejection of leave must be for a rational reason which properly bears on the protection of the public: *X v Secretary of State for Justice* [2009] EWHC 2465 (Admin).
56 Who delegates these powers to the Mental Health Casework Section at the Ministry of Justice.

restrictive aspects have, by analogy, caused criminal practitioners to consider that a hospital order with restriction is akin to a life sentence.

22.32

Whilst the restriction order is in place, the powers of section 42 of the Mental Health Act 1983 apply. Those powers include recalling a person to hospital. For the recall to be in accordance with Article 5(1) it is necessary for there to be up-to-date medical evidence which shows that something has happened since leaving hospital.[57]

TRANSFER FROM PRISON TO HOSPITAL

22.33

Sections 47 to 53 make provision for the transfer of prisoners (including civil prisoners and other detainees) from prison to hospital. Such transfers engage a number of different rights under the ECHR. To keep a prisoner in a prison setting when they require admission to hospital may amount to inhuman or degrading treatment or punishment which is contrary to Article 3 of the ECHR.[58] A breach of Article 8 of the EHCR may also be established[59] as may an Article 5(1) breach.[60]

Parole and licence conditions

22.34

It is not unusual for prisoners with mental health or capacity issues to be released with licence conditions. Some prisoners are released following a parole process. It is not uncommon for those parole processes to hear and consider evidence which relates to the mental health of a prisoner and how it relates to their risk of re-offending. The rules of evidence before the Parole Board are flexible. In some cases, a psychologist or psychiatrist member of the Board will be appointed to hear a case where it is thought that their specialist expertise is required.[61] That specialist member may lead the questioning of certain witnesses.[62] Where the Parole Board hears from expert witnesses instructed on behalf of the prisoner, it must specify why they took a different view to that expert if they reject their

57 See judgment of Toulson LJ in *MM v The Secretary of State for the Home Department* [2007] EWCA Civ 687.

58 See *R v Drew* [2003] UKHL 25 at [17]–[18].

59 If it is established that it amounts to interference with mental and physical integrity.

60 If it is established that there is an excessive delay between a transfer from the prison estate to a hospital. See *Pankiewicz v Poland* (Application no 34151/04), 12 February 2008; *Brand v The Netherlands* (Application no 49902/99), 10 November 2004.

61 See Oral Hearing Guidance at [3.17].

62 Ibid at [4.45].

analysis.[63] The failure to give reasons for rejecting expert evidence can result in a decision being quashed.[64]

Prisoners who lack the mental capacity to conduct their parole process

22.35

The participation of prisoners who lacked the mental capacity to conduct their parole processes was given little thought ahead of recent litigation *in EG, R (On the Application Of) v The Parole Board of England and Wales.*[65] That litigation led to a change (mid-proceedings) to the provision of the Parole Board Rules 2019 and the provisions contained within Rule 10 which allow the appointment of a representative for a prisoner who lacks the capacity to appoint a representative. The Administrative Court has interpreted this provision widely as allowing the appointment of a litigation friend. The Official Solicitor for England and Wales has agreed to be appointed in this role at least twice since the rule came into force.

Licence conditions

22.36

The Licence Conditions Policy Framework published[66] by the Ministry of Justice makes, surprisingly, no particular reference to the mental capacity of offenders released on licence. However, specific provision is made for the release on licence of those offenders to whom the Mental Health Act 1983 applies.[67]

22.37

Despite this, there is a requirement that licence conditions are explained to prisoners prior to their release, especially when disability may impact upon their understanding.[68] Undoubtedly, there would be a question as to whether it was lawful to recall a prisoner on the basis of the breach of a licence condition they could not understand. Similarly, the mental health and capacity of an offender would be relevant factor when considering whether it is necessary to recall them to prison.[69] Particular considerations apply when a person with extant licence conditions appears before the Court of Protection. In those

63 Ibid at [6.29].

64 See the judgment of HHJ Jarman QC in *The Queen (On the Application of Steven Stokes) v Parole Board of England and Wales v Secretary of State for Justice* [2020] EWHC 1885 (Admin) and Steven Kovats QC in *PL v Parole Board of England and Wales* [2019] EWHC 3306 (Admin).

65 *EG, R (On the Application Of) v The Parole Board of England and Wales* [2020] EWHC 1457 (Admin).

66 July 2021.

67 Ibid at [3.58]–[3.59].

68 Ibid at [3.54].

69 *The Queen on the application of Michael Goldsworthy v Secretary of State for Justice v Parole Board for England and Wales* [2017] EWHC 2822 (Admin).

circumstances, the Court of Protection may be denied the opportunity to make a decision on behalf of a person who lacks capacity because it is specified by a licence condition. For example, a licence condition may specify whether a person is able to access the internet, the Court of Protection could not make a decision which conflicted with that licence condition. Similarly, where an offender appears before the Court of Protection, careful consideration will need to be given as to what information is made public and what remains confidential.[70]

THE FUTURE

22.38

A comprehensive, single piece of legislation which addresses the compendium of issues which arise when a person with mental health or capacity issues interacts with the criminal justice system would appear to be unlikely. However, incremental change and a greater awareness is more likely. The Equality and Human Rights Commission's report,[71] the Advocates' Gateway[72] and the joint thematic inspection of the criminal justice journey for individuals with mental health needs and disorders[73] all point to a system which will change.

22.39

To what extent the criminal justice system will reform to meet the needs of persons with mental health and mental capacity issues remains to be seen. Reform of the Mental Health Act is underway and the role of the Court of Protection in preventing offending following *JB* will be explored in coming years.[74] The challenge for legislators and the courts will be to build a modern system which allows all the constituent parts of the system to function in such a way which properly supports people with mental health and capacity issues. Likewise, for professionals to have the confidence to communicate with those people and secure their rights within disparate systems and different courts.

---

70 See *A Local Authority v P (by his Litigation Friend, the Official Solicitor), National Probation Service* [2019] EWCOP 67.

71 *Inclusive Justice: A System Designed for All.*

72 Available at: www.theadvocatesgateway.org/.

73 Available at: www.justiceinspectorates.gov.uk/cjji/wp-content/uploads/sites/2/2021/11/Mental-health-joint-thematic-report.pdf.

74 *A Local Authority v JB (Rev 1)* [2021] UKSC 52.

23 Children

Joanne Cecil

INTRODUCTION

23.1

Children are fully fledged rightsholders, not merely beneficiaries of protection. They occupy a special status within the law. This is reflected in this chapter appearing in Part 3. In reality, of course, the issues relating to children arise across throughout the criminal justice process but given those around the age of responsibility and issues of how children might participate in any trial, it remains here.

23.2

This chapter does not attempt to traverse the plethora of human rights instruments but instead will focus on those most frequently invoked and where the advent of human rights has had a marked impact, namely the development and use of rights under the European Convention on Human Rights (ECHR) and those found within the UN Convention on the Rights of the Child (UNCRC), arguably the most influential international instrument within the UK regarding the rights of children.

23.3

The case of *T and V The United Kingdom*,[1] has perhaps had the most substantial impact on the development of the criminal law with regard to child defendants in England and Wales from a human rights perspective – influencing issues relating to minimum age of responsibility, effective participation, sentencing, the removal of tariff setting by the Executive, reporting restrictions and lifelong anonymity.

23.4

Despite court and judicial system efforts to accommodate the young people brought through it, to bend rigid criminal proceedings into a just process and to realise the rights of children in conflict with the law doubt remains as to the way in which children and young people who offend are dealt with in this country. Although many measures have been set in place to try and make proceedings appear 'fair', the question remains whether a young child, whose mind is not

1 *T and V The United Kingdom* (2000) 30 EHRR 121.

yet fully developed, can ever properly engage in the austere processes we deploy. There can be no doubt that children are poorly served from initial contact with the criminal justice through to sentencing and beyond.

THE ECHR, THE UNCRC AND OTHER INTERNATIONAL INSTRUMENTS

23.5

The legal landscape in England and Wales has been influenced by several its international obligations, most significantly by the ECHR and the UNCRC.[2] The ECHR applies equally to adults and children but does not contain a definition of a child and does not distinguish between adults and children. States are, however, obliged to secure rights under the Convention to 'everyone' within its jurisdiction (Article 1) and to ensure that those rights are enjoyed 'without discrimination on any ground', including grounds of age (Article 14). Strasbourg jurisprudence in the area of criminal justice and more generally aligns with the UNCRC, with a person below 18 years of age defined as a child

23.6

The United Nations Declaration on the Rights of the Child 1959 and the UNCRC require that a child enjoys special protection.[3] The guiding principle for safeguarding and promoting the welfare of children is found in Article 3 of UNCRC. This states that 'In all actions concerning children, whether undertaken by public or private social welfare institutions, courts of law, administrative authorities or legislative bodies, the *best interests* of the child should be of primary consideration' (emphasis added).[4] The essential safeguards in the UNCRC concerning children in conflict with the law are supplemented by many other specific instruments.[5] In 2010, the Committee of Ministers of the Council of Europe issued Guidelines on 'Child-friendly Justice'. The Guidelines set out a definition of the term:

> 'Child-friendly justice' refers to justice systems which guarantee the respect and the effective implementation of all children's rights at the highest attainable level, bearing in mind the principles listed below and giving due consideration to the child's level of maturity and understanding and the circumstances of the case. It is, in particular, justice that is accessible, age appropriate, speedy, diligent, adapted to

2 Adopted and opened for signature, ratification and accession by General Assembly Resolution 44/25 of 20 November 1989. Entered into force 2 September 1990, in accordance with Art 49.

3 For discussion, see *(HC) v SSHD* [2013] EWHC 982 Admin.

4 See also Art 37 on detention and Art 40 concerning juvenile justice.

5 See, eg, *The United Nations Standard Minimum Rules for the Administration of Juvenile Justice* (the Beijing Rules 1985), *The United Nations Guidelines for the Prevention of Juvenile Delinquency* (the Riyadh Guidelines), *The United Nations Rules for the Protection of Juveniles Deprived of Their Liberty* (the Havana Rules), *The UN Guidelines for Action on Children in the Criminal Justice System* (the Vienna Guidelines 1997) and *The UN Model Strategies and Practical Measures on the Elimination of Violence against Children in the Field of Crime Prevention and Criminal Justice* (2014).

and focused on the needs and rights of the child, respecting the rights of the child including the rights to due process, to participate in and to understand the proceedings, to respect for private and family life and to integrity and dignity.

THE DEFINITION OF A CHILD

23.7

The UNCRC defines a child as 'every human being below the age of 18 years unless under the law applicable to the child, majority is attained earlier' (Article 1). In the UK, the age of majority aligns with this at 18; however, the legal framework is more complicated. For example, some domestic legislation mirrors the international provisions, such as the Children Act 1989. Others, primarily in the criminal sphere, draw a distinction between a child (under 14) and 'young person'.[6] Conflicting terminology arises in the Codes of Practice of the Police and Criminal Evidence Act 1984 (PACE 1984) and section 29(1) of the Magistrates Courts Act. In those provisions, the term 'juvenile' is used to refer to those young people under 18 years of age. The most recent Sentencing Act 2020 uses a variety of terms including 'child', young offender', 'person under 18' and 'offender aged under 18'. The Sentencing Council uses 'children and young people' for those offenders aged under 18,[7] with the Judicial College adopting the term 'youth defendants' (Youths in the Crown Court, August 2022) while noting the inconsistency across the legislative landscape.

23.8

Historically, as discussed further below, inconsistency in definition and an evolving concept of childhood has resulted in lacunae within the law, specifically for those children aged over 16 but who had not attained adulthood, namely those of 17 years of age.[8] Terminology is important, both regarding the rights, entitlements, duties and obligations that flow. 'Children' occupy a special status within the law, and with that a host of additional domestic and international protections but also in engendering cultural change. One only has to consider the term 'delinquent'. A child-centred approach requires identification of that person as a 'child'.

23.9

On the international plane, the term 'children in conflict with the law' encompasses those under the age of 18 who encounter the justice system as a result of being suspected or accused of committing an offence. This terminology

6 See, eg, the Children and Young Persons Act 1933, s 107(1) and the Children and Young Persons Act 1969, s 70(1).

7 *Sentencing Children and Young People – Overarching Principles*, effective from 1 June 2017.

8 See *R(ota HC) v SSHD* [2013] EWHC 982 Admin considering the position regarding provisions contained in PACE Codes of Practice and the lacuna relating to the requirement for an appropriate adult in the police station.

has been adopted in other jurisdictions including by the Scottish Government[9] and by the Inns of Court College of Advocacy in its guidance for practitioners who prosecute or defend children and young people in the criminal justice system.

THE AGE OF CRIMINAL RESPONSIBILITY

23.10

England, Wales and Northern Ireland remain outliers in terms of the prevailing laws on the age of criminal responsibility, setting the age at which a child can be prosecuted for a criminal offence at just 10 years.[10] This is now the lowest level in Western Europe. Although previously Switzerland and Scotland set it lower, at ages seven and eight respectively, this has now changed, with the former revising the minimum age to 10, so on a par with England and Wales, and the latter raising the age to 12.[11] The average age of criminal responsibility within Europe is 14 years of age, with Switzerland (and Ireland in some limited exceptions) being the only other country with a minimum age of 10.[12]

23.11

There is no specified minimum age of criminal responsibility (MACR) in international human rights instruments. The UN Standard Minimum Rules for the Administration of Juvenile Justice (the Beijing Rules)[13] which, as the title suggests, represented the minimum conditions deemed acceptable by the UN for the treatment of children in the criminal justice system, preceded the UNCRC and provides some guidance regarding relevant considerations as to age threshold. Although the Beijing Rules are not binding on the UK, they run alongside the UNCRC, which has adopted many of its provisions. In addition to dealing with several basic principles, the Beijing Rules recommend that the age of criminal responsibility should not be set 'at too low an age level' and simply refers to 'bearing in mind the facts of emotional, mental and intellectual maturity'. The commentary to Rule 4 provides some further elucidation in drawing the parallels between criminal responsibility and the realisation of other social, economic and political rights and responsibilities:

> The minimum age of criminal responsibility differs widely owing to history and culture. The modern approach would be to consider whether a child can live up to the moral and psychological components of criminal responsibility; that is, whether a child, by virtue of her or

9 Working with Children in Conflict with the Law 2021 (Scottish Government, 2021).

10 Section 50 of the Children and Young Persons Act 1933; see also the Crime and Disorder Act 1998, s 34 abolishing '*doli incapax*', the rebuttal presumption that a child aged 10 or over is incapable of committing an offence. The age of criminal responsibility having been raised in England and Wales from the age of eight in 1963.

11 Age of Criminal Responsibility (Scotland) Act 2019.

12 Child Rights International Network, Minimum age of Responsibility in Europe.

13 Approved by the UN Seventh Congress on 6 September 1986.

> his individual discernment and understanding, can be held responsible for essentially anti-social behaviour. If the age of criminal responsibility is fixed too low or if there is no lower age limit at all, the notion of responsibility would become meaningless. In general, the is a close relationship between the notion of responsibility for delinquent or criminal behaviour and other social rights and responsibilities (such as marital status, civil majority, etc.).[14]

23.12

Similarly, Article 40(3)(a) of the UNCRC does not suggest or specify any age, nor give any indication as to how low would be 'too low' for these purposes. Article 40(3) of the UNCRC requires signatories to:

> seek to promote the establishment of laws, procedures, authorities and institutions specifically applicable to children alleged as, accused of, or recognized as having infringed the penal law, and, in particular: (a) The establishment of a minimum age below which children shall be presumed not to have the capacity to infringe the penal law; and (b) whenever appropriate and desirable, measures for dealing with such children without resorting to judicial proceedings, providing that human rights and legal safeguards are fully respected.

23.13

The age of criminal responsibility was considered by the Strasbourg Court in 1999 in *T and V v The United Kingdom*,[15] the well-known case concerning two defendants who had been charged with the murder of Jamie Bulger, a toddler. The boys were both aged 10 at the time of the offences and just 11 at the time of their trials. A challenge was brought on the basis that it violated Article 3 of the ECHR in that the threshold age for criminal responsibility could amount to inhuman or degrading treatment.

23.14

The Court referred to the absence (at that time) of a prevailing standard across the European jurisdictions for a common age of criminal responsibility. It noted that the age of 10 was not so young as to disproportionately differ from the various ages in other European countries. There was, in other words, nothing to suggest that treating a 10-year-old as having the same criminal responsibility and culpability as an adult was, in itself, a violation of the child's rights, though this did not mean that the justices were united in considering this age of responsibility as unproblematic.

---

14 The UN Standard Minimum Rules for the Administration of Juvenile Justice (the Beijing Rules), Commentary, Rule 4.

15 *T and V v The United Kingdom* (2000) 30 EHRR 121.

23.15

Such was the strength of feeling on this point that five of the 17 judges issued dissenting opinions to the effect that the age of responsibility in this case was so low as to be a violation of Article 3, the right to protection from torture or cruel and inhumane treatment. The majority, however, did not agree, and the conclusion of the Court was that the attribution of criminal responsibility to the applicants did not, in itself give rise to any such breach. This was not without controversy domestically. Shortly after the Joint Committee on Human Rights recommended that Parliament reconsidered and raised the age of criminal responsibility to 12. This was rejected by the Government at the time.[16] Since then there have been repeated calls for an increase in the age threshold for criminal responsibility.[17]

23.16

Internationally, the UNCRC has similarly continued to express concerns including recommending in 2002 that the UK should raise it 'considerably'.[18] In 2007, it declared that an age of criminal responsibility of younger than 12 years is not 'internationally acceptable' and constituted a bare minimum. In addition it recommended that the threshold be raised to 14 or 16 to contribute to a juvenile justice system which accords with the requirements of Article 40(3)(b) of the UNCRC.[19] The criticisms were repeated in 2016, with a recommendation to raise the minimum age in 'in accordance with acceptable international standards'.[20] This followed a joint submission by the UK Children's Commissioners to the UNCRC in May 2016, calling for the UK and devolved governments to raise the minimum age of criminal responsibility 'as a matter of urgency'.[21] The Children and Young People's Commissioner for Scotland urged an incremental increase towards a minimum age of criminal responsibility of 14 or 16 years.

23.17

A Private Members Bill to raise the age of criminal responsibility has been introduced by Lord Dholakia, Liberal Democrat and is, at the time of writing, in its Second Reading in the House of Lords.[22] This follows an earlier failed attempt by Lord Dholakia in 2016.[23]

---

16 *Joint Committee Report on the UN Convention on the Rights of the Child*, 10th Report of 2002–2003, HL 117 HC 81.

17 See, eg, *The Age of Criminal Responsibility, Briefing Paper Number 7687*, 15 August 2016, T McGuinness, House of Commons Library.

18 See note 4 above, at [59] and [62(a)].

19 United Nations Committee on the Rights of the Child (2007) *General Comment No 10* at [32].

20 UN Committee on the Rights of the Child, *Concluding observations on the fifth periodic report of the United Kingdom of Great Britain and Northern Ireland*, CRC/C/GBR/CO/5, 12 July 2016 at [79].

21 UN Committee on the Rights of the Child, *Examination of the Fifth Periodic Report of the United Kingdom of Great Britain and Northern Ireland – UK Children's Commissioners' Recommendations*, May 2016.

22 HL Bill 90, *Age of Criminal Responsibility Bill* [HL] – Parliamentary Bills – UK Parliament.

23 See, eg, Response of Lord Faulks on behalf of the Government to the Second Reading of Lord Dholakia's Age of Criminal Responsibility Bill, HL Deb 29 January 2016 c1574–75.

DIVERSION AND OUT OF COURT DISPOSALS

23.18

Much of the trajectory of courtroom practice since *T and V* has been towards a more robust framework for the disposal of matters involving very young offenders. Domestic case law has dealt with the obligations owed by the courts towards children on several occasions. *R v G and another*[24] revised the approach to take to the concept of recklessness and concerned a pair of defendants aged 11 and 12 who had set fire to some newspapers in the back of a shop, thrown them under some dustbins (apparently expecting that the newspapers would simply burn out) and thereby started a fire which spread and caused approximately £1 million of damage.

23.19

The House of Lords considered and unanimously overruled the previous prevailing authority of *R v Caldwell*,[25] observing that it was not clearly blameworthy to do something involving risk of injury to another if one genuinely did not perceive the risk[26] – which plainly a child might not – and concluding that the age and maturity of the defendants (certainly where they were children) was a relevant consideration for the purposes of deciding whether or not they had behaved recklessly. In the words of Lord Bingham, 'it is neither moral nor just to convict a defendant (least of all a child) on the strength of what someone else would have apprehended if the defendant himself had no such apprehension'.[27]

23.20

Indeed, all parts of the criminal justice system are, albeit somewhat lately, moving to contend with their obligations to children and young people as users of the court. Significant work has been undertaken to provide guidance on diversion and/or decisions to prosecute. That is beyond the scope of this chapter, however this includes specialist guidance from the Ministry of Justice, CPS, Police, YOT, Youth Justice Board and other involved agencies.

23.21

Fundamentally, there is a growing recognition, supported by a sizeable body of evidence, that the criminalising of children and young people is of itself undesirable, and should be avoided unless absolutely necessary. Evidence and research gathered by, for example, the Youth Justice Board for England and Wales (a non-departmental public body responsible for overseeing youth justice) stresses that it is preferable where possible to divert young people with problematic conduct away from judicial criminal disposals, which overall

---

24 *R v G and another* [2003] UKHL 1; [2004] 1 AC 1034.

25 *R v Caldwell* [1982] AC 341.

26 Other than for reasons of self-induced intoxication

27 *The Age of Criminal Responsibility, Briefing Paper Number 7687*, 15 August 2016, T McGuinness, House of Commons Library at [32]–[33].

make children more likely to reoffend rather than less. This accords with the underlying principles in the UNCRC which places a duty to promote measures without recourse to 'judicial proceedings'.[28]

FAIR TRIAL, ARTICLE 6 AND EFFECTIVE PARTICIPATION[29]

23.22

Robert Thomson and Jon Venables were both aged 10 at the time they committed their offence and just 11 at the time of their trial and conviction for the murder of James Bulger, a toddler. They were tried in an adult Crown Court, in the full glare of the media and in the full face of public hostility. In view of their youth, several modifications were made by the Crown Court, notionally to ensure they could participate as effectively as possible in proceedings. For example, they were seated next to social workers in a specially raised dock, within 'whispering distance' [30] of their parents and lawyers (with whom they were also permitted to interact in a special 'play area' during adjournments). Hearing times were also shortened to reflect the school day.

23.23

This was, however, the first time that the Strasbourg Court had to consider how Article 6 should apply to a trial involving a child. Here they did find that the youth of the appellants had contributed to a violation, despite the 'not inconsiderable' modifications made by the Crown Court. The fact that the trial took place in public, under intense media scrutiny, formed a large part of the Court's reasoning. They concluded that where a young child is charged with a grave criminal offence, it may be necessary for steps to be taken such as to conduct the trial in private, 'so as to reduce as far as possible the child's feeling of intimidation and inhibition',[31] or possibly to limit the amount of press reporting.

23.24

The judgment in *T and V* resulted in the promulgation by the then Lord Chief Justice, Lord Bingham, of a specific practice direction to ensure compliance with a child's right to a fair trial. This required significant adaptations and minimum standards of practice to guarantee a child's effective participation. This practice direction has been modified over the years, reflecting the increased appreciation of the unique issues faced when trying children. These have continually stressed the need to take account of a child's relative lack of emotional maturity, intellectual development and their overall wellbeing. Increasingly when dealing with young defendants and witnesses the Courts have adopted methods such as the use of pre-trial familiarisation visits, the removal of wigs and gowns and a

---

28 UNCRC, art 40(3)(b).

29 See also Chapter 24.

30 *T and V v The United Kingdom* [2000] 30 EHRR 121 at [90].

31 Ibid at [87].

general reduction in the formality of proceedings for the benefit of any children and young people involved.

23.25

Even these measures have not always been enough, however, to allay the concerns of the Strasbourg Court. Notably, in *SC v United Kingdom,*[32] an 11-year-old defendant was convicted of robbing an 87-year old woman and was sentenced to two-and-a-half year's detention following a trial in the Crown Court. Experts who had assessed the defendant before his trial had formed the view that he had a significant degree of learning difficulty and a low intellectual level for his age, severely limiting his understanding of the trial process. The court, rejecting submissions from his counsel that trying him would amount to an abuse of process, and finding that the defendant was fit to plead, nevertheless attempted to make proceedings as informal as possible for his benefit.

23.26

The Strasbourg Court recognised that the defendant did not need to understand every single point of law or technicality of proceedings to be said to have 'participated effectively' in his trial. Nevertheless, they noted that, although the defendant appeared to understand that what he did was wrong, his understanding of the consequences flowing from his actions was extremely limited. Of particular concern to the Strasbourg Court was the defendant's apparent lack of understanding that he could receive a custodial sentence for his offence; following sentence, when he was taken below stairs to the cells, he appeared to be confused and frightened, having apparently been under the impression that he would be returning home to his foster father. This ultimately led the Strasbourg Court to conclude that, notwithstanding the measures taken by the Crown Court, the defendant's Article 6 rights had been violated by the trial he had received.

23.27

One of the most significant advances in this regard in ensuring the effective participation of child defendant's came in 2013, when children were recognised as 'vulnerable people in court' and a section on intermediaries was introduced. The Criminal Procedure Rules 2020 (Part 18), as amended by the Criminal Procedure (Amendment) Rules 2021, provide special measures to assist and facilitate a defendant under the age of 18 to participate in their trial, and to give evidence, including by the appointment of an intermediary.[33] The Consolidated

---

32 *SC v United Kingdom* (2005) 40 EHRR 10.

33 See, however, *R v Cox (Practice Note)* [2012] EWCA Crim 549; [2012] 2 Cr App R 6 where, although it was determined that it would be desirable to use an intermediary, it did not follow that the trial should be stopped when it was impossible to find one. Rather, it was for the judge to make an informal assessment of whether the trial could proceed fairly without one. See also *R (P) v Barking Youth Court* [2002] 2 Cr App R 19, DC, and *DPP v P* [2007] EWCHC 949 (Admin); 1 WLR 1005, DC, re: exceptional circumstances when a stay might be imposed in advance of hearing any evidence at trial, again leaving the question of a child's level of understanding to be determined by the court. If the court/judge decides that the child cannot understand, or take an effective role in proceedings, it should consider moving to a trial under s 4A of the Criminal Procedure (Insanity) Act 1964, namely whether the child did the act alleged.

Criminal Procedure Rules and Practice Directions[34] generally sets out the court's duty to adapt to assist the young who are by definition vulnerable, and underline that it is the duty of the parties and of the court to identify the needs of witnesses and, by implication, defendants at an early stage.[35] This is to ensure appropriate treatment and questioning, especially where the court directs that the latter be through an intermediary.[36]

23.28

The statutory power to appoint an intermediary for a defendant giving evidence under section 33BA of the Youth Justice and Criminal Evidence Act 1999 is not yet in force. The power of a judge to grant an intermediary is therefore governed by the inherent power of the court at common law as recognised in *C v Sevenoaks Youth Court*.[37] To refuse an intermediary, where required, would breach the defendant's Article 6 rights as it would impede their ability to effectively participate. Where a defendant is not able to effectively participate in their trial, the case must be stayed as an abuse of process.[38] This power is rarely exercised and has a degree of overlap with issues relating to fitness to plead. Guidance can be found in the lead cases of *R v Dean Thomas*[39] and *TI v Bromley Youth Court*.[40] In *TI*, the Court noted that:

> The essential point is that any defendant in any criminal proceedings must have a fair trial. Where a defendant cannot participate effectively in the proceedings, whether in whole or in part, he will not have a fair trial. Particular problems may arise in cases involving vulnerable young defendants and a court must be vigilant to consider how issues of concentration and understanding may affect such a defendant's ability to participate in his trial. We note also that, where the defendant is under 18, the court is under a duty to 'have regard to the welfare of the child or young person' pursuant to Section 44(1) of the Children and Young Persons Act 1933. This statutory duty essentially is mirrored by the provisions of Article 3(1) of the UN Convention on the Rights of the Child identifying the rights of the child as being a primary consideration for any court taking a step in respect of a child.[41]

23.29

None of the judgments given above, however, mean that the trial of a defendant who is a youth, or with limited mental capacity, will necessarily lead to a breach of Article 6 even when modifications are not deployed.

34 The Criminal Procedure Rules 2020.
35 Ibid, r 13(2)(b) and (3).
36 Ibid, r 3.8(6).
37 *C v Sevenoaks Youth Court* [2009] EWHC 3088 (Admin).
38 *R (P) v West London Youth Court* [2005] EWHC 2583 (Admin).
39 *R v Dean Thomas* [2020] EWCA Crim 117
40 *TI v Bromley Youth Court* [2020] EWHC 1204 (Admin)
41 Ibid at [43].

23.30

R v Grant-Murray (Janelle) and others[42] concerned multiple defendants involved in a joint-enterprise murder and GBH trial as a result of a spontaneous altercation with a rival gang. At the time of the offences, one defendant was aged 14 while the other two were 13. The Crown Court, over a long and complex case, therefore had to consider not only how to tailor proceedings to accommodate their youth (including considering whether an intermediary would be required), but also how this affected any directions to the jury on joint enterprise, given that two of the defendants also had significant cognitive and developmental difficulties, falling in the lowest percentile. In short, limited modifications were made and limited consideration given to the fact that they were young children in lengthy criminal proceedings. It was submitted that the relevant *Criminal Practice Directions for Vulnerable Defendants* had not been followed and that they had been unable to effectively participate. Although an intermediary had been available to one defendant, there was a failure to comply with the ground rules which resulted in the impermissible use of non-literal language, complex vocabulary, failure to signpost, lengthy and multiple-part questions, tagged questions and statements used as questions.

23.31

Exceptionally, the EHRC intervened asserting that there was a systemic problem in many trials leading to a lack of support for vulnerable defendants in court, a lack of adherence to the practice directions and insufficient training for both practitioners and judges. Whilst the application to appeal was dismissed, the court made important comments on the training of practitioners representing children and vulnerable defendants in the criminal courts and resulted in procedural changes to ensure that practice directions relating to vulnerable defendants are properly considered.

23.32

A concurrent challenge to conviction was also made on the basis of the joint enterprise directions provided to the jury, which although correct in what was understood to be the law at the time, had later been found to be wrong in the case of *R v Jogee* by the Supreme Court.[43] Namely, that mere foresight of an accomplice's intention is not enough to prove guilt against a secondary party to an offence and that intention to commit the crime was the true determinant of liability for all those involved in an offence. Specific arguments were advanced regarding its application to children and that the trial judge ought to have directed the jury as to how to properly assess the reaction and responses of defendants in those particular circumstances and with those particular conditions, rather than giving a standard joint-enterprise direction. This included arguments based upon emerging science regarding adolescent brain development, as discussed further below.

42 *R v Grant-Murray (Janelle) and others* [2017] EWCA Crim 1228.
43 *R v Jogee* [2016] UKSC 8.

23.33

This argument (amongst others) was rejected by the Court of Appeal on the basis that the jury had been made aware of the defendants' youth, deficits and reasoning during the evidence, and that 'experienced trial counsel, including leading counsel, did not think that specifically tailored directions were appropriate'.[44] It is questionable whether the issue was even considered.

23.34

One specific aspect which has continued to be met with a degree of resistance is the placement of children in the dock. Although there have been instances of good practice it is still the norm in serious offending in hearings and trials in the Crown Court for children to remain in the dock.[45] In *Grant-Murray*, all six defendants in the trial sat in the dock, with no supporting adults, for the duration of the trial. An incident arose with one defendant setting fire to another's hair in the ante room to the dock. There had been no consideration of the relevant practice direction. Whilst the appeal court found that it was 'regrettable'[46] that a discussion about where the defendants should sit did not happen in open court, it went on to find that this did not render the convictions unsafe. In this respect the lessons of *T and V* have not been learned. Not only does this impact on effective participation, but also issues of prejudice. There has arguably been a growing momentum in recent years for change from stakeholders across the criminal justice system, including some of the senior judiciary.[47]

23.35

Notwithstanding these provisions, as with many areas relating to children in conflict with the law, implementation is poor, with inconsistent decision making and concerns about resource constraints impermissibly informing decisions.[48] There remains an uneasy tension between the findings of the Strasbourg Court, the evolution of courtroom procedure for young court users and the continued trial of youths in the Crown Court.

44 Ibid at [100]–[104].

45 *R v Grant-Murray (Janelle) and others* [2017] EWCA Crim 1228.

46 Ibid at [157].

47 See, eg, The Howard League (2020) 'What if the Dock Was Abolished in Criminal Courts?' referencing comments of the then Lord Chief Justice, Lord Thomas, regarding magistrates' courts; and J Blackstock (2015) 'In the Dock: Reassessing the Use of the Dock in Criminal Trials', in JUSTICE, 1 July 2015. Available at: https://justice.org.uk/in-the-dock/.

48 See, eg, the Law Commission report 'Unfitness to Plead (Law Com No 364) and C Taylor *Review of the Youth Justice System in England and Wales* (London: Ministry of Justice 2016). Available at: https://assets.publishing.service.gov.uk/government/uploads/system/uploads/attachment_data/file/577103/youth-justice-review-final-report.pdf.

ADOLESCENT BRAIN DEVELOPMENT: IMPLICATIONS FROM A HUMAN RIGHTS PERSPECTIVE, CULPABILITY, FORESIGHT AND REHABILITATION

23.36

Many developments in the UK are being driven by an increasing awareness and understanding of neurological development, brain functioning and comparative deficits into early adulthood and up to the age of 25. There is a strong base of emerging evidence highlighting consistent and universal differences in the judgment and consequential thinking processes between children and young people and adults. Although young offenders may know the difference between right and wrong, they may not fully appreciate risk, understand the consequences of their violent or disruptive actions, the processes they then go through in court or in custody, or have the means to address their behaviour.

23.37

Issues of adolescent development have traditionally been conceptualised in terms of youth and maturity as established features of mitigation; however, this is changing. The intrinsic characteristics of children from a scientific developmental perspective has been recognised by the United States Supreme Court in a trilogy of seminal judgments.[49] In each of these cases the Court drew upon scientific studies on adolescent brain development in concluding that adolescents, by virtue of their inherent psychological and neurobiological immaturity, are not as responsible for their behaviour as adults. Specific areas of developmental delay are relevant to the question of capacity and criminal responsibility:

> One of the key distinctions they draw is between cognition (generally present in adolescents) and judgment (often considered to be lacking), with the latter taken to include the ability to 'imagine alternative courses of action, think of potential consequences of these hypothetical actions, estimate probabilities of their occurrence, weigh desirability in accordance with one's preferences, and engage in comparative deliberations about alternatives and consequences.[50]

23.38

Most recently a line of authorities has sought to deal with the somewhat arbitrary issue of those who are 18 and over at the point of commission of an offence. The crossing of the age threshold into adulthood at 18:

---

49 *Roper v Simmons* 543 US 551 (2005), *Graham v Florida* 130 S Ct 2011 (2010), *Miller v Alabama*, 132 S Ct 2455, 2460 (2012).

50 C Walsh (2011) 'Youth Justice and Neuroscience: A Dual-Use Dilemma' 51(1) *The British Journal of Criminology* 21–39.

has many legal consequences, but it does not present a cliff edge for the purposes of sentencing … Full maturity and all the attributes of adulthood are not magically conferred on young people on their 18th birthdays. The youth and maturity of an offender will be factors that inform any sentencing decision, even if an offender has passed his or her 18th birthday.[51]

51 *R v Clarke* [2018] EWCA Crim 185.

Part 4

Trial and sentence

24 Participation and a fair and impartial tribunal

Peter Carter KC

CONSTITUENT FEATURES OF A FAIR TRIAL

24.1

A fair trial is identified by a number of features. These constituent features have developed over time and are an amalgam of common law, statute and international law standards (some of which have been incorporated into domestic law by statute).

24.2

A fair trial includes rights which protect an accused before the 'trial' as we know it starts. The right to a fair trial has as its corollary the right not to be tried unfairly. In *R v Horseferry Road Magistrates' Court ex p Bennett* [1994] 1 AC 42, Lord Oliver said at paragraph [68] it is '... axiomatic that a person charged with having committed a criminal offence should receive a fair trial and that, if he cannot be tried fairly for that offence, he should not be tried at all'. It is a substantive right engaged throughout the criminal process.

24.3

A fair trial consists of the following[1] –

(a) The presumption of innocence

(b) No punishment without law. The law must be ascertainable. Courts cannot create new offences,[2] nor can the executive do so under the guise of the prerogative.[3]

(c) The accused must be informed at the time of arrest and/or charge of the offence alleged.

(d) Freedom from discrimination or profiling

(e) The right to legal representation of the accused's choice, including during pre-charge interviews, or the right to represent themselves.

---

1 See Fair Trials International's Fair Trials Guide – The right to a fair trial | Fair Trials | Fairness, equality, justice; and Amnesty International's Fair Trial Manual – Amnesty International.

2 *R v Jones* [2006] UKHL 16; [2006] 2 WLR 772 at [61] citing *Knuller (Publishing, Printing and Promotions) Ltd v Director of Public Prosecutions* [1973] AC 435.

3 *R v Jones*, ibid at [22].

(f) The right to attend court hearings and be present throughout.

(g) Open and public hearings.

(h) The right to challenge the evidence of prosecution witnesses, embracing the right to notice in advance of the evidence to be relied upon by the prosecution.

(i) Time and facilities for the accused to prepare and present a defence on equivalent terms to those of the prosecution.

(j) The accused's right not to be forced to give evidence against themself, and the prohibition of coercion and torture of the accused or of witnesses.

(k) The right to apply for bail pending and during trial.

(l) Access to an interpreter for those accused who are not sufficiently fluent in, or comprehending of, English.

(m) The right to be informed of material in the hands of the prosecution which undermines the prosecution case or assists that of the accused.

(n) Special consideration for the vulnerable accused.

(o) Trial by an impartial tribunal.

(p) Protection from the prosecution abusing the process of the criminal courts.

(q) Protection from the admission of unfairly obtained evidence.

(r) Sentence on conviction which is in accordance with law and which is not cruel or inhumane.

(s) A right of appeal against conviction and sentence.

Most of these rights are qualified or curtailed in certain circumstances – see below paragraphs **24.4** to **24.35**.

WHERE THE CONSTITUENT FEATURES OF A FAIR TRIAL ARE FOUND

24.4

The Criminal Procedure Rules 2020[4] begin with the 'Overriding Objective' of the CrimPR 'code':

> **The overriding objective**
>
> 1.1. (1) The overriding objective of this procedural code is that criminal cases be dealt with justly.
>
> (2) Dealing with a criminal case justly includes—

4 The Criminal Procedure Rules 2020 (SI 2020/759) as amended.

(a) acquitting the innocent and convicting the guilty;

(b) treating all participants with politeness and respect;

(c) dealing with the prosecution and the defence fairly;

(d) recognising the rights of a defendant, particularly those under Article 6 of the European Convention on Human Rights;

(e) respecting the interests of witnesses, victims and jurors and keeping them informed of the progress of the case;

(f) dealing with the case efficiently and expeditiously;

(g) ensuring that appropriate information is available to the court when bail and sentence are considered; and

(h) dealing with the case in ways that take into account—

 (i) the gravity of the offence alleged,

 (ii) the complexity of what is in issue,

 (iii) the severity of the consequences for the defendant and others affected, and

 (iv) the needs of other cases.

The inclusion of Article 6 of the ECHR expressly incorporates an accused's right to a fair trial. The Criminal Procedure Rules do not prescribe nor even identify what is included in the Article 6 rights. It is to be assumed the omission is a recognition that the constituents of a fair trial are sufficiently understood and embedded not to require elaboration in the Rules.

24.5

Article 6 of the ECHR has been incorporated into domestic law by sections 1 to 4 of, and Schedule 1 to, the Human Rights Act 1998 (HRA) –

> 1. In the determination of his civil rights and obligations or of any criminal charge against him, everyone is entitled to a fair and public hearing within a reasonable time by an independent and impartial tribunal established by law. Judgment shall be pronounced publicly but the press and public may be excluded from all or part of the trial in the interests of morals, public order or national security in a democratic society, where the interests of juveniles or the protection of the private life of the parties so require, or to the extent strictly necessary in the opinion of the court in special circumstances where publicity would prejudice the interests of justice.
>
> 2. Everyone charged with a criminal offence shall be presumed innocent until proved guilty according to law.
>
> 3. Everyone charged with a criminal offence has the following minimum rights:

(a) to be informed promptly, in a language which he understands and in detail, of the nature and cause of the accusation against him;

(b) to have adequate time and facilities for the preparation of his defence;

(c) to defend himself in person or through legal assistance of his own choosing or, if he has not sufficient means to pay for legal assistance, to be given it free when the interests of justice so require;

(d) to examine or have examined witnesses against him and to obtain the attendance and examination of witnesses on his behalf under the same conditions as witnesses against him;

(e) to have the free assistance of an interpreter if he cannot understand or speak the language used in court.

24.6

Article 7 of the European Convention on Human Rights (ECHR),[5] also incorporated into domestic law by the HRA 1998, provides –

> 1. No one shall be held guilty of any criminal offence on account of any act or omission which did not constitute a criminal offence under national or international law at the time when it was committed. Nor shall a heavier penalty be imposed than the one that was applicable at the time the criminal offence was committed.
>
> 2. This article shall not prejudice the trial and punishment of any person for any act or omission which, at the time when it was committed, was criminal according to the general principles of law recognised by civilised nations.

24.7

Article 14 of the International Covenant on Civil and Political Rights (ICCPR)[6] sets out similar but slightly more expanded rights than those in Articles 6 and 7 of the ECHR.

> 1. All persons shall be equal before the courts and tribunals. In the determination of any criminal charge against him, or of his rights and obligations in a suit at law, everyone shall be entitled to a fair and public hearing by a competent, independent and impartial tribunal established by law. The press and the public may be excluded from all or part of a trial for reasons of morals, public order (*ordre public*) or national security in a democratic society, or when the interest of the private lives of the

---

5 For a more detailed guide see Guide on Article 7 – No punishment without law: the principle that only the law can define a crime and prescribe a penalty (coe.int).

6 Adopted and opened for signature, ratification and accession by General Assembly Resolution 2200A (XXI) of 16 December 1966, which entered into force on 23 March 1976.

parties so requires, or to the extent strictly necessary in the opinion of the court in special circumstances where publicity would prejudice the interests of justice; but any judgement rendered in a criminal case or in a suit at law shall be made public except where the interest of juvenile persons otherwise requires or the proceedings concern matrimonial disputes or the guardianship of children.

2. Everyone charged with a criminal offence shall have the right to be presumed innocent until proved guilty according to law.

3. In the determination of any criminal charge against him, everyone shall be entitled to the following minimum guarantees, in full equality:

(a) To be informed promptly and in detail in a language which he understands of the nature and cause of the charge against him;

(b) To have adequate time and facilities for the preparation of his defence and to communicate with counsel of his own choosing;

(c) To be tried without undue delay;

(d) To be tried in his presence, and to defend himself in person or through legal assistance of his own choosing; to be informed, if he does not have legal assistance, of this right; and to have legal assistance assigned to him, in any case where the interests of justice so require, and without payment by him in any such case if he does not have sufficient means to pay for it;

(e) To examine, or have examined, the witnesses against him and to obtain the attendance and examination of witnesses on his behalf under the same conditions as witnesses against him;

(f) To have the free assistance of an interpreter if he cannot understand or speak the language used in court;

(g) Not to be compelled to testify against himself or to confess guilt.

4. In the case of juvenile persons, the procedure shall be such as will take account of their age and the desirability of promoting their rehabilitation.

5. Everyone convicted of a crime shall have the right to his conviction and sentence being reviewed by a higher tribunal according to law.

6. When a person has by a final decision been convicted of a criminal offence and when subsequently his conviction has been reversed or he has been pardoned on the ground that a new or newly discovered fact shows conclusively that there has been a miscarriage of justice, the person who has suffered punishment as a result of such conviction shall be compensated according to law, unless it is proved that the non-disclosure of the unknown fact in time is wholly or partly attributable to him.

> 7. No one shall be liable to be tried or punished again for an offence for which he has already been finally convicted or acquitted in accordance with the law and penal procedure of each country.

24.8

Lord Hoffmann indicated how the right to a fair trial fits within our criminal procedure. When considering, in *R v Lyons* [2003] AC 976, the test to be applied when determining an appeal against conviction, he said:

> The question in this appeal is whether the appellants had a fair trial. Strictly speaking, it is whether their convictions are unsafe. That is the word used by section 2(1)(a) of the Criminal Appeal Act 1968 (as substituted by section 2(1) of the Criminal Appeal Act 1995) to state the only ground upon which the Court of Appeal is permitted and required to allow an appeal against a conviction on indictment. But unsafe does not mean only that the accused might not have committed the offence. It can also mean that whether he did so or not, he was not convicted according to law. As Rose LJ said in *R v Mullen* [2000] QB 520, 540: 'for a conviction to be safe, it must be lawful.' And what the law requires, among other things, is that the accused should have had a fair trial'.[7]

24.9

Historical trials under English law now seem unfair. Until 1894 an accused could not give evidence in their own defence. Changes in the rights and privileges of victims, witnesses and accused have developed sometimes in advance of, and sometimes in response to, internationally prescribed standards. Victims and accused are treated as citizens not as subjects and the right to a fair trial applies irrespective of nationality or status. Lord Bingham in *The Rule of Law* said, 'The right to a fair trial is a cardinal requirement of the rule of law … fairness is a constantly evolving concept'[8] and he quoted from *R v Horseferry Road Magistrates' Court ex p Bennett* [1994] 1 AC 42, at paragraph [68], that it is 'axiomatic that a person charged with having committed a criminal offence should receive a fair trial and that, if he cannot be tried fairly for that offence, he should not be tried at all' (*per* Lord Oliver).[9]

24.10

Fair trial standards are set out in international instruments, but their status in trials depends on domestic law. Sometimes, as with the HRA, an international convention is incorporated in part into domestic law by statute. But international conventions not incorporated into domestic law have limited impact on how courts interpret and apply the right to a fair trial. There is a common law presumption that Parliament does not intend to legislate inconsistently with

7 *R v Lyons* [2003] AC 976 at [21]
8 T Bingham, The Rule of Law (Harmondsworth, Penguin, 2011).
9 Chapter 9, pp 90 and 96.

its international obligations. Where legislation is unspecific or ambiguous, conventions can be used to interpret the legislation so as to make it compatible with those international instruments. Section 3(1) of the HRA provides:

> So far as it is possible to do so, primary legislation and subordinate legislation must be read and given effect in a way which is compatible with the Convention rights.

24.11

The extent of the limitation of this ability of courts to colour the interpretation of statutes to make them compatible with the Convention is reinforced by section 3(2) which provides that section 3(1) does not affect incompatible legislation. These provisions in the HRA 1998 apply only to the ECHR. They do not form overriding rules of interpretation and do not apply to other international conventions. There are no provisions in the Interpretation Act 1978[10] dealing with how courts interpret treaties and international conventions to which the UK is a party. That is a matter of established practice. In *R v Lyons*[11] Lord Bingham said:

> 13. … rules of international law not incorporated into national law confer no rights on individuals directly enforceable in national courts. But although international and national law differ in their content and their fields of application they should be seen as complementary and not as alien or antagonistic systems. Even before the Human Rights Act 1998 the convention [*sc. ECHR*] exerted a persuasive and pervasive influence on judicial decision-making in this country, affecting the interpretation of ambiguous statutory provisions, guiding the exercise of discretions, bearing on the development of the common law.
>
> 14. … however, … a convention duty, even if found to exist, cannot override an express and applicable provision of domestic statutory law. Whether the Court of Appeal was (and the House is) subject to such a constraint is in my view the central issue in this case.

24.12

In the same case Lord Hoffmann said:

> 27. In other words, the Convention is an international treaty and the ECtHR is an international court with jurisdiction under international law to interpret and apply it. But the question of whether the appellants' convictions were unsafe is a matter of English law. And it is firmly established that international treaties do not form part of English law and that English courts have no jurisdiction to interpret or apply them:

10 As amended by the European Union Withdrawal (Consequential Modifications) (EU Exit) Regulations 2020 (SI 2020/1447).

11 *R v Lyons* [2002] UKHL 44; [2003] 1 AC 976.

> *JH Rayner (Mincing Lane) Ltd v Department of Trade and Industry* [1990] 2 AC 418. Parliament may pass a law which mirrors the terms of the treaty and in that sense incorporates the treaty into English law. But even then, the metaphor of incorporation may be misleading. It is not the treaty but the statute which forms part of English law. And English courts will not (unless the statute expressly so provides) be bound to give effect to interpretations of the treaty by an international court, even though the United Kingdom is bound by international law to do so. Of course there is a strong presumption in favour of interpreting English law (whether common law or statute) in a way which does not place the United Kingdom in breach of an international obligation. As Lord Goff of Chieveley said in *Attorney-General v Guardian Newspapers Ltd (No. 2)* [1990] 1 AC 109, 283:
>
> 'I conceive it to be my duty, when I am free to do so, to interpret the law in accordance with the obligations of the Crown under [the Convention].'
>
> 28. But for present purposes the important words are 'when I am free to do so'. The sovereign legislator in the United Kingdom is Parliament. If Parliament has plainly laid down the law, it is the duty of the courts to apply it, whether that would involve the Crown in breach of an international treaty or not.

RESTRICTIONS AND CURTAILMENTS OF THE RIGHTS UNDERPINNING A FAIR TRIAL

24.13

The rights set out in **24.3** above must be adapted to the circumstances of our criminal justice system. Few of the rights are absolute.

The presumption of innocence

24.14

There are circumstances in which a legal (or persuasive) burden is placed on the accused by statute. An example is the defence of diminished responsibility to a charge of murder provided by section 2(2) of the Homicide Act 1957. Other cases require an accused to prove a specific exception.[12] Where a legal burden is placed on the accused, the standard of proof is the balance of probabilities, rather than the higher burden placed on the prosecution. In other cases where a burden is placed on an accused, that has been interpreted as a requirement that the defence provide some evidence of the issue (as part of their case or that of

12 *R v Hunt* [1987] AC 352.

the prosecution), which it is for the prosecution then to disprove. This is known as an 'evidential burden'. Whether a legal or evidential burden is imposed depends on whether the wording of the statute enables the court to construe it so that an unfair burden is not placed on an accused.[13] Presumptions of fact are permissible against an accused, provided that the statutory provision is clear and does not amount to an unfair reversal of the burden of proof.[14]

No punishment without law

24.15

There is a paradox that judges are required to explain the law in clear terms to a jury, whereas an accused is presumed to know it. Consistently with Article 7 of the ECHR, courts can interpret the ingredients of an offence to update the circumstances to which the law applies. In *R v R*,[15] the House of Lords decided that the long-established presumption that a man could not rape his wife was no longer the law. This decision was approved by the European Court of Human Rights (ECtHR)[16] on the basis that Article 7 did not prevent the evolution of the law in ways which could be anticipated.

The accused must be informed at the time of arrest and/or charge of the offence alleged

24.16

Sometimes that is impractical, eg because the suspect is violent or too intoxicated to comprehend.

Freedom from discrimination or profiling

24.17

See the case of Colin Stagg[17] in which Ognall J excluded from Stagg's trial at the Central Criminal Court the 'honey trap' evidence of an undercover officer under section 78 of the Police and Criminal Evidence Act (PACE) 1984 on the grounds of fairness, forcing the prosecution to offer no evidence. His trial was to be predicated on a police investigation based on profiling which involved deception by an undercover officer.

---

13 *Sheldrake v DPP* [2004] UKHL 43; [2005] 1 AC 264 at para [51].

14 Ibid.

15 *R v R* [1992] 1 AC 599.

16 *SW v UK, CR v UK* (1996) 21 EHRR 363. See also *Ivey v Genting Casinos* [2017] UKSC 67; [2017] 3 WLR 1212 on the change to the test of dishonesty.

17 Who is Colin Stagg? Man wrongly accused of Rachel Nickell murder | ITV News London.

The right to legal representation of the accused's choice, including during pre-charge interviews, or the accused's right to represent themself

24.18

Legal aid provisions restrict the seniority of the lawyer who can be instructed, depending on the nature of the case. Accused persons do not have a right to the lawyer of their choice if that lawyer is unavailable at the time the instructions are sent and/or the case is to be tried. An accused's right to defend themself should they desire is an established right. Should an accused exercise that right, there are restrictions on an accused cross-examining complainants and vulnerable witnesses in certain types of cases. In such cases the court can appoint a lawyer to act on the accused's behalf and cross examine the witness(es).

The right to attend court hearings and be present throughout

24.19

This is subject to the overriding objective of the Criminal Procedure Rules, which may require a case to be continued in the temporary absence of an ill or disruptive accused.

Open and public hearings

24.20

There are very limited circumstances, based on the interests of national security, in which a case can be conducted in whole or in part in the absence of the media and the public.[18] This exceptional procedure was approved by the ECtHR in *Yam v UK*.[19] Judgment must be given in public, even if it is a truncated version of a fuller judgment *in camera*.

The right to challenge the evidence of prosecution witnesses

24.21

An accused is entitled to advance notice of the evidence to be given, but not necessarily the identity of the witness. Undercover police officers are often permitted to conceal their names in their witness statements, and when they give evidence, under the provisions of Part 3 of the Coroners and Justice Act 2009. Particularly vulnerable witnesses may also be given similar protection (eg those at risk of violent reprisals).

---

18 *R (Yam) v Central Criminal Court* [2015] UKSC 76; [2016] AC 771.
19 *Yam v UK* (2020) 71 EHRR 4.

Time and facilities for the accused to prepare and present a defence on equivalent terms to those of the prosecution to present its evidence

24.22

An accused in custody cannot realistically have the same facilities as the prosecutor and is dependent on whether legal aid provision is adequate to enable his lawyers to find witnesses and to instruct competent experts where appropriate.

Right not to be forced to give evidence against themself, and the prohibition of coercion and torture of the accused or of witnesses

24.23

Section 76 of PACE 1984 protects an accused against evidence of an admission which was or may have been obtained by oppression (including torture) or as a consequence of 'anything said or done which was likely, in the circumstances existing at the time to render unreliable any confession made by him as a consequence thereof'. The burden of persuasion to exclude otherwise admissible evidence is on the accused unless it is self-evident.[20]

24.24

An accused cannot be compelled to provide evidence either in interview to the prosecuting authority or in court. However, sections 34 and 35 of the Criminal Justice and Public Order Act 1994 allow a court to draw adverse inferences from a failure to give an explanation in interview which is relied on by the accused in court or from a failure to give evidence in the trial.

The right to apply for bail pending and during trial

24.25

This is not a right to be granted bail. Section 4(1) of the Bail Act 1976 creates a rebuttable presumption in favour of bail. Section 22 of the Prosecution of Offences Act 1985 requires courts to grant bail where the prosecution has failed to comply with time limits and failed to justify the delay. Section 25 of the Criminal Justice and Public Order Act 1994 creates a presumption against bail for those facing charges of homicide, rape and some other offences contrary to the Sexual Offences Act 2003 and in respect of an accused who has previously been convicted of one of those offences.

---

20 *Canale* (1990) 91 Cr App R 1.

Access to an interpreter for those accused who are not sufficiently fluent in, or comprehending of, English

24.26

There is no exception to this right.

The right to be informed of material in the hands of the prosecution which undermines the prosecution case or assists that of the accused

24.27

Often the most time-consuming and difficult part of a criminal trial is dealing with unused, especially digital, material. Complexity or limits on resources do not provide justification for the failure to provide an accused with material which could undermine the prosecution or support the defence, the absence of which material makes, or would make, a conviction unsafe for the purposes of the Criminal Appeal Act as set out at **24.8** above.

Special consideration for vulnerable accused

24.28

Some special measures are available for accused to assist them in giving evidence. Section 33A of the Youth Justice and Criminal Evidence Act 1999 allows vulnerable accused to give evidence via a video link and CrimPR 18(f) provides a process for enabling accused to give evidence with the assistance of an intermediary.

Trial by an impartial tribunal

24.29

Impartiality is not the same trial by 'peers'. Blackstone spoke lyrically of the right to a jury trial:[21]

> The trial by jury, or the country, *per patriam*, is also that trial by the peers of every Englishman, which, as the great bulwark of his liberties, is secured by the great charter … So that the liberties of England cannot but subsist, so long as this palladium remains sacred and inviolate; not only from open attacks, (which none will be so hardy as to make) but also from all secret machinations, which may sap and undermine it; by introducing new and arbitrary methods of trial.

21 *Blackstone's Commentaries* (9th edn, 1783) vol IV, pp 349–50.

24.30

In fact, most criminal cases are tried not by jury but by district judges or lay justices. In jury trials an accused has little say in the composition of the jury. Peremptory challenges to jurors no longer exist and there is limited enthusiasm in the judiciary for interfering with the random process of jury selection so as to ensure at least one of the jurors shares some of the characteristics of the accused.[22]

24.31

The importance of impartiality of an appeal court is demonstrated by the *Pinochet* case[23] in which the link between one of the Law Lords and an NGO was sufficient to require a re-hearing by a different panel.

Protection from the prosecution abusing the process of the criminal courts

24.32

In extreme cases a prosecution will be stopped due to some conduct of the state which is unconscionable in a democratic society. Examples are kidnapping of the accused to secure their presence in the jurisdiction, or torture of a third party to obtain evidence.[24] An alternative is where the conduct of the state (and in particular of the prosecution) has made it impossible for the accused to have a fair trial. An example is where the prosecution has destroyed relevant evidence which could assist the accused's case.

Protection from the admission of unfairly obtained evidence

24.33

Relevant evidence can be excluded by applying the tests in sections 76 and 78 of PACE 1984. The test is not whether the evidence was obtained unfairly – it is whether it has an unfair effect on the trial as a whole, including whether the jury think it has that effect. In extreme cases the way evidence was obtained can amount to an abuse of process resulting in the prosecution being stayed.

---

22 *Smith* [2003] EWCA Crim 283; [2003] 1 WLR 2229; and *Bridge* [2019] EWCA Crim 2220.

23 *Pinochet, In re* [1999] UKHL 1; [2000] 1 AC 119.

24 *A v Secretary of State for Home Department* [2005] UKHL 71; [2006] 2 AC 221; *Beckford* [1996] 1 Cr App R 94; *Crawley* [2014] EWCA Crim 1028; [2014] 2 Cr App R 16.

Sentence on conviction which is in accordance with law and which is not cruel or inhumane

24.34

Sentencing Guidelines (now under s 59 of the Sentencing Act 2020) have created a structured approach to sentencing with a view to achieving consistency. However, the degrading conditions in which many prisoners (remand as well as convicted) must live do not feature in sentencing policy and Lord Woolf's injunction to restrict sentences of imprisonment because of overcrowding no longer seems to carry weight.[25] Only in the light of the Covid-19 pandemic has leniency due to intolerable prison conditions temporarily surfaced.[26]

A right of appeal against conviction and sentence

24.35

There is no right to an appeal hearing. The Criminal Appeal Act 1968 provides a right to apply for leave to appeal. Post-conviction, the persuasive burden of overturning a conviction or reducing a sentence is on the accused. In the case of sentence, an appeal will succeed only if the sentence was wrong in law or manifestly excessive.

---

25 *Kefford* [2002] EWCA Crim 519; [2002] 2 Cr App R (S) 106.
26 *Manning* [2020] EWCA Crim 592; [2020] 2 Cr App R (S) 46.

25 The burden and standard of proof and Article 6 of the ECHR

Peta-Louise Bagott

OVERVIEW

25.1

There is an inherent tension in criminal proceedings: the more serious the crime, the greater the public interest in securing a conviction. Central to attenuating the danger that stems from this tension are the burden and standard of proof and the fairness of proceedings. The right to a fair trial enshrined in Article 6 of the European Convention of Human Rights (ECHR), which includes the presumption of innocence, is relevant to the application of the burden and standard of proof.

25.2

In the context of the burden of proof, it could be argued that the courts' interpretation of the right to a fair trial in Article 6, including the presumption of innocence in Article 6(2), conflicts with the text of the Convention right and also the jurisprudence from the European Court of Human Rights (ECtHR). It appears that Article 6 has been treated as a qualified right, when it should serve as an unqualified right, since the Human Rights Act (HRA) 1998 came into force. Despite this, it has been taken as read that the correct legal test, and reasoning, has been applied by the appellate courts by judges and advocates alike. The difference between a qualified right and an absolute right and how the courts have fallen into error is analysed at **25.6–25.8** and **25.9–25.15** below. Qualified rights, such as the right to privacy contained in Article 8, can be lawfully interfered with when it is necessary and proportionate to the aim pursued. A proportionality assessment is the key to deciding whether the right has been violated. Article 6 is absolute and cannot be interfered with in this way. This is what distinguishes it from a qualified right. The approach taken by the appellate courts to submissions on Article 6 and, in particular, on Article 6(2), are considered at **25.18–25.33** below, in the context of reversing the burden of proof. It is arguable from the authorities that the courts have treated Article 6 as a qualified right and undertaken a proportionality assessment to determine whether they deem that a violation has occurred. While the outcomes of the cases considered are consistent with the ECtHR jurisprudence – that reversing the burden of proof does not, without more, violate the presumption of innocence – the legal bases justifying the courts' approach to reverse burdens arguably conflict with the text of Article 6 and the ECtHR's own approach to determining violations. It may be argued that the approach of the highest courts in England and Wales to Article 6 is indicative of the courts being willing to treat it as a qualified right that can be lawfully interfered with when it is proportionate to do so. The courts' may be confronted with submissions that they have fallen into error as to how Article 6 should be interpreted and applied, and that their approach has set a precedent for the further erosion of the right to a fair trial in future cases.

25.3

The courts' approach to the standard of proof has been less contentious. While the standard of proof required in criminal proceedings has not been the subject of much discussion in the ECtHR jurisprudence, the Court has made it clear that 'any doubt should benefit the accused'; see **25.30** *et seq.*[1] Domestic courts have not strayed from this.

THE BURDEN OF PROOF

25.4

Before considering the domestic courts' approach to the burden of proof and Article 6, it is necessary to examine the difference between qualified and unqualified rights to give proper context to the case law of England and Wales.

Article 8

25.5

Article 8 is an example of a qualified right.[2] The text of Article 8(1) provides that 'everyone has the right to respect for his private and family life, his home and his correspondence'. However, Article 8(2) qualifies this in the following way:

> There shall be no interference by a public authority with the exercise of this right *except such as is in accordance with the law and is necessary* in a democratic society in the interests of national security, public safety or the economic well-being of the country, for the prevention of disorder or crime, for the protection of health or morals, or for the protection of the rights and freedoms of others [emphasis added].

1 *Barberà and Others v Spain* (1989) 11 EHRR 360 at [77].

2 Other qualified rights are Articles 9–11 (freedom of thought, conscience and religion; freedom of expression; freedom of assembly and association).

25.6

This provision contains specific exceptions to the right guaranteed. These limitations may only be justified if they are 'in accordance with the law' and 'necessary in a democratic society'. The first component requires the following: there must be a specific legal rule or regime which authorises interference with the right; the citizen must have adequate access to this law; and the law must be formulated with sufficient precision to allow the citizen to foresee the circumstances in which the law would, or might, be applied.[3] Even if a measure has been taken in pursuit of one of the legitimate interests listed, the second component requires that it must be 'necessary'. This is satisfied if the interference arises out of a pressing social need and it is proportionate to the legitimate aim pursued.[4] A restriction is generally considered to be disproportionate if a less intrusive measure exists that may achieve the same goal.[5] If a right has been infringed, it will not be considered to be disproportionate if it is restricted in its application and effect, and there are safeguards in domestic law to ensure that an individual is not subjected to arbitrary treatment.[6] They are qualified by the need to protect the rights and freedoms of others, as these can trump an individual's right to privacy. Therefore, a qualified right contains an express provision that allows the right to be lawfully interfered with when it is proportionate to the aim pursued.

25.7

When Article 8 challenges are considered by the ECtHR, the following approach is taken: first, the court must determine whether the right is engaged, ie whether there has been a *prima facie* violation of the right (Article 8(1)); and second, the court must consider whether that right has been unlawfully infringed, ie whether the violation can be justified pursuant to a lawful derogation of the right (Article 8(2)).[7]

Article 6 and the presumption of innocence

25.8

Article 6 itself is not a qualified right. It does not contain a general express provision that qualifies the right to a fair trial in the same way as Articles 8 to 11. As such, there is no provision that permits it to be lawfully interfered with, regardless of any pressing social need and regardless of the proportionality of interference relative to the legitimate aim pursued. Public interest concerns cannot justify measures that curtail this right.[8]

---

3 *Sunday Times v United Kingdom* (1979) 2 EHRR 245; *Malone v United Kingdom* (1984) 7 EHRR 14.

4 *Sunday Times v United Kingdom* (1979) 2 EHRR 245.

5 *Campbell v United Kingdom* (1993) 15 EHRR 137.

6 *MS v Sweden* (1997) 3 BHRC 248.

7 See, eg, *Kilin v Russia* [2021] ECHR 384.

8 *Bykov v Russia* [2009] ECHR 441, [93]; *Zaichenko v Russia* [2010] ECHR 185; *Jalloh v Germany* (2006) 44 EHRR 32. This was endorsed in *Ibrahim and Others v United Kingdom* (2016) 61 EHRR 9 at [252].

25.9

Article 6(2) embodies the principle of the presumption of innocence, which requires that neither the judge nor the jury should start with the preconceived idea that the accused has committed the offence; it requires that the overall burden of proving the accused's guilt is on the prosecution; any doubt should be resolved in favour of the accused.[9]

25.10

The ECtHR authorities confirm that a different approach is taken with absolute rights and qualified rights. Article 6 and its constituent element Article 6(2) is an example of this. In the context of reversing the burden of proof, *Salabiaku v France* established that:

> Presumptions of fact or of law operate in every legal system. Clearly, the Convention does not prohibit such presumptions in principle. It does, however, require the Contracting States to remain within certain limits in this respect as regards criminal law… Article 6(2) does not therefore regard presumptions of fact or of law provided for in the criminal law with indifference. *It requires States to confine them within reasonable limits which take into account the importance of what is at stake and maintain the rights of the defence.*[10]

25.11

It is clear from the text of Article 6(2) that the presumption of innocence is absolute. States cannot exceed the 'reasonable limits' of Article 6(2). Reversing the burden of proof does not exceed them. This is because the starting point remains that the accused is innocent, the overall burden of proving guilt remains on the prosecution and any doubt is resolved in favour of the accused.[11] The 'reasonable limits' test does not equate to the proportionality test that applies to qualified rights – in *Salabiaku*, the Court did not purport to apply 'proportionality' principles. *Salabiaku* cannot be interpreted as qualifying Article 6(2), thereby making it a derogable right.[12] If this were the case, the ECtHR itself would have lowered the threshold of legal protections afforded to the accused under the Convention. It is clear from the Court's jurisprudence that it has not done so.

25.12

Lingens v Austria (1982) 4 EHRR 373 is an example of the differences in the approach taken towards Article 6 as an absolute right and Article 10 as a qualified right. In this case, violations of both rights were alleged. The accused had published an article that was alleged to be defamatory. The issues included (1) the reversal of the burden of proof, such that the accused had to prove his statement was true in order to rely on the statutory defence; and (2) the

---

9 *Barberà and Others v Spain* (1989) 11 EHRR 360 at [77].

10 *Salabiaku v France* (1991) EHRR 379, [28] (emphasis added).

11 *Barberà*, para 77; *Radio France v France* (2000) 40 EHRR 29 at [24].

12 See, eg, Arts 8–11.

curtailing of his right to freedom of expression. The appellant challenged the reverse burden of proof imposed by the statute, which stated that it was a defence to the defamation charge to show that the statement published was in fact true.[13] The Court held that presumption of innocence in Article 6(2) was not engaged as the overall burden of establishing guilt remained with the prosecution.[14] The accused remained innocent until proven guilty, as required by the Convention. While the interests of the victim were considered,[15] the presumption of innocence was not qualified by the need to protect the rights and freedoms of others. The right was absolute and was treated as such. There was no discussion of whether reversing the burden was proportionate to the aims pursued. In contrast, the Court's reasoning on the alleged violation of Article 10(1) considered whether the right was engaged, and then whether interference with this right could be justified on the basis of necessity or proportionality. The legal tests applied to the different rights show that there are different considerations and issues in play.

25.13

The *travaux préparatoires* confirm that states had no intention of creating a right to a fair trial that was qualified, and could be lawfully interfered with by the need to protect the rights and freedoms of others.[16] It is for this reason that states codified due process rights – to ensure that the accused's fundamental rights are the general public interest.[17] Reading a general qualification into the text of Article 6 would offend not only the text of the provision, but also the state parties' intention.

Article 6 in domestic criminal law

25.14

The burden of proof contains two elements: the legal burden (or the persuasive burden) and the evidential burden. The leading case on the burden of proof in criminal cases is *Woolmington v DPP*.[18] The general rule is that the prosecution bears the burden to prove an accused's guilt. This is often referred to as the

---

13 *Lingens v Austria* (1982) 4 EHRR 373 at [390].

14 Ibid at [390]–[391].

15 Ibid at [391].

16 Council of Europe, *Collected Edition of the 'Travaux Préparatories' of the European Convention on Human Rights* (Martinus Nijhoff, 1977).

17 *Ibid*. The ECHR, as a treaty, is subject to the general rules of interpretation for treaties laid down in Arts 31–33 of the Vienna Convention on the Law of Treaties. Article 31(1) provides that a treaty shall be interpreted 'in good faith in accordance with the ordinary meaning to be given to the terms of the treaty in their context and in light of its object and purpose'. This requires the direct wishes of the state parties be considered, in addition to the goals set for the treaty regime as a whole. See *Al-Saadoon and Mufdhi v United Kingdom* (2010) 51 EHRR 9, para 127. See, further, O Ammann, 'The Interpretative Methods of International Law: What Are They, and Why Use Them?' in O Ammann (ed) *Domestic Courts and the Interpretation of International Law* (Brill, 2020); S Dothan, 'The Three Traditional Approaches to Treaty Interpretation: A Current Application to the European Court of Human Rights' (2019) 42 *Fordham International Law Review* 766–93; I Buffard and K Zemanek, 'The "Object and Purpose" of a Treaty: An Enigma?' (1998) 3 *Austrian Review of International Law* 311–43, 326.

18 *Woolmington v DPP* [1935] AC 462, p 841.

'golden thread' of criminal law.[19] However, there are exceptions to this. Express or implied statutory provisions can reverse the onus onto the defence and require the defendant to bear either a legal or evidential burden of proof. This area has provided fertile ground for Article 6(2) challenges and is a good example of court's approach to alleged violations of this right. It requires careful consideration in light of the above as Article 6, and vicariously Article 6(2), has been interpreted as a qualified right to which a proportionality assessment can be applied.

Has Article 6 has been misunderstood?

25.15

The HRA incorporates Article 6(2) of the ECHR into criminal law. It provides that 'everyone charged with a criminal offence shall be presumed innocent until proved guilty according to law'. The HRA brings this the binding nature of this Convention right. The starting point under section 2 of the HRA is that a court must consider any judgment, decision, declaration, or advisory opinion of the ECtHR when a Convention right is in issue. It is important to bear this in mind, as it is evident that the authorities have veered away from the ECtHR jurisprudence and instead give the domestic interpretation of Article 6 primacy. This trend has caused the courts to move towards the application of an erroneous domesticised construction of Article 6.

25.16

Brown v Stott and *R v Lambert* were two of the first HRA litigation cases before the appellate courts.[20] In both the Privy Council and the House of Lords, the Court found that, in accordance with the ECtHR's jurisprudence, Article 6 was not an absolute right.[21] In *Brown,* Lord Bingham concluded that:

> [l]imited qualification of these rights is acceptable if reasonably directed by national authorities towards a clear and proper public objective and if representing no greater qualification than the situation calls for.[22]

25.17

This was endorsed by the House of Lords in *Lambert,* where it was found that:

> … the article 6(2) right is not absolute and unqualified, the test to be applied is whether the modification or limitation of that right pursues a legitimate aim and whether it satisfies the principle of proportionality.[23]

---

19 Ibid.
20 *Brown v Stott* [2001] 2 WLR 817; *R v Lambert* [2001] UKHL 37.
21 Ibid, see pp 836B and 851H; Ibid at [88].
22 Ibid p 836B.
23 *R v Lambert* [2001] UKHL 37 at [88].

25.18

On the basis of these statements, one would be forgiven for thinking that Article 6 contained an express provision allowing for a fair trial, and the presumption of innocence, it to be lawfully interfered with. It is spoken about as if it were a qualified right. Despite both the text of Article 6(2) and the ECtHR jurisprudence contradicting this, the suggestion is that Article 6 can be derogated from when a legitimate aim is pursued, providing its proportionate. This neatly captures the Court's error.

25.19

Shortly after, the Court of Appeal in *R v Forbes* sought to distance itself from this position by reaffirming that Article 6 was, in fact, an absolute right.[24] However, it relied on *Brown* to say that the constituent elements of Article 6, one of which is the presumption of innocence in Article 6(2), were 'not absolute'.[25] It is interesting that it did not cite a single ECtHR authority for this proposition and there is no analysis as to why this conclusion is consistent with the same. Lord Steyn in *R v A* tried to clarify the position in stating that:

> It is well established that the guarantee of a fair trial under article 6 is absolute: a conviction obtained in breach of it cannot stand. The only balancing permitted is in respect of what the concept of a fair trial entails: here account may be taken of the familiar triangulation of interests of the accused, the victim and society in this context proportionality has a role to play.[26]

25.20

The difficulty with this assertion is that it implies that a proportionality test can, and should, be applied to an absolute right. It suggests is that if the balance falls in favour of the victim and society as a whole, the accused's right to a fair trial can be interfered with. This would be to treat Article 6 as a qualified right. Therefore, the statement is inherently contradictory: a right cannot be absolute but also derogable when it is necessary and proportionate to the aim pursued. Perhaps the use of the word 'proportionality' was in error. However, as it has specific legal connotations in the context of Convention rights litigation, it is difficult to see how this could be chalked down to a simple oversight or clumsy language.

25.21

The Privy Council again in *McIntosh v HM Advocate* relied on *Brown* to assert that 'it is plain that [article 6(2)] is not absolute but equally plain that encroachments on the presumption are not to be uncritically accepted'.[27] The Council then proceeded to cite a passage from *Salabiaku* which states

24 *R v Forbes* [2001] 1 AC 473; [2001] 1 Cr App R 31 at [24].
25 Ibid.
26 *R v A* [2001] UKHL 25 at [38] [citations omitted].
27 *McIntosh v HM Advocate* [2001] UKPC D 1 at [30].

that presumptions must be confined within 'reasonable limits'. The reference to 'reasonable limits' appears to have been interpreted as being a reference to the proportionality requirement. Given that *Salabiaku* does not support this proposition and no proportionality assessment was carried out in that case the Privy Council rooted its understanding of the right in the domestic authorities' interpretation of it.

25.22

The trend of blindly relying on the domestic court's conception of Article 6 continued in *SL (A juvenile) v DPP*.[28] The appellant argued that the burden on the defendant to show a good reason or lawful authority for carrying a bladed article in a public place violated the presumption of innocence in Article 6(2).[29] Once again, authorities stating that Article 6 was not absolute and could be derogated from when it was necessary and proportionate to the legitimate aim pursued were touted as the legal basis for this.[30] This is reiterated by the approach taken in *R v Matthews (Mark Anthony)*:

> The reason for which an accused has a bladed article in a public place is something peculiarly within the knowledge of the accused. We are accordingly quite satisfied that there is an objective justification for some derogation from the presumption of innocence...[31]

25.23

Reversing the burden of proof in these circumstances does not constitute a limitation of the right enshrined in Article 6(2). There is no derogation from the presumption of innocence by requiring an accused to provide an explanation as they are still presumed innocent until the prosecution can prove otherwise; the burden of proof remained on the prosecution; any doubt would be resolved in favour of the accused. Yet the rhetoric is that the presumption of innocence can be interfered with in the same way as qualified rights.

25.24

In *Attorney General's Reference (No 1 of 2004)*,[32] a five-judge court was convened to consider issues relating to reverse burdens and preparatory hearings. The Court considered that there was a 'need for guidance' as the considerable number of authorities conflicted on reverse burdens and Article 6.[33] A trend towards the 'aggressive' application of Article 6 to reverse burden provisions was identified.[34] In response, the Court noted that the extent of Article 6 litigation was 'disturbing' because the provision 'did no more than reflect the requirements

28 *SL (A juvenile) v DPP* [2001] EWHC Admin 882; [2002] 1 Cr App R 32.
29 See the Criminal Justice Act 1988, s 139.
30 *SL (A juvenile) v DPP* [2001] EWHC Admin 882; [2002] 1 Cr App R 32 at [12]–[20].
31 *R v Matthews (Mark Anthony)* [2003] EWCA Crim 813; [2004] QB 690 at [16].
32 *Attorney General's Reference (No 1 of 2004)* [2004] EWCA Crim 1025.
33 Ibid at [9].
34 Ibid at [14].

of fairness which have long been part of English law'.[35] The Court gave general guidance on Article 6 litigation. It did not address whether the Convention right and its components were absolute and, if they were, whether the law had taken a wrong turn in its application of Article 6, and, if so, in what respect.

25.25

In *R v Williams (Orette)*,[36] the Court of Appeal did not take the opportunity to clarify the status and application of Article 6 as an unqualified right. The point on appeal was whether section 1(5) of the Firearms Act 1982 derogated from the presumption of innocence in Article 6(2) by placing the burden on a defendant to prove that they did not know, or had no reason to suspect, that the firearm was readily convertible into a firearm within the provisions of section 1.[37] The Court found that the central issue to the appeal was:

> Is the derogation from the presumption of innocence justified as representing a reasonable and proportionate response, balancing the importance of what is at stake for the public with the maintenance of the normal rights of the defendant?[38]

25.26

This single question appears to encapsulate the apparent error in the application of Article 6. It permits the presumption of innocence in Article 6(2) to be qualified by the need to protect the rights and freedoms of others.

25.27

The Court made no reference to the absolute nature of the Article 6 right in *R v Foye*[39] in finding that there was no justification for departing from the decision in *R v Lambert (Steven)*[40] that the reverse burden of proof applicable to the partial defence of diminished responsibility was not incompatible with the presumption of innocence in Article 6. The Court of Appeal asked itself two questions: first, whether Article 6(2) was engaged; if so, second, whether the relevant statutory provision was proportionate and therefore a 'justified modification' of the right.[41] This follows the two-step assessment used by the ECtHR for qualified rights. As with *R v Williams (Orette)*, the second question appears to show that the Court of Appeal erroneously treated Article 6 as a qualified right.

---

35 Ibid.

36 *R v Williams (Orette)* [2012] EWCA Crim 2162.

37 The Firearms Act 1982, s 1(1) reads: 'Subject to any exemption under this Act, it is an offence for a person— (a) to have in his possession, or to purchase or acquire, a firearm to which this section applies without holding a firearm certificate in force at the time, or otherwise than as authorised by such a certificate; (b) to have in his possession, or to purchase or acquire, any ammunition to which this section applies without holding a firearm certificate in force at the time, or otherwise than as authorised by such a certificate, or in quantities in excess of those so authorised.'

38 *R v Williams (Orette)* [2012] EWCA Crim 2162; [2013] 1 WLR 1200 at [31].

39 *R v Foye* [2013] EWCA Crim 475.

40 *R v Lambert (Steven)* [2002] QB 1112.

41 *R v Foye* at [28].

25.28

It is arguable that, when the above authorities are considered, Article 6 and with it the presumption of innocence in Article 6(2), has been interpreted and applied as a qualified right. The 'reasonable limits' test in *Salabiaku* has erroneously been applied as a proportionality requirement. As a result, the appellate courts' understanding is that the right to a fair trial can be lawfully interfered with when it is necessary and proportionate. Given the unambiguous text of Article 6 and the object and purpose of the right, it is unclear how this interpretation of how the Article should be applied evolved. More than 20 years after *Brown* and *Lambert* it does not appear that the legal basis on which the courts have decided Article 6 and Article 6(2) violations in the context of the burden of proof has been scrutinised. If the Court has erred over the years, the effect is that the protection afforded to the accused enshrined in Article 6 has been reduced in a way that cannot be justified by the right itself.

THE STANDARD OF PROOF

The standard applied by the ECtHR

25.29

The standard of proof in criminal proceedings is not prescribed in Article 6. The ECtHR jurisprudence has not explored it any great depth either. One explanation for this could be that the standard is so well established that it has simply never been challenged.[42] It is, however, implicit in other cases that when the prosecution bears the burden of proof, the standard of proof is beyond reasonable doubt.[43] The ECtHR has not declared that the standard of proof is an Article 6 issue, although the ECtHR has never specifically engaged with that question. In England and Wales criminal courts have relied on well-established domestic principles.

The standard applied by the domestic courts

25.30

Where the burden lies on the prosecution, the prosecution must satisfy magistrates or a jury of the defendant's guilt beyond reasonable doubt.[44] The direction given has evolved to avoid difficulties juries encounter with the concept of beyond reasonable doubt,[45] with juries now being directed to consider whether they are 'satisfied so that they are sure' of a defendant's guilt. While they do not need to be 'certain',[46] the Court of Appeal has disapproved of phases such as 'reasonably

42 *Barberà and Others v Spain* at [77].

43 *Austria v Italy* (1963) YBVI 740 at [784]; *Ireland v United Kingdom* (1980) 2 EHRR 25; *Goodman v Ireland* (1993) 16 EHRR CD26.

44 *Woolmington v DPP*; *R v Bracewell* (1978) 68 Cr App R 44.

45 *R v Majid (Abdul)* [2009] EWCA Crim 2563.

46 *R v Bracewell* (1978) 68 Cr App R 44; *R v JL* [2017] EWCA Crim 621.

sure' and 'pretty sure'.[47] Judges have been advised to avoid trying to define 'sure' and 'reasonable doubt' any further.[48] In *Bentley (Deceased)*,[49] the Court of Appeal confirmed that a jury should be directed that if, on reviewing all of the evidence, they were unsure or had any reasonable doubt as to the defendant's guilt, this should be resolved in the defendant's favour. Where the burden is on the prosecution and a judge has to decide an issue of fact in a criminal trial, the standard of proof is also beyond reasonable doubt.[50]

25.31

Attention should be paid to the fact the criminal standard of proof can be applied to proceedings that are civil in nature, and not criminal within the meaning of Article 6. For example, in *Gough v Chief Constable of Derbyshire*, the Court of Appeal found that the criminal standard of proof applied to football banning orders under section 14B of the Football Spectators Act 1989.[51] Applying the criminal standard was also found to be appropriate where a possible consequence of breaching an order was a custodial sentence.[52] If the burden of proof lies with the defence, the standard of proof required is that used in civil proceedings: the balance of probabilities.[53] The courts confirmed this in the cases concerning the legal burden vesting in the accused (see **25.15–25.20**, above).

47 *R v Woods* [1961] Crim LR 324; *R v Law* [1961] Crim LR 52.
48 *R v Ching* (1976) 63 Cr App R7.
49 *Bentley (Deceased)* [2001] 1 Cr App R 21.
50 *R v Ewing (Terence Patrick)* (1983) 77 Cr App R 47.
51 *Gough v Chief Constable of Derbyshire* [2002] 2 All ER 985 at [89]–[90].
52 *Clingham v Royal Borough of Kensington and Chelsea* [2002] UKHL 39, [37]; *R v Crown Court at Manchester (ex parte McCann)* [2002] UKHL 39 at [83].
53 *R v Carr-Briant* [1944] 29 Cr App R 76. See more recently, *MK v R (Maione)* [2018] EWCA Crim 667.

26 Self-incrimination and the right to silence

Miriam Smith

OVERVIEW

26.1

The 'right to silence' and 'privilege against self-incrimination' are distinct but related concepts. Lord Mustill stated in *R v Director of Serious Fraud Office, ex parte Smith*:

> This expression [the right to silence] arouses strong but unfocused feelings. In truth it does not denote any single right, but rather refers to a disparate group of immunities, which differ in nature, origin, incidence and importance, and also as to the extent to which they have already been encroached upon by statute.[1]

26.2

The rights to silence and not to incriminate oneself have long been essential and fundamental elements of the criminal justice system in England and Wales. However, they are not absolute rights. Just as with other areas of criminal law and procedure, Article 6 has had a significant influence on the precise nature and scope of these rights and principles and their development in domestic law.

26.3

Whilst the twin rights are not specifically mentioned in Article 6, it is well established that they are implicit in it since they are 'standards which lie at the heart of the notion of a fair procedure under Article 6'.[2] These principles are closely linked to the presumption of innocence and their rationale lies in protecting the accused against improper compulsion by the authorities and fulfilment, more broadly, of the aims of Article 6.

1 *R v Director of Serious Fraud Office, ex parte Smith* [1993] AC 1 at [30]–[31].
2 *Murray v United Kingdom* (1996) 22 EHRR 29 at [45]; *Saunders v UK* (1997) 23 EHRR 313 at [68].

RIGHT TO SILENCE

Law of the European Court of Human Rights

26.4

It is clear from ECtHR case law that permitting the tribunal of fact to draw an adverse inference from the defendant's silence does not, in and of itself, violate Article 6. In *Condron v UK*,[3] the Court accepted that the right to silence could not prevent the defendant's silence being taken into account in assessing the persuasiveness of the prosecution evidence in cases which clearly call for an explanation by the defendant. The Court emphasised, however, that fair procedure under Article 6 required 'particular caution' by the domestic court before relying on silence and the trial judge's direction to the jury on the drawing of adverse inferences is particularly important in this regard.

26.5

Necessarily, each case requires a direction tailored to its facts. Guidance as to the content of such directions may be found in the Crown Court Compendium, Part 1. This draws on relevant case law and the earlier specimen direction (concerning s 34 of the Criminal Justice and Public Order Act 1994) which was approved by the ECtHR in *Beckles v UK*.[4] Failure to give a proper direction will not necessarily give rise to a breach of Article 6 nor render a conviction unsafe: each case turns on its facts and whether there is a breach of Article 6 as a result of misdirecting a jury is a matter to be determined in light of all the circumstances of the case.[5]

Common law

26.6

Prior to the Criminal Justice and Public Order Act 1994 (CJPOA), it was firmly established at common law that adverse inferences were not generally permitted to be drawn from the exercise of the right to silence by a defendant at trial.[6] Indeed, it was considered a misdirection for a judge to invite the jury to draw such an inference since it may have appeared that the jury was being invited to disregard the defence put forward because the accused had exercised their right to silence.

26.7

However, it is not entirely accurate to say that silence went without comment. Indeed, it was possible for the judge to make limited comment on the defendant's silence notwithstanding it might have had the effect of being prejudicial. In

3 *Condron v UK* (2001) 31 EHRR 1.
4 *Beckles v UK* (2003) 36 EHRR 13.
5 *R v Chenia* [2002] EWCA Crim 2345; [2003] 2 Cr App R 6.
6 *R v Gilbert* (1977) 66 Cr App R 237; R v Alladice (1988) 87 Cr App R 380.

Gilbert, the Court of Appeal considered that it may not be a misdirection simply to say to the jury, '"This defence was first put forward at this trial" or words to that effect'. Stronger comment was permitted where the defence case involved asserting facts that were at odds with the prosecution case or additional to it and within the defendant's own knowledge.[7]

STATUTORY EXCEPTIONS

Criminal Justice and Public Order Act 1994

26.8

The right to silence at common law has been restricted by the enactment of the CJPOA. The effect of sections 34 to 38 of the CJPOA is to expand the circumstances in which adverse inferences may permissibly be drawn by the tribunal of fact from the defendant's silence at the police station and at trial. Where the statutory scheme does not apply, the common law rule still applies.[8]

26.9

Under the CJPOA, in specified circumstances an adverse inference may be drawn from:

- a failure to mention, when questioned or charged, facts later relied upon in court (s 34);
- a failure to give evidence at trial (s 35);
- a failure to account for objects, substances or marks (s 36); and
- a failure to account for presence at a particular place (s 37).

26.10

How far reaching the restrictions brought about by these provisions has been a matter of varying express and implied comment by the appellate courts. Lord Bingham CJ stated in *Bowden*[9] that the 'object of these sections was to weaken the protection which criminal defendants had previously enjoyed against the drawing of inferences adverse to them from such failures and refusals in the circumstances specified'. However, in *McGarry*,[10] the Court of Appeal considered that the CJPOA derogated from the established common law rule 'only and in a limited way'.

26.11

Lord Bingham CJ recognised in *Bowden* that since these provisions 'restrict rights recognised at common law as appropriate to protect defendants against the risk of injustice, they should not be construed more widely than the

7 *R v Martinez-Tobon* [1994] 1 WLR 388.
8 *R v McGarry* [1998] EWCA Crim 2364; [1999] 1 WLR 1500.
9 *R v Bowden* [1999] EWCA Crim 331; [1999] 1 WLR 823 at 827.
10 *R v McGarry* [1998] EWCA Crim 2364; [1999] 1 WLR 1500; [1999] 1 Cr App R 377.

statutory language requires'. Similarly, their Lordships in *R v Webber (Robert)*[11] recognised the scope for these provisions to be 'an instrument of unfairness or abuse' and emphasised the importance of statutory safeguards being observed and jury directions being carefully framed.

Section 34 of the Criminal Justice and Public Order Act 1994

26.12

Section 34 permits the tribunal of fact to draw such inferences 'as appear proper' from the accused's failure to mention when questioned under caution or when charged facts which are later relied upon in their defence at trial, which they could reasonably have been expected to mention, provided that the conditions in section 34(1) are satisfied and that the two questions of fact which arise as a result (Is there some fact which the defendant has relied on in his defence? Did the defendant fail to mention it to the constable when he was being questioned in accordance with the section?) are resolved against the accused.[12]

26.13

What is 'reasonable' in the context of what facts an accused could reasonably have been expected to mention depends on all the circumstances. In *Howell*, Laws LJ stated:

> The kind of circumstance which may most likely justify silence will be such matters as the suspect's condition (ill-health, in particular mental disability; confusion; intoxication; shock, and so forth – of course we are not laying down an authoritative list), or [their] inability genuinely to recollect events without reference to documents which are not to hand, or communication with other persons who may be able to assist with [their] recollection. There must always be soundly based objective reasons for silence, sufficiently cogently and telling to weigh in the balance against the clear public interest in an account being given by the suspect to the police.[13]

26.14

The principal purpose behind section 34 is to deter late fabrication and to encourage early disclosure of genuine defences. In *Brizzalari*,[14] the Court of Appeal observed that the mischief at which the provision was primarily directed was the 'positive defence' following a 'no comment' interview and/or the '"ambush" defence'. It may be considered there are compelling arguments for an adverse inference to be drawn in such circumstances. For example, the public interest in reasonable disclosure by the accused of what they have to say

11 *R v Webber* (Robert) [2004] UKHL 1; [2004] 1 WLR 404 at [27].
12 *R v Argent* [1996] EWCA Crim 1728; [1997] 2 Cr App R 27.
13 *R v Howell* [2003] EWCA Crim 1; [2005] 1 Cr App R 1 at [24].
14 *R v Brizzalari* [2004] EWCA Crim 310 at [57].

when faced with a factual accusation is undermined where the accused can systematically avoid adverse comment at their trial. In addition, where at trial an accused provides an account or relies on a particular fact which was previously withheld, it may be too late for it to be countered by the prosecution.

26.15

Given this, section 34 is generally seen to apply where a particular fact is advanced by the defence which is suspicious by reason of it not being put forward at an early opportunity. The obvious inference is that the 'fact' now advanced is untrue. The Court of Appeal has repeatedly discouraged an approach which over-formalises common sense' and over-complicates trials and summings-up by invoking section 34 unless the merits of the case require it.[15]

26.16

An inference under section 34 may form part of the case to answer and be part of the case which results in a conviction. However, under section 38(3), neither the case to answer nor the conviction should be based solely on an inference drawn from the accused's failure to mention when questioned under caution, or when charged, facts which are later relied upon in court. This subsection was prompted by the principle in *Murray* that the accused should not be convicted solely or mainly on an inference from silence.[16]

26.17

By section 34(2A), no inference may be drawn unless the defendant has first been given an opportunity to consult a solicitor prior to being questioned or charged. This subsection was inserted by s 58 of the Youth Justice and Criminal Evidence Act 1999 to ensure compliance with *Murray,* which held that there was a breach of Article 6 as a result of denying the applicant access to legal advice in circumstances where inferences could be drawn from their silence during police questioning. In order to be valid, any waiver of the right to legal advice should be 'voluntary, informed and unequivocal'.[17]

26.18

Often a defendant cites advice from their legal representative as the reason for remaining silent in interview. This issue has been the subject of numerous decisions by domestic courts and the ECtHR, in itself suggestive of the difficulty with such a situation. Lord Woolf CJ described the position in such cases as 'singularly delicate',[18] recognising the clear competing considerations:

> On the one hand the Courts have not unreasonably wanted to avoid defendants driving a coach and horses through s. 34 and by so doing defeating the statutory objective. Such an explanation is very easy for

15 *R v Maguire* [2008] EWCA Crim 1028 at [10].
16 *R v Murray* (1996) 22 EHRR 29.
17 *Saunders* [2012] EWCA Crim 1380; [2012] 2 Cr App R 26.
18 *R v Beckles* [2004] EWCA Crim 2766; [2005] 1 WLR 2829 at [43].

a defendant to advance and difficult to investigate because of legal professional privilege. On the other hand, it is of the greatest importance that defendants should be able to be advised by their lawyer without their having to reveal the terms of that advice if they act in accordance with that advice.

26.19

As with any other reason for remaining silent, reliance on legal advice is a matter for the tribunal of fact to examine and the ultimate question remains whether the facts relied upon at trial were facts which the defendant could reasonably have been expected to mention when questioned or charged. In making that assessment, the question for the tribunal of fact is whether the legal advice is the true reason for the defendant remaining silent when questioned or charged).[19] Put another way, the question is whether the defendant remained silent 'not because of [the] advice but because [they] had no or no satisfactory explanation to give'.[20] Conversations between the defendant and their lawyer are subject to legal professional privilege. A defendant who wishes to explain the reasons for silence following legal advice is not obliged to waive privilege, but they may find it difficult to explain their reasons for silence without doing so. If privilege is not waived, it must be respected.[21] Privilege will be waived if the defendant and/or their lawyer give evidence of the content or the reason for the advice. In such circumstances, privilege will not be waived generally but only to the extent of 'opening up questions which properly go to whether such reason can be the true explanation for [the defendant's] silence'.[22] A defendant may therefore be asked questions about recent fabrication and what they told their lawyer of the facts now relied upon at trial. The ECtHR in *Condron*[23] observed that a defendant who chooses to make the content of their lawyer's advice part of their defence at trial cannot complain that the CJPOA overrode the confidentiality of these discussions.

26.20

Care is required in the wording of any direction to the jury where section 34 is relied upon. Guidance as to the content of the direction can be found in the Crown Court Compendium, Part 1. Whether it is necessary to give a direction to the jury in circumstances where the judge concludes that the requirements of section 34 have not been met but the jury has nevertheless been made aware of the defendant's failure to answer questions is open to debate. On the one hand, as held in *McGarry*,[24] such a direction is important to ensure that the jury is not left in 'no-man's land' between the common law rule and the statutory exception without guidance as to how to deal with the defendant's silence.

19 *R v Betts* [2001] EWCA Crim 224; [2001] 2 Cr App R 16 at [53] approved in *Hoare* [2004] EWCA Crim 784; [2005] 1 WLR 1804 at [54]–[55].

20 *Hoare* at [51].

21 *Beckles* at [43].

22 *R v Seaton* [2010] EWCA Crim 1989; [2011] 1 WLR 623 at [43].

23 *R v Condron* (2001) 31 EHRR 1.

24 *R v McGarry* [1998] EWCA Crim 2364; [1999] 1 WLR 1500.

On the other hand, such a direction only serves to remind the jury of the defendant's failure to answer questions and therefore its inclusion may be more prejudicial to the defendant than not giving the direction at all.[25]

Section 35 of the Criminal Justice and Public Order Act 1994

26.21

Under section 35, inferences from the defendant's failure to give evidence at trial are permissible. Accordingly, the CJPOA repealed section 1(b) of the Criminal Evidence Act 1898 which provided that the defendant's failure to testify was not to be made the subject of any comment by the prosecution. Section 35 provides that unless the defendant's guilt is not in issue or it appears to the court that their physical or mental condition makes it undesirable for them to give evidence, the tribunal of fact may draw such inferences 'as appear proper' from the accused's failure to give evidence or their refusal without good cause to answer any questions.

26.22

In answering whether it appears to the court to be undesirable for the defendant to give evidence, the judge has a broad discretion.[26] and a wide margin of appreciation.[27] The authorities suggest that this discretion will be exercised bearing in mind the general desirability for a defendant to testify.

26.23

Notwithstanding the wording of section 35(1)(b), the Court of Appeal in *D*[28] stated that the exception is not limited to cases where a defendant will suffer an adverse impact on his health or condition: the Court recognised that there may be circumstances, unrelated to damage to health, in which it would not be just, and so would be undesirable, to permit an inference to be drawn. In exercising its discretion the court should take into account all the circumstances of the case[29] and is entitled to weigh in the balance matters such as the defendant's ability to give a clear account of their defence at various pre-trial stages,[30] the nature and significance of the area in which the defendant could give evidence,[31] the availability of mitigating measures, such as the use of an intermediary, by which vulnerable defendants can be assisted in giving evidence and protected from unfair or oppressive cross examination,[32] and the anticipated approach of a fair-minded jury.[33] Each case turns on its facts and there is not, at least at

---

25 *R v Thomas* [2002] EWCA Crim 1308; *R v Jama* [2008] EWCA Crim 2861.
26 *R v Friend* [1997] EWCA Crim 816; [1997] 1 WLR 1433; *R v Burnett* [2016] EWCA Crim 1941.
27 *R v D* [2013] EWCA Crim 465; [2014] 1 WLR 525.
28 Ibid at [52].
29 *R v Tabbakh* [2009] EWCA Crim 464.
30 *R v Friend* [1997] EWCA Crim 816; [1997] 1 WLR 1433.
31 *R v D* [2013] EWCA Crim 465; [2014] 1 WLR 525.
32 *R v Burnett* [2016] EWCA Crim 1941.
33 *R v D* [2013] EWCA Crim 465; [2014] 1 WLR 525.

present, a blanket approach nor a more generous approach to be taken in the case of defendants who are young or who have mental difficulties.[34] The Court in *Friend* noted that it will be a rare case that it is considered 'undesirable' for a defendant to give evidence.[35] Notwithstanding the judge's broad discretion, on a practical level the issue will not arise in the category of cases where a defendant is found to be unfit to plead and so does not give evidence. Where no adverse inference arises, for example because the court concludes it would be undesirable for the defendant to give evidence, the jury must be properly directed about this.

26.24

A refusal to answer questions will be taken to be without good cause unless the defendant is entitled to refuse to answer questions on grounds of privilege, due to statutory entitlement or at the discretion of the court (s 35(5)). Subject to these arguably very limited exceptions, a defendant risks the drawing of inferences unless they answer all proper questions and a judge may remind the defendant of this duty.[36] In *Cowan,*[37] the Court of Appeal rejected the suggestion that inferences under section 35 should be confined to exceptional cases and stated that its plain wording indicated that it was not limited to exceptional cases, rather the exceptional cases were those dealt with by the exceptions in which the provisions for drawing an inference were not to be invoked. The Court in *Cowan* held that even if none of the exceptions applies, it is open to a court to decline to draw an inference from the defendant's silence although for a judge to direct a jury against drawing such an inference would require 'some evidential basis for doing so or some exceptional factors in the case making that a fair course to take'.

26.25

As a precondition to reliance on section 35, the court is obliged to satisfy itself that defendants who have not indicated that they intend to give evidence know that they are entitled to do so and understand the consequences of declining to do so (s 35(2) and (3)). The judge must ask the relevant questions of the defendant or the defendant's advocate. This remains the case even if the defendant has deliberately absented themself from trial thereby preventing their advocate from taking instructions.[38] This mandatory requirement stems from the fact that the right to give evidence in one's own defence is an essential aspect of a fair trial. In *Wright,*[39] the Privy Council, considering an identical provision to section 35, observed that the decision to give evidence is 'probably the most significant decision which a defendant has to make in the course of [their] criminal trial' and therefore one which 'will almost invariably be the subject of close consideration by [them] in conjunction with [their] advisers'.

34 Ibid at [57].
35 *R v Friend* [1997] EWCA Crim 816; [1997] 1 WLR 1433.
36 *R v Ackinclose* [1996] Crim LR 747.
37 *R v Cowan* [1996] QB 373; [1996] 1 Cr App R 1.
38 *R v Gough* [2001] EWCA Crim 2545; [2002] 2 Cr App R 8.
39 *R v Wright* [2016] UKPC 18.

26.26

Before an adverse inference is drawn, the tribunal of fact must themselves be satisfied the prosecution case calls for an answer and the defendant is the person to give it.[40] It is not sufficient that the judge has concluded following the close of the prosecution case that the case is fit to be left to the jury. On one view this goes beyond the strict requirements of section 35, but it ensures conformity with the requirement of section 38(3) that there cannot be a case to answer, and the defendant cannot be convicted, solely on an inference drawn from a failure to give evidence or refusal to answer questions. The tribunal of fact must also be satisfied before drawing an adverse inference that the defendant's silence can only sensibly be attributed to them having no answer or none that would stand up to cross examination. In many cases, it will be difficult for a reason for the failure to be advanced without evidence.

26.27

The effect of section 35 is that the tribunal of fact may regard the inference from the defendant's failure to give evidence as, in effect, a further evidential factor which lends support to the prosecution case.[41] The nature of the inference available will depend on the strength of the prosecution case and the way in which the evidence has developed. In the Northern Irish case of *Murray v DPP*, Lord Slynn observed:

> if parts of the prosecution case had so little evidential value that they called for no answer, a failure to deal with those specific matters cannot justify an inference of guilt. On the other hand, if aspects of the evidence taken alone or in combination with other facts clearly call for an explanation which the accused ought to be in a position to give, if an explanation exists, then a failure to give any explanation may as a matter of common sense allow the drawing of an inference that there is no explanation and that the accused is guilty.[42]

26.28

Whilst section 35 has made inroads into the previously established common law rule, the Court of Appeal in *Cowan*[43] held that it does preserve the right to silence. The Court firmly rejected the suggestion that the requirement that the defendant give evidence 'on pain of an adverse inference being drawn' puts a burden on them to give evidence in order to avoid a conviction. This is due, in particular, to the fact that the burden of proving guilt remains on the prosecution throughout, the prosecution has to establish a *prima facie* case before any question of the defendant giving evidence is raised, and the tribunal of fact is expressly precluded from being convicted solely because of an inference drawn from the defendant's silence.

---

40 *R v Cowan* [1996] QB 373; [1996] 1 Cr App R 1; *R v Murray* (1996) 22 EHRR 29.

41 Ibid at 379C.

42 *Murray v DPP* [1994] 1 WLR 1.

43 *Cowan* [1996] QB 373; [1996] 1 Cr App R 1.

Sections 36 and 37 of the Criminal Justice and Public Order Act 1994

26.29

Sections 36 and 37 of the CJOPA 1994 permit the tribunal of fact to draw such inferences 'as appear proper' from the accused's failure account for objects, substances, marks and presence at a particular place, provided certain conditions are satisfied. In particular, the effect of section 36(4) and section 37(3) is that adverse inferences may not be drawn under these sections unless when a constable requests the accused to account for the object, substance, mark or presence they also give the accused a 'special warning' (ie explain to the accused in ordinary language what the effect of the sections would be if they failed or refused to comply with that request), the terms of which are provided in PACE Code C.[44]

26.30

These sections are fairly restrictive. Crucially, they only permit inferences to be drawn in respect of the state or location of the accused at the time of arrest. The state or location of the accused at other times, for example at the scene of the alleged offence or another suspicious location but where no arrest takes place cannot give rise to inferences under these sections.

26.31

Sections 36 and 37 do not require a finding, comparable to section 34(1), that the defendant could reasonably have been expected to account for objects, substances, marks or presence as requested by the officer. Accordingly, sections 36 and 37 do not invite comparison between the account given in interview and evidence given at trial. In *Compton*,[45] the Court held in relation to section 36 that the sole question for the tribunal of fact is whether the defendant did 'account' for the matter requested by the officer. This must apply equally to section 37.

26.32

As with the other subsections, inferences under sections 36 and 37 may form part of the case to answer or the case which results in a conviction but neither a case to answer nor a conviction can be founded solely on an inference drawn from the accused's failure to account for objects, substances, marks or presence at a particular place.

---

44 PACE Code C is one of the Codes of Practice which regulate police powers and protect public rights which are required to be published by the Home Office under the Police and Criminal Evidence Act 1984. It provides the requirements for the detention, treatment and questioning of suspects not related to terrorism in police custody.

45 *Compton* [2002] EWCA Crim 2835 at [32].

26.33

Directions in relation to section 34 are relevant to the judge's task under section 36.[46] In *Compton*, Buxton LJ held in relation to section 36 that the most crucial point is that the jury must be directed that they can only hold against the defendant a failure to give an explanation if they are sure that they had no acceptable explanation to offer. Where the defendant states that they remained silent and did not account for the matter requested by the officer on the advice of their solicitor, the direction to the jury should be in the same terms as under section 34.

PRIVILEGE AGAINST SELF-INCRIMINATION

26.34

Long established at common law, the privilege against self-incrimination entitles a person to refuse to answer questions or to provide documents or objects if to do so would carry a real or appreciable risk of its use in a prosecution against them.[47]

26.35

In the context of Article 6, the trigger for the privilege is that a person is 'charged' with a criminal offence. This has a particular meaning in ECtHR jurisprudence, that is that the person has been substantially affected by an allegation and they have become, in effect, a suspect (see *Ambrose v Harris*).[48] The right applies to criminal proceedings in respect of all types of cases, regardless of complexity or seriousness.[49] Significantly, the privilege against self-incrimination does not protect the accused from compulsory questioning or the making of an incriminating statement *per se*. It is the obtaining of evidence by coercion or oppression[50] and the use of such evidence in criminal proceedings to incriminate the accused,[51] which may infringe Article 6 and thus is the focus of the right.

26.36

As with the right to silence, the right not to incriminate oneself is not absolute and so direct compulsion does not necessarily result in a violation of Article 6. In considering whether there has been a violation of Article 6, the ECtHR has applied a test to establish whether the 'essence of the right' has been infringed. Such an approach necessarily involves consideration of the facts and circumstances of each case rather than a blanket approach. In determining whether the essence of the right has been infringed, the following criteria are

46 Ibid at [36].
47 *Rio Tinto Zinc Corporation v Westinghouse Electric Corporation* [1978] AC 547.
48 *Ambrose v Harris* [2011] UKSC 43; [2011] 1 WLR 2435 at [62]–[63].
49 *Saunders* at [74].
50 *Ibrahim v UK* (2015) 61 EHRR 9.
51 *Saunders* at [67].

considered: the nature and degree of compulsion used to obtain the evidence; the weight of the public interest in the investigation and punishment of the offence at issue; the existence of any relevant safeguards in the procedure; and the use to which the material so obtained was put.[52]

26.37

The privilege against self-incrimination is not confined to admissions of wrongdoing or directly incriminating statements but includes any statement which may later be deployed in criminal proceedings in support of the prosecution case.[53,54] The rationale behind this is that evidence obtained under compulsion, which may be of a non-incriminating nature such as exculpatory comments or information on questions of fact, may nevertheless be deployed in support of the prosecution case to contradict or cast doubt upon other statements made by the accused at the pre-trial stage or in evidence.

26.38

However, in *Saunders*,[55] the ECtHR held that the privilege against self-incrimination does not extend to and thus prevent the use in criminal proceedings of certain material obtained from the accused under compulsion such as documents acquired pursuant to a warrant or samples of breath, blood, urine or bodily tissue. The Court drew a distinction with compelled statements on the basis that these types of material came into existence independently of the will of the accused at a time before any compulsory discovery process was initiated. In drawing this distinction, the Court did not address its earlier decision in *Funke v France*[56] where it found a violation of Article 6 even though it concerned (according to the distinction in *Saunders v UK*) documents of an independent existence. The applicant in *Funke* had been convicted of failing to produce bank statements to the French customs authorities on request and the criminal proceedings for non-production were intended to compel cooperation in a prosecution to be brought for offences contrary to certain financial regulations. The effect of the decision in *Saunders v UK* must be that *Funke* was not correctly decided, particularly since *Saunders v UK* was subsequently confirmed in *L v UK*[57] and applied in *Jalloh*.

26.39

Saunders has had significant impact on domestic law. Amongst other things, it showed that the use in criminal proceedings of material obtained by statutory compulsion in the course of non-criminal proceedings would likely infringe the privilege against self-incrimination under Article 6. As a result of *Saunders v UK* and no doubt in anticipation of the coming into force of the Human Rights Act 1998, Parliament enacted section 59 and Schedule 3 to the Youth

52 *Jalloh v Germany* (2007) 44 EHRR 32 at [117].
53 *Ibrahim* at [268].
54 *Zaichenko v Russia* [2010] ECHR 185 at [52]–[60].
55 *Saunders* at [69].
56 *Funke v France* (1993) 16 EHRR 297.
57 *L v UK* [2000] 2 FLR 322.

Justice and Criminal Evidence Act 1999 which inserted provisions into a number of different statutes and orders concerned with fraud-related or similar investigations, providing immunity against the use in criminal proceedings of material obtained by statutory compulsion in the course of non-criminal proceedings. Notably, these provisions provide immunity only in respect of the use of answers and statements made in response to compulsory questioning under the relevant powers. They do not restrict the use of pre-existing documents disclosed under compulsion. Presumably the scope of these provisions reflected Parliament's understanding of the scope of the privilege in light of *Saunders*, rather than *Funke*. Had Parliament considered that the privilege did extend to the kind of 'independent' documents in issue in *Funke*, then it could have made these immunity provisions more extensive.

26.40

The principle that evidence existing independently of the will of the accused does not normally engage the privilege against self-incrimination is also now clearly established at common law (*R (River East Supplies Ltd) v Crown Court at Nottingham*. In *Kearns*,[58] Aikens J stated:

> There is a distinction between the compulsory production of documents or other material which have an existence independent of the will of the suspect or accused person and statements that [they have] had to make under compulsion. In the former case there is no infringement of the right to silence and the right not to incriminate oneself. In the latter case there could be, depending on the circumstances.

26.41

Parliament may, expressly or by necessary implication, limit, amend or exclude the common law privilege against self-incrimination.[59] Accordingly, and notwithstanding the privilege, particular individuals may be required to answer questions or provide information or documents in specific situations notwithstanding this may incriminate them.

26.42

There is no Parliamentary consistency of practice where the privilege has been abrogated. A statute which provides for an obligation to provide information or to answer questions may say that no privilege against self-incrimination may be claimed. Statute may, at the same time, prevent the use in subsequent criminal proceedings of the potentially incriminating information, or answers provided, as a form of protection.

Examples of where the privilege has been *expressly* abrogated include:

- Theft Act 1968, s 31;

---

58 *Kearns* at [53].

59 *Bishopsgate Investment Management Ltd (In Liquidation) v Maxwell (No 1)* [1993] Ch 1.

- Senior Courts Act 1981, s 72;
- Children Act 1989, s 98; and
- Fraud Act 2006, s 13.

Examples of where the privilege has been *impliedly* abrogated include:

- Insolvency Act 1986, ss 235 and 236 (considered in *Bishopsgate*); and
- Terrorism Act 2000, Sch 7 (considered by the Supreme Court in *Beghal v DPP*[60] and the ECtHR in *Beghal v UK*[61]).

26.43

There is no Parliamentary consistency of practice where the privilege has been abrogated. A statute which provides for an obligation to provide information or to answer questions may say that no privilege against self-incrimination may be claimed. Statute may, at the same time, prevent the use in subsequent criminal proceedings of the potentially incriminating information, or answers provided, as a form of protection. An example of both provisions featuring is in section 31 of the Theft Act 1968.

26.44

Alternatively, statute may closely limit the use in subsequent criminal proceedings of the information or answers provided. An example of this is found in section 98 of the Children Act 1989, which states a statement or admission potentially in breach of the privilege may only be admissible in evidence against its maker, their spouse or civil partner in proceedings for an offence other than perjury.

26.45

Statute may expressly provide that answers may be used in evidence to support a subsequent prosecution. For example, section 12 of the Road Traffic Offenders Act 1988 provides that in specified circumstances and in prosecutions for specified offences a statement made by the accused in response to a requirement under section 172(2) of the Road Traffic Act 1988 to give information as to the identity of a driver of a particular vehicle on a particular occasion may be used by the prosecution as evidence that the accused was the driver of the vehicle on that occasion. Use of answers to support a subsequent prosecution in these circumstances has been found not to violate Article 6.[62] In reaching that decision in *O'Halloran*, which concerned a conviction for speeding, the ECtHR placed particular emphasis on the 'special nature' of the regulatory regime to which owners and drivers of vehicles were subject and the limited nature of the information sought by a notice under section 172.

---

60 *Beghal v DPP* [2015] UKSC 49; [2016] AC 88.

61 *Beghal v UK* [2019] EHCR 181.

62 *Brown v Stott* [2003] 1 AC 681, approved in *O'Halloran v UK* (2008) 46 EHRR 21.

26.46

Statute may intend to impose an unqualified obligation to answer questions or provide information and contain none of these stipulations. This is the case in sections 235 and 236 of the Insolvency Act 1986.

26.47

The power, under section 78 of the Police and Criminal Evidence Act 1984, to exclude unfair evidence on which the prosecution proposes to rely is one safeguard which can be invoked by a defendant, particularly where statute does not preclude reliance upon answers or information obtained by compulsion in a subsequent prosecution. The circumstances in which evidence is obtained is a central consideration in the exercise of the power under section 78 and so evidence obtained by compulsion would appear to be a classic class of evidence which it would be unfair to admit at trial.

26.48

The role of section 78 was the subject of much discussion by the Supreme Court in *Beghal*. Lord Hughes and Lord Hodges considered section 78 provided a 'powerful reason' why the risk of prosecution based upon answers to questioning under Schedule 7 to the Terrorism Act 2000 is not a real and appreciable one. Their Lordships stated that whilst the 'mere fact that prosecution is not the purpose of such questioning does not sufficiently reduce the risk, the provisions of section 78 of the Police and Criminal Evidence Act 1984 in practice do'. In essence, their Lordships considered the outcome of the application of section 78 was 'inevitable' since they could not see a situation in which answers obtained under these compulsory powers would not fall to be excluded by the trial judge and in any event the power must be exercised in accordance with Article 6. However, in his dissenting judgment, Lord Kerr disagreed as to the inevitability of the application of section 78: he doubted that incriminating responses given under compulsion would be excluded if, for instance, they corroborated or reinforced other evidence which directly implicated the defendant. Lord Kerr also alluded to the fact that a court may not exclude independently discovered evidence relied upon by the prosecution which is found in consequence of the incriminating answers given. There is no 'fruits of the poisonous tree' doctrine in English law or under Article 6 which, for example, extends the exclusionary rule on confessions or unfair evidence so as to render all evidence obtained in consequence inadmissible.[63] Accordingly, even if a defendant successfully invokes section 78 and excludes a self-incriminating answer, there is no guarantee that they will not be prosecuted on the strength of it. There is, therefore, a compelling argument that the risk of prosecution is capable of being real in some cases.

63 *HM Advocate v P* [2011] UKSC 44; [2011] 1 WLR 2497.

26.49

Whilst this discussion is largely academic in the context of Schedule 7 of the Terrorism Act 2000 (para 5A of Schedule 7 now expressly provides that answers or information obtained under the Schedule 7 compulsory powers are inadmissible except in specified proceedings or circumstances, and came into effect on 13 August 2020), it is demonstrative of tensions in domestic law and unresolved questions generally. The difficulty is that there cannot be a blanket approach in cases of this kind, so resolution, based on widely applicable principle, is unlikely to come quickly.

27 Admissibility of evidence

Deanna Heer KC and Dominic Lewis

OVERVIEW

27.1

The touchstone of admissibility in criminal, and indeed civil proceedings, is relevance. Only relevant evidence is admissible. However, not all relevant evidence will be admissible. In the criminal law in particular, a number of exclusionary rules have developed which restrict the use of otherwise admissible evidence. While many of these rules developed through the common law, they can now be viewed through the prism of human rights, in particular the Article 6 right to a fair trial. However, Article 6 itself lays down no rules of evidence, which are primarily a matter for the domestic courts: *Schenk v Switzerland*.[1]

27.2

Various categories of admissibility argument are considered below. In general terms, however, similar principles will apply. The modern criminal court will consider the impact on the fairness of the proceedings of the admission of evidence, howsoever obtained. Regardless of which Convention right is alleged to have been breached in obtaining the evidence, the question for the court will ultimately turn on whether, if the evidence were to be admitted, the proceedings as a whole would remain compatible with the Article 6 right to a fair trial. Accordingly, with limited exceptions, the question of whether or not there has been a breach of a Convention right will not be determinative of whether evidence obtained as a result of that breach will be admitted in criminal proceedings.

EVIDENCE OBTAINED IN BREACH OF ARTICLE 3

27.3

The exceptions to the rule expressed above concern evidence obtained in breach of Article 3: 'No one shall be subjected to torture or to inhuman or degrading treatment or punishment.'

1 *Schenk v Switzerland* (1991) 13 EHRR 242.

Torture

27.4

The use of torture for the purpose of securing evidence (usually by confession) has been proscribed in this country since the mid-seventeenth century. Further, it is now settled law that the state may not rely upon evidence which has or may have been procured by torture *by officials of a foreign state* without the complicity of the British authorities. There is thus a general rule that evidence obtained by torture is inadmissible in judicial proceedings: *A v Secretary of State for the Home Department (No 2).*[2]

27.5

The rationale for this absolute rule does not rest on the proposition that involuntary statements (whether made by defendants or third parties) are inherently unreliable. While that has traditionally been one of the relevant considerations for courts in rejecting the admission of such evidence – and indeed remains so – the objection runs deeper than that.

Lord Bingham in *A* explained that third-party torture evidence fell to be excluded as 'unreliable, unfair, offensive to ordinary standards of humanity and decency and incompatible with the principles which should animate a tribunal seeking to administer justice' [at 52]. Lord Hoffmann observed that: 'The use of torture is dishonourable. It corrupts and degrades the state which uses it and the legal system which accepts it' [at 82]. He reasoned that the rule against the admission of evidence obtained by torture much exclude statements obtained by torture anywhere, 'since the stain attaching to such evidence will defile an English court whatever the nationality of the torturer' [at 91]. Lord Hope noted that: 'The use of such evidence is excluded not on grounds of its unreliability – if that was the only objection to it, it would go to its weight, not to its admissibility – but on grounds of its barbarism, its illegality and its humanity' [at 112].

The test to be applied

27.6

As to the test that should be applied by a court when assessing whether evidence has been obtained by torture, Lord Hope [at 118][3] provided the opinion adopted by the majority: the court (in that case, SIAC[4]) should refuse to admit evidence if it concludes on the balance of probabilities that the evidence was obtained by torture.

2 *A v Secretary of State for the Home Department (No 2)* [2005] UKHL 71.

3 Ibid.

4 Special Immigration Appeals Commission, which deals with appeals against UK government decisions over refusing or removing British citizenship, deportations from the UK and denial of entry to the UK, including on national security grounds.

27.7

However, in the context of criminal proceedings, that test will not suffice. In a series of judgments, the ECtHR has made it clear that evidence ought not to be admitted if the court concludes that there is a real risk that it was obtained by torture: see *Othman v United Kingdom*,[5] *El Haski v Belgium*.[6] The burden of establishing such a risk falls on the individual, but plainly in practice the more difficult task where there is some evidence to support the individual's case on this issue is likely to be that of the state in rebutting any such contention.

What level of ill-treatment is required?

27.8

As to what level of ill-treatment is required to render evidence inadmissible under the principle against torture, the prevailing view of the House of Lords was that inhuman or degrading treatment falling short of torture would not fall within the exclusionary rule. That conclusion has now been superseded by the ECtHR and can no longer be considered good law. In *El Haski* the court concluded:

> The use in criminal proceedings of statements obtained as a result of a person's treatment in breach of art. 3 – irrespective of the classification of that treatment as torture, inhuman or degrading treatment – makes the proceedings as a whole automatically unfair and in breach of art. 6.[7]

What material is covered by the exclusionary rule?

27.9

In *Jalloh v Germany*,[8] the court held that incriminating evidence – whether in the form of a confession or real evidence – which had been obtained as a result of acts of violence in breach of Article 3, should never be relied upon as proof of guilt, irrespective of its probative value.

27.10

In *Gäfgen v Germany*,[9] the ECtHR was required to consider the subtler question of whether the admission of evidence obtained as a result of a confession, which had itself been obtained through threats of 'immediate and significant ill treatment', rendered the trial as a whole unfair. In that case no actual violence was found to have been used. The statements made under threat of violence had

---

5 *Othman v United Kingdom* (2012) 55 EHRR 1 at 273.
6 *El Haski v Belgium* (2013) 56 EHRR 31.
7 Ibid at [85].
8 *Jalloh v Germany* (2007) 44 EHRR 32.
9 *Gäfgen v Germany* (2011) 52 EHRR 1.

been excluded from the trial, but the evidence derived from searches conducted in reliance on those statements was admitted.

27.11

The court found that the threats amounted to a breach of Article 3 and went on to consider the impact of that conduct on the fairness of the trial process. It referred to its decision in *Jalloh* but noted that the question of whether the use of real evidence obtained as a result of an act qualifying as inhuman treatment contrary to Article 3 but falling short of torture would always render a trial unfair had not yet been settled. [10]

27.12

The court noted that, unlike Article 3, Article 6 does not enshrine an absolute right. It discussed the possible impact of admitting evidence obtained as a result of Article 3 breaches amounting to an incentive for law enforcement officers to use such methods, notwithstanding the absolute prohibition. It noted that the repression of such conduct might require the exclusion of evidence thereby obtained from the trial process, even though that evidence was more remote than evidence extracted immediately as a consequence of a violation of Article 3. However, it ultimately concluded:

> … both a criminal trial's fairness and the effective protection of the absolute prohibition under Article 3 in that context are only at stake if it has been shown that the breach of Article 3 had a bearing on the outcome of the proceedings against the defendant, that is, had an impact on his or her conviction or sentence.[11]

27.13

The court went on to note that the basis of the conviction in that case was not the real evidence, but the defendant's full confession at his trial: 'It can thus be said there was a break in the causal chain leading from the prohibited methods of investigation to the applicant's conviction and sentence in respect of the impugned real evidence.'[12] Accordingly, the trial as a whole was held not to be unfair.[13]

27.14

Gäfgen is plainly a case that turns on its own facts, but the principle that emerges approximates to the following: that where real evidence has been obtained as a result (whether direct or indirect) of ill-treatment which amounts to a breach of Article 3, the admission of that evidence is likely to render the trial as a whole

---

10 Ibid at [73].
11 Ibid at [178].
12 Ibid at [180].
13 Put another way, had the defendant remained silent at trial, or denied his guilt, it seems unlikely that the reasoning of the ECtHR could have been relied upon to uphold any resulting conviction.

unfair in a case in which there is a causal connection between that evidence and the conviction.

Disclosure of material obtained in breach of Article 3

27.15

It is worth noting that while the state is precluded from placing any reliance on material obtained in breach of Article 3, the proper exercise of its disclosure function may well require such material to be disclosed, if it may assist the individual who is engaged in litigation *against* the state. That is the position in SIAC,[14] and while that regime is obviously in many ways *sui generis*, there would appear to be no reason why the principle that *exculpatory* material obtained in breach of Article 3 should be disclosed ought not to apply in criminal proceedings. The practical consequence of such a disclosure quandary arising would likely be a PII hearing and disclosure of a gist.

Interplay with section 76(2) of the Police and Criminal Evidence Act 1984 – exclusion of confessions obtained by oppression etc.

27.16

The exclusionary rule in section 76(2) of the Police and Criminal Evidence Act 1984 (PACE) covers a broader range of conduct than the case law discussed above. Under section 76(8) 'oppression' is defined as *including* torture, inhuman or degrading treatment, and the use or threat of violence (whether or not it amounts to torture). That is clearly not intended to be an exhaustive list: 'oppression' is not confined to conduct that would violate Article 3 and it has previously been held that the word should be given its ordinary dictionary meaning.[15] While shouting by the police during interview may amount to oppression,[16] the bar for contending that robust questioning amounts to oppression is likely to be relatively high.

27.17

Under sections 76(4)–(6) of PACE, evidence discovered as a result of an inadmissible confession may be adduced at trial, provided that the manner in which that evidence was discovered (ie as a result of the excluded confession) may not be admitted in evidence.

14 See SIAC Practice Note dated 5 October 2016, at §13.

15 'The Oxford English Dictionary *as its third definition of the word runs as follows:* "Exercise of authority or power in a burdensome, harsh, or wrongful manner; unjust or cruel treatment of subjects, inferiors, etc.; the imposition of unreasonable or unjust burdens"' [*per* Lord Lane CJ, at p 142]: *R v Fulling* [1987] QB 426.

16 See *R v Paris* (1993) 97 Cr App R 99.

EVIDENCE OBTAINED IN BREACH OF ARTICLE 8

27.18

Where the circumstances in 27.6 to 27.14 (above) do not apply, evidence obtained unlawfully (ie, in breach of a Convention right) will not automatically be ruled inadmissible. The approach of the courts when determining the impact of any breach of a Convention right on the fairness of criminal proceedings will be similar to that adopted where a breach of one of the PACE Codes of Practice is alleged. Where the admission of evidence would lead to unfairness, the court has the power to exclude it, but the fact that evidence was obtained unlawfully does not of itself render that evidence inadmissible in criminal proceedings. The case law is this area typically concerns evidence obtained in breach of Article 8 (eg, by unauthorised audio eavesdropping device,[17] telephone intercept,[18] or covert surveillance[19]). Similar principles are likely to apply to the use of emerging technology – for example automated facial recognition technology.[20]

27.19

The case of *Khan v UK*[21] serves as a convenient illustration of the interplay between Article 6 and other Convention rights. In that case, the ECtHR found a breach of the defendant's Article 8 right to respect for his private life where the police used a secret listening device to obtain evidence against him, where there was no statutory system to regulate the use of covert listening devices and the relevant Home Office guidelines were neither legally binding nor directly publicly accessible. The interference with the defendant's Article 8 right was therefore not 'in accordance with the law'. The evidence obtained using the devices was, in effect, the only evidence against the defendant, and upon it being ruled admissible by the trial judge he pleaded guilty to a serious Class A drugs importation offence. The defendant was awarded damages for the breach of Article 8, but his conviction was held to be safe: there had been no violation of his Article 6 right to a fair trial. When considering whether any breach of Article 6 was established, the central question was 'whether the proceedings as a whole were fair'.[22] The ECtHR concluded that they were, because, had the domestic courts (both at first instance and on appeal) considered that the admission of the evidence would have given rise to substantive unfairness, they would have had a discretion to exclude it under section 78 of PACE.[23]

17 See eg, *Khan v UK* (2001) 31 EHRR 45.
18 See eg, *R v P & others* [2002] 1 AC 146, where in fact no breach of Article 8 was established.
19 See eg, *R v Button* [2005] EWCA Crim 516; *R v Loveridge & others* [2001] 2 Cr App R 591; *R v Mason & others* [2002] 2 Cr App R 628. Cf *Allan v UK* (2003) EHRR 12.
20 See eg, *R (oAo Bridges) v Chief Constable of South Wales Police & others* [2020] EWCA Civ 1058.
21 *Khan v UK* (2001) 31 EHRR 45.
22 Ibid at [38].
23 Ibid at [39]–[40].

27.20

Similarly, in *PG v UK,*[24] the ECtHR found a breach of Article 8 after covert listening devices were installed in a suspect's house and in a police cell in which the suspects were detained. Such activity did not constitute a criminal offence in domestic law but the undoubted interference with the suspects' Article 8 rights was not 'in accordance with law' as there was no statutory authority for the interference. However, the admission of evidence from the covert devices did not render the proceedings as a whole unfair, and the convictions were safe. Of relevance was the fact that the product of the eavesdropping was not the only evidence against the defendants and (more fundamentally) the ability of the domestic courts to exclude the evidence if they considered that its admission would have given rise to 'substantive unfairness'. Therefore section 78 of PACE operates to protect the rights of defendants so that the approach of domestic courts to evidence obtained in breach of Article 8 is compliant with Article 6.

27.21

The approach of the ECtHR outlined above is mirrored in the approach of domestic courts to the admissibility of evidence obtained in breach of Article 8. Lord Hobhouse, delivering the leading judgment in *R v P and others*[25] explained:

> The critical question is the fairness of the trial. Questions of the admissibility of evidence are not governed by Article 8. The fair use of intercept evidence at a trial is not a breach of Article 6 even if the evidence was unlawfully obtained.

And, in discussing the ECtHR's decision in *Khan*:

> It should be noted that the ECtHR again emphasised that the defendant is not entitled to have the unlawfully obtained evidence excluded simply because it has been so obtained. What he [is] entitled to is an opportunity to challenge its use and admission in evidence and a judicial assessment of the effect of its admission upon the fairness of the trial as is provided for by s.78.

RIGHT TO EXAMINE WITNESSES UNDER ARTICLE 6

27.22

Article 6 guarantees the right to a fair trial. The minimum rights set out in Article 6(3)(a)–(e) are aspects of that general right and should not be considered exhaustive.[26] In terms of admissibility of evidence, the right of the accused to examine or have examined witnesses against them under Article 6(3)(d) has

24 *PG v UK* (2008) 46 EHRR 51.
25 *R v P and others* [2002] 1 AC 146, HL.
26 *Artico v Italy* 3 EHRR 1; *Edwards v UK* 15 EHRR 417; *Foucher v France* 25 EHRR 234.

been the subject of considerable European jurisprudence. That jurisprudence falls into two categories: hearsay and anonymous witnesses. In relation to each of these, similar principles apply.

Hearsay evidence

27.23

In *Kostovski v The Netherlands*,[27] the ECtHR reiterated that questions of admissibility of evidence were primarily a matter for the national courts and that the task of the ECtHR was to consider the overall fairness of the trial. In respect of Article 6(3)(d) it held: 'As a rule, these rights require that an accused should be given an adequate and proper opportunity to challenge and question a witness against him, either at the time the witness was making his statement or at some later stage of the proceedings.' Successive cases before the European Court led to the development of the so-called 'sole or decisive rule' starting with *Doorson v The Netherlands*[28] and culminating in a decision by the Chamber of the ECtHR in *Al-Khawaja v UK*[29] to the effect that, in the absence of special circumstances, there were unlikely to be any counterbalancing measures which would be sufficient to justify the introduction of untested evidence which is the sole or decisive evidence in the case.[30]

27.24

The UK appealed to the Grand Chamber and, in the meantime, the Supreme Court, considering the case of *R v Horncastle and others*,[31] declined to follow the Strasbourg jurisprudence. Lord Phillips, in a comprehensive review of the case law identified that the 'sole or decisive rule' had emerged from an *obiter* observation in *Doorson* without explanation or qualification and without a full consideration of the available safeguards, including the statutory code set out in the Criminal Justice Act 2003 which, he said, struck the correct balance between the rights of the accused and the rights of victims and witnesses even where the evidence was sole or decisive.

27.25

Having considered the Supreme Court ruling, in *Al-Khawaja v UK*,[32] the Grand Chamber of the ECtHR qualified the Chamber's decision, holding that there were two requirements which flowed from the general proposition that an accused should be given an adequate and proper opportunity to challenge and question a witness against him. First, there must be a good reason for the non-

27 *Kostovski v The Netherlands* (1990) 12 EHRR 434.

28 *Doorson v The Netherlands* (1996) 22 EHRR 330.

29 *Al-Khawaja v UK* (2009) 49 EHRR 1.

30 See also, *Luca v Italy* (2003) 36 EHRR 46; *Van Mechelen v The Netherlands* (1997) 25 EHRR 647; *PS v Germany* (2001) 36 EHRR 61 and, in respect of the untested evidence of a co-defendant, *Kaste and Mathisen v Norway* (2009) 48 EHRR 3.

31 *R v Horncastle and others* [2009] UKSC 14.

32 *Al-Khawaja v UK* (2012) 54 EHRR 23.

attendance of a witness. Secondly, when a conviction was based solely or to a decisive degree on depositions made by a person whom the accused has had no opportunity to examine or have examined, the rights of the defence *may* be restricted to an extent that is incompatible with the guarantees provided by Article 6. The reason for the witness's absence was a preliminary question which should be examined before any consideration of whether the evidence was sole or decisive. The Court acknowledged that there may be a number of reasons why a witness was absent but considered only two in the context of the case. Plainly the death of a witness would constitute a good reason. Absence due to fear of testifying required closer examination. Where the fear was attributable to the defendant, it would be appropriate to allow the evidence to be adduced even if it was the sole or decisive evidence in the case. To hold otherwise would subvert the integrity of the proceedings. Where there was a more general fear of testifying, the trial Court would be required to conduct appropriate enquiries to determine whether there were objective grounds for the fear and whether those objective grounds were supported by evidence. Allowing a witness statement to be admitted in *lieu* of live evidence had to be seen as a measure of last resort and the trial Court must be satisfied that all available alternatives, such as witness anonymity or special measures to protect the witness, would be inappropriate or impractical. As to the second question, the word 'decisive' should be narrowly construed. It meant more than merely probative and indicated evidence of such significance or importance as was likely to be determinative of the outcome of the case. But the sole or decisive rule should not be applied inflexibly. The admission of evidence which is sole or decisive will not inevitably result in a breach of Article 6; the central question will be whether there were sufficient counterbalancing measures to secure the defendant's rights under Article 6. The ECtHR considered that the safeguards set out in the Criminal Justice Acts of 1988 and 2003 together with section 78 of PACE and the common law were, in principle, strong safeguards to ensure fairness; the question in an individual case will be how those safeguards are applied.

27.26

In *Horncastle v UK,*[33] the ECtHR applied the principles set out in *Al-Khawaja* and, considering the domestic case of *R v Riat and others,*[34] rejected the applicant's argument that any decisive evidence must be shown to be reliable or, at the very least, shown not to be unreliable to any significant extent before it could be admitted.

27.27

In *Schatschaschwili v Germany,*[35] the ECtHR clarified that the lack of a good reason for the failure to secure the attendance of a witness was not in itself determinative, although it would be a very important factor to be weighed in

33 *Horncastle v UK* (2015) 60 EHRR 31.
34 *R v Riat and others* [2012] EWCA Crim 1509.
35 *Schatschaschwili v Germany* (2016) 63 EHRR 14.

the balance and one that may tip the balance in favour of finding a breach of Article 6.The trial Court was required to have made reasonable efforts to secure the attendance of the witness. Further, the Court would consider whether there existed sufficient counterbalancing safeguards even where the evidence was neither sole nor decisive; the extent of the counterbalancing measures necessary to ensure that the trial is fair will depend on the weight of the evidence. Such measures included not just procedural safeguards but also evidential matters such as the existence of corroboration and the ability of the accused to give evidence. The principles identified in *Al-Khawaja*[36] and *Schatschaschwili* are equally applicable where the witness is available but refuses to give evidence: see *NK v Germany* and *Price v UK*.[37]

Anonymous witnesses

27.28

In *R v Davis,*[38] the House of Lords held that, under common law principles the introduction of evidence from anonymous witnesses whose evidence was 'sole and decisive' without sufficient safeguards for the defendant fell foul of Article 6. Lord Mance referred to the line of European jurisprudence set out above, starting with *Kostovski v Netherlands*[39] which established that Article 6(3)(d) was applicable to anonymous witness evidence and referred to *Doorson v The Netherlands*, [40] in which the Court stated:

> It is true that Article 6 does not explicitly require the interests of witnesses in general, and those of victims called upon to testify in particular, to be taken into consideration. However, their life, liberty or security of person may be at stake, as may interests coming generally within the ambit of Article 8 of the Convention. Such interests of witnesses and victims are in principle protected by other, substantive provisions of the Convention, which imply that Contracting States should organise their criminal proceedings in such a way that those interests are not unjustifiably imperilled. Against this background, principles of fair trial also require that in appropriate cases the interests of the defence are balanced against those of witnesses or victims called upon to testify …

The Court also referred to *PS v Germany*[41] in which it stated:

> In appropriate cases, principles of fair trial require that the interests of the defence are balanced against those of witnesses or victims called upon to testify, in particular where life, liberty or security of person are

36 *Al-Khawaja v UK* (2012) 54 EHRR 23.
37 *NK v Germany* (2019) 68 EHRR 9; *Price v UK* (2017) 64 EHRR 17.
38 *R v Davis* [2008] UKHL 36.
39 *Kostovski v Netherlands* (1990) 12 EHRR 434.
40 *Doorson v The Netherlands* (1996) 22 EHRR 330.
41 *PS v Germany* (2001) 36 EHRR 61.

at stake, or interests coming generally within the ambit of Art. 8 of the Convention.

27.29

Whilst accepting that these cases established that the use of anonymous evidence was not under all circumstances incompatible with Article 6, Lord Mance nevertheless doubted that the Court's use of the word '*require*' in the above cases was intended to suggest that there was an obligation for national legal systems to provide for anonymous witnesses in all circumstances. He referred to the 'sole or decisive test' first referred to in *Doorson* (above) observing that, in practice, where the Strasbourg Court had found a violation of the right to a fair trial, it had commonly done so by reference to a conjunction of considerations, not merely because the conviction was based solely or decisively on anonymous evidence. In the present case, the House of Lords found that the combination of the fact that the anonymous evidence was sole or decisive and the degree to which procedures to protect the anonymity of the witness had hampered the defence was unfair, and that any further relaxation of the basic common law rule requiring witnesses on issues in dispute to be identified and cross-examined with knowledge of their identity was a matter for Parliament and not the Courts. Very quickly the government introduced the Criminal Evidence (Witness Anonymity) Act 2008, subsequently replaced by sections 86 to 93 of the Coroners and Justice Act 2009, which provides a statutory code governing the admissibility of anonymous evidence in which there is no absolute prohibition on the introduction of anonymous evidence that is sole or decisive, but simply a statutory requirement for the Court to have regard to that factor amongst others.

Entrapment/agents provocateurs

27.30

This topic is often considered from the perspective of abuse of process, but where such an argument fails, the issue may instead give rise to an application to exclude evidence. Where the commission of an offence has been incited by an undercover officer, there will have been a breach of Article 6. See *Teixeira De Castro v Portugal*,[42] in which the ECtHR, stated that, although the rise in organised crime required appropriate measures to be taken, the right to fair administration of justice nevertheless holds such a prominent place that it cannot be sacrificed for the sake of expedience. Relying on *Kostovski v The Netherlands*[43] it stated that the Convention did not preclude reliance on anonymous informants in appropriate circumstances; nevertheless, the use of undercover agents had to be restricted and appropriate safeguards put in place. The Court stated that it was necessary to determine whether the actions of the police had gone beyond that of an undercover agent and found that there

42 *Teixeira De Castro v Portugal* (1999) 28 EHRR 101.
43 *Kostovski v The Netherlands* (1990) 12 EHRR 434.

had been a breach where there was no evidence that the applicant had been predisposed to commit the offence, the officers had gone beyond an essentially passive role and their evidence had been the main evidence against the accused.

27.31

In *R v Loosely*,[44] the House of Lords held that there was no appreciable difference between the position at common law in England and the ruling in *Teixeira*. Although evidence of entrapment did not provide the accused with a substantive defence in English law, there were nevertheless two available remedies: a stay of the proceedings as an abuse of process or, where that failed, an application to exclude the evidence under section 78 of PACE. In deciding whether there was entrapment, their Lordships doubted the relevance of the defendant's predisposition to commit the offence, since the essence of entrapment was the misuse of State power. Lord Nicholls expressed this as a consideration of whether the police did no more than present the defendant with an unexceptional opportunity to commit a crime rather than whether the police had gone beyond an essentially passive role. Other factors to be considered included the nature of the crime and the reason for the operation, the extent of police participation, proportionality and the degree of supervision of the police actions, which in the UK may be different from the judicial oversight in other European countries but had the same purpose.

27.32

In *Ramanauskas v Lithuania*,[45] the ECtHR built on the *Texeira* ruling that the use of sources such as anonymous informants to found a conviction was acceptable only if adequate and sufficient safeguards against abuse were in place. In particular, there needed to be 'a clear and foreseeable procedure for authorising, implementing and supervising the investigative measures in question'. The Court described police incitement as occurring where the officers involved '… do not confine themselves to investigating criminal activity in an essentially passive manner but exert such an influence on the subject as to incite the commission of an offence that would otherwise not have been committed, in order to make it possible to establish the offence, that is, to provide evidence and institute a prosecution'. It went on to state that where the disclosed material did not enable the Court to determine whether there was incitement, it was obliged to examine the procedure whereby the plea of incitement was determined in order to ensure that the rights of the defendant were adequately protected, in particular, the right to adversarial proceedings and to equality of arms. The Court said:

> It falls to the prosecution to prove that there was no incitement, provided that the defendant's allegations are not wholly improbable. In the absence of any such proof, it is the task of the judicial authorities to examine the facts of the case and to take the necessary steps to

---

44 *R v Loosely* [2001] UKHL 53.

45 *Ramanauskas v Lithuania* (2010) 51 EHRR 11.

uncover the truth in order to determine whether there was any incitement. Should they find that there was, they must draw inferences in accordance with the Convention.

27.33

Ramanauskas was relied upon by the applicant in *R v Syed*,[46] who argued that in the light of subsequent Strasbourg developments postdating *Loosely*, a new approach was required placing the burden of proof on the prosecution to show that there had been no incitement. The Court of Appeal held that *Loosely* remained compliant with the requirements of Article 6. It declined, however, finally to determine where the burden of proof lay, holding that it was irrelevant to the present case; in respect of an application to stay proceedings, the burden was on the accused to make good the charge of abuse. The Court found the key passage in *Ramanauskas* difficult to follow. Further exploration of the burden of proof in the Strasbourg jurisprudence, it said, would have to await a case where it was necessary for the decision.

46 *R v Syed* [2018] EWCA Crim 2809.

28 Vulnerable Witnesses

Mary Prior KC and Miriam Smith

OVERVIEW

28.1

In recent years there has been a drive by Parliament and the criminal courts to ensure that vulnerable witnesses are not subjected to unnecessary trauma while they are involved in the criminal justice system. It is arguable that there has been a greater emphasis on the rights of vulnerable witnesses than on vulnerable defendants giving evidence. The right to a fair trial is enshrined in the law of England and Wales though Article 6 (see Chapter 24), the common law and statute. Article 6 is engaged when steps are taken to assist witnesses in a way which may be argued to interfere with the rights of defendants and when defendants seek assistance in the forensic process to ensure fairness. In this chapter the relevant measures available to assist vulnerable witnesses are considered generally, with human rights commentary overlaid, so that the commentary may be seen in context without cross-referencing to other works being necessary.

28.2

Part II of the Youth Justice and Criminal Evidence Act 1999 (YJCEA 1999) introduced a range of measures intended to assist child and other vulnerable witnesses, including those with physical or mental disabilities, to give evidence in criminal proceedings in England and Wales (YJCEA 1999, s 68(6)). The availability of such 'special measures' for witnesses did not begin with this legislation, but it significantly expanded previous statutory provisions (which generally applied only to children) and the limited protections that were available for adult witnesses.

28.3

The approach to and treatment of vulnerable witnesses and defendants have changed considerably since the introduction of the YJCEA 1999. Over 20 years on, the habitual use of special measures in court remains a constantly evolving process. The prevailing view now is that the procedures of an adversarial trial must be adapted to the needs of child and other vulnerable witnesses and not the other way around: *R v Lubemba*.[1] However, the Court of Appeal has emphasised that the overall responsibility of the court for the fairness of the trial has not been altered by the wide and increased availability of special measures: *R v Cox*.[2]

1 *R v Lubemba* [2014] EWCA Crim 2064 at [45].
2 *R v Cox* [2012] EWCA Crim 549; [2012] 2 Cr App R 6 (63) at [29].

ELIGIBILITY FOR SPECIAL MEASURES

28.4

Sections 16 to 17 of the YJCEA 1999, as amended by the Coroners and Justice Act 2009 (CAJA 2009), provide the eligibility criteria for special measures for witnesses. These provisions apply equally to all witnesses, whether called by the defence or the prosecution (s 19(1)). However, they do not apply to the accused: Parliament's clear intention in sections 16(1) and 17(1) was to exclude the accused from those entitled to the special measures scheme set out in the Act.

28.5

The following persons are automatically eligible for special measures:

- witnesses under the age of 18 (s 16(1)(a));
- (adult) complainants of sexual offences, offences under sections 1 and 2 of the Modern Slavery Act 2015 or any offence where it is alleged that the accused's behaviour amounted to domestic abuse within the meaning of section 1 of the Domestic Abuse Act 2021, unless they inform the court they do not wish to be so eligible (s 17(4) and (s 4A));
- any witness in a case involving a "relevant offence", currently defined to include homicide offences and various offences against the person involving a firearm or knife and various other firearms and weapons-related offences, unless they inform the court they do not wish to be so eligible (s 17(5) and Sch 1A).

28.6

A witness is also eligible for special measures if, taking into account any views expressed by them, the court is satisfied that the quality of their evidence is likely to be diminished by reason of:

- suffering from a mental disorder, having a significant impairment of intelligence and social functioning, having a physical disability or suffering from a physical disorder (s 16(1)(b) and (2)); or
- fear or distress in connection with testifying in the proceedings (s 17(1)), taking into account the matters specified in s 17(2).

28.7

Once the court has determined that a witness is eligible for assistance, the court must determine whether any of the special measures available for that witness would, in its opinion, be likely to improve the quality of evidence given by the witness (YJCEA 1999, s 19(2)(a)). If so, the court must then determine which special measures would be likely to maximise the quality of the evidence given by the witness so far as practicable and give a direction accordingly for the measure(s) to apply to evidence given by the witness (s 19(2)(b)). In determining whether any special measure(s) would or would not be likely to improve or maximise the quality of the evidence given by the witness, the court must consider all the circumstances of the case including any views expressed by the witness and whether the measure(s) might tend to inhibit such evidence being effectively tested by a party to the proceedings (s 19(3)).

28.8

The procedure for making an application for a special measures direction is set out in section 19 of the YJCEA and in Part 18 of the Criminal Procedure Rules 2020, as amended. Even where eligibility is automatic, applications must still be made. The court may also raise, of its own motion, whether a special measures direction should be made.

RANGE OF SPECIAL MEASURES AVAILABLE

28.9

Sections 18 and 23 to 30 of the YJCEA 1999,[3] provide a range of special measures which a court can direct for eligible witnesses to ensure effective participation in a trial. These measures are available in all criminal courts.

28.10

Measures presently available include:

- screening the witness from the accused whilst they give evidence (s 23);
- giving evidence via live link from a room in the courthouse or another location, with or without a witness supporter present (s 24);
- excluding certain persons from the court room for the duration of the witness' evidence (only available where the proceedings relate to a sexual offence, an offence under sections 1 or 2 of the Modern Slavery Act 2015, an offence where it is alleged that the accused's behaviour amounted to domestic abuse within the meaning of section 1 of the Domestic Abuse Act 2021, or where it appears to the court that there are reasonable grounds for believing that any person other than the accused has sought, or will seek, to intimidate the witness in connection with testifying in the proceedings) (s 25);
- removal of wigs and gowns whilst the witness gives evidence (s 26);
- a video recorded interview with a police officer or social worker constituting evidence-in-chief, provided the witness is available for cross-examination unless the parties agree it is not necessary for the witness to be called (s 27);

3 As amended by the Coroners and Justice Act 2009 and the Domestic Abuse Act 2021.

- video recorded cross-examination and re-examination, where the evidence-in-chief has already been video recorded and will be admitted into evidence (s 28);
- examination of the witness, however and wherever conducted, through an intermediary (only available for witnesses under the age of 18 or suffering from a physical or mental condition) (s 29); and
- provision of aids to communication (only available for witnesses under the age of 18 or suffering from a physical or mental condition) (s 30).

28.11

Special measures may be complemented by other available protective procedures such as the prohibition on an accused charged with particular offences cross-examining particular witnesses including the complainant (see YJCEA, ss 34–38), witness anonymity orders (see CAJA 2009, Ch 2, Pt III), reporting restrictions in respect of adult witnesses (see YJCEA 1999, s 46) and lifetime anonymity of complainants in sex offence cases (Sexual Offences (Amendment) Act 1992, s 1).

GROUND RULES HEARINGS

28.12

In *Lubemba* (above), the Court of Appeal indicated that, save in exceptional circumstances, ground rules hearings should be held in every case involving a vulnerable witness to make directions for their fair treatment and participation. It is clear from the Crim PR (CrimPD I, 3E) that such hearings should also take place for cases involving vulnerable defendants. The ground rules hearing should cover, amongst other matters, the general care of the witness; if, when and where the witness is to be shown their video interview; when, where and how the parties (and the judge if identified) intend to introduce themselves to the witness; the length of questioning, frequency of breaks and the nature of the questions to be asked; how and when any limitations on questioning will be explained to the jury. The Advocate's Gateway provides a toolkit with a checklist for these hearings.

DIRECTIONS TO THE JURY ABOUT SPECIAL MEASURES

28.13

Where a witness in a trial on indictment gives evidence in accordance with a special measures direction, the judge must give a warning to the jury to ensure that it does not prejudice the accused (YJCEA 1999, s 32). This warning should be given immediately before the witness gives evidence, when it is more likely to impress itself on the jury and may be repeated in the summing-up;

R v Brown.[4] The Crown Court Compendium provides advice to judges in this regard as well as model directions. It states that the purpose of a direction is to explain what is to happen or has happened and to ensure that there is no prejudice to the defendant and so the direction should give an explanation about the purpose of presenting evidence with special measures. At the same time, the trial judge should, if applicable, also direct the jury in general terms that limitations have been placed on the defence advocate in cross-examination: *R v YGM.*[5] If any specific issues of content have been identified that the defence advocate cannot explore the judge may wish to direct the jury about them after cross-examination is completed, but in any event the judge should direct the jury about them in summing-up.

28.14

If a special measures warning is given when the witness gives evidence or on the first occasion that the special measure is used, it need not be repeated for subsequent witnesses giving evidence by the same means and/or in summing up when it may give the matter more emphasis in a way which is detrimental to the defendant.[6] Failure to give the warning required by statute in appropriate terms, either when the witness gives evidence or in summing up, does not necessarily render a conviction unsafe.[7] Similarly, failure to direct the jury about limitations placed on the defence advocate in cross-examination may not render a conviction unsafe.[8]

COMPLIANCE WITH ARTICLE 6 ECHR

28.15

Several special measures available within the YJCEA 1999 regime have been considered by domestic appellate courts in the context of the accused's right to a fair trial under Article 6.

28.16

A direction made under section 23 of the YJCEA that a witness be screened from the accused whilst they give evidence would not, in itself, breach Article 6. However, an issue may arise in relation to anonymous witnesses. In *X v United Kingdom,*[9] the Commission found that a complaint under Article 6(1) and (3)(d) concerning the use of screens to shield anonymous witnesses from the accused, the public and the media due to intimidation was manifestly ill-founded. However, this was in circumstances where the anonymous evidence was far from the only item of evidence on which the trial court based its decision to

4 *R v Brown* [2004] EWCA Crim 1620.
5 *R v YGM* [2018] EWCA Crim 2458 at [21].
6 *R v Brown* at [21].
7 *R v PR* [2010] EWCA Crim 2741 at [53]–[54].
8 *R v YGM* [2018] EWCA Crim 2458.
9 *X v United Kingdom* (1992) 15 EHRR CD113 (Application no 20657/92), 1 January 1993.

convict and this evidence did not implicate the applicant. In *R v Davis*,[10] the appellant was convicted of murdering two men by shooting them at the party. He was identified by three witnesses who gave evidence anonymously, from behind screens, because they had refused out of fear to testify if their identities were disclosed. In contrast to *X*, the House of Lords held this procedure was contrary to Article 6(3)(d) and in breach of common law fairness. The accused's defence, which went to the probability and credibility of the witnesses, was gravely hampered by the protective measures used.

28.17

A direction made under section 25 of the YJCEA that a witness' evidence be heard in private[11] would not breach an accused's right to a fair and public hearing since Article 6(1) provided that press and public may be excluded when such measure was "strictly necessary" so as not to prejudice the interests of justice; *R v Richards*.[12]

28.18

A direction made under section 27 of the YJCEA that a video recorded interview be admitted as a witness' examination-in-chief is compatible with Article 6 provided the defence has adequate and proper opportunity to challenge and question the witness at some stage: *R v Camberwell Green Youth Court, ex parte D and G*.[13] The statutory discretions to exclude all or part of a video interview in the interests of justice (s 27(2)) and to permit the witness to give evidence in the court room and expand on the video recorded interview if it is in the interests of justice (s 27(7)) also protect an accused's rights under Article 6.[14] Further, the general rule that child witnesses are automatically eligible for special measures does not contravene Article 6. Under s 27(4) of the YJCEA 1999 it is possible for a video interview to be admitted where the witness is not available for cross examination. Unless the hearsay provisions in sections 114 to 117 of the CJA apply, admission of a video interview, in these circumstances, could give rise to difficulties in relation to Article 6.

SPECIAL MEASURES AVAILABLE FOR THE ACCUSED

28.19

The accused is expressly excluded from access to the special measures regime set out in ss 23 to 30 YJCEA, resulting in disparity in treatment between witnesses and defendants. In *ex parte D and G*, their Lordships recognised the

---

10 *R v Davis* [2008] UKHL 36; [2008] 1 AC 1128.

11 The public gallery was cleared of members of the public but not the Press.

12 *R v Richards* (1999) 163 JP 246.

13 *R v Camberwell Green Youth Court, ex parte D and G* [2005] UKHL 4; [2005] 2 Cr App R 1 at [12]–[15], [49]–[53].

14 Ibid at [33], [51].

'very real problems' arising from the disparity between child witnesses and child defendants but nevertheless stated that the fact an accused may need assistance to give their best evidence did not justify excluding methods by which others may give their best evidence.

28.20

Despite this, the court has an inherent jurisdiction to modify orthodox procedures to ensure a fair trial and effective participation of an accused in the proceedings. This provides the route to special measures for child and vulnerable defendants who were initially (see below) or still are excluded from the statutory regime. In *R v SH*,[15] a case involving a defendant with limited IQ, poor comprehension, and an inability to read or write, the Court of Appeal considered that as a matter of principle a trial judge has a discretion to give special assistance to a defendant. Such measures would extend to permitting the accused to have the assistance of a person acting in the role equivalent to an interpreter whilst giving evidence to assist the accused to understand the nature of the question being asked; reading a detailed defence statement to the jury to assist the defendant to put a coherent account before them where it was apparent that he had difficulty recalling facts; and permitting leading questions to be asked based on that statement or other document setting out a coherent account he gave in the past where it was apparent that he had difficulty recalling facts.[16] In *R (C) v Sevenoaks Youth Court*,[17] the Divisional Court held the court's inherent powers to ensure a fair trial also included a power to appoint an intermediary to help the accused during the trial itself and in preparation for it. However, the court's inherent jurisdiction has generally been viewed as limited, and not extending for example to permitting a defendant to testify by live link or video recorded interview (cf *Ukpabio*[18]). Some years after the YJCEA, Parliament made provision – albeit on a very limited basis – for access to special measures for child and vulnerable defendants across criminal courts.

28.21

First, the Police and Justice Act 2006 inserted new sections 33A, 33B and 33C into the YJCEA to permit the court, on application by the defence, to direct, that the accused give evidence via a live link. These new provisions came into force in January 2007. The procedure for making such an application is set out in Part 18 of the Crim PR. In order for such a direction to be made, the court must be satisfied that it is in the interests of justice for the accused to give evidence via a live link, and:

(a) if the accused is under the age of 18, that their ability to participate effectively in the proceedings as a witness giving oral evidence is compromised by their level of intellectual ability or social functioning and the live link would enable the accused to participate more effectively as a

15 *R v SH* [2003] EWCA Crim 1208.
16 Ibid at [25], [28] and [29].
17 *R (C) v Sevenoaks Youth Court* [2009] EWHC 3088 (Admin); [2010] 1 All ER 735.
18 *Ukpabio* [2007] EWCA Crim 2108.

witness, whether by improving the quality of their evidence or otherwise (s 33A(4)); or

(b) if the accused is aged 18 or over, that they are unable to participate effectively in the proceedings as a witness giving oral evidence because they suffer from a mental disorder (within the meaning of the Mental Health Act 1983) or otherwise have a significant impairment of intelligence and social function and the live link would enable the accused to participate more effectively as a witness, whether by improving the quality of their evidence or otherwise (s 33A(5)).

28.22

Where a direction has been made for the accused to give evidence via a live link, they must give all their evidence by this means including any cross-examination (s 33A(6)). However, the court has a discretion to discharge the direction at any time before or during the hearing in which it applies if it appears to be in the interests of justice to do so (s 33A(7)). The Explanatory Notes accompanying the inserted section state this includes where an accused finds that giving evidence via a live link is very difficult and believes that giving evidence in open court would allow them to give a better quality of evidence. The court may exercise this discretion of its own motion or on application (s 33A(7)).

28.23

Section 33A plainly draws a distinction between child and adult defendants and imposes a lower threshold for use of a live link by a child defendant. The Explanatory Notes accompanying the inserted section states this 'lower threshold for child defendants recognises that it may be more common for juveniles to experience difficulties during the trial through limited intelligence and social development, than it went on for adults'. However, the Explanatory Notes go on to state that s 33A(4) 'is aimed at juvenile defendants with a low level of intelligence or a particular problem in dealing with social situations and is not intended to operate merely because an accused is a juvenile and is nervous, for example'.

28.24

Second, section 104 of the CAJA 2009 would insert new sections 33BA and 33BB into the YJCEA to put on a statutory footing the courts' power to direct that the accused give evidence through an intermediary. However, these provisions are not yet in force. They are unlikely to be implemented: the Law Commission has urged that sections 33BA and 33BB not be implemented as enacted because they do not adequately protect the child or disabled defendant's right to participate effectively in the trial.[19]

19 Unfitness to Plead, Law Com No 364 (January 2016), vol 1, para 2.65.

28.25

Accordingly, at present the court must rely on its inherent jurisdiction should it wish to make a direction for an intermediary to be appointed to assist the accused. Crim PR, Part 18 sets out the procedure to be followed. There is no presumption that an accused assessed as being in need of an intermediary will be so assisted nor is appointment mandatory where an intermediary would improve the trial process: *R v Cox* (above). The decision to appoint an intermediary is fact sensitive and calls for an assessment of the relevant circumstances of the accused and the circumstances of the particular trial. The court may exercise its inherent powers to appoint an intermediary to assist a defendant with a particular part or parts of the trial, such as the defendant's evidence, or for the entire trial. The Criminal Practice Direction observes that the appointment of an intermediary for the defendant's evidence will be rare and that it will be exceptionally rare for an order to be made for the appointment of an intermediary for the duration of a trial (see CrimPD I, 3F.12). However, it does not follow that there is a high hurdle to overcome if an intermediary is necessary for the accused to participate effectively in the trial process: *R v Thomas*.[20]

28.26

The absence of an appropriate intermediary for an accused assessed as being in need of one does not necessarily render a trial unfair and thus the proceedings an abuse of process. In such a situation, the trial judge must make an informed assessment of whether it is possible to have a fair trial in the absence of an intermediary by adapting procedures in the ordinary trial process as appropriate, for example shorter periods of evidence, taking frequent breaks to enable the accused to relax and for defence counsel to summarise the evidence and take instructions, ensuring questions to witnesses are phrased simply and answers are given in short sentences.[21]

COMPLIANCE WITH ARTICLE 6 ECHR

28.27

It is apparent from the wording of the statutory provisions considered above that there is asymmetry in the approach to, and treatment of, child and vulnerable witnesses and defendants in England and Wales in relation to special measures. Most obviously, there are fewer special measures available to defendants than for witnesses. Child defendants are not automatically eligible for special measures by virtue of their age, whereas child witnesses are. Defendants with a mental disorder or learning difficulty have to overcome additional eligibility criteria to access special measures to witnesses in a similar position. Physically disabled witnesses are entitled to special measures in particular circumstances, but there is no equivalent for defendants with physical disabilities. Further, child defendants

20 [2020] EWCA Crim 117; [2020] 4 WLR 66.
21 *R v Cox* at [21], [29]–[30].

are precluded from accessing special measures in cases of fear or where there is a risk of intimidation for instance by co-defendants.

28.28

The differing statutory criteria for special measures as between child and adult defendants, and child and adult witnesses, has prompted much criticism. Commentators have argued that this inequality may contravene Article 6(3)(d).[22] In *R (OP) v Secretary of State for Justice*,[23] Rafferty LJ recognised "the risk of unfairness or at its lowest a perceived risk of unfairness" due to the inequality of arms. In relation to intermediaries, the Law Commission has stated that a statutory entitlement for a defendant to be appointed an intermediary in appropriate circumstances is 'essential' to rectify the 'inequity' of the comparative positions of defendants and witnesses, to ensure compliance with section 20 of the Equality Act 2010 and Articles 12(3) and 13 of the UN Convention on the Rights of Persons with Disabilities and to provide a proper framework for what has become a practical reality by the exercise of inherent jurisdiction.[24]

28.29

Despite increased appreciation over recent years of the needs of young and vulnerable persons involved in criminal trials and the requirement for significant adaptations and minimum standards of practice to ensure effective participation (see below), it remains to be seen whether Parliament will create parity between affected witnesses and defendants in relation to special measures.

OTHER ADAPTATIONS IN PROCEEDINGS FOR DEFENDANTS

28.30

The current Criminal Practice Direction (CrimPD I, 3G) provides a number of 'modifications' for use prior to and during any trial, sentencing or appeal hearing. Whilst these adaptations complement the special measures available to child and vulnerable defendants, they also go far beyond them in that they are not focussed solely on the trial and giving evidence but comprehension of and engagement in the proceedings more generally. This stems from the requirement in the Criminal Practice Direction that the court 'take "every reasonable step' to encourage and facilitate … the participation of any person, including the defendant (CrimPR 3.8(3)(a) and (b))' which includes enabling 'a defendant to give their best evidence … comprehend the proceedings and engage fully with [their] defence' (CrimPD I, 3D.2). The Practice Direction further states that the pre-trial and trial process should, so far as necessary, be adapted to meet those ends and notes that regard should be had to the welfare of a young defendant

22 See, eg, Laura C H Hoyano, 'Coroners and Justice Act 2009 – Special Measures Directions Take Two: Entrenching Unequal Access to Justice?' [2010] Crim LR 345.

23 *R (OP) v Secretary of State for Justice* [2014] EWHC 1944 (Admin); [2014] 1 Cr App R 7 (70) at [46].

24 Unfitness to Plead, Law Com No 364 (January 2016), vol 1, at paras 2.31 to 2.37.

as required by section 44 of the Children and Young Persons Act 1933, and generally to Crim PR, Parts 1 and 3 (the overriding objective and the courts' powers of case management).

28.31

The Criminal Practice Direction sets out the following modifications, which appear from its language to be mandatory:

- If a vulnerable defendant, especially one who is young, is to be tried with one who is not, the court should consider at the Plea and Trial Preparation Hearing (in the Crown Court) or case management hearing (in a magistrates' court) whether the vulnerable defendant should be tried on his own if the court is satisfied that a fair trial cannot be achieved by use of appropriate special measures or other support for a vulnerable defendant (CrimPD I, 3G.1).
- If the defendant's use of the live link is being considered, they should have an opportunity to have a practice session (3G.4).
- If the case has attracted or may attract widespread public or media interest, the assistance of the police should be enlisted to try to ensure that the defendant is not exposed to intimidation, vilification or abuse when attending court (3G.5).
- Subject to appropriate security arrangements, the proceedings should, if practicable, be held in a courtroom where all participants are on the same or almost the same level (3G.7).
- Subject to appropriate security arrangements, a vulnerable defendant, especially if young, should if they wish be permitted to sit with members of their family (or others in a like relationship) and with some other suitable supporting adult such as a social worker, and in a place which permits easy and informal communication with their legal representatives (3G.8).
- The court should ensure that a suitable supporting adult is available throughout the course of the proceedings for a vulnerable defendant (3G.8).
- At the beginning of proceedings, the court should explain what is to take place to a vulnerable defendant in terms they can understand and, in the Crown Court, it should ensure the role of the jury has been explained. The court should remind those representing the accused, the supporting adult and any intermediary of their respective responsibilities to explain each step as it happens and to ensure that the vulnerable defendant has understood. Throughout the trial the court should continue to ensure, by any appropriate means, that the defendant understands what is happening and what has been said by those on the bench, the advocates and witnesses (3G.9).
- The trial should be conducted according to a timetable which takes full account of a vulnerable defendant's ability to concentrate and with frequent and regular breaks, if necessary (3G.10).

- The court should ensure, so far as practicable, that the whole trial is conducted in clear language that the accused can understand and that evidence-in-chief and cross-examination are conducted using questions that are short and clear. The conclusions of the 'ground rules' hearing should be followed, and advocates should use and follow the advocates' 'toolkits' (3G.10).
- In the Crown Court, the court should consider whether robes and wigs should be worn taking into account the wishes of a vulnerable defendant (and any vulnerable witness) (3G.12).

28.32

In addition, the court may:

- Arrange a visit, out of court hours and before the trial, sentencing or appeal hearing, to the courtroom in which that hearing is to take place so that the vulnerable defendant can familiarise themselves with it (3G.2).
- Restrict attendance by members of the public in the courtroom to a small number, perhaps limited to those with an immediate and direct interest in the outcome (3G.13).
- Restrict the number of reporters attending in the courtroom to such number as is judged practicable and desirable (3G.13).

29 Article 7: No punishment without law

Tony Vaughan and Sophie Nandy

OVERVIEW

29.1

Under Article 7 of the European Convention on Human Rights (ECHR), only the law can define a crime and prescribe a penalty; and criminal penalties must not be heavier than those that applied at the time the crime was committed. Article 7 ECHR provides:

> No punishment without law
>
> 1. No one shall be held guilty of any criminal offence on account of any act or omission which did not constitute a criminal offence under national or international law at the time when it was committed. Nor shall a heavier penalty be imposed than the one that was applicable at the time the criminal offence was committed.
> 2. This article shall not prejudice the trial and punishment of any person for any act or omission which, at the time when it was committed, was criminal according to the general principles of law recognised by civilised nations.

29.2

Pursuant to Article 15(2) ECHR, no derogation is permitted from Article 7 in times of war or other public emergency.

29.3

This chapter considers the applicability of Article 7. It then examines the twin 'guiding principles' non-retrospectivity and legality (comprising legal certainty, accessibility and foreseeability).[1]

1 *R v Rimmington; R v Goldstein* [2005] UKHL 63, [2006] 1 AC 459 [33]–[37].

APPLICABILITY OF ARTICLE 7

Personal criminal liability established

29.4

Article 7 is engaged only where a person has been found guilty of, or found personally liable for, a criminal offence. As such, in *Lukanov v Bulgaria*,[2] the European Commission on Human Rights decided that Article 7 did not apply as the 'proceedings instituted against the applicant ha[d] not yet been terminated' therefore the Applicant had not been found guilty of a criminal offence. Furthermore, in *X v the Netherlands*,[3] the Commission found that the applicant had wrongly invoked Article 7 when challenging his extradition to stand trial for alleged offences in the Netherlands. The Commission reasoned that the concept of 'guilt' in Article 7, although autonomous, 'cannot cover the decision on extradition which may lead to a conviction'.[4]

29.5

In *GIEM SRL and Others v Italy*,[5] the Grand Chamber made an important distinction between the necessity of prior establishment of 'personal criminal liability'[6] and a formal criminal court conviction.[7] Whilst the former is necessary to engage Article 7, the latter is not mandatory:[8] 'complian[ce] with Article 7… does not require that all disputes … must necessarily be dealt with in the context of criminal proceedings *stricto sensu*'.[9] The court must ensure that the finding of criminal liability is compliant with the safeguards contained in Article 7 and that its originating proceedings are compliant with Article 6.[10]

'Criminal offence'

29.6

Article 7 only applies to conduct which amounts to a 'criminal offence' as defined in the Strasbourg case law. In *Engel and Others v the Netherlands* (1976) 1 EHRR 647 the Court ruled that the charge or offence must be 'criminal' within the meaning of Article 6 based on the following three considerations (the *Engel* criteria):[11]

2 *Lukanov v Bulgaria* (Application no 21915/93) 12 January 1995 at [6].
3 *X v the Netherlands* (Application no 7512/76), 6 July 1976.
4 Ibid, p 185. See also *Varvara v Italy* (Application no 17475/09), 24 March 2014 at [71].
5 GIEM SRL and Others v Italy (Application no 1828/06), 28 June 2018.
6 Ibid at [251].
7 Ibid at [252].
8 Ibid.
9 Ibid at [253].
10 Ibid at [252].
11 Ibid at [82].

(a) whether the provision(s) defining the offence charged, belong, according to the legal system of the respondent State, to criminal law, disciplinary law or both concurrently …

(b) the very nature of the offence [which] is a factor of greater import;[12]

(c) the degree of severity of the penalty that the person concerned risks incurring.

Concept of a 'penalty'

29.7

The concept of 'penalty' found in Article 7 possesses an autonomous meaning.[13] In determining whether the penalty imposed falls within Article 7, the Court will look 'behind appearances' to the substance of the measure.[14] Whether the penalty has been imposed following a conviction for a criminal offence is merely one criterion to be considered among others; and the absence thereof does not prevent the applicability of Article 7.[15] Other factors include:[16]

(a) the nature and purpose of the relevant measure;

(b) the characterisation of the measure under national law;

(c) procedures for making and implementing the measure; and

(d) the severity of the measure.

29.8

Because Article 7 only applies to provisions 'defining offences and the penalties for them', it does not apply to procedural law. However, the Court looks to substance over form. In *Scoppola v Italy*,[17] the Grand Chamber found that 'the classification in domestic law of the legislation concerned cannot be decisive'. Given that the domestic procedural rule involved in *Scoppola* was related entirely to the length of sentence, it thus fell within the scope of Article 7 as a 'provision of substantive criminal law'.[18]

---

12 The greater importance of the second criterion was reaffirmed in *Jussila v Finland* (2007) 45 EHRR 39 at [38].

13 *GIEM SRL and Others v Italy (*Application no 1828/06) and two others, 28 June 2018 at [210].

14 Ibid. See also *Welch v United Kingdom* (1995) 20 EHRR 247 at [27]–[28]; *Jamil v France* (Application no 15917/89), 8 June 1995 at [30].

15 *GIEM SRL v Italy,* [215]–[217].

16 Ibid at [211]; *Welch v the United Kingdom* at [28], *Jamil v France at* [31]; *Kafkaris v Cyprus* (2009) 49 EHRR 35 at [142], *Del Rio Prada v Spain* at [82].

17 *Scoppola v Italy (No 2)* (2010) 51 EHRR 12.

18 Ibid at [111]–[113]. Limitation periods were characterised as procedural in *Coeme and Others v Belgium* (Application nos 32492/96, 32547/96, 32548/96), 22 June 2000 at [149].

29.9

Further, Article 7 does not apply to measures relating to the execution or implementation of a penalty, which is not a 'penalty' for the purposes of that article. The House of Lords emphasised this distinction in *R (Uttley) v Home Secretary.*[19] Before 1983, U had committed multiple sexual offences, three of which were rapes for which the maximum sentence was life imprisonment. U was prosecuted for these offences in 1995. The basis for his appeal was that, under the previous regime, he would have been released on remission after serving two-thirds of his sentence, subject to good behaviour. Following the change in the law, he would be released on licence at the two-thirds point of his sentence, with the terms of his licence applying until the three-quarter point of his sentence. U contended that the new regime resulted in the 12-year sentence imposing a heavier penalty than would have applied under the old regime and that Article 7(1) had been breached. The House of Lords rejected that argument. Lord Phillips ruled that the applicable 'penalty' was the maximum sentence which *could* have been imposed 'under the law in force at the time that his offence was committed',[20] which was life imprisonment. Therefore, the 12-year sentence imposed was a 'manifestly … less heavy penalty than life imprisonment' and U's argument was therefore 'manifestly unsound'.[21] His application to Strasbourg was declared inadmissible.[22]

29.10

A number of other cases have addressed the distinction between a penalty and an executing or implementing measure in the following contexts:

- *Sentence remission*: *Kafkaris v Cyprus*[23] – 'although the changes in prison legislation and in the conditions of release may have rendered the applicant's imprisonment effectively harsher, these changes cannot be construed as imposing a heavier 'penalty' … issues relating to release policies, the manner of their implementation and the reasoning behind them fall within the power of the member States … determining their own criminal policy'. [24]
- *Legislative amendment on the conditions for release on parole*: in *Hogben v the United Kingdom*[25], whilst the sudden change in UK parole policy which delayed eligibility for parole resulted in an 'effectively harsher' imprisonment than if the applicant were eligible at an earlier stage, the matter related to the execution of the penalty, not the penalty.
- *Redefinition or modification of the 'penalty'*:

19 *R (Uttley) v Home Secretary* [2004] UKHL 38, [2004] 1 WLR 2278.
20 Ibid at [21].
21 Ibid at [23].
22 *Uttley v United Kingdom* (Application no 36946/03), 29 November 2005. *Uttley* was approved in *Abedin v United Kingdom* (an admissibility decision) (2021) 72 EHRR SE6 at [36].
23 *Kafkaris v Cyprus* (2009) 49 EHRR 35 at [152].
24 See also *Grava v Italy* (Application no 43522/98), 10 July 2003 at [49].
25 *Hogben v the United Kingdom* (Application no 11653/85), 3 March 1986.

- Significantly, in *Kafkaris*,[26] the court found that the interpretation and application of regulations relating to execution of a penalty may at the relevant time go beyond mere execution. In that case, concerning the execution of a penalty of life sentence, the court found that the distinction was not 'immediately apparent'.
- The Court in *Del Rio Prada v Spain*[27] explored this dilemma further when finding that: 'the court does not rule out the possibility that measures taken by the legislature, the administrative authorities or the courts after the final sentence has been imposed or while the sentence is being served may result in the *redefinition* or *modification* of the scope of the 'penalty' imposed by the trial court. When that happens, the Court considers that the measures concerned should fall within the scope of the prohibition of the retroactive application of penalties enshrined in art. 7(1)' (emphasis added). The test to be applied by the court when considering whether the measure taken during the execution of the penalty concerns solely the execution or impacts the scope, is:

  > what the 'penalty' imposed actually entailed under the domestic law in force at the material time … what its intrinsic nature was … it must have regard to the domestic law as a whole and the way it was applied at the material time.[28]

  The court decided that a case-law doctrine, resulting in any remissions for work done in detention ceasing to apply to the applicant's 30-year sentence, rendered it a measure which fell within scope of Article 7(1).[29]

29.11

Measures which have been found to constitute penalties within Article 7 have included:

- A confiscation order relating to proceeds of a criminal offence: *Welch v the United Kingdom*.[30]
- Imprisonment in default of fine (where insolvency of debtor had not been demonstrated): *Jamil v France*.[31]
- A preventive detention order issued by the trial court after conviction for serious offences for preventive and punitive purposes, of unlimited duration: *M v Germany*.[32]

---

26 Kafkaris (above) at [149].
27 *Del Rio Prada v Spain* (2014) 58 EHRR 37 at [89].
28 Ibid at [90].
29 Ibid at [109]–[110].
30 *Welch v the United Kingdom* (1995) 20 EHRR 247 at [29]–[35].
31 *Jamil v France* (Application no 15917/89), 8 June 1995 at [32].
32 *M v Germany* (2010) 51 EHRR 41 at [123]–[133].

- Expulsion and 10-year prohibition of residence in place of a prison sentence: *Gurguchiani v Spain*.[33]

29.12

Measures which have been found not to constitute penalties have included:

- Preventative measures (eg mandatory hospitalisation of a person who lacks criminal responsibility) *Berland v France*.[34]
- Trial court ordered preventive detention after conviction for serious criminal offences for purpose of treating prisoner's mental disorder: *Ilnseher v Germany*.[35]
- Inclusion of person on police or judicial register of sexual or violent offenders: *Adamson v the United Kingdom*.[36]
- Detention with view to preventing person engaging in unlawful activities: *Lawless v Ireland (No 3)*.[37]

Only the law can define a crime and prescribe a penalty: legal certainty, accessibility and foreseeability

29.13

Turning to the substantive protections contained in Article 7, the principle that only the law can define a crime and prescribe a penalty entails two main strands. First, it is well-established in Strasbourg case law that Article 7 encompasses the principle of *nullum crimen, nulla poena sine lege* (no punishment without law). This principle requires that, at the time that the accused performed the acts resulting in their prosecution and conviction, there was a legal provision making the act punishable, and that the penalty does not exceed the limits set by the provision.[38] This strand has also been described as reflecting the principle of legal certainty.[39]

29.14

Secondly, Article 7 consists of the 'quality of law' requirements of accessibility and foreseeability.[40] The requirement of accessibility is that the elements of the offence must be defined with precision.[41] As to foreseeability, 'this requirement

33 *Gurguchiani v Spain* (Application no 16012/06), 15 December 2009 at [40].

34 *Berland v France* [2018] 12 WLUK 770 at [39]–[47].

35 *Ilnseher v Germany* [2018] 12 WLUK 770 at [210]–[236].

36 *Adamson v the United Kingdom* (1999) 28 EHRR CD 209, CD211.

37 *Lawless v Ireland (No 3)* (1961) 1 EHRR 15 at [19].

38 *Coeme and others v Belgium* (Application nos 32492/96, 32547/96, 32548/96), 22 June 2000 at [145]; *Brumarescu v Romania* (2001) 33 EHRR 35 §61; *Del Rio Prada v Spain* at [80]; See also *Achour v France* (2007) 45 EHRR 2 at [43]; *R v Rimmington; R v Goldstein* [2005] UKHL 63; [2006] 2 All ER 257.

39 *Rimmington*, ibid.

40 *Del Rio Prada v Spain* (2014) 58 EHRR 37 at [145].

41 See also *G v France* (1996) 21 EHRR 288 at [25]; *Custers, Deveaux and Turk v Denmark* (Application nos 11843/03) and two others, 9 May 2006 at [82]; *Korbely v Hungary* (2010) 50 EHRR 48 at [74]–[75]; *Vasiliauskas v Lithuania* (2016) 62 EHRR 31, [167]–[168], *Kononov v Latvia* (2011) 52 EHRR 21 at [234]–[239], [244], *Kokkinakis v Greece* (1993) 17 EHRR 397 at [40].

is satisfied where the individual can know from the wording of the relevant provision (art. 7) and, if need be, with the assistance of the courts' interpretation of it, what acts and omissions will make him criminally liable' (*Cantoni v France*).[42] The requirement has been said to be satisfied where the individual is able, if necessary with 'appropriate advice… to foresee, to a degree that is reasonable in the circumstances, the consequences which a given action may entail' (*Chauvy and others v France*).[43] However, in *Kokkinakis v Greece*,[44] it was acknowledged that 'many laws are inevitably couched in terms which, to a greater or lesser extent, are vague' due to 'the need to avoid excessive rigidity and to keep pace with changing circumstances.[45] Where there is a 'penumbra of doubt' in a case where the facts are borderline, this does not necessarily mean that the provision infringes Article 7, as long as the provision 'proves to be sufficiently clear in the large majority of cases'.[46]

29.15

The Grand Chamber has ruled that use of the terms 'blanket reference' or 'legislation by reference' to statutory provisions as a technique to criminalise certain behaviours does not necessarily infringe Article 7.[47] However it must be ensured that read together, both the referencing provision and the referenced provision allow the individual to foresee (with appropriate legal advice if necessary) the conduct which entails criminal liability.[48] The court has also underlined 'that however clearly drafted a legal provision may be … there is an inevitable element of judicial interpretation. There will always be a need for elucidation of doubtful points and for adaptation to changing circumstances'.[49] Where a provision is constructed in vague terms, it is permissible in terms of Article 7 for the interpretation and application of the provision to a be 'question[s] of practice'.[50] This is subject to the proviso that the interpretation is 'consistent with the essence of the offence',[51] considering whether the interpretation is covered by the text of the provision in the context of the statutory instrument, as well as the reasonableness of the interpretation.[52]

42 *Cantoni v France* (1996) ECHR 52, at [29]. See also *Kafkaris v Cyprus* (2009) 49 EHRR 35 at [140], *Del Rio Prada v Spain* (2014) 58 EHRR 37 at [79], *GIEM SRL and others v Italy* (Application no 1828/06), 28 June 2018 at [242], [246].

43 'Appropriate advice' means legal advice: *Chauvy and others v France* (2005) 41 EHRR 29, [43]–[45]. See also *Jorgic v France* [2007] ECHR 583 at [113].

44 *Kokkinakis v Greece* at [40].

45 See also *Cantoni v France* [1996] ECHR 52 at [31].

46 Ibid at [32]. See also *Liivik v Estonia* [2009] ECHR 989, [96]–[104], *Georgouleas and Nestoras v Greece* (Application nos 44612/13 and 45831/13), 28 May 2020 at [66].

47 *Advisory Opinion concerning the use of the 'blanket reference' etc* (Request no P16-2019-001) 29 May 2000 at [74].

48 Ibid.

49 *Kafkaris v Cyprus* (2009) 49 EHRR 35 at [142]. See also *SW v the United Kingdom* (1995) 21 EHRR 363 at [36], *Streletz Kessler and Krenz v Germany* (2001) 33 EHRR 31, at [50], *Kononov v Latvia* (Application no 36376/04), 17 May 2010 at [185]. See also *R v Rimmington* at [35].

50 *R v Rimmington* Ibid.

51 *Jorgic v Germany* (Application no 74613/01), 12 July 2007 at [104].

52 Ibid at [105]. See also *SW v the United Kingdom* (1995) 21 EHRR 363 at [43].

29.16

It nevertheless remains the case that, if a law is not sufficiently accessible, foreseeable and precise, it may not constitute 'law' for the purposes of Article 7 (*Del Rio Prada v Spain*[53]). The following sources of law establishing criminal offences have been held to be sufficiently accessible, foreseeable and precise to be treated as 'law' for the purposes of Article 7:

(a) Judicial law-making: 'Article 7 … cannot be read as outlawing the gradual clarification of the rules of criminal liability through judicial interpretation from case to case, provided that the resultant development is consistent with the essence of the offence and could reasonably be foreseen'.[54]

(b) Prison rules;[55]

(c) Non-codified constitutional customs;[56]

(d) 'Domestic law as a whole and the way it was applied at the material time'.[57]

29.17

State practice which is incompatible with the domestic constitution as well as statute law, and which infringes international human rights obligations, or practices which empty legislation of its substance will not be classified as 'law' for the purposes of Article 7.[58]

29.18

In England and Wales, offences which have been held to meet the standard for accessibility and foreseeability, and therefore legal certainty, include obscenity: *R v Perrin*;[59] perverting the court of justice: *R v Cotter*;[60] materially contributing to the extent of insolvency by gambling: *R v Muhamad*;[61] gross negligence manslaughter: *R v Misra*;[62] public nuisance: *R v Goldstein*;[63] possessing a document or record containing information likely to be useful to be useful to a person committing or preparing an act of terrorism: *R v K*;[64] collecting or making a record of information of a kind likely to be useful to a person committing or preparing an act of terrorism and selling and distributing terrorist publications: *R v Brown*;[65] encouraging or assisting offences believing

53 *Del Rio Prada v Spain* (2014) 58 EHRR 37 at [91].

54 Ibid at [36], [41]–[43].

55 *Kafkaris v Cyprus* (2009) 49 EHRR 35 at [145]–[146]. In that case the Prison Regulations related to 'the execution of the life sentence imposed by the court … the assessment of a possible remission of … sentence on the ground of good conduct and diligence' (at [145]).

56 *Advisory Opinion concerning the use of the 'blanket reference' etc* (Request no P16-2019-001) 29 May 2000 at [69].

57 *Kafkaris v Cyprus* at [146]. See also *Del Rio Prada v Spain* (2014) 58 EHRR 37, [90].

58 *Streletz, Kessler and Krenz v Germany* (2001) 33 EHRR 31, [87]–[88], [100], [103].

59 *R v Perrin* [2002] EWCA Crim 747.

60 *R v Cotter* [2002] EWCA Crim 1033 [25]–[36]; [2002] 2 Cr App R 29.

61 *R v Muhamad* [2002] EWCA Crim 1856 at [29]; [2003] QB 1031.

62 *R v Misra* [2004] EWCA Crim 2375 [62]–[64]; [2005] 1 Cr App Rep 328.

63 *R v Goldstein* [2005] UKHL 63 [32]–[37], [2006] 1 AC 459.

64 *R v K* [2008] EWCA Crim 185; [2008] 3 All ER 526.

65 *R v Brown* [2011] EWCA Crim 2751 at [31]–[32]; [2012] 2 Cr App Rep (S) 39.

that one or more would be committed: *R v S*;[66] murder through participation in the show trial of the political opponents of a totalitarian regime, resulting in the conviction and execution of those opponents: *Polednova v Czech Republic*;[67] conduct prejudicial to military discipline: *R v Armstrong*;[68] and the export of waste contrary to regulations: *R v Ideal Waste Paper Co Ltd*.[69]

Principle of non-retroactivity of criminal law

29.19

It is well-established that Article 7 'unconditionally prohibits the retrospective application of the criminal law where it is to an accused's disadvantage'.[70] In *R v Rimmington*, the House of Lords said: 'The essential thrust of [article 7] is to prohibit the creation of offences, whether by legislation or the incremental development of the common law, which have retrospective application.'[71]

29.20

In a case involving a continuing *actus reus* spanning conduct both before and after the enactment of retrospective criminal law, the Strasbourg Court held in *Rohlena v the Czech Republic*,[72] that perpetrating domestic abuse over a period of six years could constitute a single criminal act: 'whose classification in Czech criminal law had to be assessed under the rules in force at the time of completion of the last occurrence of the offence, provided that the acts committed under any previous law would have been punishable also under older law'.[73]

29.21

As regards sentencing, a criminal penalty cannot be imposed if it is more severe than that which would have been applied at the time the offence was committed. This is also known as the *lex gravior* principle. In *Del Rio Prada* (above) it was held that legislative, administrative or judicial action resulting in redefinition or modification of the original penalty, where that action is taken following imposition of the final sentence or during the time the offender is serving their sentence, should engage the non-retroactivity principle.[74] As noted above, the non-retroactivity principle was encapsulated by the House of Lords in *Uttley* as precluding the imposition of a sentence which exceeds the maximum that applied at the time the offence was committed.[75] Lords Rodger and Carswell took the view that, 'the object of [article 7] appears to have been to prevent a

66 *R v S* [2011] EWCA Crim 2872; [2012] 1 WLR 1700.

67 *Polednova v Czech Republic* (Application no 2615/10), 21 June 2011.

68 *R v Armstrong* [2012] EWCA Crim 83.

69 *R v Ideal Waste Paper Co Ltd* [2011] EWCA Crim 3237 [42]–[44], [46], [2012] Env LR 19.

70 *Del Rio Prada v Spain* (2014) 58 EHRR 37 at [116]. See also *Kokkinakis v Greece* (1993) 17 EHRR 397 at [52].

71 *R v Misra* [2005] 1 Cr App R 328; [2004] EWCA Crim 2375 at [29], approved in *R v Rimmington; R v Goldstein* [2005] UKHL 63; [2005] 3 WLR 982 at [33].

72 *Rohlena v the Czech Republic* (59552/08) (ECtHR 27 January 2015).

73 Ibid at [61] and see [62].

74 *Del Rio Prada v Spain* at [89].

75 *Uttley* at [21] *per* Lord Phillips.

sentence being imposed which could not have been imposed at the time of the offence, because the maximum was then lower'.[76]

29.22

The corollary of the non-retroactivity and *lex gravior* principle is that if provision is made by law for a lighter penalty, subsequent to the commission of the offence, the offender shall benefit from the lighter penalty (*R v Docherty*[77]). The Strasbourg Court has held that, 'application of a criminal law providing for a more lenient penalty, even one enacted after the commission of the offence, has become a fundamental principle of law' (*Scoppola v Italy (No 2)*[78]). This is also the 'longstanding common law practice'.[79] It was significant, in *Scoppola*, that the legislation of the respondent State had recognised that principle since 1930. The Commission has noted that, whilst the observations made by the court in *Scoppola* were phrased generally,[80] the principle had been subsequently developed and applied.[81] The UK Supreme Court has resisted the invitation to approve the further principle articulated in *Scoppola* that, 'where there are differences between the criminal law in force at the time of the commission of the offence *and subsequent criminal laws enacted before a final judgment is rendered*, the courts must apply the law whose provisions are most favourable to the defendant'.[82]

29.23

In *R v H and others*,[83] the Court of Appeal gave detailed guidance as to the impact of the non-retroactivity principle in the context of sentencing those convicted of historic sexual offences. The court dealt with the issue of criminal conduct that 'span[s] different legislative provisions governing the substantive law of sexual crime, and variations in the maximum penalties' involving at least eight different sets of legislation.[84] During the relevant period, there were a variety of sentencing regimes and legislative provisions dealing with the release of prisoners serving custodial penalties. The Court's primary conclusions of principle were as follows (the context-specific sentencing guidance are omitted):

(a) Sentence will be imposed at the date of the sentencing hearing, on the basis of the legislative provisions then current, and by measured reference to any definitive sentencing guidelines relevant to the situation revealed by the established facts.

(b) Although sentence must be limited to the maximum sentence at the date when the offence was committed, it is wholly unrealistic

76 This summary of their joint view was articulated by Lord Judge CJ in *R v H & others* [2011] EWCA Crim 2753, [2012] 1 WLR 1416 at [18].

77 *R v Docherty* [2016] UKSC 62, [2017] 1 WLR 181.

78 *Scoppola v Italy (No 2)* (2010) 51 EHRR 12 at [107].

79 *Docherty* at [42].

80 *Advisory Opinion concerning the use of the 'blanket reference'* at [82].

81 Ibid. Discussed in *Gouarre Patte v Andorra* (33427/10) (ECtHR, 12 January 2016), [28]–[36]; *Koprivnikar v Slovenia* (Application no 67503/13), 24 January 2017 at [59].

82 *Docherty* at [39]–[40].

83 *R v H and others* [2011] EWCA Crim 2753; [2012] 1 WLR 1416.

84 Ibid at [10].

to attempt an assessment of sentence by seeking to identify in 2011 what the sentence for the individual offence was likely to have been if the offence had come to light at or shortly after the date when it was committed. Similarly, if maximum sentences have been reduced, as in some instances, for example theft, they have, the more severe attitude to the offence in earlier years, even if it could be established, should not apply.

(c) [T]he particular circumstances in which the offence was committed and its seriousness must be the main focus. Due allowance for the passage of time may be appropriate. The date may have a considerable bearing on the offender's culpability … .

29.24

The Court of Appeal explored the scope of the principle (*a*) in *R v Shah (Amar Abbas)*[85] in which the appellant argued that the requirement to treat the sentencing guidance in force on the date of sentencing as a 'starting point' implied a degree of flexibility.[86] The starting point for sentencing murder had been increased from 15 years to 25 years following the introduction of paragraph 5A of Schedule 21 to the CJA 2003, which applied to offences committed on or after 2 March 2010.[87] He argued that as a consequence of sentencing 'old manslaughter' committed before 2 March 2010 on the basis of the old 'starting point', he 'would or might be dealt with comparatively more harshly than a person sentenced for murder'.[88] The appellant's attempt to expand the nature of the 'starting point' was ultimately rejected by the Court of Appeal. It was held that, whilst the sentencing guidelines in force on the sentencing date should apply, sentencing remained subject to the maximum sentence applicable on the date the offence was committed.[89]

29.25

In *R v L*,[90] the Court of Appeal addressed the correct approach to sentencing an adult in relation to sexual offences committed as a teenager. The offender challenged the 30-month term of imprisonment imposed on the grounds that the sentencing powers of the trial judge were limited by the maximum sentence of six months for consecutive terms available at the time for an offender who was 14-years-old at the date of the offence.[91] The Court summarised the following principles to be applied in these circumstances:

(a) The general principle: 'the relevant maximum penalty is the maximum penalty available for the *offence* at the date of the commission of the offence'.[92]

85 *R v Shah (Amar Abbas)* [2018] EWCA Crim 249, [2018] 2 Cr App R (S) 8.
86 Ibid at [21].
87 Ibid at [18].
88 Ibid at [23].
89 Ibid at [28].
90 *R v L [*2017] EWCA Crim 43; [2017] 1 Cr App R (S) 51.
91 Ibid at [8].
92 Ibid at [14]

(b) Exception applies where, at the time of commission of the offence, no form of custodial sentence could have been imposed on the offender.

(c) The exception is not to facilitate a 'broader inquiry'. If custody is available at the time of commission of the offence for the offender, the offender's age at that time is solely relevant to the assessment of the offender's culpability. The statutory maximum for the offence is the sole constraint on the sentencing court.[93]

The fact that the sentencing court had at least one custodial penalty available to it was sufficient 'to satisfy the requirements of and the principles of common law fairness' regardless of the nature or maximum length.[94]

29.26

In *R (Khan) v Secretary of State for Justice*,[95] the claimant challenged the lawfulness of legislation amending the release on licence provisions for terrorist offenders[96] on the grounds of incompatibility with Articles 5, 7 and 14 of the ECHR. Under the old regime applicable at the sentencing date, the claimant would automatically have been released halfway through his sentence;[97] whereas, pursuant to the amendments, the issue of release was referred to the Parole Board at the two-thirds point of the sentence. Khan challenged the amendments, *inter alia,* on the grounds of lack of certainty and foreseeability. Reliance was placed on *Rio Del Prado* (above). The High Court dismissed the claim, reasoning that *Del Rio Prada* was 'specifically geared to the facts of the case',[98] and that the nine-year increase in sentence for Ms Del Rio Prada[99] stemming from the change in caselaw doctrine had obliterated any distinction between 'penalty' and 'execution', therefore constituting a redefinition of the penalty imposed.[100] In light of this, the High Court in *Khan* decided that the claimant's position was more akin to that of the applicants in the *Hogben v United Kingdom*, and the *Uttley* domestic and Strasbourg decisions (among others). The High Court relied fundamentally on the principle that 'a change to the administration of a penalty, by an alteration to the early release provisions … will not engage article 7'.[101]

93 Ibid in full.
94 Ibid at [15].
95 *R (Khan) v Secretary of State for Justice* [2020] EWHC 2084 (Admin), [2020] 1 WLR 3932.
96 Terrorist Offenders (Restriction of Early Release) Act 2020, s 1(2), amending CJA 2003, s 247A.
97 Ibid at [10].
98 Ibid at [102] citing *R (Abedin) v Secretary of State for Justice* [2015] EWHC 782 (Admin) at [17].
99 *R (Khan) v Secretary of State for Justice* at [90].
100 Ibid at [104]–[105].
101 Ibid at [95]–[96]. See also *Hogben v United Kingdom* (1986) 46 DR 231 [3]–[4]; *R (Uttley) v Secretary of State for the Home Department* [2004] UKHL 38; [2004] 1 WLR 2278 [38], [43]; *Uttley v the United Kingdom* (Admissibility Decision) (2005) ECHR 855; (Application no 36946/03) 29 November 2005, p 8; *R (Robinson) v Secretary of State for Justice* [2010] EWCA Civ 848; [2010] 1 WLR 2380; *R (Salami) v Parole Board* [2010] 1 WLR 2380; [2010] EWCA Civ 848 [22]; *R (Abedin) v Secretary of State for Justice* [2015] EWHC 782 (Admin) [17]–[18]; [2015] 2 WLUK 54, *Abedin v the United Kingdom* (2021) 72 EHRR SE6 [32]–[36].

30 Article 8: Right to respect for private and family life

Tony Vaughan with Emma Fitzsimmons

INTRODUCTION

30.1

Article 8 of the European Convention on Human Rights (ECHR) is a qualified right which, by sub-paragraph (1), guarantees the right to 'respect' for a person's private and family life, their home and their correspondence. The circumstances in which those interests can be interfered with are set out in sub-paragraph (2). Article 8 provides:

> Right to respect for private and family life
>
> 1. Everyone has the right to respect for his private and family life, his home and his correspondence.
> 2. There shall be no interference by a public authority with the exercise of this right except such as is in accordance with the law and is necessary in a democratic society in the interests of national security, public safety or the economic well-being of the country, for the prevention of disorder or crime, for the protection of health or morals, or for the protection of the rights and freedoms of others.

30.2

In *R v G*,[1] Lord Hoffmann said that, 'prosecutorial policy and sentencing do not fall under article 8 … if the offence in question is a justifiable interference with private life'. These observations are fundamentally based on the important public interest in prosecuting criminal conduct, ensuring 'public safety' and 'the prevention of disorder or crime'. On the face of it, Lord Hoffmann's words suggest a limited role for Article 8 of the ECHR to be deployed in the criminal trial and sentencing process since it may be thought that these important public interests will invariably justify any interference with Article 8(1) rights. However, whether a particular measure does so will always be context and fact specific. Thus, in the absence of authority to the contrary, the question of whether an interference with Article 8(1) rights occasioned by a particular measure within the criminal justice process will need to be carefully considered from first principles, which are set out in the first part of this chapter. In practice,

1 *R v G* [2008] UKHL 37; [2009] 1 AC 92 at [10].

Article 8 remains potentially relevant in a number of contexts which may bear on trial and sentence; these are touched upon in the second part of this chapter.

GENERAL PRINCIPLES

30.3

When analysing whether any act or measure violates Article 8 of the ECHR, a well-established sequence of questions falls to be addressed, namely:

(a) Will the proposed measure be an interference by a public authority with the exercise of the applicant's right to respect for his private, family life, home or correspondence (etc)?

(b) If so, will such interference have consequences of such gravity as potentially to engage the operation of Article 8?

(c) If so, is such interference in accordance with the law?

(d) If so, is such interference necessary in a democratic society in the interests of national security, public safety or the economic well-being of the country, for the prevention of disorder or crime, for the protection of health or morals, or for the protection of the rights and freedoms of others?

(e) Is such interference proportionate to the legitimate public end sought to be achieved?[2]

30.4

Each of the elements of Article 8 of the ECHR has an autonomous meaning in the Strasbourg case law. As such, domestic law cannot limit the scope or meaning of Article 8 as defined under the Convention jurisprudence. Article 8 entails primarily a negative obligation to refrain from unjustifiably interfering with Article 8(1) interests.[3] However, it may also impose positive obligations that are inherent in effective respect for the protected interests, such as a positive obligation to ensure adequate protection to individuals against crimes which would interfere with private life and physical integrity.[4] In order to answer questions (a) and (b), above, it is important to understand the nature of the interests which the state must respect.

---

2 *R (Razgar) v Secretary of State for the Home Department* [2004] UKHL 27; [2004] 2 AC 368 at [17]; *HH v Italian Prosecutor* [2012] UKSC 25 at [30].

3 *Kroon v Netherlands* (1995) 19 EHRR 263 at [31].

4 See, eg *G v United Kingdom* (Application No 37334/08), 30 August 2011, at [38]; *R v G* [2008] UKHL 37 at [54].

PRIVATE LIFE

30.5

The concept of 'private life' is broadly defined and encompasses a person's social, personal and professional life. In *Niemietz v Germany*,[5] the Strasbourg Court ruled that it was not 'possible or necessary to attempt an exhaustive definition of the notion of "private life"...'. It would be 'too restrictive to limit the notion to an "inner circle" in which the individual may live his own personal life as he chooses and to exclude therefrom entirely the outside world'. To exclude 'professional activities' from the scope of Article 8 could lead to unequal treatment. In *Pretty v UK*,[6] the Court noted that, 'gender identification, name and sexual orientation and sexual life fall within the personal sphere protected by Article 8'.[7] Also included within the scope of Article 8 is 'the ability to conduct one's life in a manner of one's own choosing', including the pursuit of 'activities perceived to be of a physically or morally harmful or dangerous nature for the individual concerned'. Article 8 ensures that the individual has a space within which they can 'pursue the development and fulfilment of his personality'.[8]

PHYSICAL, PSYCHOLOGICAL OR MORAL INTEGRITY

30.6

A person's physical and psychological integrity and, more broadly, their health, falls within the concept of private life.[9] Article 8 entails a positive obligation to provide 'effective protection' against serious physical harm by private individuals. In *MC v Bulgaria*,[10] the ECtHR observed:

> While the choice of the means to secure compliance with Art.8 in the sphere of protection against acts of individuals is in principle within the State's margin of appreciation, effective deterrence against grave acts such as rape, where fundamental values and essential aspects of private life are at stake, requires efficient criminal law provisions. Children and other vulnerable individuals, in particular, are entitled to effective protection.[11]

5 *Niemietz v Germany* (1992) 16 EHRR 97 at [29].

6 *Pretty v UK* (2002) EHRR 1 at [61]–[62].

7 See also *Peck v the United Kingdom* (2003) 36 EHRR 41 [57].

8 *A-MV v Finland* (2018) 66 EHRR 22 at [76].

9 *Z v Finland* (1998) 25 EHRR 371 at [71]; *Bensaid v United Kingdom* (2001) 33 EHRR 10 at [47]; *Razgar*, above; *Pretty* at [61].

10 *MC v Bulgaria* (2005) 40 EHRR 20 at [150] and [185].

11 See also *X and Y v the Netherlands* (1986) 8 EHRR 235, [22]–[23]; *Milicevic v Montenegro* (Application no 27821/16), 6 November 2018 at [54]–[56]; *Jankovic v Croatia* [2011] 1 FLR 407.

30.7

Equally, in *Nicolae Virgilu Tanase v Romania*,[12] the Court noted: 'Not every act or measure of a private individual which adversely affects the physical and psychological integrity of another will interfere' with Article 8.

PRIVACY

30.8

The mere storing of data relating to the private life of an individual amounts to an interference within the meaning of Article 8,[13] whether or not the stored data is subsequently used.[14] Whether the personal data relates to a person's private life depends on the context, the nature of the records, and how those records are to be used.[15] Article 8 regards the protection of personal data as of fundamental importance.[16] There may be a positive obligation to provide access to personal data by way of an 'effective and accessible procedure', such as where this is required to enable an individual 'to effectively counter any allegations of his or her collaboration with the security services'[17] or to 'receive information necessary to know and to understand their childhood and early development'.[18]

30.9

In order to ascertain whether the notions of 'private life' and 'correspondence' are applicable, the ECtHR has, on several occasions, examined whether individuals had a reasonable expectation that their privacy would be respected and protected; whilst this consideration is significant, it is 'not necessarily conclusive'.[19] Interaction, even in a public context, may fall within the scope of private life. Publication of a photo may thus intrude upon a person's private life even where that person is a public figure.[20] The concept of privacy under Article 8(1) also, in principle, encompasses the right to one's image, photographs and writing; and to protection of individual reputation. Secret surveillance necessarily interferes with individual privacy; whether it is lawful depends on the extent and effectiveness of available safeguards, the necessity and proportionality of the measure, and provided that the secrecy of the surveillance does not render the measure effectively unchallengeable.[21]

---

12 *Nicolae Virgilu Tanase v Romania* (Application no 41720/13), 25 June 2019 at [128]–[132].
13 *Leander v Sweden* (1987) 9 EHRR 433 at [48].
14 *Amann v Switzerland* (2000) 30 EHRR 843 at [69].
15 *Friedl* (1996) 21 EHRR 83 at [49]–[51] and *Peck v United Kingdom* (2003) 36 EHRR 41 at [59].
16 *Z v Finland* (1998) 25 EHRR 371 at [95].
17 *Joanna Szulc v Poland* (Application no 43932/08), 13 November 2012 at [87].
18 *Yonchev v Bulgaria* (Application no 12504/09), December 2017 at [49]–[53].
19 *Benedik v Slovenia* (Application no 62357/14), 24 April 2018 at [101].
20 *Von Hannover v Germany (No 2)* (2012) 55 EHRR 15 at [95].
21 *Kennedy v United Kingdom* (2011) 52 EHRR 4 at [124]; *Big Brother Watch v United Kingdom* (2022) 74 EHRR 17; *Klass v Germany* (1979–80) 2 EHRR 214 at [36]; *Varga v Slovakia* (Application no 58361/12), 20 July 2021, at [151]–[162].

FAMILY LIFE

30.10

The existence of 'family life' is essentially a question of fact depending on the existence of close personal ties.[22] Article 8 protects family life arising from lawful and genuine marriage,[23] and between a parent and their minor child,[24] as well as family life arising from lawful adoption.[25] Other non-marriage based relationships may also be covered by Article 8 depending on the facts.[26] Article 8 protects not only currently existing family life but also entails a positive obligation to protect the future development of a real family life.[27] Applying this principle, the Grand Chamber in *Dickson v United Kingdom*,[28] accepted that the refusal of artificial insemination facilities to a serving prisoner and his wife engaged their right to respect for family and private life.

HOME

30.11

Whether a place is a 'home' for the purposes of Article 8(1) is a question of fact which depends on the existence of 'sufficient and continuous links' with a specific place, whether or not lawfully occupied.[29] In *Chiragov v Armenia*,[30] the applicants' 'home' was a village from which they had been forcibly displaced during a war many years prior, in which applicants had 'long-established lives and homes'. By contrast, in *Loizidou v Turkey*,[31] an area where the applicant planned to build a residential home and where she grew up was not her 'home', even though she had grown up and her family had roots there. In *Buck v Germany*,[32] the Court held that the term 'home' may extend to a professional person's office.'

CORRESPONDENCE

30.12

Article 8 covers correspondence between an individual and a lawyer, even where the lawyer has not yet been formally instructed.[33] The prevention or

22 *Lebbink v Netherlands* (2005) 40 EHRR 18 at [33].
23 *Abdulaziz, Cabales and Balkandali v United Kingdom* (1985) 7 EHRR 330.
24 *Berrehab v Netherlands* (1988) 11 EHRR 322 at [21]; *Ahmut v Netherlands* (1997) 24 EHRR 62 at [60].
25 *Pini v Romania* (2005) 40 EHRR 13; *Marckx v Belgium* (1979–1980) 2 EHRR 330 at [31]; *Johnston and Others v Ireland* (Application no 9697/82), 18 December 1986 at [56].
26 *Van der Heijden v Netherlands* (2013) 57 EHRR 13 at [50]; *Marckx v Belgium; Evans v United Kingdom* (2008) 46 EHRR 34 at [45].
27 *Sen v Netherlands* (2003) 36 EHRR 7 at [40].
28 *Dickson v United Kingdom* (2008) 46 EHRR 41 at [65]–[66].
29 *Prokopovich v Russia* (2006) 43 EHRR 10 at [36].
30 *Chiragov v Armenia* (2016) 63 EHRR 9 at [206].
31 *Loizidou v Turkey* (1997) 23 EHRR 513 at [66].
32 *Buck v Germany* (2006) 42 EHRR 21 at [31]–[32].
33 *Schonenberger and Durmaz v Switzerland* (1988) 11 EHRR 202 at [29]. See also: *Campbell v the United Kingdom* (1993) 15 EHRR 137 at [48]; and *Michaud v France* (2014) 59 EHRR 9 at [117]–[119].

delay of prisoner's letters by the prison authorities constituted an interference with Article 8 in *Silver v United Kingdom*.[34] However, the Court said that when considering whether the interference was 'necessary', regard had to be paid to the 'ordinary and reasonable requirements of imprisonment … some measure of control over prisoners' correspondence is called for'.[35] A wide-ranging search of a lawyer's office pursuant to a broadly framed warrant to search and seize documents relating to a specific person was a disproportionate interference with the lawyer's correspondence in *Niemietz v Germany*.[36]

'IN ACCORDANCE WITH THE LAW'

30.13

The words 'in accordance with the law' in Article 8(2) of the ECHR require both that a measure that interferes with Article 8(1) interests has some basis in domestic law and that it be compatible with the rule of law. In relation to the latter concept – as it has been interpreted in ECHR jurisprudence – the Strasbourg Court has consistently recognised that the domestic law be adequately accessible and foreseeable before it can constitute 'law' for the purposes of Article 8(2). In relation to foreseeability:

> a norm cannot be regarded as a 'law' unless it is formulated with sufficient precision to enable the citizen to regulate his conduct: he must be able – if need be with appropriate advice – to foresee, to a degree that is reasonable in the circumstances, the consequences which a given action may entail… A law which confers discretion must indicate the scope of that discretion.[37]

30.14

It is inherent in the requirement of foreseeability that the applicable 'law' offers sufficient protection against arbitrary interference by the state with Convention rights[38] and that that state interference with individual rights should be subject to effective control.[39] Article 8 also entails minimum procedural requirements, notably that an applicant may be entitled to a degree of involvement in the decision making process to a sufficient degree 'to provide him with the requisite protection of his interests'.[40]

---

34 *Silver v United Kingdom* (1983) 5 EHRR 347 at [84].

35 Ibid at [96].

36 *Niemietz v Germany* (1992) 16 EHRR 97 at [32].

37 *Silver v United Kingdom* (1983) 5 EHRR 347 at [85]–[88]; see also *S v United Kingdom* (2009) 48 EHRR 50 at [95]–[96]; *Fernandez Martinez v Spain* (Application no 56030/07), 12 June 2014 at [117].

38 *Kruslin v France* (1990) 12 EHRR 547 at [33]–[35].

39 *Klass v Germany* (1978) 2 EHRR 214 at [55].

40 *Petrov and X v Russia* (2019) 69 EHRR 10 at [101]; *R (B) v Stafford Crown Court* [2006] EWHC 1645 (Admin) at [22]–[25]. In the *Stafford Crown Court* case, an application for judicial review of the Crown Court's refusal to require service of an application for summons of the NHS trust to produce the claimant's medical record was granted, where the absence of provision in the Criminal Procedure Rules for such service meant that no account was taken of the views of affected persons whose privacy was being interfered with: [22]–[25].

NECESSITY AND PROPORTIONALITY

30.15

It is for the State to demonstrate that the interference with Article 8(1) rights pursued one or more of the legitimate aims specified in Article 8(2) and that the State had any of those aims in mind as the intended justification for the interference.[41]

In determining whether the impugned measure was 'necessary in a democratic society', the court is required to consider whether, in all the circumstances, the reasons adduced to justify them were relevant and sufficient, and whether the measures were proportionate to the legitimate aims pursued.[42,43]

ARTICLE 8 IN THE CONTEXT OF TRIAL

30.16

This section addresses two contexts (non-exhaustive) in which Article 8 ECHR has been used at the trial stage or on an appeal against conviction, notably to contend that:

(a) evidence should be excluded under section 78 of the Police and Criminal Evidence Act 1984 or that its admission would amount to an abuse of process; and

(b) the trial or conviction, and/or a decision whether to prosecute is incompatible with Article 8.

Exclusion of evidence under PACE section 78 and abuse of process

30.17

In a case pre-dating the Human Rights Act 1998, (HRA), Lord Nolan said in *R v Khan*,[44] that a breach of Article 8 of the ECHR is a matter which 'may be relevant to the exercise of the section 78 power', albeit that the 'determinative factor' was the effect of the breach on the fairness of the proceedings as a whole. Notwithstanding that the Crown Court is prohibited from acting inconsistently with Convention rights by section 6 of the HRA,[45] Lord Nolan's summary of the relevance of Article 8 ECHR to a section 78 application reflects the approach taken by the courts, as set out below.

---

41 *Kilin v Russia* (Application no 10271/12), 11 May 2021 at [61].

42 *Z v Finland,* ibid at [94]; *Dudgeon v United Kingdom* (1982) 4 EHRR 149 at [51]–[53]; *MA v Denmark* (Application no 6697/18), 9 July 2021 at [140]–[163].

43 These concepts have been the subject of much case law. For further reading, see Article 8 of the ECHR Guide (available online) for further detail.

44 *R v Khan* [1997] AC 558, 581–582.

45 Section 6(1) provides: 'It is unlawful for a public authority to act in a way which is incompatible with a Convention right.' 'Public authority' includes a court (s 6(3)(a)).

30.18

As regards abuse of process, arguments raising Article 8 may relate to either of the two categories of abuse, ie (1) where the court concludes that the accused cannot have a fair trial; and (2) where it would offend the court's sense of justice and propriety to try the accused in all the circumstances.[46] The second category encompasses unlawful conduct[47] and 'behaviour that threatens either basic human rights or the rule of law'[48] and therefore potentially applies to a case involving a breach of the ECHR. In the context of criminal trials, appeals against conviction and challenges to decisions to prosecute, the authorities have focused on the impact of Article 8 violations on the fairness of the proceedings, rather than on abuse of process.

30.19

In *R v Khan* (above) the defendant appealed against conviction, *inter alia*, on the grounds that, under section 78 of PACE, the trial judge should have excluded a covert voice recording in which he made incriminating statements. The Crown conceded that a listening device had been installed by means of civil trespass occasioning some damage to the defendant's property. The House of Lords accepted that a breach of Article 8 'may be relevant' to the exercise of the section 78 power, but that the 'determinative factor' was the effect of the breach on the fairness of the proceedings as a whole.[49] The House of Lords ultimately decided that there was no unfairness, but noted that the case had only come before the House of Lords because of the lack of a statutory system for regulating the use of surveillance devices by police.[50] The position of Liberty, the Intervener, was that section 78 provided a sufficient remedy to examine the significance of the Article 8 breach to the fairness of the proceedings.[51]

30.20

Mr Khan applied to the ECtHR, which ultimately treated the lack of such a system of statutory regulation as rendering the interference with the defendant's Article 8 rights 'not in accordance with the law' and thus in violation of Article 8.[52] In subsequent cases, the ECtHR also ruled that the reliance by the police on material obtained from covert listening devices which had been installed without the applicants' knowledge was 'not in accordance with the law' because of a lack of a statutory system of regulation of such measures, and therefore unjustifiably interfered with their Article 8 right to privacy.[53]

---

46 *R v Maxwell* [2010] UKSC 48, [2011] 1 WLR 1837 at [22]; *R v Horseferry Road Magistrates' Court, ex parte Bennett* [1994] 1 AC 42 at 61H.

47 *R v Crawley* [2014] EWCA Crim 1028, [2014] Cr App R 16 at [17].

48 *Ex parte Bennett* at 61H.

49 Lord Nolan, pp. 581–582.

50 Ibid at 582.

51 Ibid at 579E–F.

52 *Khan v UK* (2001) 31 EHRR 45 at [28].

53 *Chalkley v UK* (2003) 37 EHRR 30 at [25]; *PG v UK* (2008) 46 EHRR 51 at [35]–[38].

30.21

Through the Regulation of Investigatory Powers Act 2000 (RIPA), Parliament sought to address this *lacuna* in regulatory oversight. Subsequent challenges to decisions of the trial judge to reject section 78 applications made in respect of covert surveillance have, in the main, been unsuccessful. *R v Khan*,[54] concerned a trial judge's decision to admit into evidence recordings of conversations between two appellants which took place in a police van. Due to limited direct evidence, authorisation had been obtained in accordance with RIPA 2000 to carry out 'directed surveillance' prior to the arrests. The Court of Appeal considered how the wording of section 28(2) and (3) of RIPA 2000 satisfied the requirements of Article 8 and found that surveillance was conducted in good faith, albeit that it was, 'conducted in circumstances in which the investigating officers negligently failed to have proper regard to the limits of their authorisation'; accordingly, a violation of Article 8 was found. However, the Court of Appeal found that the violation 'sa[id] nothing about the fairness of the appellants' trial' and there was no misrepresentation, entrapment or trickery, oppression or coercion. Furthermore, there had been no limit to the appellants' right to challenge or explain the evidence. In concluding that the trial judge had been correct to admit the recording, the court also considered the 'seriousness of the crime under investigation and the potential danger to the victim'.[55]

30.22

In *R v Turner*,[56] the defendant appealed against conviction on the basis that the trial judge erred in rejecting the submission that the indictment ought to be stayed as an abuse of process due to the use of intrusive covert surveillance at the home of the appellant, which had recorded privileged material;[57] in the alternative the trial judge should have excluded the surveillance evidence under section 78, which had entailed a breach of Article 8. The intrusive covert surveillance at the appellant's home had been authorised by the Chief Constable and approved by the Surveillance Commissioner. The Court of Appeal noted that the recording 'provided clear evidence that the appellant had killed the deceased …'. The abuse of process submission was rejected. The Court of Appeal held that the section 78/Article 8 argument had been 'doomed to failure': as authorisation and approval had been obtained, there was no failure to disclose material which would have been helpful to the appellant, and no unfairness. 'The only unfairness was that the appellant chose to say things that he did because he did not realise that they were being recorded.'[58]

30.23

In *R v King*,[59] the Court of Appeal re-stated the principle that evidence obtained by means of covert audio equipment will be admissible, and that any violation

54 *R v Khan* [2013] EWCA Crim 2230.
55 *PG v UK* at [45]–[56].
56 *R v Turner* [2013] EWCA Crim 642.
57 There was no suggestion that a violation of Article 8 ECHR was relevant to 'category 2' abuse.
58 Ibid at [30].
59 *R v King* [2012] EWCA Crim 805 at [22].

of Article 8 rights will not automatically lead to exclusion of the evidence obtained under section 78 of PACE. The effect of the breach depends on whether the breach prevents a fair trial. The Court confirmed that breaches of the PACE 1984 Codes of Practice are relevant to the issue of fairness. The issue of the fairness of admitting surveillance evidence became intertwined with the issue of whether the investigating officers had acted in deliberate breach of section 30 of PACE 1984. The Detective Inspector had issued a written decision before the arrests stating that the two defendants were to be placed together in a police vehicle with recording facilities. The decision did not mention the section 30 duty. The court found that whilst 'the deliberate flouting of a statutory duty for the purpose only of creating an opportunity for a covert recording may, depending upon the circumstances, result in the exclusion of evidence', the trial judge had been right to reject the section 78 application, the following factors being instructive:

(a) there had been no evidence before the trial judge indicating that the investigating officers had deliberately been dilatory in order to obtain the recording;

(b) the court noted that it had never been asked to consider an admissibility challenge to evidence on the basis of an alleged breach of section 30;

(c) whilst the two were under arrest, they were under the supervision of police officers who, as instructed, did not engage them in conversation concerning their arrest;

(d) the placement of the two in the same vehicle provided only the opportunity for them to speak, in the belief no one could overhear;

(e) there was no trick or subterfuge to lead the two to believe that had to respond to arrests;

(f) although the covert recording occurred before interview under caution, this placed them at no greater disadvantage.[60]

30.24

In *Perry v United Kingdom*,[61] the ECtHR ruled that evidence had been obtained covertly in breach of PACE Codes of Practice in at least three respects: the breaches were 'not in accordance with the law' and were thereby in violation of Article 8. The Court emphasised that issues relating to the fairness of the use of evidence obtained in violation of that article had to be distinguished from the question of the lawfulness of the interference with 'private life'. Such issues were relevant to Article 6 rather than Article 8.[62]

60 Ibid at [20], [21], [26].
61 *Perry v United Kingdom* (2004) 39 EHRR 3 at [42]–[49].
62 Ibid at [48].

Prosecuting and/or convicting would violate Article 8 of the ECHR

30.25

Even if evidence obtained in violation of Article 8 cannot properly be excluded under section 78, to what extent is there scope to challenge the propriety of the proceedings themselves, whether *via* abuse of process, or an application for judicial review of the CPS decision to continue the prosecution?

30.26

The case of *SXH v CPS (United Nations High Commissioner for Refugees Intervening)*,[63] suggests that either approach is likely to face difficulties. *SXH* was prosecuted for possession of false identity documents, contrary to section 25(1) of the Identity Cards Act 2006; but the charge was discontinued after she was granted refugee status. She sued the CPS for damages, including arising from her detention on remand and on the basis that the CPS decision to prosecute the claimant had violated Article 8. The Court dismissed her appeal, ruling that the decision to prosecute did not engage Article 8. Lord Toulson, giving the leading judgment, considered *R v G (Secretary of State for the Home Department intervening)* and *G v United Kingdom*[64] and noted the absence of any reported case in which it had been held that the institution of criminal proceedings for a matter 'which is properly the subject of criminal law may be open to challenge on article 8 grounds …'.[65] Echoing the approach of Lord Hoffmann in *R v G*, Lord Toulson considered that such would be illogical:

> [I]f the matter is properly the subject of the criminal law, it is a matter for the processes of the criminal law. The criminalisation of conduct may amount to interference with article 8 rights; and that will depend on the nature of the conduct. If the criminalisation does not amount to an unjustifiable interference with respect for an activity protected by article 8, no more does a decision to prosecute for that conduct. The consequences will be matters for the determination of the court.[66]

30.27

At the same time, Lord Kerr's concurring opinion (*obiter*) lends support to the view that an ongoing decision to prosecute may be challenged if it violates the defendant's Article 8 rights. He noted that there may be a failure to have respect for the defendant's right to a private life if the prosecution is aware or ought to have become aware that the basis for a proposed prosecution no longer obtains or a complete defence is available to the defendant.

---

63 *SXH v CPS (United Nations High Commissioner for Refugees Intervening)* [2017] UKSC 30.

64 *R v G (Secretary of State for the Home Department intervening)* [2009] AC 92 and *G v United Kingdom* [2011] 53 EHRR SE25.

65 *SXH v CPS* at [32].

66 Ibid.

30.28

Article 8 was unsuccessfully relied upon in *Henderson v Metropolitan Police Commissioner*,[67] an appeal by way of case stated from a magistrates' court decision granting the police's application for the destruction of dog under the Dangerous Dogs Act 1991. It was undisputed that in some circumstances the destruction of a dog would be an interference with the owner's Article 8 rights. The destruction of a pit bull terrier is highly likely to be justified under Article 8(2) unless it is found not to be a danger to public safety. *Locus standi* was to be restricted to owners or those in charge of the dog at the time able to demonstrate an Article 8 right. Standing would not extend to someone seeking to give the dog a home absent a destruction order.[68]

30.29

By contrast, *R (Waxman) v CPS*,[69] successfully challenged a CPS decision not to prosecute F for harassment on the grounds that the state owed her a duty under Article 8 to protect her 'physical and moral integrity'; the CPS failure to prosecute 'involved a failure in its duty to her'. Article 8 imposes a positive duty on the state to 'maintain and operate an adequate system for affording protection against acts of violence by private individuals'.[70] It further noted that, while the failure of the state was less severe than in *Jankovic* and *A*, it had still breached its duty under Article 8. The *Hajduova* decision underlined 'that there may be a breach of the state's positive duty under Article 8 without there being a fundamental failure of the system'.

30.30

In *R v Pearce*,[71] one of the grounds of appeal against conviction was that the trial judge erred in permitting the prosecution to treat the appellant's 15/16 year-old daughter and partner of 19 years as hostile witnesses without taking proper account of the Article 8 rights of those involved. [72]The appellant argued that a marriage certificate should not 'be the touchstone of compellability'. The Court of Appeal dismissed the appeal and adopted a strict approach to the construction of section 80(3) of PACE 1984: 'wife or husband of a person charged'. The Court agreed that a wider approach would raise the possibility of 'serious limitations being placed upon society's power to enforce the criminal law' if the appellant's construction were correct.[73] The court agreed that in any case, the interference was covered by Article 8(2) in that the interference was in accordance with the law and could be regarded as necessary in a democratic society for the prevention of crime, taking into the wording found in the Contempt of Court Act 1981.

---

67 *Henderson v Metropolitan Police Commissioner* [2018] EWHC 666 (Admin).

68 Ibid at [29]–[30].

69 *R (Waxman) v CPS* [2012] EWHC 133 (Admin).

70 Ibid at [21], referring to cases including *Jankovic v Croatia*; *A v Croatia* [2011] 1 FLR 407 and *Hajduova v Slovakia* [2011] 53 EHRR 8 at [24].

71 *R v Pearce* [2001] EWCA Crim 2834.

72 See also *R v Suski* [2016] EWCA Crim 24.

73 Ibid at [12].

ARTICLE 8 AND SENTENCING

30.31

The sentencing of a defendant who has a family inevitably engages not only a primary carer's Article 8 right to a family life but also that of her family including any dependent child or children.[74] In *R v Petherick*, the Court of Appeal gave extensive guidance as to the impact of Article 8 when the courts are considering sentencing a primary carer of minor children to a term of imprisonment.[75] However, notably, the Court did not endorse the proposition – which by then was established at the level of the Supreme Court[76] – that the interests of affected children had to be a primary (although not the paramount) consideration. Subsequent authority has not gone further and applied the principle that the best interests of affected children are a primary consideration. The Joint Committee on Human Rights tabled amendments to the Police, Crime, Sentencing and Courts Bill 2021 which would require judges to consider pre-sentence reports including information about children before sentencing a mother; to take into account the best interests of the child; and require the government to gather and publish data on children born in prison and separated from their mothers in prison.[77] The government did not adopt the proposals.

74 *R v Petherick* [2012] EWCA Crim 2214.

75 Ibid at [18]–[25].

76 *HH v Deputy Prosecutor of the Italian Republic, Genoa* [2012] UKSC 25; *ZH (Tanzania) v SSHD* [2011] UKSC 4. See also, subsequently, *JR38's application for Judicial Review (Northern Ireland)* [2015] UKSC 42; [2016] AC 1131 at [78].

77 'Children of mothers in prison and the right to family life: The Police, Crime, Sentencing and Courts Bill', Joint Committee on Human Rights, 12 May 2021.

31 Article 9: Freedom of thought, conscience and religion

Will Durrands

BACKGROUND

31.1

There are many examples of historical attempts at protecting religious freedoms. *Cuius regio, eius religio*[1] was a principle of European international law originating in the wake of the Protestant Reformation and the wars that followed which addressed the freedom of religion for states, but not individuals.

31.2

Article X of the *Declaration of the Rights of Man and of the Citizen* drafted in 1789 in the early stages of the French Revolution by the National Constituent Assembly as a proto constitution developed the point further. With assistance from Thomas Jefferson, it stated that no man was to be 'disquieted' on account of his religious views provided they did not disturb public order – an early case of a qualified right. The First Amendment to the US Constitution, adopted two years later, is one of the first examples of a legal protection of freedom of religion without reference to a specific religion, it prevented government from making laws that might prohibit the free establishment or exercise of religion by an individual.

31.3

The persecution of various religious groups before and during the Second World War and the later prosecution of the perpetrators of human rights abuses established a clear need for religious freedoms to be enshrined in the ECHR. Whilst Article 9 is not as frequently relied upon as Articles 6, 10 and 11 in the criminal context, there remain circumstances where its impact is felt in these courts.

1 'Whose realm, their religion'.

ARTICLE 9

31.4

Article 9 reads as follows:

> 1 Everyone has the right to freedom of thought, conscience and religion; this right includes freedom to change his religion or belief and freedom, either alone or in community with others and in public or private, to manifest his religion or belief, in worship, teaching, practice and observance.
>
> 2 Freedom to manifest one's religion or beliefs shall be subject only to such limitations as are prescribed by law and are necessary in a democratic society in the interests of public safety, for the protection of public order, health or morals, or for the protection of the rights and freedoms of others.

PROTECTED ENTITIES

31.5

Article 9 guarantees everyone the general right to freedom of thought, conscience and religion. This right primarily protects individuals but also protects associations with religious or philosophical aims that are capable of exercising the right to freedom of religion.[2] Freedom of conscience is not a right that can be exercised by non-individuals[3] and profit-making corporate bodies cannot rely on any of the rights enshrined by Article 9.[4]

BELIEF

31.6

Article 9 applies equally to both religious and non-religious beliefs. In order for a doctrine to benefit from the protections of Article 9 and qualify as a *belief* it must:

(a) attain a certain level of cogency, seriousness, cohesion and importance;

(b) be worthy of respect in a democratic society, not incompatible with human dignity and not conflict with the fundamental rights of others; and

(c) concern a weighty and substantial aspect of human life and behaviour.[5]

---

2 *Institut de Pretrês Francais v Turkey* (Application no 26308/95), 19 January 1998; 92 BDR 15 at [20].

3 *Kontakt-Information-Therapie and Hagen v Austria* (Application no 11921/86), 12 October 1988; 57 DR 81 at [88].

4 *X v Switzerland* (Application no 7865/77), 27 February 1979; 16 DR 85 at [87].

5 *Campbell and Cosans v United Kingdom* (1982) 4 EHRR 293 at [36].

31.7

Accordingly, idealism alone does not qualify for Article 9 protection as a 'belief'. The distinction is often difficult to define: by way of example, the ECHR has found that veganism[6] and pacifism[7] meet the criteria for protection as a belief.

MANIFESTATION

31.8

Article 9 guarantees a general internal freedom of thought, conscience and religion. This is an absolute right. In contrast, freedom to manifest one's beliefs is qualified. Manifestation of a belief includes worship, teaching, rites and rituals, through public manifestation: rights extend only to behaviour linked intimately with an individual's belief. It is not within the Court's remit to evaluate the legitimacy of a belief, but it may make factual findings on whether a belief is genuine and sincere if appropriate.[8]

31.9

The Commission explained the distinction between circumstances when one might meet the criteria for 'manifestation' in the case of *Eweida v UK*.[9]

> Even where the belief in question attains the required level of cogency and importance, it cannot be said that every act which is in some way inspired, motivated or influenced by it constitutes a 'manifestation' of the belief. Thus, for example, acts or omissions which do not directly express the belief concerned or which are only remotely connected to a precept of faith fall outside the protection of art.9(1). In order to count as a 'manifestation' within the meaning of art.9, the act in question must be intimately linked to the religion or belief. An example would be an act of worship or devotion which forms part of the practice of a religion or belief in a generally recognised form. However, the manifestation of religion or belief is not limited to such acts; the existence of a sufficiently close and direct nexus between the act and the underlying belief must be determined on the facts of each case. In particular, there is no requirement on the applicant to establish that he or she acted in fulfilment of a duty mandated by the religion in question.

31.10

An example of this in practice may be taken from the case of *Arrowsmith v UK*.[10] which saw the appellant convicted under sections 1 and 2 of the Incitement to

---

6 *H v United Kingdom* (Application no 18187/91), 10 February 1993; 16 EHRR CD 44.
7 *Arrowsmith v United Kingdom* (Application no 7050/75), 16 May 1977; 19 DR 5 at [19].
8 *X v United Kingdom* (Application no 7291/75), 4 October 1977; 11 DR 55.
9 *Eweida v UK* (2013) 57 EHRR 8 at [82].
10 *Arrowsmith v United Kingdom* at [19].

Disaffection Act 1934 after leaflets were distributed to British soldiers soon to be deployed to Northern Ireland. The leaflets sought to persuade the soldiers to resist their deployment, with the appellant arguing that the publications were a manifestation of their pacifist ideas.

31.11

The Commission held that the leaflets were a political challenge to the British Government's policy in Northern Ireland rather than a *manifestation* of pacifism. Whilst there was sometimes a fine line to be drawn, it was noted by the Commission that in the circumstances of this case, the publications failed to convey central pacifist principles that political objectives should be secured by non-violent means.

31.12

In *Pretty v UK*,[11] little argument focused on Article 9. The Court's finding shows the significance of 'manifestation' (and the importance of considering the interplay with other rights):

> One may accept that Mrs Pretty has a sincere belief in the virtue of assisted suicide. She is free to hold and express that belief. But her belief cannot found a requirement that her husband should be absolved from the consequences of conduct which, although it would be consistent with her belief, is proscribed by the criminal law. And if she were able to establish an infringement of her right, the justification shown by the state in relation to Article 8 would still defeat it.[12]

Protest

31.13

Direct action protesters primarily cite their rights under Articles 10 and 11 to demonstrate; see Chapters 32 and 33. Whilst some activists may be motivated by their religious beliefs or conscience to act, rarely does their direct action constitute a manifestation of those beliefs capable of Article 9 protection.

31.14

The case of *Halcrow, Grace and Mead v CPS*,[13] is an exception to that assumption. The case centred on the control of entry to the inner stone circle of Stonehenge and touching the stones. The appellants argued that they attended Stonehenge in February 2018 to worship at 'their temple'; they bypassed barriers and began to sing, chant and touch the stones, leaving after about 10 minutes. This was repeated in May 2018. The appellants were convicted of five offences of

11 *Pretty v UK* [2002] 35 EHRR 1.
12 Ibid at [31].
13 *Halcrow, Grace and Mead v CPS* [2021] EWHC 483 (Admin).

breaching the Stonehenge Regulations 1997[14] and were each given conditional discharges. The appeal was ultimately unsuccessful (see 31.28 below) but the Court found that the appellants' conduct engaged Article 9 in that their direct actions were a manifestation of their pagan beliefs.

Manifestation: limitations

31.15

Any interference with the right to manifest a religion or a belief must be justified under Article 9(2), accordingly if curtailing these rights is not prescribed by law and not necessary in a democratic society in pursuit of a legitimate aim[15] then the interference will be unlawful. Equally, if an interference is on the face of it pursuant to the permitted limitations in Article 9(2) but is otherwise a disproportionate infringement on an individual's rights, it will be unlawful.

31.16

Whether there has been an interference is largely fact specific, Lord Nicholls in *R (on the application of Williamson) v Secretary of State for Education and Employment*,[16] stated that the test is whether there has been a 'material interference … to an extent which was significant in practice' to an individual's freedom to manifest their beliefs.

PRESCRIBED BY LAW

31.17

This initial check on whether a limitation is legitimate applies both to legislative provision and to any body of case law from domestic courts applying that legislation.[17]

NECESSARY IN A DEMOCRATIC SOCIETY

31.18

'Necessary' requires a 'pressing social need'[18] to be identified as the motive for the provision in question.

---

14 Made pursuant to the Ancient Monuments and Archaeological Areas Act 1979, s 19.

15 *Svyato Mykhaylivska Parafiya v Ukraine* (Application no 77703/01), 14 June 2007 at [132] and [137]: an interference that does not pursue one of the specified aims can never be justified.

16 *R (on the application of Williamson) v Secretary of State for Education and Employment* [2005] UKHL 15; [2005] 2 AC 246, at [39].

17 Any interference prescribed by case law must be adequately accessible and formulated in with sufficient precision to allow an individual to regulate their conduct: see *Svyato-Mykhaylivska Parafiya* (ibid.) for an example of where the law was not sufficiently foreseeable.

18 *ISKCON v United Kingdom* (Application no 20490/92), 8 March 2004; 76-A DR 90 at [106].

IN PURSUIT OF A LEGITIMATE AIM

31.19

Whilst the identified legitimate aims set out in Article 9(2) are strictly exhaustive, the Commission has in practice granted a very wide margin of appreciation in relation to Article 9 reflecting the variety in domestic constitutions and affording a 'special importance' to national decision making.[19]

Protection of public health/safety

31.20

Examples of where Article 9 interference has been justified under this heading are various and include the application of legislation that required the wearing of a motorcycle crash helmet[20] and a refusal to allow druidic ritual at Stonehenge.[21]

31.21

A number of religious groups claim that the use of some prohibited substances is central to their beliefs and that the consumption (or importation for consumption) of drugs is 'manifestation' pursuant to Article 9. Two notable groups are the União do Vegetal (UDV) and Rastafarians.

31.22

UDV has sought to argue[22] that their ritualistic consumption and importation of hoasca[23] (vegetal) with the active ingredient DMT (a Class A controlled substance) was a core aspect of their declared objective to 'contribute to the spiritual development of the human being and the improvement of his or her intellectual qualities and moral virtues'.

31.23

UDV applied for a judicial review of the Secretary of State's decision to refuse the group a licence to produce, supply or possess vegetal pursuant to section 7 of the Misuse of Drugs Act 1971. It was accepted by the Secretary of State that the consumption of vegetal was a manifestation of religion pursuant to Article 9. The sole issue was whether the refusal of the licence was a legitimate and proportionate limitation of UDV's rights in the interests of public safety and the protection of health. Despite assertions as to the limited evidence of any health complications associated with long term vegetal use and the permissible consumption of vegetal in Brazil and the USA[24] the claim was unsuccessful

19 *Sahin v Turkey* (2007) 44 EHRR 5 at [109].

20 *X v United Kingdom* (Application no 7992/77), 12 July 1978; 14 DR 234.

21 *Chappell v United Kingdom* (Application no 12587/86), 18 January 2001; 53 DR 241 at [247].

22 *Beneficent Spiritist Center Uniao Do Vegetal v Secretary of State for the Home Department* [2017] EWHC 1963 (Admin).

23 Lso, known as ayahuasca, consumed as a tea.

24 See para [13] of the judgment.

and the interference with the manifestation of UDV's beliefs permissible under Article 9.

31.24

In *R v Taylor*,[25] T was arrested on his way into the Rastafarian Temple in Kennington, London. T was searched and found to be in possession of over 60 wraps of herbal cannabis and £295 cash. On arrest he said, 'I'm a Rasta. It's part of my religion.' Later in his police interview under caution he said that the cannabis was to be used in a regular act of worship within the temple where each of the attendants were to be given an equal amount of the drug: his explanation for the multiple wraps. T was charged with and ultimately pleaded guilty to possession of a controlled drug of Class B with intent to supply after an adverse ruling by the judge that T's Article 9 rights had not been infringed. T appealed against his conviction on Article 9 grounds. To the Court of Appeal's surprise, the Crown conceded that that all the cannabis in T's possession would be exclusively for religious purposes.

31.25

T submitted that the judge's approach was flawed in that he failed to hear evidence or make findings in relation to a number of issues – such as the impact of cannabis on health – which he argued would have informed any decision as to whether any infringement on T's Article 9 rights was a reasonable response to legitimate aims. It was also argued that the final issue of proportionality of any response ought to have been left to the jury. The Court rejected these arguments, finding no need for a jury to hear the 'merits or demerits of cannabis' and concluded that the relevant provisions of the Misuse of Drugs Act 1971 were compatible with Article 9(2).

To ensure public order

31.26

The Commission in *X v Germany* [26] held that states have a fairly wide remit to 'put limits on the manner in which individuals may behave in public places'. Here, X was free to express his disagreement with union attitudes to abortion in correspondence with public officials. He was not free to compare the unions to the Nazi Party.

31.27

In one of many cases balancing the access to, and preservation of, Stonehenge, the Commission in *Pendragon v UK* [27] held that a four-day restriction preventing

25 *R v Taylor* [2001] EWCA Crim 2263.
26 *X v Germany* (Application no 12230/86) 5 July 1977; 11 EHRR 101 at 102.
27 *Pendragon* v UK (1999) 27 EHRR CD179.

a Druidic Summer Solstice festival from being held was a legitimate and proportionate Article 9 interference to ensure public order at the site.

To protect the rights of others

31.28

The appeal of *Halcrow* (above)[28] failed after the Court found that interference with the appellants' rights to worship unrestricted at Stonehenge was proportionate when balanced against the 'general interest of the community to see Stonehenge preserved for present and future generations':

> This is because it would have meant in practice that access to the stone circle would have had to be lifted as and when any person chose to walk into the stone circle, so long as they were protesting or exercising religious rights. Such access would inevitably have an adverse effect on Stonehenge to the detriment of current and future generations.

31.29

Notwithstanding the Court's finding in favour of the appellants in each prerequisite aspect of behaviour before it qualifies for Article 9 protection, this case serves as a prime example that manifestation of religious belief is not absolute and the interpretation of limitations can be broad.

31.30

A similar example of this limitation may be seen in the case of *Connolly v DPP*.[29] C was a Roman Catholic who had sent photos of aborted foetuses to three pharmacies that sold the morning-after pill. She was convicted of three offences contrary to the Malicious Communications Act 1988. On appeal it was held that interference with her Article 9 rights was justified as necessary in a democratic society to protect the rights of others not to suffer distress and anxiety.

31.31

The case of *R (Williamson) v Secretary of State for Education* (above) was an unsuccessful challenge to the prohibition of corporal punishment in schools by a number of headmasters from private Christian schools. W sought to argue that schools ought to be allowed to beat pupils (with their parents' permission), as corporal punishment was a doctrine advocated in the Bible. The House of Lords concluded (1) that corporal punishment was not a *manifestation* of Christianity;

---

28 See para [49]. It is understood that the case is neither the subject of a domestic appeal nor an application to the Commission.

29 *Connolly v DPP* [2007] EWHC 237 (Admin). The judgment focuses primarily on C's Article 10 rights (see Chapter 32), although Lord Justice Dyson reached conclusions in relation to Art 9(2) by analogy with Art 10(2).

and (2) in any event, interference was necessary in a democratic society for the protection of the rights and freedoms of others.

Other examples

Religious dress

31.32

Religious dress is acknowledged as a statutory defence to the offence of Possession of a Bladed Article. Section 139(5)(b) states that it is not an offence to carry a bladed article if it is being carried for 'religious reasons'. The defendant bears the burden of proof (to the civil standard) to show the religious reasons for carrying the article – an example of this may be the Sikh practice of carrying a kirpan.

31.33

In the case of *R v D*,[30] the Court held that D was free to wear a niqab throughout her trial save when giving evidence. Religious dress in Court has since been addressed in the Equal Treatment Benchbook which, in the context of criminal cases; gives the following guidance:[31]

(a) any issue regarding the wearing of the veil ought to be addressed at a pre-trial directions hearing;

(b) the identity of a witness/appellant/defendant can be established in private by a female member of staff, avoiding the need for removal of the veil in open court;

(c) justification of removing the veil when giving evidence requires close scrutiny; removal is not always essential for the tribunal to assess the evidence given;

(d) if removal is felt necessary, steps must be taken to minimise discomfort/concern, including screening and limiting the number of people in the public gallery; and

(e) in jury trials, the approach in *D* might be appropriate.

31.34

Various adjustments and practices for court participants of different denominations when taking the oath are discussed in Chapter 9 of the Equal Treatment Bench Book.

---

30 *R v D* [2013] 9 WLUK 348; [2013] Eq LR 1034.

31 See www.sentencingcouncil.org.uk/wp-content/uploads/Equal-Treatment-Bench-Book.pdf; Chapter 9, para 22 et seq.

Samples of Bodily Fluid

31.35

A Muslim prisoner who had been fasting and not drinking water for religious reasons was wrongly convicted (in internal prison proceedings) for failing to provide a sample for a mandatory drug test after being unable to supply sufficient urine for the test.[32] It is unclear whether a similar defence might be available to a defendant charged with failure to provide a sample pursuant to section 7 of the Road Traffic Act 1988. It is submitted that should a detainee be unable to provide sufficient urine for a sample in a situation analogous to this case, the appropriate course of action would be to seek a blood or breath sample as an alternative.

31.36

Jehovah's Witnesses do not accept blood transfusions, believing that blood is sacred and represents God. Whilst there is considerable variation in personal choice, there is no general doctrine prohibiting Jehovah's Witnesses from giving blood samples as these are not destined for transfusion. Care must be given to any sample taken from a detainee in these situations and specimens treated with respect and disposed of with care. Notwithstanding this, it is submitted that any lack of care with a sample freely given would lead to an Article 9 argument which might have bearing on criminal proceedings.

SENTENCING

31.37

Section 66 of the Sentencing Act 2020 reflects the heightened status of religious beliefs that are targeted by offenders. As with offending motivated by race and hostility or related to sexuality, any offending that targets a victim's actual or presumed membership of a religious group attracts an uplift in sentencing by the Courts.

32 *R. (on the application of Bashir) v Independent Adjudicator* [2011] EWHC 1108 (Admin): the conviction arose from the applicant's failure to obey a lawful order: Prison Rules 1999, r 51(22).

32 Article 10: Freedom of expression

Tom Wainwright

OVERVIEW

32.1

Article 10 of the European Convention on Human Rights (ECHR) provides:

> (1) Everyone has the right to freedom of expression. This right shall include freedom to hold opinions and to receive and impart information and ideas without interference by public authority and regardless of frontiers. This article shall not prevent States from requiring the licensing of broadcasting, television or cinema enterprises.
>
> (2) The exercise of these freedoms, since it carries with it duties and responsibilities, may be subject to such formalities, conditions, restrictions or penalties as are prescribed by law and are necessary in a democratic society, in the interests of national security, territorial integrity or public safety, for the prevention of disorder or crime, for the protection of health or morals, for the protection of the reputation or rights of others, for preventing the disclosure of information received in confidence, or for maintaining the authority and impartiality of the judiciary.

32.2

Freedom of expression constitutes 'one of the essential foundations of a democratic society'[1] and is 'one of the basic conditions for its progress and for the development of every [person]'.[2] In *DPP v Ziegler*,[3] the High Court summarised some of the essential bases for the importance of Article 10 including that:

- it is important for the autonomy of the individual and their self-fulfilment;
- it is conducive to the discovery of truth in the 'marketplace of ideas': 'History teaches that what may begin as a heresy (for example the idea that the earth revolves around the sun) may end up as accepted fact and indeed the orthodoxy';

1 *Sunday Times v UK (No 2)* 14 EHRR 229 at [50].
2 *Handyside v UK* (1979–1980) 1 EHRR 737.
3 *DPP v Ziegler* [2019] 1 Cr App R 32.

- it is essential to the proper functioning of a democratic society: 'A self-governing people must have access to different ideas and opinions so that they can effectively participate in a democracy on an informed basis'; and
- it helps to maintain social peace by permitting people a 'safety valve' to let off steam: 'In this way it is hoped that peaceful and orderly change will take place in a democratic society, thus eliminating, or at least reducing, the risk of violence and disorder.'[4]

32.3

The interplay between Article 10 and the criminal law raises some of the most interesting questions in criminal jurisprudence, seeking as it does to determine the boundaries of free speech. Although the common law recognised the importance of freedom of speech,[5] the coming into force of the Human Rights Act 1999 (HRA) forced the courts to confront and identify the extent to which the criminal justice system will restrict what people say or how they say it. As a result, Article 10 has had a very significant impact on criminal justice.

CONTENT OF FREE SPEECH

32.4

Freedom of expression applies not only to information or ideas that are favourably received or regarded with indifference. It extends to those which 'offend, shock or disturb'.[6] 'Such are the demands of that pluralism, tolerance and broad-mindedness without which there is no democratic society.'[7]

32.5

In *Redmond-Bate v DPP*, Lord Justice Sedley railed against a submission that freedom of expression was limited to speech which was unobjectionable:

> That will not do. Free speech includes not only the offensive but the irritating, the contentious, the eccentric, the heretical, the unwelcome and the provocative provided it does not tend to provoke violence. Freedom only to speak inoffensively is not worth having. What Speaker's Corner (where the law applies as fully as anywhere else) demonstrates is the tolerance which is both extended by the law to opinion of every kind and expected by the law in the conduct of those who disagree, even strongly, with what they hear. From the condemnation of Socrates to the persecution of modem writers and journalists, our world has seen too many examples of State control of unofficial ideas. A central purpose of the European Convention on Human Rights has been to

4 *Handyside v UK* at [49].
5 *Derbyshire CC v Times Newspapers* [1995] AC 534.
6 *Sunday Times v UK (No 2)* 14 EHRR 229 at [50].
7 *Handyside v UK* at [49].

> set close limits to any such assumed power. We in this country continue to owe a debt to the jury which in 1670 refused to convict the Quakers William Penn and William Mead for preaching ideas which offended against State orthodoxy.[8]

32.6

Similar points have been strongly emphasised in other cases:

> ...it must be recognised that legitimate protest can be offensive at least to some – and on occasions must be, if it is to have impact. Moreover, the right to freedom of expression would be unacceptably devalued if it did no more than protect those holding popular, mainstream views; it must plainly extend beyond that so that minority views can be freely expressed, even if distasteful.[9]

> ... a freedom which is restricted to what judges think to be responsible or in the public interest is no freedom. Freedom means the right to publish things which government and judges, however well motivated, think should not be published. It means the right to say things which 'right-thinking people' regard as dangerous or irresponsible.[10]

32.7

Where the expression in question relates to 'a debate on a matter of general concern and constitutes political and militant expression ... a high level of protection of the right to freedom of expression is required'.[11] A person taking part in such debates is allowed to have recourse to a degree of exaggeration or provocation and to make 'somewhat immoderate statements'. [12] Satire is an important form of artistic expression and social commentary which has a natural tendency to provoke and agitate and any attempt to restrict it should be examined with particular care.[13]

32.8

Politicians are expected to have a thicker skin than private individuals when it comes to criticism or mockery. In particular, those who have themselves used virulent speech and demonstrated extremist views must accept that they have exposed themselves to harsh challenge and therefore have to display a higher level of forbearance.[14] A politician 'inevitably and knowingly lays himself open to close scrutiny of his every word and deed by both journalists and the public at large, and he must consequently display a greater degree of tolerance'.

---

8 *Redmond-Bate v Director of Public Prosecutions* (2000) HRLR 249 at [20].
9 *Abdul v DPP* [2011] HRLR 16.
10 *R v Central Independent Television plc* [1994] Fam 192, 202–203.
11 *Lindon and others v France* (2008) 46 EHRR 35 at [48].
12 Ibid at [56].
13 *Eon v France* (Application no 26118/10), 14 March 2013.
14 *Lindon and others v France* at [56].

32.9

Particular importance is also attached to press reporting. In *Jersild v Denmark*,[15] the European Court quashed the conviction of a journalist for broadcasting an interview with three members of a far right group, in which they used offensive language and expressed racist views. The intention of the programme was not to endorse but to expose and ridicule those views, and to raise the growth of such groups as a matter of social concern. The court held that:

> Not only does the press have the task of imparting such information and ideas: the public also has a right to receive them. Were it otherwise, the press would be unable to play its vital role of 'public watchdog'.[16]
>
> …it is of great importance that the media are not discouraged, for fear of criminal or other sanctions, from imparting opinions on issues of public concern.[17]

Journalistic freedom covers a degree of exaggeration and provocation, although it must not overstep certain bounds including those relating to the rights and reputation of others.[18]

32.10

Section 12 of the HRA, requires that courts have particular regard to the importance of the Convention right to freedom of expression and, where the proceedings relate to journalistic, literary and artistic material, the extent to which the material will be published.

LIMITATIONS ON FREE SPEECH

32.11

Where rights under Article 10 of the ECHR are engaged, restrictions on that right must be 'narrowly construed' and the justification for any criminal sanction must be 'convincingly established'.[19] In *Alekhina v Russia,* the court stated that there is 'little scope under Article 10(2) of the Convention for restrictions on political speech or debates on questions of public interest'.[20] The court further observed that '… according to international standards for the protection of freedom of expression, restrictions on such freedom in the form of criminal sanctions are only acceptable in cases of incitement to hatred'.[21] Where such statements are made which are alleged to have stirred up violence, hatred or intolerance, the court must consider:

---

15 *Jersild v Denmark* (1995) 19 EHRR 1.
16 *Lindon and others v France* at [31].
17 Ibid at [44].
18 *Fressoz v France* (2001) 31 EHRR 2.
19 *Sunday Times v UK (No 2)* 14 EHRR 229.
20 *Alekhina v Russia* (2019) 68 EHRR 14 at [212].
21 Ibid at [223].

- whether the statements were made against a tense political or social background: the presence of such a background has generally led the European Court to accept that some form of interference with such statements was justified;
- whether the statements, fairly construed and seen in their immediate or wider context, could be seen as a direct or indirect call for violence or as a justification of violence, hatred or intolerance: the European Court has been particularly sensitive towards sweeping statements attacking entire ethnic, religious or other groups or casting them in a negative light; or
- the manner in which statements were made and their capacity, directly or indirectly, to lead to harmful consequences.[22]

32.12

Not entirely consistently with this jurisprudence, in *Pwr v DPP*, the High Court concluded that:

> …the ECtHR does not, for article 10 purposes, prescribe any bright line between speech that incites to violence and other speech. Although the State may be afforded a wider margin of appreciation for criminal laws which regulate the former, the latter may still be the subject of a criminal offence so long as what is provided is 'appropriate' and 'without excess'.[23]

32.13

The effect on those affected by totalitarian communist rule in Eastern Europe, of displaying a symbol associated with that regime, was not sufficient to determine the limits of freedom of expression. In *Vajnaj v Hungary* it was held that:

> In the Court's view, a legal system which applies restrictions on human rights in order to satisfy the dictates of public feeling – real or imaginary – cannot be regarded as meeting the pressing social needs recognised in a democratic society, since that society must remain reasonable in its judgement. To hold otherwise would mean that freedom of speech and opinion is subjected to the heckler's veto.[24]

32.14

In terms of the limits which may be placed on protests, the Court of Appeal in *Tabernacle v SSD*, observed that:

> Rights worth having are unruly things. Demonstrations and protests are liable to be a nuisance. They are liable to be inconvenient and tiresome,

22 Ibid at [218]–[220].
23 *PWR v DPP* [2020] EWHC 798 (Admin) at [36].
24 *Vajnai v Hungary* (2010) 50 EHRR 44 at [57]

> or at least perceived as such by others who are out of sympathy with them.[25]

The State must recognise that any demonstration in a public place may cause 'a certain level of disruption to ordinary life' and encounter hostility. Public authorities must therefore show a certain degree of tolerance to protests.[26]

32.15

As well as the restrictions under Article 10(2), the right to freedom of expression is also subject to Article 17 of the ECHR which states that:

> Nothing in this Convention may be interpreted as implying for any State, group or person any right to engage in any activity or perform any act aimed at the destruction of any of the rights and freedoms set forth herein or at their limitation to a greater extent than is provided for in the Convention.

Therefore, for example, where a member of an extreme far right party displayed a poster calling for the removal of all Muslims from the United Kingdom, his actions were incompatible with the Convention values of tolerance, social peace and non-discrimination and he was not entitled to the protections of Article 10.[27]

FORMS OF EXPRESSION

32.16

Freedom of expression includes participating in a demonstration and therefore the right to protest is protected under Article 10.[28] This protection extends beyond simple speeches and placards. In *Roberts & Others* , the Court of Appeal confirmed that:

> … there is no doubt that direct action protests fall within the scope of Articles 10 and 11 …[29]

when dealing with three defendants convicted of public nuisance having sat on top of lorries for two to three days in a protest against hydraulic fracturing. Similarly, obstructing a fox hunt, breaking into a construction site to impede engineering work[30] and obstructing a grouse hunt[31] have been found to be expressions of opinion within Article 10. In *Drieman v Norway*,[32] the European

25 *Tabernacle v SSD* [2009] EWCA Civ 23 at [43].
26 *Kudrevicius v Lithuania* (2016) 62 EHRR 34.
27 *Norwood v UK* (2005) 40 EHRR 11.
28 *Steel v UK* [1999] 28 EHRR 603.
29 *Roberts & Others* [2019] 1 WLR 2577 at [39].
30 *Hashman and Harrup v UK* (Application no 25594/94), 25 November 1999.
31 *Steel and others v UK* [1999] 28 EHRR 603.
32 *Drieman v Norway* (Application no 33678/96), 4 May 2000.

Court proceeded on the assumption that physically obstructing a whale-hunting ship could come within Article 10, although it may not enjoy the same degree of protection as political speech or debate. In *Ziegler v DPP*,[33] the Supreme Court held that deliberately obstructive action by protestors, even where it had more than a minimal impact on others, could still be protected by the right to freedom of expression.

32.17

The courts have acknowledged that in some cases the 'manner and form' of a protest can constitute the actual 'nature and quality' of the protest. Therefore, the Aldermaston Women's Peace Camp which had been taking place monthly since 1985 had acquired a 'symbolic force inseparable from the protestors' message and was 'the very witness of their beliefs'. In *Tabernacle v Secretary of State for the Defence*,[34] a byelaw which prohibited camping near the nuclear weapons site which was the focus of the protest and which would effectively have brought the camp to an end, was held unjustly to interfere with the Article 10 (and 11) rights of the participants even though there would have been other ways of carrying out the demonstration.[35] Article 10 does not bestow any 'freedom of forum' and does not require:

> …the automatic creation of rights of entry to private property, or even, necessarily, to all publicly owned property (Government offices and ministries, for instance). Where however the bar on access to property has the effect of preventing any effective exercise of freedom of expression or it can be said that the essence of the right has been destroyed, the Court would not exclude that a positive obligation could arise for the State to protect the enjoyment of Convention rights by regulating property rights.[36]

32.18

Even where a protest takes place in property or on land to which the public enjoys free entry, such as a church, exercising free speech may require respect for prescribed rules of conduct depending on the nature and function of the place.[37] In *DPP v Cuciurean*,[38] the High Court held that neither Articles 10 nor 11 includes the right to protest on privately owned land or upon publicly owned land from which the public is generally excluded, other than in the most extreme circumstances.

---

33 *Ziegler v DPP* [2021] 2 Cr App R 19.
34 *Tabernacle v Secretary of State for the Defence* [2009] EWCA Civ 23.
35 See also *Frumkin v Russia* (2016) 63 EHRR 18.
36 *Appleby v UK* (2003) 37 EHRR 38.
37 *Alekhina v Russia* (2019) 68 EHRR 14.
38 *DPP v Cuciurean* [2022] EWHC 736 (Admin); [2022] 2 Cr App R 8.

32.19

In *Gough v UK*,[39] the European Court held that being naked in public in order to express an opinion as to the inoffensive nature of the human body was a form of expression covered by Article 10 of the European Convention.

32.20

A call for boycotts may come under Article 10, even though it combines an expression of opinion with incitement to differential treatment. If it amounts to a call to discriminate it will go beyond the exercise of freedom of expression, but this will not always be the case and any purported justification for interfering with political discourse must be properly analysed.[40]

DEFENCE, INTERPRETATION OR ABUSE OF PROCESS?

32.21

In *Dehal v CPS*,[41] Moses J held that in any case in which Article 10 was engaged, as well as proving the elements of the offence, the prosecution also had to prove that a prosecution was necessary and proportionate in accordance with the right to Freedom of Expression. However, in *Bauer v DPP*,[42] Moses LJ held that 'whatever the merits' of *Dehal*, it did not mean that in a case of an alleged aggravated trespass arising out of a protest, the prosecution had to prove anything more than the elements of the offence.

32.22

The final nail in the coffin for this argument appeared to have been hammered in by the High Court in *James v DPP* in which the High Court held that *Dehal* was wrongly decided and should not be followed:

> The proportionality, for the purposes of articles 10 or 11, of a decision to prosecute is simply not an issue for the trial Courts to deal with.[43]

A decision to prosecute could only be adjudicated on by a criminal court if, exceptionally, it amounted to an abuse of the court's process.[44] Instead, the elements of the offence had to be interpreted in a way which ensured compliance with Article 10.

39 *Gough v UK*, *The Times*, 3 December 2014.
40 *Baldassi and others v France* (Applications nos 15271/16 et seq), 11 June 2020.
41 *Dehal v CPS* [2005] EWHC 2154 (Admin).
42 *Bauer v DPP* [2013] 1 WLR 3617.
43 *James v DPP* [2016] 1 WLR 2118 at [25].
44 Disproportionality would not amount to an abuse of process (Brown [2022] 1 Cr App R 18).

32.23

Then, in *Ziegler v DPP*, the coffin was apparently prised open again by the Supreme Court, when Lord Hamblen and Lord Stephens observed that arrest, prosecution, conviction and sentence were all separate restrictions on Article 10, the proportionality of each being a fact-specific enquiry requiring the evaluation of the circumstances in the individual case. They went on to hold that:

> In a criminal case the prosecution has the burden of proving to the criminal standard all the facts upon which it relies to establish to the same standard that the interference with the arts 10 and 11 rights of the protesters was proportionate. If the facts are established then a judge, as in this case, or a jury, should evaluate those facts to determine whether or not they are sure that the interference was proportionate.[45]

32.24

However, in *DPP v Cuciurean* (above) the High Court held that the passage in *Ziegler* (above) was limited to the offence of obstructing the highway and did not provide a general 'proportionality defence'. It is difficult to see how the passage is limited to obstructing the highway given, for example, its reference to a jury who would not determine the summary only offence of obstructing the highway. Nonetheless, *Cuciurean* was approved by the Court of Appeal in *AG Ref No 1 of 2022*[46] and by the Supreme Court of Northern Ireland in *AGNI Ref – Abortion Services (Safe Access Zones) (Northern Ireland) Bill.*[47]

INDIVIDUAL OFFENCES

32.25

Following *Cuciurean and AG Ref No 1 of 2022*,[48] the position reverts to that set out in *James v DPP* (above). Broadly, there are some offences whose wording allows a proportionality assessment (often, but not always, those which have a lawful or reasonable excuse defence) and others which have been pre-determined to always be proportionate by Parliament. The Court of Appeal in *AG Ref No 1 of 2022* then somewhat muddied the waters by observing that not all offences could be placed into these two categories and that there may be some instances in which a free-standing proportionality assessment would need to be read in, using section 3 of the Human Rights Act 1998, else a declaration of incompatibility may arise at the appellate stage. The Supreme Court of Northern Ireland agreed in *AGNI Ref – Abortion Services (Safe Access Zones) (Northern Ireland) Bill*,[49] holding that:

45 *Ziegler v DPP* at [60].

46 By a Court of Appeal whose constitution included the two judges who decided *Cuciurean*.

47 *AGNI Ref – Abortion Services (Safe Access Zones) (Northern Ireland) Bill* [2022] UKSC 32.

48 *AG Ref No 1 of 2022* [2023] 1 Cr App R 1.

49 *AGNI Ref – Abortion Services (Safe Access Zones) (Northern Ireland) Bill* [2022] UKSC 32.

It is important not to make the mistake of supposing that all offences can be placed into one of those categories, or to suppose that a reference to lawful or reasonable excuse in the definition of an offence necessarily means, in cases concerned with protests, that an assessment of proportionality can or should be carried out. The position is more nuanced than that.[50]

There would be some protest-related offences for which Convention rights would not be engaged, for example if the conduct in question involved violent intentions. In other cases, the other ingredients of the offence would strike the appropriate balance and no further proportionality assessment would be required.

32.26

In the first category identified in *James v DPP*, a number of offences have been identified as requiring a proportionality assessment to be carried out since the coming into force of the HRA. For example, when dealing with offences involving 'threatening, abusive or insulting' words or behaviour under sections 4, 4A or 5 of the Public Order Act 1986, what amounts to a threat, abuse or an insult must take into account the importance of freedom of expression and the fact that Article 10 can protect offensive and distasteful speech.[51] It must also be taken into account in assessing whether the defendant's conduct was reasonable for the purposes of the defence under sections 4A or 5.[52]

32.27

In relation to offences under section 5 of the Public Order Act 1986, the courts have identified the following factors as potentially relevant to the question of proportionality:[53]

- whether the behaviour went beyond legitimate protest;
- whether the behaviour had not formed part of an open expression of opinion on a matter of public interest, but had become disproportionate and unreasonable;
- whether the defendant knew the likely effect of their conduct upon witnesses;
- whether the accused deliberately chose to desecrate a symbol of very considerable importance to many;
- whether the defendant was aware of the likely effect of their conduct;
- whether the method of protest had anything to do with conveying a message or expressing an opinion or was simply a gratuitous and calculated insult;

50 Ibid at [53].

51 *Hammond v DPP* [2004] EWHC 69 (Admin) at [21].

52 *Norwood v DPP* [2003] EWHC 1564 (Admin), *Hammond v DPP* ibid at [22], *James v DPP* [2016] 1 WLR 2118 at [34].

53 *Percy v DPP* [2001] EWHC Admin 1125 *and Abdul v DPP* [2011] EWHC 247 (Admin).

- whether protesters entered into a dialogue with the police beforehand;
- whether protesters had cooperated with the police;
- whether warnings to the protesters about their actions had been disregarded; and
- the level of harassment, alarm or distress caused.

32.28

The High Court in *James v DPP* held that in relation to an offence of failing to comply with a direction imposed on a public assembly under section 14 of the Public Order Act 1986, the defendant's rights under Articles 10 (and 11) were protected because:

1. The officer must have reasonable grounds for believing that the assembly may result in serious disorder.
2. The conditions imposed must genuinely and reasonably appear necessary to the officer to prevent that serious disorder.

This leaves open the possibility of a breach with someone's Article 10 rights where the order itself is lawful but is implemented in a disproportionate manner. In addition, following *Ziegler v DPP*,[54] it fails to account for the fact that even where an arrest may be considered necessary and proportionate, this does not necessarily mean that prosecution and conviction are justified. At that later stage:

> The police's perception and the police action are but two of the factors to be considered. It may have looked one way at the time to the police (on which basis their actions could be proportionate) but at trial the facts established may be different (and on that basis the interference involved in a conviction could be disproportionate).

32.29

In *Ziegler v DPP*, the Supreme Court reinstated the acquittals of four defendants after their not guilty verdicts for obstructing the highway[55] were quashed by the High Court. The legislation provided that the prosecution had to prove that a person did not have a 'lawful excuse' for the obstruction and a series of authorities prior to *Ziegler* had established that protesting could amount to lawful use of the highway if it was reasonable and proportionate. Whether it did so required an assessment under Article 10 as to whether the restriction of a conviction was necessary and proportionate in pursuit of a legitimate aim.

32.30

Factors to be taken into account in such an assessment include, but are not limited to:

54 *Ziegler v DPP* at [57],

55 Highways Act 1980, s 137.

- the extent to which the continuation of the protest would breach domestic law, including the nature and extent of any actual or potential breaches;
- the importance of the precise location to the protesters;
- the duration of the protest;
- the degree to which the protesters occupy the land;
- the extent of the actual interference the protest causes to the rights of others, including the property rights of the owners of the land, and the rights of any members of the public;
- whether the views giving rise to the protest relate to very important issues and whether they are views which many would see as being of considerable breadth, depth and relevance;
- whether the protesters believed in the views they were expressing;
- the place where the obstruction occurs: an obstruction can have different impacts depending on the commercial or residential nature of the location of the highway;
- the extent of the actual interference the protest causes to the rights of others: the extent of the actual interference can depend on whether alternative routes were used or could have been used;
- whether the obstruction was targeted at the object of the protest; and
- prior notification to and co-operation with the police may also be relevant factors in relation to an evaluation of proportionality; however, prior notification, co-operation with the police, and that there is a domestic legal requirement for prior notification, must not encroach on the essence of the rights.[56]

32.31

In *AG Ref No 1 of 2022*, the Court of Appeal held that, for offences of criminal damage, it would not be necessary to carry out a proportionality assessment in cases involving:

- private property, where the damage was more than 'trivial'; or
- public property, where the damage was more than 'significant' or was inflicted 'violently'.

In the second category set out in *James v DPP*, the courts have held that if the elements of the offence are proved, the restrictions imposed by the criminal law are necessary and proportionate. For example, in *Bauer v DPP*, it was held that once the elements of aggravated trespass are made out, there could be no question of the defendants' actions being justifiable as an exercise of their

56 *Ziegler v DPP* at [72]–[78].

right to freedom of expression.[57] This was confirmed by the Supreme Court in *Richardson v DPP*, in which it was held that:

> Of course a person minded to protest about something has [Article 10 and 11] rights. But the ordinary civil law of trespass constitutes a limitation on the exercise of this right which is according to law and unchallengeably proportionate. Put shortly, article 10 does not confer a licence to trespass on other people's property in order to give voice to one's views.[58]

32.32

Similarly, in *Coltman*,[59] Article 10 was held simply not to apply to an offence of 'computer hacking'[60] even where the unauthorised access had been obtained in order to expose a matter of public importance. In *R v Brown*,[61] the Court endorsed a concession that Articles 10 and 11 did not provide a defence in relation to the common law offence of public nuisance and no proportionality assessment was required. However, this may have been in the belief that there was no 'lawful excuse' defence to the common law offence, which does not appear to be correct.[62] The new statutory offence of public nuisance in section 78 of the Police, Crime, Sentencing and Courts Act 2022 contains an explicit reasonable excuse defence.

32.33

Leaving aside criminal proceedings arising from protests, Article 10 has also been considered in relation to other offences, including obscenity. In *Handyside v UK* (above) the defendant's conviction under the Obscene Publications Act 1959 was found to engage Article 10 but the interference was considered to be justified in pursuit of protesting morals under Article 10(2). The requirements of morality varied from time to time and from place to place. Individual states had a margin of appreciation in determining where the appropriate boundary lay and could take into account factors such as the intended audience of the publication.

32.34

In relation to prosecutions for unauthorised disclosure of secret services material, if there were:

> a sweeping, blanket ban permitting of no exceptions, [this] would be inconsistent with the general right guaranteed by article 10(1) and

57 Criminal Justice and Public Order Act 1994, s 68.
58 *Richardson v DPP* [2014] AC 635 at [4]. Referred to in *Cuciurean* at [78].
59 *Coltman* [2018] EWCA Crim 2059; [2019] 2 Cr App R 35.
60 Computer Misuse Act 1990, s 1.
61 *R v Brown* [2022] EWCA Crim 6; [2022] 1 Cr App R 18.
62 See Law Commission 'Simplification of Criminal Law: Public Nuisance and Outraging Public Decency', 3.39–3.40.

> would not survive the rigorous and particular scrutiny required to give effect to article 10(2).[63]

However, the safeguards built into and surrounding the Official Secrets Act 1989 meant that a prosecution for breaching the Act was a proportionate interference with a defendant's Article 10 rights.

32.35

Whilst Article 10 means that a person cannot be convicted simply because they publish something expressing a controversial political or religious view, this does not amount to an exemption from the criminal law. Therefore, where a person published an item which, to their knowledge, carried a real risk that it would be understood by a significant number of readers as encouraging the unlawful commission of terrorist offences, freedom of speech did not mean that they were entitled to be acquitted of an offence under section 2 of the Terrorism Act 2006 because they were expressing political or religious views.[64]

---

63 *Shayler* [2002] 2 WLR 754 at [36].
64 *Faraz* [2013] 1 Cr App R 29.

33 Article 11: Freedom of assembly and association

Andrew Johnson and Chris Jenkins

OVERVIEW

33.1

> The right to demonstrate and the right to protest on matters of public concern…are rights which it is in the public interest that individuals should possess; and, indeed, that they should exercise without impediment so long as no wrongful act is done. It is often the only means by which grievances can be brought to the knowledge of those in authority – at any rate with such impact as to gain a remedy. Our history is full of warnings against suppression of these rights.[1]

33.2

The rights of free assembly and association are enshrined within Article 11 of the European Court of Human Rights (ECHR). They are rights that are recognised as being a fundamental feature of democratic society, and are protected not just in Europe, but in democracies across the world.[2] They are not only fundamental rights, but broad rights, too; whether it be people gathering in Clapham Common to emphasise the need to ensure women's safety in public spaces,[3] or individuals gluing themselves to the M25 in protest against the government's response to the climate crisis,[4] the activities of people seeking to exercise their Article 11 rights are rarely far from the public eye.

33.3

Article 11 rights are often exercised in protest action which frequently brings these rights into potential conflict with domestic criminal law. The courts have to balance these competing laws.

1 *Pitt v Hubbard* [1975] 3 WLR 201 at p 178.
2 See, eg, the First Amendment of the United States Constitution.
3 Protest calling for changes to the law to keep women safe following the murder of Sarah Everard; see, eg, *The Guardian*, 13 March 2021.
4 Protest by 'Insulate Britain'; see, eg, *The Telegraph*, 20 September 2021.

ARTICLE 11

Article 11: Freedom of Assembly and Association

1. Everyone has the right to freedom of peaceful assembly and to freedom of association with others, including the right to form and join trade unions for the protection of his interests.

2. No restrictions shall be placed on the exercise of these rights other than such as are prescribed by law and are necessary in a democratic society in the interests of national security or public safety, for the prevention of disorder or crime, for the protection of health or morals or for the protection of the rights and freedoms of others. This article shall not prevent the imposition of lawful restrictions on the exercise of these rights by members of the armed forces, of the police or of the administration of the State.

33.4

Previously, the rights enshrined in Article 11 had been protected under the common law of England and Wales. The ratification of the ECHR by the UK codified those rights, and enabled citizens of the UK to seek a remedy for a breach of their Article 11 rights before the European Court of Human Rights (ECtHR) in Strasbourg. The Human Rights Act 1999 (HRA) incorporated Article 11 directly into the law of England and Wales:

(a) the primary and secondary legislation of England and Wales, so far as it is possible to do so, must be read and given effect to in a way that is compatible with Article 11;[5] and

(b) it is unlawful for any public authority – including a court – to act in a way which is incompatible with Article 11.[6]

POTENTIAL CONFLICT BETWEEN ARTICLE 11 AND THE CRIMINAL LAW OF ENGLAND AND WALES

33.5

While it encompasses both the freedom of assembly and freedom of association, the rights under Article 11 most frequently cross swords with domestic criminal law in the context of protest action. Criminal offences that may potentially be committed by individuals protesting in the course of exercising their Article 11 rights include the following small selection:

(a) wilful obstruction of the highway;[7]

---

5 HRA, s 3(1).
6 HRA, s 6(1).
7 Highways Act 1980, s 137(1).

(b) criminal damage;[8]

(c) public order offences;[9] and

(d) offences relating to the obstruction of police constables and resisting arrest.[10]

33.6

Covid-19 led to new criminal offences being introduced to prevent non-essential public gatherings. These often came into direct conflict with Article 11 rights. For example, during the main phases of the pandemic, the Health Protection (Coronavirus) Regulations 2020[11] prohibited people from leaving their house without reasonable excuse and prevented assemblies of more than six people.

APPROACH TAKEN BY THE COURT WHEN DETERMINING WHETHER AN INDIVIDUAL'S RIGHTS UNDER ARTICLE 11 MAY POTENTIALLY PROVIDE A DEFENCE TO CRIMINAL CONDUCT

33.7

When considering whether an individual's rights under Article 11 may potentially provide a defence to a criminal charge, so as to provide the individual with a 'lawful excuse' for their conduct, the court should embark upon the following five-step enquiry:[12]

(a) Is what the defendant did in exercise of one of the rights in Article 11?

(b) If so, is there an interference by a public authority with that right?

(c) If there is an interference, is it 'prescribed by law'?

(d) If so, is the interference in pursuit of a legitimate aim as set out in Article 11(2)?

(e) If so, is the interference 'necessary in a democratic society' to achieve that legitimate aim?

8 Criminal Damage Act 1971, s 1(1).
9 Public Order Act 1986.
10 Police Act 1996, s 89(2).
11 Health Protection (Coronavirus) Regulations 2020 (SI 2020/129).
12 See, eg, *DPP v Ziegler* [2019] EWHC 71 (Admin) at [63], adopted by the Supreme Court in *DPP v Ziegler* [2021] UKSC 23 at [16].

IS WHAT THE DEFENDANT DID IN EXERCISE OF ONE OF THE RIGHTS IN ARTICLE 11?

33.8

The first issue that must be resolved is whether the defendant's conduct was in exercise of one of the rights in Article 11.

Freedom of assembly

33.9

The term 'assembly' is not defined in the ECHR. Indeed, the ECtHR has sought to refrain from offering a precise definition of the term 'assembly' for fear of it being restrictively interpreted,[13] beyond simply stating that the importance of Article 11 in a democratic society is such that the term 'assembly' should not be restrictively interpreted.[14] That said, the ECtHR has provided some assistance as to what is, in principle, capable of constituting an 'assembly'. The term has been ruled to include:

(a) static meetings and public processions;[15]

(b) public and private meetings;[16] and

(c) not only meetings of a political nature, but also social,[17] cultural[18] and religious[19] meetings.

33.10

The protections under Article 11 are limited to 'peaceful' assemblies. Assemblies where the organisers and/or participants engage in violent conduct or seek to pursue aims which reject the foundations of a democratic society, fall outside the protection of Article 11.[20] However, it is not uncommon for predominantly peaceful assemblies to feature discrete instances of violence. In these circumstances, any discrete acts of violence do not deprive the wider assembly of the protection of Article 11. The courts, when considering whether an individual was engaging Article 11 rights in such circumstances, will consider whether the individual had remained peaceful in their behaviour.[21]

13 *Navalnyy v Russia* [2018] ECHR 1062 at [98].

14 *Kudrevičius and Others v Lithuania* [2015] ECHR 906 at [91].

15 *Djavit An v Turkey* [2003] ECHR 91 at [53].

16 Ibid at [56].

17 *Emin Huseynov v Azerbaijan* [2015] ECHR 470 at [91].

18 *The Gypsy Council and Others v the United Kingdom* (Application no 66336/01), 18 January 2001.

19 *Barankevich v Russia* [2007] ECHR 648 at [15].

20 *Kudrevičius and Others v Lithuania* at [92].

21 *Primov and Others v Russia* [2014] ECHR 605 at [155].

33.11

A further feature of the rights enshrined under Article 11 is the right of individuals and organisers to choose the time, place and modalities of the assembly.[22] For example, in *Hall v Mayor of London*,[23] it was acknowledged by Lord Neuberger, with whom Arden and Stanley Burnton LJJ agreed:

> The right to express views publicly … and the right of the defendants to assemble for the purpose of expressing and discussing those views, extends … to the location where they wish to express and exchange their views.

This is a crucial aspect of the rights contained within Article 11 because the time, location or manner of assembly may have a particular symbolic force, and courts recognise that 'the purpose of an assembly is often linked to a certain location and/or time, to allow it to take place within sight and sound of its target object and at a time when the message may have the strongest impact'.[24]

33.12

However, the distinction between the essence of a protest and the manner and form of its exercise has to be treated with care;[25] it is not correct to say that Article 11 guarantees a right to 'freedom of forum' for an assembly and it does not, for example, provide a right of entry to privately-owned property. In some cases, the purpose of an assembly may be linked to its particular time and location, but in others the importance of this link may be insubstantial.

Association

33.13

An 'association', similarly, is not defined in statute, but it has been broadly held to require a voluntary grouping of individuals for a common goal.[26] Article 11, in this respect, does not relate to a right simply to share the company of others on a social basis, for example; it concerns the right of an individual to form or be affiliated with a particular group or organisation which is pursuing particular aims.[27] For an 'association' to fall within the ambit of Article 11, it needs to be a private organisation, as distinct from a public one. Factors that will be relevant to assessing whether an 'association' is private or a public include:

- whether it was founded by individuals or the legislature;
- whether it remained integrated within the structure of the State;

22 *Sáska v Hungary* [2012] ECHR 1981 at [21].
23 *Hall v Mayor of London* [2010] EWCA Civ 817 at [37].
24 *Lashmankin v Russia* [2017] ECHR 130 at [405].
25 *Tabernacle v Secretary of State for Defence* [2009] EWCA Civ 23.
26 *Young, James and Webster v the United Kingdom* [1981] ECHR 4 at [167].
27 *McFeeley v the United Kingdom* [1984] ECHR 23 at [114].

- whether it was invested with administrative, rule-making and disciplinary power; and
- whether it pursued an aim which was in the general interest.

IS THERE AN INTERFERENCE BY A PUBLIC AUTHORITY WITH AN INDIVIDUAL'S ARTICLE 11 RIGHTS?

33.14

If the court does conclude that an individual was engaging their Article 11 rights, the next issue will be to consider whether there has been an interference with those rights by a public authority. The wording of Article 11(2) makes it plain that the right to free assembly and association is not unqualified. This is a theme that has been repeatedly emphasised by the courts:

> [The rights contained within Article 11] do not comprise a 'trump card' – they are not absolute rights, but freedoms the exercise of which carries duties and responsibilities, and they may be the subject of such limitations as are prescribed by law and are necessary in a democratic society.[28]

33.15

A public authority's interference with Article 11 rights can encompass restrictions taken before, during or after an assembly.[29] These restrictions can take a variety of forms, of which the following are merely a few examples:

(a) In respect of an interference arising before an assembly, the ECtHR has held that a refusal by Turkish and Turkish-Cypriot authorities to allow an individual to travel to southern Cyprus to participate in an assembly amounted to an interference with their Article 11 rights.[30]

(b) The use of force by police against protesters, or the police arresting protesters, is a common example of an interference arising during an assembly.[31]

(c) Finally, the charging of an individual with a criminal offence, or a sentence that is subsequently imposed for such an offence, is capable of amounting to an interference with Article 11 rights after an assembly has taken place.[32]

28 *Buchanan v CPS* [2018] EWHC 1773 (Admin).
29 *Kudrevičius and Others v Lithuania* at [100].
30 *Djavit An v Turkey* [2003] ECHR 91.
31 *Laguna Guzman v Spain* [2020] ECHR 670 at [42].
32 *Ezelin v France* [1991] ECHR 29 at [39].

IS THE INTERFERENCE PRESCRIBED BY LAW?

33.16

Perhaps unsurprisingly, given the fundamental role that Article 11 rights play in a democratic society, public authorities do not have an unfettered right to interfere with an individual's right to freedom of assembly and association. In order for a public authority's interference to be lawful in principle, the interference must be 'prescribed by law'. There are three elements to this, all of which, when combined, serve to protect individuals exercising their Article 11 rights from spurious or nebulous interference by the state:[33]

33.17

First, there must be a legal basis for the intervention in domestic law. *Djavit An v Turkey* provides an example of an intervention which did not have any legal basis. The case concerned the decision of the Turkish and Turkish-Cypriot authorities to refuse to permit the applicant to cross the 'green line' from the Turkish Republic of Northern Cyprus into southern Cyprus to engage in peaceful assembly with Greek Cypriots. In fact, there was no law regulating the issuance of permits to Turkish Cypriots living in Northern Cyprus to travel into southern Cyprus for the purpose of engaging in peaceful assembly. For that reason, the ECtHR concluded that 'the manner in which restrictions were imposed on the applicant's exercise of his freedom of assembly was not "prescribed by law" within the meaning of [Article 11(2)] of the Convention'.[34] Second, the law in question must be accessible. Third, the consequences of breaching the law must be readily foreseeable. It should be stressed that this latter requirement does not require the consequences of a given action to be foreseeable with absolute certainty, but the law in question must be 'formulated with sufficient precision to enable the citizen – if need be, with appropriate advice – to foresee, to a degree that is reasonable in the circumstances, the consequences which a given action may entail'.[35]

IS THE INTERFERENCE IN PURSUIT OF A LEGITIMATE AIM?

33.18

Article 11(2) further requires that for an interference with an individual's Article 11 rights to be lawful, it must be in pursuit of a legitimate aim. The factors which are capable of amounting to legitimate aims are set out in the body of Article 11(2) and include:

- national security or public safety;

33 See eg, *Rotaru v Romania* [2000] ECHR 192 at [52].
34 *Djavit An v Turkey* [2003] ECHR 91 at [67].
35 *Kudrevičius and Others v Lithuania* [2015] ECHR 906 at [109].

- the prevention of disorder or crime;
- the protection of health and morals; and
- the protection of the rights and freedoms of others.

IS THE INTERFERENCE NECESSARY IN A DEMOCRATIC SOCIETY?

33.19

If the previous four questions have been answered in the affirmative, then the court must consider whether the interference is 'necessary in a democratic society'. It is this question which requires the court to carry out an assessment of the proportionality of the public authority's interference with an individual's Article 11 rights and, in turn, requires the consideration of the following four further questions:

- Is the aim sufficiently important to justify interference with a fundamental right?
- Is there a rational connection between the means chosen and the aim in view?
- Are there less restrictive alternative means available to achieve that aim?
- Is there a fair balance between the rights of the individual and the general interest of the community, including the rights of others?

In most cases, the answers to the first three of these questions are likely to be self-evident. It is the final question – whether a fair balance has been struck between the different rights and interests at stake – upon which the bulk of cases involving the interplay between criminal conduct and Article 11 rights will turn.

33.20

This issue was considered at length by the Supreme Court in the case of *DPP v Ziegler*,[36] in which the court undertook a detailed analysis of the approach that should be taken when considering the proportionality of a public authority's interference with an individual's Article 11 rights. The appellants in *Ziegler* were opponents of the arms trade and sought to protest the Defence and Security International Arms Fair that was being hosted at London's Excel Centre in September 2017. The appellants' conduct consisted of blocking an approach road leading to the Excel Centre by lying on the carriageway and attaching themselves to two lock boxes situated on either side of the road. The attending police officers attempted to persuade the appellants to remove themselves from the road voluntarily and, when those efforts failed, the appellants were arrested. In total, the carriageway was blocked for between 90 and 100 minutes. The

36 *DPP v Ziegler* [2021] UKSC 23. See also Chapter 32 (from 32.2).

appellants were all charged with offences under section 137 of the Highways Act 1980 relating to their wilful obstruction of the highway.

33.21

The appellants were initially acquitted at trial. The district judge ruled that the prosecution had failed to prove that the appellants' actions – which he considered to be 'limited, targeted and peaceful' – were unreasonable. The case was stated. The Divisional Court ruled that the district judge had erred, and directed that convictions be entered and the case be remitted to the magistrates' court for sentencing.[37] Two questions of general public importance were certified for the Supreme Court, the second of which required the court to consider the proper approach to the question of in what circumstances an intervention would be deemed to be 'necessary in a democratic society'. The court, in doing so, set out a number of factors that will inform a trial court's assessment of proportionality when considering whether a fair balance has been struck between the different rights and interests at stake.

Must proportionality be proved?

33.22

In *DPP v Cuciurean*,[38] the Divisional Court – in an approach subsequently approved by the Court of Appeal in in *Attorney-General's Reference (No 1 of 2022)*[39] held that *Ziegler* did not mean that in all prosecutions for offences arising out of non-violent protests, the prosecution was required to prove the proportionality of a conviction with Convention rights. In the Reference, the Court of Appeal concluded this was correct.

33.23

The Divisional Court in *Cuciurean* also accepted the prosecution contention that where the elements of an offence of aggravated trespass were proved, there was no need for an independent consideration of the proportionality of the conviction – it fell into the category of offences where proof of the specific ingredients of the offence proved that the conduct concerned was beyond was reasonable for the purposes of the exercise of Convention rights. In contrast, some offences – such as the wilful obstruction of the highway – provide a defence which enabled assessment of proportionality on the particular facts of the case. In the Reference, the Court of Appeal recognised the potential for a middle ground of cases in which the ingredients of an offence were not sufficient to render a conviction inherently proportionate, but where a defence which enabled proportionality to be considered was not available, and in such cases it would be necessary to consider whether the offence could

37 *DPP v Ziegler* [2019] EWHC 71 (Admin).

38 *DPP v Cuciurean* [2022] EWHC 736 (Admin).

39 *Attorney-General's Reference (No 1 of 2022)* [2022] EWCA Crim 1259.

be interpreted through section 3 of the HRA, or alternatively whether a declaration of incompatibility was required (see 32.26).

33.24

In the Reference, the Court of Appeal concluded that while criminal damage was not an offence for which no fact-specific assessment was required, the prosecution of any case which reached the Crown Court, which would involve damage exceeding £5,000 in value, would inevitably not infringe Convention rights.

What factors will be relevant when assessing proportionality?

33.25

The courts have made plain that it is impossible to provide an exhaustive list of factors that will be relevant when assessing proportionality; it is an inherently fact-sensitive enquiry, and the examination of the factors 'must be open textured without being given any pre-ordained weight'.[40] *Ziegler* summarises the case law and provides non-exhaustive factors that will often be relevant when conducting an assessment of proportionality:[41]

(a) the extent to which the continuation of the protest would breach domestic law;[42]

(b) the importance of the precise location to the protesters;[43]

(c) the duration of the protest;[44]

(d) the degree to which the protesters occupy the land;[45]

(e) the extent of the actual interference the protest causes to the rights of others, including the property rights of the owners of the land and the rights of any members of the public;[46]

(f) whether the views giving rise to the protest relate to 'very important issues' and whether they are 'views which many would see as being of considerable breadth, depth and relevance';[47]

(g) whether the protesters 'believed in the views they were expressing';[48]

(h) whether the obstruction was targeted at the object of the protest;[49] and

40 Ibid at [71].
41 Ibid at [71]–[78].
42 *City of London Corpn v Samede* [2012] EWCA Civ 160 at [39].
43 Ibid.
44 Ibid.
45 Ibid.
46 Ibid.
47 Ibid at [40].
48 Ibid at [41].
49 *Kudrevičius and Others v Lithuania* at [171].

(i) whether there was prior notification to, and co-operation with, the police, especially if the protest is likely to be contentious or to provoke disorder.[50]

The extent to which the continuation of the protest would breach domestic law

33.26

When assessing the proportionality of the interference, the court should consider the extent to which the continuation of the protest would breach domestic law. It will be common in criminal matters arising from protest action for an assembly, and its continuation, to amount to a *prima facie* breach of domestic law. For example, a protest on a public road potentially involves the commission of an offence of wilful obstruction of a highway contrary to section 137 of the Highways Act 1980. However, this fact alone will not necessarily render any intervention with the individual's Article 11 rights proportionate. The Supreme Court in *Ziegler* noted that if a protest is peaceful, then no other offences, such as resisting arrest or assaulting a police officer, will have been committed, and that the absence of any other breaches of domestic law can be factored into the court's assessment of proportionality.[51]

The importance of the precise location to the protesters

33.27

As detailed above in 33.9, the rights to freedom of assembly and association include a right to select the time, location and modalities of the assembly, within the limits of Article 11(2). In *Ziegler*, for example, the appellants advanced that there was a particular 'symbolic force' to the location of their protest, specifically an approach road to the Excel Centre where the Defence and Security International Arms Fair which formed the basis of their protest was taking place.

The duration of the protest

33.28

The length of the protest is also a factor that will often be of some relevance to the court's assessment of proportionality; in some circumstances, the longer a protest goes on, the more proportionate interference by a public authority may become.

50 *DPP v Ziegler* [2021] at [78].
51 Ibid at [77].

The degree to which protesters occupy the land and the extent of the actual interference the protest caused to others

33.29

Although these factors were identified as separate factors by the court in *City of London Corpn v Samede*,[52] in fact, they will often be closely linked; the greater the degree to which the protesters occupy the land in question, the greater the likely interference to the rights of others the protest will cause.

33.30

The Supreme Court in *Ziegler* addressed at length the question of how purposeful disruption which had a more than *de minimis* impact on the rights of others ought to affect the court's assessment of proportionality. In *Ziegler*, the appellants' protest had involved the obstruction of one of the carriageways leading up to the venue of the arms fair. The Divisional Court, in explaining why it considered the district judge's assessment of proportionality to have been wrong, noted that it did not consider a fair balance to have been struck between the rights of the appellants and the rights of others, in light of the fact that 'the ability of other members of the public to go about their lawful business was completely prevented by the physical conduct of these respondents for a significant period of time'. The effect of the Divisional Court's decision was that deliberately obstructive conduct could not constitute a lawful excuse for the purposes of section 137 of the Highways Act 1980, where the impact on other highway users was more than *de minimis*. The Supreme Court reviewed the ECtHR case law[53] and rejected the Divisional Court's approach:

> 'Disruption is not determinative of proportionality … intentional action by protesters to disrupt by obstructing others enjoys the guarantees of articles 10 and 11, but both disruption and whether it is intentional are relevant factors in relation to an evaluation of proportionality … intentional action even with an effect that is more than de minimis does not automatically lead to the conclusion that any interference with the protesters' article 10 and 11 rights is proportionate.'[54]

Whether the views giving rise to the protest relate to 'very important issues'

33.31

The court is entitled to take into account the general character of the views which give rise to the basis of the protest when conducting an assessment of

52 *City of London Corpn v Samede* [2012] EWCA Civ 160.

53 *Steel v United Kingdom* (2005) 41 EHRR 22; *Hashman and Harrup v United Kingdom* [1999] ECHR 133; *Kudrevičius and Others v Lithuania* [2015] ECHR 906.

54 *DPP v Ziegler* [2021] at [67].

proportionality: 'political and economic views are at the top end of the scale, and pornography and vapid tittle-tattle is towards the bottom'.[55] However, even though the broad character of the expression can be taken into account, particular care must be taken when assessing the views being expressed in the course of particular protest action, and the court must not adjudicate on the merits of the particular protest. Accordingly, while the court is entitled to attribute some weight to the general nature of the protest, 'it cannot be a factor which trumps all others, and indeed it is unlikely to be a particularly weighty factor: otherwise, judges would find themselves according greater protection to views which they think important, or with which they agree'.[56]

Whether the protesters believe in the views they were expressing

33.32

The court may take into account whether the protesters believed in the views they were expressing when assessing the proportionality of the interference with Article 11 rights. However, it is difficult to imagine a situation in which it would be proportionate for protesters to interfere with the rights of others based upon views in which they did not believe.[57]

Whether the obstruction was targeted at the object of the protest

33.33

The courts may consider interference with Article 11 rights to be more proportionate in cases where the obstruction has not been targeted at the object of the protest. For example, in *Kudrevičius v Lithuania*, the ECtHR took into account the fact that the applicants' obstruction of one of the three main roads in Lithuania had no direct connection with the target of their protest (which was aimed at highlighting a perceived lack of government action regarding the decrease in price of a number of agricultural products).[58] This can be contrasted with the protest action in *Ziegler*, where the obstruction was targeted to prevent vehicles being able to access the Defence and Security International Arms Fair.

Prior notification and co-operation with the police

33.34

In *Ziegler*, the Supreme Court noted that this factor may be relevant, particularly where the protest action is expected to be contentious or to provoke disorder.[59]

55 *City of London Corpn v Samede* [2012] EWCA Civ 160 at [41].
56 Ibid.
57 Ibid at [72].
58 *Kudrevičius and Others v Lithuania* at [171].
59 *DPP v Ziegler* [2021] at [78].

This does not necessarily require the police to be notified of the exact nature of the protest. If the police have been made aware that some form of protest action is likely to be taking place and are then in a position to implement general preventative measures, notification and co-operation may be relevant.[60] However, even though this may be capable of being a relevant factor, it must not encroach upon the essence of the rights protected under Article 11.[61]

The proportionality assessment

33.35

The court's assessment of proportionality is inherently fact sensitive and will normally require the court to balance a number of competing factors when reaching an ultimate decision on whether the public authority's interference was proportionate. It is for the prosecution to prove to the usual criminal standard (ie so the tribunal of fact is sure) all the facts upon which it relies to establish, to the same standard, that the interference with the individual's Article 11 rights was proportionate. If the facts are so established, then the tribunal of fact must then evaluate those facts to determine whether they are sure that they interference was proportionate.[62] The tribunal of fact's assessment of proportionality must exclude any facts or inferences which have not been proved to the criminal standard.

THE TEST TO BE APPLIED BY AN APPELLATE COURT WHEN ASSESSING A STATUTORY DEFENCE OF 'LAWFUL EXCUSE' WHEN CONVENTION RIGHTS ARE ENGAGED IN A CRIMINAL MATTER

33.36

This was the first certified question considered by the Supreme Court in *Ziegler* (above). The majority, led by Lord Hamblen and Lord Stephens, and with whom Lady Arden largely concurred, ruled that when assessing the decision of a trial court in respect of a statutory defence of 'lawful excuse' when Convention rights are engaged in a criminal matter the approach should be to determine whether the trial court made an error of law material to the decision reached which is apparent on the face of the case, or if the decision is one which no reasonable court, properly instructed as to the relevant law, could have reached on the facts found.[63] As in cases such as these, where the statutory defence relies upon the trial court conducting an assessment of proportionality, the

60 *Balcik v Turkey* [2007] ECHR 1002 at [51].
61 *DB v Chief Constable of the Police Service of Northern Ireland* [2017] UKSC 7.
62 *DPP v Ziegler* [2021] at [60].
63 Ibid at [54].

test for the appellate court to consider is whether there is an 'error or flaw in the reasoning on the face of the case which undermines the cogency of the conclusion on proportionality. That assessment falls to be made based on the primary and secondary findings set out in the case stated, unless there was no evidence for them, or they were findings which no reasonable tribunal could have reached'.[64]

64 Ibid.

34 Human rights and sentencing

Dr Lyndon Harris

INTRODUCTION

34.1

Under section 6 of the Human Rights Act 1999 (HRA), sentencing courts must exercise their procedural and substantive powers in a manner that is compatible with rights under the European Convention on Human Rights (ECHR). Sentencing law, procedure and practice varies considerably among Convention states. The Strasbourg jurisprudence operates in two strands: (1) broad principles which may be of some utility to domestic sentencing courts; and (2) specific decisions as to the legality of specific practices in Convention states, which generally have limited relevance beyond the State in question.

34.2

Article 6 applies throughout criminal proceedings, including the sentencing *process* and the determination of confiscation proceedings.[1] Generally, however, the *execution* of a sentence does not fall within the ambit of Article 6.[2] Thus, there is a general right to challenge a sentence. This applies equally to 'minor' (or regulatory) offences for which imprisonment is not available.[3]

SENTENCING IN ENGLAND AND WALES

34.3

In brief terms, the sentencing system in England and Wales operates a limiting retributivist scheme, whereby the dominant principle is retributive proportionality; thereafter, consequentialist considerations operate further to inform the sentencing outcome. In practical terms what this means is that the dominant principle requires the sentence to be in proportion to the seriousness of the conviction offence(s): the more serious the offence, the more severe the penalty.

1 See eg, *Phillips v The United Kingdom* (Application no 41087/98), 5 July 2001.
2 See eg, *A v Austria* (Application no 16266/90), 23 April 2004.
3 See eg *Ozturk v Germany* (1984) 6 EHRR 409.

34.4

That principle, however, is imprecise. There is no mathematical formula by which the seriousness of an offence may be compared with the severity of a sentence (usually, imprisonment): a sentence cannot be objectively tested to determine whether it conforms with the governing principle. Rather, it is an exercise of judgement, thus, there is a range of sentences which are 'not wrong', rather than a single correct sentence. It therefore follows that the principles establish a range of sentences which will be proportionate to the seriousness of the offence.

34.5

Within that range of sentences, the consequentialist considerations can inform the sentencing outcome. These are 'forward-looking' and involve considerations of the likelihood of recidivism, the need for deterrence and reparation to the victim(s). These considerations may only inform the sentencing outcome within the range set by the governing principle – that the sentence must be in proportion to the seriousness of the offence(s); they cannot take a sentence outside of that range.

34.6

The relevant provisions of the Sentencing Act 2020 are as follows.

> s 63 Assessing seriousness
>
> Where a court is considering the seriousness of any offence, it must consider—
>
> (a) the offender's culpability in committing the offence, and
>
> (b) any harm which the offence—
>
> (i) caused,
>
> (ii) was intended to cause, or
>
> (iii) might foreseeably have caused.
>
> S 57 Purposes of sentencing: adults
>
> (1) This section applies where—
>
> (a) a court is dealing with an offender for an offence, and
>
> (b) the offender is aged 18 or over when convicted.
>
> (2) The court must have regard to the following purposes of sentencing—
>
> (a) the punishment of offenders,
>
> (b) the reduction of crime (including its reduction by deterrence),
>
> (c) the reform and rehabilitation of offenders,
>
> (d) the protection of the public, and

(e) the making of reparation by offenders to persons affected by their offences.

(3) Subsection (1) does not apply—

(a) to an offence in relation to which a mandatory sentence requirement applies (see section 399), or

(b) in relation to making any of the following under Part 3 of the Mental Health Act 1983—

(i) a hospital order (with or without a restriction order),

(ii) an interim hospital order,

(iii) a hospital direction, or

(iv) a limitation direction.

34.7

It follows from the above that sentencing *quantum* in England and Wales is vague. Further, the punitiveness of a Convention state's sentencing regime is a matter for the individual state. Convention rights do not guarantee either a general right to challenge the severity of a sentence or provide a basis for which, generally and without more, a sentence can be said to be incompatible with the Convention. There are, however, ways in which the severity of a sentence can be challenged via the Convention. These are explored below.

ARTICLE 3

34.8

The text of Article 3 states:

> **Prohibition of torture**
>
> No one shall be subjected to torture or to inhuman or degrading treatment or punishment.

Article 3 is primarily relevant to sentencing in two respects: (1) disproportionality of sentence; and (2) whole life sentences and other irreducible terms. In order to fall within Article 3, the treatment complained of must 'attain a minimum level of severity'.[4] Various forms of treatment have since been found to violate Article 3. However, there is little clear guidance as to where that level lies.

4 *Ireland v United Kingdom* (1979–80) 2 EHRR 25.

Disproportionality of sentence

34.9

Disproportionality of sentence is most commonly raised in domestic courts as a mitigating factor. The argument, in a nutshell, is that there are factors that are particular to the offender that result in the otherwise proportionate sentence being disproportionate. On occasion it will be said this amounts to an Article 3 violation; in some circumstances it will merely be advanced as mitigation. The obvious factor is ill-health (which brings with it a consideration of advanced age[5]).

34.10

The leading case is *R v Bernard*,[6] in which the Court of Appeal (Criminal Division) identified the following four principles:

(a) a medical condition which might at some unspecified future date affect either life expectancy or the prison authorities' ability to treat the prisoner satisfactorily is not a reason to reduce an otherwise appropriate sentence (although it might be a matter for the Home Secretary to consider in relation to his powers of release);

(b) the fact that an offender was HIV positive or otherwise had a reduced life expectancy was not generally a factor which should affect sentence;

(c) a serious medical condition, even when it was difficult to treat in prison, would not automatically entitle an offender to a lesser sentence than would otherwise be appropriate;

(d) an offender's serious medical condition might enable a court, as an act of mercy in the exceptional circumstances of a particular case, rather than by virtue of any general principle, to impose a lesser sentence than would otherwise be appropriate.

34.11

In *R v Qazi; R v Hussain*,[7] the court held that a State party to the Convention has to accord a minimum humane level of treatment to those imprisoned but it was the primary responsibility of the State to ensure compliance with Article 3 and to accord a minimum humane level of treatment lies with the executive branch of the State, because that branch of the State is responsible for prisons.

34.12

The court in *R v Hall*,[8] summarised the position thus: medical needs of prisoners are well-understood in prison administrations: there are sophisticated

5 As to advanced age, see *R v Clarke; R v Cooper* [2017] EWCA Crim 393; [2017] 2 Cr App R (S) 18.
6 *R v Bernard* [1997] 1 Cr App R (S) 135.
7 *R v Qazi; R v Hussain* [2010] EWCA Crim 2579; [2011] 2 Cr App R (S) 8.
8 *R v Hall* [2013] EWCA Crim 82; [2013] 2 Cr App R (S) 68.

arrangements to ensure prisoners' needs are ordinarily met by the relevant primary care trust in close collaboration with the prison authorities. Medical care was ordinarily provided in prison. In exceptional and extreme circumstances, the Lord Chancellor might advise the exercise of the power to release under the prerogative. Therefore, a court passing sentence ought not to concern itself with the adequacy of arrangements in any individual case, except where the mere fact of imprisonment would inevitably expose the prisoner to inhuman or degrading treatment contrary to Article 3.

34.13

This is the position. Health can bring a particular case within Article 3; however, this is principally a matter for the executive rather than a sentencing court. There may be extreme cases in which submissions to a sentencing court, properly evidenced, may result in the sentencing court taking an exceptional course.

LIFE SENTENCES

34.14

With whole life terms, there has been what has been described as a 'dialogue' between the European Court of Human Rights (ECtHR) and domestic courts regarding the legality of indeterminate sentences with no possibility of release. The Court has considered whether such a sentence is lawful *per se*, and whether a sentence without the possibility of review is lawful. This dialogue came to a head in *Vinter v UK*.[9] The Fourth Section (by a 4:3 majority) held that the whole life order imposed in England and Wales for offences of murder did not violate Article 3; the minority agreed that the lack of a review mechanism rendered the sentence incompatible with Article 3. The Grand Chamber held that the issue was whether the law provided for:

> … a review which allow[ed] the domestic authorities to consider whether any changes in the life prisoner were so significant, and such progress towards rehabilitation [had] been made in the course of the sentence, as to mean that continued detention [could] no longer be justified on legitimate penological grounds … .[10]

The method of compassionate release said by the domestic courts to render the sentence compatible with Article 3, '… was not what was meant by a "prospect of release" in *Kafkaris*'. Further, there must be both a prospect of release and a possibility of review in order for a life sentence to be compatible with Article 3.

9 *Vinter v UK* (2016) 63 EHRR 1.
10 Ibid at [127].

34.15

Following *Vinter*, the Court of Appeal (Criminal Division) further considered the issue in *Attorney General's Reference (No 69 of 2013)*.[11] The court held that the whole life order was not incompatible with Article 3 and that the ECtHR had, in effect, misunderstood the statutory regime and the related guidance. The court stated that there was a possibility of release where exceptional circumstances were present and that although the Indeterminate Sentences Manual indicated that this would apply to cases of compassionate release on health grounds, the Secretary of State in exercising the power of release was not confined to the policy in the manual and would be bound to consider all relevant circumstances.

34.16

In the subsequent case of *Hutchinson v UK*, the Grand Chamber held that the UK whole life sentence did comply with Article 3:

> … following the Grand Chamber's judgment in which it expressed doubts about the clarity of domestic law, the national court has specifically addressed those doubts and set out an unequivocal statement of the legal position, the Court must accept the national court's interpretation of domestic law.[12]

Thus, the position is settled, for now. The whole life order is compatible with Article 3, provided the mechanism for review remains as set out in *Attorney General's Reference (No 69 of 2013)*.

ARTICLES 5 AND 14

34.17

Articles 5 and 14 state:

> **ARTICLE 5**
>
> **Right to liberty and security**
>
> 1. Everyone has the right to liberty and security of person. No one shall be deprived of his liberty save in the following cases and in accordance with a procedure prescribed by law:
>
> (a) the lawful detention of a person after conviction by a competent court;

11 *Attorney General's Reference (No 69 of 2013)* [2014] EWCA Crim 188; [2014] 1 WLR 3964.
12 *Hutchinson v UK* (2017) 43 BHRC 667.

(b) the lawful arrest or detention of a person for non- compliance with the lawful order of a court or in order to secure the fulfilment of any obligation prescribed by law;

(c) the lawful arrest or detention of a person effected for the purpose of bringing him before the competent legal authority on reasonable suspicion of having committed an offence or when it is reasonably considered necessary to prevent his committing an offence or fleeing after having done so;

(d) the detention of a minor by lawful order for the purpose of educational supervision or his lawful detention for the purpose of bringing him before the competent legal authority;

(e) the lawful detention of persons for the prevention of the spreading of infectious diseases, of persons of unsound mind, alcoholics or drug addicts or vagrants;

(f) the lawful arrest or detention of a person to prevent his effecting an unauthorised entry into the country or of a person against whom action is being taken with a view to deportation or extradition.'

[…]

ARTICLE 14

Prohibition of discrimination

The enjoyment of the rights and freedoms set forth in this Convention shall be secured without discrimination on any ground such as sex, race, colour, language, religion, political or other opinion, national or social origin, association with a national minority, property, birth or other status.

Article 5

34.18

The 'dangerousness' life sentence available under the Sentencing Act 2020 is imposed on a joint preventive/punitive basis: the seriousness of the offence justifies a life sentence and the offender poses a significant risk of serious harm to members of the public. The minimum term must be set by reference to the principle of proportionality (ie it must be proportionate to the seriousness of the offence). The mechanism for release is a consideration by the Parole Board at the expiry of the minimum term, but the sentence is indeterminate and thus release is discretionary. The ECtHR's approach to such hybrid sentences has been to ensure that there are periodic reviews of the sentence, in particular, with reference to the individual's characteristics that render them 'dangerous' such that the preventive sentence is justified.[13] Similar considerations apply to

13 See eg, *Winterwerp v Netherlands* (1979–1980) 2 EHRR 387 at [55].

so-called therapeutic sentences such as hospital orders under the Mental Health Act 1983.[14]

Article 14

34.19

Challenges have been brought to the legality of sentences on the basis of discrimination; it has been said that a particular sentence (and its effect) discriminates against a particular group and thus is incompatible with Convention rights. Challenges tend to come in the form of the 'other status' category in Article 14. 'Other status' has been given a broad definition;[15] this has not been limited to personal characteristics which are innate or inherently linked to personal identity.[16]

34.20

An applicant must demonstrate that they fall within the 'other status' category and that they were in a relatively similar/analogous (but not identical) position to those treated differently.[17] In *R (Stott) v Secretary of State for Justice*,[18] the defendant had been sentenced to an extended determinate sentence (which involved serving two-thirds of the custodial term before consideration of release by the Parole Board. The applicant contended that had he been sentenced to a life sentence, his eligibility for consideration of release would have been at the half-way point of the sentence; thus, he was in a worse position despite having been sentenced to a less-severe sentence and this constituted discrimination within the meaning of Articles 5 and 14. The Court held:

- by a 3:2 majority, there was no unlawful discrimination;
- by 4:1, the differential treatment fell within Article 14;
- by 3:2, extended sentence prisoners were not in an analogous situation to life sentence prisoners due to the relevant differences between the two sentence types; and
- by 3:2, that there was an objective justification for the differential treatment.

34.21

The details of the judgment bear close reading; the various dissenting opinions illustrate that this is an area which may provide further ground for litigation. The decision was based in part on a comparison between the different regimes: extended sentences, determinate sentences and indeterminate sentences. It is

14 See eg, *X v UK* (1982) 4 EHRR 188.
15 *Carson and Others v UK* (Application no 42184/05), 16 March 2010.
16 *Clift v UK (*Application no 7205/07), 13 July 2020.
17 Ibid at [66].
18 *R (Stott) v Secretary of State for Justice* [2018] UKSC 59; [2020] AC 51.

arguable that this is perhaps to misunderstand the sentencing system. Although it has many different parts, it must surely be viewed as a single regime and there must be some coherence between the different parts. Of course, proper deference must be paid to the legislature who has the right to choose different considerations and aims to pursue; however, the decision in Stott arguably arrives at its conclusion by a slightly treacherous route. It may have been more convincing to find that the differential treatment is justified because a life sentence is not necessary where it is not known when the risk will abate but, where this can be assessed, an extended sentence (with the requirement to spend longer in custody) is justified.

34.22

Challenges to prison policy are beyond the scope of this chapter. However, *Alexandru Enache v Romania* is worthy of note: female offenders with young children could defer custodial sentences until their child's first birthday; the Court held that there was no Article 14 violation, due to the 'specific features' of motherhood.[19] However, in *Ēcis v Latvia*, a blanket ban on male prisoners obtaining prison leave was incompatible with Articles 14 and 8 on grounds of sex.[20]

ARTICLE 7

34.23

The text of Article 7 is set out at 29.1 (above). Article 7 contains two dominant concepts relevant to sentencing: (1) the concept of a 'penalty'; and (2) the scope of the prohibition on retrospectivity.

Penalty

34.24

The concept of a 'penalty' is autonomous and thus courts are obliged to look beyond the *prima facie* description and appearance in domestic law to ascertain whether something is a penalty (and thus falls within the scope of Article 7 protection).[21] One key consideration is whether there is a criminal conviction which led to the imposition of the measure; however, this is not determinative.[22]

Other factors are relevant to this determination, including the nature and the aim of the measure in question in addition to its severity, its classification in domestic law and the procedures associated with its imposition and enforcement.[23]

---

19 *Alexandru Enache v Romania* (Application no 16986/12), 3 October 2017.
20 Ēcis v Latvia (Application no 12879/09), 10 January 2019.
21 *GIEM SRL and Others v Italy* (1828/06, 34163/07 and 19029/11), 28 June 2018 at [210].
22 Ibid, at [215]–[219].
23 See also *Welch v UK* (Application no 17440/90), 9 February 1995 at [28]; and *Del Río Prada v Spain* (Application no 42750/09), 10 July 2012 at [82].

Severity will not be decisive, however, because many non-criminal measures of a preventive nature can have a substantial impact on the person concerned.

34.25

Welch is important: the ECtHR held that a confiscation order imposed upon conviction was a penalty for Article 7 purposes. The confiscation regime is compensatory and preventive in nature, in seeking to remove the proceeds of criminal activity from a convicted person; however, the Court noted at [29] that it was irrelevant that the statutory 'presumptions' (*sic*) may affect proceeds or property unrelated to the offence: a confiscation order was dependent on a criminal conviction.[24]

34.26

Preventive detention imposed following a conviction, notwithstanding the overt preventive nature of the measure, was held to be a penalty.[25] Although in England and Wales we treat preventive custodial sentences (life sentences, extended determinate sentences and previously, longer than commensurate sentences, to name a few) as 'sentences' such that there is no question that the Article 7 protections apply, this has continued relevance as Parliament continues to legislate on a preventive basis (eg changing release regimes and providing new sentence types grounded in prevention rather than punishment).

34.27

By contrast, the inclusion of an individual on a 'register' (eg of sexual offenders) for preventive and deterrent purposes is not a penalty for these purposes as they operate 'completely separately' to the sentencing regime.[26] While there is some similarity between this and, for example, the imposition of behaviour orders such as the sexual harm prevention order, the obvious distinction is that the latter arises as a part of the sentencing process and involves the exercise of the sentencing judge's discretion.

SCOPE OF PROHIBITION ON RETROSPECTIVITY

34.28

The prohibition on the retrospective application of legislation has been an area rich in case law. The meaning of '[n]or shall a heavier penalty be imposed than the one that was applicable at the time the criminal offence was committed' has been litigated both in the domestic and Strasbourg courts on numerous

---

24 *Welch* was decided in relation to a previous confiscation regime, but the same principles apply under the Proceeds of Crime Act 2002. By contrast, a purely preventive 'confiscation order' not contingent upon a criminal conviction will not fall within the definition of a penalty: see eg, *M v Italy* (Application no 12386/86),15 April 1991.

25 See *M v Germany* (Application no 19359/04), 17 December 2009.

26 See eg, *Adamson v UK* (Application no 42293/98), 26 January 1999 at [1] and *Gardel v France* (Application no 16428/05), 17 December 2009 at [39]–[47].

occasions. Specifically, the debate has focused on the words '… than the one that was applicable at the time …" – in essence, it requires a comparison between the sentence imposed by the sentencing court and the sentence that was 'applicable' at the time the offence was committed. The rationale is obvious and grounded in fairness, accessibility and foreseeability.[27] To criminalise conduct and impose criminal liability retrospectively or to increase a penalty and impose that penalty retrospectively offend against that principle. But what is permitted? As noted above, the issue has been extensively litigated. In outline, where the sentence imposed was available at the time of the commission of the offence, there will not be a breach of Article 7.

34.29

In *Coeme v Belgium*,[28] the Court held that a penalty imposed after a trial that was higher than would have been imposed at the time of the offence, but within the limits of the law at that time, involved no breach of Article 7: the court must '… verify that … the punishment imposed did not exceed the limits fixed by [the] provision [in force at the time]'. This approach was endorsed by the House of Lords in *R (Uttley) v Secretary of State for the Home Department*[29] (see 29.9).

34.30

The position remains clear: if the sentence imposed is within the limits of the law at the time of the commission of the offence, then there will be no Article 7 violation on that basis. Article 7 does not prohibit, in principle, the application of case law developed long after the offence was committed, provided that it was reasonably foreseeable under the law applicable at the time: (see 29.3).

34.31

What is the position where subsequent changes are imposed to the execution of a sentence, however? In both *Kafkaris* and *Uttley*, the courts expressly considered a change to a sentence during its execution. In *Uttley*, Baroness Hale considered the conversion of a sentence of custody to one involving hard labour. She stated that this might be sufficient to amount to the retrospective imposition of a penalty heavier than that which was applicable at the time of the offence.

34.32

In *Del Rio Prada*[30] (see 29.10 and following, above), the ECtHR stated, in the context of an 'early release' regime, that such changes (while different to the position in *Kafkaris*, where that was held to concern the execution of the sentence) concerned the penalty but could not violate Article 7 because they

27 In *Kafkaris v Cyprus* [2009] 49 EHRR 35 at [137]–[140] the court observed, in Art 7(1), 'law' implies qualitative requirements, including accessibility and foreseeability. Those requirements had to be satisfied when considering the definition of a criminal offence and the penalty that the offence carried.

28 *Coeme v Belgium* (Application nos 32492/96, 32547/96, 32548/96, 33209/96 and 33210/96) at [145].

29 *R (Uttley) v Secretary of State for the Home Department* [2004] UKHL 38; [2004] 1 WLR 2278; see also *Kafkaris v Cyprus* [2009] 49 EHRR 35.

30 *Del Rio Prada* (2014) 58 EHRR 37 at [71].

always operated to the offender's benefit. In essence, the sentence entitled the state to detain the offender for its full term and any reduction from that was not more severe (ie heavier) than the original penalty. This has since been put into operation in England and Wales, most recently through the Terrorist Offenders (Restriction of Early Release) Act 2020. That Act delayed the release of certain offenders from the half-way point of their sentence to the two-thirds point, operating retrospectively with any sentenced prisoner who had not yet been released. In *Del Rio Prada*, however, the ECtHR held that there had been a violation of Article 7 where remissions to the offender's sentence had been made in a way not consistent with the case law at the time of the offence but rather based on a Supreme Court decision in which the court had departed from previous decisions in circumstances where that departure was not foreseeable. Thus, retrospective changes to the execution of the sentence are permissible, even where they appear to be adverse to the offender, provided they: (i) remain within the scope of the original sentence; (ii) do not amount to a heavier penalty than that capable of being imposed at the time of the commission of the offence; and (iii) are foreseeable.

ARTICLE 8

34.33

The text of Article 8 is set out in 30.1 above. Article 8 has a clear relevance to sentencing, both to the offender directly and to their dependants. It is a qualified right and may be interfered with where it serves a legitimate aim (see Chapter 30). A criminal conviction provides the State with the lawful ability to interfere with that right (although there are of course limits) – the requirement for proportionality in sentencing was recognised by the Council of Europe in its 1992 paper, Consistency in Sentencing, recommendation 92(17)). It is clear, then, that the offender's Article 8 rights are of limited utility in reducing or avoiding a custodial sentence. There are examples of cases in the domestic courts where reference is made, obliquely or otherwise, to such rights as a reason to avoid or reduce an immediate custodial sentence; however, it is perhaps better to see this as an exercise of the principle of parsimony rather than Article 8 in operation (see Sentencing Act 2020, s 231).

34.34

R v Petherick[31] is one of the best-known decisions concerning what is termed the 'collateral impact' of a sentence (see 30.31 and following). The Court in *Petherick* made a number of observations about the effect of an immediate custodial sentence:

(a) the sentencing of a defendant inevitably engages not only their own Article 8 family life rights but also those of their family: and that includes

31 *R v Petherick* [2012] EWCA Crim 2214; [2013] 1 Cr App R (S) 116.

(but is not limited to) any dependent child or children, or any one for whom they act as a carer, whether or not there is a marital or parental link;

(b) imprisonment has a number of consequences: a family is likely to be deprived of its breadwinner, the family home may be lost and schools may have to be changed;

(c) three questions should be asked:

  (i) is there an interference with family life?

  (ii) is it in accordance with law and in pursuit of a legitimate aim within Article 8(2)?

  (iii) is the interference proportionate given the balance between the various factors?

(d) long before the HRA 1998, the domestic courts recognised the importance of dependent children and the effect of imprisonment: that was reflected in the Convention rights and also the sentencing guidelines, which included reference to having a sole or primary caring responsibility for a dependent relative;

(e) sentencing courts ought to be informed about the domestic circumstances of the defendant to enable any effect upon the family life of others to be taken into consideration;

(f) the legitimate aims of sentencing which have to be balanced against the effect that a sentence often inevitably has on the family life of others, include the need of society to punish serious crime, the interest of victims that punishment should constitute just deserts, the needs of society for appropriate deterrence and the requirement that there ought not to be unjustified disparity between different defendants convicted of similar crimes;

(g) where the case stands on the cusp of custody, the balance is likely to be a fine one: in that kind of case the interference with the family life of one or more entirely innocent children can sometimes tip the scales and mean that a custodial sentence, otherwise proportionate, may become disproportionate;

(h) the likelihood, however, of the interference with family life which is inherent in a sentence of imprisonment being disproportionate is inevitably progressively reduced as the seriousness of the offence increases; and

(i) in a case where custody cannot proportionately be avoided, the effect on children or other family members might afford grounds for mitigating the length of sentence, but it may not do so.

34.35

Petherick has been applied in numerous subsequent cases and, in part, has been incorporated into the Sentencing Council's Definitive Guideline on the

Imposition of Community and Custodial Sentences (which guides the decision on whether to impose a suspended sentence order or whether an offence crosses the custody threshold).[32] The position can therefore be summarised shortly:

(a) the Article 8 rights of the offender are relevant, but are unlikely to make a substantial difference to the sentence imposed in the absence of other material factors;

(b) the Article 8 rights of any dependent relatives, principally children, may be a powerful factor in the sentencing decision; however, this will be particularly so where the case is either on the cusp of the custody threshold or where the sentence is of a length that may be suspended;

(c) evidence should be placed before the sentencing court as to the effect of imprisonment upon dependants; and

(d) having dependent relatives is not a 'get out of jail free card' and the sentencing court will need to make a judgement in each individual case, weighing the relevant factors and coming to an appropriate conclusion.

32 There is a growing body of academic research which documents the effects of imprisonment on dependent children. In particular, the work of Shona Minson in relation to the maternal imprisonment should be considered; Shona Minson, 'Direct Harms and Social Consequences: An Analysis of the Impact of Maternal Imprisonment on Dependent Children in England and Wales' (2019) 19(5) *Criminology and Criminal Justice* 519.

35 Restraint and confiscation

Nathaniel Rudolf KC

INTRODUCTION

35.1

The application of human rights principles is as relevant in the consideration of restraint and confiscation proceedings and orders as it is in any other part of the criminal case process. That is, in large part, because there are common international standards which encourage the confiscation of property linked to the commission of serious crime.[1] Therefore, any such deprivation must be in accordance with human rights, the other relevant common international standard.

35.2

This chapter will consider restraint and confiscation orders together with enforcement for their non-compliance. It is therefore limited to Part 2 of the Proceeds of Crime Act 2002 (POCA).[2]

35.3

Although restraint orders might be said to be civil in nature[3] the same human rights considerations apply. In *R v S*, the Court of Appeal said:

> The provisions of art.1 Protocol 1 and of arts 6 and 8 of the European Convention on Human Rights are obviously relevant context here.[4]

The availability of public funding means that the provisions that prevent a person using their own property appear unlikely to engage the Convention.[5] In relation to confiscation, the Divisional Court in *R (Lloyd) v Bow Street Magistrates' Court,* made it clear it was 'now clearly established that Art.6.1 applies to all stages of criminal proceedings ... That includes any confiscation proceedings'.[6]

1 *Gogitidze v Georgia* (Application no 36862/05), 12 May 2015 at [105].
2 Issues under predecessor regimes (the Criminal Justice Act 1988 and the Drug Trafficking Act 1994) are likely to be the same; but there are differences in the statutory schemes.
3 *Re O* [1991] 2 WLR 475 p 528 (a decision under the Criminal Justice Act 1988 which reposed the power to make restraint orders in the High Court rather than the Crown Court where it lies under POCA).
4 *R v S* [2020] 1 Cr App R 13 at [33].
5 *See R v Luckhurst* [2022] UKSC 23, at [48].
6 *R (Lloyd) v Bow Street Magistrates' Court* [2004] 1 Cr App R 11.

35.4

POCA's legislative scheme is compliant with the human rights of those subjected to its application. POCA continues the adversarial nature of the criminal trial process where arguments can be put before the court[7] and defendants are entitled to be present and represented.[8] It imposes obligations upon the prosecution by reference to pleading its case (s 16); third-party rights can be accommodated at that stage (s 10A); and any outcome must be a confiscation order that is proportionate (s 6(5)(b)). In seeking restraint orders, especially *ex parte*, the prosecution has a high standard to meet to ensure the court is aware of all relevant material[9] (it must put its 'defence hat on' and tell the judge that which the defence would in seeking to oppose the making of an order) and the Court of Appeal (Criminal Division) has concluded that the disclosure of material that might undermine the case for the prosecution or assist that of the defence applies to confiscation as much as the trial process.[10] Defendant and third-party rights are catered for at all stages by reference to the ability to 'intervene' and seek to vary or discharge a restraint order (s 42).

35.5

The principal rights engaged are Article 6(1) and 'Article One of Protocol No 1 – Right to Property' (A1P1). That is because there is a process that is required to be fair and the whole exercise relates to the potential for the confiscation of property. That is so even though confiscation orders are orders against people in a sum of money; rather than directed against property, albeit based upon such property. Other human rights aspects may be engaged from time to time at discrete stages. These are separately dealt with below.

35.6

Article 6(1) permits States to have recourse to presumptions. A presumption, in certain cases, that property is the proceeds of crime will not offend the Convention.[11] Thus, the assumptions in cases involving a defendant with a criminal lifestyle in section 10 of POCA are, in themselves, not offensive to the application of human rights. That is especially so as, in section 10(6), there is a process that can lead to the disapplication of the assumptions by the court.[12] Article 6(1) also permits reverse burdens. The requirement that a person shows that their assets are at a level less than the benefit figure is also not offensive to the application of human rights.[13] However, the application of the concept of proportionality that has forced its way to the front of any consideration of these topics from a human rights perspective.

7 *Veits v Estonia* (Application no 12951/11), 15 January 2015 at [72] and [74].
8 *Butler v UK* (Application no 41661/98) 26 April 1995.
9 See eg, *Barnes v Eastenders Cash & Carry plc* [2015] AC 1 at [120].
10 *R v Onuigbo* [2014] EWCA Crim 65 at [58].
11 *Salabiaku v France* (Application no 10519/83), 7 October 1988 at [28].
12 *Phillips v UK* (Application no 41087/98), 5 July 2001 at [43].
13 *Grayson v UK* (Application no 19955/05), 23 September 2008 at [45]–[49].

35.7

A1P1 states:

> **Article 1 of Protocol No. 1 – Right to property**
>
> 1. Every natural or legal person is entitled to the peaceful enjoyment of his possessions. No one shall be deprived of his possessions except in the public interest and subject to the conditions provided for by law and by the general principles of international law.
>
> 2. The preceding provisions shall not, however, in any way impair the right of a State to enforce such laws as it deems necessary to control the use of property in accordance with the general interest or to secure the payment of taxes or other contributions or penalties.

Nothing, therefore, in A1P1 prevents a state using property for the payment of penalties. What is required is a proportionate relationship between the means employed to meet the desired aim.[14]

35.8

The legislative aim of POCA is to deprive criminals of the benefit of their offending. To that direct and unequivocal end, the provisions of POCA are to be employed. Proportionality, as a concept, is not geared towards considering the effect upon a defendant of a confiscation order (save where it coincides with an order that offends the legislative aim). In *R v Ahmad and Fields* [2015] AC 299 the Supreme Court stated:

> 38. When faced with an issue of interpretation of the 2002 Act, the court must, of course, arrive at a conclusion based both on the words of the statute and on legal principles, but it is also very important to bear in mind the overall aim of the statute, the need for practicality, and Convention rights. The overall aim of the statute is to recover assets acquired through criminal activity, both because it is wrong for criminals to retain the proceeds of crime and in order to show that crime does not pay. Practicality involves ensuring that, so far as is consistent with the wording of the statute and other legal principles, the recovery process, both in terms of any hearing and in terms of physically locating and confiscating the assets in question, is as simple, as predictable, and as effective, as possible. Defendants are entitled to their Convention rights, in particular to a fair trial under article 6 and are only to be deprived of assets in accordance with A1P1.

---

14 *Phillips v UK* at [51]–[52].

RESTRAINT ORDERS

The making of a restraint order

35.9

In *Director of the Serious Fraud Office v O'Brien* the Supreme Court stated:

> 35. A restraint order under section 41 of POCA is an interim remedy. Its aim is to prevent the disposal of realisable assets during a criminal investigation or criminal proceedings. Under section 41(7) the court may make such order as it believes is appropriate for the purpose of ensuring that the restraint order is effective. This may include, for example, an order requiring disclosure of assets by the person against whom the restraint order is made.[15]

35.10

To Article 6 and A1P1 can be added Article 8 given that restraint orders, almost always impact upon those who are entirely innocent of any wrongdoing but who can be grossly affected by the order. An investigation into a person whose family is suddenly unable to deal with its own property plainly engages the family members' human rights.

35.11

Section 40 of POCA sets out the conditions that must be fulfilled before a court can make a restraint order. There are five situations that are catered for, mainly, but not exclusively, dependent upon the stage of the investigation or proceedings and whether it is reasonable to consider that the defendant has benefited from criminal conduct.

35.12

The relevant parts of section 41 of POCA follow:

> **41. Restraint orders**
>
> (1) If any condition set out in section 40 is satisfied the Crown Court may make an order (a restraint order) prohibiting any specified person from dealing with any realisable property held by him.
>
> (2) A restraint order may provide that it applies—
>
> (a) to all realisable property held by the specified person whether or not the property is described in the order;
>
> (b) to realisable property transferred to the specified person after the order is made.

15 *Director of the Serious Fraud Office v O'Brien* [2014] AC 1246.

…

(7) The court may make such order as it believes is appropriate for the purpose of ensuring that the restraint order is effective.

…

(7B) The court—

(a) must include in the order a requirement for the applicant for the order to report to the court on the progress of the investigation at such times and in such manner as the order may specify (a 'reporting requirement'), and

(b) must discharge the order if proceedings for the offence are not started within a reasonable time (and this duty applies whether or not an application to discharge the order is made under section 42(3)).

35.13

Section 42 contains detailed provisions for applications to discharge or vary restraint orders. This includes by 'any person affected' by a restraint order. Access to the court in this way is, for the reasons set out above, one reason why this part of the scheme is compliant with human rights standards, as is the reporting requirement.

35.14

In particular, the making of a restraint order is subject to what has become known as the 'legislative steer' contained within section 69 of POCA. This section is critical as it provides the Crown Court with the direction required to take account of both a defendant's Article 6 rights and the rights generally of persons under A1P1. The peculiar situation of selling property prior to the making of any confiscation order is directly addressed.

35.15

Drawing the threads together, a restraint order properly made under section 41 of POCA, if the conditions in section 40 are met, will not, of itself, breach Article 6 or A1P1. However, the greatest care must be taken to ensure that third-party rights are protected and that a restraint order is in place to cover the appropriate proportion (amount) of a person's assets for the shortest time that is properly permissible.

35.16

Where human rights will come into sharp focus is on the issues of delay and whether proceedings have been started (or are likely to be concluded) within a 'reasonable time'. In *R v S*, the Court of Appeal (Criminal Division) said, in discussing the statutory purpose of section 42(7) of POCA, that A1P1,

Article 6 and Article 8 were 'obviously relevant' when the Crown Court had to decide whether to apply the mandatory requirement to discharge a restraint (particularly and all assets order) if the circumstances arose.[16] The underlying rationale of section 69, as confirmed in *R v Waya,* is that criminals should not profit from their crimes: 'and a restraint order is thus a means of furthering that particular public interest'.[17] Section 42(7) was to be read without any gloss: 'It is then for the court to decide, having regard to all the circumstances of the particular case, whether or not the proceedings have been started within a reasonable time.'[18] The Court stated:

> Just what those circumstances are, and the weight to be ascribed to them, will necessarily vary from case to case. It is not possible to identify by way of exhaustive list just what the relevant circumstances will be in every case. But in the ordinary way, we suggest, the following, in no particular order, at least will usually be likely to be relevant (there may of course, we stress, be others in any given case) where s.42(7) is under consideration:
>
> (1) the length of time that has elapsed since the restraint order was made;
>
> (2) the reasons and explanations advanced for such lapse of time;
>
> (3) the length (and depth) of the investigation before the restraint order was made;
>
> (4) the nature and extent of the restraint order made;
>
> (5) the nature and complexity of the investigation and of the potential proceedings; and
>
> (6) the degree of assistance or of obstruction to the investigation.[19]

35.17

Although the list is non-exhaustive, it is concerned with the investigation into, as opposed to the impact upon, a person or their family. However, in any given case such considerations may have considerable weight, making what might otherwise be a reasonable time unreasonable. Section 42(7) allows the Crown Court to make any other order to ensure the restraint order is effective. Traditionally, disclosure orders have been used, requiring a person or persons to set out their assets. It can also include a repatriation order requiring assets (except land) to be returned to the UK. Such orders, of themselves, are human rights compliant. The position will depend on the individual facts of cases: if repatriating property causes insuperable difficulties that can be measured then A1P1 or Article 8 may be offended. A disclosure order, however, must not require a person to incriminate themself so as to expose them to a risk of

16 *R v S* [2020] 1 Cr App R 13 at [33].
17 *R v Waya* [2012] UKSC 51; [2013] 2 Cr App R (S) 20 at [37].
18 Ibid, at [38].
19 Ibid, at [39].

prosecution after being compelled to provide information. Any order should have a condition attached to it expressly setting that out.[20] Although decided under the common law, it reflects the position under Article 6(1).

Breach of a restraint order

35.18

Breach of a restraint order or any ancillary order made under section 41(7) is a civil contempt of court. In *O'Brien*. the Supreme Court said:

> POCA does not provide that it is an offence to disobey or obstruct a restraint order or a receivership order, but the Crown Court has an inherent power to treat such behaviour as contempt of court, for which it may impose punishment under section 45 of the Senior Courts Act 1981.[21]

CONFISCATION

Overview

35.19

As set out above, Part 2 of POCA is a regime which of itself is compliant with human rights principles. The key is to avoid a human rights breach on the facts of particular cases.

Presence of defendant

35.20

A number of sections of POCA deal with confiscation in a defendant's absence. With absconders the Crown Court has the jurisdiction to deal with confiscation applying section 6 but applying the protections found in section 28.[22] This will not offend against Article 6. Neither it seems, necessarily, will involuntary absence (although this is fact dependent). In *R v Bhanji*,[23] the defendant was unable to attend due to chronic illness. The confiscation order was upheld on the basis that their case was sufficiently before the court for it to make a fair assessment. However, where the state deports a defendant and refuses to allow them to participate this is likely to be a breach of Article 6.[24]

---

20 *Re O* [1991] 2 WLR 475, p 529.

21 *R v* O'Brien at [36].

22 *R v Okedare (No 2)* [2014] 1 WLR 4088.

23 *R v Bhanji* [2011] EWCA Crim 1198.

24 *R v Gavin; Tasie* [2011] 1 Cr App R (S) 126.

The making of a confiscation order

35.21

The key provision under which confiscation orders are made is section 6 of POCA:

> 6. Making of order
>
> ...
>
> (4) The court must proceed as follows—
>
> (a) it must decide whether the defendant has a criminal lifestyle;
>
> (b) if it decides that he has a criminal lifestyle it must decide whether he has benefited from his general criminal conduct;
>
> (c) if it decides that he does not have a criminal lifestyle it must decide whether he has benefited from his particular criminal conduct.
>
> (5) If the court decides under subsection (4)(b) or (c) that the defendant has benefited from the conduct referred to it must—
>
> (a) decide the recoverable amount, and
>
> (b) make an order (a confiscation order) requiring him to pay that amount.
>
> Paragraph (b) applies only if, or to the extent that, it would not be disproportionate to require the defendant to pay the recoverable amount.
>
> ...

35.22

For an analysis of how the exercise should be conducted, see the decision of the House of Lords in *R v May*,[25] approved by the Supreme Court in *R v Ahmad; Fields*.[26]

35.23

As set out above, the assumptions in section 10 of POCA are compliant with Article 6. They may be disapplied on the facts of any individual case. Section 6(4) is therefore compliant. Equally, as we have seen, the reverse burden upon a defendant to show their assets are less than the benefit figure is also compliant with Article 6. That is sufficient to deal with section 6(5)(a) as, by section 7, if a defendant can show the available amount is less than the benefit figure, the confiscation order will be made in the lower sum. It is important to consider the position of tainted gifts since, by section 9(1) the available amount is the

25 *R v May* [2008] 1 AC 1028.

26 *R v Ahmad; Fields* [2015] 2 AC 299 at [39].

total of the defendant's free property (s 82) together with the value of any tainted gifts made (ss 78, 79 and 81).

35.24

What is critical is the concept of proportionality. It is against the legislative aims that the answer to the question of whether a confiscation order would be disproportionate must be tested. Its most well-known exposition, which led to the addition of the words at the end of section 6(5)(b) of POCA, is found in *R v Waya*.[27] The Supreme Court held that a court must not make any order that is disproportionate as it would violate A1P1; the Court stated:

> To make a confiscation order in his case, when he has restored to the loser any proceeds of crime which he had ever had, is disproportionate. It would not achieve the statutory objective of removing his proceeds of crime but would simply be an additional financial penalty.[28]

The Court held there may be other examples of where an order may be disproportionate.

35.25

The next example of that is *R v Ahmad; Fields* [2015] AC 299 where the Supreme Court considered cases of 'joint benefit'. There the Court held that it would be disproportionate for the state to recover the same benefit twice:

> … where a finding of joint obtaining is made, whether against a single defendant or more than one, the confiscation order should be made for the whole value of the benefit thus obtained, but should provide that it is not to be enforced to the extent that a sum has been recovered by way of satisfaction of another confiscation order made in relation to the same joint benefit.[29]

Any order that contains a joint benefit with another defendant ought to be drafted in the terms set out by the Supreme Court to prohibit double recovery. Different considerations may apply, however, where there is a mixture of joint benefit from an offence and benefit from general criminal conduct which is unique to an individual defendant.[30]

35.26

The most up-to-date position is governed by *R v Andrewes*[31] where the defendant had obtained employment by lying about his qualifications but had gone on to give full service for his salary. The case is useful for drawing together the threads of what is, but also what is not, meant by proportionality:

---

27 *R v Waya* [2013] 1 AC 294 at [1]–[35] should be read to understand how the jurisprudence has developed in relation to proportionality since 2013.

28 Ibid, at [28].

29 *R v Ahmad; Fields* at [74].

30 See eg, *R v Lowther* [2020] EWCA Crim 1387 [72]–[80].

31 *R v Andrewes* [2022] UKSC 24.

> Although the certified question set out in para 2 refers to both section 6(5) of POCA and A1P1 of the ECHR, it is clear that the proviso in section 6(5) embraces A1P1. They are not laying down two independent tests. We can therefore focus simply on the proviso in section 6(5) … There is a legitimate aim of stripping a criminal of the fruits of crime, confiscation is a rational means of achieving that aim, and there are no less intrusive means of doing so. It follows that the sole … issue is … whether the measure is a proportionate means of achieving a legitimate aim, here of stripping the criminal of the fruits of crime. The disproportionality proviso to section 6(5) is focused on that crucial issue is asking precisely the same question. Is the confiscation of the sum in question (the recoverable amount) a proportionate way of stripping the criminal of the fruits of crime?[32]

35.27

On the facts of that case the Supreme Court, disagreeing with the Court of Appeal, held in 'CV fraud' cases there was a 'middle way' that was proportionate in stripping the defendant of the fruit of their crime, namely the difference between the higher earnings actually obtained through fraud, and the lower earnings they would have obtained had they not used it.[33] Each case will need to be decided on its own facts and it is for the prosecution to prove what the proportionate order should be.[34]

35.28

Finally, there is the concept of tainted gifts, created to prevent defendants from giving away property to avoid the effects of confiscation. As stated above, the value of the tainted gift is included within the available amount. In *R v Box*, the Court of Appeal considered proportionality where the value of tainted gifts would otherwise fall to be included within the confiscation order. The Court said that there might be some exceptional cases where a tainted gift leads to '… an order [which] will not recover the proceeds of crime and will simply lead to a sentence of imprisonment being served which the defendant in question can do nothing about …'. In such circumstances the protection of an inadequacy finding is limited by section 23. There is '… no warrant for creating a discretion to abrogate it. In such a case, the order may on those grounds be held to be disproportionate.'[35]

The imposition of a default term of imprisonment

35.29

Where a court makes a confiscation order it must order a term of imprisonment to be served in default of payment. Section 35(2A) of POCA contains a table

---

32 Ibid, at [38].
33 Ibid, at [45].
34 Ibid, at [39].
35 *R v Box* [2018] 4 WLR 134 at [21].

setting out the maximum terms dependent upon the value of the confiscation order made.

35.30

Guidance as to the imposition of the default term and the importance of proportionality was given in *R v Castillo*. Although this pre-dated changes to *maxima* the principles still appear applicable. The Court said '... in this context too proportionality ... commands some attention especially in the top bracket where there is no maximum amount for the confiscation order'. The Court noted that '[a] sum of £2 million to £3 million is not far above the top bracket's floor of £1 million when one considers that the same bracket would contain an order for, say, £100 million'. Proportionality 'does not define the right order' but 'some heed should be paid to the fact' that the same maximum term would apply for a much greater order. Although this pre-dated changes to *maxima*, the principles still appear applicable. The Court said '... in this context too proportionality ... commands some attention especially in the top bracket where there is no maximum amount for the confiscation order'.[36]

35.31

There are limits to the importance of proportionality at this stage. The Divisional Court in *Collins v DPP*,[37] pointed out that proportionality is built into POCA when an order is made by section 6(5)(b). When a magistrates' court is considering whether to impose the default term, a determination as to proportionality has already been made. The magistrates' court gives credit for sums paid under section 79(2) of the Magistrates' Courts 1980 and makes determinations as to wilful or culpable neglect and the sufficiency of other means of enforcement required by section 82(4). That makes the magistrates' decision proportionate.

35.32

Once, therefore, the Crown Court has imposed a lawful default term in line with the guidance in *Castillo* it will be proportionate. That, subject to considerations of Article 6, also applies to a proper decision of a magistrates' court when it comes to the enforcement of the default term.

The enforcement of a confiscation order

35.33

'Enforcement' of a confiscation order traditionally arises in one of two ways. First, an enforcement receiver may be appointed by the Crown Court (on the application of the prosecutor (POCA, s 50)) to realise the assets of the defendant and/or the free property held by a tainted gift recipient. Any receiver appointed

---

36 *R v Castillo* [2012] 2 Cr App R (S) 36 at [12], [14].
37 *Collins v DPP* [2021] 1 WLR 3391 at [32].

will always be subject to the superintendence of the court. Both a defendant and any party affected are able to make representations and ask for property to be excluded from the ambit of the confiscation. Provided the process is undertaken properly it is unlikely that any human rights considerations will arise. Second, the default term may be activated by a warrant of commitment by a magistrates' court in relation to any outstanding sum. For a full analysis of the process, see *R (Gibson) v Secretary of State for Justice*.[38]

The substantial human rights issues that arise from time to time are delay and its consequences. In *R (on the application of O'Connell) v Westminster Magistrates' Court*, the Divisional Court considered the lines of authority that had emerged. In that case a confiscation order was imposed in 2003 with a default term of 10 years. The prosecutor sought to activate it in 2017. The magistrates' court activated the term and Mr O'Connell appealed. The Divisional Court concluded that the question was:

> … whether, in the circumstances which now prevail, it would be so unjust and disproportionate to require an offender to suffer the consequences of failure to satisfy the confiscation order, which was one of the consequences of his proved criminal conduct, that an application that he should do so should be refused. If that is so it is likely that the court will find that the reasonable time right has been violated and that the remedy will be a stay.[39]

35.34

The Court held[40] that the enforcing court must consider whether the imposition of the default sentence would violate the reasonable time right under the ECHR and, if so, what remedy should be granted to vindicate that right. The court was not considering traditional abuse of process but whether the imposition of a prison sentence after a long delay was lawful in this sense. The following matters are relevant:

(a) prosecutorial misconduct (by culpable delay or otherwise); this will be highly relevant and may be decisive; however, it is not a condition precedent to declining to impose a default term;

(b) delay being caused by the defendant leaving the jurisdiction, failing to pay and failing to inform the prosecutor where they were;

(c) the outcome of any inadequacy application or the defendant invoking the statutory remedies to prevent injustice; and

(d) the court cannot grant the warrant unless it:

    (i) is satisfied the default is due to the offender's wilful refusal or culpable neglect; and

38 *R (Gibson) v Secretary of State for Justice* [2018] 1 WLR 629, SC.
39 *R (on the application of O'Connell) v Westminster Magistrates' Court* [2017] EWHC 3120 at [34].
40 Ibid, at [36].

(ii) has considered or tried all other methods of enforcing payment of the sum and the court finds they are inappropriate or have been unsuccessful.

The defendant has a right to be heard on those questions and to give evidence about them. The grant of a warrant is not a punishment for not paying the order, or for not paying it sooner. It is a means of enforcement.[41]

35.35

The court held:[42]

> In deciding whether it would actually be unjust and disproportionate to impose the sentence of imprisonment the court must look at the detailed facts and circumstances of the particular case ....

Each case will be looked at on its own facts with the principles above being applied. It will not be sufficient to point to the delay in and of itself. Evidence of effect of imprisonment will be critical to the determination of whether there is a violation of the reasonable time guarantee and, if so, what the consequences ought to be. There are occasions, although they will be extremely rare, where enforcement both as to the activation of the default term and recovery of sums owed might fall foul of Article 6.

41 The principles are set out in *R v Harrow Justices, ex parte DPP* [1991] 1 WLR 395.

42 *R (on the application of O'Connell) v Westminster Magistrates' Court* at [43].

Index

[All references are to paragraph number.]